17,49

Teaching
English
Abroad

VACATION WORK
PUBLICATIONS

This edition first published in Great Britain 2010 by
Crimson Publishing, a division of Crimson Business Ltd
Westminster House
Kew Road
Richmond
Surrey
TW9 2ND

First published 1991
Tenth edition 2010

TEACHING ENGLISH ABROAD
by Susan Griffith
Editorial assistant Samantha Harper

© Crimson Publishing, 2010

A catalogue record for this book is available from the British Library.

ISBN 978 1 85458 556 1

Printed and bound by Ashford Colour Press, Gosport, Hants

Eckersley Oxford

Eckersley Oxford is one of the oldest language schools in the UK, having been founded in 1955 by the eponymous John Eckersley. Eckersley Oxford is accredited by the British Council and is a Trinity College London CertTESOL course provider. It is a member of English UK and has been awarded an A rating on the UK Border Agency Register of Sponsors.

The school is situated in a quiet pedestrian street in the heart of the city, close to the Ashmolean Museum, theatres, historic pubs and colleges. With 11 classrooms, Eckersley Oxford welcomes up to 160 full-time students from all over the world at any time. Many of the rooms have interactive whiteboards, laptops and projectors installed, and the 21st century setting is continued elsewhere in the school. There is a brand new digital language laboratory where the students can also check e-mails and there is wireless internet access throughout the school.

The students' room is equipped with a television and games including table tennis, a keyboard and guitar as well as a kitchen, where students often prepare meals for the popular international lunches! There is also a screen projector for watching films. One of the unusual features of the school is the roof garden, where students and staff can sit and relax and there are even classes held outside.

The staff at Eckersley Oxford are dedicated to providing a great service in a great city and celebrating a proud tradition with a very contemporary outlook, embodied in the school strap line, 'Our Past Building Your Future'.

Bridge Recruitment for EOD

English Opens Doors is a volunteer programme sponsored by the United Nations and run by the Chilean Ministry of Education. The programme's aim is to match native English speaking volunteers with Chilean English teachers in schools across the country. Volunteers live with a Chilean host family and co-teach English classes, helping to lead activities that focus on speaking and pronunciation. Bridge TEFL recruits teachers for these positions for placement in the Patagonia region of Chile.

Sarah Athanas volunteered for English Opens Doors in 2007-2008 through BridgeTEFL. She was placed in the Patagonia Region of Aysén, one of Chile's least-populated regions. Here she talks about her experience living at the bottom of the world.

'Volunteering in Patagonia through the English Opens Doors Program was definitely one of the hardest and best things I've ever done. I was placed in a public school that had limited resources and staff. My classroom was often cold in the winter and my students crowded around the woodstove to keep warm. In the beginning, it was scary and overwhelming to stand up in front of a room full of energetic and mischievous kids. I didn't think I'd ever learn their names, much less teach them English! Eventually we got used to each other and I really became attached to my students. I will never forget the ways they thanked me—by carrying my bag down the hallway or giving me a hug after class. I think they taught me much more than I could have ever taught them!

I had heard lots of things about Patagonia before I went there. Everyone talks about the harsh beauty of the Patagonian landscape, and I wanted to see it for myself. What I hadn't heard much about are the people who live there. What I discovered from living there is that the people of Patagonia are astoundingly warm and kind. I have never been welcomed into the homes of so many strangers. There is a special pride and self-sufficiency in these people that you have to admire. Anyone who can make Patagonia their home is a special person.'

Sarah summarises what she liked best about volunteering:

'When you volunteer anywhere, whether it is Chilean Patagonia or New York City, you will be taken out of your comfort zone and you will have to push yourself to new limits. You also will not earn any money. You may not be able to buy lots of souvenirs or new clothes, or even go out for nice dinners. What happens under these circumstances is really special. You start to live by your actions and the relationships that you form with people. Nothing else matters. And chances are that when you go back to earning a paycheck, the lessons you learned as a volunteer will stay with you. That is the transformative power of volunteering.'

For more information on teaching in Patagonia, Chile, visit www.BridgeTEFL.com.

CONTENTS

PREFACE

Those of us who speak English as a first language tend to take for granted how universally dominant it has become. As the global language of pop songs, air traffic control, computer games and most of facebook it has infiltrated other languages. For whatever reason – the influence of the internet, globalisation of marketing, because it sounds so damn cool – languages around the world are increasingly peppered with anglicisms. An ability to teach the English language is highly valued and the most globally mobile skill there is. English teaching institutes are always opening in new corners of the world from Georgia in the Caucasus to Macau in the South China Sea, and in a thousand more familiar places from Bordeaux to Buenos Aires.

On the one hand *Teaching English Abroad* is not aimed primarily at the professional teacher who already has access to a wide range of information on working abroad. Neither is it intended to encourage people to bluster their way into jobs abroad on the insufficient grounds that they are native speakers of the language. Between these two extremes, countless ordinary people have the appropriate backgrounds and personalities to become successful teachers of their native language. The beauty of English teaching is that it is accessible to so many.

No average profile of the travelling teacher can be identified. For this tenth edition, I have received enthusiastic feedback from many world-roaming teachers, including a recent Bath University graduate who funded a year in Berlin through his teaching, an early retired telecommunications worker who is teaching in Athens on the strength of a TEFL certificate he obtained in Corinth, a free spirit from Cambridge who while spending a few months living by a lake in Guatemala volunteered to teach children through a local charity, a journalist couple from Australia taking a prolonged career break in northern Italy, a gap year student who taught at a Buddhist nunnery in the Himalayas, an American in Paris, and people of all stages of life teaching English in China. There is a continuing trend for older candidates to be attracted to the idea of obtaining a TEFL certificate before embarking on a teaching experience abroad. Other noticeable developments for this edition include a huge increase from Portugal to Taiwan in the teaching of English to children as young as kindergarten age.

The TEFL industry has spawned many hundreds of specialist websites that cover teacher training forums, provide interactive exercises for students and publicise current vacancies worldwide. Some might wonder what a book can add. I have tried to create a hand-held tool that makes it possible for the reader to compare at a glance destinations for teachers, institute requirements, visa regulations, possible problems and rewards. This book aims for clarity to help make sense of the overwhelming clutter of unsifted information online.

Note that the hundreds of language schools and teaching organisations around the world that submitted details of their teaching vacancies for 2011 have not paid to be included in this book. Shaded text headed by a company name has been supplied by the relevant company, whereas boxed first-hand accounts by named teachers have been freely shared with readers. It is beyond the scope of the author to investigate every school included, so it is the readers' responsibility to carry out their own checks on prospective employers.

In addition to all the hard information and listings of actual vacancies, this book tries to convey a flavour of life as a teacher abroad, by including first-hand descriptions of everything from banquet-induced hangovers in China to tips for renting accommodation in Buenos Aires. My aim from the first edition has been to make the information as concrete as possible, to cut the waffle. This book can be the stepping stone to a brilliant year or two of adventure abroad.

Susan Griffith
Cambridge
September 2010

ACKNOWLEDGEMENTS

The new revised edition of *Teaching English Abroad* would not have been possible without the help of scores of English teachers and the people who employ them. They have generously shared their wealth of information, insights and anecdotes. As well as all the people who helped with the nine previous editions the following should be thanked for their contributions, some of them substantial, to the research for this updated edition:

Peter Beech, Sara Breese, Paul Carey, Tom Clark, Deryn Collins, Jain Cook, Sheila Corwin, Barbara Darragh, Melanie Drake, Melissa Evans, Dilys Ewart, Ed Flok, Steph Fuccio, Minna Graber, Tom Grundy, Andy Heath, Nino Hunter, Kit Kidner, Annette Kunigagon, Philip Lee, Anna Ling, Jerry Melinn, Lizzi Middleton, Alexandra Neuman, Geoff Nunney, Aidan O'Toole, Ian Parr, Denley Pike, Gemma Pirelli, James Robinson, Mary Rose, Antoinette Sarpong, Jeff Saunders, Don Sloan, Charlotte Steggall, Samantha Thornley, Phil Tompkins, Melanie Twinning, Sab Will, Craig Wilson.

NOTE: The opinions expressed in the case studies shown with a grey background are entirely those of the featured organisation.

While every effort has been made to ensure that the information contained in this book was correct at the time of going to press, details are bound to change, especially those pertaining to visa requirements for teachers, exchange rates and the conditions offered by the schools listed in the country directories. Readers are invited to write to Susan Griffith, Crimson Publishing, Westminster House, Kew Road, Richmond, Surrey TW9 2ND; info@crimsonpublishing.co.uk with any comments or corrections. The best contributions will be rewarded with a free copy of the next edition or any other Crimson title of their choice.

NOTE: Most wages and prices are given in local currencies. For conversion to sterling and US dollars, use www.oanda.com.

British Council offices abroad are frequently referred to in these chapters. The Council's up-to-date address book can be accessed on http://www.britishcouncil.org/new/contact-us/.

PART 1
INTRODUCTION

INTRODUCTION

The British Council estimates that the number of English language learners will peak in the next decade at a staggering two billion. The statistics illustrate the extent to which English dominates our globalised world: three-quarters of the world's mail is written in English, 80% of the world's electronically stored information is in English and well over a third of users of the internet communicate in the language you are reading at this moment. Mind-boggling statistics aside, the demand for instruction at all levels given by people who happen to speak English as their mother tongue is enormous and set to continue increasing for the foreseeable future.

Just as Latin was the lingua franca of Europe in the Middle Ages, now it is English that is the language used to communicate between persons not sharing a mother tongue. When the newly liberated nations of eastern Europe sloughed off Russian, they turned in very large measure to English rather than to the other main European languages. In fact, countries as far-flung as Cambodia, Namibia and Turkmenistan are busy making English one of the keystones of their educational systems. In German-speaking Switzerland, there are signs that English is replacing French as the preferred second language at school. English is the international language of science, of air traffic control, and to a very large extent of trade and export. This is bad news for all those Germans, Swedes and French Canadians who would like to market their language skills to fund a short or long stay abroad. But it is English speakers, mainly from Britain, Ireland, North America, Australia and New Zealand who accidentally find themselves in possession of such a sought-after commodity.

SOME DEFINITIONS

The commonly used acronyms ELT, TEFL, TESL and TESOL can be confusing, especially since they are often used interchangeably. ELT, which stands for English Language Teaching, has come to be the mainstream expression in the UK (preferred by such august bodies as the University of Cambridge and by the publishers of the main journal in the field). But most people still refer to TEFL (pronounced 'teffle'), Teaching English as a Foreign Language. TESL stands for Teaching English as a Second Language, and TESOL means Teaching English to Speakers of Other Languages. People learn English as a second language when they need to use it in their day-to-day lives, for example emigrants to the UK and the USA or inhabitants of ex-colonies where English retains official status and may well be the medium of instruction in schools. (English is the official or joint-official language in more than 75 countries.)

As this book is for people who want to travel abroad to teach, the term TEFL is mainly used here, as well as ELT. Teachers of English as a Second Language (ESL) are usually involved with multicultural education. In the USA, the vast majority of English language teaching is of ESL because of the huge demand for English among those people who have emigrated to the USA and whose first language is not English. Therefore the term ESL dominates in American contexts, even when (technically) EFL is meant.

The acronym TESOL covers both situations, yet it is not widely used apart from in institutions, which favour the Trinity College London qualifications known as the Certificate and Licentiate Diploma in TESOL (see Training section later) and also in the context of the American organisation TESOL Inc., which is the largest English teachers' organisation in the world, claiming more than 13,000 members.

There is no shortage of other acronyms and sub-categories in the world of TEFL. One of the main ones is ESP which means English for Specific Purposes. ESP aims to match language teaching with the needs of various professions such as business, banking, tourism, medicine, aviation, science, technology, secretaries, etc. Business English is probably the most important in this category (and 'English for Shopping' as sometimes offered in Japan is the least important). Because a great many learners are motivated by a desire to use English at work, they want their teachers to adopt a functional rather than a structural approach. In other words they want to have lessons in which they can pretend to be telephoning a client, recommending, applying, advising, agreeing, complaining and so on. They are certainly not interested in the subjunctive.

EAP stands for English for Academic Purposes, i.e. English at an advanced level usually taught to students who are planning to study at foreign universities or English-medium institutions in their own country. EAP is largely in the hands of government-funded programmes, such as those run by the British Council.

Note that the acronym TOEFL can cause confusion. The Test of English as a Foreign Language is a US-based standardised test administered to language learners. Passing a TOEFL exam is widely held to be a reliable indicator of how well an individual can communicate in English. The focus of many language schools abroad is to prepare candidates for the exam, and so may advertise for teachers with 'TOEFL' experience. The UK counterpart, sponsored by the British Council and Cambridge ESOL is IELTS (International English Language Testing System).

SCOPE OF OPPORTUNITIES

The range of locations and situations in which English is in demand covers an enormous spectrum. If TEFL is booming in Kazakhstan and Laos and Guatemala, there can be few corners of the world to which English has not penetrated. English has been called a 'barometer of Western influence' and only a handful of countries in the world have rejected Western influence outright (such as Bhutan and North Korea) and which therefore have no call for EFL teachers. More important nations with their own native English speaking population (such as India) are also not promising destinations for the aspiring teacher.

Many years have passed since the arrival of the single European market, which precipitated the greatest expansion of the English language than ever before in Europe's history. There has been an enormous increase in demand, especially from companies and professionals eager to participate in an integrated Europe. At least one German-based multinational has gone so far as to decree that all operations will be conducted in English. The attraction of European Union countries for British and Irish teachers is enhanced by the fact that they have the legal right to work.

The kinds of people who want to learn English are as numerous as the places in which they live. The recent worldwide recession has seen corporations from Moscow to Madrid cutting back on training budgets as a cost-cutting exercise. Yet in many cases demand has held up despite this. In an even more competitive market, a command of English is considered so essential that individuals are prepared to fund themselves and their children. The area of the industry which seems to be booming almost everywhere is the teaching of children (known as Young Learners or YL in the trade). Kids as young as three years are being sent to private English classes to improve their career prospects.

People around the world can think of a dozen reasons why they need to sign up for private English lessons:

- A Taiwanese student dreams of studying at UCLA.
- A Polish bus driver, proud to be from a member state of the EU, wants to work in Denmark where he will be able to communicate in English.
- The wife of the Peruvian ambassador in Islamabad wants to be able to speak English at official functions.

i-to-i

Meet i-to-i's official Teach in China Blogger!

*TEFL novice **Craig Barber**, 22, kept members of i-to-i's TEFL community, Chalkboard, as well as the wider world, updated with his experience of teaching in Shanghai over the course of his five-month internship. Craig, who is originally from West Yorkshire, jetted out to China in August 2009 with 50 other interns after completing i-to-i's comprehensive 120-hour Combined TEFL Course. During the course (included in the internship package) he gained a great footing in TEFL theory with a 100-hour online course and put that theory into practice on an action-packed 20-hour weekend course.*

Craig, who had just finished studying at university, had never travelled outside of Europe before, but that didn't put him off. Before leaving he wrote on his blog, which can be found at www.tefl-chalkboard.com/craigbarber: 'In just a few weeks' time I will be stood in front of a class of students potentially 100 strong! Despite this my overwhelming feelings are that of excitement and anticipation. I always planned to go travelling after university and now it's just around the corner.'

He's now put the skills learnt on the theory element of the internship into practice teaching kids at a kindergarten. Over the course of the internship he gained hundreds of hours of teaching practice, as well as earning cash to fund further adventures in this amazing country.

Speaking on his first day, he said:

> *My first day of teaching ever went much better than I thought it would, it was actually quite fun! The lessons that I had planned went quite well and I had a Chinese teacher in the class with me which made it much easier. I left the school after my first 8 hours feeling uplifted and pleased with myself.*

To read the latest update from Craig's adventure, go to www.tefl-chalkboard.com/craigbarber. To join Craig in getting TEFL qualified, racking up 300 hours of teaching experience over five months in China, just visit www.onlinetefl.com/teaching-internships/china/ or contact i-to-i's TEFL team on 0800 093 2552/0800 352 1793.

- A Greek secondary school student has to pass her English exams in order to proceed to the next year and, like most of her classmates, attends a private tutorial college for English lessons.
- A Turkish youth wants to be able to flirt with tourists from northern Europe.
- A Mexican waiter wants to get a job in the Acapulco Hilton.
- A Saudi engineer has to be able to read reports and manuals in English for his job.

The list is open-ended, and prospects for hopeful teachers are therefore excellent. There are also hundreds of international schools throughout the world where English is the medium of instruction for all subjects and there may be specific EFL vacancies. These will be of most interest to certified teachers who wish to work abroad.

But the situation is not all rosy for the prospective teacher. As the profile of the English language has risen, so has the profile of the profession which teaches it, and the number of qualified and experienced English teachers has increased along with the rise in demand. The difficult employment situation for new graduates in the UK and elsewhere has prompted some to look abroad, and to equip themselves with a TEFL certificate in order to get some work experience on their CV. The explosion in the availability of training courses means that a much higher proportion of job-seekers have a TEFL certificate than was the case a decade ago, and (quite rightly) foreign language schools are becoming more selective when hiring staff.

People who cruise into a country expecting to be hired as an EFL teacher simply on the basis of being a native speaker are in most cases (though not quite all) in for a nasty shock. Employers at all levels will ask for evidence of the ability to teach their language or at least a university degree as proof of a sound educational background. Certainly without a degree, a TEFL qualification or any relevant experience, the scope of opportunities shrinks drastically.

WHO IS ELIGIBLE TO TEACH?

Anyone who can speak English fluently and has a lively positive personality has a fighting chance of finding an opening as a teacher somewhere. Geordies, Tasmanians and Alabamans have all been known to be hired as English teachers (not to mention Norwegians and North Africans), though most employers favour native speakers of English without a heavy regional accent. Depending on the economic and cultural orientation of a country, schools will prefer British English or North American English. For obvious geopolitical reasons Europe and Africa incline towards Britain while Latin America and the Far East incline towards the USA and Canada. Many other countries have no decided preference, for example Indonesia and Turkey. Clear diction is usually more important than accent. On the American English versus British English debate, **Sab Will**, Course Director of TEFL Paris training courses says:

> *I'm not convinced it's a major concern. There are certainly French who find one flavour (or should that be 'flavor'?) easier to understand than the other, and some people want to be taught mainly in one 'accent' based on their intended future use of English. But overall I think it all evens out. Most students are happy with a friendly, competent and enthusiastic teacher who is able to adapt to their needs and supply them with materials and learning situations relevant to their situation. In relation to that, the origin of the teacher pales in comparison. Of course the teacher should be able to 'neutralise' their accent if necessary, whatever their origins, so that the student has a model which will be understood throughout the English-speaking world.*

English language teaching is an industry which is seldom regulated, giving rise to the host of cowboy schools which are mentioned (usually disparagingly) throughout this book. The other side of the coin is the proliferation of cowboy teachers, who have no feel for language, no interest in their pupils and no qualms about ripping them off. The issue of qualifications must be considered carefully. It is obviously unwise to assume that fluency in English is a sufficient qualification to turn someone into an EFL teacher. Many experienced teachers of English come to feel very strongly that untrained teachers do a disservice both to their pupils and to their language. Certainly anyone who is serious about going abroad to teach English should turn to the relevant chapter to consider the training options. As Groucho Marx said, who would want to belong to a club that would want him as a member if he has no formal qualifications or experience? Among the army of teachers-cum-travellers, there are undoubtedly some lazy, spiritless and ungrammatical native speakers of English who have bluffed their way into a teaching job. Most books and journals about language teaching are unanimous in their condemnation of such amateurs. Yet there are some excellent teachers who have learned how to teach by practising rather than by studying. For certain kinds of teaching jobs, a background in business and commerce might be far more useful than any paper qualifications in teaching. Therefore we have not excluded the unqualified teacher-traveller from our account. As long as they take their responsibilities seriously and bear in mind that their pupils have entrusted them with significant quantities of time and money to help them learn, they need not bring the EFL profession into disrepute. Some untrained teachers we talked to during the research for this book found the responsibility so unnerving that they promptly enrolled in a TEFL course before unleashing themselves on an unsuspecting language-learning public.

Non-native speakers should not assume that their services will not be in demand outside their home countries. **Richard Ridha Guellala** was born in Holland, raised in Tunisia and partly educated in England, and now has one of the most highly respected qualifications in TEFL, the Cambridge Diploma. While teaching in Thailand, he wrote:

> *Most non-native speakers think that a position as an EFL teacher is impossible for them. However I came to the conclusion that even unqualified non-native speakers are often hired by Asian schools, as long as they project a professional image during the interview, speak clearly, are well-groomed, know the basics of English grammar and are fluent in the language. Scandinavians and Dutch are sometimes even more successful in finding teaching jobs at top schools than native speakers. True, we non-native speakers possess a rather 'heavy' or 'funny' accent but, believe it or not, some Asian employers favour our accents to the native speaker's because we speak more slowly and use very simple basic vocabulary.*

At an extreme opposite from the casual teacher-traveller is the teacher who makes ELT a career. Only a minority of people teaching English abroad are professional teachers. Career prospects in ELT are in fact not very encouraging. After teachers have achieved a certain level of training and experience, they can aspire to work for International House and then for the British Council. From there, they might become a director of studies at a private language institute, although one is unlikely to become a director without a primary interest in business and administration.

THE OLDER TEACHER

An increasing number of early-retired and other mature people is becoming interested in teaching English abroad for a year or two. Although it may be true that in certain contexts, language institutes are more inclined to employ a bright young graduate, if only for reasons of image and marketing, there are plenty of others who will value maturity, especially the growing number of establishments specialising in teaching young children. **Peter Beech**, Director of Anglo-Hellenic in Corinth, Greece, which trains and places teachers in jobs, has noticed an increasing interest from people who have already had a career in the UK, in teaching or in any field, who want to move abroad.

Whereas few companies openly impose an upper age limit, some age discrimination does regrettably take place, more noticeable in some countries than in others. For older job-seekers it will be a matter of spreading their net as widely as possible by contacting as many relevant organisations, including voluntary ones, as possible. Older applicants may have to work harder to demonstrate enthusiasm, energy and adaptability to prospective employers; but this should be no bar to someone committed to creating adventures later in life.

Australian journalists **Alexandra Neuman** and **John Carey**, aged 49 and 50, respectively, decided that having worked for 30 odd years it was time to do something different. They didn't want to do the sensible thing and wait till retirement so started saving and planning, and after a couple of years had saved enough to fund a year in Italy. At first Alex didn't work but when they decided to extend their stay, she needed to find work. The only work available was teaching English, which is what she is doing right now in the lovely town of Bergamo:

JERRY MELINN enjoyed teaching English at an institute in Athens through Anglo-Hellenic so much that he has signed on for another year:

I suppose you could say I don't fit the profile of a TEFL teacher. Usually they are unattached, young and out to see the world after finishing their university studies. I worked in the telecommunications industry in Ireland for almost 40 years and took advantage of an early retirement scheme when I was 56 years old. I didn't want to stop working and, as my four children were grown up, I decided with the agreement of my wife, to try my hand at teaching English in Greece. I was interested in Greece because we have friends here and had been coming to Greece on holidays for many years.

It won't matter what you read, who you speak to or how much planning you do once you arrive, your experience will be completely different. I have yet to meet one person who had a similar experience to mine, so above all you must bring with you tolerance, flexibility and an upbeat attitude. The rewards are well worth it. I love living here, I have never met such kindness and I know bureaucracy is terrible and I get paid badly but as I sit looking out of my hilltop apartment to the snow-capped Alps and the grapes ripening on the vine just below my bedroom window I think life is pretty wonderful!

WHAT EMPLOYERS ARE LOOKING FOR

Between the dodgy operators and the British Council is a vast middle ground of respectable English teaching establishments. Many would prefer to hire only qualified staff, yet they are not always available. On the whole these schools are looking for teachers with a good educational background, clear correct speech, familiarity with the main issues and approaches to TEFL, and an outgoing personality.

A bachelor's degree and/or TEFL certificate is no guarantee of ability as **Marta Eleniak** observed in Spain, where she taught during her gap year (after doing a one-week introductory TEFL course):

I've seen graduate teachers make such a mockery of the enterprise that it's almost criminal. TEFL is creative teaching. Forget about your educational experiences. In TEFL you have got to be able to do an impression of a chicken, you've got to be a performer. And you have to be flexible. If the pupils are falling asleep, conduct a short aerobics class and change tack to something more interesting. A good teacher builds a rapport with the class, and is enthusiastic, patient, imaginative and genuinely interested in the welfare of the pupils.

A sophisticated knowledge of English grammar is not needed, since in most cases, native speakers are hired to encourage conversation and practise pronunciation, leaving the grammar lessons to local teachers. On the other hand, a basic grasp is necessary if only to keep up with your pupils.

MOTIVES FOR TEACHING ENGLISH

There are perhaps five main types of individual to be found teaching English from Tarragona to Taipei:

- The serious career teacher.
- The student of the prevailing language and culture who teaches in order to fund a longer stay.

- The long-term traveller who wants to prolong and fund his or her travels.
- The philanthropic or religious person sponsored by an aid organisation, charity or mission society.
- The misfit or oddball, perhaps fleeing unhappiness at home.

Experienced English teacher **Deryn Collins** wrote from Spain, identifying just three types of folk who teach abroad:

> *There are people who want to learn about how others live and take part, those who want to put a year out on their CV and those who leave their homeland because they cannot live with their 'own'. Which means you will on occasion work with a weirdo or maybe you are that weirdo. But mostly the mix of personalities is a marvellous thing. You can find good friends in teachers' rooms – some might even find love!*

In many countries, English teaching is the most easily attainable employment, in fact the only available employment for foreigners. Anyone who wants to transcend the status of mere tourist in a country such as Thailand, Bolivia or Japan will probably be attracted to the idea of teaching English. The assumption behind some thinking at the snobbish end of the EFL spectrum is that people who do it for only a year or two as a means to an end (e.g. learning Chinese, studying Italian art, eating French food) are necessarily inadequate teachers.

There are small pockets of people (mainly in the Far East) whose sole ambition is to earn as much money as possible to pay off student debts or fund further world travels. These are seldom good teachers if only because they take on so many hours of teaching that they can't possibly prepare properly for their lessons. But for most teachers, making a lot of money is not a priority or, if it was at the outset, they are soon disillusioned.

Salaries in popular tourist destinations (such as Paris, Barcelona, Chiang Mai) may actually be lower than in less appealing neighbouring towns, even though the cost of living is higher. Pay scales are relatively meaningless out of context. For example, the high salaries paid in Japan are usually eaten up by high rents and other expenses, at least in the first year. When converted into sterling a salary in Romania might sound pitiful but will be perfectly adequate there. In some countries such as Bolivia and Kenya, a TEFL salary may not be enough to fund anything beyond a very spartan lifestyle, and savings from home are essential to fund any travelling. Yet the majority of people who spend time abroad teaching English are able to afford to live comfortably and have an enjoyable time without feeling pinched, although they end up saving little.

RED TAPE

The European Union (EU) now consists of the UK, Ireland, the Netherlands, Belgium, Luxembourg, Denmark, Sweden, Finland, Austria, Estonia, Latvia, Lithuania, Poland, Czech Republic, Slovakia, Hungary, Slovenia, Malta, Bulgaria, Romania, the Greek populated area of Cyprus, France, Germany, Italy, Greece, Spain and Portugal, the latter six of which have enormous EFL markets. Within the EU, the red tape should be minimal for all nationals of member states who wish to work in any capacity (though the relevant sections of the country chapters make it clear that this is not always the case). Outside the EU, legislation varies from country to country. In theory there is also 'free reciprocity of labour' within the European Economic Area. The EEA takes in those western European countries that have decided to stay outside the Union, viz. Iceland, Liechtenstein, Norway and Switzerland.

All of this means that British and Irish nationals have a significant advantage over Americans, Canadians, Australians, New Zealanders and South Africans when job-hunting in Europe. Although not impossible for other nationalities, it is very difficult for them to find an employer willing to undertake the task of proving to the authorities that no EU national is available or able to do the job. **Brian Komyathy** from Long Island, New York, was disappointed when he made enquiries about moving to an EU country:

> *European walls of regulations do not exactly bespeak, 'Americans welcome aboard'. I'm technically eligible to acquire Irish and hence EU citizenship through my grandparents, so as soon as various documentary records are located and processed I'll not have the problems I do now. A slew of phone calls convinced me of the necessity of taking this course.*

Other Americans find ingenious ways to stay just about legal. **Rachel Beebe** worked in Portugal using *recibos verdes* (green receipts), which are intended for use by temporary workers in the country. In some cases non-Europeans with a student visa are permitted to work up to a certain number of hours (see chapter on France, for example). International and student exchange organisations may be able to assist. Some US-based organisations co-operate with partner agencies in various countries to place native speaker teachers in schools or institutes, often as volunteers or as live-in tutors. For particulars, see the chapter *Finding a Job, Opportunities for North Americans*.

The immigration authorities of many countries accord English teachers special status, recognising that their own nationals cannot compete as they can for other jobs. Other countries may lack the mechanism for granting work visas to English teachers and so will often turn a blind eye to those who teach on tourist visas, since everyone knows that locals are not being deprived of jobs, rather they're being given an advantage by having the chance to learn English.

Some organisations have developed a study-and-teach solution. While you are learning Russian in Moscow or Spanish in Caracas, you do some English tutoring on the side. Since your status is primarily as a student, it is unnecessary to obtain a full work authorisation. Teachers who find a job before leaving home can usually sort out their visas or at least set the wheels in motion before arrival, which greatly simplifies matters. You can only start the process after finding an employer willing to sponsor your application, preferably one who is familiar with the processes. There is no point applying to the embassy or consulate until you have found an employer. The majority of countries will process visas only when they are applied for from outside the country. So if you have to visit your chosen country on a tourist visa in order to find a job (which is the usual process), you will have to leave the country to apply for the work visa, though often this can be done from a neighbouring country rather than your country of residence. The restrictions and procedures for obtaining the appropriate documentation to teach legally are set out in Part 2 of this book, country by country.

STAYING ON THE RIGHT SIDE OF THE LAW
Prospective teachers should contact the relevant consulate for the official line. If you do get tangled up in red tape, always remain patient with consular officials. If things seem to be grinding to a halt, it may be helpful to pester them, provided this is done with unfailing politeness.

REWARDS AND RISKS

The rewards of teaching abroad are mostly self-evident: the chance to become integrated in a foreign culture, the pleasure of making communication possible for your students, the interesting characters and lifestyles you will encounter, a feeling of increased self-reliance, a better perspective on your own culture and your own habits, a base for foreign travel, a good suntan... and so on.

Yasmin Peiris, away from home for the first time and teaching in China, sums up the highs and lows:

> *Looking back on the last 12 months, some experiences stand out very clearly. Unfortunately, that includes times when you fall ill or feel homesick, or even feel lonely. Homesickness is natural and is a phase that passes very quickly. This is my first time away from home and I feel like the past year has been a massive achievement personally and professionally. It's been great having my own apartment, making friends from all over the world, learning Chinese, and more importantly, realising my own strengths, limits and skills through my time here. The work experience gained and the friendships made will be the most precious souvenir – that I know won't get lost or confiscated by customs. I already knew that I had to come into this experience with an open mind, and I'm glad I did because China surprised me at every turn, constantly giving me something weird or wonderful to write home about.*

Good teachers often find their classes positively fun and place a high value on the relationships they form with their students. Teaching is a lot of fun when it's done right. One-to-one teaching can also be enjoyable since you have a better chance to get to know your students or clients. (By the same token, it can be a miserable experience if you don't get on, since there is no escape from the intimacy of the arrangement.) Off-site teaching provides glimpses into a variety of workplaces and private homes, perhaps even resulting in hospitality and friendship with your students.

As competition for jobs has increased, working conditions have not improved. There is a growing tendency for EFL teachers to be offered non-contract freelance work, with no guarantee of hours, making it necessary for them to work for more than one employer in order to make a living. Job security is a scarce commodity. Part-time freelancers of course miss out on all the benefits of full-time work such as bonuses, holiday pay, help with accommodation in some cases, and so on.

Uninitiated teachers run the risk of finding themselves working for a shark or a cowboy who doesn't care a fig about the quality of teaching or the satisfaction of the teachers, as long as pupils keep signing up and paying their fees. 'Client satisfaction' is their only criterion of success; business takes complete precedence over education. Exploitation of teachers is not uncommon since the profession is hampered by a lack of both regulation and unionisation.

The job of teaching English is demanding; it demands energy, enthusiasm and imagination, which are not always easy to produce when confronted with a room full of stonily silent faces. Instead of the thrill of communication, the drudgery of language drills begins to dominate. Instead of the pleasure of exchanging views with people of a different culture, teachers become weighed down by sheaves of photocopies and visual aids. Like most jobs when done right, teaching English is no piece of cake and is at times discouraging, but invariably it has its golden moments. It offers opportunities for creativity, learning about other cultures and attitudes, making friends and of course travelling. Not a bad job in many ways.

Roberta Wedge writes amusingly on a possible spin-off from a teaching contract abroad:

> *TEFL is one of the most sex-balanced job fields I know (though the Director of Studies is usually a man) and, for those who are interested, the possibilities of finding your one true love appear to be high. 'Thrown together in an isolated Spanish village, eating tapas in the bar, hammering out lesson plans together – we found we have so much in common.' And a year later they were married. (A true story.)*

On a more serious note, teachers should inform themselves about the political situation before offering their EFL services and take stock of their particular sensitivities concerning issues such as political freedom, democracy, human rights, religion, and so on. To take a couple of examples, teachers in China have been shocked by the overt racism. For instance a Ghanaian teacher working in a small city not that far from Beijing had to get used to the local people coming up to him to rub his skin to see if the black would come off. In the Central Asian Republics, home to ethnically diverse populations, certain groups are treated shamefully. If you are concerned by these matters, check the US-biased Freedom House website at www.freedomhouse.org for updates. Additional insight can be gained from Reporters Sans Frontieres (Reporters without Borders) at www.rsf.org. With regard to 'press freedom' their Worldwide Press Freedom Index rates countries according to the liberality of their press.

TRAINING

TEFL Training

I did my TEFL course with TEFL Training. It comprised a distance learning course and a weekend workshop which I did in Southampton. Shortly after completing the course I moved to Japan with my Japanese girlfriend and I got a job with an English language school called Nichibei.

After one year I decided to apply for a job at the British Council in Osaka. I'd heard they paid well and that it was one of the best places to teach. Normally they require a minimum of 5 years' teaching experience but I thought there would be no harm in trying anyway. I spoke to the head teacher and managed to arrange an interview. Much to my surprise I was offered a job on a part-time contract.

After one year I got a job with OTC in Osaka. OTC employs teachers and sends them out to different clients. Usually you teach at a school in the day time and at a business in the evening. They are a well-run organisation who treats their staff very well. I gained lots of experience at OTC. I taught at junior and senior high schools, about 20 different companies including some famous names like Nintendo (at their head quarters in Kyoto).

With all this experience on my resum I found that prospective employers were often keen to interview me when I sent them my CV but more so in Asia than in the UK. I decided to come back to the UK. My experiences teaching in Japan had enabled me to have a lot of fun, boost my confidence and set my sights on higher goals for the future. On returning to Brighton I got a TEFL job with EC that paid L15 an hour. I had never imagined myself earning so much in the UK. The summer after I got another job with a school in Brighton on a similar wage and the summer after that I got a job with GEOS in Bangkok, Thailand.

I think the TESOL certificate I did with TEFL Training was very helpful in landing certain jobs. Pound for pound it is probably one of the best investments I ever made. After 9 years of TEFLing I've come to realise how lucky I am to be a native English speaker. It's a passport to working and living in almost any country you choose and earning a good (local) wage. The TESOL certificate helps you to utilize this innate advantage and acquire numerous skills and experiences that can be very helpful in any other career you decide to embark on in the future.

I am actually dyslexic and my spelling has always been quite bad. However, I've found there are many English teachers who also struggle with spelling on occasion. I would recommend anyone to do this course and have a go at TEFL teaching. It's lots of fun!

Tom Brown

THE VALUE OF ELT QUALIFICATIONS

Training in teaching English as a foreign language is not absolutely essential for successful job-hunting; but it makes the task easier by an order of magnitude. Anyone with the Cambridge

Certificate (CELTA) or the Trinity Certificate in TESOL (both discussed in detail below) is in a much stronger position to get a job in any country where English is widely taught. These certificate courses provide a rigorous introduction to teaching English in just one month full-time (admittedly at considerable expense) or part-time over a period of months, and so anyone interested in spending some time teaching abroad should seriously consider enrolling in a certificate course. There are numerous other kinds of qualifications available, some obtainable after a weekend course and others after years of university study; many are described briefly in the Directory of Training Courses below.

However, the Cambridge and Trinity certificates should not be thought of as a magical passport to work. Increasingly, even certificate-holders are having to struggle to find a decent job, mainly because so many more people now have the qualification than a decade ago. Many language schools, especially in France and Germany, will not want to hire a novice teacher and are unlikely to be tempted to take on anyone who does not present a dynamic and energetic image. Still, the certificate training continues to give applicants an important edge over the competition.

Global TESOL College

28 May 2010
Global TESOL College

To the Staff of Global TESOL College:

As a participant in this year's course, held in Toronto, I personally congratulate all of you, especially the instructor, Loren Yaremchuk, on the fantastic assemblage of strategies, techniques and effective tacit. The reason behind this letter is precisely for that reason, as an aspiring ESL instructor, upon completing your course, I find myself in a better position in presenting material in a more effective, professional and meaningful way than I would have ever known via the academic route. The reasons for this are two fold.

Firstly, my university courses have been strictly theoretical in scope. At the University of Toronto, there is not a single course in the ESL course calendar that I can think of that clearly outlines, as your manual does, ways a teacher can go about handling the class's attention while at the same time making the students feel English can be accessible. I am aware that not even a Practicum, whereby ESL instructors are given class exposure, provides the necessary tool for a lasting impression on the teacher to do good for the students' sake. Only, perhaps, years of exposure can bring this out fully. But more importantly, in the five days, this student can honestly say, I can pinpoint the whats and hows of a solid and caring teacher.

Secondly, despite the manual's focus on teaching strictly conversational English, these last five days have brought forth concrete methods enabling me to look out for real life examples and how to incorporate them into a more persuasive lesson plan. This will prove to be the most useful in the long term. So, thank you once again and hopefully the Global TESOL College will branch out further and one day be taught at a university/college level.

Sincerely,

Nikola A Pavic
Toronto, Ontario, Canada
Advanced TESOL Certificate Program Graduate

Increasing your marketability is not the only reason to get some training. The assumption that just because you can speak a language you can teach is simply false. There may be plenty of people who have a natural flair for teaching and who can do an excellent job without the benefit of a certificate or any other ELT qualification. (As mentioned earlier, the term ELT has come to be preferred to TEFL in many contexts.) There are, however, many other people who, when faced with a class full of eager adolescents, would not have a clue where to begin. Doing a TEFL course cannot fail to increase your confidence and provide you with a range of ideas on how to teach and (just as important) how not to teach. Even a short introductory course can usually illustrate methods of making lessons interesting and of introducing the range of teaching materials and approaches available to the novice teacher. What is needed more than theory or academic attainment, is an ability to entertain and to dramatise, but not without a framework into which your classroom efforts can be placed.

A perpetual problem which a TEFL course solves is the general level of ignorance of grammar among native speakers. Native-speaker teachers often find that their pupils, who are much better informed on English grammar than they are, can easily catch them out with questions about verb tenses and subjunctives, causing embarrassment all round. Some training courses can also introduce you to the cultural barriers you can expect to encounter and the specific language-learning difficulties experienced by various nationalities (many of which will be touched on in the country chapters).

Some go so far as to see training almost as a moral obligation. Completely untrained teachers may end up being responsible for teaching people who have paid a great deal of money for expert instruction. This is of special concern in countries which have been inundated with 'tourist-teachers', while the ministries of education may be struggling to create all-graduate teaching professions. If you happen not to be a natural in the classroom, you may well fail to teach anything much to your pupils, whether they be young children in Hong Kong or businessmen in Portugal.

Not satisfied that a one-week course was enough to qualify him as a teacher, **Ian Abbott** went on to do the Cambridge Certificate at International House in Rome and summarises his view of TEFL training:

I wouldn't recommend teaching English as a foreign language without investing in a course first. You've got to remember that the people coming along to your lessons are desperate to learn your language and it is costing them a small fortune. It is only fair that you know what you are doing and can in the end take that money without guilt, knowing you haven't ripped them off to increase your travel funds.

One of the practical advantages of joining a TEFL course is that many training centres have contacts with recruitment agencies or language schools abroad and can advise on, if not find, a job abroad for you at the end of the course. Training centres differ enormously on how much help they can offer. If the 'after-sales service' is important to you, shop around before choosing which training course to patronise.

Even in countries where it may be commonplace to work without a formal TEFL qualification (for example Thailand and Japan), teachers who lack a specific grounding in TEFL will often be at a disadvantage. In some cases, the jobs available to the unqualified tend to be at the cowboy end of the market and may therefore offer exploitative conditions. In some countries (such as Turkey) a TEFL certificate is a prerequisite for a work visa, which is yet another justification for doing some formal training before setting off.

Hamburg School of English

The CELTA Teacher Training Centre in Hamburg has been offering high-quality, small-sized courses since 2003, training around 60 teachers each year. If you could ask them, what would they say about our course?

- I would recommend this class to anyone who is serious about advancing their career in EFL just because of the amount of practice and knowledge they would stand to gain by taking it.

- Do it! It's very hard work but you get so much out of it.

- I can't imagine how I taught without it - it really opened my eyes to the needs of students and the resources available and also what I am capable of!

- Before teaching practice I felt I was given a great amount of support.

- (The course is) great - I think you guys are great tutors!

We consider it part of our job to provide you during your training with the best set of resources to help you develop yourself as a teacher, but we also never forget that the richest resource available is you, and the rich experience of teaching and learning that you already have within you.

After a CELTA course with us, teachers go on to posts internationally, from working one-to-one in Berlin to teaching groups of 100-400 people in China, from preparing students for language exams to helping politicians hone their presentation skills.

The possible contexts for teaching English are unlimited and so we cannot afford to restrict your development by adhering to dogmatic beliefs of what "best practice" may be; it is much more important to appreciatively explore and critically appraise actions taken in the classroom, so that, once you leave us, you are well-equipped to continue developing and adapting. Teaching is, after all, learning.

RANGE OF COURSES

There is a bewildering array of courses available, at vastly different levels and costs, so it is wise to carry out some careful research before choosing. The British Council publishes introductory information on its website (see www.britishcouncil.org/teacherrecruitment-tefl-qualifications.htm). If you need help funding a training course, you may be eligible for a Professional and Career Development Loan, which is a bank loan where the government covers the interest for the duration of the course and for the first month after the course finishes. After that you have to pay it back in the normal way; further details can be found at www.direct.gov.uk/cdl or by phoning 0800 585505. Unfortunately, due to a change in UK government funding for adult courses in 2010, TEFL training courses are not currently eligible for funding for the next academic year (2010–2011).

When choosing a course, it is worth asking certain questions that will indicate how useful the qualification will be at the end of it, such as, is there any external validation of the course and how much opportunity is there for teaching practice. Also find out what size a class you will be in (10–12 is much better than 15–20) and what qualifications and experience the tutors have. Cactus TEFL (www.cactustefl.com) is a mine of information about all things TEFL-related. It offers a useful advice, orientation and admissions service for prospective TEFL teachers. The online and telephone support offers personal guidance on courses, and allows you to apply directly to a wide range of TEFL course providers worldwide. Cactus also has a jobs site at www.cactustefl.com/jobs/index.php. The Directory of Training Courses in this chapter organises the courses available under various headings the 100+ hour certificate courses externally validated by the University of Cambridge and Trinity College London, 'Academic and Other Recognised Courses', which are primarily full academic courses offered at universities (this list is far from comprehensive), a few 'Distance Learning' courses, 'Short Introductory Courses in the UK' and, finally, a selection of courses offered worldwide: 'Training Courses in North America' and 'Training Courses Worldwide'.

Kristall International

Kristall International has been providing training and education courses since 1982. These have included management development for companies, consultancy for educational and adventure courses and assessment for university students on their school teaching practices.

For the past 19 years Kristall has been the forerunner in fast-track TEFL courses around the UK and abroad. The courses are carefully structured to bring the best out of participants by building on positives, in small groups of two or more. The aim is to develop teaching skills and techniques in a fun and informative way. Through watching teachers in action, Kristall's staff show participants how to plan lessons and use language books to gain ideas and teaching structures. The approach gives participants the confidence to teach conversational English, helping them create a keen and enthusiastic classroom environment or teaching one-on-one, and giving them the passion to learn more about grammar.

The end product gives participants access to work in the UK or abroad and a Kristall TEFL certificate. Participants will find work in the UK either privately or in institutions. Work abroad has always been a main attraction in Spain, Thailand, Japan, France and other countries.

Kristall also provides English language tuition on a homestay basis close to the ancient Welsh capital of Carmarthen, situated in 13 acres of hillside with picturesque rivers and close to sandy beaches. Specialist tuition is available on a one-to-one or small group basis.

For more information, call 01994 231145 (24 hours) or e-mail info@tefl-course.net (www.tefl-course.net).

CERTIFICATE COURSES

The most useful qualification for anyone intending to spend a year or more abroad as an English teacher is a Certificate in English language teaching validated by one of the two examination bodies active in the field of ELT: University of Cambridge ESOL Examinations and Trinity College London. The Certificate qualification is acquired after an intensive 120–130-hour course offered full-time over one month or part-time over several months.

Most centres expect applicants to have the equivalent of university entrance qualifications, i.e. three GCSEs and two A levels and some require a degree. Admission to the course is at the discretion of the course organiser after a sometimes lengthy selection process. Places on courses at the well-established centres may be difficult to get because of high demand, especially in summer, so early application is advised.

Applicants must be able to demonstrate a suitable level of language awareness and convince the interviewer that they have potential to develop as a teacher. Past academic achievement is less important than aptitude; even a PhD does not guarantee acceptance. Most schools will send you a task sheet or grammar research activity as part of the application. Sample questions might be 'How would you convey the idea of regret to a language learner?' or 'Describe the difference in meaning between "I don't really like beetroot" and "I really don't like beetroot"'.

Courses are not cheap but should be viewed as an investment and a potential passport to a worthwhile profession in many different countries. In fact, prices have not risen much over the past few years, with many centres trying to survive amid keen competition. The range is about £900 to £1,200 for a full-time course. Most centres include the validation body's fee, variously called assessment, moderation or examination fee, which in 2010 was £110 for Trinity, and just over £100 for Cambridge, though potentially quite a bit more (e.g. €250) for courses abroad.

Many colleges of further education offer the Trinity or Cambridge certificate part-time and these are usually less expensive. Timetables for part-time courses vary, but the norm is to attend classes one or two evenings a week for one or two terms of the academic year plus occasional full days for teaching observation and practice. Once accepted onto a certificate course, you will usually be given a pre-course task to familiarise yourself with some key concepts and issues before the course begins. Full-time courses are very intensive and 100% attendance is expected, so you need to be in a position to dedicate yourself completely to the task in hand for four weeks. The standard of teaching is high, the course rigorous and demanding and the emphasis is on the practice of any theory taught. One of the requirements is that participants teach a minimum of six hours of observed lessons to authentic English language students.

Trinity's CertTESOL and the Cambridge CELTA are accredited by the UK Qualifications and Curriculum Authority, the national body for the regulation of vocational qualifications outside the higher education sector. On the National Qualifications Framework both certificates have recently been upgraded from a level 4 to a level 5, which is considered equivalent in difficulty to the second year of an undergraduate degree course.

International House Barcelona

I had been working for several years as a massage therapist in London, and I really wanted to expand upon my teaching qualifications and experience in another field. Several of my friends were working as English Teachers in Spain at the time, and they suggested I look into getting a qualification in English Teaching.

It was one of the best decisions I ever made in my life!

I took my time researching various language academies and institutes, in a number of cities across Europe. International House (IH) in Barcelona ticked all the boxes - I love Spain, and had been to Barcelona several times on holiday (what an amazing city it is!).

IH offers a superb training in English Teaching, and is authorized and accredited to run the Cambridge University teaching diplomas (CELTA and DELTA) - internationally recognized, and respected as one of the best qualifications around.

The course provided everything I was hoping for, and more. At IH, they not only tutor you in becoming an English Teacher, but they also help to instill and nurture an invaluable set of skills around group facilitation and training delivery.

From Day One, I felt supported and encouraged to learn, grow and evolve as a teacher. The tutors were enthusiastic, knowledgeable, happy to help and advise, and provided informed and invaluable insights into our Teaching Practice sessions. Our fellow trainee teachers were also a great source of inspiration - we were encouraged to observe each other and offer both motivational and developmental feedback to one another. We also learned how to "reflect" objectively upon our own Teaching Practice sessions, and how to bring awareness and sensitivity to the preparation and planning of our lessons. Creativity, integrity and authenticity were encouraged at every moment, and I loved the fact that the course focused our awareness on the needs of the students, as well as the skills of the teacher - a lesson for life.

Because of the high regard held world-wide for the CELTA, I had offers of work almost straight away, as did most of my fellow trainees. I now live in Spain, and am thoroughly enjoying teaching English in Barcelona.

Thank you International House!

Mark

Norwich Institute for Language Education

Do you want to travel the world?

Just graduated and wondering what to do? Thinking of a mid-life career change? A CELTA course could be the answer. If travel broadens the mind, then living and working as a teacher in another country opens the mind - to other people, other ways of life and other languages. The global spread of English provides the ideal opportunity not just for travel but for a deeper engagement in another culture.

What is CELTA?

If you look at advertisements in the educational press, you'll see that CELTA is a passport to teaching posts all over the world. After a year or two of teaching English in Spain or Korea or Costa Rica, many former CELTA trainees move on to non-teaching jobs, but the experience they have gained stays with them, to say nothing of the transferable skills they have acquired in the classroom. For others, CELTA proves to be the gateway to successful careers in English language teaching as Directors of Studies, textbook writers or teacher trainers.

Some advertisements claim that you can learn to teach English on a weekend course. Of course this isn't possible, but the CELTA course (usually a highly intensive four weeks) can equip you with the confidence, resources and resourcefulness that you'll need to stand up in front of a class - and then to continue learning how to teach. CELTA is the most widely recognised initial training course for teachers of English as Foreign Language (EFL). The general aim of CELTA is to develop basic practical awareness - a combination of language awareness and classroom skills. It's a full-time commitment for four weeks, but a really worthwhile investment.

CELTA at NILE

NILE, the only CELTA centre in East Anglia, has been delivering CELTA courses since 2006, with a 99% pass rate. We receive regular updates from former trainees, who keep us informed about the travel and experience they have enjoyed since doing the course. Here's a typical example: 'I don't know how to express my feelings to thank you for your attention and support! I do admire the professional staff at NILE. I was really lucky to spend the whole month growing with professionals.'

CAMBRIDGE CELTA

Cambridge CELTA (Certificate in English Language Teaching to Adults) has established itself as the passport to teaching opportunities overseas. It has a rock-solid reputation in the international teaching community and high levels of recognition among employers around the world. CELTA is administered and regulated by University of Cambridge ESOL Examinations (Cambridge ESOL, 1 Hills Road, Cambridge CB1 2EU; 01223 553355; ESOLHelpdesk@CambridgeESOL.org; www.cambridgeESOL. org) and is sometimes referred to simply as the Cambridge Certificate. Many believe that CELTA is the most reliable route to jobs with better rates of pay and with employers who are willing to give more support to novice teachers.

You don't have to stay in the UK to take CELTA. Administered and regulated by University of Cambridge ESOL Examinations, CELTA courses are offered at more than 280 centres worldwide. For example, the British Council runs courses in Milan, Naples, Kuwait, Kiev, Dhaka, Mumbai, Casablanca and many others; CELTA courses are offered by 17 centres in Australia, nine in New Zealand and holding steady in North America so that there are now nine CELTA course providers in the USA and six in Canada. A full list is available at the Cambridge ESOL website – www.CambridgeESOL.org/teaching.

Securing a place on a CELTA course isn't automatic. Course providers are selective in order to ensure standards are kept high – and as a result, the pass rate is usually at least 90%. Grades available are Pass, Pass 'B' and Pass 'A', giving candidates the chance to distinguish themselves. CELTA provides a foundation of theory but focuses on effective teaching skills and practical tools for teaching English to adult learners. You'll gain hands-on teaching practice and the experience and support to build confidence in the classroom.

Many teachers believe that a CELTA plus some teaching experience is the perfect recipe for securing a good teaching job, as **Doug Burgess** wrote while teaching in Chile:

If you are interested in job security and acquiring a work visa, it is highly advisable that you complete the CELTA and try to get some experience as it will give you flexibility and options when you are here so that you can have the most comfortable and enjoyable time possible.

Some people have voiced surprise that a course which qualifies people to teach only adults is still so dominant, when much of the demand for English comes from young learners. Cambridge ESOL also offers an equivalent course for people who want to teach young learners – CELTYL (Certificate in English Language Teaching to Young Learners) at a selected number of centres in the UK and abroad.

TRINITY COLLEGE LONDON

The other principal initial Certificate in TESOL is awarded by Trinity College London (89 Albert Embankment, London SE1 7TP; 020 7820 6100; tesol@trinitycollege.co.uk; www.trinitycollege.co.uk). When job details in this book and elsewhere say 'Cambridge or equivalent', they are referring primarily to the Trinity qualifications, which are regarded as having equal academic standing. The Trinity Certificate (CertTESOL) has international recognition and is highly regarded by employers in the UK and around the world. Currently there are more than 100 centres worldwide offering CertTESOL training full or part-time. Nearly a third are outside the UK, with four centres in Spain and New Zealand and centres in other countries such as Canada, Hong Kong, Czech Republic, Hungary, Ireland, Italy, Japan and Uruguay.

Trinity stipulates a minimum of 130 hours offered intensively over a minimum of four and often five weeks or part-time over a longer period. All intensive courses must have a pre-course learning component in addition to the minimum hours. The course content includes grammar and phonology, a range of teaching approaches and methodologies, classroom management and motivation, hands-on experience of teaching aids (from blackboards to computers), introduction to the learning of an unknown language (in which trainees receive four hours' instruction and lesson planning). In addition, they must complete a minimum of six hours of observed and assessed teaching practice and spend at least four further hours observing experienced teachers of English.

The CertTESOL is accepted by the British Council as an appropriate initial TESOL qualification in its accredited English language teaching organisations in the UK and its own teaching centres overseas. All courses meet the core Trinity requirements but there are variations in course delivery across the different providers to reflect the best of their in-house practice and philosophy. Trinity

Trinity College London

Pippa remembers her time at Trinity College London:

I got good grades for my four A-levels and wanted to take a year out abroad. I did some research on the net – found out a bit about teaching English ('TESOL') – but realised that a weekend course wouldn't be cheap, or actually give me the qualification for a decent job. I looked into online teacher training – but I really wanted the experience of meeting other would-be teachers and experienced trainers.

I therefore chose a 5-week intensive Trinity CertTESOL course – I could have done it part-time, but I was in a hurry! I was warned about how very intensive it would be – how I should tell my friends that I'd be really busy for five weeks... and sure enough when I was accepted for the course I had to start reading straightaway and some written tasks to complete beforehand.

The course itself was an extraordinary experience. I started (and finished!) by feeling very enthusiastic and energetic. There were written assignments ('journals') to prepare over the four weeks and I was corrected on my grammar, punctuation and spelling, which was a surprise at first. I had to plan my time carefully – what I would do in the evenings and at the weekend, how much I could read. The most demanding but exciting part was the teaching practice with real students from different nationalities. It had never occurred to me I would feel so nervous. The first time I stood up in front of them I realised they expected to learn something from me, and I kept forgetting that there was no point in explaining difficult words or ideas in English – I had to learn very specific techniques to teach my own language.

Overall...

- My own communication skills improved enormously.
- My students were very kind and I learnt to respect their feelings.
- The other trainees were (all bar one) very supportive.
- I learnt to manage a heavy workload, and my own time, in and out of school.
- I feel I developed as a teacher and as a person – all in 5 weeks!

also works closely with QuiTE – Quality in TESOL Education (www.quality-tesol-ed.org.uk) to ensure that its qualifications are in line with those of other comparable awarding bodies – principally Cambridge ESOL. The Trinity CertTESOL can also be taken as an integral module within a bachelor's degree programme at some universities such as Central Lancashire (Preston) and the Open University.

CHOOSING A COURSE

It is up to prospective trainees to weigh up the pros and cons of the courses available to them and to establish how rigorously each course under consideration is monitored. One reservation that a few employers abroad have expressed is that the proliferation of providers of certificate courses, whether on behalf of Cambridge, Trinity or independents, has made it more difficult to maintain a uniform standard, especially since so much of the assessment of candidates is subjective. The general de-

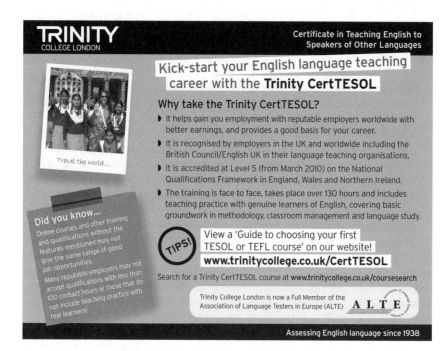

cline in standards of literacy in Britain and North America has also prompted some to complain of a decline in quality of TEFL training.

When it comes to workload, trainees in both CELTA and Trinity TESOL courses complain of a punishing schedule. But most come away claiming that the course elements are superb. At the time, participants sometimes feel as though they are drowning in information, but realise that the course has to pack a great deal of material into four brief weeks. When trying to identify differences between them, one view is that the CELTA concentrates more on the structure of language and classroom management, and Trinity on the use of authentic materials and practical teaching techniques. The majority who go on to teach abroad are very grateful for the training it gave them, as in the case of **Andrew Sykes**, teaching in Bordeaux:

> *As for the certificate course that I did at Leeds Metropolitan University, it was certainly one of the most stimulating, challenging and interesting things I have ever studied for. Initially I felt a bit out of place – I had a background of science A levels, a maths degree and 2 years as a (failed) accountant. The course was professionally run and there were good teacher-student relations. Most people had never taught anybody anything before in their life, but we were gradually eased into teaching by the supportive teaching staff who were refreshingly (and diplomatically) critical when required to be. A criticism which some students had was that there wasn't enough feedback about what was expected to gain a pass, let alone achieve an A or B. The best recommendation for the course is perhaps that I would never have felt comfortable teaching without it.*

So even if your social life disappears for a month and all you can talk about at weekends is phrasal verbs and English idioms, the consensus is that it is worthwhile.

Many certificate courses are offered by independent companies outside the Cambridge and Trinity folds and these are more difficult to assess. For many, one of the key factors will be cost. Generic certificate courses are available in dozens of countries and the cheapest ones are offered in the cheapest countries. **James Clarke** and his girlfriend **Sally** were looking for a course for under $1,000 inclusive in South America and ended up at one in Peru, which has since gone out of business, though that did not prevent them for thinking it gave them a good grounding:

We took (and both passed) a TEFL training course in Trujillo Peru which cost $900 for 4 weeks including a homestay and all food – much cheaper than anywhere in Buenos Aires where we had been before. It was a very good experience, with only one other student on the course, unlike a rival course we observed in Cusco, Peru, where there were maybe 14 students. Every day of the first week we observed 4 hours of classes (with participation) as well as 4 hours of theory from 9am to 1pm. The 2nd week, the observation turned into actual teaching of the classes with the same theory lessons. The 3rd week was observation of a higher standard of classes and then the 4th week was teaching, but 4 hours per day instead of 2 hours in the 2nd week. We taught grammar, conversation and pronunciation, all using games, activities, dynamics and motivational techniques using music. There was one drawback which we suspect was down to the price of the course – we did not receive any original textbooks, just photocopied pages from textbooks.

Possible advantages of doing a TEFL training course abroad are that you may already be teaching or living in that country and want to upgrade your qualifications locally; the course and cost of living may be cheaper than in your home country; and successful course participants will almost certainly be put in touch with local employers, making it much easier to land a job in that place.

Teaching practice is key. Busy colleges such as Ealing, Hammersmith and West London College offer an insight into the diversity of ELT work because they teach such a wide range of students, to whom their CELTA trainees are exposed during teaching practice sessions.

OTHER RECOGNISED QUALIFICATIONS

In 2005, Cambridge ESOL introduced the Teaching Knowledge Test (TKT), a new accessible test about teaching English to speakers of other languages, delivered to international standards. The test, which can be taken by both practising and aspiring teachers, involves three modules that cover the background to language learning and teaching, planning lessons/using resources and managing the teaching and learning process. TEFL training centres worldwide are offering short courses to candidates who want to prepare for TKT, which is more accessible than CELTA and does not include teaching practice as part of the assessment. A new module of interest to current teachers with no formal qualifications is called TKT Practical which requires no course work but an assessment of practical teaching abilities. Further information is available at www.cambridgeesol.org/TKT.

Beyond CELTA is the Diploma. Whereas CELTA is considered an initial qualification, the Diploma (as distinct from any old diploma with a lower case) is an in-service course for experienced English language teachers. The Cambridge Diploma in English Language Teaching to Adults (DELTA) and the Trinity Diploma (Dip TESOL) are high-level qualifications usually open to graduates who have at least two years of recent ELT classroom experience. The Diploma course is available intensively over a minimum of eight weeks but more usually part-time over several months or a year. A Distance DELTA option supported by International House (IH) and the British Council is increasingly popular (www.the-distancedelta.com) because it can be combined with full-time teaching work. The fees of £2,200 are sometimes subsidised by employers. DTE(E)LLS focuses on teaching English as a second language and replaces the Cambridge ESOL Certificate in Further Education Teaching.

Universities (especially the former polytechnics) from Brighton to Belfast offer their own certificate or diploma in TEFL. Most are one- or two-year courses, full or part-time, and tend to be more theoretical than Cambridge and Trinity courses. It is important to do some research before committing yourself to a course so that you are sure that the qualification you obtain will be recognised by employers both in the UK and overseas. Once again find out if there is some form of external assessment and whether the course includes a reasonable amount of teaching practice.

Stephen Curry felt let down by the course he chose:

> *I called my local university to see what courses were available and was advised that they could provide a course consisting of two modules, one from the PGCE and one from the MEd programme which would be equivalent in status to a one-month certificate and would be 'recognised'. The course of study took from May to February to complete. It was a lot of hard work, research based and absolutely no fun whatsoever. I did the course on the understanding that it would lead to a stand-alone TEFL certificate. I have since tried to get the university to confirm in writing that this module carries the recognition they claimed it would but they now say that they cannot do this. Unfortunately it was not until the latter stages of the course that I (and others) began to see that the eventual outcome would be a qualification that was unlikely to be recognised in the eyes of anyone outside the university, let alone as being equivalent to the Cambridge/Trinity certificate.*

A number of undergraduate institutions offer TESL as part of an undergraduate course; the weighty *UCAS Handbook* lists all university courses in the UK and can be consulted online at www.ucas.com, or in any careers or general library. MA courses in ELT and Applied Linguistics are offered at dozens of universities and colleges. Some offer a master's by distance learning aimed at practising ELT teachers worldwide. Arguably, there is a world oversupply of MAs, however, an MA is a pre-requisite for many posts in some countries, especially in the Middle East.

INTRODUCTORY COURSES

Although the Cambridge and Trinity certificates are sometimes referred to as 'introductory courses', there are many cheaper, shorter and less rigorous introductions to the subject. With the dramatic rise in the popularity of certificate courses there has been a decline in what might be considered as more amateurish courses, though these do have a role to play, for example for school leavers who would not be accepted onto a Certificate course or for the curious who do not want to commit themselves to a month-long course or pay £900.

Because there are some commercial enterprises and 'cowboy' operators cashing in on the EFL boom, standards vary and course literature should be studied carefully before choosing. Most people who have done a TEFL training course claim that the most worthwhile part is the actual teaching practice, preferably to living breathing foreigners rather than 'peer-teaching' in mock lessons to fellow participants. The fact is that most short introductory courses do not allow for much chance to do teaching practice. On the other hand they can provide lots of original lesson ideas and some hand out useful manuals full of lesson plans. The more upmarket introductory courses often present themselves as an opportunity to sample the field to see whether you want to go on to do a certificate course at a later stage. Others make their course sound as if it alone will be sufficient to open doors worldwide. It would be unreasonable to expect a weekend or five-day course to equip anyone to teach, but most participants do find them helpful. After seeing an advertisement in the New York subway advertising for English teachers, **Roger Blake** was prompted to seek out some training. Back in England, Roger, who admits to being a not particularly academic type, enjoyed the 'crash' weekend training he did with i-to-i so much that he enrolled in a home-study module of a further 20 hours. Later when he was asking about local teaching possibilities at the British Council in Addis Ababa, he felt more confident being able to show two course certificates.

The majority of residential courses last a weekend or for four to five days and cost between £200 and £500, not counting accommodation. Almost all will issue some kind of certificate which can sometimes be used to impress prospective employers. Anyone who wants a job after doing a short course should aim to do it in the spring when the majority of jobs are advertised for the following academic year. Many people who complete an introductory or 'taster' course go on to do an intensive certificate, often at the same centre.

A number of private language centres offer their own short courses in TEFL, which may focus on their own method, developed specifically with the chain of schools in mind (for example Berlitz) or may offer a more general introduction.

Anyone who wishes to specialise in the highly marketable field of Business English should enquire about specialist courses such as the Further Certificate for Teachers of Business English (FCTBE) validated by the London Chamber of Commerce & Industry (LCCI) and offered by several companies involved in this market, such as Inlingua Teacher Training in Cheltenham.

TEFL England

ODLQC accredited; SQA Approved; ILA Approved

TEFL England is one of the foremost providers of TEFL courses and because it is run by experienced TEFL professionals, you can be sure that the advice you receive is sound. TEFL England runs a range of TEFL courses to suit the individual and you can mix short classroom courses with more intensive online courses providing you with the certification and training you need to get started in TEFL. Classroom courses are available over weekends and during the week at locations throughout England. TEFL England also provides a FREE job service, giving you over-the-phone careers advice and contacts in countries worldwide. Check the website for latest vacancies and opportunities (0871 221 8335; info@teflengland.co.uk; www.teflengland.co.uk).

DISTANCE LEARNING

Some practising teachers of English who want to obtain a qualification are attracted to the idea of self-study by distance learning, partly because it will be cheaper than a conventional course and because it can be done in the candidate's own time and/or in any part of the world. Course providers are making increased use of electronic communications, doing away not only with the necessity of having physical access to a training course but of being dependent on the post, often unreliable in distant parts of the world. Some companies are delivering complete courses online, for example i-to-i, which for some years has been offering intensive weekend courses around the UK (www.onlinetefl.com).

Typically, distance courses at the professional end of the spectrum involve at least 150 hours of home study. Some 'hybrid' courses offer distance learning in combination with a residential element. A new entrant to the profession is faced with a bewildering array of distance courses to choose from but does not always possess the knowledge or experience to judge between them.

University of Manchester

The School of Education at the University of Manchester in the UK was one of the first university departments in the world to offer a professional qualification in TESOL, which it began back in 1962. At that time it was a diploma, but a master's qualification soon followed. The courses have always been influential and innovative, and since the 1980s the degree has been offered both as on-site and as a distance learning version. The university prides itself on the reflective approach that is developed at Manchester and its courses are designed for people who want to progress in their profession – those who may have had a number of years of experience and are now seeking new ways of working, new ways of engaging in their practice. Graduates from these courses may continue as class teachers, but many go on to take other roles in the profession including design, book publishing, running their own schools, researching and other roles.

A further aspect of the courses at Manchester is their engagement with a wide variety of new technologies in education. These feature very strongly in the MA in Educational Technology and TESOL, but are also a required component on the MA TESOL in which all students take at least one baseline module in this area. Other features of the courses include modules in the field of intercultural language education, the psychology of language education and teacher education. Manchester also believes that its assessment processes reflect good practice in the field, and, as well as writing essays about their own teaching, course participants are also asked to do presentations and engage in enquiry-based learning. Quite often coursework ends up being published in a variety of different places.

Whether you choose to study face to face at Manchester or in context via distance learning, the coverage of subjects and topic areas are the same and the university increasingly brings its on-site and distance students together using a range of educational technologies. The students consider the uses of technology in teaching very innovative. All of the members of the academic staff are active in the profession, attending conferences, being active in teacher organisations like IATEFL and TESOL as well as more specialist organisations such as EuroCALL. For more information on the range of activities and publications, visit the Manchester Uni blog: http://edtechandttesol.info.

A number of accrediting bodies and monitoring organisations exists, but competition between them does not make the task much easier. It is strongly recommended that you ensure that the certificate course for which you are applying is accredited by an independent body, for example ODLQC (Open & Distance Learning Quality Council; www.odlqc.org.uk), which was originally set up by the UK government in 1968 but is now independent.

As a part of the general move within the profession to monitor standards and offer assurances of quality, the College of Teachers (www.collegeofteachers.ac.uk) is an important awarding body though recently some TESOL distance course providers have changed their allegiance.

The International Accreditation of TESOL Qualifying Organisations (IATQuO) is another monitoring organisation, which has been run by an individual in Bristol since 2005 and is gradually expanding its inspection role; details from IATQuO (Park View, Alveston Road, Bristol BS32 4PH; ADMoller@aol.com; www.iatquo.org).

ACTDEC, the Accreditation Council for TESOL Distance Education Courses, was established in 1993 to improve on standards of distance TESOL/TEFL programmes. A copy of the ACTDEC code of practice and other details, including a list of accredited members can be viewed online at www.ACTDEC.org.uk.

A NOTE ABOUT ACCREDITATION

Various accrediting bodies boldly display their logos on the websites of various course providers. It is always a wise precaution to investigate as deeply as possible. In some cases providers of distance learning courses club together to set up their own agency to accredit their own courses. In other cases, providers need only pay a subscription fee to be 'accredited' without any process of impartial inspection. Another trick is that some dodgy schools falsely claim to be accredited by a certain body. For example IATQuO publishes a list of companies making fraudulent claims (www.iatquo.org/LIST.htm). So it is prudent to be sceptical.

People considering the distance learning route to TEFL training should be cautious. The most obvious disadvantage is the lack of face-to-face teaching practice, though some courses do provide opportunities for blocks of teaching practice and others provide plenty of tutor feedback. A new development for the distance student of TESOL is that they may be able to get actual teaching practice online or via Skype. If you are not satisfied with the course but have paid your money (typically £400+ for a certificate course), you have little recourse. One way of ascertaining the worth of a distance learning course you may be considering is to ask to be put in touch with past students. For example, Global English asks its students to complete appraisal forms, many of which are very positive, such as this one filled out by **Glyn Askey** from Yorkshire:

> *Having had an interest in TEFL for some time, I required a course which would give me an insight into TEFL at an affordable cost. I found that the Global English course made you think from the outset about your students, your lesson planning and the methods of teaching... A well put together course and positive friendly feedback.*

Details of introductory, internet and distance training courses both in Britain and abroad are provided in the Directory of Training Courses which follows.

TRAINING IN THE USA

Most TESL training in the USA is integrated into university degree courses in Applied Linguistics at both the undergraduate and graduate levels. Until a decade or two ago, there were virtually no short intensive courses in TEFL available in North America. That has now changed. In addition to the Cambridge centres in the USA, there are a number of independent TEFL training organisations offering four-week intensive courses (see Directory of Training Courses below). The major providers like Transworld are well connected with language schools abroad (particularly in Latin America and the Far East). Competition is keen among the schools, and prices fairly consistent at about $2,300–$2,800 for a four-week course, with the odd course available for less than $2,000.

The American Language Institute in San Diego has been praised by its graduates, like **Bryson Patterson** writing from Costa Rica:

> *The amTEFL course is a solid teacher training programme encompassing methodology, live classroom practice, grammar and job placement. A day at the amTEFL begins with four hours of methodology (the theory and practice of second language acquisition). Trainees are then instructed in the ins and outs of lesson planning, and annual planning. Mock classes are video taped, helping students to evaluate their own performance. Afternoons are spent working as assistants for mentor teachers in live EFL classrooms and rotating through all the levels of EFL classes at the ALI.*

If one of your main criteria is the after-course job advice, make sure you investigate properly. **Melanie Twinning** felt let down by the choice she made:

> *Despite being at least $1,000 more expensive than the competition, the course I chose really didn't do everything they promised. They have really no job placement to speak of and the man in charge of job placement is actually rather mean. Luckily I had your book and a bit of confidence and was able to find positions on my own but if you're paying $3,000 for a TEFL course I think you should get what they promise. I have to say the course itself was incredibly well done and the director is phenomenal. They just won't help you at all unless you are going to Korea.*

Increasingly, American universities and colleges are offering intensive TESL training including one-semester courses. It is easier to get practical experience of teaching English (without a qualification) by joining one of the many voluntary ESL programmes found in almost every American city, run by community colleges, civic organisations and literacy groups. For a first hand account see the chapter on North America at the end of this book. ProLiteracy Worldwide (www.proliteracy.org) operates in most states and offers volunteer tutors a 12-hour tutor training workshop and publishes specialist ESL materials.

ESLFocus.com

Catering to ESL/EFL/TESOL professionals, students, teachers, travelers, job-hunters, writers, and organizations, ESLFocus.com is the most comprehensive ESL and travel magazine on-line. While centered on a library of premium-quality, original editorials and articles unavailable elsewhere, the site hosts enhanced features, among them a full-featured ESL Job Board, a comprehensive Worldwide Directory of ESL organizations and institutes numbering over ten thousand, and a large, full-featured reader Forum.

The site's centerpiece is its growing library of original articles written by experts and teachers from around the world, which include valuable up-to-date information on topics ranging from current TESOL practices to casual trips abroad with a TESOL theme to current events of interest to the industry and casual reader alike. A regularly updated front page roster of headline links keeps readers in touch with ESL around the world, and an ESL and travel links feature points readers to news, educational, and community websites of interest to the site's demographic.

ESLFocus.com also hosts a Resources channel hosting content ranging from lesson planning to travel tips, and the site solicits and accepts independent content, whether as press release, resource, teaching asset or editorial article. A Store advises prominent independent ESL resources available from popular sources, and a community ESL Wiki is planned to open at the site later in 2010.

ESLFocus.com is the most comprehensive single source for such a wide variety of quality content – for the first time, readers have access to a Directory of schools and colleges world-wide and an indexed, searchable, global ESL Job Bank at the same site they can consume original, premium content on the ESL and travel experience. ESLFocus seeks user participation on a variety of levels, and parties are encouraged to make contact to learn more. Writers are especially encouraged to participate and may contact the site in order to arrange an introduction and discuss remuneration.

The ESL industry and public are encouraged to visit and all standard features come free of any charge. Organizations may create a simple log-in account and post details of their school or firm in the Worldwide Directory, and place their help-wanted advertisements – presently free of charge up to four listings – in the Job Board, currently listing nearly six hundred advertisements.

The site also includes an RSS feed, and accepts paid advertiser banners in all common sizes and types. Interested parties are encouraged to contact jhlane@eslfocus.com. Visit ESLFocus.com today for more.

DIRECTORY OF TRAINING COURSES

CAMBRIDGE CERTIFICATE (CELTA) COURSES IN THE UK

ACTION ENGLISH LANGUAGE TRAINING LLP: Leeds; ✆ 0113 244 9403; www.aelt.co.uk; full-time; rough frequency 12 per year.

Action English

Action English is a small and friendly training centre in the heart of Leeds which runs TEFL training courses leading to the internationally recognised Cambridge CELTA qualification. It offers four-week, intensive CELTA courses throughout the year, and a part-time course which runs from September to March. It can also prepare teachers for TKT and provide short, tailored courses for overseas teachers. Accommodation is available locally in self-catering flats or in a home stay.

A relatively new school, Action English takes a fresh, personal approach to training and teaching. The owner-directors, Sarah and Claire, bring years of experience to their training programmes, having worked overseas and in various institutions in the UK including higher education. They have established good contacts with local EFL and ESOL employers, and many ex-trainees have found work in the region, though most prefer to teach abroad. In recent years, they have found jobs as diverse as working with Voluntary Service Overseas, teaching children in a missionary school in Sri Lanka and teaching English for Academic Purposes in a Chinese university.

As well as TEFL courses, Action English caters for English language learners. It offers general English at various levels, IELTS preparation and tailored English classes for small groups and one-to-one clients. Some of these classes are now being taught by 'graduates' from Action English CELTA courses. There are also classes for beginners and learners with literacy needs: these are taught by volunteer teachers, many of whom have also trained on Action English CELTA courses.

As for the quality of the courses, feedback from course members speak for itself:

A well organized course run by absolute professionals!

(November 2009)

It was a very intense experience but very beneficial. Thank you for the very good tutoring and all your effort!

(January 2010)

I think your teaching and your commitment to teaching is of the very highest standard I've come across and I want to thank you for the huge effort you've put into this - thanks for an excellent course!

(April 2010)

ANGLIA RUSKIN UNIVERSITY: Cambridge; ✆ 01223 363271; www.anglia,ac.uk.

ANGLO-CONTINENTAL TEACHER TRAINING CENTRE: Bournemouth; ✆ 01202 557414; www.anglo-continental.com; full and part-time; rough frequency 5 per year.

BASIL PATERSON COLLEGE: Edinburgh; ✆ 0131 225 3802; www.basilpaterson.co.uk; full-time; rough frequency 8 per year.

BELFAST METROPOLITAN COLLEGE: Belfast; ✆ 028 9026 5142; www.belfastmet.ac.uk; part-time; rough frequency 2 per year.

BELL LANGUAGE SCHOOL: Cambridge; ✆ 01223 278804; www.bell-centres.com/celta. 3 full-time, £1150; Part-time course offered at Bedgebury, Kent.

BLACKBURN COLLEGE: Blackburn; ✆ 01254 292903; www.blackburn.ac.uk; part-time.

BOLTON COMMUNITY COLLEGE: Bolton; ✆ 01204 907333; www.bolton-community-college. ac.uk; part-time.

BRASSHOUSE CENTRE: Birmingham; ✆ 0121 3030114; www.birmingham.gov.uk/brasshouse; part and full-time; rough frequency 1 per year.

BRITISH STUDY CENTRES: Oxford; ✆ 01865 246620; full-time; rough frequency 12 per year.

BROMLEY COLLEGE OF FURTHER & HIGHER EDUCATION Bromley (Kent); ✆ 020 8295 7000, ext 7127; www.Bromley.ac.uk; part-time.

BROOKLANDS COLLEGE: Weybridge (Surrey); ✆ 01932 797774; www.brooklands.ac.uk; full and part-time; rough frequency 1 per year.

CANTERBURY CHRIST CHURCH UNIVERSITY: Canterbury; ✆ 01227 767700, ext 2129; www.canterbury.ac.uk; full and part-time; rough frequency 1 per year.

CARDIFF COLLEGE INTERNATIONAL: Cardiff; ✆ 02920 908033; www.glan-hafren.ac.uk; 1 full-time, 2 part-time per year; £1,200.

CILC (Cheltenham International Language Centre): Cheltenham (Gloucestershire); ✆ 01242 714092; www.glos.ac.uk/cilc; full-time; rough frequency 3 per year.

CITY COLLEGE HANDSWORTH: Birmingham; ✆ 0121 204 0000; www.citycol.ac.uk; part-time.

CITY OF BATH COLLEGE: Bath; ✆ 01225 312191; www.citybathcoll.ac.uk; Full-time in summer, and part-time, £1,155.

CITY OF BRISTOL COLLEGE: Bristol; ✆ 0117 312 5886; www.cityofbristol.ac.uk; part-time.

CONCORDE INTERNATIONAL STUDY CENTRE: Canterbury; ✆ 01227 451035; www. concorde-international.com; full-time, 6 per year.

EALING, HAMMERSMITH & WEST LONDON COLLEGE: London; ✆ 0800 980 2185/2175; www.wlc.ac.uk; Full-time 7 times a year and part-time.

EMBASSY CES NEWNHAM: Cambridge; ✆ 01223 345650; www.embassyces.com; Full-time; roughly 4 per year.

ENGLISH LANGUAGE HOUSE: Milton Keynes; ✆ 01908 694357; www.englishlanguagehouse. co.uk; full and part-time; rough frequency 5 per year.

GLOUCESTER COLLEGE: Cheltenham; ✆ 01242 532144; www.gloscat.ac.uk; full and part-time; rough frequency 2 per year.

GREENWICH COMMUNITY COLLEGE: London; ✆ 020 8316 6610; www.gcc.ac.uk; full and part-time; rough frequency 6 per year.

INTENSIVE SCHOOL OF ENGLISH & BUSINESS COMMUNICATION: Brighton; ✆ 01273 384800; www.ise.uk.com; full and part-time; rough frequency 5 per year.

INTERNATIONAL HOUSE BELFAST: ✆ 028 9033 0700; www.ihbelfast.com.

INTERNATIONAL HOUSE LONDON: London; © 020 7611 2414; www.ihlondon.com; full and part-time; rough frequency 11 per year.

International House London

Jessica Mendes Rego did her CELTA at IH London in January 2009.

After I graduated in 2007, I worked in finance in central London for two years. Despite the whole economic crisis and talk of how difficult it is for young people to find a job these days, I decided to quit my job and do my CELTA at International House. Bored of the office life and wanting something 'more', I decided to take the risk - a choice which I have no regrets about and which has proved to be one of the best decisions I have made in my life!

I truly enjoyed the CELTA. The course was really well-designed and organized, the tutors were extremely knowledgeable, helpful and fun, and overall it was a fantastic experience.

Throughout the course I discovered what it means to be a good teacher and how important it is to deliver high quality lessons to your students. The CELTA taught me how to prepare lessons adequately, manage my class effectively and deal with unexpected situations when teaching. I also became aware of the value of cooperation and teamwork, and I made some lifelong friendships during my time at IH London.

Having a CELTA resulted in lots of new opportunities in my life. Part of the fun after I'd qualified was spending time just hunting for jobs in exciting, faraway places - there are so many posts out there for English teachers and the CELTA is highly regarded anywhere in the world - the opportunities it provides are endless. It's the best qualification to have whether you simply want to travel and be a globe trotter for a while or whether you decide to make a career of it. It gives you choice - and that gives you freedom. I would recommend it to anyone!

Last October I took up a position teaching children in Taipei, Taiwan and what a fantastic experience it has been - and still continues to be! Taipei is a wonderful city and I am really enjoying my time here. Not only do I enjoy teaching English but I've also had the opportunity to do some travelling in Taiwan, learn Mandarin and become immersed in the Taiwanese culture, which is absolutely fascinating. I have also found that wherever you go there are foreigners doing the same as you and it is easy to make friends, which brings you 'a bit of home' - vital for keeping homesickness at bay!

Looking ahead to the future, I have also had job offers in Prague and Costa Rica and I am already excited about the prospect of teaching somewhere else in the world in the next few years...!

TRAINING

DIRECTORY OF TRAINING COURSES

INTERNATIONAL HOUSE NEWCASTLE UPON TYNE: Newcastle; © 0191 232 9551; www. ihnewcastle.com; full-time; rough frequency 6 per year.

International House Newcastle

I took the CELTA course in March 2010 at International House Newcastle. The course was an amazing opportunity to develop solid skills in teaching English to speakers of other languages. I found it incredibly intensive, but hugely rewarding. Teaching practice sessions began on the second day - and whilst this was at first a daunting prospect (!) - each lesson I taught provided a great learning experience - tutor and peer feedback was always very useful and it really felt like all students were making visible progress with each lesson they delivered.

The input sessions were always engaging and informative and gave invaluable insights into diverse aspects of teaching, covering everything from lesson planning, to learning styles, the role of the teacher to specific learner needs, to phonetics and alternative teaching approaches. The course tutors were really supportive but also very inspiring throughout the course. For me, this was the best learning experience I'd had in years.

Following the completion of the course I was offered a teaching position at International House, which I am really enjoying. I still often refer to my notes from the course throughout my teaching week - looking at everything from my own self-evaluation exercises, to individual input sessions on skills, grammar lessons, etc. The course tutors also made lots of recommendations for further reading - and I have found these books really useful now that I'm teaching full-time.

I have recently been offered a position at a language school overseas, and therefore had to give my first interview for a teaching position. Whilst some of the interview questions were challenging, I felt confident in talking about TEFL practice as I could continually draw upon my experience of the CELTA at IH Newcastle.

Hannah Barnes, Teacher

ITTC: Bournemouth; © 01202 397721; www.ittc.co.uk; full-time; rough frequency 12 per year; £1,187.

LANGUAGE LINK TRAINING: London; © 020 7370 4755; www.languagelink.co.uk; full and part-time; rough frequency 7 per year.

LTC ENGLISH ACADEMY: Hove (East Sussex); © 01273 735975; www.ltc-brighton.com; full-time; rough frequency 5 per year.

MANCHESTER ACADEMY TEACHER TRAINING (UK) LTD: Manchester; © 0161 2375619; www.manacad.co.uk; full and part-time; rough frequency 11 per year.

NEWCASTLE COLLEGE: Newcastle; © 0191 200 4467; www.ncl-coll.ac.uk; part-time.

NEW COLLEGE NOTTINGHAM: Nottingham; © 0115 910 4595; www.ncn.ac.uk; part-time. Also offers PTLLS (preparing to Teach in the Lifelong Learning Sector).

ITTC

I originally come from Canada, but came to England in 2002 and got work in an office. The monotony got to me and I searched around for a CELTA course and decided on ITTC. I'm glad I chose ITTC as the course was so practical and the tutors on the course were really good role models who tried to get the best out of everyone.

I was lucky to be offered work at BEET/ITTC straight after the course, and I worked the whole summer for them before I went to teach overseas. I've taught in private language schools, I've set up and organised English immersion camps for teenagers where I had to design the whole course as well as produce materials, I've worked in secondary schools overseas and also trained up to be an examiner for English language examinations. So far I've spent time in Switzerland, Italy and Colombia, and I come back to England regularly to work on summer programmes.

Having the CELTA has given me an opportunity to use my brain more than I ever did working in an office. I love working with people from different cultures, and it has also allowed me to learn other languages more easily. I still don't like being asked to teach areas I haven't been trained for and I'm not much of a disciplinarian - but this hasn't really been a problem, as my students always seem so motivated.

Lisa D - a not so average CELTA candidate wrote this while in Bournemouth, but who knows where she is now!

New College Nottingham

CELTA kick-starts Craig's career

A CELTA qualification can really improve your skills and increase your chances of employment, as **Craig** found out when he completed the intensive Cambridge CELTA/PTLLS course at New College Nottingham:

' I had taught conversational English classes in schools and businesses in Japan, but enrolled at New College Nottingham because I realised the need to gain a recognised qualification to build my TEFL career.

' It was the best move I have ever made. The course has brought so much to both my teaching and my career; I have learned how to plan and organise lessons, teaching techniques and methodologies, and have had the opportunity to observe experienced teachers in the classroom. I still use many of the techniques I learnt at college.

' Upon returning to Japan I felt energised and my teaching was much more effective. Teaching became enjoyable again.

' For anyone thinking about a career in TEFL/TESOL I cannot recommend the course at New College Nottingham more highly.'

For an information pack and application form call New College Nottingham on 0115 910 4595, email rose.underwood@ncn.ac.uk, or visit www.ncn.ac.uk

NILE: Norwich; ✆ 01603 664473; www.nile-elt.com; full-time; rough frequency 8 per year.

OXFORD AND CHERWELL VALLEY COLLEGE: Oxford; ✆ 01865 551828; www.ocvc.ac.uk/about-teacher-training; part and full-time; rough frequency 4 per year.

OXFORD HOUSE COLLEGE: London; ✆ 020 7580 9785; www.oxfordhousecollege.co.uk; part and full-time; rough frequency 12 per year.

RANDOLPH SCHOOL OF ENGLISH: Edinburgh; ✆ 0131 226 5004; www.randolph.org.uk; part and full-time; rough frequency 9 per year.

READING OPEN CENTRE: English Language & Teacher Training Centre, Reading (Berkshire); ✆ 0118 9391833; www.efl-reading.co.uk; semi-intensive; rough frequency 3 per year.

ST GILES INTERNATIONAL LONDON HIGHGATE: London; ✆ 020 8340 0828; www.stgiles-international.com/teacher-training; full-time; rough frequency 10 per year.

SAXONCOURT TEACHER TRAINING: London ✆ 020 7499 8533; www.saxoncourt.com; full and part-time; rough frequency 12 per year.

SKOLA TEACHER TRAINING: London; ✆ 020 7287 3126; www.skola.co.uk; Part-time; 3 times a year, £999.

SOLIHULL COLLEGE: Solihull; ✆ 0121 6787277; www.solihull.ac.uk; part-time.

SOUTH THAMES COLLEGE: London SW18; ✆ 020 8918 7366; www.south-thames.ac.uk; part-time.

STANTON TEACHER TRAINING: London; ✆ 020 7221 7259; www.stanton-school.co.uk; full-time; rough frequency 12 per year.

STEVENSON COLLEGE: Edinburgh; ✆ 0131 535 4600; www.stevenson.ac.uk; part-time.

STOKE-ON-TRENT COLLEGE: Stoke-on-Trent; ✆ 01782 603637; www.stokecoll.ac.uk; full-time; rough frequency 1 per year.

STUDIO SCHOOL: Cambridge; ✆ 01223 369701; www.studiocambridge.co.uk; full-time; rough frequency 2 per year.

SUSSEX DOWNS COLLEGE: Eastbourne; ✆ 01323 637232/08452 601608; www.sussex-downs.ac.uk; intensive course offered over 22 days in the summer; also part-time, £947.

TORBAY LANGUAGE CENTRE: Devon; ✆ 01803 558555; www.lalschools.com/torbay; full-time; rough frequency 5 per year; £1,100.

UNIVERSITY OF GLASGOW, EFL Unit: Glasgow; ✆ 0141 330 6521; www.gla.ac.uk/efl.

UNIVERSITY OF SHEFFIELD, ENGLISH LANGUAGE TEACHING CENTRE: Sheffield; ✆ 0114 222 1799; www.sheffield.ac.uk/eltc.

WALTHAM FOREST COLLEGE: London; ✆ 020 8501 8091; www.waltham.ac.uk; part-time.

WESTMINSTER KINGSWAY COLLEGE: London SW1; ✆ 020 7802 8813; www.westking. ac.uk; full-time; rough frequency 1 per year.

CAMBRIDGE CERTIFICATE (CELTA) COURSES ABROAD

The following centres, listed alphabetically by country, offer the Cambridge Certificate in English Language Teaching to Adults.

AUSTRALIA

AUSTRALIAN TESOL TRAINING CENTRE (ATTC): Sydney; ✆ 2 8252 2821; www.attc.edu.au; full and part-time; rough frequency 12 per year; also offered at ATTC Brisbane.

CURTIN UNIVERSITY: Perth; ✆ 8 9266 4224; www.celta.curtin.edu.au; full-time; rough frequency 2 per year.

HOLMESGLEN LANGUAGE CENTRE: Chadstone (Victoria); ✆ 3 9564 1819; www.holmesglen. vic.edu.au; full and part-time; rough frequency 4 per year.

HOLMES INSTITUTE TEACHER TRAINING: Melbourne; ✆ 3 9662 2055; www.holmesinstitute. edu.au; full-time; rough frequency 6 per year.

INSEARCH UNIVERSITY OF TECHNOLOGY, SYDNEY (UTS): Sydney; ✆ 2 9218 8646; www. insearch.edu.au/courses/celta; full and part-time; rough frequency 4 per year.

INSTITUTE OF CONTINUING & TESOL EDUCATION (ICTE): Brisbane; ✆ 7 3346 6770; www. icte.uq.edu.au; full and part-time; rough frequency 4 per year.

INTERNATIONAL HOUSE SYDNEY: Sydney; ✆ 2 9279 0733; www.training.ihsydney.com; 4 full-time courses per year, 3 part-time; A$2,700 plus $250 Cambridge assessment fee.

KAPLAN INTERNATIONAL COLLEGE: Cairns; ✆ 7 4031 3466; www.kaplaninternational.com; full-time; 3 times per year; A$2,750.

LA TROBE UNIVERSITY LANGUAGE CENTRE: Melbourne; ✆ 3 9479 1722; www.latrobe.edu. au; full-time; rough frequency 6 per year.

MILNER INTERNATIONAL COLLEGE OF ENGLISH: Perth; ✆ 8 9325 5444; www.milner. wa.edu.au/CELTA; full and part-time; rough frequency 6 per year.

PHOENIX ENGLISH LANGUAGE ACADEMY: Perth; ✆ 8 9227 5538; www.phoenixela.com.au; full-time; rough frequency 6 per year.

RMIT ENGLISH WORLDWIDE: Melbourne; ✆ 3 9657 5876; www.rmitenglishworldwide.com; full and part-time; rough frequency 3 per year.

SOUTH AUSTRALIAN COLLEGE OF ENGLISH (SACE Adelaide): Adelaide; ✆ 8 8410 5222; www.sacecoll.sa.edu.au; full-time; rough frequency 4 per year.

TASMANIAN COLLEGE OF ENGLISH (SACE Hobart and SACE Whitsunday): Tasmania; ✆ 3 6231 9911; www.tas.sace.com.au; full-time; rough frequency 4 per year.

UNIVERSITY OF TASMANIA ENGLISH LANGUAGE CENTRE: Hobart; ✆ 3 6226 2590; www. international.utas.edu.au; once a year full-time and part-time; A$2,500.

AUSTRIA

BFI VIENNA: Vienna; ✆ 1 811 78 10152; www.bfi.at/english/courses/celta; full-time 2 per year.

BANGLADESH

BRITISH COUNCIL BANGLADESH: Dhaka; ✆ 2 911 6171/6145; www.britishcouncil.org/bangladesh; full-time; rough frequency 1 per year.

BRAZIL

BRITANNIA INTERNATIONAL ENGLISH: Ipanema, Rio de Janeiro; ✆ 21 2511 0940; www.britannia.com.br; full-time and part-time; R$3,816 (£1,425).

S B C I RIO DE JANEIRO: Rio de Janeiro; ✆ 21 2528 1104; www.culturainglesa.net; full-time.

SEVEN ENGLISH: Sao Paulo; ✆ 2533 36111; www.sevenidiomas.com.br; full-time and part-time both twice a year; R$2,420 (US$1,320) plus US$160 Cambridge fee.

SOCIEDADE BRASILEIRA DE CULTURA INGLESA: Recife; ✆ 81 3228 6649; www.culturainglesa.com.br; full-time; rough frequency 1 per year; also offered in Rio, Tambauzinho and Mirrasol.

UP LANGUAGE CONSULTANTS: Terreo; ✆ 11 5105 0200; www.uplanguage.com.br; full-time.

BULGARIA

AVO-BELL SCHOOL OF ENGLISH: Sofia; ✆ +3592 943 00 68/+3592 943 3943; www.avo-bell.com; full-time; rough frequency 4 per year.

CANADA

GLOBAL VILLAGE: Calgary; ✆ 403 543 7300; www.celtacalgary.ca; full-time 3 times a year, part-time offered twice a year; C$2,500.

GLOBAL VILLAGE: Vancouver; ✆ 604 684 1010; www.gvenglish.com; part and full-time; rough frequency 6 per year.

INTERNATIONAL HOUSE: Toronto; ✆ 416 322 3405; www.sol-group.net; 3 part-time courses offered per year, C$2,500.

INTERNATIONAL LANGUAGE INSTITUTE: Halifax; ✆ 902 429 3636; teach@ili.ca; www.celta.ca; full-time monthly; C$2,300.

INTERNATIONAL LANGUAGE SCHOOLS OF CANADA – MONTREAL: Montreal; ✆ 514 876 4572; www.celta.ilsc.ca; full-time; rough frequency 6 per year.

LANGUAGE STUDIES CANADA: Toronto; ✆ 416 488 2200; www.lsc-canada.com; full-time; rough frequency 9 per year.

CHINA

INTENSIVE SCHOOL OF ENGLISH: Wuhan; see entry for ISE in listings of CELTA courses in the UK.

LANGUAGE LINK CHINA TRADE CENTER: Beijing; ✆ 10 5169 5591/92/93; www.language-link.com.cn; full-time; rough frequency 8 per year.

SYDNEY INSTITUTE OF LANGUAGE AND COMMERCE (SILC): Shanghai; ✆ 21 6998 0003; www.insearch.edu.au/international./silc; course run once a year in August by Insearch in Sydney (entry above).

COLOMBIA

BRITISH COUNCIL BOGOTÁ: Bogotá; ✆ +571 325 9090; www.britishcouncil.org/colombia; full-time; rough frequency 5 per year.

INTERNATIONAL HOUSE BOGOTÁ: Bogotá; ✆ 1 336 4747; www.ihbogota.com; full-time twice a year; $1,500.

COSTA RICA

INSTITUTO BRITANICO: San José; ✆ +506 283 7059 ext 110; www.institutobritanico.co.cr; full-time; rough frequency 3 per year.

CZECH REPUBLIC

AKCENT INTERNATIONAL HOUSE: Prague; ℭ 261109; www.akcent.cz; full and part-time; rough frequency 10 per year; also offered in Bratislava from time to time.
MASARYK UNIVERSITY: Brno; ℭ 549 497785; part-time.

ILC France-IH Paris

Lynsey Hodkinson from Perth (UK) Michael Gleeson from Christchurch (New Zealand) and Eleanor Hickey from Leeds (UK) did the CELTA course at ILC France-IH Paris, and now work at the school.

Why did you want to do the CELTA course?

Lynsey: The CELTA offered a well-rounded introduction to teaching English and the possibility to travel and work. The intensive element gave me confidence that can't be obtained through part-time or distance learning.
Michael: I had just left a career in the army in New Zealand and saw the CELTA as an opportunity for a new way of life in France.
Eleanor: I had some hands-on experience as an assistant teaching English to teenagers in France. I enjoyed it, but felt training was essential if I was to teach well.

Why did you choose to do the course at ILC France-IH Paris?

Lynsey: ILC France-IH Paris was my first choice; I wanted to teach abroad. Doing the course outside your own country shows prospective employers you can operate in a new environment.
Michael: I had heard of International House and felt confident that the course would be well run. The centre was situated in the heart of Paris too.
Eleanor: A friend had trained at ILC France-IH Paris & recommended it. I knew it would be challenging, but rewarding.

How did you benefit from the course?

Lynsey: I gained confidence, awareness and understanding of the English language and learnt different teaching methods.
Michael: The tutors had lots of experience to share and the course structure, with morning seminars and afternoon teaching practice, really helped learning.
Eleanor: I especially liked feedback immediately after teaching practice. It allowed all the trainees to develop their skills.

Who would you recommend to do the CELTA course?

Lynsey: I recommend the course to individuals who are thinking about travelling or relocating to another country, considering a career change or a new challenge.
Michael: I liked the fact that there were people from different backgrounds on the course, all really keen to learn and teach.
Eleanor: People who are genuinely interested in teaching and who recognise that it's a full-time job.

EGYPT

BRITISH COUNCIL: Cairo; ℭ 2 300 1666; www.britishcouncil.org/egypt; full-time; frequency 4 per year; 10,000 Egyptian pounds ($1,750/£1,200).

FRANCE

ILC FRANCE (INTERNATIONAL LANGUAGE CENTRE): Paris; ℭ 1 44 41 80 20; www.ilcfrance.com; full-time; rough frequency 9 per year.
TRANSFER: Paris; ℭ 1 42 66 14 11; www.transfer.fr; full-time; rough frequency 4 per year.

GERMANY

BERLIN SCHOOL OF ENGLISH: Berlin; ✆ 30 229 0456; www.berlin.school-of-english.de; 8 full-time per year and two part-time; €1,500.

HAMBURG SCHOOL OF ENGLISH: Hamburg; ✆ 40 480 21 19; www.hamburg.school-of-english.de; full and part-time 7 per year; €1,500.

MUNCHNER VOLKSHOCHSCHULE: Harthausen, Munich; ✆ 8106 300631; www.mvhs.de.celta; full and part-time; rough frequency 2 per year; €1,550.

GREECE

CELT: Athens; ✆ 210 330 2406; www.celt.edu.gr; €1,450; also offers its own certificate course.

STUDY SPACE: Thessaloniki; ✆ 2310 269697; www.studyspace.gr.

HUNGARY

INTERNATIONAL HOUSE: Budapest; ✆ 1 345 7046; www.ih.hu; full and part-time; 8 full-time, 2 part-time per year; £749–£849.

INDIA

THE BRITISH COUNCIL ENGLISH LANGUAGE TEACHING CENTRE: New Delhi; ✆ +91 11 4219 9000; www.britishcouncil.org/india; full-time 6 times a year, including those offered in Mumbai and Chennai; Rs105,000 (£1,550).

INDONESIA

THE BRITISH INSTITUTE (TBI): Jakarta; ✆ +62 21 300 27988; www.tbi.co.id; full and part-time; rough frequency 2 per year.

IRELAND

INTERNATIONAL HOUSE: Dublin; ✆ 1 4759011/1 4759013; www.ihdublin.com; 9 full-time and 1 part-time course; €1,610 full-time, €1,695 part-time.

UNIVERSITY COLLEGE CORK, Language Centre: Cork; ✆ 21 490 2043/490 3883; www.ucc.ie/Esol; part-time and one intensive course in August; €1,680.

ITALY

BRITISH COUNCIL: Milan; ✆ 02 772 22242; www.britishcouncil.it.

BRITISH COUNCIL: Naples; ✆ 081 578 82 47; www.britishcouncil.it; full-time; rough frequency 1 per year.

THE CAMBRIDGE SCHOOL: Verona; ✆ 045 800 3154; www.cambridgeschool.it; full and part-time; rough frequency 2 per year.

INTERNATIONAL HOUSE: Milan; ✆ 02 527 9124; www.ihmilano.it; full and part-time; rough frequency 2 per year.

INTERNATIONAL HOUSE PALERMO: Palermo; ✆ 091 584954; www.ihpalermo.it; full-time; rough frequency 1 per year.

INTERNATIONAL HOUSE ROME/ACCADEMIA BRITANNICA: Rome; ✆ 06 704 76 894; www.ihromamz.it; full-time and semi-intensive 6 per year.

TEACHERTRAINING: Milan; ✆ 328 887 3365; www.teachertraining.it; full and part-time; rough frequency 5 per year.

International House Rome and Palermo

Rome

I can tell you only positive things about the course. Personally, it gave me exactly what I needed: a lot of practical knowledge about teaching. That's the best thing about it, I think: it really enables you to perform in a classroom. It was hard work but all that stress that I was so worried about at the beginning was successfully relieved by our tutors' extremely professional and supportive attitude. Working in a small Teaching Practice group was a great experience as well. A little more teaching practice would have been fine as many of us had the impression of having to stop just when we started to enjoy teaching and feel more confident about it. Anyway, it was a wonderful experience, you all did an excellent job and all I can say is just carry on like this!

Viktoria Szabo, CELTA course, International House, Rome

Palermo

IH Palermo offers CELTA teacher training in a four-week intensive format, and is the first approved Cambridge ESOL centre in Sicily. IH Palermo has been offering the CELTA programme since 2002 and has the most cost-effective CELTA training in southern Italy. Each year it welcomes candidates from all over the world. Applicants have ranged in age from 20 to 70 and come from a variety of backgrounds - recent university graduates; individuals planning to teach and travel overseas; teachers looking to improve their teaching style and to add new skills to their repertoire; retired teachers seeking a challenge to win. The four-week Cambridge CELTA course is very intensive. The attendance requirement is 100% and in addition to the 10:00 to 18:00 workdays at International House Palermo, you will need most evenings and weekends for homework tasks, written assignments, lesson planning and preparation. The course is demanding and challenging, but most trainees enjoy and thrive on the work. As a CELTA trainee, you will be working in large, modern classrooms, and you will have access to a quiet workroom for lesson preparation and self-study. IH Palermo has materials for your exclusive use as a CELTA trainee, including a variety of up-to-date books on methodology, grammar, and activity books for use in the classroom. Additionally, you will have access to other areas open to students at International House Palermo, such as the recreation area and the computer laboratory. For more information, visit the IH website. Registrations are open for the CELTA course to be held in June 2011.

www.ihpalermo.it

JAPAN

LANGUAGE RESOURCES: Kobe; ✆ 78 382 0394; www.languageresources.org; part-time.

KOREA

THE BRITISH COUNCIL: Seoul; ✆ 2 3702 0646; www.britishcouncil.org/korea.htm; full-time; rough frequency 2 per year; 2,500,000 won (£1,375/$2,000).

LEBANON

ALLC INTERNATIONAL HOUSE BEIRUT: Beirut; ✆ 1 500 978; www.allcs.edu.lb; full-time; rough frequency 2 per year in the summer; $1,600.

Teachertraining.it

I came to the CELTA certification at teachertraining.it in Milan with a hopeful eye on the possibility of a new career. I left with the assurance of one. For this I offer my thanks to the team of tutors, each coming to the table with their own brilliant style of teaching and the generosity to share their methods. As teachers they bring an inexhaustible amount of patience, dedication and passion. As mentors they offer understanding, accessibility and encouragement. This, mixed with creativity, good humor and a contagious enjoyment of the work have made the training a truly life-changing experience.

Georgia Graham (USA)

After two great years working in publishing, I decided to take the plunge and fulfil a long term ambition and move to Italy to teach English. I was really excited about my career change and completing the course at teachertraining.it but I also felt nervous about whether I'd be able to teach and also whether I'd like it. From day one, I knew I'd made the right decision. The course at teachertraining.it was practical and very hands on. I learnt a huge amount on the course and I felt constantly challenged. The tutors were great and really knew how to get the best out of us. I would definitely recommend the teachertraining.it course to anyone who wants to teach English in Italy.

Caroline Jordan (UK)

I was working in a bank when I decided to do the CELTA course at teachertraining.it in Milan. It was a very enriching experience in all senses: international environment, professional and friendly tutors, realistic approach to teaching. We were given constant feedback on our progress that helped me reflect on my teaching and become more self-confident. I highly recommend it to everyone starting a career in teaching or looking for a career break like me.

Ileana Constantin (Romania)

MALAYSIA

THE BRITISH COUNCIL LANGUAGE CENTRE: Kuala Lumpur; ✆ 3 2723 7900; www.british-council.org/malaysia; Part-time over 20 weeks (every Sunday) or 10 weeks (Tuesdays and Thursdays); 8,000 ringgits (£1,660).

MALTA

NSTS ENGLISH LANGUAGE INSTITUTE: Valletta; +356 2558 8500; www.nsts.org; full-time; rough frequency 2 per year.

MOROCCO

BRITISH COUNCIL CASABLANCA: Casablanca; ✆ 22520990; www.britishcouncil.org/morocco-english-teach-celta.htm; full-time; rough frequency 1 per year; 2,100 dirhams (£1,570).

THE NETHERLANDS

BRITISH LANGUAGE TRAINING CENTRE: Amsterdam; ✆ 020 622 3634; www.bltc.nl; full and part-time; rough frequency 1 per year.
BRITISH SCHOOL NETHERLANDS: Den Haag; ✆ 070 315 40 80; www.britishschool.nl.

NEW ZEALAND

ASPECT EDUCATION: Christchurch; ✆ 3 379 5452; www.kaplanaspect.com; full-time: rough frequency 2 per year.

AUCKLAND LANGUAGE CENTRE: Auckland; ✆ 9 303 1962; www.learnenglish.co.nz; full-time; rough frequency 4 per year.

CHRISTCHURCH COLLEGE OF ENGLISH: Christchurch; ✆ 3 343 3790; www.ccel.co.nz; full-time; rough frequency 5 per year.

CHRISTCHURCH POLYTECHNIC INSTITUTE OF TECHNOLOGY: Christchurch; ✆ 3 940 8296; www.cpit.ac.nz; part-time.

LANGUAGES INTERNATIONAL: Auckland; ✆ 9 309 0615; www.languages.ac.nz; full-time; rough frequency 6 per year.

ROTORUA ENGLISH LANGUAGE ACADEMY: Rotorua; ✆ 7 349 0473; www.rela.co.nz; full-time; rough frequency 2 per year.

UNIVERSITY OF WAIKATO LANGUAGE INSTITUTE: Hamilton; ✆ 7 858 5600; www.waikato. ac.nz; full-time; rough frequency 4 per year.

OMAN

BRITISH COUNCIL OMAN: Qaboos; ✆ 2468 1000; www.britishcouncil.org/me-oman.

CALEDONIAN COLLEGE OF ENGINEERING: Seeb; ✆ 24536165 ext 376; www.cce.edu.om; full-time; rough frequency 2 per year.

POLAND

BRITISH COUNCIL KRAKOW: Krakow; ✆ 12 428 5936; www.britishcouncil.org/poland-celta-krakow.htm.

ELS-BELL SCHOOL OF ENGLISH: Warsaw; ✆ 22 621 3836; www.bellschools.pl; 2 full-time in summer and 2 part-time; 4,900 zloty (£990).

INTERNATIONAL HOUSE INTEGRA: Katowice; ✆ 32 259 99 97; www.ih.com.pl.

INTERNATIONAL HOUSE WROCLAW: Wroclaw; ✆ 71 78 17 290; www.ttcentre.ih.com.pl; full-time; rough frequency 3 per year.

PORTUGAL

INTERNATIONAL HOUSE LISBON: Lisbon; ✆ 21 315 1493/4/6; www.ihlisbon.com; full and part-time; rough frequency 10 per year.

RUSSIA

BKC-INTERNATIONAL HOUSE MOSCOW: Moscow; www.bkcih-moscow.com; full-time; rough frequency 7 per year; £995.

SINGAPORE

THE BRITISH COUNCIL SINGAPORE: Napier Road; ✆ 64721010; www.britishcouncil.org/singapore; part-time.

SOUTH AFRICA

GOOD HOPE STUDIES: Cape Town; ✆ 21 683 1399; www.ghs.co.za; full-time; rough frequency 8 per year.

INTERNATIONAL HOUSE JOHANNESBURG: Johannesburg; ✆ 11 339 1051; www.ih johannesburg.co.za; full-time; rough frequency 10 per year.

International House Lisbon

Taking the CELTA course at IH Lisbon has been a life-changing experience. It is, without a doubt, an incredibly intense course, but ultimately, very rewarding. No sooner have you observed a veteran teacher in the classroom, than you are teaching your first class. The tutors, however, provide you with all the advice, support and encouragement you need to get through those first few nerve-wracking lessons. Feedback is constant, fair and endlessly helpful. In addition, all the reference materials you could possibly need are either located in the school library, or accessible from the computer room. IH Lisbon provided me with the solid foundations on which to start my teaching career, and I would highly recommend the school to anyone wishing to undertake the CELTA certificate.

Louise Marques

Good Hope Studies

The driver eased the Audi down the wrong side of a traffic-clogged street, then turned through a red light onto the wrong side of a crossing street. A traffic cop looked studiously away. This was Moscow, and I was on my way to teach English to the driver's VIP boss... Eyebrows were raised when I traded a career in finance for the joys of teaching English. But I've never looked back. Teaching has taken me to the high Caucasus mountains, the banks of the Volga, and the beautiful town squares of Poland. I have met teachers from many walks of life - former translators, former school teachers, former pilots, actors, lawyers... all have found their niche in English teaching.

But first there was CELTA. It is by far the most-recognised qualification around and has definitely helped open the doors of top language schools to me. The course itself was very intensive (read late night lesson planning) - but intensive in a thrilling, inspiring way! I couldn't have asked for better tutors than Justin and Carrey.

... on the car sped. Outside the temperature was minus 22, and even the light felt brittle. It was wonderful, but a far cry from Cape Town with its long sandy beaches and perfect summer days. Cape Town has lured me now. In September, I watch the whales blowing on my way to work. At weekends there are hikes in the mountains. Everything's more casual here. Last month I was at a jazz concert in a scrapyard; last Sunday I ambled through autumn vineyards! I've adopted the Cape Town sandals and shorts. I smile. And no, I don't have any exciting rides down the wrong side of the road. Thankfully!

SPAIN

CAMBRIDGE SCHOOL: Barcelona; © 93 870 2001; www.cambridgeschool.com; full-time; rough frequency 6 per year.
CAMPBELL COLLEGE: Valencia; © 96 362 8983; www.campbellcollege.com.

CLIC INTERNATIONAL HOUSE: Seville; ✆ 95 450 0316; www.tefl.es; full-time; rough frequency 12 per year; €1,490 plus €520 for 4 weeks' accommodation.

HYLAND LANGUAGE CENTRE: Madrid; ✆ 91 431 9757; www.hylandmadrid.com; 2 full-time (July and September) and part-time from January; €1,500.

INSTITUTO DE IDIOMAS: Santiago; ✆ 981 563 100; www.usc.es; full-time; rough frequency 2 per year.

INTERNATIONAL HOUSE BARCELONA: Barcelona; ✆ 93 268 4511; www.ihes.com/bcn; full and part-time; rough frequency 10 per year.

INTERNATIONAL HOUSE MADRID: Madrid; ✆ 91 319 7224 or 90 214 1517; www.ihmadrid training.com/allaboutcelta/; full and part-time; rough frequency 7 per year; €1,530.

INTERNATIONAL HOUSE PALMA: Palma; ✆ 971 726408; www.ihes.com/pal; full-time; rough frequency 7 per year.

LEWIS SCHOOL OF LANGUAGES: Barcelona; ✆ 93 411 1333; www.tesol-spain.com; full-time; rough frequency 8 per year.

UNIVERSITY OF SANTIAGO DE COMPOSTELO: La Coruna; ✆ 981 563100 ext. 16599; www.usc.es/idiomas/celta; full-time July and September; €1,400.

SWITZERLAND

BELL SWITZERLAND: Geneva; ✆ 22 749 16 16; www.bell-school.ch; full and part-time; rough frequency 1 per year.

FLYING TEACHERS: Zurich; ✆ 44 1 350 3344; www.flyingteachers.biz; full-time; rough frequency 4 per year; SFr3,950 (£2,350).

THAILAND

ECC (THAILAND): Bangkok; ✆ 2 655 1236; www.eccthai.com; full-time; rough frequency 8 per year; $1,600; also offered in Phuket and Chiang Mai.

INTERNATIONAL HOUSE BANGKOK: Bangkok; ✆ 2 632679; www.ihbangkok.com; also offered in Chiang Mai.

Campbell College Valencia

Before the course

I thought the application procedure at Campbell College was very efficient. Some of the language tasks were challenging but it gave me a very clear idea of what to expect. It helped me focus on what I really needed to learn before starting the course. I was also provided with useful material to help me prepare for the course as well as a useful supplementary booklist. All in all, I think I was extremely well prepared for the course.

David, UK

On the course

Teaching practice was the most interesting yet challenging area of the course. Here, I feel I was given excellent guidance and support from tutors throughout the course at both elementary and upper-intermediate levels. Once I had finished my teaching practice session, I particularly enjoyed reading tutor's appraisals of my lessons. Without doubt, I learnt a lot from these and they certainly helped me plan future lessons.

My mid-course tutorial really helped me evaluate my progress on the course and put things into perspective; it focussed on key areas and ways to help me improve further.

By the end of the course at Campbell College my teaching was a lot more effective, my lessons were well-structured with a clear purpose and suitable learning objectives.

Verónique, Belgium

After the course

The whole experience was really brilliant. I really loved the course and have learnt so much – I didn't think it was possible to take so much on board in just 4 weeks. Now I feel really confident that I can plan my lessons on my own and teach EFL anywhere in the world. I believe in fact that I can do quite a good job too! I was extremely impressed with both centre and the tutors. Moreover, I feel everything I have learnt at Campbell College in Valencia will be invaluable for my future teaching career.

Abby, Canada

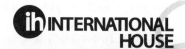

TURKEY

BILKENT UNIVERSITY: Ankara; ✆ 312 290 1912; www.bilkent.edu.tr/~busel; part-time.

TRAINING

DIRECTORY OF TRAINING COURSES

47

BRITISH SIDE: Istanbul; ✆ 212 327 9403; www.britishside.com; 2 full-time in summer, 1 part-time in autumn; 2,300 Turkish lira (£1,000).

INTERNATIONAL TRAINING INSTITUTE: Levent, Istanbul; ✆ 212 283 6466 or 26; www.iti-istanbul.com; full and part-time; rough frequency 5 per year.

IZMIR UNIVERSITY OF ECONOMICS: Izmir; ✆ 232 279 2525; www.ieu.edu.tr; full-time; rough frequency 1 per year.

UKRAINE

BRITISH COUNCIL KIEV: Kiev; ✆ 44 490 5600/99 792 2832; www.britishcouncil.org/ukraine; full-time in July (plus August course in Odessa); 10,000 hryvnia (£850).

INTERNATIONAL HOUSE KYIV: Kiev; ✆ 44 238 9870; www.ih.kiev.ua; full-time; rough frequency 3 per year.

UNITED ARAB EMIRATES

THE BRITISH COUNCIL, ABU DHABI: Abu Dhabi; ✆ 2 691 0600; www.britishcouncil.org/me; full and part-time, 1 per year; also in Sharjah and Dubai.

HIGHER COLLEGES OF TECHNOLOGY: Many locations; ✆ 2681 2070; www.hct.ac.ae.

INTERNATIONAL HOUSE DUBAI: Dubai; ✆ 4321 3121; www.ihdubai.com.

UNIVERSITY OF WOLLONGONG: Dubai; ✆ 4 395 4422; www.uowdubai.ac.ae; full and part-time; rough frequency 1 per year.

USA

CY-FAIR COLLEGE: Cypress; ✆ 832 482 1024; www.lonestar.edu/celta; full and part-time; rough frequency 3 per year.

DENVER BRIDGE-LINGUATEC: Denver; ✆ 303 777 7783 ext 862; www.bridgetefl.com; full-time; rough frequency 6 per year.

INTERCULTURAL COMMUNICATIONS COLLEGE: Honolulu; ✆ 808 946 2445; www.icchawaii.edu; full-time; rough frequency 3 per year.

ST GILES INTERNATIONAL: San Francisco; ✆ 415 788 3552; www.stgiles-usa.com; full-time; rough frequency 8 per year.

TEACHING HOUSE BOSTON: Boston; ✆ 617 963 0215; www.teachinghouse.com; full and part-time; rough frequency: 8 full-time courses per year and 2 part-time courses per year.

TEACHING HOUSE MIAMI: Miami; ✆ 305 508 4904; www.teachinghouse.com; full-time; rough frequency 2 per year.

TEACHING HOUSE NEW YORK: New York; ✆ 212 732 0277; www.teachinghouse.com; full and part-time; rough frequency 28 per year.

TEACHING HOUSE SAN DIEGO: San Diego; ✆ 619 320 6192; www.teachinghouse.com; full-time; 4 courses per year.

VIETNAM

APOLLO EDUCATION: Hanoi and Ho Chi Minh City; ✆ +844 943 2053; www.apolloedutrain.com; $1,500.

INTERNATIONAL LANGUAGE ACADEMY (ILA): Ho Chi Minh City; ✆ 8 3838 6788, ext 1924; www.ilavietnam.com; full-time; rough frequency 9 per year.

LANGUAGE LINK VIETNAM: Hanoi; ✆ 4 3974 4999; www.llv.edu.vn; full-time; rough frequency 4 per year.

TRINITY COLLEGE LONDON CERTIFICATE (TESOL)
COURSES IN THE UK

ABERYSTWYTH UNIVERSITY: Aberystwyth, Wales; ℂ 01970 622545; www.aber.ac.uk/tesol; full-time; rough frequency 2 per year; £1,300.

BASINGSTOKE COLLEGE OF TECHNOLOGY: Basingstoke, Hants; ℂ 01256 306350; www.bcot.ac.uk; full-time and part-time; rough frequency 1 per year.

BRACKNELL & WOKINGHAM COLLEGE: Bracknell, Berkshire; ℂ 01344 401638; www.bracknell.ac.uk; full-time and part-time; once each per year.

Teaching House, New York

Teaching House opened its doors in 2007 with the goal of providing the highest quality EFL/ESL teacher training in the USA. In less than three years, it has become the largest CELTA centre in North America and has trained roughly 1,500 teachers, hundreds of whom have kept in touch, reporting on their experiences in education around the world and how the Teaching House CELTA prepared them for their dream job.

Marian wrote the following while she was working in Colombia. She is now teaching ESL in New York City and working towards her master's degree in Bilingual Education:

'I got my CELTA in December 2007 and headed down to Bogotá. I was able to get a job quickly at International House Bogotá. IH is a nice place to get on your feet and meet others in the city (with your CELTA you are more or less guaranteed work).'

Katy writes about her experience living and teaching in Turkey:

'I began applying for jobs while I was still studying at Teaching House and flew out to start the job within two weeks of finishing my CELTA. In retrospect, doing my CELTA and moving to Istanbul were two of the best decisions I've made in my life.'

Kate describes her experience seeking her dream job in India:

'I work at a private school called Primrose School, which has a very progressive view about education for India. I teach three classes of English everyday but I also teach music, art, photography and yoga! It is certainly a diverse job and it keeps me quite busy. I love it so much! I know my CELTA helped prepare me greatly for this job. This school is not a language institute; it is just a normal primary and secondary school. English is widely spoken in India therefore it does not have a market for English teachers like other Asian countries. Just when I was about to throw in the towel on India, I found a listing on the school's website by doing one last random Google search. Even in a country like this where it may seem like an ESL job is nonexistent, if you are persistent, you will find your dream job. So don't give up!'

Finally, **Cory** recounts his experience finding a TEFL job in China:

'I found my current job while still in the United States. After completing my CELTA, I applied to 60 universities around China. The experience that I received while teaching during the CELTA program helped me immensely. On my first day of class in China, I knew exactly what I was doing and how I should do it. This allowed me to remain calm and confident in my ability to teach the class. All of this I owe to the CELTA program that I completed through Teaching House.'

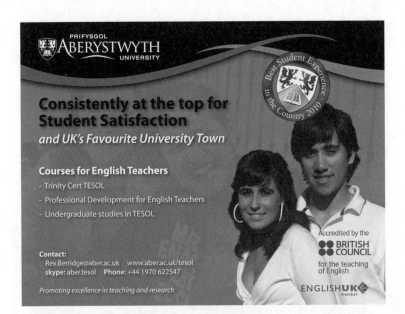

Aberystwyth University

Teach English and travel

With a passport and a recognised certificate in English language teaching you can see the world. Living among the people, being accepted as a teacher and a respected member of the community, you will see a side of the culture that you never knew existed. Stay for a few years and become a local, or take a short contract and move on again. The world becomes smaller and more accessible when you have the skills to work your way around it.

A full CertTESOL course can be as short as 5 weeks, and your rewards will be a certificate that you can use across the world, and a set of skills that will make you confident and capable in the classroom.

TESOL training at Aberystwyth

The Trinity CertTESOL is one of the two major international qualifications of the profession, recognised worldwide. Aberystwyth University is the only centre in Wales that offers this course. Applicants enrolling for the summer courses can qualify in time to teach overseas this summer or get away to a warm climate for the winter.

Set in a small town on the warm west coast of Wales, Aberystwyth University has the benefits of a beautiful location and excellent learning resources. No wonder that it was voted the best in the country for student satisfaction in 2010, and ranked by the International Student Barometer 2009 as number 1 of 123 Higher Education institutions worldwide for 'good place to be' and 'overall student satisfaction'.

The International English Centre IEC has over two decades' experience of training English language teachers. You develop your teaching skills with classes of international students, and expert trainers guide you through the whole process. The IEC is a small, friendly team, with huge student support.

CITY COLLEGE PLYMOUTH: Plymouth; ✆ 01752 305859; www.cityplym.ac.uk; Part-time; 1 per year.

COLCHESTER INSTITUTE: Colchester; ✆ 01206 712487; www.colchester.ac.uk; full-time, also part-time (twice of 8 weeks, once of 21 weeks); £1,155.

DARLINGTON COLLEGE OF TECHNOLOGY: Durham; ✆ 01325 503275; www.darlington. ac.uk; part-time.

EAST BERKSHIRE COLLEGE LANGLEY: Slough, Berkshire; ✆ 01753 793000; www.eastberks. ac.uk; part-time.

GATESHEAD COLLEGE: Gateshead, Tyne and Wear; ✆ 0191 490 0300; www.gateshead. ac.uk; part-time over 33 weeks.

GOLDERS GREEN COLLEGE TEACHER TRAINING CENTRE: London; ✆ 0208 731 0963; www.englishlanguagecollege.co.uk; full-time; 9 times per year; part-time twice.

Golders Green College

Trinity CertTESOL courses at Golders Green College, London

Michael Langton completed the CertTESOL course at Golders Green College in 2010. This is what he said on completing it:

I'd been thinking of doing this course for years before – I'm glad I finally did, and I'm really glad I chose to do it at Golders Green College. Having completed the course – although it was really hard work, I'm sad it's over! I sort of wish it kept going! I enjoyed all of it – particularly learning new things every day, about the English language and also about how to teach it; making new friends with fellow trainees; and the teaching practice with the foreign students, who were so great.

The students were SO friendly and enthusiastic – it made teaching practice such a positive and fun experience. I looked forward to it every time. The tutors were really friendly and extremely kind and helpful; they had great senses of humour, and encyclopaedic knowledge, which was really good for them as teacher-trainers, but they were also great English teachers in their own right. There was a really positive atmosphere, and so many interesting lessons given by the different trainers, almost every hour of every day was something new – it was a really engrossing, intense 5 weeks, where I learnt so much, and made some really good, new friends.

The Unknown Language part of the course at the beginning was surprising in lots of different ways – I learnt a lot more from this experience than I would have been able to anticipate. It was a very useful way of teaching us many things, and fun too. It will help me immensely and completely in the future – I wouldn't be able to teach English without it, and now because of the course I have the possible opportunity of teaching almost anywhere in the world!

I would absolutely recommend the course. It's a really stimulating and enriching experience – the training, the content, the tutors, fellow trainees, the students you get to teach, and all the different challenges, make it so worthwhile.

To experience Golders Green CertTESOL for yourself contact the Director of Studies, Karen Aldwell, at tesol@goldersgreencollege.co.uk or call 0208 731 0963.

ILS: English, Notinghiam; © 0115 969 2424; www.ilsenglish.com; 9 full-time courses per year, £950.

INLINGUA: Cheltenham; © 01242 250493; www.inlingua-cheltenham.co.uk; Full-time; 5 times a year.

ILS English

It's amazing to think that a one-month intensive language teaching programme could lead to so much.

... that's what **David Cockayne** says about his Trinity CertTESOL programme he carried out at ILS English in Nottingham.

Following his BA in International Business from Nottingham Business School, David carried out various English language contracts in China and South Korea and soon realized his heart was in teaching and not the cut-throat world of business. David soon felt the need to study for an internationally recognised teaching certificate. After considerable research he decided that the Trinity CertTESOL offered a more rigorous programme than the CELTA.

When David applied for the CertTESOL with ILS English he said of the Course Director, Steve Button, 'His level of knowledge, professionalism and communication was first class and I felt that I would gain a great deal from the ILS instructors. The course not only taught me so much about teaching approaches and methodologies, but it also enabled me to vastly expand my knowledge and understanding of the English language.'

Shortly after David found a teaching job in Catalunya. Everything ILS had prepared him for was immediately put to the test. 'However, after just 6 months, I became the temporary Director of Studies (DoS). Through hard work and dedication, I was then offered the full-time position of DoS with funding made available for me to undertake the DELTA qualification!'

David was later offered the opportunity to move into higher education at a University in China, 'A 3-year contract was too good to turn down. My position at the University has enabled me to see the importance of relevant, professional language tuition in modern day education, whilst allowing me to incorporate skills in teaching approaches, methodologies and the use of learner technologies in the classroom, skills all developed initially through the Trinity programme.'

INTERNATIONAL HOUSE BRISTOL: Bristol; © 0117 9090 911; www.ihbristol.com; full-time; rough frequency 4 per year.

IH Bristol

It was in September 2009 that I found myself, all of a sudden, at Bergamo train station in Lombardy, North Italy, bound for Lecco, a small town on the foot of the trailing leg of Lake Como. And as I stood alone on that platform in the early evening sunshine, with barely a word of the mother-tongue and not entirely sure whether I definitely had somewhere to stay when I arrived there, I reflected on how I had got myself into this situation.

It had all started on November 2nd 2008 and I was sat with my fellow fresh Tefl-ites awaiting the beginning of our 5 week TESOL guidance into the heady world of international EFL teaching. To cut a long story short, the course was as challenging and fulfilling as anything I had ever done. Along the way, amongst other things, I taught students from no less than 20 different countries, learnt rudimentary Japanese, taught, reflected, analysed, learnt about different languages & cultures, taught again, made a facebook-page-worth of new friends, played the most international games of football ever, taught again and had a marvellous time whilst doing it all.

As chance would have it, I was soon offered a job at the very place where I had received my expert guidance; The Language Project, Bristol (now IH Bristol). What followed remains the happiest period of my tax-paying life I have ever had. TEFL teaching was, without a doubt, the shoe that fitted. So why, 8 blissful months down the line, did I find myself alone on a train platform in North Italy? I had caught the bug.

Now at the end of my 8 month tenure here in Italy I have had a chance to reflect once again on how it has developed me as a teacher. Teaching abroad swept me, as it has swept countless before me, out of a comfort zone and into a situation which has unequivocally allowed a deeper connection with the plight of the language learner. I was the fish out of water this time. Professionally, it has stretched and challenged me, with my having to integrate and, perhaps more essentially, assimilate into a new professional set up and 'way of doing things'; less skills-based and more grammar-focused lessons, variable hours, different protocol and standards expected from a foreign employer etc. It has been tough at times indeed, and a zeal for the job at hand, i.e. teaching, is essential. But, in short, by making the idealistic and slightly naïve leap into the unknown of international EFL teaching, I have come out head and shoulders a more fulfilled and, dare I say, better teacher than when I stood, alone and discombobulated on the platform of Bergamo train station.

So go home and spin that globe and decide where it is you'd like to go next.

Dominic Harris

INTERNATIONAL TRAINING NETWORK: Christchurch, Dorset; ✆ 01202 475956; www.itnuk. com; full and part-time; rough frequency 3 per year; Christian organisation; £990 plus £110 Trinity moderation fee.

ISIS GREENWICH SCHOOL OF ENGLISH: London; ✆ 0208 293 1444; www.isisgroup.co.uk; full-time; rough frequency 9 per year.

KENT SCHOOL OF ENGLISH: Broadstairs, Kent; ✆ 01843 874 870; www.kentschoolofenglish. com; full-time.

LANGSIDE COLLEGE GLASGOW: ✆ 0141 272 3776; www.langside.ac.uk; full and part-time; rough frequency 3 per year.

THE LANGUAGE INSTITUTE/TLI ENGLISH LANGUAGE TRAINING: Edinburgh; ✆ 0131 226 6975; www.tlieurope.com; full time; rough frequency 4 per year; £995.

Oxford TEFL

I fell into EFL in London at the end of the 80s to make a bit of extra cash and meet people from all over the planet. It was a short-term thing. More than 20 years ago now. I came to Barcelona in 1990, trained with Duncan Foord, and liked the experience so much that, together, we went on to form Oxford TEFL back in 1998.

The view from the other side of the desk was interesting and fulfilling, but distanced me from the reason I'd stayed in EFL – the students, and I went back to the itinerant life of a freelance EFL teacher.

So, why do I still do it?

Because I still get a huge, life-affirming kick out of it. Out of seeing the expression on a student's face when they can finally use a piece of language that was giving them problems. Out of working on a presentation, and seeing them gain confidence, realising it's not going to be the drama they thought it was. Out of adapting my style to different people and different technologies.

These are the tangible moments, ones any teacher would mention. But there are others. We get insights into many different types of business, from tiny companies that operate out of a back room, to multi-nationals. I've worked with advertisers, publishers, genome researchers, pilots, lawyers, opera-house managers, actors and many more. And have picked up from them all notions of their own fields. There can be few jobs that give you that kind of wide-ranging contact.

I've seen them on good days and bad, when they were celebrating getting a new contract or worrying about their next pay-cheque. And all of this has given me insight into the human mind that I doubt a psychology degree would have done.

We know we're not in this for the money, but we also know that there are different kinds of wealth; living on the shores of the Med since 1990, getting to know hundreds of people, and really feeling that my work can make a difference, has made me feel far richer than if I'd stayed in London and caught the Northern Line every day to 'the office'.

That's why I'll be getting out of bed on Monday morning with, if not a smile on my face, something not far off.

www.oxfordtefl.com

LANGUAGES TRAINING & DEVELOPMENT: Witney, Oxfordshire; ✆ 01993 708637; www. ltdoxford.com; full-time; rough frequency 6–12 per year.

MANCHESTER COLLEGE OF ARTS & TECHNOLOGY: Manchester; ✆ 0161 953 5995; www. mancat.ac.uk; 2 full-time and 1 part-time per year.

NORTHAMPTON COLLEGE: Northampton; ✆ 01604 736225; www.northamptoncollege. ac.uk; Part-time 1 per year.

NORTHBROOK COLLEGE: Northbrook, Sussex; ✆ 0845 155 60 60; www.northbrook.ac.uk; part-time twice a year (evenings for 13 weeks); £901 (ask about discounts if on benefit).

OXFORD TEFL LONDON: London WC1; www.oxfordtefl.com; Full-time and part-time throughout the year; £905.

ST BRELADE'S COLLEGE: St. Aubin, Jersey; ✆ 01534 741305; www.st-brelades-college. co.uk; full-time; rough frequency 2 per year; £1,000 plus £150 for books and exam fee.

ST GEORGE INTERNATIONAL: London; ✆ 020 7299 1700; www.tesoltraining.co.uk; 11 full-time and 4 part-time per year.

St George International

I completed my TESOL certificate at St George International one cold snowy day in January 2009, after a challenging but very rewarding four week course with a great bunch of people. It was definitely the best January I have ever spent in my career since leaving university 25 years ago. I had previously worked in retail and construction management, but wanted to find a more fulfilling and enjoyable career – and I have!

After qualifying, I found a job very quickly and have been teaching in a school in Central London since then. I was amazed how relevant all of the course was, and how easy it was to move on from the training classroom to the real McCoy. My next step is to start teaching business classes, where I will be using my industry experience to help students to learn Business English.

SGI prepared me well before starting the course, so I knew exactly what to expect and there were no surprises during the well coordinated course. It did require a lot of time commitment, but the four weeks passed in a very enjoyable flash of learning, comprehension and presentation. I think the best part was probably teaching a group of genuine students on the first afternoon. This represented a microcosm of the course as a whole: learn something, put it into practice, and observe others doing the same.

The whole course ran like a well-oiled machine, with mentors and coaches providing positive support and enthusiasm in copious doses. The other trainees were all really interesting and there was a great spirit of helping each other through the course. The best thing about the course is, without doubt, the professionalism of the SGI team.

Telford Wallace

ST GILES LONDON CENTRAL: London; ✆ 020 7837 0404; www.stgiles-international.com; full-time; rough frequency 9 per year.

SHEFFIELD HALLAM UNIVERSITY TESOL CENTRE: Sheffield; ✆ 0114 225 5515; www.shu. ac.uk/tesol/teaching; 4 full-time and 3 part-time courses offered per year.

SIDMOUTH INTERNATIONAL SCHOOL: Sidmouth, Devon; © 01395 516754; efl@sidmouth-int.co.uk; www.sidmouth-int.co.uk; full-time; rough frequency 3 per year; £1,045 including moderation fee; accommodation arranged on request.

SOUTH ESSEX COLLEGE: Southend-on-Sea, Essex; © 01702 220400; www.southessex.ac.uk; part-time twice a year.

SUSSEX LANGUAGE INSTITUTE: University of Sussex, Brighton;© 01273 678006; www.sussex.ac.uk; full-time; rough frequency 3–4 per year

SUTTON COLLEGE OF LEARNING FOR ADULTS: Sutton, Surrey; © 020 8770 6901; www.scola.ac.uk; Part-time 1 per year.

TEFL LAB LONDON: London WC1;© 0800 022 4186; www.tefllab.co.uk; full time.

THE INSTITUTE: London N2;© 020 8829 4141; www.hgsi.ac.uk; 3–4 times a year; part-time; £950.

UNIVERSAL LANGUAGE TRAINING (ULT): Woking, Surrey; © 01983 853808; www.universal-language.co.uk; full-time monthly and part-time 2 per year.

UNIVERSITY OF CHICHESTER: Bognor Regis Campus, West Sussex; © 01243 812194; www.chiuni.ac.uk; Part-time for 8 weeks; £1,110.

UNIVERSITY OF WOLVERHAMPTON: Wolverhampton; © 01902 322484; www.wlv.ac.uk; Part-time 1 per year.

Sidmouth International School

Sidmouth International School, Sidmouth, Devon, offers four-week intensive full-time Trinity College London CertTESOL courses. The centre also runs LTCL Diploma courses with discount for successful CertTESOL trainees. The teacher-training team has worked together for a number of years and includes several of its own successful CertTESOL and LTCL Diploma candidates, who can bring a genuine empathy to the training – so successful Trinity College CertTESOL courses have been run since the centre was established in 1994. Sidmouth International School has links with teaching organisations overseas and is happy to help with advice and work placement for teachers planning to travel abroad to work. The school also has close links with language schools in the south-west of England and can help teachers returning to the UK in their search for fixed-term summer contracts or longer-term employment.

- Full-time intensive four-week courses starting in February, May and October.

- Over 90% pass rate for trainees with wide range of educational and occupational backgrounds.

- Excellent record of employment for successful trainees in UK and overseas.

- Post course guidance on professional development for teachers (including discount on diploma courses).

- Blended learning, part-time LTCL Diploma TESOL courses for teachers in UK and overseas (please enquire for annual dates and fees).

For more information contact the Head of Teacher Training, Sidmouth International School, May Cottage, Sidmouth, Devon EX10 8EN (01395 516754; efl@sidmouth-int.co.uk).

TRINITY COLLEGE LONDON CERTIFICATE (TESOL) COURSES ABROAD

CANADA

COVENTRY HOUSE INTERNATIONAL: Ontario; ℂ 416 929 0227; www.study-at-coventry. com; full-time; rough frequency 2 per year; C$999 (with discount).

CZECH REPUBLIC

OXFORD TEFL: Prague; ℂ 226 211 900; www.teflprague.com; full-time; rough frequency 10 per year, €1,300.

HONG KONG

ENGLISH FOR ASIA: Sheung Wan, Hong Kong; ℂ 2366 3792; www.englishforasia.com; full and part-time; rough frequency 10–12 per year.

Atlantic School of English

Grace Evans of West Cork is a past graduate of Atlantic School of English – the only school in Ireland approved by Trinity College London – and has never looked back since she received her CertTESOL certification in 2004.

"Completing my TESOL certificate opened up a world of possibilities to me; quite literally. I don't know if it was sipping a Belgian beer, bungee jumping in Queensland, riding a rickshaw in Calcutta or posing in front of the Sydney Opera House when it hit me that I have the best passport in the world. Unlike many people I know, I haven't had to leave places before I'm ready because of finances – regardless of where I am in the world someone always wants to learn English and people will always pay for that skill.

I've had the privilege of meeting triple the number of people that the average person meets in their life. Finding a job has never been an issue since I did my TESOL certificate. I have not only met these people but I've been able to immerse myself in their cultures through living in different countries rather than passing through like the average tourist does every day."

Atlantic School of English & Active Leisure
Schull
Co Cork
Ireland
www.atlantic-english.com
info@atlantic-english.com
Tel: +353 28 28943

Trinity CertTESOL at Byron

Wondering how to fill your school or university gap year? Are you looking for a career change?

Given today's difficult job market it's refreshing to know that there is a way you can step into employment immediately following a training course. Teaching English is a huge business which is further expanding, especially in the Far East. An absolute requirement for teachers is a qualification which is recognised internationally. Following the successful passing of the Trinity College CertTESOL you will be equipped to travel the world literally walking into a job.

Now you can study for this internationally recognized qualification in Italy's stunning and fascinating capital city. Experience Italian culture and gain an understanding of working and living abroad while training on a high quality course offered by Byron Language Development, a well-established and prestigious language school situated in Rome's historic centre.

The Byron Language Development CertTESOL course offers:

- 4-week, 140 hour intensive course
- Ongoing assessment and external moderation by Trinity College
- Guided lesson planning with trainers and fellow trainees
- 6 hours of teaching practice with groups of real students at different levels
- A one-to-one teaching experience with a selected student, and based on the Learner Profile Case Study of the same student
- Extra input sessions on Business English, Teaching Young Learners and career guidance

'Everybody at Byron was really friendly, and the course tutors were very supportive and approachable. I really enjoyed the course and would recommend it to anybody with a genuine interest in teaching – it's worth it.'
Iris Gordon-Bouvier

'Earning my TESOL Certificate was one of the biggest challenges that I have faced, yet I am so happy that I decided to take it on at Byron. The instruction was fantastic and by the time I had finished I felt confident and thoroughly prepared to begin my teaching career.'
Kristine Masters

About Byron

Byron Language Development is located in Rome's historic quarter of Testaccio, a stones throw from the graves of Keats and Shelley and the Circus Maximus. It is a leader in the market of Business English and Management training serving the demanding business community in the city.

Our success is reflected in the quality, seriousness and reliability of our staff, and in the subsequent achievements of the students who attend our courses.

www.byronschool.it

Oxford TEFL, Prague

Prague is my home

The Golden City. The City of 100 Spires. Praha. Whatever you wish to call it, Prague is home. I arrived here in August of 2009. I did my TEFL certificate at OxfordTEFL. They offered the Trinity CertTESOL, one of the two most prestigious TEFL certificates in the world. I loved the flexibility this offered but I ultimately chose the OxfordTEFL program because of how professional and helpful they were. The month long course certainly wasn't easy but the long hours and the teacher's focused training definitely put me in a position to succeed as I transitioned into this new field. These were people who truly cared about my growth and development as a teacher.

And even better, by doing my TEFL training in Prague I was able to conduct a local job search instead of an all-internet one. During my training course I was able to arrange several interviews by submitting a plethora of applications. These interviews were friendly, comfortable and, for me, successful. I ended up in the enviable position of having several offers to choose between. I chose a well known business-focused school for several reasons. Better pay. Well organized. My business background (I have an MBA). But at the time the most compelling reason was that they offered to help with my visa.

Let me be clear, getting a visa and a work permit here are much easier than they are in some other countries (Italy, Greece, Ireland, etc.) if you aren't EU. But even though it's easier in the Czech Republic, it's still a minor bureaucratic nightmare. Fortunately, most places are willing to provide you some assistance with this process. Mine did more than most, since it provided an in-house expert who handled all the details for me. I merely had to take a couple trips to Vienna to finalize everything (and believe me I wasn't complaining about being 'forced' to visit Vienna).

Teaching itself has turned out to be the most pleasantly surprising part of this decision. I've always enjoyed teaching but I moved here to travel and see the world. Teaching was just the most logical way to facilitate my globe-trotting ambitions. But it has become a job that I truly enjoy. My students are all dedicated and eager to learn. Most are friendly, open and excited to work with a native speaker. English is valuable to them in both their careers and their personal lives and knowing that I'm helping them improve their lives gives a deeper meaning to my job. The nice thing about Czech students is that most of them have had English (especially grammar) since they were children. Because of this, most of my time is spent improving their vocabulary and fixing pronunciation mistakes. And since the best way to do this is through somewhat structured conversation, I'm often getting paid to talk with interesting people. Not a bad situation.

But for all this, my favorite thing about being here is still Prague itself. The majestic castles. The towering cathedrals. The lovely parks (and the equally lovely beer gardens inside them). The efficient metro. The relaxed environment that permeates everything. The language that's so different that even the simple act of ordering lunch can become an interesting challenge. It's all wonderful. But what I love most is the mystery and the adventure that every new day here holds.

They say 'home is where the heart is' and that's why I say Prague is home to me.

Luke Brazell

INDONESIA

IALF BALI (INDONESIA AUSTRALIA LANGUAGE FOUNDATION): Bali; ℂ 361 225243; www. tesolbali.com; full-time; rough frequency 4 per year; $1,800.

IRELAND

ATLANTIC SCHOOL OF ENGLISH AND ACTIVE LEISURE: Schull, County Cork; ℂ 28 28943; www.atlantic-english.com; full-time; rough frequency 3 per year.

ITALY

BYRON LANGUAGE DEVELOPMENT: Rome; ℂ 06 42873419; www.byronschool.it; 5 per year.
VICTORIA INTERNATIONAL SCHOOL: Turin; ℂ 01119701242; v.i.s@fastwebnet.it.

NEW ZEALAND

ALPHA EDUCATIONAL INSTITUTE: Christchurch; ℂ 3 359 1525; www.alpha.school.nz; full-time; rough frequency 2 per year.
EDENZ COLLEGES: Auckland; ℂ 9 920 5920; www.teachertraining.co.nz; full and part-time; rough frequency 5 per year.
ENGLISH LANGUAGE ACADEMY: Auckland; ℂ 9 919 7695; www.ela.auckland.ac.nz; full and part-time 1 per year.
INTERNATIONAL PACIFIC COLLEGE: Queenstown; ℂ 6 354 0922; www.ipc.ac.nz/index.php; full-time 1 per year.

PARAGUAY

STAEL RUFFINELLI DE ORTIZ – ENGLISH: Asuncion; ℂ 21 226062/207017; www.stael.edu. py; part-time 1 per year.

SPAIN

CHESTER SCHOOL OF ENGLISH: Madrid; ℂ 91 401 97 29; www.chester.es; full-time; rough frequency 5 per year.
THE LANGUAGE INSTITUTE: Pontevedra; ℂ 986 104763/862461; www.tlieurope.com; full-time; rough frequency 4 per year.
OXFORD TEFL: Barcelona; ℂ 93 458 0111; www.oxfordtefl.com; full-time; rough frequency 12 per year.
UNIVERSAL LANGUAGE TRAINING (ULT): Woking; ℂ 01483 770911 or 01983 853808; www. universal-language.co.uk; TEFL training centre which offers summer school in Zamora.

URUGUAY

DICKENS INSTITUTE: Montevideo; ℂ 2 710 7555; www.dickens.edu.uy; part-time.

SHORT INTRODUCTORY COURSES

BERLITZ WORLDWIDE: http://careerservices.berlitz.com; all newly hired teachers (who must be university graduates) must join free 2-week training in-house in the Berlitz method.
EF ENGLISH FIRST TEACHER TRAINING: Cambridge/Brighton; ℂ 0207 341 8777; www. ef.com/master/tl/professional-development; approx £530 for 1 week, £1,010 for 2 weeks; cost varies depending on location.
INTENSIVE SCHOOL OF ENGLISH AND BUSINESS COMMUNICATIONS: Brighton, UK; ℂ 01273 384800; www.ise.uk.com; £250; frequency 1 per year; also offers CELTA in Wuhan China.
INTENSIVE TRAINING COURSES (ITC): Darlington, Co. Durham, UK; ℂ 0845 644 5464; www. tefl.co.uk; £210; various locations; frequency most weekends all year; optional part 2 is a distance component costing a further £135.

i-to-i: Leeds, UK; ✆ 0800 093 2552; 0800 352 1793; www.i-to-i.com or www.teflcourses.com; from £179; various locations; frequency most weekends all year.

ITTC: Bournemouth, UK; ✆ 01202 397721; www.ittc.co.uk; TEFL Taster day £55 including lunch; frequency 10 per year.

KRISTAL INTERNATIONAL, Camarthan, UK; ✆ 01944 231145; www.tefl-course.net; modularised 30-hour courses which combine on-site and home study. Weekend courses offered in various UK locations. Prices from £229 for Module 1.

NORTHAMPTON COLLEGE: Northampton, UK; ✆ 0845 300 44 01; www.northamptoncollege.ac.uk; £90; frequency 1 per year.

SAXONCOURT TEACHER TRAINING: London; ✆ 020 7499 8533; www.saxoncourt.com; several 1-week courses throughout the year; £300.

SUSSEX DOWNS COLLEGE: Sussex, UK; ✆ 01323 637 111; www.sussexdowns.ac.uk; TEFL taster day 1 per year, £18.

SUSSEX LANGUAGE INSTITUTE: Sussex, UK; ✆ 01273 873234; www.sussex.ac.uk; £225; frequency 1 per year.

TEFL England: info@teflengland.co.uk. Trading name of TEFL Scotland (next entry).

TEFL Scotland: ✆ 0871 221 8335; info@teflscotland.co.uk; www.teflscotland.co.uk. 20-hour weekend TEFL courses throughout Scotland with online additions.

TEFL TIME: Sussex, UK; ✆ 01903 708178; www.tefltime.com; £189 for weekend courses, often held at the Holiday Inn at King's Cross; frequency 9 per year.

TEFL TRAINING: Oxon, UK; ✆ 01608 811048; www.tefltraining.co.uk; from £210; various locations; frequency most weekends all year.

DISTANCE LEARNING ONLINE COURSES

LinguaEdge

Ruth Hergens recalls her online training with LinguaEdge:

I wanted to teach English overseas and had done some research into TESOL certificate courses. The courses I found were time-intensive, expensive, and located far from the town I live in. However, the more research I did, the more I found out that an expensive, on-site course was no longer a hard requirement. I also found that online courses didn't always have the best reputation. However, the LinguaEdge online TESOL Certification really changed my concept of just how effective a good online course can be. The context was interactive and kept me engaged and learning actively throughout the course. Visuals, learning activities, video clips, and current content made sure that what I was learning was both effective and 'hands-on'.

My other concern about online learning was that it had the potential to be a passive, solitary experience. However, the LinguaEdge course quickly changed my thinking about this as well. I was assigned a course 'tutor', who not only graded my written assignments, but gave me detailed comments, suggestions, and leads on resources that expanded my knowledge of the material.

In short, taking the LinguaEdge online TESOL Teacher Certificate course not only saved me time and money, but I learned so much that when I got the overseas teaching job I wanted I was able to walk into my first class confident and prepared.

www.linguaedge.com

AMERICAN TESOL INSTITUTE: Tempa, FL, USA; ✆ 813 975 7404; www.americantesol.com; from US $ 295.

EUROLINK COURSES: Sheffield, UK; ✆ 0114 262 1522; www.eurolinkcourses.co.uk; £600 in instalments/£540 if paid in full; offers optional practical teaching placement; cost with practical teaching placement is £1,095 in instalments/£1,020 if paid in full.

GLOBAL ENGLISH: Exeter, Devon, UK; ✆ 01392 411999; www.global-english.com; from £195; offers specialist components in Young Learners and Business English; teaching practice can be arranged in Portugal, Thailand and Italy.

ICAL: London, UK; ✆ 0845 310 4104; www.teacher-training.net; £135; offers practical teaching placement; cost is £395.

i-to-i: Leeds, UK; ✆ 0800 093 3148 or 0113 204 4610; www.i-to-i.com, www.onlinetefl.com; from £143.

INTESOL WORLDWIDE: 4 Higher Downs, Knutsford, Cheshire WA16 8AW, UK; ✆ 0800 567 7189/01565 621661; www.intesoltesoltraining.com; accredited by a national awarding body; online and offsite courses from £395 to £895; offers teaching practice in accredited schools; accredited for quality of service with a money back guarantee by ODLQC; branches worldwide.

INTESOL WORLDWIDE

After researching various TESOL courses I decided to train with INTESOL because they ran a distance learning course that was affordable and gave me the flexibility to complete the work over a long period of time. My only dilemma was whether this qualification would be accepted worldwide and stand up against the well known Trinity and Cambridge TEFL certificates. Lynda Hazelwood, the Course Director at INTESOL, assured me that the qualification was accredited through the correct channels and that I shouldn't find any difficulties finding excellent contracts with the INTESOL Certificate in TESOL.

I found the course easy to follow, and if I needed help with anything I just needed to pick up the phone and ask for advice. The course materials were interesting and gave me the knowledge that I needed to begin Teaching English as a Second Language.

I qualified as an ESOL Teacher with INTESOL in 1998 and immediately found employment with a Language School in my home town of Plymouth. Since that time I've worked in numerous language schools teaching English at master's level, including schools in foreign countries such as Thailand and France. The INTESOL Certificate in TESOL has been invaluable and has enabled me to travel and work, as well as helping me to secure employment within the national education system in England.

Recently I called Lynda Hazelwood with a request for my course results module by module because a school that I was applying to work with was requesting them. Considering that I took the qualification over 10 years ago now, I was amazed when Lynda gave me my results immediately over the phone from her database. This is just one example of how well INTESOL is run as an organisation and how they are there to support any of their students not just when they take the qualification but throughout their career. And... I got the job!'

Esther Knight

LANGUAGES TRAINING & DEVELOPMENT: Witney, Oxfordshire, England; ✆ 01993 708637; www.ltdoxford.com; £350; does not offer practical teaching placement.

LINGUAEDGE: Beverly Hills, CA, USA; ✆ 888 944 3343; www.linguaedge.com; 50-, 100- or 150-hour online courses. Optional 20-hour teaching practicum available.

LONDON TEACHER TRAINING COLLEGE: London; ✆ 020 8133 2027; www.teachenglish. co.uk; £175; offers practical teaching placement; cost with practical teaching placement is £255.

NORWOOD ENGLISH: Laois, Eire; ✆ 57 8756325; www.norwoodenglish.com; from £160; does not offer practical teaching placement.

TEFLSTOP: www.teflstop.com; part of INTESOL WORLDWIDE (above); new accredited online course aimed at backpackers; £195; optional extra of doing teaching practice via Skype; assistance given on finding jobs at a large language chain in Turkey and to graduates in North America who are looking for online teaching jobs.

TEFL TRAINING: Oxon, UK; ✆ 01608 811048; www.tefltraining.co.uk; £395 if paid in full/£420 in instalments.

TRAINING LINK ONLINE: Sheffield, UK; ✆ 0114 235 2245; www.traininglinkonline.co.uk; £525 if paid in full/£585 in instalments; offers practical teaching placement.

UNIVERSITY OF BIRMINGHAM: Birmingham, UK; ✆ 0121 414 5695/6; www.cels.bham. ac.uk; does not offer practical teaching placement.

WORDS LANGUAGE SERVICES: Dublin, Ireland; ✆ +353 1 6610240; www.wls.ie; £325; does not offer practical teaching placement.

ACADEMIC COURSES

This represents a small selection of university courses in TEFL/TESL in the UK. On the UCAS.com site, you can search by subject and find courses in TEFL/TESOL usually offered in combination with another subject such as a modern language or tourism.

ANGLIA RUSKIN UNIVERSITY: East Road, Cambridge CB1 1PT; ✆ 01245 493131; efl@anglia. ac.uk; www.anglia.ac.uk; offer BA in English Language teaching and an MA in Applied Linguistics and TESOL.

ASTON UNIVERSITY: Languages and Social Sciences Unit, Aston Triangle, Birmingham B4 7ET; ✆ 0121 204 3762; lss_pgadmissions@aston.ac.uk; www.aston.ac.uk; MSc in Teaching English to Speakers of Other Languages (TESOL), MSc in Teaching English for Specific Purposes (TESP), MSc in Teaching English to Young Learners (TEYL), MSc in Educational Management in TESOL (EMT), part-time, 2–5 years, £6,950; MA in TESOL studies, MA in TESOL and Translation, MA in Applied Linguistics, all £3,630.

CANTERBURY CHRIST CHURCH UNIVERSITY COLLEGE: North Holmes Road, Canterbury CT1 1QU; ✆ 01227 767700 (Department of English and Language Studies); languagestudies@ canterbury.ac.uk; www.canterbury.ac.uk; offers Diploma/MA in TESOL; full (12 months) or part-time; also offers the CELTA (see entry).

LONDON METROPOLITAN UNIVERSITY: 166–220 Holloway Road, London N7 8DB; ✆ 020 7133 4202; humanities@londonmet.ac.uk/admissions@londonmet.ac.uk; www.london-met.ac.uk; MA International ELT & Applied Language Studies (for experienced teachers); MA TEFL (for newly qualified teachers). Full-time one-year course; fees £4,050 for EU students or £7,155 for non-EU students.

MIDDLESEX UNIVERSITY: The Burroughs, London NW4 4BT; ✆ 020 8411 5555; enquiries@ mdx.ac.uk; www.mdx.ac.uk; BA (Hons) in Teaching English as a Foreign Language.

UNIVERSITY OF BEDFORDSHIRE: Park Square, Luton, Bedfordshire LU1 3JU; ✆ 01234 400400; www.beds.ac.uk; BA (Hons) in English Language Studies with Teaching English as a Foreign Language (TEFL), BA (Hons) in English Language for Business, BA (Hons)/ Diploma in English for International Communication, MA in Applied Linguistics (TEFL), TEFL Certificate (summer school), TEFL Certificate (part-time evening).

UNIVERSITY OF BIRMINGHAM: Centre for English Language Studies, Westmere, Edgbaston Park Road, Edgbaston, Birmingham B15 2TT; ✆ 0121 414 3239/5696; cels@bham. ac.uk; www.cels.bham.ac.uk; the Centre for English Language Studies specialises in language research, training and consultancy; CELS is part of the Department of English at the University of Birmingham; the department holds the highest possible ratings for both research and teaching, offers full-time or part-time courses on campus in TEFL/TESL, Applied Linguistics, English for Specific Purposes, Language and Lexicography, Special Applications of Linguistics, Translation Studies, Applied Corpus Linguistics, Critical Discourse, Culture and Communication; also offers distance learning courses in TEFL/TESL, Translation Studies and Applied Linguistics in addition to Postgraduate Research Degrees by distance learning; all campus-based courses last for one year and begin in October. Distance learning MA courses begin in April and October and typically take 30 months; possibility to study part-time, one term per year; accommodation available on campus; contact CELS administrator via www.cels.bham.ac.uk.

UNIVERSITY OF BRIGHTON: School of Languages, Falmer, Brighton, East Sussex BN1 9PH; ✆ 01273 643336; a.pickering@brighton.ac.uk; www.bton.ac.uk; offers Diploma and MA in TESOL; 1 year full-time or part-time; these are both post-graduate courses; applicants must have some English teaching experience for the MA and 2 years for the Diploma; also offers a MA in English Language Teaching, 1 year full-time or part-time, for teachers with a limited amount of experience.

UNIVERSITY OF CENTRAL LANCASHIRE: School of Languages and International Studies, Preston, PR1 2HE; ✆ 01772 893136; cenquiries@uclan.ac.uk; www.uclan.ac.uk; BA (Hons) in Teaching English to Speakers of Other Languages, BA (Hons) in TESOL and Modern Languages, MA in TESOL and Applied Linguistics.

UNIVERSITY OF EDINBURGH: Institute for Applied Language Studies (IALS), 21 Hill Place, Edinburgh EH8 9DP; ✆ 0131 650 6200; ials.enquiries@ed.ac.uk; www.ials.ed.ac.uk; offers short intensive EFL teacher development courses of between 1 and 3 weeks' duration in July/August.

UNIVERSITY OF ESSEX: International Academy, Wivenhoe Park, Colchester, Essex CO4 3SQ; ✆ 01206 872217; dilly@essex.ac.uk; www.essex.ac.uk/internationalacademy. MA TESOL/ Diploma TESOL/Certificate TESOL; the modular MA TESOL (180 credits) can be taken either within 1 year or over a period of 6 years with exit points at Diploma (120 credits) or Certificate (60 credits); also providing CELTA training in conjunction with Santiago de Compostela in Spain and specialist tailor made programmes.

UNIVERSITY OF EXETER: School of Education and Lifelong Learning, St Luke's Campus, Heavitree Road, Exeter EX1 2LU; ✆ 01392 264837; ed-student@exeter.ac.uk; EdD/PhD/MPhil/ MEd/PgDip/PgCertTESOL, full-time, part-time and intensive summer study.

UNIVERSITY OF MANCHESTER: Postgraduate Admissions Office, School of Education, Faculty of Humanities, Oxford Road, Manchester M13 9PL; ✆ 0161 275 3463; education-enquiries@manchester.ac.uk; www.manchester.ac.uk; offers MA TESOL or MA Educational Technology and TESOL in 3 modes of study: 1 year full-time (onsite), UK/EU £3,466 and Overseas £11,300; 27 months part-time (onsite), EU/UK £1,733; and 3 years distance, £2,100 a year; entry requirements include 3 years' teaching experience; the university also offers an introduction to TESOL as part of an undergraduate degree (one term).

UNIVERSITY OF READING: Department of Applied Linguistics, School of Languages and European Studies, Whiteknights, PO Box 218, Reading RG6 6AA; ✆ 0118 378 8123; languages@reading.ac.uk; www.rdg.ac.uk/app_ling; MA ELT in both campus-based and distance-study modes, with an additional study track for novice teachers; also, MA in Applied Linguistics, BA in Applied English Language Studies.

UNIVERSITY OF STIRLING/CELT:, Institute of Education (CELT), Stirling FK9 4LA; ✆ 01786 467934; celt@stir.ac.uk; www.celt.stir.ac.uk; MSc in TESOL (Teaching English to Speakers of Other Languages); MSc in TESOL and CALL (Computer Assisted Language Learning); and PhD and EdD in TESOL Education available; General English, IELTS Preparation, English for University Study, Short Courses for Teachers, and a Summer School in August are also offered.

UNIVERSITY OF SUSSEX: Admissions, Sussex House, Falmer, Brighton, East Sussex BN1 9RH; ✆ 01273 678416; UG.Admissions@sussex.ac.uk (for bachelor's degree programme) or PG.Admissions@sussex.ac.uk (for master's programmes); www.sussex.ac.uk; BA in English Language Teaching; 3- or 4-year joint major in ELT with English, English Language, Language(s) or Linguistics; includes opportunity to take Trinity TESOL Certificate as part of degree; MA in English Language Teaching; MA in International English Language Teaching and a Post-graduate Diploma in ELT (full-time 1 year, part-time 2 years).

UNIVERSITY OF WARWICK: Centre for Applied Linguistics, Coventry CV4 7AL; ✆ 024 7652 3200; appling@warwick.ac.uk; www2.warwick.ac.uk/fac/soc/al/; MA in ELT/ESP/English for Young Learners (all post-experience), English Language Teaching (Studies and Methods) (less than 2 years' experience), ELT (Multimedia) (either pre- or post-experience); one-term Post-graduate Certificate in any of the MA specialisms (January to March), 2 terms for a Post-graduate Diploma.

TRAINING COURSES IN NORTH AMERICA

American TESOL Institute

www.AmericanTESOL.com

Schools and universities abroad are actively seeking ESL Teachers who speak the 'American' dialect.

Why?

Blame Satellite TV and the internet. Students all over the world are exposed to 'American' English at every waking moment. Consequently, there is a world of work for American English speakers. North American ESL professionals are in big demand in Asia including Korea, Taiwan, China, and Thailand. The same is true for the Middle East. Saudi Arabia leads the pack followed by Kuwait, the United Arab Emirates, and the Sultanate of Oman. There are also growing opportunities in Central and Latin America.

The first step is to get certified to teach English as a Second Language from a reputable school, such as the American TESOL Institute, based in Tampa, Florida, USA. ATI offers all of its courses online, as well, allowing students to obtain the credentials to teach ESL no matter where they are.

Once you have your TESOL Certificate in hand, ATI has a job placement programme to assist graduates to secure a good position teaching abroad. Most seasoned ESL professionals will tell you: 'The learning experience just begins when you set foot in a new and exciting land. The sun never sets on your teaching opportunities.'

USA

AMERICAN LANGUAGE INSTITUTE: San Diego State University, 5250 Campanile Drive San Diego, CA 92182 1914; ✆ 619 594 5907; ali@mail.sdsu.edu or rhillier@mail.sdsu.edu; www.americanlanguage.com; well-known AMTEFL Certificate validated by SDSU Dept of Education (3 graduate credits); 4 weeks, 130 hours, offered 4 times a year (spring and summer); $2,650; dormitory/homestay/apartment accommodation can be arranged through the ALI housing office.

BOSTON ACADEMY OF ENGLISH: 59 Temple Place, 2nd Floor, Boston, MA 02111; 617–338 6243; info@bostonacademyofenglish.com; www.bostonacademyofenglish.com; 4 weeks intensive 120-hour CTEFL course, $2,450; part-time over 12 weeks, $2,300.

BOSTON LANGUAGE INSTITUTE: 648 Beacon St, Boston, MA 02215; ✆ 617 262 3500; info@teflcertificate.com; www.teflcertificate.com; intensive 4-week TEFL Certificate course (120 hours) offered monthly; 12-week Saturday programmes also offered 3 times a year; special TEFL Certificate Programme for Non-Native Speakers of English also offered: course includes additional training on pronunciation, American culture and other relevant topics; tuition of $2,795 includes fees, all study materials and lifetime job assistance.

BostonTEFL.com: admin@bostontefl.com; www.bostontefl.com; basic online training course ($295) can be supplemented by a 20-hour face-to-face weekend course (together $785) and a further opportunity to obtain 2 weeks teaching practice overseas ($1,745).

GLOBAL TEFL: ✆ 312 209 3660; mail@globaltefl.org; www.globaltefl.org; Full-time SIT TESOL Certificate courses offered by freelance certified trainers Ron and Ellen Bradley and other SIT certified trainers in Chicago, California, Grand Junction, Colorado, and Boston; Part-time courses offered at some locations; $2,295 inclusive; (for further details of course see website).

HAMLINE UNIVERSITY: TEFL Certificate Program, School of Education, 1536 Hewitt Avenue, St. Paul, MN 55104; ✆ 651 523 2429; education@hamline.edu; www.hamline.edu; intensive 1-month courses in July and January and part-time extensive courses autumn and spring; current tuition $3,230; focus is on developing communicative language teaching strategies; ongoing career counselling provided. Graduate credit granted; course can be used towards Hamline's MA in ESL; advanced TEFL option offered.

MIDWEST TEACHER TRAINING PROGRAM: 19 N. Pinckney Street, Madison, WI 53703 USA; ✆ 800 765 8577 or ✆ 608 257 8476; info@mttp.com; www.mttp.com; practical, hands-on 5-week TEFL Certificate Course (130 hours including 10 hours of teaching practice) in a progressive university city; 4 times a year; tuition and course materials $2,595; housing arranged if needed; integrated with an ESL school providing an international environment; job placement assistance including resource library, job search workshop and personal résumé editing; grads have found jobs in 40 countries.

OXFORD SEMINARS: Santa Monica and New York; ✆ +1 800 779 1779; www.oxfordseminars.com; TESOL/TESL courses held in cities around the USA, usually on university/college campuses; 60 hours over 3 consecutive weekends; US$1,095.

SCHOOL OF TEACHING ENGLISH AS A SECOND LANGUAGE: (affiliate programme with Seattle University College of Education), 9620 Stone Avenue. N., Suite 101, Seattle, WA 98103; ✆ 206 781 8607; STESLinfo@seattleu.edu; www.schooloftesl.com; 12-credit, 4-week intensive courses (monthly), non-intensive evening classes (quarterly), and online classes (quarterly); $233 per credit, 2010 academic year; accommodation available on request; classes carry college credit and can be used as a portion of master's degrees at Seattle University (except online classes); counselling, monthly employment seminars, graduates' networking services and an onsite ESOL class.

TRANSWORLD SCHOOLS: TESOL Certificate (Teaching English to Speakers of Other Languages) training courses at Transworld Schools, 701 Sutter Street, 6th Floor, San Francisco, CA 94109; ✆ 1 888 588 8335/415 928 2835; transwd@aol.com; www.transworldschools.com; Comprehensive TESOL Certificate (4 weeks full-time, 14 weeks part-time, $2,000); TESOL Certificate (3 weeks full-time, 10 weeks part-time $1,800); Intensive TESOL Certificate (for experienced ESOL teachers – 2 weeks full-time; 7 weeks part-time, $1,600); Advanced TESOL Certificate (for experienced ESOL teachers – 1 week full-time; 4 weeks part-time, $900); Online TESOL Certificate with 1 week on-site residency $1,200; all courses internationally recognised; approved by State of California, BPPVE (Bureau for Private Post-secondary Education) and accredited by ACCET, Continuing Education Credits awarded; high quality training, low tuition, and lifetime job placement worldwide; accommodation ($165–$250 per week); courses include evaluated Teaching Practice, teaching children and adults, grammar, Business English, TOEFL and syllabus design. Facilities include multimedia lab, video and internet.

WASHINGTON ACADEMY OF LANGUAGES: TESL Graduate Certificate/Endorsement Program, 2 Nickerson St., Suite 201, Seattle, WA 98109; ✆ 206 682 4463 or toll-free ✆ 888 682 4463; info@wal.org; www.wal.org; Graduate TEFL Certificate offered in conjunction with Seattle Pacific University; 8 courses for total of 24 quarter credits; offered intensively as 8-week summer course, online or in evening classes over academic year; tuition for each course is $510.

WESTERN WASHINGTON UNIVERSITY TESOL PROGRAM: Bellingham, WA 98225; ✆ 360 650 4949; Trish.Skillman@wwu.edu; ww.wce.wwu.edu/Resources/TESOL; Full-time and part-time university courses starting in September, with a summer intensive option; interdisciplinary course work and practical experience lead to a certificate of achievement and a supporting endorsement in teaching ESL; distance education and overseas practicum experiences in Mexico available; fees $1,950–$2,200.

CANADA

Note that the website of TESL Canada (www.tesl.ca) has links to a large number of approved teacher training programmes across Canada.

ARCHER COLLEGE VANCOUVER: 525 Dunsmuir St, Unit 200, Vancouver, BC V6B 1Y4; ✆ 604 608 0538; VancouverESL@ArcherEducation.com; www.archereducation.com; TESL Canada recognised courses offered full-time for 1 month, or part-time over 14 weeks; all courses include practicum and are offered year-round.

TRANSWORLD SCHOOLS

TRANSWORLD SCHOOLS (San Francisco, California, USA) is a private vocational training school offering internationally recognized TESOL Certificate (Teaching English to Speakers of Other Languages) training courses and English language programs. All courses are Approved by the State of California, BPPVE (Bureau of Private Postsecondary and Vocational Education) and award Continuing Education Credits. Transworld Schools is accredited by ACCET (Accrediting Council of Continuing education and Training) and as such, is required to meet the highest industry standards.

Transworld Schools successfully places more than 90% of its TESOL graduates in schools and universities worldwide. The school also contracts with overseas English Language Programs, universities and governments to provide comprehensive program management, curriculum design, and teacher hire.

Transworld Schools offers the following full and part-time courses both on-site and online:

- Comprehensive TESOL Certificate: 4 weeks full-time, 14 weeks part-time, 140 hours, $2,000
- TESOL Certificate: 3 weeks full-time, 10 weeks part-time, 105 hours, $1,800
- Intensive TESOL Certificate (for experienced ESOL teachers): 2 weeks full-time, 7 weeks part-time, 70 hours, $1,600
- Advanced TESOL Certificate (for experienced and/or certified teachers): 1 week full-time, 4 weeks part-time, 35 hours, $900
- Online TESOL Certificate: 4 modules, 100 hours, 1 week on-site teaching practicum residency, $1200.

Transworld Schools offers affordable, high quality training, and provides frequent tuition scholarships upon approval. Graduates receive lifetime job placement assistance. All TESOL Certification courses include evaluated teaching practice with international students, grammar, language skills, teaching techniques and lesson planning, Business English, teaching children and adults, and Computer Assisted Language Learning. Advanced TESOL certification includes TOEFL preparation training and test, syllabus and curriculum design, and methods and approaches.

Transworld Schools is located in downtown San Francisco. The school provides a multi-media computer lab, plus video and internet access. Student accommodation is located within 5 minutes walk in downtown San Francisco, and prices range from $175 to $250 per week. The school is authorized under federal law to enroll non-immigrant foreign students and issue the 1-20 form for student visa application. Transworld Schools publishes the online magazines ESLFocus.com and EnglishTeen.com as resources for ESOL teachers and international students.

Transworld Schools, 701 Sutter Street, 6th Floor, San Francisco CA 94109. 415-928-2835. Fax:415-928-0261. E-mail: Transwd@aol.com Website: www.TransworldSchools.com.

GLOBAL TESOL: 10037 B-82 Ave, Edmonton, Alberta T6E 1Z2, Canada; ✆ +1 888 270 2941/780 438 5704; info@globaltesol.com; www.globaltesol.com; office/training centres across Canada, and in many countries worldwide; world's largest TESOL Certificate and Diploma granting programme as described in a free Travel-and-Teach information package; 40,000 graduates teaching English in 85 countries; range of Canada Government certified TESOL Certificate and Diploma courses held regularly in cities throughout Canada and other countries; 5-day intensive format, or online and correspondence study options available worldwide; overseas job guaranteed; prices range from C$695 to C$3,495; famous for its 16 specialisation course options; 120-hour to 600-hour programme available; other courses offered online or by correspondence include Teaching Business English, Teaching TOEFL Preparation, Teaching Grammar, Teaching Children, Teaching Adults, Tourism English, Teaching CALL Computer English and more; accommodation can be arranged; franchises available, e-mail for details.

The Bridge IDELT™

As the employment slump continues and more and more people look for work teaching English overseas, getting a recognised certification in Teaching English as a Foreign Language (i.e. TEFL) becomes more and more important. Here **Brett Windhausen** talks about his decision to take Bridge TEFL's International Diploma in English Language Teaching™.

I took the IDELT course because I wanted to learn the skills I'd need to know how to teach effectively, English in particular. Due to my Linguistics degree, I had plenty of background knowledge in SLA, and I had some experience with teaching from the freelance tutoring, but I felt I needed a particular set of skills to be able to teach well. Unfortunately, before I took the course, it would've been difficult to even elucidate what skills I might've thought necessary, which is why the course was valuable to me – it taught me not only what skills are necessary for a teacher, but how to utilize them as well.

On completing the IDELT™ course, Brett landed a job with JET, the Japanese Teacher Exchange Program, and plans to teach in Japan for 1-3 years.

I think having the IDELT certificate made me a more competitive candidate, and likely gave a substantial boost to my ability to land the position. Had I not had the certificate, I would've been much less confident not only in my ability to get selected for the position (which is highly competitive), but also in my ability to perform well in the job once it started. Furthermore, I now feel that though I am still far from the perfect teacher, I at least have a solid grounding in the fundamentals and a lack of nervousness about being able to teach well, which I needed to be able to grow and hone my skills as an educator.

In general, most salaried teaching jobs require some form of certification in order to teach English as a foreign language. Native speakers may be able to secure a job as a tutor or as a teacher at a private school without a certificate; however, this type of employment is often difficult to secure before leaving your home country.

Most TEFL teacher certification courses are about 120-140 hours in duration and can be taken on-site, online, or as a combination of the two. When choosing a course, be sure to check for accreditation and references to make sure you are getting a legitimate certification. For more information on the Bridge IDELT™ teacher certification course, visit www.BridgeTEFL.com.

GLOBAL VILLAGE ENGLISH CENTRES: Calgary and Vancouver; info@gvenglish.com; www. gvenglish.com; TESOL Diploma course; 180 classes over 8 weeks, offered 5 times a year in Calgary; C$2,665; also offer the CELTA.

INTERNATIONAL HOUSE VANCOUVER, 200–215 West Broadway, Vancouver, BC V6H 167; ✆ 604 739 9836; http://tesl-vancouver.com; IH Career College offers IH Certificate (130 hours and online) starting monthly. C$1,400 (C$950 online).

OXFORD SEMINARS: 131 Bloor St. West, Suite 200–390, Toronto, ON M5S 1R8 and 10405 Jasper Ave, Suite 16–21, Edmonton, AB T5J 3S2; ✆ +1 800 269 6719; info@oxfordseminars. com; www.oxfordseminars.com; 60-hour course held over 3 consecutive weekends; C$995 (plus GST) with various discounts available such as C$100 off for early booking.

PEAK TESOL: Rocky Mountain School District 6; ✆ +1 877 427 5114 or ✆ 0250 427 5114; peak.tesol@gmail.com or gabbot@rmbc6.ca; www.sd6.bc.ca/peaktesol; 50 hours of in-class training with 50 hours of distance-learning; the course includes supervised practice teaching with real international students; C$1,250.

TRAINING COURSES WORLDWIDE

WORLDWIDE

BRIDGE-LINGUATEC: Head office: 915 South Colorado Blvd, Denver, Colorado 80246; ✆ 303 785 8864; toll free (USA and Canada): ✆ +1 888 827 4757/0800 028 8051 (UK); www. bridgetefl.com; intensive 140-hour TEFL courses offered in centres in Argentina, Brazil, Chile, Peru, China, Costa Rica, Czech Republic, Greece, Italy, Mexico, Spain, Thailand, Turkey and Vietnam; all courses cost US$1,995 including registration fee, tuition and books; also offers 2 week residential plus 80 hours online course ($1,495).

International House Vancouver

You have to do your homework before you start your teacher training. I wanted a course that would include a teaching practicum and give me a solid foundation, and I also wanted a credential that would be portable. My research led me to International House Vancouver, and they made my decision an easy one. They offer CELTA and the International House Certificate in Teaching Languages (IHCTL), both of which are well recognized around the world and by TESL Canada.

The instructors were excellent and knowledgeable, but I had my doubts that you could truly get ready to teach in just one month, but part way through the program I had a eureka moment. One morning, as part of our training, we went to observe a typical ESL class in the school. It was readily apparent that the integrated skills approach that is at the core of the IH program really works. Another important aspect of the course was the instructor feedback right after each teaching practice. It was extremely useful to have this prompt feedback while the lesson was still fresh. In retrospect I really liked the fact that the course was so intensive and immersive. The course gave me confidence and the essential tools needed to get started in a great new career.

Tony Madson

GLOBAL TESOL COLLEGE: main website: www.globaltesol.com and headquarters in Canada: 7712, 104 St, Edmonton, Alberta T6E 4C5; in North America: ✆ +1 888 270 2941/+1 780 438 5704; tesol@globaltesol.com; US-East in North America: ✆ +1 866 837 6565; tesol@tesolworld.com; US-West in North America: ✆ +1 888 837 6587; info@globaltesol usa.com; Australia: ✆ +61 7 3221 5100; teachenglish@sarinarusso.com.au; China: +86 134 0508 0034; info@teflcoursechina.com; Greece: ✆ +30 274 302 9012; Georgia@ globaltesol.gr; for accommodation: info@linguisticlab.com; India: ✆ +91 172 2692682; info@tesolindia.com; Malaysia: ✆ +6085 413778; joanne@globaltesol.com.my; Mexico: ✆ +52 818 368 2410; linda@engcanada.com; New Zealand: nz@globaltesol.co.nz; Phil-ippines: ✆ +632 910 1438; global@edulynxcorp.com; Singapore: ✆ +65 6221 3957; info@globalelt.org; Taiwan: ✆ +886 2 2369 1181 (24 hrs); anne@globaltesol.com.

SIT (SCHOOL FOR INTERNATIONAL TRAINING) GRADUATE INSTITUTE: Kipling Road, PO Box 676, Brattleboro, VT 05302; ✆ 800 257 7751; tesolcert@sit.edu; www.sit.edu/tesolcert; Full-time; 130-hour SIT TESOL Certificate course offered in various locations in the US and worldwide including Chicago, IL and Rohnert Park, CA (see Global TEFL above under USA), Quito (Ecuador), Oaxaca (Mexico), Bangkok and Chiang Mai (Thailand), Guatemala City and Quetzeltanango (Guatemala), Kharviv (Ukraine) and others; fees vary from $1,400 in Thailand to $2,295 in the US.

TEFL INTERNATIONAL: admin@teflinternational.org.uk; www.teflinternational.org.uk; USA Head office: 1200 Belle Passi Rd. Woodburn, OR 97071; TEFL International TESOL Certifi-cate, 120-hour including observed Teaching Practice; available worldwide – full-time, Part-time and Distance Learning; Special Projects with guaranteed work or internship (including volunteer projects); TEFL International World Wide Locations: Buenos Aires, Beijing, Hong Kong, Shanghai, Zhuhai, Manuel Antonio, Prague, Alexandria, Brittany, Corinth, Calcutta, Florence, Rome, Tokyo, Kathmandu, Cebu (Philippines), Lubin, Seoul, Barcelona, Seville, Ban Phe, Chiang Mai and Phuket, London, New York, Woodburn, Ho Chi Minh City; most centres offer the course every month; prices vary slightly from US$1,390 to US$1,790, but with regular specials and discount programmes.

ARGENTINA

EBC SERVICIOS LINGÜÍSTICOS: Anchorena 1676, 1425 Capital Federal, Buenos Aires; ✆ 800 845 6719 (UK, free); ✆ +1 888 393 4015 (US free); info@ebc-tefl-course.com; www. ebc-tefl-course.com; US$1,559.

ÍBERO SPANISH SCHOOL:, 150 Uruguay Street, Buenos Aires; ✆ +54 11 5218 0240; info@ iberospanish.com, info@iberotefl.com; www.iberospanish.com, www.iberotefl.com; inten-sive 4-week TEFL certificate courses offered monthly; $870 plus course materials costing $45; can be combined with 3 weeks Spanish tuition for $ 1,240; followed by optional 4-day trip to Iguazu Falls.

TEFL INTERNATIONAL: Recoleta Institute, Ayacucho 1571, Buenos Aires; ✆ +5411 6380 3134; admin@teflinternational.org.uk; www.teflinternational.org.uk; 120-hour TESOL; monthly start dates; course fee $1,790.

AUSTRALIA

AUSTRALIAN TESOL TRAINING CENTRE (ATTC): Sydney: Level 1, 31 Market Street, Sydney, NSW 2000; ✆ +61 2 9389 0249; Brisbane: Level 1, 295 Ann Street, Brisbane, QLD 4001; ✆ +61 7 3229 0350; train@attc.edu.au; www.attc.edu.au. CELTA centres that offer Foundation in TESOL course (4 weeks) full and part-time courses throughout the year; accommodation service available; internet enrolment $1,500.

ENGLISH LANGUAGE SERVICES: Adelaide Institute of Technical and Further Education (part of the Government Department of Education, Training and Employment), 5th Floor,

International House Sol Group

Andrea receives a letter from a former student at International House Sol Group:

Hello Andrea!!!

How are you?? I hope all is well.

I must first apologize since it has taken me so long to update you on my situation here. Although incredibly busy, everything since I have got to Paris has been fantastic.

Very soon after I got here I had two interviews - one with a craigslist guy (not a school - more of a company) and secondly with Nadia from ELS (the person you connected me with).

I want to take this opportunity to say thank you so much for all of your effort and time you put into helping me find a job. I have accepted a position with ELS and I really enjoy it. I have signed a contract working towards a full-time position with them until December (short contracts I think are quite common with the crisis). Regardless, if they like me and all else goes right around December they will extend my contract. For now, I love the school. Great people, super resources and very secure (the French socialist system only adds to my enthusiasm - a lot of health coverage, 5 weeks' paid vacation and pretty good pay). I was working two jobs, but have now moved fully to the ELS school since they have increased my hours and offer me lots of security.

On that note, I would like to thank you once more for being so wonderful, hardworking and helpful during my training at IH and more importantly during the hunt for a job in Paris. I still can't believe that all of this has material-ized so perfectly. I would like to stress that you greatly contributed to my success here. Sending my contact to Nadia has made things fantastic, easy and very relieving. So... THANK YOU!!!!!

I will keep you updated as things move along here. As I have already men-tioned the school is great and I think will only get better.

Okay Andrea have a wonderful day, and let's keep in touch.

Oh yes... I cannot stress the value of the IH TESL teacher training pro-gram. It has allowed me to utilize my skills in a way that I know the people I am working for and the students I am teaching are obviously noticing and crediting me on... awesome.

Sincerely,

Julie Gorecki

Renaissance Centre, 127 Rundle Mall, Adelaide, South Australia 5000; ✆ 8 8207 8805; els.tesol@tafesa.edu.au; http://els.sa.edu.au; Certificate IV in TESOL; 315 curriculum hour course AUS $3,300; TESOL for overseas teachers and TESOL online.

GLOBAL TESOL AUSTRALIA: Sarina Russo Centre, 82 Ann Street, Brisbane, Queensland 4000; ✆ +61 7 3221 5100; teachenglish@sarinarusso.com.au; www.globaltesol.com; 120-hour to 600-hour programmes available; tuition fees AUS $995–AS $2,300; all courses can be completed in-class, online or by correspondence; job overseas guaranteed.

TEACH INTERNATIONAL: Head Office, Level 2, 370 George Street, Brisbane, Queensland 4000; ✆ +61 7 3211 4633 ext 4; www.teachinternational.com; Foundation in TESOL, 100 hours, AUS $1,695; Certificate III in TESOL, 110 hours, AUS $2,295, and Certificate IV in TESOL, 220 hours, AUS $2,995, accredited by Australian government; offered throughout the year.

BULGARIA

TEFL VARNA: Varna, 3 Tcar Asen Street, info@TEFLVarna-bg.com; www.teflvarna-bg.com; 4 week, 120+ hour intensive course; over 12 hours of teaching practice, observed by teacher-trainers; approximately 10 courses per year; course fee €1,150; job assistance provided.

CAMBODIA

CamTEFL: Conversations with Foreigners (CWF), Corner St 478 and St 155, Toul Tumpung, Phnom Penh; info@camtefl.org; www.camtefl.org; 4-week accredited TEFL certificate course run on a not-for-profit basis; CamTEFL courses are scheduled to fit with volunteering at the school; cost is US$1,450.

LANGUAGECORPS ASIA CO LTD: Phnom Penh, Cambodia; ✆ +855 23 211 087; +1 508 471 4852 (US); 0203 287 4853 (UK); www.languagecorpsasia.com; also in Thailand and Vietnam; 4 Week 144-hour TESOL courses available monthly in Cambodia, Thailand, Vietnam and special China/Taiwan programmes; $1,750 includes initial 2 weeks academic instruction at Panasastra University in Cambodia followed by final 2 weeks in country of choice with 20 hours of local language classes, 15 hours of teaching practice, and daily lesson planning and materials development workshops; also includes 3-day excursion to Angkor Wat; job placement assistance is provided in each country.

CHILE

THE TEFL ACADEMY: Av. Las Urbinas 68, Providencia, Santiago; ✆ +560 245 36740; info@tefl-academy.com; www.tefl-academy.com; 120-hour certificate course; offered monthly; US $1,499; life-long job assistance.

CHINA

BUSINESS ENGLISH SOLUTIONS INTERNATIONAL, LLC: Zhejiang China and 510 West Deming Place, Chicago IL 60614; ✆ 773 572 2473 (Chicago); ✆ +86 13757252787 (China); Info@journeyeast.org; www.Journeyeast.org; TEFL Certification and iTEFL (Intensive TEFL China Certification); US $1,800–$2,800 including accommodation; ESL Job Placement Service.

TEFL INTERNATIONAL: At Gateway Language Village, Xiangzhou Culture Plaza, Ningxi Road, Zhuhai; ✆ 756 229 8967; admin@teflinternational.org.uk; www.teflinternational.org.uk; 120-hour accredited TESOL certificate course; good job and internship prospects all over China with the job placement assistance programme; course runs monthly and costs US$1,590 (including accommodation).

COLOMBIA

ISSO – INTERNATIONAL STUDENT SERVICES ORG: Calle 24N #5 BN-63, ✆ +57 2 680 2001; also in Bogotá: Cra. 15 # 95–35; ✆ 2 218 1679; teflestudiosexterior.com; www.estudiosexterior.com; training centres in Bogotá, Cali, Medellin and Barranquilla. 3 courses offered – TEFL, TEYL and TKT (preparation course); accredited by Colombian Ministry of Education and in association with ILAC (International Language Academy of Canada); course includes 10 hours of class observation and 10 hours of teaching practice.

COSTA RICA

CENTRO ESPIRAL MANA/TESOL TRAINING COSTA RICA, El INVU: de Peñas Blancas, Via San Carlos, Alajuela; ✆ 506 468 0020 or in USA: ✆ 585 200 3091; tesoltrainingcosta rica@hotmail.com; www.tesoltrainingcostarica.org; School for International Training's TESOL Certificate Course; 1-month intensive, 3-month extensive; US $1,950 tuition, US $600 room and board in local homes or rented houses plus materials; other teacher training and training of trainer courses designed and delivered based on demand.

COSTA RICA TEFL: Heredia and Playa Samara; info@costaricatefl.com; www.costaricatefl.com; offers 10 TEFL Certification courses per year, 160 hours' contact time; costs $1,350, including job placement assistance, course materials, course portfolio and text and access to local cultural events as well as a 10% discount on Spanish classes at Intercultura; the core instructors all have Masters degrees and/or higher in Education and in teaching English as a second or foreign language with more than 22 years of professional teaching experience; Heredia courses affiliated to Intercultura Costa Rica; www.interculturacostarica.com; see entry in Central America chapter.

TEFL INTERNATIONAL: TEFL International, S.A. Apartado #161 Quepos, 6350 Costa Rica; admin@teflinternational.org.uk; www.teflinternational.org.uk; 120-hour TESOL; optional Spanish as a Second Language Course; monthly start dates; course fee $1,690.

CYPRUS

INTESOL: Limassol; UK office: ✆ 1565 631 366; info@intesolinternational.com; www. intesolinternational.com; 4-week TESOL course with teaching practice; lifetime job guidance.

PAPANTONIOU INSTITUTE: 30a Ippocratous, Nicosia 2122; ✆ +357 22455724; papanto-niouinstitute@yahoo.co.uk; www.papantoniou-institute.com; 6-week teaching refresher courses and 8-week TEFL courses, with monthly start dates; validated by IATQI and ASET/ CIACQ; full range of LTTC and LCCI courses.

CZECH REPUBLIC

BOHEMIA TEFL: Pražská 24, IGY Centrum, 370 04 České Budějovice; ✆ +420 387 426 753/✆ 734 481 587; info@tefl-course.eu; www.tefl-course.eu; 2 or 4 week courses (65 or 130 hours) with minimum 10 hours observed teaching practice; free organised activities during the course from adventure sports to beer tours; job assistance on completion of the course.

THE CALEDONIAN SCHOOL: Vltavská 24, 150 00 Prague 5; ✆ 2 5731 3650; jobs@caledonian school.com; www.caledonianschool.com; 4-week intensive TEFL course in Prague; visa assistance; job guarantee available (see website for further details).

ITC INTERNATIONAL TEFL CERTIFICATE: Frantiska Křížka 1, Prague 7 170 00; ✆ 224817530; info@itc-training.com; ITC trains English speakers during a 4-week intensive course offered monthly which includes Business English; tuition is US $1,440 (Prague only), which includes registration, lifetime TEFL career and job guidance, course manual, all materials, and housing and visa help; ITC is a member of IATEFL, College of Teachers (UK), and TESOL; contact info@itc-training.com or apply online at www.itc-training.com.

TEFL INTERNATIONAL: Prague – new centre from May 2010; admin@teflinternational.org.uk; www.teflinternational.org.uk; 120-hour TESOL; optional Czech Language Course; monthly start dates; from $1,490.

TEFL: Worldwide Prague. Freyova ul. 12/1, 190 00 Prague; ✆ +420 603 486 830; info@ teflworldwideprague.com; www.teflworldwideprague.com; British and American owned school offering 4-week TEFL course in Prague; courses offered monthly; job assistance worldwide.

ECUADOR

CENTRO DE ESTUDIOS INTERAMERICANOS/CEDEI: Casilla 597, Cuenca; ✆ 7 283 9003; info @cedei.org; www.cedei.org; summer TEFL programme, $3,225 including accommodation.

EGYPT

AMERICAN UNIVERSITY IN CAIRO: PO Box 74 New Cairo 11835; ✆ 2 2797 4978; teflinfo@ aucegypt.edu; www.aucegypt.edu; US enquiries to 420 Fifth Avenue, 3rd Floor, New York, NY 10018 2729; ✆ 212 730 8800; offers MA in Teaching English as a Foreign Language (MA/TEFL); American-style education in an overseas setting.

TEFL INTERNATIONAL: 4,Shohdy Basha Street, Stanly, Alexandria; admin@teflinternational.org. uk; www.teflinternational.org.uk; 120-hour TESOL; monthly start dates; course fee $1,690; optional teaching Internship programme with Arabic language and cultural programme, 10 weeks US$1,990 (incl. accommodation); steady supply of jobs in Cairo.

FRANCE

TEFL INTERNATIONAL: Association Camina Kergall, 22570 Plèlauff, Britanny; admin@teflinter- national.org.uk; www.teflinternational.org.uk; 120-hour TESOL; monthly start dates; course fee €1,590.

TEFL PARIS: 8 rue des Carmes, 75005 Paris; 143 25 7966; www.teflparis.com; 4-week cer- tificate course operating since 2004. 8 times a year. €1,200 plus accommodation €320– €400.

GERMANY

LANGUAGE SPECIALISTS INTERNATIONAL: Pfalzburger Strasse 83, 10719 Berlin; ✆ 30 3450 2180; info@lsi-berlin.de; www.tefl-germany.com; 4-week TESOL courses run every month; €1,375.

GREECE

ANGLO-HELLENIC TEACHER TRAINING: PO Box 263, Corinth 20100; ✆ 27410 53511; info@ teflcorinth.com; www.teflcorinth.com. Delivers training course for TEFL International (see entry below).

CELT: Athens; ✆ 210 330 2406; www.celt.edu.gr; €1,450; 100+ hour Certificate course; also offer CELTA course, €1,300.

TEFL INTERNATIONAL: TEFL certificate offered every month; 120 hours full-time over 4 weeks, 10 hours observed teaching practice; all tutors are Britons or Americans resident in Greece and experienced teachers with MAs in ELT; cost €1,670; accommodation in furnished apartment, €350 single, €250 shared; extensive optional social programme; help with job placement via Anglo-Hellenic Teacher Recruitment (see Greece chapter); range of short teacher development courses including preparation course for the Cambridge ESOL TKT; 30 hours full-time over 1 week, or weekend options (see www.tkt.gr); €275.

TEFL INTERNATIONAL: 45 Kyprou Street, Corinth, 20100 Peloponnese; admin@teflinterna- tional.org.uk; www.teflinternational.org.uk; 120-hour TESOL; monthly start dates; course fee €1,590; English teaching jobs in Greece service available.

VIA LINGUA CRETE Chrysanthou Episkopou 48, Chania 73 132; 28210 574 38; crete@vialingua. org; www.vialingua.org. Offered monthly €1325 plus €300 shared accommodation.

HONG KONG

CHINESE UNIVERSITY OF HONG KONG: 23/F, Tower, B, School of Continuing and Professional Studies, The Chinese University of Hong Kong, Mongkok Town Centre, 90 Shantung Street,

TEFL Worldwide

Ginny Thompson remembers her experiences from the October 2006 course with TEFL Worldwide:

When I think back about my two years living abroad, it's amazing to realize how much my four-week experience with TEFL Worldwide Prague has impacted my life. With a bag packed for only those four weeks, I arrived in Prague with an open mind and a desire to experience a life and culture outside of the States. Little did I know, I would end up living in the Czech Republic for two years, working in Spain, South Korea and Peru, traveling the world, developing lifelong friendships and most importantly experiencing illuminating growth.

Although I had traveled and studied abroad before, I still arrived in Prague full of anxiety, a pounding heart and thoughts like, 'How can I possibly teach English to someone who doesn't understand English?' These thoughts were quickly comforted by a lovely welcome to the city from TEFL Worldwide Prague from the moment I arrived at my accommodation. It was reassuring to arrive in a completely foreign place and feel so well cared for and encouraged by TEFL Worldwide to truly make the most of my certification experience. The instructors were patient, competent and extremely knowledgeable in the TEFL field. As I had never taught a class before in my life I was shocked at how by the end of the four weeks I felt confident to walk into any classroom anywhere in the world and teach an engaging, successful lesson.

I will always treasure memories like cooking dinner with friends while laughing over creative lesson ideas, the smile on my Czech student's face when she finally understood a grammar point, and the clinking of champagne glasses at the end of an incredible experience. TEFL Worldwide provided a program that not only gave me an excellent skill-set but also the freedom to be creative in my teaching, the support to find a job and home, and the encouragement to go out and explore the world. I've always said the most difficult part of leaving your comfort zone and moving abroad is that initial decision to pack your bags and get on a plane. After that first step, the world you enter will be an exciting, adventure filled place full of experiences you can't even imagine. From then on your world will expand horizons beyond horizons and you will be so thankful you took that initial risk. TEFL Worldwide Prague welcomed me into that world, taught me to embrace it and will forever hold a special place in my heart www.teflworldwideprague.com.

Mongkok, Kowloon; ✆ 2209 0235; http://english.scs.cuhk.edu.hk/scs/course/lang/eng/ab/doc/071-393000-01?disp=en; two courses on offer: Diploma Programme in Teaching English as a Second Language, 10 months, tuition fee HK$13,500 plus HK$100 enrolment fee; Master of Arts Programme in Teaching English to Speakers of Other Languages (jointly organised by School of Continuing and Professional Studies, The Chinese University of Hong Kong and Lancaster University), 2 years, tuition fee HK$ 89,800 plus HK$200 enrolment fee; contact Carol To, Programme Coordinator.

HUNGARY

VIA LINGUA BUDAPEST: Tavasz u. 3, 1033 Budapest; ✆ +36 1 368 11 56; Budapest@via lingua.org; www.vialingua.org; 4-week intensive Certificate in TEFL course.

INDIA

TEFL INTERNATIONAL: Golpark, Kolkata, Bengal; admin@teflinternational.org.uk; www.teflinter national.org.uk; 120-hour TESOL; monthly start dates; course fee $1,490; internship, volunteering and paid teaching work arranged.

IRELAND

ALPHA COLLEGE OF ENGLISH: 4, North Great George's Street, Dublin 1; ✆ 1 8747024; admin@alphacollege.com; www.alphacollege.com.

CENTRE OF ENGLISH STUDIES: 31, Dame Street, Dublin 2; ✆ 1 6714233; info@ces-schools. com; www.ces-schools.com.

CLARE LANGUAGE CENTRE: Erasmus Smith Building, College Road, Ennis, Co Clare; ✆ 65 6841681; clarelc@iol.ie; www.clarelc.ie.

CORK LANGUAGE CENTRE INTERNATIONAL: Wellington House, 16, St Patrick's Place, Wellington Road, Cork; ✆ 21 4551661; info@corklanguagecentre.ie; www.corklanguagecentre.ie.

DORSET COLLEGE: 66 Lower Dorset St, Dublin 1; ✆ 1 8309677; info@dorset-college.ie; www.dorset-college.ie.

DUBLIN SCHOOL OF ENGLISH: Dollard House, 2–5 Wellington Quay, Temple Bar, Dublin 2; ✆ 1 6773322; admin@dse.ie; www.dse.ie.

GALWAY LANGUAGE CENTRE: The Bridge Mills, Galway; ✆ 91 566468; info@galway language.com; www.galwaylanguage.com.

INTERNATIONAL HOUSE DUBLIN: 66, Lower Camden Street, Dublin 2; ✆ 1 4759011/3; info@ihdublin.com; www.ihdublin.com.

NORTH MON LANGUAGE INSTITUTE: North Monastery Road, Cork; ✆ 21 4394458; info@ nmli.ie; www.nmli.ie.

U-LEARN: 6 Gardiner Place, Dublin 1; ✆ 1 8787 339; info@u-learn.ie; www.u-learn.ie.

MEI-RELSA: 1 Lower Pembroke Street, Dublin 2; ✆ 1 618 0910; ✆ 1 618 0909; brian. burns@mei.ie; www.mei.ie; is an association of recognised schools and a representative body (similar to English UK); many MEI-RELSA schools provide teacher training courses (TEFL) and ACELS-accredited courses.

Other course providers in the Republic of Ireland include:

INTERNATIONAL TEFL COLLEGE OF IRELAND: 29 Northumberland Avenue, Dun Laoghaire, Co. Dublin; ✆ 1 280 7001; info@itci.ie; www.itci.ie; 100-hour TEFL training courses; several courses run throughout the academic year (September to May); €500; teaching practice with foreign students free of charge.

ISRAEL

TASP (TEACH AND STUDY PROGRAM): Kadima, Israel; ✆ 9 899 5644; www.tasp.org.il; MA in Teaching English as a Foreign Language combined with 15 hours a week of interning in schools and Hebrew language classes; US contact: Jewish Federation of Greater Los Angeles (Talia Scharlin, TScharlin@JewishLA.org); from US $11,000 per year.

ITALY

ACLE (ASSOCIAZIONE CULTURALE LINGUISTICA EDUCATIONAL): Via Roma, 54, 18038 Sanremo; ✆ 0184 506070; info@acle.org; www.acle.org; 5–6 day intensive TEFL-TP (Through Theatre and Play) introductory course with full board and lodging included; €150 course fee; successful students work as paid tutors, teaching English at camps throughout Italy (see Italy chapter); this project offers a combination of theory plus invaluable practical

MEI

Ireland as quality English language destination: English Language Schools in Ireland have been offering English language programmes to international schools since the early 1960s. It was then a small industry, more or less a cottage industry, but grew throughout the years as the country developed and industrialised. It is now a thriving sector with international students from every corner of the globe studying in all parts of Ireland. In 2008 approximately 116,000 students chose Ireland as their destination for international programmes.

The quality sector of the industry is represented by **Marketing English in Ireland (MEI)** (www.mei.ie), a collection of approximately 60 quality organisations dedicated to attracting students who wish to study intensive courses in Ireland. Member schools of MEI offer programmes to adults, young adults and juniors for seasonal or year-round courses. In MEI schools teacher qualifications, facilities, premises, training programmes and accommodation facilities have all been certified by the Irish Government Department of Education & Skills, ensuring that they are all of the highest level of quality. MEI schools do short-term programmes, year-round programmes, academic-year programmes (High School), closed programmes, international examination preparation and – with the MEI Foundation Course – work with third level institutions to groom students for entry to university programmes in Irish Colleges. Accommodation is arranged in residences, apartments or host family accommodation.

All these programmes of quality standard are offered in a setting of great charm and warmth. Whether it be in the city or countryside Ireland offers unique possibilities for the international student to savour a pace and a rhythm of life that makes learning a pleasure. As a destination of quality education Ireland offers the international student all the facilities necessary for the attainment of perfection.

experience with emphasis on drama and child-centred learning activities; tutors receive an introductory TEFL Certificate at the end of the working period.

INTERLINGUE LANGUAGE SYSTEM: Via Ennio Quirino Visconti 20, 00193 Rome; ✆ 06 321 5740/321 0317; info@interlingue-it.com; www.interlingue-it.com; TEFL International PELT Certificate courses run monthly (tefl.rome@interlingue-it.com; www.teflinternationalrome. it). €1,300 without accommodation; accommodation from €400; jobs often available for the best students on the courses.

TEACHING ENGLISH IN ITALY: Florence; www.teachingenglishinitaly.com. 4-week intensive courses offered monthly in Florence, US $500 deposit plus €1,190. Online course also offered which can be supplemented with Teaching Practice Programme in Florence lasting 1 or 2 weeks.

THE LEARNING CENTER OF TUSCANY, LLC: Viale Corsica, 15c/17a, Florence 50134; ✆ 39 055 051 5035; Cell USA ✆ 1 831 917 4752; www.learningcentertuscany.com; CTEFL school affiliated with TEFL International, offering a 4-week course in the basic methods of English language teaching, mainly for native English speakers; offered monthly; deposit of €500 plus €960.

VIA LINGUA FLORENCE, Via Brunelleschi 1 50123 Florence; ✆ 055 283161; florence@vialingua.org; www.cteflflorence.com; TEFL Certificate moderated by ELT Institute, Hunter College, City University of New York; 1-month intensive; approximately 10 a year; course fee €1,175.

JAPAN

TEFL INTERNATIONAL: Watanabe Students House, 18–15 Kamiyama-cho, Shibuya, Tokyo; admin@teflinternational.org.uk; www.teflinternational.org.uk; 120-hour TESOL; monthly start dates; course fee US$2,290; paid teaching work arranged.

MEXICO

DUNHAM INSTITUTE: Avenida Zaragoza 23, Chiapa de Corzo, Chiapas; © 961 61 61498; academic-coordinator@dunhaminstitute.com; www.dunhaminstitute.com; 4-week TEFL course in conjunction with Spanish courses and language exchange and tutoring of local students; minimum commitment 8 weeks if tutoring local students or 5 months if teaching in schools; US$1,500 includes free homestay with local family.

INTERNATIONAL TEACHER TRAINING ORGANIZATION: Madero No. 469, Guadalajara, Jalisco 44100; © 52 33 3658 3224/03614 3800; toll-free from UK: © 800 404 9800; toll-free from USA: © +1 866 514 7479; info@www.teflcertificatecourses.com; www.teflcertificatecourses.com/guadalajara.html; offered monthly; US$1,400.

TEACHERS LATIN AMERICA: Avenida Cuauhtemoc 793, Colonia Narvarte, DF; © 55 52564108; teachers@innovative-english.com; www.innovative-english.com; 80-hour plus TEFL Certificate Programme; 40 hours in-class study, 10–20 hours of instructor-assessed student teaching and at least 25 additional hours of self-study on grammar, lesson planning, etc. US$1,190 including accommodation; job assistance throughout Latin America; TEFL online certificate course US$350.

PERU

MÁXIMO NIVEL EXECUTIVE LANGUAGE CENTER; Avenida El Sol 612, Cusco (Peru) and Antiguo Higueron 100 metros sur 50 metros este, San Pedro, San Jose (Costa Rica); © +51 84 25 7200; info@maximonivel.net; www.maximonivel.net; 150-hour TEFL/TESOL Certificate (over 4 weeks) for US$1,600 offered monthly except December; 50-hour TEIB (Teaching English for International Business) Certificate and TIEEP (Teaching International English Exam Preparation) Certificate (over 6 days), US$400 each; rough frequency 4 times a year; housing arranged with families, in shared apartments, hostels, etc. from US$225 for 4 weeks; lifetime job-finding assistance; an average of 5 graduates are employed by Máximo Nivel each month.

SEPA DEL PERU: (Servicios Educativos Peruanos Americanos del Peru), Puente Bolognesi 114–116, Arequipa; © 54 222390; educationalexcellence@gmail.com or sepa@perupass.com; www.perupass.com (click on the logo of SEPA del Peru); 13-week TEFL training and volunteer teaching programme ('World's Toughest TEFL/TESOL Program'); monthly start dates; US$2,955; possibility of extra Spanish classes (US$75 for 10 hours per week); homestay or alternative accommodation (US$40–$65 a week).

PORTUGAL

INTERNATIONAL HOUSE LISBON: Rua Marques Sá da Bandeira 16, 1050–148 Lisbon; © 21 315 1493/4/6; ttraining@ihlisbon.com; 4 week (120 hours) CELTA courses (€1,450); also part-time DELTA course (200 hours) and IH Younger Learners Certificate (€725).

SOUTH AFRICA

TEACHERS SA/ONE WORLD LANGUAGE SCHOOL: 5th Floor, 50 Long Street, Cape Town 8001; © 21 422 4493; info@teacherssa.co.za; www.teachersSA.co.za; entry-level TEFL courses focusing on the fundamentals of communicative language teaching; run throughout the year; courses run in Cape Town and Pretoria.

SPAIN

CANTERBURY TEFL: Calle covarrubias 22, 2° Derecha, 28010 Madrid; ✆ 91 125 01 09; www.canterburytefl.com; 40 hours of teaching theory supplemented by 40 hours of lesson planning, 20 hours class observation and 20 hours paid internship. Course fee €1,275 reduced by €280 for paid teaching.

EBC SERVICIOS LINGÜÍSTICOS: Orense 16, 2E, 28020 Madrid; ✆ 91 555 3975; info@ebc-tefl-course.com; www. ebc-tefl-course.com; offered monthly; approx £915/€1,175.

EUROPE TEFL TEACHER TRAINING: Salvador Espriu 91, 08005 Barcelona; ✆ 932 215 515 info@europetefl.com; www.europetefl.com; 4-week intensive full-time; TEFL courses run throughout the year in Barcelona, Seville, and many other locations in Europe and Latin America; €1,300, including all course materials, expert job guidance, alumni network and more; accommodation in the city centre and close to the schools can be arranged, €400–500 a month; contact: Kevin Cline.

INTERNATIONAL HOUSE BARCELONA: Calle Trafalgar 14, 08010 Barcelona; ✆ 93 268 4511; training@bcn.ihes.com; www.ihes.com/bcn; Business English Teachers course, 36 hours over 2 weeks, July only, €450; also, Director of Studies Training Course and Trainer Training Course, both 1 week in July, €425; and the International Diploma in Language Teaching Management (IDLTM), 2-week on-site course in July followed by 8 months of on-line assignments, €2,950; help given with finding accommodation.

ITC INTERNATIONAL TEFL CERTIFICATE BARCELONA/MADRID: See entry under heading Czech Republic above.

TEFL INTERNATIONAL: In Seville, Granada and Barcelona. admin@teflinternational.org.uk; www.teflinternational.org.uk; 120-hour TESOL; monthly start dates; course fee from €1,390.

TtMADRID: Calle General Yague 70, 1°, 28020 Madrid; ✆ +34 91 572 1999; info@ttmadrid.com; www.ttmadrid.com; 4-week intensive courses accredited by IATQUO; courses run monthly; course fee €1,275; participants must be at least 21 and have a degree or equivalent work experience; assistance with accommodation; interviews with top teaching agencies arranged on graduation with members of their agency group; course emphasis on teaching Business English; real teaching experience with adults and elective inputs on how to teach children; small, intimate groups with complete support during and after the course.

THAILAND

AYC INTERCULTURAL PROGRAMS: 9/197, 7th Floor, GOT Building Soi Ratchadaphisek 29, Ratchadaphisek Road, Chatuchak, Bangkok, 10900; ✆ +66 2556 1533 38; gettesol@aycthailand.com; www.aycthailand.com, www.gettesol.com; 120 hour TESOL certification validated by INTESOL; course runs every month and costs US$899; job guarantee for native English speakers under 52 years of age, holding a bachelor's degree.

CHICHESTER COLLEGE, THAILAND: 1st Fl., Muangthai Phatra Complex, 252/193 Rachadapisek Rd., Bangkok 10320; ✆ 2 693 2901; www.chichester.ac.th; TESOL certificate and diploma courses in cooperation with Chichester College UK; certificate runs 10 weeks part-time 5 times a year, or 4 weeks full-time (offered monthly); TESOL diploma course runs over 6 months beginning October and April; US$1,490 for full-time Certificate course, US$890 for part-time; US$1,800 for Diploma; accommodation offered at a private lodge near the Chichester Training Centre in Bangkok, and provided at a special subsidised rate of US$100 for the entire duration of the full-time course only; graduates are provided teaching placements in Thailand or Cambodia.

PARADISE TEFL THAILAND: ✆ +66 846 161609; info@teachinparadise.com; www.teach-inparadise.com; 4-week courses in Chiang Mai in Northern Thailand; 4-week Certificate

Canterbury TEFL

Receive your Advanced TESOL Certificate in Madrid, Spain

Canterbury Tefl has been certifying teachers for over 10 years with 1,500 graduates to date, becoming one of the most innovative and hands-on Tefl courses to be found. As an important complement to classroom instruction the company provides the highest amount of required teaching hours in the field with its 'paid practicum module'. The course has the double advantage of being accredited by one of the most prestigious organisations in education, the College of Teachers of London, while constantly implementing new ideas.

In March 2010, Canterbury launched a new feature in the course that highlights its philosophy of combining excellent classroom instruction with the immediate application of the concepts taught. Students participate with trained instructors in teaching school groups for five days at its second training facility in the province of Leon. This part of the programme is presently being expanded to include adult and business groups.

Canterbury Tefl provides guaranteed teaching jobs for all graduates at both its institutes in Madrid: Canterbury English and Canterbury Consulting Spain, which have been providing language services since 1994. Both are official test centres for the Toeic and Toefl Exams by ETS (provider of the GMAT and SAT exams), Extracurricular English course centres for the University of Alcala de Henares' 'Instituto Franklin', and Members of the Madrid Chamber of Commerce.

Canterbury Tefl offers the possibility for experienced graduates to work in the Spanish school system, in association with the organisation UCETAM, which is responsible for placing English teaching assistants in over 100 schools in and around Madrid. In the summer Canterbury helps with placement in English camps that it runs directly or in many other camps that have come to rely on its graduates. For more information, visit www.canterburytefl.com.

course (120 hours) plus 2-week and weekend intro course. 4-week course costs 40,000 Baht (£600) including guaranteed job placement.

THE TEFL INSTITUTE: United Educational Consultants Co. Ltd, 4th Floor, Silom Plaza, Silom Road corner Narathiwat Road, Bangkok 10500; ℂ 2 233 2388; info@teflthai.com; www.teflthai.com; 120 hours over 5 weeks with more than 20 start dates throughout the year; 44,500 Baht; course earns eligible graduates 9 US graduate credits in education, US Master's degree can be completed in 1 year while teaching in Thailand, also offers graduate diploma in teaching, 3.5 year part-time Bachelor degree in education, and weekend study for 1.5-year dual US and Thai accredited master's degree (www.uecthai.com), including required Thai teaching licence.

TEFL INTERNATIONAL: 38/53–55 Moo 1, Klaeng, Muang Rayong 21160; ℂ 38 652 280; admin@teflinternational.org.uk; www.teflinternational.org.uk; 120-hour TESOL certificate course at Ban Phe, Chiang Mai and Phuket; £875 includes accommodation; job and volunteering prospects arranged throughout Thailand.

TEXT AND TALK ACADEMY: 1960 Phaholyothin Road (opposite Mayo Hospital), Lardyao, Chatuchak, Bangkok 10900; ℂ +662 561 3443; info@TEFLTeachThai.com; www.tefl-teach-thai.com; 4 and 6 week certificate courses (about US$1,395), upgrade and refresher course, 16 week diploma course, 8 week TEYL course, 8 week advanced skills course and home study course.

FINDING A JOB

You have only two choices: to search for a job from afar or go to the country of your choice and look around. Having a job arranged before departure obviously removes much of the uncertainty and anxiety of leaving home for an extended period. It also allows the possibility of preparing in appropriate ways: sorting out the right visa, researching the course books in use, etc. Others prefer to meet their employer and inspect the school before signing a contract. It is always an advantage to meet or make contact with other teachers to get the real lowdown on a particular employer and place, rather than accepting a job in complete ignorance of the prevailing conditions. But of course this is not always feasible.

Employers usually choose their staff several months before they are needed, so most schools advertise between April and July for jobs starting in September. If you want to look for a job in person, you will either have to go on a reconnaissance mission well in advance of your proposed starting date or take your chances of finding a last-minute vacancy.

FINDING A JOB IN ADVANCE
There are three ways of finding a teaching job in advance

- *By answering an online advertisement*
- *Using a recruitment agency or the large international English teaching organisations such as International House*
- *Conducting a speculative job search, i.e. making contact by e-mail or letter with all the schools whose addresses you can find in this book or on the internet.*

TEFL WEBSITES

For schools, a website advert offers an easy and instantaneous means of publicising a vacancy to an international audience. Teachers looking for employment can use search engines to look for all pages with references to EFL, English language schools and recruitment. CVs can be e-mailed quickly and cheaply to advertising schools, who can then use e-mail themselves to chase up references. The internet has very quickly taken over as the primary means of recruitment.

Arguably it has become a little too easy to advertise and answer job adverts online. At the press of a button, your CV can be clogging up dozens, nay, hundreds of computers. It is interesting to remark that some of the schools that corresponded with this book for the current edition said that they seemed to get a more reliable brand of teacher from readers of this book and that they are more impressed with a job-seeker who goes to the trouble of assimilating the information in a book than the ones who spend their days skating over the internet. But basically, recruitment via the internet is here to stay.

While opening up an enormous range of possibilities, the internet can be a bewildering place to job-hunt. A host of websites promises to provide free online recruitment services for English teachers. Because many sites are struggling on the margins, they often seem to offer more than they can deliver and you may find that the number and range of jobs posted are disappointing. You would hope that a site with a name like 'eflteachingjobs.com' would have more than unpromising links such as 'TV Cabinets for Teachers' and some general waffle.

But everywhere you look on the internet, potentially useful links can be found. More than 100 websites are devoted to EFL/ESL jobs, many in Asia. For many years Dave Sperling's 'Dave's ESL

Cafe' (www.eslcafe.com) dominated the field and it is still the first port of call for many to check job vacancies and investigate further. Often the job discussion forums are invaluable, for example if you are considering signing a contract with a training company in Kazakhstan; although some of these forums tend to be quite a few years old. In any case 'Dave' provides a mind-boggling amount of material and many links to specific institutes and chains in each country.

Another key international site is www.tefl.com, which has gained in authority and popularity over the last couple of years. When subscribing (for free), you can specify whether you want to be notified of vacancies by e-mail on a daily or weekly basis. The site claims to have more than 18,000 registered employers. At the time of writing the countries with the most vacancies listed were China (35) and Spain (32).

It is possible to register your details as a job-seeker. **Fergus Cooney** learned the hard way not to be too general:

> *I posted a message simply stating 'Qualified teacher seeking job'. Within two days I was inundated with many dozens of replies requesting my CV and, more surprisingly with job offers everywhere, although the majority were from Korea, Taiwan and China. 'Jackpot', I thought (I have since realised that many schools/agents must have an automatic reply system which e-mails those who advertise in the way I did). I quickly began sifting through them, but not as quickly as they kept arriving in my inbox. Before a few more days had passed, I had become utterly confused and had forgotten which school was which, so I deleted them all, got a new e-mail address and posted a second, more specific message on Dave's.*

These two giants of the TESL world (eslcafe.com and tefl.com) have pushed some other rivals out of business. Note that the website www.onestopenglish.com (maintained by the educational publisher Macmillan) publishes an annotated links page to a range of ELT job sites, many of which are now defunct.

Here is a brief survey of some of the key recruitment sites:

- http://tesljobs.com – dated vacancies with archive of older postings, country by country, Afghanistan to Yemen.
- http://youcanteachenglish.com/jobs – admirably clear list of worldwide vacancies with dates and e-mail addresses.
- www.linguistic-funland.com/tesljob.html – links to independent TEFL training courses worldwide and some job vacancies.
- www.ihworld.com – International House maintains clear website with links to its 1,400 affiliated schools worldwide with e-mail addresses of directors and directors of studies. The recruitment and training sections of the website are accessible to all.
- www.tefl.net/esl-jobs/index.htm – more limited choice than some, but carries some up-to-date vacancies.
- www.eslbase.com – reasonably reliable links to language schools, country by country.
- www.Totalesl.com – part of the Icon Group of Thailand (www.icongroupthailand.com), which also owns Tesall.com and ESL Job Feed. Strongest in vacancies in Asia.
- www.tefljobs.co.uk – an offshoot of seasonworkers.com based in Scotland. Has a handful of job postings, mainly in the UK.
- www.tefllogue.com – discursive site with links to blogs and other sites that might be useful (but no current vacancies).
- http://jobs.guardian.co.uk/jobs/education/tefl – job vacancy listings on the *Guardian* Unlimited website. In the olden days the Tuesday *Guardian* was a primary source of TEFL job ads but the online version is a shadow of its former self (only one advertiser outside the UK at the time of writing). www.guardian.co.uk/education/tefl has an archive of relevant articles and a directory provided by country-by-country experts.

- www.teflscotland.co.uk and www.teflengland.co.uk – some current vacancies; contact details available to trainees on their TEFL training course.
- www.footprintsrecruiting.com – Vancouver-based recruitment service showing the range of vacancies in Korea, Taiwan, China, Chile, etc. that they are trying to fill.
- www.cactusteachers.com – for TEFL articles, information and advice for practising TEFL teachers, especially on admission to all post-initial training and teacher development courses. Its job site has next to nothing.

Other websites that are country-specific, e.g. www.ohayosensei.com (jobs in Japan) or www.ajarn.com (teaching in Thailand) are listed in the relevant country chapters.

TEFL Scotland

ODLQC accredited; SQA approved; ILA approved

I had just started work as an architect before I was made redundant and was one of the many victims of the recession. I knew there wouldn't be any meaningful jobs here in the UK so I decided to go to Japan and spend a year or two there doing something useful rather than kicking my heels in the UK waiting for the recession to end. I took a 20-hour weekend TEFL course with TEFL Scotland. I had never taught before so wasn't sure what to expect, but the course was so full-on and fun that the time flew by and before I knew it I was delivering mini-lessons to others in the group. I met loads of others from the course, from quite a wide background, and I am still in touch with some of them nearly 2 years on. I learnt loads about how to teach and what to teach in such a short space of time and by the end of it I was sure I actually wanted to go to Japan to teach English and more to the point I felt that I could do it. Having done a bit of grammar on the course, I felt I had to do more so I signed up for the online grammar course. I did it in my own time (which I had loads of) and had it finished pretty quickly. Knowing the grammar was really useful, because the students all knew it! And my confidence in the grammar really grew during my first year of teaching.

Getting the job in Japan was the next step and TEFL Scotland helped me out with the application to Japan. There was a bit of paperwork and the odd trip to an embassy and an interview of course, but the whole process was done in about two months and then I was off. I am now in my second year of teaching English in Japan! I never expected to like teaching so much, but the skills I learnt on the course have really allowed me to develop over the year or so I have been in Japan. I know that I will return to the UK and continue my career as an architect, but not just yet.

Mike Gilchrist

TEFL Scotland is the largest provider of TEFL courses in Scotland and because it is run by experienced TEFL professionals, you can be sure that the advice you receive is sound. TEFL Scotland offers a wide range of TEFL courses to suit and you can mix short classroom courses with more intensive online courses providing you with the certification and training you need to get started in TEFL. Classroom TEFL courses are available throughout Scotland from Dumfries to Stornoway.

TEFL Scotland also provides a FREE job service giving you over-the-phone careers advice and contacts in many countries worldwide. Check the website for latest vacancies and opportunities and funding on courses (0871 221 8335; info@teflscotland.co.uk; www.teflscotland.co.uk)

RECRUITMENT FAIRS

In an ideal world, prospective teachers could meet a range of employers all at once. Certified class-room teachers looking for vacancies in international schools have access to this kind of event (see section on Certified Teachers below). But it is not very common in TEFL. The energetic **Aidan O'Toole**, long resident of Andalucia, describes the advantages of the annual job fair he has spearheaded in Cordoba, where Spanish language schools can meet job-seekers in May:

> *Last year was the first Spain-wise recruitment fair which was a success with 226 teachers attending and 60 FECEI language schools. Each side invests a small amount of money into getting a job, which is far more efficient than teachers flying out from England for just one or two interviews. The chance to meet face to face is tremendously useful for both sides. Of course tefl.com (and similar) have trans-formed the recruitment process and the typed CV and letter box seem to belong to another era. But it is just too easy for newly qualified teachers to lean on the wrong button on their computer and send out hundreds of CVs, sometimes in answer to adverts they haven't even read.*

Aidan thinks that meeting a range of job-seekers makes it much easier for language school owners to spot the best candidates than rifling through a pile of CVs from new CELTA graduates. Meeting face to face also allows candidates who do not fit the perfect profile a chance to shine.

The only other job fairs we have heard of specifically for TEFL teachers take place in Shanghai (see China chapter).

RECRUITMENT ORGANISATIONS

Major providers of ELT and teacher placement organisations of various kinds may be able to assist prospective teachers in English-speaking countries to find teaching jobs. Some are international educational foundations; some are voluntary organisations such as VSO or charities; some are major chains of commercial language schools; and others are small agencies which serve as intermediar-ies between independent language schools abroad and prospective teachers. The companies and organisations listed in this chapter have been assigned to the following categories (though there is some blurring of distinctions):

- International ELT organisations (including the major language school chains).
- Commercial recruitment agencies.
- Voluntary, gap year and religious organisations.
- North American organisations, which cater primarily (though not exclusively) to citizens of the USA and Canada.
- Placement Services for British and American state-qualified teachers.

Note that agencies and organisations that operate only in one country or one region are described in the country chapters in the second part of this book.

It is hardly worthwhile for a family-run language school in northern Greece or southern Brazil to pay the high costs which most agencies charge schools just to obtain one or two native-speaker teachers. Vacancies that are filled with the help of agencies and recruitment consultants tend to be at the elite end of the ELT market. Jobs advertised by agencies are usually for specialised or high-level positions, for example in corporations with in-house EFL programmes or foreign governments.

HOW AGENCIES WORK

Agencies make their money by charging client employers; the service to teachers is usually free of charge. By law in the UK, no fee can be charged to job-seekers either before or after placement, except if a package of services is sold alongside (e.g. insurance, visas, travel, etc.) Note that different rules apply in other countries, so that placement fees are the norm in the USA. Some of the best recruitment organisations to deal with are ones that specialise in a single country and are located in situ, such as English Educational Services in Madrid or Cambridge Teachers Recruitment in Athens (see Spain and Greece chapters). They tend to have more first-hand knowledge of their client schools.

Bear in mind that the use of an intermediary by foreign language institutes is no guarantee of anything. Particularly in the American context, small independent recruiters are sometimes trying to fill vacancies that no-one in the country who is familiar with the employer would deign to fill. As the American **Rusty Holmes** said of his employer in Taiwan, 'The school was so bad it had to recruit from America.' If you are in any doubt about the reliability of an agency or the client he/she represents, it is a sensible precaution to search online and ask for the name of one or more previous teachers whom you can ask for a first-hand account. It is a bad sign if the agency is unable or reluctant to oblige.

The hiring of teachers for chain schools abroad is done either at a local level especially when they are franchises (so direct applications are always worthwhile) or centrally, if the school has trouble filling vacancies.

One way in which recruitment agencies work is to create a database of teachers' CVs and to try to match these with suitable vacancies as they occur. In order to be registered with such an agency it is almost always essential to have a relevant qualification, often at least the Cambridge or Trinity Certificate. Smaller agencies may have fewer vacancies on their books but they can often offer a more personal service. A good agency will provide a full briefing and information pack on the school in particular and the country in general, and will make sure that the contract offered is a reasonable one.

Volunteer English teachers are in demand by dozens of commercial sending agencies which routinely charge volunteers £500–£2,000 for placement and related services. Before her final year at university, **Susannah Kerr** took up one of these placements in Thailand which she found to be less structured than the agency literature had promised. She felt that the school to which she was assigned did not really need English-speaking volunteers and she suspected that they invited foreigners merely as status symbols. With hindsight she felt that she had been naïve to assume that the school would be grateful for her efforts. She was allowed to teach whatever she liked, so naturally she concentrated on spoken English and taught no grammar and only occasional writing exercises. She was given no lesson plans and was not required to prepare the students for exams. When the teachers saw that the volunteers were coping, they took a holiday.

THE BRITISH COUNCIL

The British Council (www.britishcouncil.org) is the largest ELT (English Language Teaching) employer in the world. The Council represents the elite end of the English language teaching industry. At its own 130 or so teaching centres in 56 countries, it offers the highest quality language teaching available in those countries and employs the best qualified teachers, so it is important to understand that the British Council will not welcome applications from very inexperienced or unqualified teachers. The British Council is a very professional organisation and jobs with it tend to come with attractive terms and conditions.

The Council's offices abroad are usually well informed about opportunities for English language teaching locally. Most maintain a list of private language schools (while making it clear that inclusion does not confer recognition), which is often a useful starting point for a job search.

The Council publishes an Address Book of its offices worldwide which is updated quarterly, and an interactive map (www.britishcouncil.org/new/articles/maps), with links to its centres around the world. The charter of the British Council defines its aims as 'to promote Britain abroad, providing access to British ideas, talents and experience in education and training, books and periodicals, the English language, the arts, the sciences and technology'. It is non-profit-making and works non-politically (although that didn't stop President Putin pressuring it to suspend operations in Russia in December 2007). It employs just over 6,000 staff overseas, a good percentage of whom are involved with the teaching of the English language in some capacity. In some countries such as Hungary the British Council has closed its teaching centre and prefers to work with local organisations to promote the teaching of English. Partly because of government cutbacks, the British Council has closed more than 30 teaching centres in the past few years. Other work that the Council carries out includes the running of libraries, the organisation of cultural tours and exchanges, etc. But language teaching and teacher recruitment remain one of its central concerns.

A useful starting place for qualified EL teachers is to request the recruitment literature, which is available free of charge from Teacher Vacancies (10 Spring Gardens, London SW1A 2BN; 020 7389 4931; teacher.vacancies@britishcouncil.org; www.britishcouncil.org/teacherrecruitment.htm).

British Council teaching centres recruit both through London and locally. They especially welcome applications from teachers with experience or an interest in specialist areas such as Young Learners, Business English, skills through English, IELTS exam preparation, etc.

Contracts are usually for two years and renewable. Although terms and conditions vary from centre to centre, the terms of employment with the British Council are generally favourable. Teachers recruited through the Teacher Recruitment Service have their airfares paid, an allowance for shipping their belongings and an attractive salary package. Many teachers value all the intangible benefits such as the security of working for an established institution, and encouragement of professional development with possible perks such as receiving a subsidy to study for a Diploma qualification or other training grants. Once you have secured one job with the Council, it is possible to move to other jobs in other places, since the Council regularly notifies its network of all vacancies.

A completely separate programme run by the British Council is the placement of language assistants in schools for an academic year. The Language Assistants Team administers exchange programmes with 18 countries worldwide. Applicants for assistant posts must be aged 20–30 and native speakers of English who have completed their secondary education and at least two years of degree-level study in the UK, usually but not necessarily in the language of the destination country. In some countries (especially China and countries in Latin America) posts are of particular interest to graduates interested in a career in TEFL. The website is open for applications from October and the deadline for submission is 1 December (for a job starting the following autumn), though the deadlines may be extended for posts in China. Contact the Assistants Team (10 Spring Gardens, London SW1A 2BN; 020 7389 4596; assistants@britishcouncil.org; www.britishcouncil.org/languageassistants). There are offices also in Scotland (British Council Scotland, The Tun, 4 Jackson's Entry, Holyrood Road, Edinburgh EH8 8PJ; 0131 524 5735); and Northern Ireland (7 Fountain Street, Belfast BT1 5EG; 028 9024 8220).

In conjunction with the BBC, the British Council also maintain a website called Teaching English (www.teachingenglish.org.uk), which is a free resource for teachers and includes lesson plans, work sheets, teaching tips, etc.

The British Council is a large and complex institution with two headquarters: one at 10 Spring Gardens, London SW1A 2BN (020 7930 8466) and the other at Bridgewater House, 58 Whitworth Street, Manchester M1 6BB (0161 957 7000). Telephone callers who do not know exactly which department they need should contact the Council's Information Centre in Manchester (0161 957 7755; general.enquiries@britishcouncil.org).

INTERNATIONAL ELT ORGANISATIONS

The Bell Educational Trust Worldwide Educational Services, Hillscross, Red Cross Lane, Cambridge CB2 0QU (01223 275500; www.bell-worldwide.com/jobs). Bell recruits teachers for ELT posts in its associated schools in Thailand (Jobs.Thailand@bell-worldwide.com), and for many current overseas projects especially in the Middle East (Bahrain, Jordan, Qatar, Saudi Arabia and Libya), Asia (China and Vietnam) and Central Europe (Poland, Romania, Bulgaria, Ukraine and Azerbaijan). Candidates will be required to have a degree and a recognised TEFL qualification.

Bénédict Network International Sarl, 3 Place Chauderon, PO Box 270, 1000 Lausanne 9, Switzerland (21 312 4728; benedcit@benedict-international.com; www.benedict-international.com). Over 50 business and language schools in Europe (mostly in Germany, Switzerland and Italy), plus several in Russia and Ecuador.

Berlitz, (http://careerservices.berlitz.com,; links to vacancies worldwide (some of them past their sell-by date). Berlitz is one of the largest language training organisations in the world with about 470 centres in 70 countries. It is also one of the oldest, founded in 1878. The company's core business is language and cultural training, and teacher vacancies occur most often in Germany, Turkey and Korea. All Berlitz teachers are native, fluent speakers and university graduates; all must undergo training in the 'Berlitz Method', a direct 'see-hear-speak' teaching approach that does not rely on translation. Berlitz is known for supervising their teachers' techniques very closely, and deviation from the method is not permitted. When Berlitz has urgent vacancies to fill, usually in southern Europe, it places an advertisement in British newspapers inviting any interested university graduates to attend interviews in London, Manchester, Edinburgh or Dublin. Usually, however, Berlitz schools abroad employ teachers directly, usually on a part-time basis initially, after they have completed a two-week Method course.

Cactus TEFL, (www.cactustefl.com) publishes a guide to working in TEFL: *The Little Book of TEFL Jobs,* which is packed with advice for the teacher searching for a job in TEFL, and advertisements from schools which regularly employ teachers. The booklet is available free as a PDF and can be downloaded from the jobs section of the website: www.cactustefl.com/jobs/index.php or requested by e-mail to info@cactustefl.com.

CfBT Education Trust, 60 Queens Road, Reading RG1 4BS (0118 902 1000; www.cfbt.com). Has offices in Brunei, Malaysia and Oman which recruit for and manage EFL/EAP/ESP/Primary/Secondary teachers and instructors for various projects and contracts. The website contains contact details for each office and information on how to apply. CfBT's International and Consultancy Group (0118 902 1613; consultancydatabase@cfbt.com), at above address, with regional bases in Africa, South East Asia and the Gulf, recruits education consultants for donor-funded projects and programmes in developing countries.

EF English First Teacher Recruitment and Training, 666 Fuzhou Road, 1st Floor, Shanghai, China 200001 (+86 21 6133 6043; efrecruitment@ef.com; www.teachenglishfirst.com and www.ef-teachers.com). Recruitment of teachers for 200 EF schools in 16 countries, primarily China, Russia, Indonesia and Saudi Arabia.

ICC – The European Language Network, Berner Heerweg 183, D-22159, Hamburg (40 645 32963; info@icc-languages.eu; www.icc-languages.eu). Umbrella organisation for adult education associations (e.g. Volkshochschulen, folk high schools or Universities of Applied Sciences) in 17 European countries cooperating in the learning and teaching of foreign languages in Europe. Can provide enquirers with a list of member organisations and contact names. The ICC runs specialist training courses for foreign language teachers in adult, continuing and vocational education. A teacher certification scheme (EUROLTA = European Certificate in Language Teaching to Adults) is also in operation.

IH World Organisation, Unity Wharf, 13 Mill Street, London SE1 2BH (020 7394 2143; worldrecruit@ihworld.co.uk; www.ihworld.com). International House (IH) is one of the largest and oldest groups of language schools, teaching English as a foreign language (and 25 modern languages) in 140 schools in more than 40 countries worldwide. IHWO Recruitment Services is based in London at the International House World Office, which is the coordinating body for all International House affiliated schools. It is responsible for managing the recruitment of teachers, trainers and senior staff for IH schools and annually expect to assist in the recruitment of between 350 and 400 teachers for International House schools worldwide. The minimum qualification requirement for teaching posts is the Cambridge CELTA, IH CYL or Trinity TESOL Certificate. All IH schools adhere to internal quality standards which provide strict guidelines on terms and conditions, working hours and working environment. For further information on teaching and senior posts abroad visit www.ihworld.com/recruitment. (Note: IH London, a language school and teacher training centre, is a separate company training directory.)

Inlingua (www.inlingua.com). International chain of 350 language centres that operate autonomously in 44 countries across Europe, Africa, Asia, North and South America. Link to jobs on website. At the time of writing there were vacancies in its schools in Italy, Spain, Syria, Ecuador and India.

Language Link, 21 Harrington Road, London SW7 3EU (020 7225 1065; recruitment@languagelink.co.uk; www.languagelink.co.uk). Training and recruitment agency which places about 200 qualified (including newly qualified) teachers in its network of affiliated schools in Russia, China, Vietnam Kazakhstan and Uzbekistan. Usually minimum qualifications are TEFL Certificate or PGCE or experience but visit the website of the country you wish to work in as the agency may be running in-service training courses over the period of the contract. Employment contracts are from 36 weeks and can be extended to 24 contact hours per week. Local pay rates. Shared apartment accommodation is usually provided at no additional cost or deduction from the salary. Interested teachers should ring to arrange an interview (in the UK or in Russia, etc.), and then send CV and photo. (See Training chapter for details of Language Link's CELTA courses.)

Marcus Evans Linguarama, 7 Elm Court, 1 Arden Street, Stratford-upon-Avon CV37 6PA (01789 203910; personnel@linguarama.com or dannycoughlan@linguarama.com; www.linguarama.com). Linguarama specialises in providing language training for professionals. Applicants for jobs in Linguarama language schools abroad must have at least a degree and a Cambridge/Trinity Certificate (or equivalent). Linguarama finds placements for 50–100 teachers and has an office in London for teacher interviews as well as the above address, which deals with vacancies at more than 20 European centres in Germany, France, Spain and Italy.

Richard Lewis Communications, Riversdown House, Warnford, Southampton, Hampshire SO32 3LH (01962 771111; www.crossculture.com). RLC has a network of offices worldwide, especially in Finland, Sweden and Germany, specialising in cross-cultural training and language teaching.

Saxoncourt, 59 South Molton Street, London W1K 5SN (020 7491 1911; recruit@saxoncourt.com; www.saxoncourt.com). One of the largest UK-based recruiters of EFL teachers, Saxoncourt places several hundred teachers per year in schools worldwide. Clients are based in Japan, Taiwan, China, Italy, Spain, Vietnam, Peru, Saudi Arabia and elsewhere. Applications are welcome, particularly from candidates with a Cambridge CELTA, Trinity TESOL or equivalent qualifications. Interviews are held in London, where possible. Interested candidates should register online at www.saxoncourt.com. The Saxoncourt website features a regularly updated current vacancies page, online registration and country-specific sections with downloadable information packs.

Saxoncourt

Saxoncourt sends teachers to Taiwan most months of the year. From initial application to arrival the company does everything it can to make the process as simple and as smooth as possible. Here's an example of a teacher who chose to work at one of our schools:

Why Taiwan?

My heart was set on Asia but I knew very little about the various cultures – no more than the vague notion I had of a continent of fireworks and festivals, of exotic sights, sounds and tastes. Friends had travelled there and come back with a host of memories. I decided to go somewhere off the beaten gap year track and ended up in Taiwan. Given the size of the island – it's barely bigger than Wales – I was surprised at how much there was to do. Besides the traditional temples and night markets, there is an abundance of outdoor pursuits and great hiking trails. I even learnt to surf!

How did your recruitment agency help you?

The process of getting there was fairly simple; passing the interview, signing a contract, and booking a plane ticket were all it took to get started. The real challenge and excitement began when I arrived, wide-eyed and slightly overwhelmed by my new surroundings.

How was the teaching?

It took a while to get used to teaching young learners and the first few weeks were tough. Yet the support from the other teachers kept me going. Before long I could see progress, and I enjoyed hearing that mirrored in the enthusiastic feedback from my British-accented students!

What are you doing now?

I'm looking for my next teaching adventure. With experience under my belt there are more opportunities open to me now, but I want to find a similarly absorbing country to explore.

Saxoncourt has over 20 years experience in teacher training and recruitment. For more information please visit www.saxoncourt.com or call 0207 491 1911.

TEFL Express

A 100 hour TEFL course led to Ho Chi Minh City, the Gobi Desert and the Great Wall... ... and an enviable career along the way.

Enda Harty's modesty belies his success. He is talented, charming and unavoidably likeable. We caught up with him as he launches the TEFL Express Online business.

Enda, tell me how your career started?

I'd finished college, done some travelling and knew I'd like to see more of the world. I did a TEFL course in 2000, though without any teaching experience or long-term plan.

It seems to have led you down an interesting road.

Yea, first stop Vietnam. My first teaching job did take a few months; an internship would have made things easier. I taught both adults and children in various centres in Vietnam and China over the next six years. My experience in reputable schools was invaluable when I moved somewhere new. In 2003 I was offered Director of Studies at Language Link, Beijing and then moved on to overseeing the running of 12 schools in China. I also developed new courses for teens which were very popular.

You enjoyed life in Asia?

Absolutely loved it! Vietnam is amazing – a unique culture and fantastic people. I had loads of fun and made great friends. China was intriguing and where most of my professional development happened. While I was based there I saw Cambodia, Laos, Mongolia, Thailand, Japan, and North Korea – deeply enriching cultural experiences, especially Laos and the Gobi desert – what a place!

I believe you got an award in China? Why did you leave?

The City of Beijing gave me a Great Wall of Friendship Award for my Contribution to Beijing's Society and Growth. They have a big emphasis on learning English. Hungry for teachers! I'd started developing more courses and was interested in broadening the availability through the web when a beautiful Spanish girl lured me to Majorca! Now I'm based between the UK, Ireland and Majorca and really excited about taking online teaching where it hasn't gone yet.

Web: www.teflexpress.co.uk
Email: info@teflexpress.co.uk
Freephone: (+44) 0800 0488861

Saxoncourt New Zealand, 138 Queen Street, Auckland, New Zealand (9 309 2201; nz@ saxoncourt.com). Recruits teachers for Taiwan, China and Japan.

Wall Street Institute (teach@wallstreetinstitute.com; www.wallstreetinstitute.com). With headquarters in Baltimore, WSI operates both company-owned and franchised centres, and employs more than 2,000 teachers in over 400 centres in 28 countries and territories in Asia (China, Indonesia, Hong Kong, South Korea, Taiwan, Thailand), Europe (France, Germany, Italy, Portugal, Spain, Switzerland, Russia, Turkey), Latin America (Argentina, Brazil, Chile, Colombia, Ecuador, Mexico, Nicaragua, Peru, Venezuela), the Middle East (Israel, Saudi

Arabia) and Africa (Morocco). The countries with almost continuous vacancies are China, Russia and Indonesia. Applicants should have at least a bachelor's degree and the appropriate professional qualifications of a CELTA or equivalent TEFL certificate. One year's teaching experience is an advantage. Due to restrictions on visa legislation in many countries within the network, WSI prefers teachers from the UK, Ireland, USA, Canada, Australia, New Zealand and South Africa. The interview process is as follows: a first-round interview is a 'get to know you' interview that will probably last around 45 minutes. Some countries will consider doing this on the phone with offshore applicants. A second-round interview will involve discussing a lesson plan created by the applicant and giving a brief teaching presentation of approximately 15 minutes. This interview will also last approximately 45 minutes. Some countries will consider doing this on the phone with offshore applicants. In this case the applicant will discuss how they would deliver a particular language point. Qualified applicants can apply online at www.wallstreetinstitute.com/jobSeekers/teaching-Staff/teachingStaff.aspx.

COMMERCIAL AGENCIES

If you have a TEFL background, you can send a CV with covering letter via e-mail or post to the relevant agencies. Agencies that specialise in a single country are not included in this chapter, but are mentioned in the country chapters.

TEFLOne (www.teflone.com). Since 2006, TEFLOne has been recruiting TEFL-certified teachers for reputable schools in China, Taiwan, Japan and South Korea; it aims to start recruiting for schools in the Middle East by the end of 2010. TEFLOne carries out the whole recruitment process from advertising to interviewing, reference checking, visa liaison and arranging arrival time. Candidates are provided with as much information and support as possible. Due to the requirements of the schools, TEFLOne can proceed only with teachers who are native English speakers from the UK, USA, Canada, South Africa, Ireland, Australia or New Zealand and holders of a recognised degree and a TEFL qualification. Most successful candidates will have completed an intensive 120-hour classroom-based TEFL course that includes at least six hours observed teaching practice. Applicant details are also added to a newsletter distribution list, which is sent out every two months by e-mail and contains information on positions in schools in Asia with articles written by teachers. Contact David Coles (david. coles@teflone.com) or Skype teflonerecruitment2.

Anglo-Pacific (Asia) Consultancy, Suite 32, Nevilles Court, Dollis Hill Lane, London NW2 6HG (020 8452 7836/020 8452 2826). Educational consultancy specialising in recruitment in Thailand, Taiwan, China, Japan and the rest of South East Asia. Also offers careers guidance to TEFL teachers returning from overseas. Welcomes approaches from graduates (or people with an HND/equivalent higher qualifications) who have a recognised TEFL certificate. Places teachers at all levels in the public and private sectors and provides teachers with background information about their destination country including teaching tips and cultural information.

Avalon School of English, 9 Great Newport Street, London WC2H 7JA (020 7240 9321/020 7379 1998; info@avalonschool.co.uk; www.avalonschool.co.uk). Candidates may be eligible for work in Avalon schools in London and worldwide.

Footprints Recruiting (www.footprintsFootprintingsrecruiting.com). A proactive and principled teacher recruitment agency based in Canada with vacancies mostly in Korea. As of 2010 it has signed an agreement with the Government of Georgia to recruit suitable English teachers for a new educational programme in the Caucasus.

HuntESL (www.huntesl.com). Online recruiter operating out of Honduras, especially active in Korea. Sister site of www.intesolinternational.com, which promotes INTESOL's TEFL training courses.

Language Solutions International, 11 Coldbath Square, London EC1R 5HL (07725 497166; barry.shorten@langsols.com or info@langsols.com; www.langsols.com). Global network of privately owned schools that specialise in teaching working adults in the energy industry; welcomes applications from highly qualified and experienced EFL teachers: Milan, Madrid, Baku (Azerbaijan), Atyrau (Kazakhstan), Algeria, Jubail Industrial City (Saudi Arabia) and Tripoli (Libya). Minimum requirement is a CELTA certificate.

Reach to Teach, head office in Albany New York state (201 467 4612; UK 0203 286 9794, Australia 2 8011 4516, New Zealand 9 889 0557; www.ReachToTeachRecruiting.com). Describes itself as one of the largest human resource companies for teachers in Asia, primarily Korea, China and Taiwan. All services are free to teachers.

Teachaway, Toronto (www.teachaway.com). Recruits for employers mainly in Korea, China, Taiwan, Saudi Arabia, UAE, Mexico.

VOLUNTARY, GAP YEAR AND RELIGIOUS ORGANISATIONS

Christians Abroad (0300 012 1201; recruit@cabroad.org.uk; www.cabroad.org.uk). Ecumenical charity providing information and advice to people of any faith or none who are thinking of working overseas, whatever their circumstances, whether short- or long-term, voluntary or paid. Occasional openings for TEFL teachers, e.g. in Tanzania.

VSO (Voluntary Service Overseas), 317 Putney Bridge Road, London SW15 2PN (020 8780 7500; enquiry@vso.org.uk; www.vso.org.uk). VSO works in more than 34 countries in Africa, Asia and the Pacific, and receives requests, including some in EFL teaching and training, for example in Ethiopia, Rwanda and Vietnam. Volunteer requirements vary but the usual commitment is two years. Most placements are for skilled and qualified professionals aged 18–75 from a variety of backgrounds. VSO recognises the Trinity TESOL and Cambridge CELTA qualifications. The VSO package for its volunteers includes airfares, medical cover, National Insurance contributions, rent-free accommodation and a modest salary in line with local pay rates. VSO also provides full in-country support including pre-departure training and briefing, basic language and cultural orientation on arrival prior to starting placement.

A number of companies charge school-leavers and others to arrange volunteer placements abroad, many of which are in schools where volunteers teach English. Several of those listed here are founder members of the Year Out Group (www.yearoutgroup.org), formed to promote well-structured gap year programmes.

Educators Abroad (www.educatorsabroad.org). Paying participants are sent to 25 countries on all continents for 4–10 weeks throughout the year to volunteer as a resource for a teacher of English in another country. Fees US $2,300–$4,200 excluding travel. Accommodation and board are provided by host schools.

Global Nomadic, London (020 7193 2652; www.globalnomadic.com). A new company that tries to minimise costs in its placements worldwide, including paid teaching in Thailand and China, and volunteer teaching in many other countries.

IST Plus, Rosedale House, Rosedale Road, Richmond, Surrey (020 8939 9057; www.istplus. com). Formerly CIEE UK, IST Plus administers the Teach in China and Teach in Thailand programmes (see respective chapters).

i-to-i, 261 Low Lane, Leeds, LS18 5NY (0800 093 3148/0113 205 4620; info@i-to-i.com; www.i-to-i.com). i-to-i offers TEFL/TESOL training, either weekend courses or distance learning, and many teaching placements worldwide for paying volunteers.

Lattitude Global Volunteer, 42 Queen's Road, Reading, Berkshire RG1 4BB (0118 959 4914; volunteer@lattitude.org.uk; www.lattitude.org.uk). Overseas volunteering opportunities for 17–25 year olds, including teaching, in many countries. Posts are for between three and 12 months (six is average) and cost the volunteer between £1,600 and £2,250 depending on the programme, plus airfare, insurance and medical costs. Board, lodging and (sometimes) a living allowance are provided. A one-week teaching skills course is mandatory for those undertaking to teach English.

Projects Abroad, Aldsworth Parade, Goring, Sussex BN12 4TX (01903 708300; info@projects-abroad.co.uk; www.projects-abroad.co.uk). Sends up to 4,000 people abroad annually on a variety of projects in developing countries, such as Bolivia, Cambodia, Mongolia and Senegal. Projects start from one month in length, with an average volunteer spending three months. Three-month placements cost between £1,395 and £2,595, depending on placement, excluding travel costs but including accommodation, food, insurance, placement and in-country support.

The Project Trust, Hebridean Centre, Ballyhough, Isle of Coll, Argyll PA78 6TE (01879 230444; info@projecttrust.org.uk; www.projecttrust.org.uk). Sends school leavers (aged 17–19) to teach (often other subjects as well as English) in schools across Central and South America, Africa and Asia. Participants must fundraise to cover part of the cost of their 12-month placement, at present £4,660.

Travellers Worldwide, 2A Caravelle House, 17/19 Goring Road, Worthing, West Sussex, BN12 4AP (01903 502595; info@travellersworldwide.com; www.travellersworldwide.com). Provides teaching as well as many other work experience and volunteer placements worldwide. Prices start from £595. Travellers also runs a weekend TEFL course in the UK, for details, see www.tefltime.com.

USIT, 19/21 Aston Quay, Dublin 2, Ireland (+353 1 602 1742; volunteer@usit.ie; www.usit.ie). In addition to the paid teaching placements USIT makes in Thailand, Taiwan, Korea and Vietnam (see country chapters), it also places paying volunteers who do not need to have qualifications to teach in Cambodia, Vietnam, Thailand, Ghana and Costa Rica. Prices are from €799 per month.

Charities and mission societies that occasionally require EFL teachers include those listed below.

Bosco Volunteer Action (BOVA) (01625 560724; http://boscovolunteeraction.co.uk). Offers opportunities to live and work alongside Catholic priests and brothers in their service to the young and the poor around the world. Some (but not all) of the volunteer opportunities involve teaching English.

Interserve, Milton Keynes (www.interserveonline.org.uk). Teaching posts in 19 countries.

OMS International, Manchester (www.omsinternational.co.uk). An evangelical, independent, Christian mission organisation that provides English lessons/camps through OMS-affiliated national churches in countries worldwide.

TeachOverseas.org, 639 N. Soldano Avenue, Azusa, California 91702, USA (toll free +1 800 895 7955; www.teachoverseas.org). Christian oragnisation that expects its volunteers to 'serve God overseas' while teaching English in one of 10 countries: Cambodia China, Czech Republic, Hungary, Kazakhstan, Kyrgyzstan, North Africa, Russia, Slovakia, and Vietnam.

OPPORTUNITIES FOR NORTH AMERICANS

Although the companies, agencies and charities listed here are based in the USA and cater primarily to North Americans, some may be in a position to help overseas applicants. Recruitment agencies in the USA have stronger links with Latin America and the Far East than with Europe. As in Britain, some organisations are involved primarily with English-medium international schools following an American curriculum, and are looking to recruit state-certified teachers; these are listed separately at the end of this section.

AIDE (Association of International Development and Exchange) (512 457 8062/1 866 6 ABROAD; reinventyourself@aideabroad.org; www.aideabroad.org). Variety of overseas placements in volunteer, internship, work, and teach abroad programmes lasting two weeks to 12 months in Argentina, Chile, China, Costa Rica, Ecuador, Guatemala, India, Peru, Spain, etc. Participants pay a programme fee to cover placement, airport pick-up, accommodation, meals, local support, medical insurance and optional language courses.

Center for Intercultural Education and Development (CIED), Georgetown University, PO Box 579400, Washington, DC 20057 9400 (http://elf.georgetown.edu). The English Language Fellow Program, administered by the CIED is a 10-month fellowship sponsored and funded by the US Department of State. Participants must be US citizens and have an MA in TESOL or a related field. Participants receive a stipend, living allowance to cover food, housing, local transportation and utilities, plus an international travel pre-departure allowance and a shipping allowance. Pre-departure briefings take place in August.

CIEE: (Council on International Educational Exchange), 300 Fore Street, Portland, ME 04101 (207 553 4000; teach@ciee.org; www.ciee.org/teach). Administers teaching in Chile, China, Spain, Dominican Republic, South Korea and Thailand. Participants are placed in local schools where they teach English and are compensated with a local salary and temporary to permanent housing.

Council for International Exchange of Scholars, 3007 Tilden St NW, Suite 5L, Washington, DC 20008 3009 (202 686 4000; scholars@iie.org; www.cies.org). The Fulbright Scholar Program, administered by the US Department of State, provides grants for teaching English in over 30 countries. A doctorate is usually required, although a master's degree is sufficient in some countries. Applicants must be US citizens.

InterExchange, 161 Sixth Avenue, New York 10013 (212 924 0446; info@interexchange.org; www.interexchange.org). Arrange homestays with 15 hours a week of English tutoring of the family in France, Spain, Italy and Germany ($695 for 1–3 months), plus paid EFL teaching posts in Chile and China and volunteer teaching in Ghana ($1,595 for 3 months). Programme fees do not include airfare.

Office of English Language Programs (OELP), US Department of State, SA 44, Room 304, 301 4th Street, SW, Washington DC 20547 (http://exchanges.state.gov/englishteaching). OELP creates and implements high-quality English language programmes in specific regions and countries around the world. OELP's programmes promote understanding of American language, society, culture, values and policies. Some Embassy Public Affairs Departments provide English language instruction as do binational centres, which work closely with American embassies. Most teachers for binational centres are hired directly by the centre in question; addresses are listed on the website given above. Teachers with an MA in TESL/TEFL may apply for the English Language Fellow Program, a 10-month fellowship programme that provides American professional expertise in teaching English as a foreign language. Qualified candidates who want to teach in US Department of State Cultural Centers should go to the website and follow the link to 'Employment Outside the United States'. The English Language Specialist programme recruits US academics in the fields of TEFL/TESL and Applied Linguistics for short-term (two to four weeks) assignments abroad.

Peace Corps, Washington, DC (1 800 424 8580; www.peacecorps.gov). TEFL has historically been one of the major programme areas of the Peace Corps, which has programmes in more than 70 countries. One-third of the nearly 8,000 volunteers who serve work in the education sector, with the majority of them in ELT. Volunteers, who must be US citizens, over age 18 and in good health, are sent on 27-month assignments. All expenses, including airfare and health insurance, are covered. Peace Corps volunteers teach at both secondary and university level, and some become involved with teacher training and curriculum development. It can take up to a year between application and departure. Education volunteers must have a college degree (not necessarily in education) and a minimum of three months' experience of ESL tutoring one-to-one or classroom teaching.

TESOL (Teachers of English to Speakers of Other Languages), Alexandria, Virginia (703 836 0774; info@tesol.org; www.tesol.org). A key organisation for professional ESL/EFL teachers worldwide, TESOL is a non-profit association offering various publications and services to 13,000+ members in 125 countries. Full individual membership costs $95 ($33 for students) per year, there is also electronic membership. Members receive a listing of job vacancies worldwide, or can search jobs online. TESOL also organises the Job MarketPlace, an ESL/EFL job fair held during TESOL's annual convention.

WorldTeach, Harvard University, Boston, Massachusetts (617 495 5527/+800 4-TEACH-0; www.worldteach.org). A private, non-profit organisation, WorldTeach provides college graduates with one-year volunteer teaching contracts (EFL or ESL) to American Samoa, Bangladesh, Costa Rica, Ecuador, Namibia, Kenya, the Marshall Islands, China, Venezuela, Chile, Pohnpei, Mongolia, Rwanda, South Africa and Guyana. Eight-week summer programmes are available in Bulgaria, China, Costa Rica, Ecuador, Poland, Namibia and South Africa. Participants pay a volunteer contribution ranging from $500 to $7,990, but several new programmes are fully funded by the host country.

CERTIFIED TEACHERS

Certified primary and secondary teachers who want to work in mainstream international schools abroad should be aware of the following agencies and organisations, which match qualified candidates with vacancies. Most of the hiring for primary and secondary schools abroad (often referred to in the American context as K-12 – kindergarten to grade 12) is done at recruitment fairs included on the list below. The files of job-seekers are added to a database that can be consulted by recruiters, who then choose whom they want to interview. Candidates who successfully land a job abroad with the help of a US agency may have to pay a placement fee of $300–$600, though in some cases the employer underwrites this expense.

Council of International Schools, 21a Lavant St, Petersfield, Hampshire GU32 3EL (01730 268244; www.cois.org). Assists only teachers who have a BEd or PGCE with at least two years' teaching experience. The agency hosts two recruitment fairs in London every year and has a searchable database online of accredited international schools.

Gabbitas Educational Consultants, London (www.gabbitasrecruitment.com). Established for 137 years, Gabbitas maintains a register of qualified and experienced teachers available for teaching posts in South America, Europe, etc. Gabbitas generally recruits subject-specialist teachers for English-medium schools.

International Schools Services, Princeton, New Jersey, USA (www.iss.edu). Offers teaching opportunities for educators in private American and international schools around the world. ISS hosts three international recruitment centres (IRCs) annually, where interviews are conducted by international school administrators. Applicants must have a bachelor's degree and relevant K-12 experience. IRC registration materials are provided on approval of application.

Queen's University, Kingston, Ontario (ed.careers@queensu.ca; http://info.educ.queensu.ca/torf/index.php). Organises the Teachers' Overseas Recruiting Fair. Registration closes in January for fair held in February for international schools. Teacher certification required plus at least two years' K-12 teaching experience.

Search Associates, British branch: David Cope, Berry House, 41 High Street, Over, Cambridge CB24 5NB, UK (01954 231130; dr.cope@virgin.net; www.search-associates.co.uk). Fully qualified primary and secondary teachers with some experience either in the UK or in a British-system international school overseas should use this contact. Teachers preferring to work in International Baccalaureate schools overseas should contact Harry Deelman, Search Associates, PO Box 168, Chiang Mai 50000, Thailand (53 244322; deelman@loxinfo.co.th; www.search-associates.com). Search Associates is not usually appropriate for TEFL teachers who have no school experience but offers information and placement assistance for teachers with at least some mainstream school experience (with pupils aged 3–18). Long-term positions only (one- to three-year contracts, renewable). Recruitment fairs for candidates seeking jobs in international schools are held annually in London, Dubai, San Francisco, Sydney and others.

Teacher Recruitment International (Aust), Sydney, Australia (2 9360 0458; www.triaust.com). Places teachers in primary and secondary school posts in international schools in Europe, Asia, the Middle East and, to a lesser extent, South America. Initial small registration fee but no placement fee.

University of Northern Iowa, Overseas Placement Service for Educators, Cedar Falls, Iowa (overseas.placement@uni.edu; www.uni.edu/placement/overseas). UNI is a non-profit organisation and it does not charge any placement fees to schools or teaching candidates. Educators must hold current certification in elementary or secondary education.

SPECULATIVE JOB HUNT

The vast majority of language schools do not publicise their vacancies internationally and instead depend on local adverts, word of mouth, personal contacts and direct approaches. Because there is quite a high turnover of staff in TEFL positions, a speculative job search has a better chance than in many other fields of employment. For a successful campaign, only two things are needed: a reasonable CV and a list of addresses of potential employers.

APPLYING IN ADVANCE

Entire books and consultancy companies are devoted to showing people how to draw up an impressive curriculum vitae (CV, or résumé as it is called in the USA). But it is really just a matter of common sense. Obviously employers will be more inclined to take seriously a well-presented document than something scribbled on the back of a dog-eared envelope. Obviously any relevant training or experience should be highlighted rather than submerged in the trivia about your schooling and hobbies. If you lack any TEFL experience, try to bring out anything in your past which demonstrates your 'people skills', such as voluntary work, group counselling, one-to-one remedial tutoring, etc. and your interest in (and ability to adapt to) foreign countries. If you are targeting one country, it would be worth drawing up a CV in the local language; **Judith Twycross** was convinced that her CV in Spanish was a great asset when looking for teaching work in Colombia. If you get the job, however, be prepared for your new employer to expect you to be able to speak the vernacular.

School websites very often have a Recruitment or 'Work for Us' icon, and increasingly applications are invited online. The necessary steps and required documents should all be explained clearly. Customs differ. In France, for example, many companies ask for a 'motivation letter'.

Attitudes and personality are probably just as important as educational achievements in TEFL, so anything which proves an aptitude for teaching and an extrovert personality will be relevant. Because this is difficult to do on paper, some eager job-hunters have gone so far as to submit a little film of themselves, preferably a snippet of teaching. A simpler alternative might be to send a photo and a cassette/CD of your speaking voice, again assuming this will be a help rather than a hindrance.

The other essential ingredient is the names and contact details of language institutes. Each of the country chapters in this book provides such a list, thoroughly updated in 2010, and recommends ways of obtaining other addresses, for example by contacting a federation of language schools (if there is one) or the British Council in your destination country. The most comprehensive source of addresses of language schools is usually the *Yellow Pages*, which in many cases can now be consulted online. Just type 'yellow pages' and your destination country into a search engine and then search for *Scuoli di Lingue* in Italy, *Jazykova Skola* in the Czech Republic and so on. Some countries are much better than others, for example, the online Portuguese Yellow Pages are very helpful whereas the Turkish are not.

Of course it has to be stressed that it is difficult, and increasingly so, to set up a firm job offer simply by correspondence. A language school would have to be fairly desperate to hire a teacher they had never met for a vacancy that had never been advertised. It is a good idea to follow up any hint of interest with a phone call. The best time to phone language school directors is six or seven weeks before the beginning of term. Perhaps the school has a contact in your country who would be willing to conduct an informal interview on their behalf. Increasingly schools are using Skype to interview prospective staff, so that they can see you as you speak.

If your credentials are not the kind to wow school directors, it might still be worth sending off a batch of warm-up letters, stating your intention to present yourself in person a couple of weeks or months hence. Even if you don't receive a reply, such a strategy may stick in the mind of employers, as an illustration of how organised and determined you are.

INTERVIEWS

Whether you are interviewed at home or abroad, slightly different rules apply. For example, smart casual dress, neither flashy nor scruffy, is appropriate in Britain, while something more formal might be called for in certain cultures such as France. Even if all your friends laugh when you pack a suit before going abroad, you may find it a genuine asset when trying to outdo the competition. As **Steven Hendry**, who has taught English both in Japan and Thailand with none of the usual advantages apart from traveller's canniness, says:

> *You may not need a tailor-made suit but you definitely need to be able to present a conservative and respectable image.*

As with the CV, so at interview. Highlight anything that is remotely connected with teaching even if it has nothing to do with the English language, and do it energetically and enthusiastically. Yet keenness will seldom be sufficient in itself. You don't have to be an intellectual to teach English; in fact the quiet bookish type is probably at a disadvantage. An amusing illustration of this is provided by **Robert Mizzi**'s description of his interview for the JET Programme in the Japan chapter.

DON'T HAVE A TEFL BACKGROUND?

Do a certain amount of research, e.g. acquaint yourself with some of the jargon such as 'notional', 'communicative-based', etc. It is not uncommon for an interviewer to ask a few basic grammar questions. To help you deal with this eventuality, see the list of recommended reading in the chapter on Preparation. Visit the ELT section of a bookshop to begin familiarising yourself with the range of materials on offer. Always have some questions ready to ask the interviewer, such as 'Do you use Cambridge or Streamline?', 'What audio materials do you have?' 'Do you encourage the use of songs?' or 'Do you teach formal grammar structures?' If you are looking for an opening in a business context, you might pick up a few tips from the section on Interviews in the chapter on Germany.

You will certainly be asked how long you intend to stay and (depending on the time of year) nothing less than nine months will be considered. They will also want to know whether you have had any experience. With luck you will be able to say truthfully that you have (at least) taught at a summer school in Britain (again, see chapter on Preparation). Some applicants who are convinced that they can do a good job make a similar claim, untruthfully, knowing that at the lower end of the TEFL spectrum this will never be checked. Similarly some candidates claim to have done a TEFL course and pretend to have left the certificate at home. A certain amount of bluffing is inevitable in most interviews, so you'll just have to decide how far you are prepared to go. Bear in mind that the true depths of your ignorance could easily be plumbed ('Ah, so you've used Cambridge. Why do you prefer it to Streamline?').

Another skill you might be tempted to exaggerate is your knowledge of the local language. **Philip Dodd** was hired by a language teaching agency in Madrid on the understanding that he could speak fluent Spanish and on his first assignment was sent out to give English lessons to a young child living in a wealthy suburb. He was greeted at the door by the mother who wished to make sure of a few things before she entrusted her precious offspring to this stranger. Not able to follow her voluble stream, Philip nodded affably and said 'si' whenever he guessed it was appropriate. After one of his affable 'si's', the woman's face turned grey and she ordered him out of her house. He still doesn't know what he said that was so shocking. On the other hand, a certain inflation of your abilities may be expected, and will be met with distortions of the truth from the employer as you both decide whether you are going to hit it off.

Of course many applicants avoid potential embarrassment at interview by preparing themselves for a stint as a teacher. If you have done a TEFL course of any description, be sure to take along the certificate, however humble the qualification. Even schools in farflung places are becoming increasingly familiar with the distinctions between various qualifications and are unlikely to confuse a Cambridge certificate with an anonymous correspondence 'certificate'. In Asia especially, nothing short of the original will do, since there are so many counterfeit copies around.

If you have a university degree, be sure to take the certificate along. Even if the interviewer is prepared to take your word for it, the school administration may need the document at a later stage either to give you a salary increment or to obtain a work permit. **Adam Hartley**, who taught English in China, hadn't realised that his MA would have earned him a higher salary; although he arranged for two separate copies to be sent from Britain, neither arrived and he had to be content with the basic salary. Americans should take along their university transcripts; any school accustomed to hiring Americans will be familiar with these. Also take along any references; something written on headed paper will always impress, even if your previous jobs were not in teaching.

Once the interviewer indicates that you are a strong contender, it is your turn to ask questions. Ask about the details of pay, hours and conditions and take notes (see the section on Contracts below). Often there are disappointing discrepancies between what is promised in the early stages and what is delivered; at least if these things have been discussed at interview, you will be in a stronger bargaining position if the conditions are not met.

Unrealistic expectations are a genuine hazard when contemplating an exciting stint of working abroad. A recruitment consultant in the field offers the following sensible advice:

Teachers should be made aware that they are being employed to do a professional job and it is hard work and long hours. They should not underestimate the cultural differences even in countries they think they know. These often lead to misunderstandings and dissatisfied teachers. I am also constantly surprised by teachers who take jobs without knowing the first thing about the place, the job, the sort of classes they will have, etc. They should make a checklist of questions and if they are making applications on their own they should ask to speak to teachers who are there at the time or who have just left.

Research is the key. You wouldn't apply for a job in the UK without knowing something about it so why do so when you're going to another country? If you are offered a job by an agent and are worried about what kind of employer the school will be, you could phone the local British Council office to find out whether the school enjoys a good local reputation. Occasionally an embassy or consulate will assist, as in the case of the US Embassy in Seoul, which keeps a file of language schools about which they have received persistent complaints. More commonly, someone will have set up a webpage where this kind of inside information can be obtained (again, common in Korea).

Professional English language teachers often try to attend a regional conference sponsored by TESOL Inc (tesol.org) or IATEFL (International Association of TEFL; iatefl.org). **Sandeha Lynch** describes the TESOL Arabia Conference he attended a couple of years ago in Al-Ain:

These are serious ELT conferences not only as marketing fairs for publishers, booksellers and software companies, but they are an open job shop for the local employers. Teachers from all over the Gulf try to get there to socialise, look for a new job or just absorb enough academic wisdom to last them another year. If teachers are looking for a job then most of the time they'll be making appointments, checking off their interview score cards and watching the clock. All of the local colleges and recruiting agencies have stands there, and they are busy from morning to night giving interviews to anyone who knows the local scene and has the right qualifications.

ON THE SPOT

It is almost impossible to fix up a job in advance in some countries, due to the way the TEFL business operates. For example, written applications to the majority of language schools in Ecuador or Peru (assuming you could compile a list of addresses) would be mostly a waste of time since the pool of expat teachers and travellers on the spot is usually sufficient. Even in countries such as Spain and Germany, for which adverts appear in the UK, the bulk of hiring is done on the spot.

When you arrive in a likely place, your initial steps might include some of the following:

- Checking craigslist, Gumtree, Kijiji or equivalent.
- Transcribing a list of schools from the *Yellow Pages*.
- Reading the classified column of the local newspapers, including the English language papers.
- Checking noticeboards in likely locations such as the British Council, US Embassy/Cultural Centres, universities, TEFL training centres, English language bookshops (where you should also check which EFL materials are stocked) or hostels which teacher-travellers frequent.

Once you have prepared a CV, e-mail it to yourself as an attachment so it will always be accessible. That way you don't have to carry it around with you and you can easily modify it in any internet café. A reconnaissance trip is a good idea if possible, although **Andrew Whitmarsh** didn't even realise he was looking for a new job, when one found him in Indonesia:

> *As often happens, I didn't find my job, my job found me. I was standing on top of a volcano in Indonesia when a gentleman in my hiking group asked me what I did for a living. Upon my reply of 'English Teacher', he declared that this was wonderful news to hear and he had just the job for me. The gentleman just happened to be the President Director of Wall Street Institute – and he needed teachers.*

With a little more purpose and a little less serendipity, **Fiona Paton** found a job teaching English in France. On her way back from a summer holiday in Spain, she broke her return journey in Vichy long enough to distribute her CV to several language schools, which resulted in a job for the academic year.

After obtaining a list of potential employers and before contacting them, get hold of a detailed map and guide to the public transport network so you can locate the schools. Phone the schools and try to arrange a meeting with the director or director of studies (DOS). Even if an initial chat does not result in a job offer, you may learn something about the local TEFL scene, which will benefit you at the next interview, especially if you ask lots of questions. You might also be able to strike up a conversation with one of the foreign teachers who could turn out to be a valuable source of information about that school in particular and the situation generally. It is very common to have to begin with just a few hours a week. Make it clear that you are prepared to stand in at short notice for an absent teacher. The longer you stay in one place, the more hours will come your way and the better your chances of securing a stable contract.

This gradual approach also gives you a chance to discover which are the cowboy schools, something which is difficult to do before you are on the scene. The British Council has called for an EU-wide recognition scheme for language schools, to force rogue schools out of business. But this is a long way off, and in the meantime disreputable schools flourish in Europe just as they do in other parts of the world. It is not always easy to distinguish them, though if a school sports a sign 'Purrfect Anglish' you are probably not going to need an MA in Applied Linguistics to get a job there. Working for a cowboy outfit may not be the end of the world, though it often spells trouble, as the chapter Problems will reveal. But without many qualifications you may not have much choice.

ADVERTISEMENTS

The monthly *EL Gazette* (www.elgazette.com) is a source of news and developments in the ELT industry for all interested individuals even though it is pitched at the professional end of the market and carries few job ads. An annual print subscription costs £33 in the UK, and £55 worldwide, though much of its content is available online. Job vacancies appear year round on the main TEFL websites, though schools that advertise in February or December are often advertising a very urgent vacancy, e.g. 'to start immediately, good salary, air fares, accommodation'; but these are exceptional.

Almost all adverts specify TEFL training/experience as a minimum requirement. But there is always a chance that this is merely rhetorical. Those who lack such a background should not feel defeated before they begin, since a TEFL background may turn out not to be essential. A carefully crafted CV and enthusiastic personality (not to mention a shortage of suitable applicants) could well persuade a school that they don't require a Cambridge or Trinity certificate with two years' experience after all.

Advertisements will sometimes include a contact name or company in the UK to which enquiries should be addressed for posts abroad. This may be a recruiting agency, TEFL training centre or a language school in the UK which is in contact with language schools abroad or it may just be an ex-employee who has agreed to do some recruitment for a commission fee. Note that none of these middle men is allowed to charge the job-seeker any fee. When discussing terms and conditions with an agent, bear in mind that the agent may be more interested in collecting a commission for finding someone to fill the vacancy than in conveying all the seamy facts.

Occasionally cases crop up of misleading or even fraudulent ads. A case a few years ago resulted in this headline in the *Times Educational Supplement*: 'Thousands conned by Botswana job hoax.' A conman placed adverts for teaching jobs in a fictitious school in Botswana, sent a letter of acceptance to all who applied and a request for $100 as a visa processing fee. Even if this sort of bare-faced fraud is rare, it is best to be sceptical when interpreting ads, including on the internet where promises of earning huge salaries, particularly in less than affluent countries, are usually pie-in-the-sky.

Based on his experience of answering advertisements placed by Turkish language schools, one experienced job-hunter has drawn up a glossary of terms, helping new applicants to 'read between the lines':

'Dollar Linked Salary' – paid in the local currency and only linked to the dollar every three or six months.
'Free Accommodation' – no way can you afford to rent a place of your own. You have no say in who your flatmates are.
'Paid Flight' – this is usually for a one-way flight.
'Leading School' – all the schools say this about themselves.
'Provides In-Service Training' – could be weekly, monthly or annually.
'Degree and Cert essential' – that's what the Ministry of Education wants. Will recruit anybody if desperate (good schools) or anybody at all (cowboys).
'Central Location' – near all the good pubs.
'Young and Dynamic Team' – be like a student again.
'Teachers are encouraged to use their own materials and be creative' – there isn't much in the way of resources.

ELT training centres often have numerous links with foreign schools and may have a noticeboard with posted vacancies. Unless you are a trainee at the relevant centre, it will probably be tricky consulting such a noticeboard, but a cooperative secretary might not mind a potential trainee consulting the board. University careers offices may also have contacts with schools abroad to which their graduates have gone in the past, so if you have a university connection, it is worth making enquiries.

FREELANCE TEACHING

Private English lessons are usually more lucrative than contract teaching simply because there is no middle man. Learners may prefer them as well, not only because of the more personal attention they receive in a private lesson but because it costs them less. As a private tutor working from your own home or visiting pupils in theirs, you can undercut the big schools with their overheads. But at the same time you deprive yourself of the advantages of working for a decent school: access to resources and equipment, in-service training, social security schemes and holiday pay. The life of a freelance teacher can be quite a lonely one. Usually teachers working for a school take on a small amount of private teaching to supplement their income, provided this is allowed in their contract. Most employers do not mind unless your private teaching is interfering with your school schedule or (obviously) if you are pinching potential clients from your employer.

Projects Abroad

Projects Abroad sends over 6,000 volunteers overseas annually, supported by 350 Projects Abroad staff on a variety of worthwhile projects in 25 countries across five continents. Choose from teaching, care, community work, conservation, medicine, veterinary medicine, physiotherapy, occupational therapy, sport, journalism, archaeology, business, law and human rights, arts and crafts, photography, drama, languages, electives and dissertation.

Projects start at a minimum of four weeks and some selected projects can accept volunteers for two weeks. Volunteers can choose their own dates for travel, with an average volunteer spending two to three months on a project. Minimum age is 16 and experience or qualifications aren't necessary. Projects start at £895 and prices include accommodation and placement, three meals a day, travel and medical insurance, 24-hour in-country staff support; airport transfers and projects can be combined.

Teaching in Peru

'I spent four amazing months teaching English to wonderful children in a school in Urubamba, Peru with Projects Abroad, which has been the most incredible experience of my life so far. The Projects Abroad staff were so helpful and caring that I never felt worried or alone which I think made my parents back home in England feel a lot better too. I was allowed two weeks' holiday allowance, which I used to travel to Buenos Aires to visit a friend, we then travelled up together through Bolivia and back into Peru. It was incredible to be able to gain an invaluable teaching experience, improve my Spanish and see more of South America as both Argentina and Bolivia were completely different to Peru, all of which I shall never forget.'

Katherine Wragg

In order to round up private pupils, you will have to sell yourself as energetically as any salesperson. Turn to the section on 'Freelance teaching' in the Spain chapter for some ideas that have worked in Spain but could work anywhere. It might be possible to persuade companies to pay you to run English classes for employees during the lunch hour or siesta (if appropriate), though you would have to be a confident teacher and dynamic salesperson to succeed. You are far more likely to find one or two pupils by word of mouth and build from there.

SELF-PROMOTION IS ESSENTIAL
Steven Hendry *plastered neatly printed bilingual notices all over town in Chiang Mai in northern Thailand.*
Ian McArthur *made a large number of posters (in Arabic and English) and painstakingly coloured in the Union Jack by hand in order to attract attention in Cairo. (Unfortunately these were such a novelty that many posters were pinched.)*

Putting a notice on appropriate noticeboards (in schools, universities, public libraries, popular supermarkets) and running an advertisement in the local paper are good ideas; you will also need a reliable mobile phone and preferably frequent access to your e-mail. These methods should put you in touch with a few hopeful language learners. Once you've made a good start, word will spread and more paying pupils will come your way, though it can be a slow process.

Counterbalancing the advantages of higher pay and a more flexible schedule are many disadvantages. Everyone, from lazy Taiwanese teenagers to busy Barcelona businessmen, cancels or postpones one-to-one lessons with irritating frequency. People who have taught in Latin countries complain that the problem is chronic. Cancellations among school and university students especially escalate at exam time. It is important to agree on a procedure for cancellations that won't leave you out of pocket. Although it is virtually impossible to arrange to be paid in advance, you can request 24 hours' notice of a cancellation and mention politely that if they fail to give due warning you will insist on being paid for the missed lesson. But you can't take too tough a line, since your clients are paying above the odds for your flexibility. Another consideration is the unpaid time spent travelling between clients' homes and workplaces.

Teaching by Skype or some other online system is now a common supplement or even full-time teaching possibility. There are even companies that recruit teachers anywhere in the world to teach remotely from their homes, for example see the US site www.gofluent.com/web/us/become-a-teacher-at-gofluent. With more and more people having fast internet connections and not enough time to attend in-person lessons, this is a growing market.

Lyndon Owen was in the vanguard of teaching by Skype:

> *I teach Business English one to one from my home in England and one of my recent students, a French professor of law, asked me to provide him with four lessons a week on the telephone. We have not finalised the details yet but since I have recently acquired Skype, I thought this might have been a cheaper medium for him once he has acquired the microphone and downloaded the free software.*

If you are more interested in integrating with a culture than in making money, exchanging conversation for board and lodging may be an appealing possibility. This can be set up by answering (or placing) small ads in appropriate places (the American Church in Paris noticeboard is famous for this). **Hannah Start**, a school-leaver from Merseyside, put up a notice at her local English language school indicating that she wanted to exchange English conversation for accommodation in Paris; a businesswoman on an intensive English course contacted her and invited her to stay with her.

PREPARATION

The preceding chapters on ELT training and job-hunting set out ways in which you can make your-self more attractive to potential employers. One of the best ways in which to prepare for a stint of teaching abroad is to teach English locally. Relevant experience can usually be gained by volunteer-ing to tutor immigrants in your home town; this is particularly feasible in the USA, where literacy programmes take place on a massive scale. It might also be a good idea to contact the director of a local commercial language school and ask to sit in on some lessons and to talk to teachers. A polite note expressing your interest in TEFL would probably meet with a positive response. EFL teachers are like everyone else; they are experts at what they do and don't mind sharing that knowledge with interested outsiders.

More prolonged exposure to TEFL can best be gained by working at a language summer school. This not only provides a chance to find out whether you will enjoy English teaching for a longer period, but may put you in touch with people who are well informed on overseas possibilities.

UK SUMMER SCHOOLS

Language courses take place throughout the British Isles in the summer, especially in tourist areas. It is estimated that there are 600–800 English language schools in operation in Britain during July and August, mainly catering for foreign students, especially from France, Spain, Italy and other EU countries, and increasingly from further afield, such as Russia and Turkey. Many of these schools advertise heavily in the spring, e.g. 'Teach English on the English Riviera'. Quality varies of course. The British Council has an accreditation scheme and a searchable database at www.educationuk. org/english allows you to search by region and type e.g. junior vacation courses in southern England. A sister organisation English UK also has links to its 400 members at www.arels.org.uk. Schools are located throughout the UK including Wales and Scotland, but are concentrated in the South East, Oxford, Cambridge and coastal resorts such as Bournemouth and Hastings. While waiting for VSO to find him a teaching placement in Mongolia, **Mr R Roy** taught English for Pilgrims (listed below), which gave him further experience at the same time as earning him a tidy sum:

> *I worked two three-week courses back to back which left me very little time to myself but also no time to spend any money and of course food and accommodation were included in the deal. It was really intense and tiring but good experience with all the visits and sports and performances and producing videos and magazines and reports. Pilgrims provided a good stock of books and equipment to help teachers prepare their lessons. I'm still in touch with them and would like to work another summer when I'm back in Britain.*

At the other end of the spectrum are the entrepreneurs who rent space (possibly ill-suited to teach-ing) and will take on almost anyone to teach. You may find yourself thrown in at the deep end with little preparation and few materials. **Marta Eleniak** was not very happy with her employer:

> *I have got nothing good to say about my employer. We were expected to do nearly everything including perform miracles, with no support and pathetic facilities. I can only liken it to being asked to entertain 200 people for 4 hours with a plastic bowl. The pupils got a raw deal too because of false promises made to them.*

She does admit though, that it was on the basis of this three-week job that she got a job in a Madrid language school.

Recruitment of summer teachers gets underway in the new year and is usually well advanced by Easter. The short-term nature of the teacher requirements means that schools sometimes have difficulties finding enough qualified staff. Wages are higher than for most seasonal summer jobs. The average starting salary for teachers is about £240 per week. Residential schools may pay less

Ardmore Group

Jude Cresswell says:

I started working for Ardmore in 2009 and have been very pleasantly surprised to find myself working for an accredited professional company with a relaxed family vibe.

For me, the ethos of teaching EFL for Ardmore is 'teamwork'. I have felt supported and valued by colleagues and admin, right from the start!

My classes are all ages and come from all over the globe. Tiny tots from Russia and lanky teenagers from Italy! We might have them just for a week or two but in that time we aim to give them not only exposure to lessons from experienced teachers but a whole 'Ardmore Experience' of activities and fun which they will remember long into their lives.

I love this job. The residential aspect means that you are always around the kids from supervising in the cafeteria to making presentations at 'graduation', so their exposure to English goes way beyond the structured lessons. I have been a teacher for over 20 years and I still enjoy the excitement of greeting a new group and seeing the happy, sometimes tearful, faces in the coach as they leave. It's good to know I have been part of a team dedicated to creating a happy memory.

Jeremy Lindon-Morris writes:

After I decided on TEFL as a new career move after a lengthy time in the travel industry, my question was for whom to work. Ardmore offered me the opportunity of a ten-week summer language school placement at a choice of superb UK locations, teaching very diverse groups of young multinational students, ranging from complete beginners through to advanced mature teenagers.

I absolutely loved my experience with Ardmore and was particularly impressed with the top quality of the teachers (university-educated, properly teacher-qualified and CRB-checked) and the fact that Ardmore produced its own series of highly customised student work books, together with an entrance and exit test to assess progress and a course graduation diploma.

Having worked in Europe teaching Business English in the main for a few years, I am now returning for my fourth consecutive Ardmore summer season. I also spend much of the off-season working for Ardmore with some EU-sponsored groups.

Under Ardmore's auspices I have had the opportunity to progress from teacher to head teacher to director of studies and to work with some very special people along the way.

if they are providing board and lodging, though some pay the same because the hours are so much longer. Since most schools are located in popular tourist destinations, private accommodation can be prohibitively expensive and the residential option attractive. Without a TEFL certificate or any TEFL background it is easier to get taken on as a non-teaching sports and activities supervisor, which at least would introduce you to the world of TEFL. EFL teachers must expect a number of extracurricular activities such as chaperoning a group of over-excited adolescents to a West End theatre or on an art gallery visit.

Some of the major language course organisations that offer a large number of summer vacancies are listed below.

Anglo Continental Educational Group, 29–35 Wimborne Road, Bournemouth BH2 6NA (01202 557414; english@anglo-continental.com; www.anglo-continental.com).

Ardmore Language Schools, Hall Place, Berkshire College, Burchetts Green, Maidenhead, Berkshire SL6 6QR (01628 826699; louise@theardmoregroup.com; www.theardmore-group.com).

Concorde International Summer Schools, Arnett House, Hawks Lane, Canterbury, Kent CT1 2NU (01227 451035; info@concorde-int.com; www.concorde-international.com).

EF Language Travel, 74 Roupell Street, London SE1 8SS (020 7341 8500); Pullens Lane, Oxford OX3 0DT (01865 759660); (oxford.recruitment@ef.com; www.ef.com/master/summerjobs).

EJO, Eagle House, Lynchborough Road, Passfield, Hants GU30 7SB (01428 751549; enquiries @ejo.co.uk; www.ejo.co.uk/employ.asp).

Embassy CES (www.embassyces.com/about/summer_jobs.aspx). Teachers and other staff needed for up to 25 summer schools.

ISIS Group

After completing my degree I found myself anxious to gain a qualification that had more practical application in the current economic climate. I discovered that gaining a qualification in TESOL would open employment doors for me worldwide, so I enrolled on a Trinity CertTESOL course at the ISIS centre, Greenwich. The level of support I received at ISIS over the four weeks was fantastic. My fellow trainees came from all walks of life, but we were all initially apprehensive about issues like standing in front of a class, dealing with students with a very low level of English, etc. The staff at ISIS guided us every step of the way and the course turned out to be one of the most rewarding, if challenging, experiences of my life. The 'small group' policy at ISIS ensured that there was always someone on hand to help me and I really felt integrated into the working life of the school.

After four weeks, not only did I feel prepared to go out into the classroom and teach, but I had also gained a really sound knowledge of contemporary TEFL issues. I have now been working at a school in the UK for the past three months and have just secured a position in Japan. It's really exciting to think I will be in Tokyo by the end of the month!

Laura James (completed the TESOL course with the ISIS group in February 2010)

International Quest Centres, 7 Trinity, 161 Old Christchurch Road Bournemouth BH1 1JU, SO14 3BQ (01202 29 68 68; jobs@internationalquest.co.uk; www.internationalquest.co.uk).

International Study Programmes, The Manor, Hazleton, Cheltenham, Gloucester GL54 4EB (01451 860379; Discover@International-Study-Programmes.org.uk; www.international-study-programmes.org.uk).

ISIS Education & Travel, 259 Greenwich High Road, London SE10 8NB (020 8293 1188; summer-recruitment@isisgroup.co.uk www.isisgroup.co.uk).

Kent School of English, 10 &12 Granville Road, Broadstairs, Kent CT10 1QD (01843 874870; enquiries@kentschool.co.uk; www.kentschoolofenglish.com).

LAL UK Summer Schools, Conway Road, Paignton, Devon TQ4 5LH (01803 558555; mark.cook@lalgroup.com; www.lalschools.com). Summer schools held in Torbay, Tavistock, Winchester, Twickenham, etc. Maximum wage of £275 for a 48-hour week.

OISE Youth Language Schools, OISE House, Binsey Lane, Oxford OX2 0EY (01865 258300; info@oise.com; www.oise.com).

Pilgrims Young Learners, 38 Binsey Lane, Oxford, OX2 0EY (01865 258332; recruitment@pilgrims.co.uk; www.pilgrimsrecruitment.co.uk).

Plus International, 8 Celbridge Mews, London W2 6EU (020 7229 4435; www.plus-ed.com). 50 summer positions in Ireland (Dublin, Maynooth and Galway).

Project International, 20 Fitzroy Square, London W1T 6EJ (020 7916 2522; info@project international.uk.com; www.projectinternational.uk.com).

Stafford House Study Holidays, 19 New Dover Road, Canterbury, Kent CT1 3AH (01227 811506; recruitment@staffordhouse.com; www.staffordhouse.co.uk). Part of Cambridge Education Group.

SUL Language Schools, 31 Southpark Road, Tywardreath, Par, Cornwall PL24 2PU (01726 814227; efl@sul-schools.com; www.sul-schools.com).

TASIS England American School, Coldharbour Lane, Thorpe, Surrey TW20 8TE (01932 565252 ext 2313; jeffbarton@tasis.com (summer programmes); www.tasis.com). Of special interest to American EFL teachers.

Thames Valley Cultural Centres, 13 Park Street, Windsor, Berkshire SL4 1LU (01753 852001; recruit@thamesvalleysummer.co.uk; www.thamesvalleysummer.com.uk).

Roberta Wedge found that working for a large summer school organisation was not only good preparation for a teaching contract in Italy, but was fun for its own sake:

The big language mills in Britain are a good way to see the country. I signed up with OISE in Exeter because I wanted to tramp the moors. It's possible to spend the whole summer jumping around fortnightly from contract to contract, all arranged ahead of time through the same organisation.

WHILE YOU'RE WAITING

After you have secured a job, there may be a considerable gap which will give you a chance to organise the practicalities of moving abroad and to prepare yourself in other ways. If you are going to a country that requires immigration procedures (the majority of cases unless you're an EU national planning to work in another member state) your employer can start the visa procedures. In addition to deciding what to take and how to get to your destination, you should think about your tax position and health insurance, plus find out as much as you can about the situation in which you will find yourself.

ELT professionals should consider joining the International Association of Teachers of English as a Foreign Language (IATEFL, Darwin College, University of Kent, Canterbury, Kent CT2 7NY; 01227 824430; generalenquiries@iatefl.org; www.iatefl.org). Membership, which costs £46 to individuals or £145 to institutions, entitles teachers to various services including six newsletters annually and access to special interest groups, conferences, workshops and symposia.

The more information you can find out about your future employer the better. **Kathy Panton** thinks that she would have been a more effective teacher in her first year in the Czech Republic if she had asked more probing questions beforehand:

> *Now that I have a better idea of what to teach I think I could handle it, but a first year teacher should ask a lot of questions; such as, what books the students have used, teacher continuity, very detailed report of what the students can do (as opposed to what they have studied), and most of all what they will be expected to accomplish during the school year. If the report is vague, I don't think anyone should take the job unless they are really confident that they'll be able to develop the framework themselves. I would look for a school that said something like, 'You'll guide the students through Hotline 1 text-book, and also give them extra vocabulary and speaking exercises to supplement the text. You'll also work with a phonics text for a few weeks, because these students have poor pronunciation. You'll probably find it useful to bring some old magazines but the school has several ESL textbooks already.' This would show that the school takes both curriculum and organisation seriously.*

An invaluable source of information is someone who has taught at the school before; ask your employer for a couple of e-mail addresses. Past teachers often pass on priceless minutiae, not only recommending pubs, bakeries, etc. but (if the accommodation is tied to the job) to arrive early and avoid the back bedroom because of the noisy plumbing or to take your wellies since winter rains turn the streets to rivers.

CONTRACTS

This is the point at which a formal contract or at least an informal agreement should be drawn up. Any employer who is reluctant to provide something in writing is definitely suspect. Horror stories abound of the young unsuspecting teacher who goes out to teach overseas and discovers no pay, no accommodation and maybe even no school. For this reason you should not only sign a contract but also have a good idea about what you are committing to.

WHAT A CONTRACT SHOULD COVER

The following items should be covered in a contract or at least given some consideration:

- ■ *Name and address of employer.*
- ■ *Details of the duties and hours of the job. (A standard load might be 24 contact teaching hours a week, plus three hours on standby to fill in for an absent teacher, fill all the board markers in the staff room, etc.)*

> - *The amount and currency of your pay. Is it adequate to live on? How often are you paid? Is any money held back? Can it be easily transferred into sterling or dollars? What arrangements are there if the exchange rate drops suddenly or the local currency is devalued?*
> - *The length of the contract and whether it is renewable.*
> - *Help with finding and paying for accommodation. If accommodation is not provided free, is your salary adequate to cover this? If it is, are utilities included? Does the organisation pay for a stay in a hotel while you look for somewhere to live? How easy is it to find accommodation in the area? If it is unfurnished what help do you get in providing furniture? Can you get a salary advance to pay for this and for any rent deposits?*
> - *Your tax liability.*
> - *Provisions for healthcare and sick pay.*
> - *Payment of pension or national insurance contributions.*
> - *Bonuses, gratuities or perks.*
> - *Days off, statutory holidays and vacation times.*
> - *Paid flights home if the contract is outside Europe, and mid-term flights if you are teaching for two years.*
> - *Luggage and surplus luggage allowance at the beginning and end of the contract.*
> - *Any probationary period and the length of notice which you and the employer must give.*
> - *Penalties for breaking the contract and circumstances under which the penalties would be waived (e.g. extreme family illness, etc.)*

Obviously any contract should be studied carefully before signing. It is a wise precaution to make a photocopy of it before returning to avoid what happened to **Belinda Michaels** whose employer in Greece refused to give her a copy when she started to dispute some points. In some cases the only contract offered will be in a foreign language (e.g. Arabic or Kazakh) and you will either have to trust your contact at the school for a translation or consider obtaining an independent English translation. **Amanda Moody** signed documents that were only in Japanese and later found out that she'd been diddled out of her end-of-year bonus.

HEALTH AND INSURANCE

Increasingly, the immigration authorities abroad will not grant a teacher a work permit until they have provided a medical certificate. Many countries such as Russia and China may insist on an HIV test and various other health checks, including for syphilis and tuberculosis. General practitioners (GPs) make a charge for carrying out these tests, whether you do it before you leave home or after arrival.

Reputable schools will make the necessary contributions into the national health insurance and social security scheme. Even if you are covered by a national scheme, however, you may find that there are exclusion clauses such as dental treatment, non-emergency treatment, prescription drugs, etc. or you may find that you are covered only while at work. Private travel insurance can be very expensive. Most insurance companies offer a standard rate that covers medical emergencies and a premium rate that covers personal baggage, cancellation, etc. On a 12-month travel policy, expect to pay roughly £20–£25 per month for barebones cover and £35–£40 for more extensive cover. Within Europe private insurance is not absolutely essential because European nationals are eligible for reciprocal emergency healthcare within the EEA. The European Health Insurance Card (EHIC) entitles EU nationals to emergency healthcare in any member state. Specialist expatriate policies might be worth investigating. Bespoke insurance policies can be drawn up by brokers such as

Campbell Irvine (www.campbellirvine.com). Off-the-peg policies are of course cheaper – try Direct Travel Insurance (www.direct-travel.co.uk) or Ace Traveller Insurance (www.aceinsure.com), which covers work and study abroad, and includes a gap year policy for people up to age 44. Policies endorsed by American Citizens Abroad in Geneva are available from Abrams Insurance Agency in Virginia (www.aia-international-insurance.com).

The EHIC is valid throughout the EEA and Switzerland. You can apply online for it at www.ehic.org. uk. Even if your employer will be paying into a health scheme, cover may not take effect immediately and it is as well to have the ordinary tourist cover for the first three months.

No matter what country you are heading for, you should obtain the Department of Health leaflet T7.1 *Health Advice for Travellers*, which is available from post offices and doctors' surgeries. Alternatively you can request a free copy on the Health Literature Line 0300 123 1002 or read it online at www.dh.gov.uk, which also has country-by-country details. Increasingly, people are carrying out their own health research on the internet; check, for example, www.fitfortravel.scot.nhs.uk and www. travelhealth.co.uk. The website of the World Health Organization (www.who.int/ith) has some information, including a listing of the very few countries in which certain vaccinations are a requirement of entry. The BBC's Health Travel Site (www.bbc.co.uk/health/travel) is a solid source of information about travel health ranging from tummy trouble to water quality and snake bites.

A company that has become one of the most authoritative sources of travellers' health information in Britain is MASTA (enquiries@masta.com; www.masta.com). It maintains a database of the latest information on the disease situation for all countries and the latest recommendations on the prevention of tropical and other diseases. This advice is provided via a personalised health brief based on your destinations and the nature of your trip, which is e-mailed to you from their website, for a charge of £3.99. Along with vaccination recommendations it also provides practical advice such as protection against malaria, information on disease outbreaks and other non-vaccine preventable health risks. Private specialist clinics abound in London but are thin on the ground elsewhere. A worldwide searchable listing of specialist travel clinics is maintained by the International Society of Travel Medicine (www.istm.org) although many countries are not included.

NATIONAL INSURANCE CONTRIBUTIONS, SOCIAL SECURITY AND PENSIONS

Nationals of the EEA countries working in another member state will be covered by European Social Security regulations. Information can be read online at dwp.gov.uk/international. Similarly, payments made in any EEA country count towards benefit entitlement when you return home. The UK also has social security agreements with other countries including Croatia, Israel, Jamaica, Turkey and the USA. The international section of the Department for Work and Pensions at Newcastle (helpline 0845 915 4811; http://dwp.gov.uk) should be able to advise. The EUlisses website (pronounced Ulysses after the hero himself; http://ec.europa.eu/employment_social/social_security_schemes/eulisses/ jetspeed) explains national social security arrangements throughout Europe.

If you don't make national insurance contributions while you are out of the UK in a country with no reciprocal agreement, you will forfeit entitlement to benefits on your return. You can decide to pay voluntary contributions at regular intervals or in a lump sum in order to retain your rights to certain benefits. Unfortunately this entitles you only to a retirement/widow's pension, and not to sickness benefit or unemployment benefit.

The question of pensions may seem irrelevant if you are just taking off for a year or two to teach English abroad. However, anyone who remains in the job for more than a couple of years should give some thought to starting or maintaining a pension. Because most English language teachers move between countries, it makes sense to pay into a personal pension scheme in your home country and also to maintain your right to a state pension by keeping up voluntary contributions. The question becomes vexed in those countries where state pension contributions are compulsory, as in Germany (see relevant chapter). Regulations of course vary from country to country so that, for instance, you are entitled to receive a pension after paying into the German scheme for five or more years but in Portugal you have to contribute for 17 years. If you pay into a scheme and leave before you are entitled to claim a pension, you will have to try to reclaim some of the money you paid in. In Germany you won't get back more than half. If you work in a number of countries you may find that you spend your retirement corresponding with national pension authorities. **John Sydes**, an expatriate teacher in Munich, has looked into the question of pensions and has been lobbying the European parliament to consider the predicament of peripatetic English teachers:

Social security regulations vary from country to country, so it is important to look into whether you will be entitled to a pension later if you intend spending any length of time in one place and have to pay pension contributions in a state scheme.

It's nice to hop around when you are young and full of energy and ideas. It's not so nice to find out that you have paid a lot of money into a scheme that won't pay you a pension later. English teachers are adventurers, but I'm afraid too many of us are forgetting a fundamental problem: how do we survive when we are old? We have managed to get the EU to realise that there is at least one group of professionals, i.e. TEFL teachers, who are living up to the European ideal of mobility of labour, but may well find they face a bureaucratic nightmare when they retire and apply for a state pension.

TAX

Calculating your liability to tax when working outside your home country is notoriously complicated so, if possible, check your position with an accountant. Everything depends on whether you fall into the category of 'resident', 'ordinarily resident' or 'domiciled'. Most EFL teachers count as domiciled in the UK since it is assumed that they will ultimately return. New legislation has removed the 'foreign earnings deduction' for UK nationals unless they are out of the country for a complete tax year. Since most teaching contracts operate from September, this means that the vast majority of EFL teachers, including teachers on high salaries in the Middle East or on the Japan Exchange and Teaching scheme which were formerly tax-free, will now be liable to UK tax. If you are out of the country for a tax year, you will be entitled to the exemption, provided no more than 62 days (i.e. one-sixth of the year) have been spent in the UK.

If the country in which you have been teaching has a double taxation agreement with Britain, you can offset tax paid abroad against your tax bill at home. But not all countries have such an agreement and it is not inconceivable that you will be taxed twice. Keep all receipts and financial documents in case you need to plead your case at a later date. For details of UK income tax while you are abroad contact HM Revenue and Customs (HMRC), Charity, Assets & Residency, St John's House, Merton Road, Bootle, Merseyside L69 9BB (0845 0700040 or from outside the UK +44 151 210 2222). HMRC has a good website if you have the patience to look for the information you need (www.hmrc.gov.uk/index.htm).

If US citizens can establish that they are resident abroad, the first $80,000 of overseas earnings is tax-exempt in the USA.

TRAVEL

London is the cheap airfare capital of the world and the number of online and office-based agencies offering discount flights to all corners of the world is seemingly endless. General websites such as www.cheapflights.co.uk, www.travelocity.com, www.expedia.com and www.opodo.com are good starting points though comparison shopping this way can be time-consuming and frustrating. Even after long hours of surfing, the lowest internet fares can often be undercut by a good agent, particularly if your proposed route is complicated, so don't hesitate to get on the phone. Alternatively, consult specialist travel magazines such as *TNT* (free in London) plus *Time Out* and the Saturday edition of *The Independent* or other national papers. The major student and youth travel agency STA Travel is usually a good starting place. For bookings and enquiries call STA Travel on 0871 230 0040 or log on at www.statravel.co.uk to find fares and check availability. You can request a quote by e-mail or make an appointment at your nearest branch.

Other reliable agencies specialising in long-haul travel include Trailfinders with 22 branches in UK cities plus Ireland and Australia (0845 058 5858 worldwide; 0845 050 5940 Europe; www.trailfinders.com.) and Travel Nation in Hove (0845 344 4225; www.travel-nation.co.uk) which is staffed by real experts who specialise in finding the best deals on round-the-world flights, discounted long-haul flights and multi-stop tickets.

Within Europe, rail is often the preferred way of travelling, especially since the months of September and June when most teachers are travelling to and from their destinations are among the most enjoyable times to travel. Good discounts are available to travellers under 26. Websites to check include www.raileurope.co.uk, www.trainseurope.co.uk (0871 700 7722) or the marvellous site for train travellers everywhere – www.seat61.com.

HOSPITALITY EXCHANGES

If you are planning to travel and conduct a speculative job hunt, you might want to take advantage of one of the hospitality exchanges that flourish over the internet, the best known of which is the Couchsurfing Project (www.couchsurfing.com). Like so many internet-based projects, the system depends on users' feedback, which means that you can check on a potential host's profile in advance and be fairly sure that dodgy hosts will be outed straightaway. Couchsurfing is so mainstream that a *Sunday Times* journalist (Fleur Brittan) has written a whole book about it called *On the Couch.*

Roving English language teacher **Bradwell Jackson** had been mulling over the possibility of travelling the world for about a decade before he finally gave up his job as a drug abuse counsellor in Florida to take off. On his earlier travels he had discovered the benefits of joining Servas (www.usservas.org in the USA; www.servasbritain.u-net.com in the UK) and two other hospitality exchange programmes Global Freeloaders (www.globalfreeloaders.com) and the Hospitality Club (www.hospitalityclub.org). His first destination was Mexico, where to his amazement he found English teaching work at the first place he happened to enquire in Mexico City:

> *I really must say right away that Servas is not simply for freeloading in people's homes. However, once you take the plunge and commit to wandering the earth, things just start to fall into place. If you belong to clubs such as Global Freeloaders, Hospitality Club, or any of the other homestay organisations, don't be surprised if the family you stay with invites you for an extended stay. The first such family I stayed with in Mexico invited me to stay for six months. All they asked is that I help with the costs of the food they prepared for me and the hot water I used.*

Bradwell has continued his couchsurfing travels in some unlikely locations. His host in Bamako, Mali, let him stay for two months in exchange for two hours of English lessons a day. He was a wealthy man who gave Bradwell all his meals, internet access, laundry and so on. He commented that 'once one lands into a dream situation like this, you are apt to feel a bit guilty, and such hospitality takes time to get used to. Still, I am certainly not complaining'. More recently, en route to his teaching job in China, he stayed with a host in Hong Kong.

MAPS AND INFORMATION

Good maps and guides always enhance one's enjoyment of a trip. Most people you will meet on the road will probably be carrying a *Rough Guide* or a *Lonely Planet*. These are both excellent series, though try not to become enslaved by their advice and preferences. Rough Guides has a series of *First Time* titles which could be of interest to gap year students including *Around the World*, *Europe*, *Africa*, *Asia* and *Latin America*. Even though so much advance information is available over the internet, nothing can compete with a proper guidebook to pore over and take away with you. If you are going to be based in a major city, buy a map ahead of time. Visit the famous travel bookshop Edward Stanford, with branches in Bristol and Manchester as well as the mother-store in Covent Garden, London; its searchable catalogue is available online at www.stanfords.co.uk. The Map Shop in Worcestershire (0800 085 4080/01684 593146; www.themapshop.co.uk) and Maps Worldwide in Wiltshire (01225 707004; www.mapsworldwide.co.uk) both do an extensive mail order business in specialised maps and guidebooks.

The Foreign & Commonwealth Office regularly updates its travel advice for every country in the world and includes risk assessments of current trouble spots. You can contact the Travel Advice Unit by phone on 0845 850 2829 or check the website (www.fco.gov.uk/travel). If you are living in a country with poor security, you might like to register your details on the FCO's LOCATE service (www. fco.gov.uk/locate) in countries where embassy officials may need to track you down in the event of an emergency.

LEARNING THE LANGUAGE

GIVE AND TAKE

Even if you will not need any knowledge of the local language in the classroom, the ability to communicate will increase your enjoyment many times over. After a long hard week of trying to din some English into your pupils' heads, you probably won't relish the prospect of struggling to convey your requests to uncomprehending shopkeepers, neighbours, etc. A refusal to try to learn some of the local language reflects badly on the teacher and reinforces the suspicion that English teachers are afflicted with cultural arrogance.

If there is time before you leave home, you might consider learning the language of the place you are going to by enrolling in a part-time or short intensive course of conversation classes at a local college of further education or using a self-study programme with books and tapes or an online course. This will also have the salutary effect of reminding you how difficult it is to learn a language. Take a good dictionary and a language course at a suitable level, for example the *Take Off In...* series from Oxford University Press (www.askoxford.com/languages) for £25, including mp3 downloads, the BBC (bbc.co.uk/languages), Linguaphone (0800 136973; linguaphone.co.uk) and Audioforum (audioforum. com). Also, check out noticeboards in local cafés etc. for adverts from young foreigners who offer conversation classes (or will swap their expertise for yours). A great resource is www.gumtree.com, which has a skills/language swap section. If you're lucky, your conversation partner might also be able to help you with advice/contacts for your trip.

Of course it is much easier to learn the language once you are there. Some employers may even offer you the chance to join language classes free of charge or swap English lessons for those in the local language; if you are particularly interested in this perk, ask about it in advance. Some cities, such as Barcelona and Istanbul, have regular informal 'English café' evenings (*intercambio* in

Spanish), although people you meet this way will be more interested in improving their English than your Spanish. Check out the site www.lingobongo.com, which focuses on language exchanges in Berlin, Madrid and other cities.

Minna Graber, who fell in love with the Romanian culture and language, is trying to improve her Romanian while teaching English in Bucharest, but her colleagues and acquaintances are not making it easy for her:

> *My main problem was that the English teaching staff were completely unable to understand that my main reason for being there was to improve my Romanian. They, in the main, refused to converse with me in anything other than English and on frequent occasions made fun of my efforts. This is despite the fact that I am at around level C1 in this languages. They seemed to believe that if you know English you don't have to learn other languages. The other assumption was that English speakers can't learn other languages. This attitude was often replicated elsewhere in the town and I had to fight quite hard to persuade my Romanian friends that I was not a walking English conversation lesson.*

Signing up for language classes on location is a good way of finding out about local teaching openings as **Till Bruckner** found:

> *The first thing I do when I arrive somewhere new is to get myself language lessons. The teacher will have met many other foreigners, have local connections and speak some English. In other words he or she is the natural starting point in your job hunt. If you make clear that you can only continue paying for your lessons if you earn money too, you've found a highly motivated ally in your search for work.*

Surprisingly, it is not always an advantage to know the language as **Jamie Masters** discovered in Crete:

> *About speaking Greek. Well, no one told me. I assumed that they'd be quite pleased to have a Greek-speaking English teacher, best of both worlds. It's useful for discipline; the kids can't talk about you behind your back; you can tell when they're cheating on their vocab tests; and, I stupidly thought, you can explain things more clearly, really get them to understand... Well, I was wrong, and was laboriously reprimanded for it when they finally worked out what I was doing. But by that time it was too late: the kids knew I could understand Greek, and so they knew they didn't have to make the effort to speak to me in English. No amount of my playing dumb worked.*

WHAT TO TAKE

The research you do on your destination will no doubt include its climate, which will help you choose an appropriate range of clothing to take. But there is probably no need to equip yourself for every eventuality. EFL teachers usually earn enough to afford to buy a warm coat or boots if required. Be sure to pack enough smart clothes to see you through the academic year; denim jeans are rarely acceptable in the classroom.

SAVE BEFOREHAND!
Even though you are expecting to earn a decent salary, you should not arrive short of money. It is usual to be paid only at the end of the first month. Plus you may need sizeable sums for rent deposits and other setting-up expenses.

A generous supply of passport photos and copies of your vital documents (birth certificate, education certificates, references) should be considered essential. Recreational reading in English may be limited, so you should take a good supply of novels, etc. It could take time to establish a busy social life, leaving more time for reading than usual. If you plan to take a laptop try to find out about the ease with which you can access the internet, which would allow you to access BBC news and sport, listen again to your favourite radio programmes and so on. An increasing number of language schools provide wifi in their staff rooms. It is less likely to be available at home, in which case you might consider taking a good short-wave radio with several bands powerful enough to pick up the BBC World Service. 'Dedicated' short-wave receivers, which are about the size of a paperback, start at £65. A further advantage of having access to the BBC is that you can tape programmes for use in the classroom. Up-to-date details of BBC World Service frequencies are available at www.bbc.co.uk/worldservice/schedules/frequencies or similarly, Voice of America's web page (www.voa.gov) has the latest listings of its broadcasting frequencies. The fantastic BBC iPlayer sadly isn't available when you're abroad at the moment, though that may change (and there are ways round it by using a secure proxy).

Find out from returned travellers what items are in short supply or very expensive. Some items that recur on teachers' lists are their favourite cosmetics, vitamin tablets, a deck of cards, ear plugs and thermal underwear.

TEACHING MATERIALS

Try to find out which course your school follows and then become familiar with it. Depending on the circumstances, there may be a shortage of materials, so again enquire in advance about the facilities. (For example, English texts being used in a few places in Cambodia dated from 1938 and contained such useful sentences as, 'I got this suit in Savile Row'.) If you are going to have to be self-reliant, you may want to contact the major EFL publishers, primarily Oxford University Press, Cambridge University Press, Longman, Heinemann, Penguin and Phoenix to request details of their course books with a sample lesson if possible, and the address of their stockist in your destination country.

Before leaving home, try to visit a specialist ELT bookshop or the EFL department of a bookshop and obtain a detailed catalogue of ELT materials. The online specialist KELTIC (www.keltic.co.uk) operates an international mail order service from Oxfordshire, offering an extensive range of materials. You can use its user-friendly website anywhere in the world to get information and advice or to order materials including the *Keltic Guide.* You can contact KELTIC by telephone (01869 363589) or e-mail (keltic@btol-uk.com).

Another major stockist is BEBC, the Bournemouth English Book Centre (Albion Close, Parkstone, Poole, Dorset BH12 3LL; 01202 712934; elt@bebc.co.uk; www.bebc.co.uk). The company supplies books, tapes, videos and ELT software by mail order to teachers worldwide. All popular ELT titles are available from BEBC's Online Bookshop (www.bebc.co.uk). The £3.50 price of a printed catalogue will be refunded with your first order. For a list of recommended titles, see the following section.

In North America those looking for TEFL titles can resort to purchasing online from Barnes and Noble (www.barnesandnoble.com) or Amazon.com. There are also a few specialist online bookstores including Alta Book Center in Utah (800 258 2375; info@altaesl.com; www.altaesl.com), which also does orthodox mail order. The publisher Delta (www.deltapublishing.com) has a series of online catalogues that may be helpful.

Here is a list of items to consider packing which most often crop up in the recommendations of teachers of conversation classes in which the main target is to get the students talking. Teachers expecting to teach at an under-resourced school might think about taking some of the following:

■ good dual language dictionary, picture dictionary

- cassettes/CDs (including pop music with clear lyrics such as the Beatles or early Billy Bragg, blank tapes/CDs (and a cassette recorder/CD player/iPlayer if necessary with spare batteries), games and activities book
- illustrated magazines such as the *National Geographic* or unusual publications, for example old comic books, teen mags or the *Big Issue* (interesting to many language learners in former communist countries)
- maps (for example of London)
- tourist guides to your home country, travel brochures, blank application forms
- flash cards (which are expensive if bought commercially; homemade ones work just as well)
- grammar exercise book
- old Cambridge exam papers (if you are going to be teaching from their suite of exams)

Postcards, balloons, stick-on stars and photos of yourself as an infant have all been used to good effect. If you know that there will be a shortage of materials, it might even be worth taking general stationery such as notebooks, carbon paper, Blutack, plastic files, large pieces of paper, coloured markers, etc. Most employers would be willing to pay the postage costs if you don't want to carry it all in your luggage. (If you are entering a country without a prearranged work visa, bear in mind that teaching aids in your luggage will alert immigration officers that you intend to work.)

Koober Grob spent an enjoyable time in Russia trying to hone the conversation skills of her highly motivated students. Her main regret was that she hadn't brought with her a 10-page list of possible discussion topics to help them practise their colloquial English, because she found that she was sometimes at a loss for topics (which may account for the conversation one day turning to chocolate-covered ants in Africa).

Richard McBrien, who taught English in China, recommends taking a collection of photos of anything in your home environment. A few rolls shot of local petrol stations, supermarkets, houses, parks, etc. can be of great interest to pupils in far-off lands. It may of course be difficult to anticipate what will excite your students' curiosity. The anthropologist Nigel Barley, who has written amusing books on his fieldwork, describes in his book *Not a Hazardous Sport* being enlisted to attend an impromptu English conversation club in a remote corner of Indonesia:

I answered questions about the royal family, traffic lights and the etiquette of eating asparagus, and gave a quick analysis of the shipbuilding industry. At the end of the evening, I fled back to the hotel.

EFL teachers cannot escape so easily, so you should be prepared to be treated like a guru of contemporary British or American culture. If you know in advance that you will have to perform in this capacity, you might get hold of *Britain* by James O'Driscoll (Oxford University Press, 2009; £25) which provides historical and cultural background of British society and institutions, as well as the private daily life of the British people.

ONLINE RESOURCES

Although TEFL and TESL teachers have been relatively slow to get net-savvy, these days more and more are getting on-line and making use of the vast number of resources available. These range from actual lesson plans and printable materials for immediate use with students to teacher forums and job sites. **Sab Will** is Course Director and main trainer on the TEFL Paris Certificate Course (teflparis.com). He has a special interest in English-learning websites and language blogs and has provided much of the information for this section. He started his first website for teachers in 1997 and currently runs hotchpotchenglish.com, which includes a teacher training forum, in-depth ELT book reviews and free interactive exercises for students.

One of the most useful types of website is that offering free teaching materials. Publisher Macmillan's *onestopenglish.com* is a good example, although practically all the major ELT publishers now offer something similar. Here you will find masses of materials, either linked in to existing coursebooks or stand-alone exercises, often with recordings, printable sheets, videos and teacher's notes.

Along the same lines are websites which are not linked to publishers but which offer very much the same thing – masses of exercises of all types. Again, there is usually a surprisingly rich free section, and a more comprehensive paying option, often aimed at organisations. The British Council's *teachingenglish.org.uk* is a good place to start, while *eslprintables.com* and *enchantedlearning.com* offer wonderful printouts and worksheets. *esl.about.com* is also well worth a look. Then there are websites which are not specifically for English teachers or learners but which house much which teachers can make use of, such as the major newspaper and television sites. Some of these, such as the BBC, Voice of America and the *Guardian* even have special sections where they have created mini-websites full of exercises for English learners based on their own up-to-date content, which is great for keeping lessons fresh and stimulating. Check out www.bbc.co.uk/worldservice/learningenglish, www1.voanews.com/learningenglish and www.guardian.co.uk/education/tefl.

Hot on the heels of the resources above comes a whole raft of websites which are not explicitly for English teaching, have no derived exercises for use in class, are not always appropriate, and yet they offer incredible potential for the innovative and adventurous English language teacher. These belong to the online world of YouTube (free videos) Flickr (free photos), Wikipedia (free knowledge) Deezer (free music), the BBC (free news) and Google Earth (free maps). Once you have learnt how to adapt real English to your classroom and to your students you will find these sites to be an absolute goldmine which will help you inject some marvellously unexpected and highly appreciated moments into your classes.

An abundance of free little programmes is available to make life easier, at least for tech-heads. With the legendary Hot Potatoes you can create your own interactive exercises such as gap-fills, crosswords and MCQs. Audacity allows you to record high-quality audio. Site Pal lets you send cute animated messages by e-mail. And Snaggit lets you grab any image, or any part of your computer screen, or the contents of an entire window, or make a video of your screen actions, in a second. With Google's Blogger you and your students can create blogs and use them to extend their English learning to their outside class activities. The virtual world 'Second Life' is being used ever more creatively by teachers to hold 'in-world' English classes in a unique, fun environment. And sites such as Amazon and eBay can be used to assess buying opportunities, read product reviews, discover the auction process and why not spend a few pennies as a group to buy something for the class! The possibilities are endless.

Last, but not least, let's mention the many teacher forums and other sources of useful information for new and experienced teachers alike. These typically cover teaching techniques, difficult situations needing solutions, or simply mention useful new teaching resources which have come to light recently. An example of this is **Sab Will**'s friendly and lighthearted hotchpotchenglish.com, and many of the above websites also include sections on teacher training and development.

In reality, there is such an enormous amount of great stuff out there that the addresses given above are given purely as examples only. The best way to discover some of them for yourself is simply to type in 'TEFL courses Paris' or 'English teacher training forum' or 'English teaching jobs Taiwan' or 'free English teaching resources' or whatever it is you're interested in and start surfing away. Googling for something specific will also provide useful leads, anything from ideas for teaching young learners (http://esl4word.wordpress.com) to preparation for IELTS (http://eflgoddess.blogspot.com). A good source of links is provided by an experienced teacher in Spain at http://eflbytes.wordpress.com.

RECOMMENDED BIBLIOGRAPHY

Oxford University Press

About to embark on her first week of lessons at a primary school in the Czech Republic, **Naomi Moir** wasn't entirely sure that the two-hour 'Teaching Young Learners' session in the penultimate week of her CELTA course had quite prepared her for the task that lay ahead.

Her class of 7-year-olds was indeed as unpredictable as she had assumed. Sometimes they came into the class full of energy and sometimes the opposite. Activities could be loved one lesson and then fall flat the next. But she quickly came to realise that what happened at the beginning of the lesson set up the way the rest of her lesson would progress. Creating an impact at the beginning, getting their attention, and getting them involved meant that the rest of the lesson often went much more smoothly. Likewise, after several weeks of lessons disintegrating as they neared the end (fading attention, chaotic departure) she came to realise that how she finished the lesson was also important - as simple as asking each child to tell her something they had learned during that lesson made them, even at such a young age, reflect and therefore learn more from the lesson.

Taking this experience, Naomi went on to author **Starting and Ending Lessons** in the **Oxford Basics for Children** series by Oxford University Press (2009). And this is really the root of the success of not only this series but of all the English Language teaching materials from Oxford University Press. The courses and resources have not only been researched and reviewed but lived and breathed. They have been written by teachers, based on their experiences in the classroom, and this is why they will work for you. The Oxford Basics are also inexpensive, so if you take nothing else before embarking on your journey to teach English abroad, pack a couple of these (see the list that follows for more titles in the series). Oh, and teabags and Marmite of course.

There is such a plethora of books and materials that the choice can be daunting to the uninitiated. Every teacher should have a basic manual of grammar handy, such as:

Oxford English Grammar Course by Michael Swan and Catherine Walter (Oxford University Press, 2011; Basic: £20 ISBN 978 019 442077 8; Intermediate: £21 ISBN 978 019 442082 2; Advanced – available September 2011). Explains the rules of grammar, shows how language works, and gives plenty of practice with CD-ROM focus on grammar and pronunciation.

Practical English Usage by Michael Swan (3rd edition, Oxford University Press, 2005; £25; ISBN 978 019 442098 3). Intermediate to Advanced. The world's most trusted reference grammar. Indispensable guide to problem points in English with explanations, sample sentences and lots of practice material.

Oxford Practice Grammar (Oxford University Press; Basic: £19; ISBN 978 019 457978 0; Intermediate: £19.50; ISBN 978 019 457980 3; Advanced: £20; ISBN 978 019 457982 7). A grammar practice series that offers a balance of explanation, practice and testing at every level. Available with Practice-Boost CD-ROMs.

Teaching Grammar by Jim Scrivener (Oxford University Press, 2003; £9.50; ISBN 978 019 442179 9).

Grammar for English Language Teachers by Martin Parrott (Cambridge University Press, 2010; £20.55).

Understanding and Using English Grammar by B Schrampfer Azar (Pearson Education, 2000; £14.60).

English Grammar in Use by Raymond Murphy (Cambridge University Press, 2004; Special price of £12 with answers available; plus supplementary exercises with answers: £9.45).

Advanced Grammar in Use by Martin Hewings (Cambridge University Press, 2005; £16.75 with answers).

English Grammar (Collins Gem, 2006; £4.99; Genuinely pocket-sized). Dubbed by at least one novice, 'the teacher's friend'.

Here is a selected list of recommended books and teaching aids which you could consider:

The Grammar Lab by K. Bourke (Oxford University Press; Book 1: £11.50; ISBN 978 019 433015 2; Book 2: £12.50; ISBN 978 019 433016 9; Book 3: £12; ISBN 978 019 433017 6). Beginner to intermediate grammar practice for children aged 9–12.

Oxford Advanced Learner's Dictionary (8th edition, Oxford University Press, 2010; £25; ISBN 978 019 4799003). The world's best selling advanced learner's dictionary. Helps develop all language skills. Available with new iWriter CD-ROM.

Oxford Learner's Thesaurus (Oxford University Press, 2008; £25; ISBN 978 019 475200 8). Upper-intermediate to advanced. Groups and defines similar words and explains the differences between them, helping the learner choose exactly the right word for the context. Comes with CD-ROM.

Word for Word by Stewart Clark and Graham Pointon (Oxford University Press, 2003; £15.50; ISBN 978 019 432755 8). Intermediate to advanced. Compares and defines about 3,000 of the most commonly confused words in English.

Collins Cobuild Advanced Learners English Dictionary (Collins, 2006; £19.50). Collins publishes a range of dictionaries for the language learner.

Cambridge Advanced Learners Dictionary (Cambridge University Press, 2008; £27). Also available as a CD-ROM (£18.45).

Freestanding by Maurice Jamall (Delta Systems; £13.95). Elementary to Upper Intermediate. Teachers' resource book suitable for children and young adults.

Grammar Practice Activities by Penny Ur (Cambridge University Press, 2009). Paperback with CD-ROM £22. Teaching classic for all levels and ages. Includes photocopiable worksheets and visuals.

More Grammar Games by M. Rinvolucri and P. Davis (Cambridge University Press, 1995; £20.85). Includes activities for all levels.

The Practice of English Language Teaching by Jeremy Harmer (4th edition, Longman, 2007). £29. A well-known core reference work for teachers from the author of *How to Teach English* (£27.70), a straightforward introduction to TEFL for new teachers.

Oxford Basics is a series of 11 short accessible books (see case study above) for teachers who are new to ELT or who are looking for new creative ways of teaching with limited resources. The series includes *Introduction to Teaching English* by Jill & Charles Hadfield (Oxford

International House *Newcastle*

- CELTA
- DELTA
- International House Certificate *Online*

tt@ihnewcastle.com
www.ihnewcastle.com
+44 (0)191 2329551

University Press, 2008; £15), a practical guide with lesson plans for new teachers of English; and *Simple Speaking Activities* by the same authors (Oxford University Press, 1999; £9.50).

The Standby Book by Seth Lindstromberg (Cambridge University Press, 1997; £19.40). Teacher's resource book of 110 language learning activities for all types of teaching situation.

Lessons from Nothing by Bruce Marsland (Cambridge University Press, 1998; £16.35). From the Cambridge Handbooks for Language Teachers series.

Children Learning English (Macmillan, 2005; £19.30). Introduces the theory behind good classroom practice with examples from around the world.

Learning Teaching (Scrivener, 2005; £21). Useful for teachers in training and as a quick resource of lively lesson ideas.

Resource Books for Teachers is another series from Oxford University Press of 30 titles giving practical advice and guidance, together with resource ideas and materials for use with secondary and adult learners. Titles include *Drama and Improvisation* by Ken Wilson (2009; £19.50) and *Teenagers* by Gordon Lewis (2007; £19.50).

Oxford Basics for Children is a series of five titles for teachers of young learners which provides adaptable teaching ideas in an easy-to-follow format. Series includes *Starting and Ending Lessons* by Naomi Moir (Oxford University Press, 2009; £9.50), *Vocabulary Activities* by Mary Slattery (2008; £9.50); *Games for Children* by Gordon Lewis with Günther Bedson (1999; £19.50) and *Storytelling with Children* by Andrew Wright (£19.50).

Ladybird Key Words Reading Scheme (Ladybird's Books for English Learning). Inexpensive series for teaching young children.

PROBLEMS

Potential problems fall into two broad categories: personal and professional. You may quickly feel settled and find your new setting fascinating but may discover that the job itself is beset with difficulties. On the other hand the teaching might suit but otherwise you feel alienated and lonely. Those who choose to uproot themselves suddenly should be fairly confident that they have enough resources to rely on themselves, and must expect some adjustment problems. Only you can assess your chances of enjoying the whole experience and of not feeling traumatised. Women may encounter special problems in countries where women have little status. An informative site is www.journeywoman.com among many others.

PROBLEMS AT WORK

Anyone who has done some language teaching will be familiar with at least some of the problems EFL teachers face. Problems encountered in a classroom of Turkish or Peruvian adolescents will be quite different from the ones experienced teaching French or Japanese business people. The country chapters attempt to identify some of the specific problems which groups of language learners present.

Although you are unlikely to be expected to entertain 200 people for four hours with a plastic bowl, there may be a fairly complete lack of facilities and resources. The teacher who has packed some of the teaching materials listed above will feel particularly grateful for his or her foresight in such circumstances. Some schools, especially at the cowboy end of the spectrum, go to the other extreme of providing very rigid lesson plans from which you are not allowed to deviate and which are likely to be uncongenial and uninspiring. Even when reasonable course texts are provided, supplementary materials for role play and games can considerably liven up classes (and teachers). You can obtain extra teaching aids after arrival from the nearest English language bookshop or make them yourself, for example tape a dialogue between yourself and an English-speaking friend or cut up magazines or use postcards to make flashcards. If the missing facilities are more basic (e.g. tables, chairs, heating, paper, pens) you will have to improvise as best you can and (if appropriate) press the administration for some equipment.

PROBLEMS WITH PUPILS

A very common problem is to find yourself in front of a class of mixed ability with incompatible aims. How do you plan a lesson that will satisfy a sophisticated business executive whose English is fairly advanced, a delinquent teenager and a housewife crippled by lack of confidence? A good school of course will stream its clients and make life easier for its teachers. But this may be left to you, in which case a set of commercially produced tests to assess level of language acquisition could come in very handy. Alternatively you can devise a simple questionnaire for the students to describe their hobbies, studies, family or whatever. This will not only display their use of English but also give you some clues about their various backgrounds. One way of coping with gross discrepancies is to divide the class into compatible groups or pairs and give tasks which work at different levels. Subdividing a class is in fact generally a good idea especially in large classes.

In some places you may even have to contend with racial or cultural friction among pupils, as **Bryn Thomas** encountered in Egypt:

> *One of the problems I found in the class was the often quite shocking displays of racism by the Egyptians towards their dark-skinned neighbours from Somalia. Vast amounts of tact and diplomacy*

were required to ensure that enough attention was given to the Somalis (who tend to be shy, quiet and highly intelligent) without upsetting the sometimes rowdy and over-enthusiastic Egyptians.

Your expectations of what teaching is supposed to achieve may be quite different from the expectations of your students. Foreign educational systems are often far more formal than their British or American counterparts and students may seem distressingly content to memorise and regurgitate, often with the sole motivation of passing an exam. But this doesn't always operate. Many teachers have had to face a class that doesn't seem to care at all about learning any English and merely wants to be entertained.

In many countries free discussion is quite alien, whether because of repressive governments or cultural taboos. It is essential to be sensitive to these cultural differences and not to expect too much of your pupils straightaway. The only way of overcoming this reluctance to express an opinion or indeed express anything at all is to involve them patiently and tactfully, again by splitting them into smaller units and asking them to come up with a joint reply.

Discipline is seldom a serious problem outside Europe; in fact liberal teachers are often taken aback by what they perceive as an excess of docility, an over-willingness to believe that 'teacher is always right'. In some cases, classes of bored and rebellious European teenagers might cause problems (especially on Fridays), or children who are being sent to English lessons after school simply as an alternative to babysitting for working mothers. Unfortunately, a couple of troublemakers can poison a class. You may even have to contend with one or two downright uncontrollable students as **Jamie Masters** did in Crete:

> *At least two of my pupils were very malevolent. There was one, Makis, who used to bring a 'prop' to every lesson, some new way of disrupting the class – an air pistol, a piece of string with a banknote tied to it, a whistle, white paint. He used to slap my cheeks, hug me and lift me off the floor, was quite open about not wanting to work… and then claimed I was picking on him when I retaliated. Well, call me a humourless unfeeling bastard, but…*

One teacher in Turkey found the majority of his students 'bouncy, bright, enthusiastic and sharp' but with one class he was always amazed that they walked upright when they got out of their chairs. It often turns out that each class develops a certain character.

Some months after Jamie Masters returned home to London, he confessed:

> *Even now you only have to say the words 'D class Mastamba' to strike terror into my heart. But the A class in the same school was a joy to teach: rowdy, yes, but I had a lot of time for them. Within a class there are different personalities of course but they tend to get subsumed into the personality of the group. So I had good classes and bad classes in all the places I taught. When I left, some classes cheered; others wept and drew hearts all over their vocab tests. The main line of demarcation may in fact be age rather than income: the younger students more or less accept that they have to work; the older ones are beginning to rebel.*

Marta Eleniak, who taught in Spain, recommends taking a hard line:

> *Be a tyrant at the start. The kids can be very wicked and take advantage of any good nature shown. Squash anyone who is late, shouts, gossips, etc. the first time or it'll never stop. The good classes make you love teaching. The bad make you feel as if you want to go back to filing.*

Each level and age group brings its own difficulties. Anyone who has no experience of dealing with young children may find it impossible to grab and hold their attention, let alone teach them any English. A lack of inhibition is very useful for teaching young children who will enjoy sing-songs, nursery rhymes, simple puzzles and games, etc. A firm hand may also be necessary if **Aine Fligg**'s experience in Hong Kong is anything to go by. She was bitten on the ankle by one of her less receptive students. When the headmaster came in and remonstrated (with Aine!), the child bit him on the nose. The brat was then incarcerated in a cupboard, and emerged somewhat subdued.

Only 18 years old himself, **Sam James** had to teach a variety of age groups in Barcelona during his gap year and despite the problems, ended up enjoying it:

> *The children I taught were fairly unruly and noisy. The teenagers were, as ever, pretty uninterested in learning, though if one struck on something they enjoyed they would work much better. Activities based on the lyrics of songs seemed to be good. They had a tendency to select answers at random in multiple choice exercises. On the other hand they were only ever loud rather than very rude or disobedient. The young children (8–12) were harder work. They tended to understand selectively, acting confused if they didn't like an instruction. Part of the problem was that the class was far too long (three hours) for children of that age and their concentration and behaviour tended to tail off as the time passed.*

Beginners of all ages progress much more rapidly than intermediate learners. Many teachers find adolescent intermediate learners the most difficult to teach. The original fun and novelty are past and they now face a long slog of consolidating vocabulary and structures. (The 'intermediate plateau' is a well-known phenomenon in language acquisition.) Adolescents may resent 'grammar games' (which are a standard part of EFL) thinking that games are suitable only for children.

The worst problem of all is to be confronted with a bored and unresponsive class. This may happen in a class of beginners who can't understand what is going on, especially a problem if you don't speak a word of their language. It can be extremely frustrating for all concerned when trying to teach some concept or new vocabulary without being able to provide the simple equivalent. If this is the case, you'll have to rely heavily on visual aids. Whole books have been written to show EFL teachers how to draw, for example *1,000+ Pictures for Teachers to Copy* by Andrew Wright (Pearson, £39.20). For a very low-level class, you may need to resort to your bilingual dictionary for lesson plans. But some enjoy the challenge: 18-year-old **Hannah Bullock** found teaching her class of Czech beginners good fun 'because each lesson was like an invigorating game of charades'. Many new teachers make the mistake of doing all the talking. During his year of teaching in Slovenia, **Adam Cook**, like many others before him, came to the conclusion that silence is one of the teacher's most effective tools.

TIPS FOR DEALING WITH A LETHARGIC CLASS
The best way to inject a little life is to get them moving around, for example get them to do a relaxation exercise or have them carry out a little survey of their neighbours and then report their findings back to the class. A reluctance to participate may be because the pupils do not see the point of it.

In many countries foreign teachers come to feel like a dancing bear or performing monkey, someone who is expected to be a cultural token and an entertainer. If the students are expecting someone to dance a jig or swing from the chandelier (so to speak) they will be understandably disappointed to be presented with someone asking them to form sentences using the present perfect. At the other extreme, it is similarly disconcerting to be treated just as a model of pronunciation, and you may begin to wonder whether your employer might be better off employing a tape recorder.

PROBLEMS WITH YOURSELF

Lessons can fizz or fizzle. The latter may be the fault of the students but more often it is down to the teacher. One of the most common traps into which inexperienced teachers fall is to dominate the class too much. Conversational English can only be acquired by endless practice and so you must allow your pupils to do most of the talking. Even if there are long pauses between your questions and their attempts to answer, the temptation to fill the silences should be avoided. Pauses have a positive role to play, allowing pupils a chance to dwell on and absorb the point you have just been illustrating. Avoid asking 'Do you understand?' since the answer is meaningless; it is much more useful to test their comprehension indirectly.

> *A native speaker's function is seldom to teach grammar, though he or she should feel comfortable naming grammatical constructions. You are not there to help the students to analyse the language but to use it and communicate with it. It has been said that grammar is the highway code, the catalogue of rules and traffic signs, quite useless in isolation from driving, which gets you where you want to go. Grammar is only the cookery book while talking is cooking for other people to understand/eat. Persuading some students whose language education has been founded on grammar rather than communication that this is the priority may be difficult, but try not to be drawn into detailed explanations of grammatical structures.*

Being utterly ignorant of grammar can result in embarrassing situations. You can only get away with bluffing for so long ('Stefan, I don't think it matters here whether or not it's a subjunctive') and irate pupils have been known to report to school directors that their teachers are grammar-illiterate. One useful trick suggested by **Roberta Wedge** is to reply, 'Very good question – we're going to deal with that in the next class.' Usually it will suffice to have studied a general grammar handbook such as *Practical English Grammar* or *Practical English Usage* (see the bibliography in the previous chapter). If you contradict yourself between one lesson and the next, and an eager student notices it, take **Richard Osborne**'s advice and say 'Ah yes, I'm sorry about that. You see, that's the way we do it at home. Bizness is often spelled with a z in Canada.'

The worst fate that can befall a teacher is to run dry, to run out of ideas and steam completely before the appointed hour has arrived. This usually happens when you fail to arrive with a structured lesson plan. It is usually a recipe for disaster to announce at the beginning of the lesson 'Tonight let's talk about our travels/hobbies/animals' or whatever. Any course book will help you to avoid grinding to a halt. Supplementary materials such as songs and games can be lifesavers in (and out) of a crisis. If you are absolutely stuck for what to talk about next, try writing the lyrics of a popular song on the board and asking the class to analyse it or even act it out (avoiding titles such as *I Want Your Body*). Apparently songs which have worked well for many teachers include George Michael's *Careless Whispers*, the Beatles' *Here Comes the Sun* and *When I'm 64* and *Perfect Day* by Lou Reed. The site http://lyricstraining.com/game2043.htm attempts to provide an easy method to learn and improve foreign languages skills through music and lyrics. Another way of stepping outside the predictability of a course book might be to teach a short poem that you like, or even a short story (e.g. by Saki) if the class is sufficiently advanced.

LESSON STRUCTURE
A very popular way to structure a lesson is in 'notions'; you take a general situation like 'praising' or 'complaining', teach some relevant vocabulary and structures and then have the class put them into practice in role-play situations. Unfortunately repetition is the key to language learning, though you have to avoid boring drills, which will kill any interest in the language.

When a lesson goes well, it can be deeply satisfying. **Philip Tompkins** did his TEFL training in Greece in 2010 and identified the high point of his teaching experiences, as sharing a joke in English with a class and all having a fit of the giggles. The low point was inadvertently using technical jargon in his first lesson which temporarily killed it dead, and being faced with blank looks.

Culture shock is experienced by most people who live in a foreign country in whatever circumstances (see below), but can be especially problematic for teachers. Unthinkingly you might choose a topic which seems neutral to you but is controversial to them. A little feature on the English pub, for example, would not be enjoyed in Saudi Arabia. A discussion about whaling might make a class of Norwegians uncomfortable. Asking questions about foreign travels would be tactless in many places where few will be able to afford international travel.

One of the more subtle problems is knowing how to approach teaching as **J. W. Arble** discovered:

I was caught up with trying to work out how to present myself to my students: whether to assume the role of friend, exotic or mentor: whether to be 'charismatic' or reserved, enthusiastic or dry, serious-minded or idiot savant. Given the limited time, I persuaded myself the aim was to make the subject interestingly different; with the hope a few might be triggered into curiosity. Less worthily, I just wanted to be liked.

One of the hardest problems to contend with is teacher burn-out. If you invariably arrive just as the class is scheduled to begin, show no enthusiasm, and glance at the clock every 90 seconds, you will not be a popular teacher. Getting hold of some new authentic materials might shore up your flagging enthusiasm for the enterprise. If not, perhaps it is time to consider going home (bearing in mind your contractual commitments).

PROBLEMS WITH EMPLOYERS

All sorts of schools break their promises about pay, perks and availability of resources. The worst disappointment of all, however, is to turn up and find that you don't have a job at all. Because schools which hire their teachers sight unseen often find themselves let down at the last moment, they may over-hire, just in the way that airlines overbook their flights in the expectation of a certain level of cancellation. Even more probable is that the school has not been able to predict the number of pupils who will enrol and decides to hire enough teachers to cover the projected maximum. Whatever the reason, it can be devastating to have the job carpet whipped from under your feet. Having a signed contract helps. It may also be a good idea to maintain contact with the school between being hired and your first day of work. If the worst does happen, you could try losing your temper, threatening to tarnish their good name, and demand a month's pay and your return airfare. Or you could try playing on the guilt of the director and ask him or her to help you get a last-minute job in another school.

Just because a school does not belong to the EFL establishment does not mean that teachers will be treated badly (and vice versa). However, the back street fly-by-night school may well cause its foreign teachers anxiety. The most common complaints revolve around wages – not enough or not often enough or both. Either you will have signed a contract (possibly in ignorance of the prevailing conditions and pay levels) or you have nothing in writing and find that your pay packet does not correspond with what you were originally promised. It is probably not advisable to take up a confrontational stance straightaway since this may be the beginning of a year of hostility and misery. Polite but persistent negotiations might prove successful. Find out if there is a relevant teachers' union, join it and ask them for advice (though EFL is notorious for being non-unionised). As the year wears on, your bargaining clout increases, especially if you are a half-decent teacher, since you will be more difficult to replace mid-term.

One recourse is to bring your employer's shortcomings to the attention of the British Council or in extreme cases of exploitation, your embassy/consulate. If you are being genuinely maltreated and you are prepared to leave the job, delivering an ultimatum and threatening to leave might work. Remember that if there are cowboy schools, there are also cowboy teachers. Many honest and responsible employers have fallen victim to unreliable and undisciplined individuals who break their promises, show up late and abuse the accommodation they are given. Try not to let your employer down unless the provocation is serious.

Language schools must function as businesses as well as educational establishments and in some case the profit motive overtakes everything else. In those cases, teachers soon realise that they matter less to the people in charge than the number and satisfaction of students. You may be asked to conduct a conversation class in a room not much smaller than the Albert Hall. Some employers leave you entirely to your own devices and even look to you for teaching ideas. Others interfere to an annoying degree; we've heard of one school director in Spain who bugged the classrooms to make sure the staff were following his idiosyncratic home-produced course outlines. **Jayne Nash** worked for a chain of schools in France that use their own method; clients learned basic phrases and words for everyday situations in parrot fashion:

The courses were aimed at local business people, therefore students learned mostly spoken English to introduce themselves, their company or product, language for meetings, telephone conversations, etc. The method seemed very effective, but can prove extremely tedious for the teacher. After you have repeated a word 10–20 times with 10 students, 4 times a day, 5 days a week...

One of the most commonly heard complaints from teachers concerns the schedule. Eager only to satisfy clients, employers tend to mess around with teachers' timetables, offering awkward combinations of hours or changing the schedule at the last moment, which is extremely stressful. A certain amount of evening work is almost inevitable in private language schools where pupils (whether of school or working age) must study English out of hours. Having to work early in the morning and then again through the evening can become exhausting after a while. It can also be annoying to have several long gruelling days a week and other days with scarcely any teaching at all (but still not days off).

H.P.W. = HOURS PER WEEK

One trick to beware of is to find that the 24 hours a week you were told you would be working actually means 32 45-minute lessons (which is much harder work than teaching 24 one-hour lessons). Even if the number of hours has not been exaggerated, you may have been deluded into thinking that a 24-hour week is quite cushy. But preparation time can easily add half as many hours again, plus if you are teaching in different locations, travel time (often unpaid) has to be taken into consideration.

In some situations teachers may be expected to participate in extra-curricular activities such as dreary drinks parties for pupils or asked to make a public speech. Make an effort to accept such invitations (especially near the beginning of your contract) or, if you must decline, do so as graciously as possible. There might also be extra duties, translating letters and documents, updating teaching materials, etc. for which you are unlikely to be paid extra.

PROBLEMS OUTSIDE WORK

Your main initial worry outside your place of employment will probably be accommodation. Once this is sorted out, either with the help of your school or on your own, and you have mastered the essentials of getting around and shopping for food, there is nothing to do but enjoy yourself, exploring your new surroundings and making friends.

CULTURE SHOCK

Enjoying yourself won't be at all easy if you are suffering from culture shock. Shock implies something which happens suddenly, but cultural disorientation more often creeps up on you. Adrenaline usually sees you through the first few weeks as you find the novelty exhilarating and challenging. You will be amazed and charmed by the odd gestures the people use or the antiquated way that things work. As time goes on, practical irritations intrude and the constant misunderstanding caused by those charming gestures – such as a nod in Greece meaning 'no' or in Japan meaning 'yes, I understand, but don't agree' – and the inconvenience of those antiquated phone boxes and buses will begin to get on your nerves. Unless you can find someone to listen sympathetically to your complaints, you may begin to think you have made a mistake in coming in the first place.

Experts say that most people who have moved abroad hit the trough after three or four months, probably just before Christmas in the case of teachers who started work in September. A holiday over Christmas may serve to calm you down or, if you go home for Christmas, may make you feel terminally homesick and not want to go back. Teachers who survive this, often find that things improve in the second term as they cease to perceive many aspects of life as 'foreign'.

The best way to avoid disappointment is to be well briefed beforehand, as emphasised in the chapter on Preparation. Gathering general information about the country and specific information about the school before arrival will obviate many of the negative feelings some EFL teachers feel. If you are the type to build up high hopes and expectations of new situations, it is wise to try to dismantle these before leaving home. English teaching is seldom glamorous.

LETTING OFF STEAM

You're likely to get depressed and disappointed at some stage, but remember not to broadcast your feelings randomly. Feeling contempt and hostility towards your host country is actually part of the process of adjusting to being abroad. But not everyone seems to appreciate that it has more to do with their own feelings than with the inadequacies (real or imagined) of the country they are in. So if you feel you have to let off steam about the local bureaucracy or the dishonesty of taxi-drivers or the way one simply cannot walk 10 yards down the pavement without people crossing the street for the express purpose of bumping into you, do remember to do it in private, in emails or when there are no local people around. This is especially important if you have colleagues who are natives of the country. They may find some of the idiosyncrasies of their culture irritating too but, unlike you, they have to live with them forever.

Some native-speaker teachers have found an unpleasant rift between local and foreign staff, which in some cases can be accounted for by the simple fact that you are being paid a lot more than they are. Sometimes new foreign teachers find their local colleagues cliquey and uncommunicative. No doubt they have seen a lot of foreigners come, and make a lot of noise, and go, and there is no particular reason why they should find the consignment you're in wildly exciting and worth getting to know.

LONELINESS

Creating a social life from scratch is difficult enough at any time, but becomes even more difficult in an alien tongue and culture. You will probably find that many of your fellow teachers are lots of fun and able to offer practical help in your first few weeks (especially any who are bilingual). If you find yourself in a one-foreigner village, surely there's another lonely teacher across the mountaintop. You could meet for a drink at the weekend to commiserate and to draw up a charter and call yourselves 'The Wonga Plateau EFL Teachers' Association' (and remember to put yourself down as founder the next time you are revising your CV). You may even want to take some positive steps to meet people and participate in activities outside the world of English language instruction. This may require uncharacteristically extrovert behaviour, but overcoming initial inhibitions almost always pays worthwhile dividends.

If you are tired of conversations about students' dullness or your director of studies' evident lunacy, you could try to meet other expatriates who are not EFL teachers. The local English language bookshop might prove a useful source of information about forthcoming events for English speakers, as will be any newspapers or magazines published in English such as the *Bulletin* in Belgium or the *Athens News* in Greece. Seek out the overseas student club if there is a university nearby (though when they discover what line of work you are in they may well have designs on you). Even the least devout teachers have found English-speaking churches to be useful for arranging social functions and offering practical advice. If there is a bar in town which models itself on a British/Irish pub or American bar, you will no doubt find a few die-hards drinking Guinness or Budweiser, who might be more than willing to befriend you.

The most obvious way to meet other foreigners is to enrol in a language course or perhaps classes in art and civilisation. Even if you are not particularly serious about pursuing language studies, language classes are the ideal place to form vital social contacts. You can also join other clubs or classes aimed at residents abroad, for example some German cities have English amateur dramatics groups.

Making friends with locals may prove more difficult, though circumstances vary enormously according to whether you live in a small town or a big city, with some gregarious colleagues or by yourself, etc. The obvious source of social contact is your students and their friends and families (bearing in mind that in certain cultures, a teacher who goes out to a bar or disco with students risks losing their respect). As long as you don't spend all your free time moping at home, you are bound to strike up conversations with the locals, whether in cafés, on buses or in shops. Admittedly these seldom go past a superficial acquaintance, but they still serve the purpose of making you feel a little more integrated in the community. Local university students will probably be more socially flexible than others and it is worth investigating the bars and cafés frequented by students. If you have a particular hobby, sport or interest, find out if there is a local club where you will meet like-minded people; join local ramblers, jazz buffs, etc. – the more obscure the more welcome you are likely to be. You only have to become friendly with one other person to open up new social horizons if you are invited to meet their friends and family. Also make an effort to organise some breaks from work. Even a couple of days by the seaside or visiting a tourist attraction in the region can revitalise your interest in being abroad and provide a refreshing break from the tyranny of the teacher's routine.

COMING HOME

For some, teaching abroad can be addictive. The prospect of returning home to scour the local job adverts becomes distinctly unappealing as they drink Retsina, eat sushi or spend the weekend at a Brazilian beach. Once you have completed one teaching contract, it will be very much easier to land the next one, and it can be exhilarating to think that you can choose to work in almost any corner of the globe. By the same token, many people who go abroad to teach English get burned out after a year or two. The majority of English teachers do not think of TEFL as a long-term proposition. They talk about their colleagues who move on to other things as getting a 'proper job', i.e. one that does not require an early start followed by a long idle morning, where shabby treatment by bosses is not the norm and where you do not have to correct anyone's phrasal verbs.

Homesickness catches up with most EFL teachers and they begin to pine for a pub or bar where repartee is quick and natural and for all the other accoutrements of the culture of their birth.

The bad news is that there are few jobs in EFL in Britain except at summer schools. Even professional English language teachers can find it difficult to land a reasonable job in the UK. American teachers will probably fare better due to the growth industry of ESL in the US, though the majority of openings are part-time with few fringe benefits and opportunities for career development. The good news is that a stint of teaching English abroad is an asset on anyone's CV/resumé. Employers of all kinds look favourably on people who have had the get-up-and-go to work at a respectable job in a foreign land. On returning home from teaching in Chile, **Heidi Resetarits** began looking for jobs and found that having international work experience on her resumé was invaluable. Potential employers were intrigued by the fact that she'd lived in Chile. Such experience can always be presented as valuable for increasing self-assurance, maturity, a knowledge of the world, communication skills and any other positive feature which comes to mind. Very few teachers have regretted their decision to travel the world, even if the specific job they did was not without its drawbacks and difficulties.

Bell Educational Trust

Bell is one of the largest British-owned providers of high-quality English language training services. Each year, 100,000 students from more than 120 countries choose to study with Bell through one of our worldwide teaching centres or e-channels.

Our mission is to change lives by providing education, training and cultural experiences for people worldwide. We can only do this because of the quality and expertise of our people.

Every single person in the Bell network plays a vital part in achieving our mission and we are committed to investing in and retaining our people, offering a full range of training and personal development opportunities alongside competitive remuneration and an attractive range of benefits.

Each year we recruit hundreds of new members of staff and we are very proud of our reputation for offering stimulating, rewarding and challenging places in which to work. We don't just believe in offering jobs - we offer careers. That's why we offer an unparalleled working environment, and one that challenges all our staff to be the very best that they can be.

Work alongside leading industry professionals, with opportunities at all levels around the globe. Joining Bell provides a world of career possibilities.

For our latest job opportunities in Saudi Arabia, Libya, the UK and other worldwide destinations and to find out more about working for Bell please visit: www.bell-worldwide.com/jobs

We also offer an excellent range of Teacher Development courses that cover all aspects of English language teaching. Courses include CELTA, Delta and residential professional teacher training.

PART 2
COUNTRY BY
COUNTRY GUIDE

Western Europe
Central And Eastern Europe
The Rest of Europe
Middle East
Africa
Asia
Latin America
Central America and the Caribbean
North America
Australasia

WESTERN EUROPE

AUSTRIA

The attraction to English in Austria is proved by the number of English bookshops with names such as the British Bookshop and Shakespeare & Co. and the popularity of English language newspapers such as *Austria Today* (www.austriatoday.at) and Austrian Times (www.austriantimes.at). The market for ELT in Austria is largely dominated by English for the business community, so teachers with any kind of experience of the business world, even if just temping in an office, have a sharp advantage over those with experience only of teaching general English.

As in Germany and Switzerland, most private language institutes depend on freelance part-time teachers drawn from the sizeable resident international community. An estimated 90% of EFL teachers in Austria are freelancers, which means that they do not have a contract with just one school and must pay tax as self-employed workers.

FINDING A JOB

The British Council in Vienna has a list of 17 English language institutes in Vienna. This list is annotated so that the kind of English tuition in which the company specialises is given, e.g. executive training, conversation classes, etc. It can be consulted online (www.britishcouncil.org/austria-english-courses-in-austria.htm).

The online *Yellow Pages* for Austria are very straightforward to use (www.gelbeseiten.at). They are fully usable in English and links to potential employers can be found under the heading 'Language Schools and Language Instruction'. Professional teachers may wish to contact and join the organisation Teachers of English in Austria (www.tea4teachers.org). Annual membership costs €33 or €22 for students and there are currently about 600 members.

Most *Volkshochschulen* offer English courses in their programmes of general adult education. The coordinating office for the provinces in Austria is situated in Vienna. Browse www.vhs.or.at/volkshochschulen for more information (there is an English summary) and www.adulteducation.at (English). The umbrella organisation is Verband Osterreichischer Volkshochschulen (Weintraubengasse 13, 1020 Vienna; 1 216 4226). See the list of employers for details about salary/working conditions for Vienna's adult education centres.

More than 200 English language teaching assistants from the UK and USA are placed in Austrian secondary schools from 1 October to 31 May by the British Council and the Fulbright Commission (Schmidgasse 14, 1080 Vienna; 1 31339). The British Council annually looks for about 120 assistants with a decent level of German to work 13 hours a week for €1,070 net per month (www.british council.org/languageassistants-austria.htm). The Fulbright Commission is responsible for recruiting American graduates with a working knowledge of German and interest in teaching for the same scheme. Detailed information and an application form (between mid-November and mid-January) can be downloaded from the Commission's website (www.fulbright.at).

New arrivals in Austria should visit a number of institutes and try to piece together a timetable. After working for three or four schools, it is better to cultivate just one or two since it is unrealistic to work for any more than this on a longer-term basis. A smart appearance and confident manner are always assets when looking for work teaching within the business community. Most Austrians will have an intermediate or higher level of English.

To give an idea of qualifications needed, MHC Business Language Training in Vienna asks for teachers who have some business background, ideally in a specialised area such as marketing, finance or law; they do not insist on a degree but welcome a teaching certificate such as the CELTA. By contrast English Connection in Salzburg requires a TEFL qualification plus at least three years' teaching experience, whereas experience and/or knowledge of business, law, medicine, tourism, etc. are seen as useful bonuses.

The rate at reputable institutes starts at €18–€20 per lesson (normally 45 minutes) and more for 60-minute lessons (€20–€30). This is none-too-generous when the high cost of living in Vienna is taken into account, although taking seminars can pay fairly well (between €300 and €400 per 7+ hour day). Life in the provinces is less expensive of course. At the interview stage, always find out whether quoted rates are gross or net, if travelling time is covered and when you will be paid. Some schools pay after the course has finished, which will leave you a pauper for an extended period.

TEACHING CHILDREN AND AT SUMMER CAMPS

The demand for teachers of children and young people is very strong in Austria as elsewhere in Europe. Summer camps provide scope for EFL teachers, as indicated in the entries for English Language Day Camps and English For Kids. Another major player is The Kids English Company (Kagraner Platz 8, 1220 Vienna; 1 263 8931; www.kidsco.at) which mounts language courses for children aged 3–10. Up to 30 native speaker teachers work at their language centre in Vienna plus teach lessons in kindergartens, private homes, etc. Recruitment takes place between May and September, and pay is generous, €28 per hour.

REGULATIONS

There is no problem with regard to regulations for British and Irish teachers; however, applications for work permits for non-EU citizens (*Beschäftigungsbewilligung*) are almost never granted. All schools claim that they will not hire a non-EU national unless they already have a work permit. According to American **Tom Clark**, who has taught English all over the world:

> *Austria is a hard nut to crack with all its red tape and its xenophobic attitude. I have been trying to find a way for seven years to get a job, preferably in Feldkirch, where my daughter lives, but it is a nightmare.*

A language institute there told him he needed to be married to an Austrian before he could be eligible for a work permit.

One complication is the reciprocal social security arrangements within the EU. Contributions into a health and pension scheme are reciprocal with the UK. Because schools have to register their staff for a social security card and also pay part of the contributions on their behalf, they are generally not willing to hire someone who is ineligible. A hefty percentage of earnings (typically 17%) will be deducted at source (or should be) of any teacher who earns more than €366 per month. The only people entitled not to have these deductions made are licensed translators (certified in Austria), who are permitted to take care of their contributions independently.

Austria (again like Germany) has many bureaucratic layers. New arrivals need to register with the police, organise a bank account (into which their wages will be paid directly) and get a tax number from the local tax office. Everyone also needs a *Meldezetel* or registration of residence.

GEOFF NUNNEY, knowing that his job at a language school in Slovakia would end with the academic year, was anxious to sort out a summer job for 2010 and had positive responses to his enquiries to summer employers in Austria, Italy and Spain, mostly sourced through this book. He accepted an invitation to Vienna, which is as accessible from where he was located in Nitra, as London is from his native Birmingham:

I walked away with the job on the day, which is a good feeling, and you couldn't wipe the smile off my face. I have got 6 weeks work with English for Kids, two in Vienna, and four in Linz. The programme is a mixture of English teaching, sports coaching and lots of things. It was quite a detailed application process: 3 lesson plans, 2 references, and then the director invited me to interview in Vienna. So I have more work than I did last summer, more time between camps and will be working in a beautiful country. Also, they pay travel expenses to Austria, and there are four days of training, before you start. It's not even the end of April, but I have my summer sorted. I can highly recommend them. The employer also responded positively to an admission of a chronic health problem I have, asked a couple of questions, not unreasonable, and checked if I have private health insurance, which I do (with Ace Travel Insurance).

LIST OF EMPLOYERS

BERLITZ AUSTRIA GmbH

Troststrasse 50, 1100 Vienna

Other branches in Vienna: Graben 13, 1010 Vienna

Mariahilferstrasse 27, 1060 Vienna; Schlosshoferstr.

13–15, 1210 Vienna

☏ +43 1 6043911

✉ birgit.seisenbacher@berlitz.at

🖥 www.berlitz.at

NUMBER OF TEACHERS: No fixed number, teachers work on a freelance basis.

PREFERENCE OF NATIONALITY: None but it is very hard for non-EU citizens to obtain work permits.

QUALIFICATIONS: Perfect command of English and a talent for teaching. Academic background is helpful but not vital. Any other background (business, engineering, IT, etc.) is welcome.

CONDITIONS OF EMPLOYMENT: Freelance contract with no fixed hours. Schools are open Monday to Friday, 8am–8pm and Saturday morning.

SALARY: Starting salary is €24 for a double unit (80 mins).

RECRUITMENT: Interviews are essential.

CONTACT: Mag. Birgit Seisenbacher, Director.

COLE ENGLISH CENTRE FOR KIDS

Weingartnerstrasse 108, 6020 Innsbruck, Tirol

☏ +43 512 571040

✉ rosie@cole.at

🖥 www.cole.at

NUMBER OF TEACHERS: 5.

PREFERENCE OF NATIONALITY: British.

QUALIFICATIONS: TEFL or PGCE with English or BA in English Language. Well spoken English.

CONDITIONS OF EMPLOYMENT: 2–4 year contract with 30 working hours per week.

FACILITIES/SUPPORT: Accommodation may be provided, depending on position. All positions come with full health insurance.

RECRUITMENT: Usually via adverts on TEFL websites. Interviews are essential and can be conducted by phone; 1 week probationary period.

CONTACT: Rosie Ladner-Cole, Proprietor.

DELPHIN SPRACHSERVICE

Getreidemarkt 17, 1060 Vienna

☏ 1 5855347

✉ ils@dolphin.at

🖥 www.dolphin.at

NUMBER OF TEACHERS: 17.

PREFERENCE OF NATIONALITY: British, Irish, American.

QUALIFICATIONS: Charisma and competence, experience and appearance, resourcefulness and reliability, diligence and dynamics.

CONDITIONS OF EMPLOYMENT: Stage 1, freelance contracts from 1 to 6 months, starting at 1 hour/week; stage 2, fixed contract (including healthcare and pension), open end, starting at 10 hours/week.

SALARY: Stage 1 €15–€35 per unit (55 mins); stage 2 €10–€25 per hour.

FACILITIES/SUPPORT: Centres provide preliminary accommodation for the first weeks and help teachers find a place on their own. Assistance with work permit only after a trial period.

RECRUITMENT: Interview essential. Face-to-face, over the phone, review of references.

CONTACT: Mag. Elke Enzlmüller, Recruitment Officer.

DIE WIENER VOLKSHOCHSCHULEN
Hollergasse 22, A – 1150 Vienna
info@vhs.at
www.vhs.at

16 Vienna Adult Education Centres (VHS, life-long learning). English courses according to CEFR levels, 60 different languages offered, European language portfolio for adults, Cambridge Exams in collaboration with British Council Vienna, TELC Certificates.

NUMBER OF TEACHERS: Varies according to demand. All teachers are freelance.

PREFERENCE OF NATIONALITY: None.

QUALIFICATIONS: EUROLTA (ICC, The European Language Network, Die Wiener Volkshochschulen), EUROLTA-EUROVOLT Diploma (ICC, The European Language Network, Die Wiener Volkshochschulen), CELTA, DELTA and/or university training, *or* varied extensive experience of language teaching in upper secondary/adult/university education (at least 2 years' work experience).

CONDITIONS OF EMPLOYMENT: Self-employed freelancers. Minimum commitment 15 weeks (one term). Teaching hours Monday–Saturday between 6am and 9pm.

SALARY: €18 per 50-minute lesson. Maximum: approx €540 per month.

FACILITIES/SUPPORT: Workshops and other in-service training courses available. Library and media facilities.

RECRUITMENT: Courses are planned 6 months in advance. European CV (google 'Europass' for information on the standard format), letter of intent and local interview essential.

ENGLISH CONNECTION
Am Rainberg 7, 5020 Salzburg
+43 (0)662 876210
office@english-connection.at
www.english-connection.at

NUMBER OF TEACHERS: 4–6 teachers of Business English.

PREFERENCE OF NATIONALITY: British, preferably resident in Austria and plan to remain medium term.

QUALIFICATIONS: TEFL qualification plus 3+ years' teaching experience. Experience and/or knowledge of business, the law, medicine, tourism, etc. very useful. Technical, chemical or engineering experience also advantageous.

CONDITIONS OF EMPLOYMENT: Freelance contract. Variable hours: 20–30 per week. Longer term fixed contract possible.

RECRUITMENT: Face-to-face interview preferred; sometimes possible in UK.

CONTACT: Jim Thomson, Course and Company Director.

ENGLISH FOR CHILDREN (EFC)/ENGLISH LANGUAGE DAY CAMP (ELDC)
Weichselweg 4, 1220 Vienna
1 958 1972 ext. 0
scott.matthews@englishforchildren.com
www.englishforchildren.com

NUMBER OF TEACHERS: EFC – varies according to need. ELDC – about 25.

PREFERENCE OF NATIONALITY: None, but must be a native English speaker.

QUALIFICATIONS: Minimum age 20. Experience of teaching children is required.

CONDITIONS OF EMPLOYMENT: EFC – freelance 10-month contract (September to June). ELDC – the summer camp runs during July for 4 weeks.

FACILITIES/SUPPORT: For the EFC programme teachers need to be living in Austria. Full training given, free of charge, before and during contract. All course materials provided. Housing not provided. ELDC – 4-week summer camp programme, lunch provided during camp days, 5 days a week, housing not provided, however relevant contacts to student housing, hostels etc. available.

RECRUITMENT: Direct applications by e-mail and telephone interviews.

CONTACT: Scott Matthews, Director.

ENGLISH FOR KIDS
Postgasse 11/19, 1010 Vienna
1 667 45 79
magik@e4kids.co.at
www.e4kids.at.

NUMBER OF TEACHERS AND CAMP COUNSELLORS:
6–8 for residential summer camp in Lachstatt near Linz in Upper Austria; 8–12 for day camps in Vienna.

PREFERENCE OF NATIONALITY: EU or others with work permit for Austria.

QUALIFICATIONS: CELTA or Trinity Certificate (minimum grade B) and some formal teaching preferred/required. Camp counsellors require no formal training/experience but must be outgoing, enjoy working with children and should like outdoor activities and sports.

CONDITIONS OF EMPLOYMENT: Duration – mid-July to end August. 2 weeks in Vienna and 3 weeks in Upper Austria. Pupil groups aged from kindergarten to age 10, and 10–15. Full-immersion courses with in-house methods following carefully planned syllabus and teachers' manual, supplemented with CD-ROMs etc.

SALARY: Varies depending on qualifications. Up to €1,650 per month gross, plus travel costs within Austria, full board and accommodation.

FACILITIES/SUPPORT: Good standard of accommodation and full board provided for teachers. Computer room, internet and video room available.

RECRUITMENT: www.e4kids.at/txt/jobs/apply/job_opportunity.html.

CONTACT: Irena Köstenbauer, Principal.

ENGLISH IS FUN CAMP
Döblinger Hauptstr. 38/3, 1190 Vienna
☎ 1 369 68 33
✆ claudia_millwisch@chello.at
🖥 www.englishisfun.at

PREFERENCE OF NATIONALITY: English native speakers (also Spanish, Italian and French native speakers). Must have permission to work in Austria.

QUALIFICATIONS: Experience of working with children needed.

CONDITIONS OF EMPLOYMENT: Hours according to demand. Freelance basis.

RECRUITMENT: Personal interviews held.

CONTACT: Claudia Millwisch, Director.

MHC BUSINESS LANGUAGE TRAINING GmbH
Wiedner Hauptstrasse 54/13A, 1040 Vienna
☎ +43 650 74 85 160
✆ office@mhc-training.com
🖥 www.mhc-training.com

NUMBER OF TEACHERS: 25.

PREFERENCE OF NATIONALITY: English, German and Eastern European language trainers and translators.

QUALIFICATIONS: MHC trainers have some business experience, ideally in a specialised area such as marketing, finance or law. A degree is not necessary, although a teaching certificate such as CELTA would be of value.

CONDITIONS OF EMPLOYMENT: Freelance, teaching 15–25 hours per week.

SALARY: €20–€30 per 60 minutes, depending on experience and development with MHC. Seminars between €300 and €400 per day (7–9 hours). Trainers are responsible for paying their own taxes (about 21%) and social security (variable).

FACILITIES/SUPPORT: Resource library, photocopying, trainer development. Assistance with finding accommodation. Trainers from non-EU countries require working papers.

RECRUITMENT: Interviews are essential and usually take place at premises. Possibility of telephone interviews if the applicant is based abroad.

CONTACT: Mark Heather, Managing Director.

MIND & MORE, MANAGEMENT AND EDUCATION SERVICES GmbH
Goldschmiedgasse 10, 3rd floor, 1010 Vienna
☎ 1 535 9695
✆ office@mindandmore.at
🖥 www.mindandmore.at

Management and Education Services is also the Representative Office of the British Open University and OU Business School in Austria, south Germany, Slovenia and Hungary.

NUMBER OF TEACHERS: About 70 language trainers in Vienna and more in many locations around the country and across the borders, plus management skills faculty trainers.

PREFERENCE OF NATIONALITY: None.

QUALIFICATIONS: Minimum university degree plus CELTA or TESOL and teaching experience; preferably also business experience.

CONDITIONS OF EMPLOYMENT: Freelance contracts. Hours vary.

SALARY: Language training – minimum rate is €22 per unit for 45-minute units/€28 for 60-minute units; more for specialised language training and seminars; market rates for management skills training.

FACILITIES/SUPPORT: Support given.

RECRUITMENT: Via internet, personal recommendations, partner institutions including British Council, BFI and related institutions. Face-to-face interview essential.

CONTACT: Tamara Weterings, Director of Studies for ELT (t.weterings@mindandmore.at).

SPIDI SPRACHENINSTITUT
Franz-Josefs-Kai 27/10, 1010 Vienna
+43 1 236 17 17 0
office@spidi.at
www.spidi.at

NUMBER OF TEACHERS: About 50 English teachers.

PREFERENCE OF NATIONALITY: EU citizens.

QUALIFICATIONS: Minimum CELTA or equivalent. Business English and ESP teaching experience preferred.

CONDITIONS OF EMPLOYMENT: Freelance. Flexible hours.

SALARY: €26–€28 per hour, depending on qualifications and experience.

FACILITIES/SUPPORT: No assistance with accommodation. Library with PCs for trainers. Monthly teacher development sessions.

RECRUITMENT: Local interview essential.

CONTACT: Jemma Jones, Director of Studies.

BENELUX

Belgium

As one of the capitals of the EU, there is a huge demand for all the principal European languages in Brussels. Yet, despite the enormous amount of language teaching in Belgium, there are also a large number of well-qualified expatriate spouses who take up teaching. This may meet some demand, but not all. To find contact details for language schools in Belgium, the online *Yellow Pages* are a useful tool. A search for 'Language Schools' in the Brussels Region on http://goldenpages.truvo.be will turn up more than 100 institutes.

Newcomer is a bi-annual publication from the publishers of the English language monthly magazine *The Bulletin*, which contains information and contact addresses of interest to the newly arrived teacher including a listing of major language schools; it can be pre-ordered for €5 (www.xpats.com/newcomer). The *Expats Directory* is an annual catalogue of useful addresses and phone numbers. Occasionally the classified ads include some requests for live-in helpers willing to teach English, or you can of course advertise yourself, though there will be plenty of competition from highly qualified teachers. The casual teacher will probably steer clear of schools that teach senior EU bureaucrats, but there are plenty of other schools. Telephone/Skype teaching has caught on in Belgium, especially among French learners of English; for example see Phone Languages (www.phonelanguages.com).

Several language teaching organisations are represented in more than one Belgian city, especially Berlitz, which employs about 225 freelance teachers in 14 branches. Linguarama Belgium also recruits freelance native speaker teachers with a TEFL teaching qualification and at least two years' experience of teaching non-native adults. CVs and letters of application can be e-mailed to personnel@linguarama.com. CLL (Centre de Langues), based in Louvain-la-Neuve, employs about 100 teachers to work on a freelance basis.

As throughout continental Europe, children attend summer camps which focus on language learning. Companies such as Kiddy & Junior Classes (part of Language Studies International) and Ski Ten International organise holiday English courses. Pro Linguis is another company that arranges week-long residential language courses in Thiaumont, a remote southern corner of Belgium near Luxembourg (+32 63 22 03 62; www.prolinguis.be), and which employs some native English speaker teachers. Courses are put on for all ages including children, so teachers may also be given pastoral duties patrolling dorms, etc.

FREELANCE TEACHING

It is quite feasible to put up notices in one of the large university towns (Brussels, Antwerp, Gent, Leuven, Liège, etc.) offering conversation practice. Almost all foreign teachers who begin to work for an institute do so on a freelance basis and will have to deal with their own tax and social security. Officially they should declare themselves *indépendants* (self-employed persons) and pay contributions that amount to up to one-third of their salary. In fact many English teachers take their gross salary without declaring it, and don't work long enough to risk being caught. Once a teacher has worked black (*en noir/in het zwart*), it is difficult to regularise his or her status, since they then have to declare all previous earnings. Therefore anyone who plans to spend more than a few months teaching in Belgium should consider this issue.

LIST OF EMPLOYERS

BERLITZ LANGUAGE CENTRES

Avenue Louise 306–310, 1050 Brussels

📞 2 626 95 93

✉ joke.vandaele@berlitz.be

NUMBER OF TEACHERS: About 225 (for Brussels, Waterloo, Nivelles, Namur, Charleroi, Liège, Antwerp, Bruges, Wevelgem, Mouscron-Tournai, Geel, Hasselt, Tienen, Mechelen).

PREFERENCE OF NATIONALITY: British or Irish.

QUALIFICATIONS: University degree.

CONDITIONS OF EMPLOYMENT: Freelance – Flexible hours (mornings, evenings plus Saturday morning).

SALARY: €15 per 40-minute teaching unit.

FACILITIES/SUPPORT: No assistance with accommodation. In-house training lasts 8 days.

RECRUITMENT: Via adverts and direct applications.

CONTACT: Joke Van Daele, Country Manager of Instruction.

CALL INTERNATIONAL

25 rue des Drapiers 25, 1050 Brussels

📞 2 644 95 95

✉ brussels@callinter.com

💻 www.callinter.com

Centres for Accelerated Language Learning in Brussels, Waterloo, Tournai and Lille.

NUMBER OF TEACHERS: 150.

PREFERENCE OF NATIONALITY: None.

QUALIFICATIONS: Degree necessary. Experience an advantage. Good communication skills needed.

CONDITIONS OF EMPLOYMENT: Freelance with a car. Flexible hours.

FACILITIES/SUPPORT: No assistance with accommodation.

RECRUITMENT: All year through.

CONTACT: Sylvie Laurent.

CLL CENTRE DE LANGUES

Place de l'Université 25, 1348 Louvain-la-Neuve

📞 10/47 06 28; 10/47 06 29

✉ jobs@cll.ucl.ac.be

💻 www.cll.be

NUMBER OF TEACHERS: 100.

PREFERENCE OF NATIONALITY: From English-speaking countries.

QUALIFICATIONS: Experience in teaching English as a foreign language and, if possible, with a degree in languages.

CONDITIONS OF EMPLOYMENT: Freelance, variable hours (daytime, evenings, Saturdays, etc.)

SALARY: €22.10–€27.50 per hour according to experience.

FACILITIES/SUPPORT: None.

RECRUITMENT: Interviews in Belgium essential, followed by an integration session.

CONTACT: Sabine Thirion, Recruiting Officer.

LANGUAGE STUDIES INTERNATIONAL SPRL

Rue du Taciturne 50, 1000 Brussels

Adult school: 📞 +32 2 217 23 73

✉ info@lsi-be.net

💻 www.lsi-be.net

Children's language school: +32 2 218 39 20/217 64 51

✉ info@kiddyclasses.net

💻 www.kiddyclasses.net

NUMBER OF TEACHERS: 30–60.

PREFERENCE OF NATIONALITY: None.

QUALIFICATIONS: For the adult school: qualified university level teachers with TEFL experience. For the children's school: qualified teachers or would-be teachers with experience in children's entertainment.

CONDITIONS OF EMPLOYMENT: Freelance, although 1–2 month contracts during the summer. Adult school hours: 9am–8pm; children's school: 9am–5pm.

SALARY: Varies.

FACILITIES/SUPPORT: None, although for the 2-month summer contract assistance is given finding accommodation.

RECRUITMENT: Via internet, newspaper, universities, company brochure. Interviews essential unless excellent references received. Interviews are carried out in Brussels.

CONTACT: Sylvaine Drablier, Director.

LC LANGUAGE CENTRE

Avenue de Broqueville, 113, 1200 Brussels

📞 2 771 71 31

✉ language.centre@skynet.be

💻 www.lclanguagecentre.com

NUMBER OF TEACHERS: 20 (for English).

PREFERENCE OF NATIONALITY: UK and USA.

QUALIFICATIONS: TEFL or TESL and experience.

CONDITIONS OF EMPLOYMENT: Freelance/flexible contracts and work hours.

SALARY: Flexible.

FACILITIES/SUPPORT: None.

RECRUITMENT: Direct application. Interview essential.

CONTACT: Annick Lombard, General Manager.

PRO LINGUIS

6717 Thiaumont

secretariat@prolinguis.be

www.prolinguis.be

NUMBER OF TEACHERS: 14 (freelancers) to work near Arlon close to the Luxembourg border.

PREFERENCE OF NATIONALITY: British.

QUALIFICATIONS: Kindergarten teacher or summer camp counsellor, primary school teacher, EFL training, BA in English or any other language, in business, law or social studies.

CONDITIONS OF EMPLOYMENT: Minimum 1-year contract, or 2-month contract in summer; 7 hours per day, 4–5 days per week.

SALARY: €90–€110 per day plus free board and lodging on campus.

RECRUITMENT: Personal contacts. Phone interviews.

CONTACT: Christiane Maillart (secretariat@prolinguis.be).

SKI TEN INTERNATIONAL

Chateau d'Emines, 45, 5080 Emines la Bruyere (Namur)

81 21 30 51

martine@ski-ten.be

www.skiten.com

NUMBER OF TEACHERS: 2 for English (plus 1 for tennis).

PREFERENCE OF NATIONALITY: None.

QUALIFICATIONS: Experience with children. Some knowledge of French useful.

CONDITIONS OF EMPLOYMENT: Student contract for July or August. 6 hours of work per day including teaching and 'animation', i.e. supervising camp activities.

SALARY: €1,000 per month.

FACILITIES/SUPPORT: Board and lodging provided at camp.

RECRUITMENT: University exchanges, word of mouth.

CONTACT: Martine Goffinet, Directrice.

Luxembourg

With only a handful of private language schools in the country, Luxembourg does not offer much scope for ELT teachers.

The national employment service (l'Administration de l'Emploi) at 10 rue Bender, L-1229 (2 478 53 00; info@adem.public.lu; www.etat.lu/ADEM) has a EURES adviser who may have information about language teaching openings.

Informal live-in tutoring jobs are possible. Luxembourg Accueil Information (10 Bisserwee, L-1238 Luxembourg-Grund; 241717; www.luxembourgaccueil.com) is a centre for new arrivals and temporary residents. It provides a range of services on its premises from October to May, including workshops and language courses, and might be able to advise on teaching and tutoring possibilities.

Inlingua has three centres in the country, in Esch-sur-Alzette and Athus, in addition to Luxembourg City (recrutement@inlingua-gr.com).

The Netherlands

Dutch people have a very high degree of competence in English after they finish their schooling. Educated Dutch people are so fluent in English that the Minister of Education once suggested that English might become the main language in Dutch universities, a suggestion which caused an understandable outcry. However, the schooling system has become increasingly international and university staff are being challenged to lecture and publish in English and to advance their English language skills.

Yvonne Dalhuijsen, project manager at UvA Talen (see list of employers), sees an increasing need for advanced levels of English within both companies and universities. She is always on the lookout for teachers who are native speakers of English.

What private language schools there are tend to provide specific training in Business English and to be looking for language trainers with extensive commercial or government experience as well as a teaching qualification and – particularly outside the capital – some fluency in Dutch. Business English, Legal English and Academic English (writing papers, abstracts, etc) are subjects in high demand. So many native English speaking citizens have settled in the Netherlands, attracted by its liberal institutions, that most companies depend on long-term freelancers.

It might also be possible to fix up some freelance lessons with university students from non-Dutch backgrounds, including Spanish, whose level of English is less advanced than their local counterparts.

The *Yellow Pages* are easy to search online (www.goudengids.nl) or for the capital Den Haag, you can look up *Taalonderwijs* (Language Training) in the online directory www.allebedrijvenindenhaag.nl. The site of VTN (Vereniging Taleninstituten Nederland) or the Dutch Association of Language Institutes links to a handful of English-teaching institutes. The British Language Training Centre in Amsterdam offers the CELTA course (see Training chapter) and may be able to give advice to qualified job-seekers and recommend other institutes to try for work. Linguarama Nederland has a sizeable operation in the business training field with centres in Amsterdam, the Hague and Soesterberg; enquiries may be sent to personnel@nl.linguarama.com. Only applicants with a full TEFL/TESOL or CELTA qualification will receive a response (www.linguarama.nl).

Outside the mainstream language institutes, it might be possible to arrange some telephone teaching. Try, for example, Dialogue Talen at Nieuwe Parklaan 44, 2597LD, The Hague (www.dialoguetalen.nl).

Another possibility for those not interested in a corporate atmosphere is the network of *Volksuniversiteit*, adult education centres. Branches that teach English can be found throughout the country, all listed at www.volksuniversiteit.nl.

LIST OF EMPLOYERS

BERLITZ LANGUAGE CENTRES
Weerdestein 205 A, 1083 GN Amsterdam
+31 20 622 13 75
info@berlitz.nl
www.berlitz.nl

NUMBER OF TEACHERS: 39.

PREFERENCE OF NATIONALITY: None.

QUALIFICATIONS: Minimum first degree.

CONDITIONS OF EMPLOYMENT: 1 year contract. Working hours are between 7.30am and 9.45pm.

SALARY: From €1,000–€2,500 per month depending on qualifications and hours worked.

RECRUITMENT: Via the website or on the spot. Interviews essential.

CONTACT: Eric Werbrouck, Manager.

BOGAERS TALENINSTITUUT B.V.
Ringbaan Zuid 42, 5022 PN, Tilburg
13 536 21 01
info@bogaerstalen.nl
www.bogaerstalen.nl

NUMBER OF TEACHERS: 5 foreign out of total of 50.

PREFERENCE OF NATIONALITY: British.

QUALIFICATIONS: Degree and TEFL certificate. Experience in teaching conversational and Business English preferred.

CONDITIONS OF EMPLOYMENT: From 1 week to 9 months.

SALARY: €22.50 per hour.

FACILITIES/SUPPORT: Will help with accommodation if needed.

RECRUITMENT: Speculative CVs and applications.

CONTACT: Marion Bernard, Training Coordinator.

PCI – PIMENTEL COMMUNICATIONS INTERNATIONAL

Bachlaan 43, 1817 GH Alkmaar

72 512 11 90/515 65 18

info@pcitalen.nl/info@pcilanguages.com

www.pcitalen.nl/www.pcilanguages.com

NUMBER OF TEACHERS: 50+.

PREFERENCE OF NATIONALITY: Mostly British, Irish or North American. Australians, New Zealanders and South Africans also welcome.

QUALIFICATIONS: Experience in business and technical English. Cross-cultural communication skills and familiarity with modern teaching methods needed.

CONDITIONS OF EMPLOYMENT: Freelancers working mostly in-company nationwide.

SALARY: starts at €27 per hour.

FACILITIES/SUPPORT: Most teachers are already living in the Netherlands.

RECRUITMENT: Advertisements, word-of-mouth and recommendations.

CONTACT: Ms Iona de Pimentel.

SUITCASE TALEN

De Paal 104 -106, 13 51 JJ Almere

36 536 74 82

info@suitcase.nl

www.suitcase.nl

NUMBER OF TEACHERS: 5 freelancers.

PREFERENCE OF NATIONALITY: British, Canadian, American or other English-speaking country.

QUALIFICATIONS: Native speakers. Pedagogical background and experience in the world of business is an advantage.

CONDITIONS OF EMPLOYMENT: Freelance. Standard length of contract normally 20 hours per month, daytime or evening.

SALARY: €30–€32.50 per hour, depending on experience.

FACILITIES/SUPPORT: No assistance with accommodation or work permits.

RECRUITMENT: Open applications. Interviews essential.

CONTACT: M E A Kwakernaak, Director.

UvA Talen

Roetersstraat 27, NL-1018 WB Amsterdam

20 525 46 37

jobs@uvatalen.nl

www.uvatalen.nl

Independent language institute, affiliated to the Universiteit van Amsterdam, and consisting of a translation agency and a training centre.

NUMBER OF TEACHERS: About 30 per year.

PREFERENCE OF NATIONALITY: None, provided native English speaker (with widely understood dialect).

QUALIFICATIONS: Experience in teaching adults and registered at the Dutch Chamber of Commerce as a freelancer. Working knowledge of Dutch and/or the level system European Framework Reference (A-B-C) is sometimes required, though not always.

CONDITIONS OF EMPLOYMENT: Freelance assignments or on a temporary contract for the duration of a course, from 2 to 20 weeks. Extensions possible.

SALARY: From €25 per hour, plus compensation for preparation work or corrections.

FACILITIES/SUPPORT: No assistance with accommodation or work permits. Project manager monitors contents of the courses and is happy to advise teachers on content and materials.

RECRUITMENT: Teachers submit CVs and cover letter; face-to-face interviews required on arrival.

CONTACT: Yvonne Dalhuijsen, Project Manager.

FRANCE

The French used to rival the English for their reluctance to learn other languages. A Frenchman abroad spoke French as stubbornly as Britons spoke English. But things have changed, especially in the business and technical community. French telephone directories contain pages of language training organisations and the law continues to put pressure on companies to provide ongoing training for staff. The Droit de Formation Continue stipulates that companies have to devote a minimum of 1.5% of their payroll to employee training. English and computing are the most popular objects of investment, and therefore many private language institutes cater purely to the business market. In fact a quick browse through the entries in the List of Employers at the end of this chapter will lead you to the conclusion that the majority of adult language training in France is business-oriented, with most of it taking place on-site and the rest taking place in business and vocational schools. In this setting the term *formateurs* or 'trainers' is often used instead of English teachers. Private training companies involved with *formation* often produce very glossy brochures which look more like the annual report of a multinational corporation than an invitation to take an evening course. Most offer one-to-one tuition.

Many of the thousands of non-profit Chambres de Commerce et d'Industrie (CCI) around France have their own Centres d'Etude des Langues. Pariglotte is the Centre de Langues in Paris (6 Av de la Porte de Champerret, 75017 Paris; www.pariglotte.fr), but there are many centres all over France (www.reseau-cel.cci.fr). In addition, a considerable number of town councils (*mairies*) offer simple English courses to locals for a reduced rate, or allow associations to offer courses using their premises, so you might be able to pick up a few hours of teaching this way.

Teaching young children is left mostly to French teachers of English, although foreign language assistants are typically placed in schools (see later). Teaching by Skype or some other on-line system is now a common supplement or even full-time teaching possibility in this growing market.

Much of the information used in the revision of this chapter in 2010 was provided by Sab Will, Director of TEFL Paris Ltd (www.teflparis.com) and resident of Paris for 15 years, for which the author is grateful.

PROSPECTS FOR TEACHERS

Advanced ELT qualifications seem to be less in demand in France than solid teaching experience, particularly in a business context. Few schools accept candidates on the basis of being a native speaker and candidates may be asked to provide an *attestation de durée d'études* to show the educational level they have reached. However, anyone who has a university degree in any subject and who can look at home in a business situation (and possesses a suit/smart clothes) has a chance of finding teaching work, particularly if they have a working knowledge of French.

All respectable language schools in France now want to see solid evidence of experience and competence, or at least a strong drive to work in the teaching field. A good CV showing past experience and a TEFL certificate from a reputable training organisation are almost guaranteed tickets at least to the interview stage.

Ironically, more 'serious' qualifications such as a BEd, PGCE or even the DELTA are not always a help. The fact is that language schools fight for contracts on price, and ordinary clients tend not to differentiate and believe language lessons are the same from whichever school. Therefore a teacher's experience and qualifications have little to do with schools winning training contracts. How much language schools have to pay teachers is a major issue. In other words, an enthusiastic new teacher clutching a shiny new TEFL Certificate may actually be more attractive than someone with a weight of experience and qualifications who expects to be paid accordingly. Salary scales are relatively fixed in France, and experience and advanced qualifications don't really give you much bargaining power. The situation is made worse by the rapidity with which language teachers move on, and language schools know that there are plenty of other good candidates hungry for work and experience, and more or less ready to work for the basic rate.

In some circles it is fashionable to learn American English which means that, despite the visa difficulties for non-EU nationals, it is possible for Americans to find work as well. Many institutes claim to have no preference as to the country of origin of their native-speaker teachers though most expect to hire foreigners already resident in France with appropriate working papers. Most French students are happy with a friendly, competent and enthusiastic teacher, whatever their nationality, who is able to adapt to their needs and supply them with materials and learning situations relevant to their situation.

FINDING A JOB

IN ADVANCE

France is such a popular and obvious destination for British and Irish people and also for North Americans that a job hunt from abroad can be disappointing. Major language teaching organisations receive speculative CVs every day and can't promise anything until they meet the applicant.

A comprehensive list of English language institutes in France is hard to come by. One source of reputable language schools is the French Training Federation (*Fédération de la Formation Profession-nelle* – FFP) (www.ffp.org). The *Pages Jaunes* (*Yellow Pages*; www.pagesjaunes.fr) are another pos-sibility, if you search under the headings 'Enseignement: Cours de Langues' or 'Ecoles de Langues'. One recent job-seeker suggests an alternative at least in Paris:

> *I got a list of schools from the British Council, as I found the Yellow Pages were basically useless. I marked on my map all the schools in each district (arrondissement) and each day visited as many schools as possible in the same district (this limits time spent on metros and also walking).*

The Centre Regional Information pour Jeunesse lists English language schools (www.crij.org), as does the Paris Anglophone website (www.paris-anglo.com), minus e-mail addresses. The Parisian Expat website has a list of companies that most often advertise for English language trainers, with links to their recruitment information (www.theparisienexpat.com/2010/05/03/english-teacher-paris-tefl).

The British Council in Paris (9 rue de Constantine, 75340 Paris; 1 49 55 73 00 www.british-council.fr) teaches English to adults, and to children and teenagers during the school holidays and may have vacancies for well-qualified teachers. Sab Will worked at the British Council for several years and says to get in you will have to convince them you are good with relevant experience and qualifications. The Council has taken over English teaching to adults from the British Institute, with which it shares the same building, and so is a major language teaching centre in Paris. It also has a useful online teaching resource centre (www.britishcouncil.org/fr/france-english-teaching-english-teaching-resources.htm) which offers a weekly collection of links to free materials from British Coun-cil websites.

The Centre International d'Etudes Pédagogiques (CIEP) in France offers thousands of assistant-ships in France for students from many different countries (1 45 07 60 00; www.ciep.fr). Under-graduates and graduates under the age of 30 (35 in the UK) can spend an academic year working as English language assistants in secondary and (increasingly) primary schools throughout France.

In return for giving conversation classes 12 hours a week, providing classroom support and teaching pupils about their country, assistants receive a gross allowance of approximately €950 a month (€770 net) for seven or nine months, beginning 1 October. Similar posts are also available in other francophone countries such as Belgium, Canada (Québec) and Switzerland.

Assistants must have a working knowledge of French so modern languages students are encouraged to apply. Applications are considered from students who have at least AS level, Higher Grade or equivalent in French. Some posts in primary schools require degree level French because any help offered by colleagues and all discussion of pupil progress, curriculum, lesson planning, etc. is likely to be in French. British applicants should contact the Language Assistants Team, British Council (10 Spring Gardens, London SW1A 2BN; 020 7389 4596; assistants@britishcouncil.org; www.britishcouncil.org/languageassistants). American students can participate in the scheme by applying through the Assistantship Program at the French Embassy in Washington; for further information contact assistant.washington-amba@diplomatie.gouv.fr or browse www.frenchculture.org/assistantshipprogram.

In some cases the description language 'assistant' is a misnomer in schools where there isn't much support from the rest of the staff. Whereas some might relish the responsibility others might find this quite isolating.

The Alliance Française (AF) is a venerable organisation, analogous to the British Council, with a large teaching operation in London and centres worldwide. Sab Will has heard favourable reports of people getting useful information or contacts from them. One of the recent TEFL Paris graduates got a job at a branch of the AF in New York.

Anyone who can converse in French might find it useful to make contact before leaving home. Most centres have a noticeboard where requests for tutors, au pairs, etc. are occasionally posted. In London, the Alliance Française of Grande Bretagne is located at 1 Dorset Square, London NW1 6PU (020 7723 6439; info@alliancefrancaise.org.uk) and in New York at 22 E. 60th St (NY 10022; 212 355 6100; languagecenter@fiaf.org; www.fiaf.org).

There is also demand for experienced English teachers from French universities, although you really need to be living in France to stand a chance of securing a job. **Michael Buxton**, who has been a native English teacher for fifteen years, taught at the University of Lyon:

EMILY SLOANE from America was posted as an assistant to a small town in Lorraine (where the quiche comes from), unknown to any English language guidebook that she could find:

I taught English to about 170 students in three different primary schools, two 45-minute sessions per class per week, for a total of 12 hours of work each week. In general, the teaching and lesson planning were thoroughly enjoyable, although I wasn't given much guidance and received no feedback throughout the year, so I'm sure the fact that I was already comfortable and experienced with teaching and working with children made a big difference in my enjoyment. The kids, although adoring and very enthusiastic, were a lot rowdier than I had expected, and I was obliged to spend a lot more time on behavior management than I'd anticipated. The kids were never mean, just excitable and chatty, especially so because my class offered a break from their usual blackboard-and-worksheet style routine. The fact that I was the only assistant in my town meant that my French improved noticeably, especially my slang and listening comprehension, although it made for some lonely weekends, because I was forced to get by in French all the time.

Today, students are much keener to communicate and the university gives them exams based around student life and the four elements speaking/listening/reading/writing. Students are also able to make use of the extremely up-to-date facilities.

The university has two/three systems of employment. Lyon 2 employs about 45 native English teachers by a system called 'vacataire', which means you need to have a principal employer. There is also another system called 'travailleurs indépendants' where the teachers can work at two/three/four universities, but are classed as self-employed and have to pay their own social security. The disadvantage of working at the university is that although they pay relatively well with good conditions of employment, they often pay late; you could be waiting for up to 6 months. Almost every day, the TESOL France jobs list sends out requests, some of them sounding desperate, for teachers. You can join for free at www.tesol-france.org/teachingjobs.php. Vacancies are notified in the university world and in the private sector, and keeping track of these is a good way to get a feel for what's available.

When applying to a training organisation, try to demonstrate your commercial flair with a polished presentation including a business-like CV (omitting your hobbies) preferably accompanied by a hand written letter in impeccable French.

Although English teachers can still get away with more relaxed dress codes and a certain 'originality' is tolerated, you will still give yourself the best chance of employment if you follow typical French conventions: dress very smartly for interviews, be positive and enthusiastic, ask questions as well as answer them, and don't sell yourself too cheaply if you have a qualification or experience which is relevant to what they are looking for. Watch out for language schools trying to make you believe that working evenings or Saturdays is absolutely normal. You may not be able to get paid more for agreeing to do this, but you might be able to negotiate other concessions, such as more time off during the week.

The technique of making a personal approach to schools in the months preceding the one in which you would like to teach is often successful. On the strength of her Cambridge Certificate from International House, **Fiona Paton** had been hoping to find teaching work in the south of France in the summer but quickly discovered that there are very few opportunities outside the academic year. On her way back to England, she disembarked from the train in the picturesque town of Vichy in the Auvergne just long enough to distribute a few self-promotional leaflets to three language schools. She was very surprised to receive a favourable reply from one of them once she was home, and so returned a few weeks later for a happy year of teaching.

Make it really easy for language schools to contact you. For about €115 you can get a rechargeable mobile phone so that potential employers can contact you no matter where you are. Feature the number prominently on all your CVs and motivational letter (often requested by employers and recruiters).Teaching English in exchange for room and board is not uncommon though is normally combined with looking after the family's children or doing some domestic chores in order to pay for studies. The strings attached to a free room should be made very clear from the outset, or the candidate (quite often a young woman) might be in for unpleasant surprise once installed if the family starts heaping on some decidedly non-linguistic tasks (ironing, washing, taking the kids to school). The British Institute in Paris has a noticeboard advertising very occasional teaching vacancies as well as live-in tutoring and au pair jobs.

While looking for something to do in her gap year, **Hannah Start** was put in touch with a French bank executive who had done an English language course in Hannah's home town and who wanted to keep up her English at home in Paris by having someone to provide live-in conversation lessons. So, in exchange for three hours of speaking English in the evening (usually over an excellent dinner), Hannah was given free accommodation in the 17th arrondissement.

ANDREW SYKES felt that he owed the success of his job-hunt to his misguided and unsuccessful accountancy training rather than to his TEFL certificate:

I wrote to more or less all the schools from your book in France and elsewhere that didn't stipulate 'experience required' and was fairly disheartened by the few, none-too-encouraging replies along the lines of 'if you're in town, give us a call.' Sitting in a very cheap hotel bedroom halfway down Italy in early November feeling sorry for myself and knowing that I was getting closer and closer to my over-draft limit and an office job back in the UK, I rang the schools that had replied and so picked up the phone and rang through to BEST in Tours. 'Drop in,' the voice said, 'and we will give you an interview'. So I jumped on the next train, met the director on Monday and was offered a job on the Tuesday morn-ing, initially on an hour-by-hour basis and then in December on a contract of 15 hours which was later increased to 20 hours a week.

OK, I was very lucky. I have since learned that the school receives several phone calls and letters per week; it's an employer's market. What got me the job was not my TEFL certificate nor my very good French. It was the fact that I was an ex-accountant. I had been one of the thousands enticed by the financial benefits of joining an accountancy firm after graduation. But I hated the job and failed my first professional exams. Ironically the experience gained during those two and a half years of hell was invaluable. Whereas in Italy they want teaching experience, in France they want business experience.

You will in the end be teaching people not objects, and any experience you can bring to the job (and especially the job interview) will help. However ashamed you may be of telling everyone in the pub back home that you were once a rat catcher, it may be invaluable if the school's main client is 'Rent-o-kil'.

TEACHING CHILDREN

The state *Education Nationale* system is highly regimented and difficult to get into without passing a very challenging test called the *CAPES*, and later on the *Aggrégation*. Native teachers might be able to find an opening in a specialised school such as a Montessori school, often run by expats. The British Council has a large and successful English teaching operation in Paris. Individual tutoring is most likely to take place on Wednesdays (when state schools are closed) and Saturdays.

If you are hoping to work with kids, for example with the British Council, you must have relevant experience, aptitude and (ideally) qualifications, as the criteria are stricter than for teaching adults. They take most new teachers on just in advance of the school year so will probably be looking to replace people around June or July ready for *la rentrée* (start of the academic year) in September. Another possibility is holiday courses, of which there are many, and for which extra teachers are needed in summer, winter and at Easter.

French kids can be rowdy, though if you have a small class, 'crowd control' shouldn't be too much of an issue. If you are having trouble managing a private class, it is difficult to complain to parents because they won't be too impressed to hear that their little cherubs are messing around and wast-ing their money.

ON THE SPOT

Prospective teachers should not automatically head for Paris but bear in mind that provincial cities have many language schools too. Due to the many French companies that have decided it is far more

SARA BREESE *described her job-hunt in Paris and the style of life teaching can pay for:*

Finding work in France is a rather arduous process; however with determination and zeal one can easily find work. I moved to Paris in September as a jeune fille au pair and doing side work teaching children English. The next year I decided to get my ESL teaching certificate at TEFL Paris which was one of the best decisions I ever made. Not only did I love the process of getting my certificate, but I also discovered a love for teaching. ESL is probably the number one industry for Anglophones and is your best investment in terms of success in the job search. In order to find a teaching job I looked in the FUSAC [mentioned below] and applied to every English teaching organisation in the magazine. After about two weeks, I received some calls asking for interviews. I interviewed with three different places, accepting a job where I still work. I am paid €20 per hour gross, 16 euros after taxes. I immediately signed a CDII which is the ideal type of contract for a Business English teacher in Paris. It translates to basically a long-term intermittent contract meaning that you will receive work when it is available but you will not stop being considered an employee.

I have not been able to save money because Paris is very expensive. I can make anywhere between €1,000 and €1,600 a month. Rent in Paris is very high and I have never heard of a teaching organisation providing housing for their teachers. When I first moved to Paris I lived in what they call a 'chambre de bonne' (maid's quarters). These are rented for about €450 per month, so as a teacher you can expect at least half your paycheque to go to rent.

cost effective to relocate in the provinces, many regional centres such as Orléans, Lyon, Marseilles, Toulouse, Lille and Rouen are crawling with medium and large international companies, all needing English-speaking staff. Not only is it hard to find work in Paris, but of course rents are very high in the capital.

If you do decide to give it a go in Paris, watch for adverts in the *métro* for English language courses, since these are usually the biggest schools and therefore have the greatest number of vacancies for teachers. Certain streets in the 8th arrondissement around the Gare St Lazare abound in language schools. With abundance also come cowboy outfits whose standards are not always what they should be. Again, schools which insist on a TEFL certificate and use a rigorous recruitment process are probably the safest bet. If you are desperate, you might want to go for less reputable or well-known schools but be ready to be disappointed.

FREELANCE TEACHING

Well-off parents of French school children often pay for private lessons for their kids. Business people with a pressing need for English, which they are reluctant to reveal to their employer, and worried exam students are other big markets for freelance English tutors. Private lessons are a very good supplement to an official contract and It is worth spending a bit of time putting notices up and spreading the word that you are available for this sort of work. Sab Will has charged €30 an hour for a minimum of two hours at a time and people seem to accept this if you can convince them you are well-qualified, experienced and pleasant to be with. By charging closer to €30 than €20 an hour you will separate yourself from those with no qualifications or experience, but you will have to deliver the goods.

Recently a new category of legal worker has been introduced, the 'Auto-entrepreneur', which is open to anyone officially based in France (i.e. with French bank account, working papers and French social security number). Individuals can set up as a one-man or one-woman company and sell their services. This is attractive to teachers because it can be accomplished quickly, including online, and also to employers because they do not have to pay social security contributions. The downside for teachers is that they become responsible for making contributions for their own pension, health insurance, taxes and so on, and of course no paid holidays or travel pass (information in English at www.anglais.urssaf.fr). But the independence is appealing and allows you to work for more than one employer much more easily.

Self-employed workers (*travailleurs indépendants*) are obliged to register at the social security office (www.urssaf.fr/general/les_urssaf/votre_urssaf/fiche.phtml). The hourly fees (*honoraires*) paid to freelance teachers should be significantly higher than to contract workers (*salariés*) since they are free of deductions. In addition to the British Institute noticeboard mentioned above, there are many other *panneaux* that might prove useful to someone looking for private tutoring. This is especially appealing to Americans who do this without worrying too much about visas.

As part of a well-organised teaching job hunt in Marseille, American **Bradwell Jackson** tried to arrange to teach some private lessons:

> *Besides searching for jobs in schools, I also tried my hand at the tutoring market. I put up petites annonces in the local boulangeries and bars, and I also put an ad in a free local paper called 13 (treize), also called Top Annonce (www.topannonces.fr). The cost of placing the ad was not free, but it wasn't expensive (maybe €10). This did turn out to be fruitful, as I did get responses. My big disadvantage was that I didn't have a cell phone, and I was told that the French are not inclined to respond to someone only by e-mail. I decided to counteract this by putting in a very low asking price, only €10 per hour. With that price, I got several responses, even with only an e-mail address advertised. The problem was that there was a time lag of two weeks between my placing the order and its appearance, by which time I had booked a plane ticket back to Mexico. I also advertised on a free website service called Kelprof (www.kelprof.com). It was indeed free, but to contact referrals you have to use a password and 08 numbers which, I learned the hard way, are very expensive.*

There are expatriate grapevines all over Paris, very helpful for finding teaching work and accommodation. The noticeboard in the foyer of the Centre d'Information et de Documentation Jeunesse (CIDJ) at 101 Quai Branly; +33 1 44 49 12 00; www.cidj.com (métro Bir-Hakeim) is good for occasional student-type jobs, but sometimes there are adverts for a *soutien scolaire en Anglais* (English tutor). It is worth arriving early to check for new notices (the hours are Monday, Tuesday and Friday 10am–6pm, Thursday 1pm–6pm and Saturday 9.30am–1pm).

The other mecca for job- and flat-hunters is the American Church at 65 Quai d'Orsay (métro Invalides), which has very active noticeboards upstairs, downstairs and outside. There is a charge for posting a notice and they are kept up to date. In the basement, the free corkboard is much more chaotic; it can take about half an hour to rummage through all the notices.

The American Cathedral in Paris (23 Avenue George V; www.americancathedral.org) near the métro stations Alma Marceau and George V, also has a noticeboard featuring employment opportunities and housing listings. The two British churches may be of assistance: St. Georges at 7 rue Auguste Vacquerie in the 16th arrondissement and St. Michael's (www.saintmichaelsparis.com) at 5 rue d'Aguesseau in the 8th (métro Madeleine). English language bookshops like the eccentric Shakespeare & Company at 37 rue de la Bâcherie opposite Notre-Dame, as well as cafés, restaurants, and bars popular with the English-speaking community (e.g. Indiana Café, the Frog pubs, Chicago Pizza Pie Factory) all distribute the free bilingual newsletter *France-USA Contacts* or *FUSAC* (www.fusac.org), which comes out the first Tuesday of the month. It comprises mainly classified adverts which are best followed up on the day the paper appears. An advert under the heading 'Work

Wanted in France' starts at €36. Sab Will recalls placing his own small ad in *FUSAC* when he first arrived in Paris and getting responses from prospective students. But it is more effective at providing ways to get into the English-speaking expat community.

It may be worth including a reminder here that anyone who advertises their services should exercise a degree of caution when arranging to meet prospective clients.

Outside the bigger cities, your chance of picking up freelance work is greatly improved. Working as a language assistant in a small town in Lorraine, **Emily Sloane** had no problem finding freelance work:

> *Through word-of-mouth and no active self-promotion, numerous townspeople contacted me about private English tutoring. By the middle of the school year I had 5 private students, whom I taught once a week each for €10, with sometimes a meal on top of that. It was nice to be able to work through more complicated material with older students and really nice to have an inside look into various French households. Plus, the tutoring sessions kept me busy. I also earned some extra cash by doing freelance writing work for the mother of one of my students, which helped to supplement my fairly meager salary and allowed me to take long and stress-free vacations during the numerous school breaks.*

REGULATIONS

EU NATIONALS

Since 2003, EU citizens have been free of the obligation to obtain residence permits to live and work in other EU countries so the *carte de séjour* is now obsolete for most. Long-stayers may choose to apply for one since it can be a useful piece of ID, but they will have to be prepared to provide a battery of translated documents.

Once you take up paid employment in France, your employer must complete all the necessary formalities for registering you with social security (*sécu*) and you will be issued with a registration card and then pay a percentage of your wages as contributions. French admin and red tape is a pain in the neck, but once you've got it over and done with you are into quite a nice system of benefits and help on anything from unemployment and housing aid to child benefit and income supplements if you don't earn much one year.

NON-EU NATIONALS

In France, it is much more difficult for Americans, Canadians, Australians and all other non-EU nationalities to get a work permit than it is for EU teachers. However, people with initiative are able to get at least some legal work, at least for a limited period. The easiest way (apart from marrying a French national) is to enrol in a French course of some sort and acquire a student visa which allows the holder to engage in up to 20 hours of paid work a week, which is a typical teaching contract anyway.

The certificate course offered by TEFL Paris (see Training directory) attracts a considerable number of Americans, some of whom go on to find teaching work in France. One of them describes the outcome of a well-organised job-hunt:

> *I recently went to Paris on the big TEFL job hunt, and thought I might share my advice on HOW TO GET A JOB. They say it's 'almost impossible' for Americans to get a work visa or a good job in France, and I'd like to prove that theory wrong. Come prepared. Get a TEFL certificate. Bring your birth certificate and CV in both French and English, handwritten cover letters in both languages, passport photos and*

college transcripts. On the third day of my search, I got an interview. A few days later, I showed up and got the job. Overall I'd say it was not NEARLY as bad as I was warned it would be. Of course, I had to go back to the US for three months to get my work visa, but there's no other way to do it, besides working illegally (something I wasn't willing to do).

Another American aged 22 took the student route, but doesn't mention what fees were payable for enrolling in a university. This advice is of use mainly to Americans who genuinely want to study for an MA:

Initially I decided to pursue a Master's degree in a French university. Luckily, I had a professor who had studied at Paris III, so I e-mailed him and asked how I could apply, but if you contact the head of the department at any Parisian university and send a proposal (CV plus motivation letter), you can ask for an application. I started this process around March/April of last year for the fall semester. Getting accepted into a French university should not be too hard if you have a bachelor's degree. It helps to speak French, but if you don't, there may be some universities with French classes or you can consider an Anglophone university such as the American University in Paris. If and when you are accepted, you will receive a letter of enrolment with which you can apply for a visa in the States. Since you can only get a student visa before going to France, this letter is very important. I received this in about June/ July. A new law requires you to go through CampusFrance (www.campusfrance.org/en/index.htm) for which you will probably need a translation of your diploma, etc. Applying for a student visa requires a lot of patience and setting up an appointment at the consulate weeks in advance. The important thing is never to get discouraged, have a lot of patience and remember – when there's a will, there's a way.

More questions on long stay student visas will be answered on the French consulate website, for example at www.consulfrance-losangeles.org. One possibility open to some Americans with Irish or Greek ancestry is to obtain an EU passport. An easier route is to teach on a voluntary or occasional basis; or you can always work on the 'black market,' which is not really easy or advisable, but is something that the French, as well as foreigners, continue to do all the same.

CONDITIONS OF WORK

Teaching 'beezneezmen' is not everyone's cup of tea, but it can be less strenuous than other kinds of teaching. Provided you do not feel intimidated by your pupils' polished manners and impeccable dress, and can keep them entertained, you will probably be a success. As mentioned above, one-to-one teaching is increasingly common – with some schools in Paris it constitutes 70% of their business – for which ELT training (including the CELTA or Trinity Certificate) does not prepare you. However, if you develop a rapport with your client, this kind of teaching can be most enjoyable as **Sara Breese** describes:

I have enjoyed teaching as most of my students are adults who have chosen to take English classes, either for pleasure or to advance their career. The majority of them are nice and very motivated, thus making my job a pleasure. The teaching is mostly one-on-one and you are allowed to teach in whichever style you please. I appreciate this freedom to be creative with my students. However, this freedom is becoming more and more rare as schools are imposing their personalised TEFL methods. I have friends who work for other companies and it makes them feel like robots repeating the same lesson over and over again. The only problems I have encountered in my time as a teacher have been in the planning. I am travelling constantly all over Paris which means your day is never dull, but also can make it rather stressful. As a mobile teacher I have to carry all of my teaching materials with me. I am often seen running through the metro with a backpack full of books, CDs and a stereo.

HAMBURG SCHOOL OF ENGLISH

Teaching is learning

Keep learning

Be a teacher

- Learn to Teach English to Speakers of Other Languages

- Gain an internationally recognised qualification issued by Cambridge ESOL

- Experience Hamburg or Berlin - two of the most attractive cities in Europe

- Take your CELTA with us

HAMBURG SCHOOL OF ENGLISH
Teacher Training Centre
Isekai 19
20249 HAMBURG
GERMANY

Tel: +49 (0)40 4326 1686
Fax: +49 (0)40 4326 1687

Email: info@hamburg.school-of-english.de
Website: http://hamburg.school-of-english.de

BERLIN SCHOOL OF ENGLISH
Teacher Training Centre
Dorotheenstr. 90
10117 BERLIN
GERMANY

Tel: +49 (0)30 229 0455
Fax: +49 (0)30 229 0471

Email: info@berlin.school-of-english.de
Website: http://berlin.school-of-english.de

BERLIN SCHOOL OF ENGLISH

As mentioned earlier, language schools which offer this facility to clients, especially those in small towns rather than big cities, may well expect you to drive, perhaps even own, a car so that you can give lessons in offices and other workplaces. Most schools pay between €18 and €25 (gross) per lesson.

Salaried teachers should be covered by a nationally agreed and widely enforced Convention Collective which makes stable contracts, sick pay, holiday pay, etc. compulsory as well as guaranteeing a monthly salary. Until recently, there were two types of typical teaching contract with French language schools. The first was a CDD (*contrat à durée déterminée*), a fixed-length contract, and a CDI (*contrat à durée indéterminée*), a permanent contract. However, because employers were obliged to pay teachers for a minimum number of hours (typically 20), during the recent downturn clients were in short supply and many teachers were being paid for 20 hours although only working for five, which meant that some schools went bust. To tackle this problem a new kind of contract has emerged and is becoming the norm: a CDII (*contrat à durée indéterminée intermittent*). This guarantees a low minimum such as 10 hours and pays an hourly rate for hours worked above that. A good language school should be able to allocate 20–25 hours a week to those who want them, but they are protected against paying for hours not taught when times are tough.

Another legislated benefit when working for a French company is that 1%–1.5% of your salary is paid into a fund for your future training. You are entitled to use this after you have worked for the company for a year or two, as Sab Will did:

> *My TEFL Diploma was paid for this way. But once I got it my employer didn't give me an extra centime more for my efforts. The three of us who had done the diploma stayed the obligatory year after the qualification and then left. So the language school lost its three most qualified teachers. Language schools that pay significantly more for experience or advanced qualifications are rare beasts.*

The annual holiday allowance for full-time teachers is five weeks plus an extra five days off.

Telephone and internet teaching are popular for their convenience and anonymity, and a growing number of companies such as Phonalangue and Telelangue specialise in this. For many people, making mistakes over the phone is less embarrassing than face to face, though the lack of personal contact is felt by some to be detrimental to the learning experience. Many have been surprised by the good results. It is not necessary to be able to speak French and possibly even an advantage to be monolingual, so you won't be tempted to break into French in frustration. The standard rate of pay for telephone teaching is about €10 for half an hour plus telephone expenses.

An unusual feature in France is that some schools calculate the salary according to a certain number of teaching hours per 9 or 12 months, and will pay overtime for hours worked in excess of this. Obviously the total can't be calculated until the end of the contract, which is a drawback for anyone considering leaving early.

Partly because of France's proximity to a seemingly inexhaustible supply of willing English teachers, working conditions in France are seldom brilliant. You can survive in France, and even Paris, on a typical 20-hour-a-week contract, but to live more than a basic existence you will need to supplement this with extra hours from somewhere else.

Although **Andrew Boyle** enjoyed his year teaching English in Lyon and the chance to become integrated into an otherwise impenetrable community, he concluded that even respectable schools treated teachers as their most expendable commodity. By contrast, **Fiona Paton** was well looked after and had no trouble finding a comfortable and affordable flat in Vichy (which is often easy in popular holiday resorts outside the summer season). Her impression was that flat-sharing is not as commonplace in France as in other countries.

EMILY SLOANE discovered that although the French do not often come across as the most approachable of people, having a slightly firmer sense of privacy than is common in some countries, they can be great company:

I joined the French Alpine Club, which had a thriving and spirited branch in my village. In addition to weekly indoor rock climbing sessions, I accompanied club members on various weekend hikes and climbing trips in the Jura and Vosges Mountains in France and Switzerland and even attended a 10-day climbing clinic in northern Provence. Learning French climbing vocabulary while suspended 100 feet above the ground, when misunderstandings could have pretty serious consequences, was an experience I won't soon forget. The club members were fantastic people who generously shared the tight space of their homemade 'camping cars' and handcrafted liqueurs. I even convinced them to dress as Americans and speak English one night at the climbing wall. In return for their effort, I provided American snacks and music and a cheat sheet of useful American slang and insults that they enthusiastically tried out on each other. Through the club I even found my very own French lover, which proved to be the most efficient way to improve my language skills.

LIST OF EMPLOYERS

ANGLESEY LANGUAGE SERVICES (ALS)
1 bis, 3 Avenue du Maréchal Foch, 78400 Chatou
- 1 34 80 65 15
- als@alschatou.com

NUMBER OF TEACHERS: 50.
PREFERENCE OF NATIONALITY: Native speakers.
QUALIFICATIONS: CELTA plus 2 years of experience preferred but possibilities for trainees.
CONDITIONS OF EMPLOYMENT: One year open contract. 15–25 hours per week. Pupils are adults and many are taught in their workplaces. Recent expansion, so group lessons at all levels offered in evenings and during the day. Some Saturday work available.
SALARY: €21.50 per hour plus 12% on top for holiday pay.
FACILITIES/SUPPORT: Some help with accommodation possible. No initial training provided but ongoing professional development provided for teachers.
RECRUITMENT: Initial contact by e-mail then one-to-one interviews held in school.
CONTACT: Mike Webster.

APPLILANGUE
16 E rue du Cap Vert, 21800 Quetigny
- 3 80 52 98 98
- contact@appli-langue.com
- www.appli-langue.com

NUMBER OF TEACHERS: 12+.
PREFERENCE OF NATIONALITY: None.
QUALIFICATIONS: TEFL diploma and/or business experience.
CONDITIONS OF EMPLOYMENT: Open-ended contracts. Hours of teaching between 8.30am and 7.30pm.
SALARY: €1,449 per month starting, less about 20% for contributions.
FACILITIES/SUPPORT: School has contact who rents rooms while teachers are looking for an apartment. Help given with work permit applications including recommending a registered translator.
RECRUITMENT: Spontaneous CVs, word of mouth from former teachers.
CONTACT: Karen Longley.

CITYLANGUES

Le Triangle de l'Arche – Bât. C, 11, cours du Triangle, La Défense 12, 92937 Paris L a Défense Cedex and 8 rue Louis Blériot, 92500 Rueil Malmaison

- 1 55 91 96 70 (Cedex)/1 47 49 79 46 (Malmaison)
- sw@citylangues.com
- www.citylangues.com

NUMBER OF TEACHERS: 25.

PREFERENCE OF NATIONALITY: None, but employ only teachers resident in Paris with French working papers.

QUALIFICATIONS: Degree and TEFL certificate.

CONDITIONS OF EMPLOYMENT: Teaching represents 72% of total paid hours as per French law.

SALARY: According to profile, graded accorded to experience.

FACILITIES/SUPPORT: No assistance with accommodation. Training available in how the French system works, emphasis on team work in school.

RECRUITMENT: Local interviews essential.

CONTACT: Stefan Wheaton, president of the Language Commission of the French Training Federation.

ENGLISH POINT

14E rue Pierre de Coubertin, Parc de Mirande, Dijon, 21000

- 380631953
- t.holland@englishpoint.fr
- www.englishpoint.fr

NUMBER OF TEACHERS: 7

PREFERENCE OF NATIONALITY: British, New Zealander, American, Canadian.

QUALIFICATIONS: Preferably a CELTA or equivalent and/or significant teaching experience plus business work experience. The majority of courses are business-based so knowledge of how a business works is essential. Also, being an objectives-based school you should be able to think from the client's perspective and adapt your teaching accordingly.

CONDITIONS OF EMPLOYMENT: Contracts are from 3 months – permanent. Teaching hours 8am–9pm, Monday–Friday (possible Saturday mornings).

SALARY: €20–24 per hour depending on age/experience/flexibility etc.

FACILITIES/SUPPORT: School can help find accommodation for teachers, from organising viewings to full accommodation management.

RECRUITMENT: Through websites, training schools, word of mouth, etc. Telephone interviews essential followed by face-to-face meeting.

CONTACT: Tony Holland, Director.

EXECUTIVE LANGUAGE SERVICES

50 rue Sainte Lazare, 75009 Paris

- 1 44 54 58 88
- info@els-france.com
- www.els-france.com.

NUMBER OF TEACHERS: Trainers for one-to-one and group tuition.

PREFERENCE OF NATIONALITY: None, but must be a native English speaker.

QUALIFICATIONS: TEFL certificate and good teaching experience of adults and professionals. A background in law, finance or business would be a plus.

CONDITIONS OF EMPLOYMENT: 1 year minimum. Full-time and part-time positions available. Team teaching in school and on-site in company premises.

FACILITIES/SUPPORT: 2 fully equipped resource centres for staff. No help with accommodation.

RECRUITMENT: Interview after CV and letter of motivation (can be interviewed by telephone). Observation of a class and demo lesson for the same class the following day.

CONTACT: N Fairbrother (nfairbrother@els-france.com).

FONTAINEBLEAU LANGUES & COMMUNICATION

47 Boulevard Marechal Foch, 77300 Fontainebleau

- 1 64 22 48 96
- contact@flc-int.com or dianne.riboh@flc-int.com
- www.flc-int.com

NUMBER OF TEACHERS: 12 English teachers, 35 in total.

PREFERENCE OF NATIONALITY: British/Irish. Australians, Canadians and Americans or other native English speakers with EU nationality or French working papers.

QUALIFICATIONS: TEFL training (e.g. CELTA). Must be dynamic, creative, versatile and able to work in a team. Previous business experience a plus.

CONDITIONS OF EMPLOYMENT: 1 year minimum. Majority of teaching takes place in company premises so owning a car is necessary (transport costs reimbursed at €0.45 approx. per km). Variety of teaching situations including groups, one-to-one lessons and Business English. Hours are grouped as much as possible between 9am and 7pm, Monday to Friday.

SALARY: Starting at €19 per hour which includes 12% holiday pay. Social security deductions are about 22%.
FACILITIES/SUPPORT: Training workshops held regularly. Large teachers' library.
RECRUITMENT: Interview essential – usually by phone.
CONTACT: Dianne Riboh, Director.

ICB EUROPE
45 rue d'Aboukir, 75002 Paris
1 44 55 38 31
naomisackville@icbeurope.com
www.icbeurope.com

NUMBER OF TEACHERS: 50.
PREFERENCE OF NATIONALITY: None but native English speaker.
QUALIFICATIONS: Prefer candidates who are TEFL/TESOL/ CELTA qualified with a couple of years of business experience, ideally within the financial/insurance sectors.
CONDITIONS OF EMPLOYMENT: Open-ended contracts. Trainers who can stay for at least 1 year are preferred. To teach during normal office hours Monday to Friday.
SALARY: Trainers who are available at all times can be guaranteed 800 teaching hours a year with an average remuneration of about €1,600 per month plus a monthly bonus programme based on student satisfaction and lesson observations. 21% deductions for tax and social security.
FACILITIES/SUPPORT: No assistance given with visas or accommodation.
RECRUITMENT: Group interview involves candidates introducing themselves, a grammar test and some group discussion about different teaching techniques. If successful at this stage the candidate then goes on to have a one-to-one interview with the owner of ICB Europe, Eric Wrobley.
CONTACT: Naomi Sackville, Recruitment Manager/ Coordinatrice Pédagogique.

ILC FRANCE – IH PARIS (INTERNATIONAL LANGUAGE CENTRE)
13 Passage Dauphine, 75006 Paris
1 44 41 80 20
info@ilcfrance.com
www.ilcfrance.com

NUMBER OF TEACHERS: 34.
QUALIFICATIONS: CELTA or approved equivalent. Experience of business world essential.

CONDITIONS OF EMPLOYMENT: Teaching hours between 8.30am and 7pm. Contracts according to French labour laws. 80% of teaching is in-company.
SALARY: Variable according to contract.
FACILITIES/SUPPORT: Assistance with finding accommodation, teacher development and training. ILC offers the CELTA course (see Training chapter).
RECRUITMENT: Spontaneous CVs and local adverts, although priority given to IH network. Interviews in Paris essential.
CONTACT: Marlene Regaya, Director.

IMPAQT
Head Office: Téléport IV, Futuropolis IV, B.P. 10186, 86962 Futurscope Cedex
5 49 49 63 80
siege@impaqt.net
www.impaQt.net

NUMBER OF TEACHERS: 30 for operations in Poitiers, Paris, Angouleme, Tours, Toulouse and Lyon.
PREFERENCE OF NATIONALITY: None.
QUALIFICATIONS: Degree, TEFL qualification and some additional experience other than in education. Minimum age 25–35, open-minded and curious with excellent communication skills and a working knowledge of French.
CONDITIONS OF EMPLOYMENT: Teaching hours are during normal office hours.
SALARY: €1,750 per month before tax.
RECRUITMENT: Usually through newspaper adverts.
CONTACT: Jane Le Goff, Director of Relations (jane@ impaqt.net).

INLINGUA PARIS
109 rue de l'Université, 75007 Paris
1 45 51 46 60
invalides@inlingua-paris.com
www.inlingua-paris.com/versionAnglaise/ emploisUk.php

NUMBER OF TEACHERS: Many teachers required for eight branches in Paris (others at Bastille, La Défense, Levallois, Roissy, Versailles, etc.).
PREFERENCE OF NATIONALITY: None.
QUALIFICATIONS: TEFL plus minimum 2 years' experience preferably with professional adults. Preferred minimum age 25. Candidates must be creative, independent, flexible, of excellent appearance and with a good cultural background.

CONDITIONS OF EMPLOYMENT: Minimum 12 months; open-ended contracts. Flexible hours, with guaranteed minimum, mostly 20–30 hours per week.

FACILITIES/SUPPORT: Assistance with accommodation, work permits and training possible.

RECRUITMENT: Interviews essential in UK or France.

LINGUARAMA
Tour Eve, 1 Place du Sud, La Défense 9, 92806 Puteaux Cedex
- 1 47 73 00 95
- paris@linguarama.com
- www.linguarama.com.

NUMBER OF TEACHERS: 30.

PREFERENCE OF NATIONALITY: None.

QUALIFICATIONS: 4-week certificate course plus 1 year's teaching experience. Driving licence useful.

CONDITIONS OF EMPLOYMENT: Full-time teachers work 25 hours per week September to June. Part-time teachers work flexible hours. Teaching is Business English, taught in-company and at school.

SALARY: Approx. €1,400 per month.

FACILITIES/SUPPORT: Advice on finding accommodation. Regular training available.

RECRUITMENT: Via Linguarama in England and also locally.

SYNDICAT MIXTE MONTAIGU-ROCHESERVIERE
35 Avenue Villebois, Mareuil, 85607 Montaigu
- 2 51 46 45 45
- smmr.anglais@cc-montaigu.fr
- www.gapyear-france.com

NUMBER OF TEACHERS: 5.

PREFERENCE OF NATIONALITY: British.

QUALIFICATIONS: Experience of and interest in teaching and a love of France.

CONDITIONS OF EMPLOYMENT: Standard contract length 9 months, to teach 20 hours per week.

SALARY: €177 per month.

FACILITIES/SUPPORT: Accommodation provided with local host families/resident project coordinator.

RECRUITMENT: UK interview essential.

CONTACT: Julie Legrée, Project Coordinator.

TEFL JOBS IN FRANCE
147 Rue Etienne Pédron, 10000 Troyes
- contact@tefljobsinfrance.com
- www.tefljobsinfrance.com

PREFERENCE OF NATIONALITY: None, but applicants must hold a European passport.

QUALIFICATIONS: Minimum experience of 1 year.

CONDITIONS OF EMPLOYMENT: Minimum contract 1 year. To work 25 hours per week, with some evening work.

SALARY: Varies according to qualifications and experience. Starting salary is approx. €1,400 per month gross.

RECRUITMENT: Interview required, can be done by phone.

CONTACT: Roy Sprenger, Director.

TELAB LANGUAGE COURSES BY TELEPHONE
Head Office, En Verdan, 71520 Saint Point
- 3 85 50 58 58
- s.evans@telab.com
- www.telab.com

NUMBER OF TEACHERS: 80.

PREFERENCE OF NATIONALITY: None but must be native English speaker, resident in France and with necessary working papers.

QUALIFICATIONS: Language teaching qualifications (TEFL or equivalent), at least 2 years' experience in teaching languages to company employees, work experience in or knowledge of a specific field (e.g. marketing, finance, medical, technical, etc.), excellent communication abilities, independent, organised and rigorous at work. Must have a computer and know how to use the internet.

CONDITIONS OF EMPLOYMENT: Teachers work from home, flexible hours between 7am and 9pm.

FACILITIES/SUPPORT: Assistance given with social security registration (about 20% of gross salary is taken at source as contributions). No help with work permits or accommodation.

RECRUITMENT: Referrals, internet, press.

CONTACT: Stephanie Evans, Manager.

TRANSFER
15 rue de Berri, 75008 Paris
- 1 56 69 22 30
- info@transfer.fr
- www.transfer.fr

ALSO: 20 rue Godot de Mauroy, 75009 Paris; 303 Square des Champs Elysees, Evry

NUMBER OF TEACHERS: 90.

PREFERENCE OF NATIONALITY: None.

QUALIFICATIONS: Either professional or technical experience (law, finance, etc.) or solid teaching experience, Cambridge CELTA or similar qualification and degree.

CONDITIONS OF EMPLOYMENT: Short-term, long-term or permanent. Teaching takes place generally from 9am to 6pm and some evenings.

SALARY: On application. About 20% deducted for tax and social security.

FACILITIES/SUPPORT: Americans must have their own work papers as no assistance is given with arranging these.

RECRUITMENT: Application and CV. Interview.

NUMBER OF TEACHERS: Varies; 68 franchised branches (e-mail addresses linked from website above).

PREFERENCE OF NATIONALITY: None.

QUALIFICATIONS: CELTA or TESOL certificate.

CONDITIONS OF EMPLOYMENT: Permanent contracts offered. To work part-time hours or full-time if necessary up to 136 hours per month.

SALARY: €1470 per month plus bonuses.

RECRUITMENT: Via local advertising and the internet. Interview not essential.

CONTACT: For Paris branch contact HR Manager, 2 Patio de la Pyramide, Puteaux 92800; +33 1 58 13 89 80; recrutement@wsiparis.com.

GERMANY

The excellent state education system in western Germany ensures that a majority of Germans have such a good grounding in English that very little teaching is done at the beginner level. However, the number of lower-level learners in the eastern part of Germany is still reasonably high. If German students want exposure to a native speaker they are far more likely to enrol in a language summer course in Britain (especially now with the pound so weak against the euro) than sign up for extra tuition at a local institute. Furthermore, many secondary schools in Germany (including the former East) employ native speakers of English to assist in classrooms (programme details below). English is also offered at *Volkshochschulen* or adult education centres where various subsidised courses are run.

Cities in the former East Germany such as Leipzig, Dresden and Erfurt are less popular destinations for job-seeking teachers than Munich, Berlin and Freiburg, and may therefore afford more opportunities, especially since provision of English in the schools lags behind that of western Germany.

The greatest demand for English in Germany continues to come from the business and professional community, although the recession has had a negative impact on demand. For example **John Sydes**, long-time resident of Munich and director of Target English (www.target-englisch.de) wrote in 2010 to say '*given the current economic situation here we should be able to cover all the courses we have with the EFL teachers who are already based in the Munich area*'. However, the economic strains are felt differently in different parts of the country and in different industries. According to **Joe Finer**, Director of Finer English which is included in this book for the first time, the impact of the recession in the state of Hesse has not been as dire as might have been expected since his clients are mainly export-driven, and so the downturn in the English language market has been negligible.

This means that there are still highly paid in-company positions for EFL and ESP teachers, and the agencies and consultancies which supply teachers to business clients have increased the number of native speaker freelance teachers they recruit. Demand is greatest outside cities such as Munich, where teachers complain about a lack of work.

PROSPECTS FOR TEACHERS

Many of the companies that market in-company English courses are desperate for good teachers and trainers, though there is no shortage of inexperienced teachers looking for teaching opportunities. Any graduate with a background in economics or business who can speak German has a good chance of finding work in a German city. A TEFL certificate and a university degree have less clout than relevant experience, as **Kevin Boyd** found when he arrived with his brand new Cambridge certificate at the beginning of the academic year:

> *I was persuaded by a teaching friend to go to Munich with him to try to get highly paid jobs together. As he spoke some German and had about a year's teaching experience, he got a job straightaway. Every school I went to in Munich just didn't want to know as I couldn't speak German and only had four weeks' teaching experience. After two days of this I decided to try my luck in Italy.*

Experience in business is often a more desirable qualification than an ELT qualification. The question is not so much whether you know what a past participle is but whether you know what an 'irrevocable letter of credit' or a 'bank giro' is. Many schools offer *Oberstufe,* advanced or specialist courses in, for example, Banking English, Business English, or for bilingual secretaries, etc. Full-time, vocationally oriented courses in languages for business and commerce are called *Berufsfachschule* and this is by far the most buoyant part of the market. For none of these is a Cambridge or Trinity Certificate or even a Diploma the most appropriate training. However, the more serious schools and the regional English Language Teachers' Associations (ELTAs) have been moving to professionalise the industry and to offer and require more training in ELT skills. Qualifications such as a degree in physics may also impress and lead to scientific translation work, according to **Penny**, a teacher in Berlin.

Very few schools are willing to consider candidates who can't speak any German. Although the 'direct method' (i.e. total immersion in English) is in use everywhere, the pupils may expect you to be able to explain things in German. Penny was not put off so easily:

> *At the beginning they all expected me to talk to them in German. True to my CELTA training I insisted on English except in emergencies and they got used to it!*

If the school prepares its students for the London Chamber of Commerce exams (LCCI), the teacher will be expected not only to understand the syllabus but to interpret and teach it with confidence. There is still a preference for British English, but the increasing number of course participants working for global or American companies prefer Canadian/American English.

Fees charged to companies by the most established and specialist teachers and trainers can be very high, which means few openings occur in this sought-after sector. These teachers also have high overheads and a staggeringly large percentage of their incomes will disappear in compulsory contributions (described below) and expenses. One further requirement of many employers is a driving licence, so that teachers can travel easily from one off-site assignment to another.

FINDING A JOB

Four hundred posts as English language classroom assistants are available at secondary schools throughout Germany. Applications are encouraged from students who have at least AS level, Higher Grade or equivalent in German. UK applicants should contact the Language Assistants Team at the British Council (10 Spring Gardens, London SW1A 2BN; 020 7389 4596; assistants@britishcouncil. org, www.britishcouncil.org/languageassistants-ela.htm). The salary is €800 a month for 12 hours of work a week. Language assistants such as **Sarah Davies** (who was sent to a small town in the east) advise against agreeing to teach in a small village where conditions may be basic and the sense of isolation strong.

American students and graduates can apply for the English Teaching Assistantships programme through the Fulbright Program (administered by the Institute of International Education, 809 UN Plaza, New York, NY 10017-3580). Candidates planning to go on to become teachers of German are strongly preferred; contractual arrangements are as above plus help with travel and insurance. University students and graduates can often find out about possible employers from their university careers office or local English schools, as happened to **Catherine Rogers**. She wrote on spec to a number of local language schools to get some experience before working abroad and ended up being interviewed by two British contacts of a government scheme for teaching English to unemployed engineers and secretaries operating in the Dresden area.

Like so many embassies, the German Embassy in London is not noted for its helpful attitude to aspiring teachers or other job-seekers. Apart from directing students to enquire about the exchange programme run by the British Council and providing addresses of the state ministries of education, it recommends applying to the Zentrale Auslands und Fachvermittlung (International Placement Services), ZAV, part of the German Federal Employment Agency (Villemombler Strasse 76, 53123 Bonn; 228 713 1330 ZAV-Bonn; Ferienbeschaeftigung@arbeitsagentur.de). All applications from abroad are handled by this office. Although people of any nationality can apply through the ZAV, only citizens of old EU countries (who have German language skills) are entitled to expect the same treatment as a German. As usual, it is much more difficult to arrange a job by sending written applications and CVs from the UK than by presenting yourself in person to language school directors and training companies, CV in hand. Determination, qualifications, experience and being on the spot are often deciding factors when an employer has to choose between large numbers of similarly qualified applicants.

The best source of language school addresses is once again the *Yellow Pages* (*Gelbe Seiten*) which can be consulted online (www.gelbeseiten.de) or try www.goyellow.de and search for *Sprachschulen*. Another way of accessing potential employers is via the local English Language Teachers Association, a branch of which can be found in most major cities. The Munich association (MELTA) is especially vigorous and carries a few job vacancies and a page of employers (www.melta.de/jobs_employers.php). There is also a forum for English teachers in Germany, including advice for 'newbies', which can be found at http://elt.yuku.com. Look for English language magazines aimed at expats and you should come across some relevant adverts. For example, the English-language magazine *Munich Found* (www.munichfound.de) carries occasional TEFL vacancies.

All the major language school chains have a significant presence in Germany including Berlitz, Inlingua (with 70 training centres), Linguarama, specialising in language training for business in eight cities, and Wall Street Institute, which keeps expanding. Rates of pay vary, however, some employers pay inexperienced teachers in the range of €12–€16 for a 45-minute lesson, whereas more senior positions are paid €18–€30+ an hour.

Throughout Germany, more than 2,000 adult education centres or *Volkshochschulen* teach the English language (among many other courses) to adults. Native speakers with teaching experience might find a role within the Deutscher Volkshochschul-Verband e.V (www.vhs.de).

One of the easiest entrées to the TEFL world is as a tutor on a language summer camp. These have mushroomed in Germany, and the demand for native English speaking staff is great. In addition to Berlitz Kids (see entry), try Camp Adventure (www.campadventure.de), Penguin Camp (www.pinguincamp.de) or Sphairos (www.sphairos.de).

INTERVIEWS

Most schools and institutes in Germany cannot, under normal operating circumstances, hire someone unseen merely on the basis of his/her CV and photo. Applicants should arrange for a face-to-face interview and should be prepared to make themselves available at a moment's notice. Professional presentation is even more important for securing work in the German business world than elsewhere. Vacancies occur throughout the year since businessmen and women are just as likely to start a course in April as in September. Germans tend to be formal, so dress appropriately and be aware of your manners at an interview. Also good references (*Zeugnisse*) are essential.

A good starting place is Frankfurt am Main, known to locals as 'Bankfurt' or 'Mainhattan'. Frankfurt has the highest concentration of major banks and financial institutions in the country and a correspondingly high number of private language schools. It is helpful, though not essential, to have some basic knowledge of German and business experience. In a job interview with a language school director, demonstrating a detailed knowledge of a handful of commonly used textbooks may be more important than business experience. A former teacher who spent two years teaching in dozens of banks and multinational companies recommends *Build Your Business Vocabulary* by J. Flower and *New International Business English* by L. Jones and R. Alexander.

You can also impress a potential employer by showing some familiarity with current major German business news (bank mergers, etc.). This can easily be done by scanning the English language press or watching the BBC's *World Business Report*. Language schools are looking for teachers who can pose intelligent questions to business students about their jobs. There is a considerable demand from the business community for guidance on conducting 'small talk' in English, which is crucial in building rapport with clients and colleagues.

NINO HUNTER decided to go to Berlin, a city which is both exquisitely trendy and reassuringly relaxed, and one that appeals most to people in search of European culture at its finest. Despite his recent degree in Modern languages from the University of Bath, he found it a struggle:

I did find it extremely difficult to find teaching posts in Berlin. I think the main reason would be the sheer number of English speakers in Berlin, many of whom wish to stay in this amazing city. Given the lack of industry, they have little alternative but to fall back on teaching English, with or without a CELTA/TEFL certificate. The English community is huge in Berlin (check the online Toytown Berlin at www.toytowngermany.com/berlin which has tons of new postings every day). There are of course a huge number of schools in Berlin but given the number of teachers and the decreasing demand over the last two years due to the global economic crisis many of them have become exceptionally picky about who they choose to take on, often asking for at least two years' experience, etc. There was a particular demand for English teachers able to teach advanced students (Cambridge levels 1 and 2) and a few schools simply wouldn't take people on who didn't have experience teaching higher level students.

All of which means that the market in Berlin is extremely saturated and sending a CV off to each and every school usually doesn't help. The best way of finding teaching positions in the city is putting on a suit and going to the schools with a CV, introducing yourself and trying your hardest not to get fobbed off by a secretary, but rather to get an actual interview where they offer you a course. This obviously requires a little courage and a fair amount of energy but is the only way of being sure your CV isn't deleted immediately and is in fact the only way I or any of my colleagues got jobs at private language schools.

The teachers at the Berlin School of English where I did my CELTA course assured me that no one would pay less than €15 for 45 minutes to a teacher with a CELTA. My first school paid me just €12 and it took me ten weeks to get up to €14, which was not at all uncommon.

Two pieces of advice I could give would be firstly to try to get on the lists for the Volkshochschulen (I think there are about seven in Berlin), as these pay more (if you have a university degree even more) and the classes are large and quite fun. I would also recommend joining ELTABB (English Language Teacher's Association (www.eltabb.com/main/index.php) which costs €40 a year but is undoubtedly the best place to network and sometimes perfect positions come up. Basically one needs to be as proactive as possible and not be too fussy. If Wall Street or Berlitz offers you a course, take it.

FREELANCE TEACHING

The majority of native speakers teaching for commercial institutes are not on contracts, but are employed on a freelance contract basis (*Honorarvertrag*) to work for between 2 and 20 hours per week. Schools employing freelance teachers are not in a position to make deductions, because they cannot know a teacher's full expenses. Teachers may also work for several different schools. Freelance teachers are responsible for paying their own tax, pension insurance contributions and (crucially) health insurance.

Upon successful completion of a Trinity TESOL certificate course in England, **Ann Barkett** from Atlanta went to Munich to look for freelance work, but found it tough going:

> *During the period December to March, I was putting up flyers for private and group lessons but received no response. I finally answered an advert for a private student whom I taught for a few weeks, but there just wasn't enough work or money coming in and I was tired of trying at that point.*

Many freelance teachers find themselves for the first time required to design an ESP course (English for Specific Purposes), individually tailored to the needs of their business students. **Nathan Edwards** found that he got better at this:

> *Experience has shown me that such a syllabus must be flexible, open to change and short-term adjustment so as to accommodate the complex and evolving needs of students who are also full-time working professionals. Students and their employers must be given the assurance of a clearly structured course outline, but this must be partly generated by an ongoing negotiated process with all the participants. Finally don't forget that the students themselves can be a valuable source of ESP course material such as authentic English e-mail messages, business letters and company brochures from their offices.*

REGULATIONS

EU nationals are free to travel to Germany to look for work, but are still subject to the labyrinthine German bureaucracy. If your German is poor or non-existent you may have to impose on the good offices of a German-speaking friend or colleague to help you since not all German civil servants speak English. Very useful guidance is available on the internet, for example on the website of the MELTA at http://elt.yuku.com where detailed information by **John Sydes**, the MELTA committee member who contributed most of the information in this section, and others go through all the necessary procedures. Also try www.expatica.com/de/main.html, which covers topics such as taxation, pensions and insurance.

The first step is to register your address with the local authority of the district you are living in (*Einwohnermeldeamt*) or at your local registry office (*Meldestelle*), as German citizens must also do. For this you will need proof that you are living locally, e.g. a copy of your contract with your landlord. You should do this within 14 days of arriving in Germany.

Only after doing this is it possible to apply for a residence permit (*Niederlassungserlaubnis*) from the residence office (*Landeseinwohneramt*) or from the aliens' authority (*Ausländerbehörde*) probably located in the *Rathaus* (town hall) or the *Kreisverwaltungsreferat* (local authority's offices). You have to go to your local authority in person with a completed residence permit application form, a valid passport and a recent passport photograph.

NON-EU NATIONALS

As a non-EU citizen, you need to find a job and to obtain a work permit before you can apply for a residence permit. Once you have found a job, you can apply for a work permit. You will need a letter from your employer stating that they will employ you through the German Employment Office (*Arbeitsamt*). The form your employer has to fill out can be downloaded from most local authority websites.

To apply for a work permit you need a valid passport, a letter from your employer stating what the position you have been offered is, what your projected income will be and the completed application form for a work permit. Once you have the work permit you can then apply for a residence permit, for which you will need:

- The completed application form.
- Valid official ID or passport.
- An up-to-date passport photograph.
- Accommodation: proof of sufficient room for all members of the family and statement of rental costs (including heating, water and electricity) and mortgage (where applicable).
- Work permit.
- Employees: proof of employment (written statement by employer or a contract).
- Self-employed applicants: statement of registration of business.
- Proof of sufficient means to support yourself.
- Detailed statement and proof of regular income (wages for the past three months, wages of spouse and children, if they have an income).
- Proof of health insurance in Germany.
- Students: statement of matriculation and proof of sufficient means to support yourself (a written statement from your parents stating they will support you is sufficient).

According to a new law (*Aufenthaltsgesetz* or *AufenthG*) that governs residence permits for non-EU citizens, applicants must prove that they have a secure and regular income which is next to impossible for freelance teachers. The only exceptions are if you can show that you can invest at least a million euros and/or create at least 10 new jobs and/or prove that the business will benefit the region economically.

German immigration laws require discretionary decisions from the individual authorities, so prospects for non-EU freelancers will differ from region to region. Only a work permit which has been issued by the district/city you live in is valid.

Americans who find an employer while still in the USA might seek advice on documentation from the Carl Duisberg Society (CDS International, New York; 212 497 3500; usabroad@cdsintl.org; www.cdsintl.org) which specialises in arranging six-month business internships.

As soon as a teacher from outside the EU obtains a promise of salaried employment, he or she should take steps to get the necessary permits. The teacher must first register his or her name and address (as for EU nationals) and then report to the *Ausländersamt* (foreigners' office). There they must present a contract or letter from a school claiming that they are the best candidate for the job (difficult). Further requirements may include a certificate of good conduct (notarised by the US Embassy for a fee), proof of address and health insurance and also a health certificate from a German doctor. If approved, a one-year residence permit will be affixed to the passport, with a hand written explanation that the bearer is allowed to work as an English teacher in private language schools only.

Unfortunately, Canadians, Australians, New Zealanders and other nationalities experience more difficulties since they require a residence visa which has been applied for in their country of origin. If within the three months of their tourist stay they manage to obtain a formal written offer of

Berlin School of English

We've been running CELTA courses since 2004 and train more than 100 teachers every year. Most of our graduates intend to work in Germany but others use the course as a stepping-stone to travelling elsewhere in the world. Recent graduates say this about us:

"The balance struck between classroom input and hands-on teaching meant the course was never abstract, completely engaging, and skills and methods discussed were always relevant. The course was intensive, but never unmanageable, and the tutors were passionate and completely expert in their field." (Kiruba)

"The constructive criticism and feedback (both peer to peer and tutor to trainee) was incredibly effective" (Chloe)

What's it like working as an English teacher in Germany? Well, nearly all of the work is on a freelance basis (often via language schools) and you will need an entrepreneurial attitude. As for the work itself, you can find yourself teaching a wide range of students and courses:

"As a result (of the course), I have been teaching English for Specific Purposes for a year now - from the energy industry and the banking sector to real estate, journalism and tourism, at all levels." (Kiruba)

"The fact that just six weeks after completing the CELTA course I was up and running in Berlin as a full time EFL teacher at companies, language schools and universities is testament to the Berlin School of English's impressive teacher-training standards." (Chloe)

What will help you be successful teaching English in Germany? A recognised qualification will certainly give you an enormous advantage over unqualified 'native speakers', but it is also important to be flexible and open-minded, curious, and committed to the quality of your work.

employment, they must return to their home country in order to apply for a working visa at the German Consulate. The application process takes up to one month and there is always a risk that the application will be refused. Successful applicants are issued with a one-year renewable work visa. Not all employers are willing to wait one month for a new teacher to begin working and may prefer to hire British or Irish teachers in the meantime.

TAX, HEALTH INSURANCE AND SOCIAL SECURITY CONTRIBUTIONS

About 95% of all the EFL teaching work in language schools and companies in Germany is offered on a freelance or self-employed basis. The hourly rates you are offered might sound good, but freelancers and self-employed teachers have to pay about 20% of their income after expenses and before tax into the German pension scheme. This is a compulsory contribution for all freelance teachers regardless of whether they already have a private pension scheme. Compulsory pension contributions and health insurance payments (also a must to obtain a work and residence permit) can easily make up 30–35% of a freelance or self-employed teacher's 'expenses', and then there is still income tax to think about. John Sydes (mentioned above) says that these 'expenses' plus rent to be paid, mean that most hard-working teachers are left with very little disposable income. **Sylvia Weismiller**, Director of Euro-Lingua, based in Freiburg, writes:

> *Yes, it's very complicated, and lots of grey areas, unenforced requirements, etc. One of my American teachers is having problems getting his permits renewed. They said if he paid his pension contributions, they would renew it. What those two have to do with each other is a mystery! However, I don't know any foreigners who pay it, even though it is an official policy.*

Sylvia also mentions solidarity tax (about 1%) and church tax (about 1%), which you can avoid by registering as an atheist. However, medical insurance can be painful, particularly if you're a woman:

> *Official health insurance depends on age, sex, etc. Also complicated. As a 40 year old female (women pay about double) I was paying €400 per month. It doesn't depend on your income. If you are a registered student however, you can get a much lower rate, I think €80 per month. As a student you can only work a limited number of hours, but as there aren't any tuition fees it's not a bad idea. There are also ex-pat programmes which charge, I believe, €90 per month. They are limited to 5 years. You have to have health insurance to get your residence permit extended.*

If you are a non-EU citizen you can ask the *Deutsche Rentenversicherung* (German pension authority) to repay the contributions you have made if you have paid into the state scheme for less than five years, i.e. have paid less than 60 pension contributions.

Foreigners working in Germany should obtain a *Lohnsteuerkarte* (tax card) if they are employees, or a *Steuernummer* (tax number) if they are self-employed or freelance from their local *Finanzamt* (tax office).

CONDITIONS OF WORK

You can almost guarantee that you will be teaching adults (since school children receive such a high standard of English tuition at school), and usually before or after office hours. Contracts for full-time work are usually at least a year long, often with a three-month probation period. But it is rare to be *Angestellt*, i.e. fully employed by a school with guaranteed minimum hours, sick pay, holiday pay, etc.

Hourly rates can be high: typically €17–€22 per lesson and double that and more for established teachers of Business English. Off-site teaching hours often incur a premium of €2–€5 to compensate for travel time, or sometimes employers pay 'three hours for two'. Freelancers who earn high incomes have normally been in Germany a long time, speak excellent German and have invested in acquiring relevant specialisations, resources, materials, etc. They have built up their clientele and reputation over years and defend their patch with understandable vigour. The majority of newcomers gain their initial experience at franchise language schools where the pay is much lower, sometimes on a par with cleaners, and where poor working conditions and no job security prevail. A 30-hour working week could consist of 40–45-minute lessons, which would be a very heavy workload.

However, after walking into a tiny English school on her street in Berlin and asking the owner if she needed any help, **Penny**, a British widow in her 50s, built up an enviable client base. She describes her experiences in Berlin:

I do two classes a week, one in the morning and one in the evenings. The morning class is made up of retired ladies who come for fun and I have difficulty keeping them speaking English. I keep reminding them that I am being paid to teach them English and not to learn German from them. We have a good relationship and go out to the cinema occasionally. The members of the evening class are slightly more serious about learning English. Some of them sometimes join in the cinema outings.

The classroom has a table with eight chairs, which limits the size of the class. There is a black board – I would dearly love a white board – and a CD/tape player. Most of my work, however, is one-to-one teaching, which I originally obtained through the school. I charge €14 and pupils come to me. Now, many pupils are recommended by a former or current pupil, so I have several German-Russians and several art historians together with some business ladies – there is a big demand for Business English.

Penny doesn't depend on her teaching, because otherwise her standard of living would be much lower than it is. If you are depending solely on one employer for your income try to find an institute which guarantees a monthly minimum number of hours. Monthly salaries for full-time *Angestellter* (employees) can be from €1,200 to €2,000 gross, with the possibility of paid overtime. Considering that a one-bedroom flat in one of the big cities can easily cost €450–€600 per month, excluding bills, salaries need to be high. Quite a few schools assist with accommodation. Teachers often turn to agencies though their fees can be very steep, as much as two or three months rent plus VAT. Try answering ads in the local paper, or look up *Wohnung* (apartments/flats) in the phone book or try the local *Mitwohnzentralen* which charges a more reasonable fee (usually one month's rent) for finding flats, though they may charge less if you end up renting a room or flat from owners who are temporarily absent. It is customary to pay your rent directly out of a bank account, so open a basic current account (*Girokonto*) as early as you can. By law, the deposit you pay (usually three months' rent) is put in a bank account, which should be a joint savings account in the tenant's and landlord's name, so that neither can withdraw money without the approval of the other.

LIST OF EMPLOYERS

ACADEMY OF BUSINESS COMMUNICATION (ABC)

ABC Franchise GmbH, Asperger Weg 14, 71732 Tamm

 7154 797 5044

info@abc-stuttgart.de

www.abc-stuttgart.de

PREFERENCE OF NATIONALITY: None.

QUALIFICATIONS: Teaching experience or business background plus university degree in any subject.

CONDITIONS OF EMPLOYMENT: Freelance only.

RECRUITMENT: Interviews preferred and are occasionally available in UK.

CONTACT: Mr Kurt Zeller, Director (kurt.zeller@abc-stuttgart.de).

ACADEMY OF EUROPEAN LANGUAGES

Prinz-Albert-Str. 73, 53113 Bonn

228 24 25 840

info@sprachakademie-bonn.de

www.sprachakademie-bonn.de.

NUMBER OF TEACHERS: 360.

PREFERENCE OF NATIONALITY: None.

QUALIFICATIONS: Advanced qualifications needed and much experience.

CONDITIONS OF EMPLOYMENT: Negotiable hours; open freelance contracts.

SALARY: €18 for a 45-minute lesson.

FACILITIES/SUPPORT: Help can be given with accommodation and work permits if necessary.

RECRUITMENT: Personal recommendations.

CONTACT: Tony Westwood, Director.

BERLIN SCHOOL OF ENGLISH
Dorotheenstrasse 90, 10117 Berlin
- 30 229 04 55
- info@berlin.school-of-english.de
- www.berlin.school-of-english.de

NUMBER OF TEACHERS: 30–40.

PREFERENCE OF NATIONALITY: None, but must be a native English speaker.

QUALIFICATIONS: University degree plus TEFL/CELTA Certificate and minimum 1 year's experience.

CONDITIONS OF EMPLOYMENT: Minimum 1 year on freelance basis. Between 16 and 30 hours per week. Focus on Business English and ESP in a diverse range of professions and industries.

SALARY: Details given at interview stage.

FACILITIES/SUPPORT: In-house training provided: accredited Cambridge CELTA Centre, regular teaching workshops and seminars, internet access for teachers, school library.

CONTACT: John Wills, School Manager.

BERLITZ DEUTSCHLAND GmbH
- http://careers.berlitz.com

Job vacancies and information about working conditions are posted on the Careers Services website (http://careers.berlitz.com/current_job_vacancies.asp). Hiring is done locally by one of the 67 schools in Germany. All contact information is provided on the above website or on www.berlitz.de. At the time of writing, more than 20 Berlitz schools had vacancies but most were open to people already residing in the vicinity or having the required documents to work in Germany (visa and work permit).

NUMBER OF TEACHERS: Varies depending on the size of the language centre. Over 1,000 instructors employed in Germany.

PREFERENCE OF NATIONALITY: Native English speakers preferred.

QUALIFICATIONS: Teaching abilities, a professional attitude, good communication skills, willing to work a flexible schedule, and preferably have a business background.

CONDITIONS OF EMPLOYMENT: Open-ended, freelance contracts. Flexible hours between 8am and 9.30pm.

FACILITIES/SUPPORT: Training in the Berlitz Method given before start. Assistance with accommodation and work permits occasionally given.

RECRUITMENT: Adverts and personal referral.

BERLITZ KIDS & TEENS – BERLITZ DEUTSCHLAND GMBH
Kurfürstendamm 203, 10719 Berlin
- +49 30 327 09 260
- guenther.bedson@berlitz.de
- www.berlitz.de

NUMBER OF TEACHERS: 250.

PREFERENCE OF NATIONALITY: Native English speakers.

QUALIFICATIONS: Experience working with children aged 7–17 and also experience of teaching English preferred.

CONDITIONS OF EMPLOYMENT: Freelance work in English holiday camps during German school holidays (Easter 1–2 weeks, summer 4–8 weeks, autumn 2–4 weeks). Camp programmes run all day from 8am to 11pm.

SALARY: €450 per week. Freelancers have to deal with tax and health insurance independently.

FACILITIES/SUPPORT: No help with accommodation. If required an employer's letter of intent can be provided to non-EU nationals. Support will be given in dealing with the German authorities.

RECRUITMENT: Advertising in local magazines and word of mouth. Interviews are desirable and can be carried out over the telephone.

CONTACT: Günther Bedson, Director.

CAMBRIDGE INSTITUT
Hildegardstr 8, 80539 München
- 89 22 11 15
- info@cambridgeinstitut.de
- www.cambridgeinstitut.de

NUMBER OF TEACHERS: Approximately 30.

PREFERENCE OF NATIONALITY: British.

QUALIFICATIONS: PGCE (preferably in modern languages) or CELTA certificate.

CONDITIONS OF EMPLOYMENT: 11-month contracts, renewable for a further 11 months. 26 hours per week. Lessons 9am–11.45am and 5.30pm–9.10pm.

SALARY: €2,100 per month less social security payment.

FACILITIES/SUPPORT: Assistance with accommodation. Induction course and ongoing workshops.

RECRUITMENT: Interview in UK or Munich essential.

CONTACT: Philip Moore, Principal.

CONTEXT SPRACHEN – UND MEDIENDIENSTE GmbH
Elisenstr 4–10, 50667 Cologne

221 925 456 12

teaching@contextinc.com

www.contextinc.com.

NUMBER OF TEACHERS: 15–20.

PREFERENCE OF NATIONALITY: None.

QUALIFICATIONS: Must be native English speakers with academic education and experience.

CONDITIONS OF EMPLOYMENT: Freelance basis. Hours vary between 8am and 8pm, Monday to Friday.

SALARY: Varies according to qualifications/experience and degree of difficulty of class taught.

FACILITIES/SUPPORT: Accommodation and visas are responsibility of teachers. Some training given.

RECRUITMENT: Newspaper adverts, followed by local interviews.

CONTACT: Wendy Lautenschlaeger, School Director.

DAVID BERRY LANGUAGES
Weinbergsweg 3, 10119 Berlin

+493044 99 025

ped@dbl-berlin.de

www.dbl-berlin.de

NUMBER OF TEACHERS: 10–15.

PREFERENCE OF NATIONALITY: None.

QUALIFICATIONS: Minimum CELTA with preferably 2 years' experience.

CONDITIONS OF EMPLOYMENT: Freelance contract with flexible working hours.

SALARY: Negotiable depending on travel/course requirements.

FACILITIES/SUPPORT: Will refer teacher to the local ELTA for help with accommodation.

RECRUITMENT: Interviews are essential.

CONTACT: David Berry-Lichtenberg, Director of Studies.

DESK
Blumenstr. 1, 80331 München

89 26 33 34

info@desk.sprachkurse.de

www.desk-sprachkurse.de

NUMBER OF TEACHERS: 30 native speakers (70 teachers in total).

PREFERENCE OF NATIONALITY: None.

QUALIFICATIONS: Degree with TEFL experience (adults).

CONDITIONS OF EMPLOYMENT: Duration of contract to suit. One of the few schools in Munich offering a full contract, rather than freelance conditions. Teaching hours mainly early mornings and evenings.

SALARY: €22 per 45-minute lesson.

FACILITIES/SUPPORT: No help with accommodation.

RECRUITMENT: CV and interview.

CONTACT: Erwin Schmidt-Achert, Owner.

DIE NEUE SCHULE
Gieselerstrasse 30a, D-10713 Berlin

30 873 03 73

info@neueschule.de

www.neueschule.de

NUMBER OF TEACHERS: 80–110.

PREFERENCE OF NATIONALITY: British, American, Irish, Canadian.

QUALIFICATIONS: Cambridge or TEFL certificate and teaching experience needed. Mostly adults (ages 25–40) in small groups of no more than 8.

CONDITIONS OF EMPLOYMENT: Open-ended freelance contracts and some employed teachers. Variable hours in the daytime (9am–3pm) and evenings (6pm–9.15pm).

SALARY: Approx. €19 per hour.

FACILITIES/SUPPORT: Help with accommodation.

RECRUITMENT: Personal interview necessary, application link on website.

ENGLISH STUDIO
Hornschuchpromenade 7, D-90762 Fürth

911 950 990 00

jobs@englishstudio.de

www.englishstudio.de

Also branches in Regensburg and Munich.

NUMBER OF TEACHERS: 15–20.

PREFERENCE OF NATIONALITY: Native English speakers. Work permit required.

QUALIFICATIONS: Minimum teaching/training qualification, e.g. PGCE, CELTA/Trinity, TEFL/TESOL certificate. Relevant business experience and commercial/industrial training experience also considered.

CONDITIONS OF EMPLOYMENT: Open-ended contract for freelancers; 24 contact hours per week; teaching hours between 7.30am and 8pm.

SALARY: Hourly rates to be negotiated.

FACILITIES/SUPPORT: May be able to advise on accommodation.

RECRUITMENT: Word of mouth. Interviews essential.

CONTACT: Thomas Hintze (thomas.hintze@english studio.de).

EURO FREMDSPRACHENSCHULE
Esplanade 36, 85049 Ingolstadt
- 841 17001
- sw@euro-ingolstadt.de
- www.euro-ingolstadt.de

State-recognised vocational language college.

NUMBER OF TEACHERS: 25.

PREFERENCE OF NATIONALITY: British, American, Canadian.

QUALIFICATIONS: At least a bachelor's degree (main focus *must* be German). PGCE preferred. At least 3 years' experience.

CONDITIONS OF EMPLOYMENT: Permanent contracts. Part-time work possible. 30 hours per week.

SALARY: Based on German state salary scale.

FACILITIES/SUPPORT: Assistance given with accommodation and work permits.

RECRUITMENT: Interview in Ingolstadt necessary.

CONTACT: Stuart Wheeler.

EURO-LINGUA
Ricarda-Huch-Str. 10, 79114 Freiburg
- 179 693 1898
- info@euro-lingua.de
- www.euro-lingua.de

NUMBER OF TEACHERS: 5.

PREFERENCE OF NATIONALITY: None, but native English speakers preferred.

QUALIFICATIONS: University degree, teaching experience, foreign language ability, preferably TOEFL or teacher training.

CONDITIONS OF EMPLOYMENT: Freelance.

SALARY: €15 per 45-minute lesson starting salary.

FACILITIES/SUPPORT: Advice given on local accommodation agencies. Non-EU teachers applying for a work permit outside Germany can be supplied with statement of projected income, etc. Support available as needed for lesson planning, books and other materials.

RECRUITMENT: Word of mouth, local ads, contact with schools abroad.

CONTACT: Sylvia Weismiller, Director.

FINER ENGLISH
Geibel Strasse 6, 34117 Kassel
- +49 561 17832
- Joefiner@aol.com
- www.Finerenglish.com

NUMBER OF TEACHERS: 10.

PREFERENCE OF NATIONALITY: British, Canadian, American.

QUALIFICATIONS: University degree plus a teaching qualification, plus at least 2 years' relevant teaching experience. However, personality is more important than a stream of qualifications.

CONDITIONS OF EMPLOYMENT: Teachers work as freelancers. School is looking for teachers able to commit for at least 1 year. Most teachers have a weekly timetable of about 17 90-minute classes.

SALARY: Teachers invoice Finer English for hours worked. Typical monthly earnings are €2,200–€3,000. Freelancers are paid in full but must organise the payment of income tax and health insurance.

FACILITIES/SUPPORT: Full teacher support provided including finding accommodation and dealing with red tape. Teachers need to arrange a medical examination with a German doctor in order to obtain medical insurance which is a pre-condition of receiving a work permit.

RECRUITMENT: Via internet. Intensive telephone interviews conducted from Kassel, Germany.

CONTACT: Joe Finer, Director.

GERMAN AMERICAN INSTITUTE TUEBINGEN
Karlstrasse 3, 72072 Tübingen
- 7071 795 260
- mail@dai-tuebingen.de
- www.dai-tuebingen.de

NUMBER OF TEACHERS: 15.

PREFERENCE OF NATIONALITY: American.

QUALIFICATIONS: Minimum bachelor's/master's degree.

CONDITIONS OF EMPLOYMENT: Freelance positions only. To work 3–9 hours per week, mostly teaching adult students.

SALARY: Hourly wage.

RECRUITMENT: Local interview required.

CONTACT: Kai Kneule, Language Program Co-ordinator (7071 795 2614; Kai.Kneule@dai-tuebingen.de).

HAMBURG SCHOOL OF ENGLISH

Main Office: Eppendorfer Landstr. 93, 20249 Hamburg

- 40 480 21 19
- info@hamburg.school-of-english.de
- www.hamburg.school-of-english.de

Teacher Training Centre: Isekai 19, 20249 Hamburg

- 40 480 21 19
- celta@hamburg.school-of-english.de
- www.hamburg.school-of-english.de

NUMBER OF TEACHERS: 60–70.

PREFERENCE OF NATIONALITY: British.

QUALIFICATIONS: University degree plus ELT certificate. Preferred minimum 1 year's experience.

CONDITIONS OF EMPLOYMENT: Minimum 1 year on freelance basis. Between 16 and 30 hours per week

SALARY: approx. €26–€38 for 90-minute teaching session.

FACILITIES/SUPPORT: Assistance given with finding accommodation and obtaining work permits. Cambridge ESOL CELTA course provider.

RECRUITMENT: Via local or telephone interviews.

HARDIE INTERNATIONAL LANGUAGE TRAINING & COACHING

Feldbank 1, 44265 Dortmund

- 231 779300
- info@hardie-iltc.com
- www.hardie-iltc.com

NUMBER OF TEACHERS: 15.

PREFERENCE OF NATIONALITY: None.

QUALIFICATIONS: Highest possible. Usually branch specialists are retrained as coaches, consultants or trainers.

CONDITIONS OF EMPLOYMENT: Open freelance contracts. Lessons take place 7 days a week between 7am and 10pm.

SALARY: Above average (depending on qualifications and experience).

FACILITIES/SUPPORT: Accommodation can be provided or at least advice given.

RECRUITMENT: Through partner organisations. Interviews compulsory and sometimes carried out in UK or by telephone.

CONTACT: James Hardie, Owner.

ICC SPRACHINSTITUT

Am Nordplatz 9, 04105 Leipzig

- 341 550 36 73
- info@icc-sprachinstitut.de
- www.icc-sprachinstitut.de

NUMBER OF TEACHERS: 42

PREFERENCE OF NATIONALITY: None.

QUALIFICATIONS: University degree, CELTA and preferably TEFL experience.

CONDITIONS OF EMPLOYMENT: Fixed term or freelance. Teaching in-company business courses, intensive and evening courses.

SALARY: €13–€16 per 45-minute lesson.

FACILITIES/SUPPORT: Assistance with accommodation and work permits (if necessary). Induction and regular training including. Good career prospects throughout the ASSET group.

RECRUITMENT: Walk-ins mainly though e-mail applications welcome. Local interview essential.

CONTACT: James Parsons, Director.

INLINGUA SPRACHSCHULE HANNOVER

Andreaestrasse 3, Ecke Schillerstrasse, D-30159 Hannover

- 511 324580
- info@inlingua-hannover.de
- www.inlingua-Hannover.de

NUMBER OF TEACHERS: 15.

PREFERENCE OF NATIONALITY: English, American, Canadian; other native English speakers.

QUALIFICATIONS: Minimum 1 year TEFL experience.

CONDITIONS OF EMPLOYMENT: Minimum 12 months. Average at least 25 school lessons (45 minutes each) per week.

SALARY: Approx. €15 per lesson.

FACILITIES/SUPPORT: Assistance finding accommodation.

RECRUITMENT: Newspaper adverts and internet.

INLINGUA SPRACHCENTER KIEL

Alter Markt 7, 24103 Kiel

- +49 431 981380
- kristin.dethlefsen@inlingua-kiel.de
- www.inlingua-kiel.de

NUMBER OF TEACHERS: Approximately 10.

PREFERENCE OF NATIONALITY: None.

QUALIFICATIONS: CELTA certificate and some teaching experience preferred.

CONDITIONS OF EMPLOYMENT: 6-month probationary period. Teaching hours Monday to Friday between 8am and 9pm and extra Saturday hours possible 8am–5pm. Full-time contract guarantees 100 teaching hours per month.

SALARY: €12 per teaching hour.

FACILITIES/SUPPORT: Information is provided about the best way to find accommodation in Kiel. Necessary paperwork is provided for non-EU employee to take to foreigners' office to obtain a work permit.

RECRUITMENT: Through online advertisements and by receiving spontaneous CVs.

CONTACT: Kristin Dethlefsen, Director of Studies.

INTERACT!

Sprachtraining – Übersetzungen – Dolmetscher, Rissener Strasse 58, 22880 Wedel/Hamburg

 +49 4103 702468

 info@interact-experts.com

NUMBER OF TEACHERS: 42.

PREFERENCE OF NATIONALITY: None.

QUALIFICATIONS: CELTA plus experience, business background.

CONDITIONS OF EMPLOYMENT: Various hours, Monday to Friday, mornings and evenings.

SALARY: Approx. € 18–20 per hour.

FACILITIES/SUPPORT: Assistance given with accommodation. Training. Access to internet/materials.

RECRUITMENT: Via adverts, agencies, internet and word of mouth.

LINGUA FRANCA

Mauer Strasse 77, 10117 Berlin

 30 8639 8080

 info@lingua-franca.de

 www.lingua-franca.de

NUMBER OF TEACHERS: 50.

PREFERENCE OF NATIONALITY: None.

QUALIFICATIONS: University degree plus TEFL experience and/or certificate. Experience in ESP preferred.

CONDITIONS OF EMPLOYMENT: Freelance only. Can generally give good teachers as many lesson hours as they want.

FACILITIES/SUPPORT: No help with accommodation. Will write the necessary letter to the employment office to support work permit application. In-house training available.

RECRUITMENT: Local interviews.

CONTACT: Charles Arrigo, Director.

MARCUS EVANS – LINGUARAMA SPRACHENINSTITUT DEUTSCHLAND

 personnel@linguarama.com

 www.linguarama.com

NUMBER OF TEACHERS: From 25 in the smaller Linguarama schools to 70 in the larger ones; Linguarama schools located in Berlin, Cologne, Düsseldorf, Frankfurt, Hamburg, Leipzig, Munich and Stuttgart. Vacancies at the time of writing in Hamburg and Bremen, and often vacancies in Munich at Sendlinger-Tor-Platz 7, 80336 Munich; 89 200 009 3 0; munich@linguarama.com.

PREFERENCE OF NATIONALITY: Native English speakers only who must have valid working papers for the EU.

QUALIFICATIONS: Minimum university degree or equivalent and a basic TEFL qualification (e.g. CELTA). Experience of teaching Business English is preferred with a keen interest in business at the minimum.

CONDITIONS OF EMPLOYMENT: Mixture of contract and freelance teachers. Freelance teachers work variable hours, usually early mornings and evenings. Contract teachers usually contracted for 1 year, extendable to 2 years, but occasionally shorter contracts available. 23 days paid holiday per 12-month contract.

SALARY: Depends on experience.

FACILITIES/SUPPORT: Contract teachers are given an initial 2-week accommodation entitlement and assistance with finding permanent accommodation. Travel expenses to the city are paid from the UK if recruitment is through head office. Help is given with obtaining a residence permit, etc. All teachers are given an induction course and paid training is held monthly.

RECRUITMENT: Usually interviews locally for freelance teachers. Contract staff are sometimes recruited locally or via Linguarama Group Personnel Department, 1 Elm Court, Arden Street, Stratford-upon-Avon CV37 6PA (see introductory section, Finding a job).

CONTACT: Danny Coughlan, Personnel Manager, Linguarama.

PET-Sprachen Bacon & Epstein
Partnerschaftsgesellschaft
Baaderstr. 3, 80469 München

✆ 89 200 620 90

✉ info@pet-sprachen.de

💻 www.pet-sprachen.de

NUMBER OF TEACHERS: 60 freelancers.

PREFERENCE OF NATIONALITY: None.

QUALIFICATIONS: TEFL qualification and/or degree preferable, as are business experience and friendly, outgoing disposition.

CONDITIONS OF EMPLOYMENT: Travelling to companies to hold in-company courses on a freelance basis.

SALARY: €21 per teaching unit (45 minutes) plus travel.

FACILITIES/SUPPORT: No assistance with accommodation. Materials support given. Teachers' workshops held.

RECRUITMENT: Direct applications. Local interviews necessary.

CONTACT: paul.bacon@pet-sprachen.de.

SPRACHZENTRUM SUD
Bahnhofplatz 2, 83607 Holzkirchen

✆ +49 8024 1733

✉ info@sprachzentrum-sued.de

💻 www.sprachzentrum-sued.de.

NUMBER OF TEACHERS: 15.

PREFERENCE OF NATIONALITY: British, Irish, American, Australian.

QUALIFICATIONS: Teaching certificate (e.g. CELTA, DELTA) or university degree. Teaching experience needed, especially in Business English.

CONDITIONS OF EMPLOYMENT: Freelance, employment possible after 1 year successful freelance.

SALARY: Between €15 and €25 per hour, depending on the qualification and contract.

RECRUITMENT: Telephone interviews possible. Candidates in Europe will be invited to interview and to teach practice lesson with volunteer students.

CONTACT: Dr. Karin Wiebalck-Zahn, Managing Director.

STEVENS ENGLISH TRAINING
Essen: Rüttenscheiderstr. 68, 45130 Essen

Cologne: Kaiser-Wilhelm-Ring 14–16, 50672 Cologne

Dortmund: Westenhellweg 112, 44137 Dortmund

Dusseldorf: Am Wehrhahn 67, 40211 Dusseldorf

Braunschweig: Petersilienstrasse 1–3, 38100 Braunschweig

Münster: Olferstrasse 6, 48153 Münster

✆ 201 8770770

✉ office@stevens-english.de

NUMBER OF TEACHERS: Approx. 80 full and part-time.

PREFERENCE OF NATIONALITY: None but should be native English speakers.

QUALIFICATIONS: TEFL certificate or business experience.

CONDITIONS OF EMPLOYMENT: 2 year contracts. Hours between 7.30am and 8.45pm Monday to Friday. 80% of teaching is in-company with high element of ESP.

SALARY: Paid on points system per 45-minute session.

FACILITIES/SUPPORT: Furnished flats available at certain locations (e.g. Essen) for trainers recruited from the UK. Extensive workshop training programme for trainers. Opportunity to take the LCCI exam 'Further Certificate in Teaching Business English' (FTBE). Extensive library of teaching materials.

RECRUITMENT: Interviews essential and regularly held in Essen. Candidates receive €100 towards travel expenses and one night's accommodation provided.

CONTACTS: Sigrid and Michael Stevens, Managing Directors.

WALL STREET INSTITUTE
ZHd. Teacher Recruitment, Rosental 5, 80331 Munich

✆ 89 552 989 0

✉ teach@wallstreetinstitute.de

💻 www.wallstreetinstitute.de

NUMBER OF TEACHERS: Approximately 150, at 27 locations.

PREFERENCE OF NATIONALITY: None, but it is easier to employ EU nationals or those who have citizenship due to visa restrictions.

QUALIFICATIONS: Teachers must be native English speakers with ESL/TEFL or equivalent qualification, experience in teaching English as a second language, ability to work within an existing, structured teaching method, excellent organisational and interpersonal skills, and be motivated, energetic and dedicated.

CONDITIONS OF EMPLOYMENT: Contracts of at least one year, usually unlimited (if residency permit has been obtained). Between 10 and 25 hours per week, plus paid overtime.

SALARY: Depends on the city. There is also the opportunity to earn bonuses and be paid commission.

FACILITIES/SUPPORT: Can help teachers find accommodation through informing them about various, reputable websites and organisations when they arrive in the city of employment. Also, if the applicant does not speak German, WSI may accompany them to the immigration office and help them register as a citizen and obtain their work permit. WSI gives a letter of intent to the employment authorities. Once the employment authorities have given their permission, the applicant receives a contract.

CONTACT: Carolyn Hutchison, Teacher Recruitment Coordination, Teacher Recruitment Coordination, WSI, Eppendorfer Landstrasse 61, 20249 Hamburg.

GREECE

The financial crisis of 2010 has not been good news for Greece's massive ELT industry. Every business is suffering at the time of writing, including private language schools, because when money is tight, language learning is one of the first things to get the chop. Public sector workers are having to accept 12% pay cuts, job losses, and an end to favourable pension payouts. On the other hand, the statistics aren't all depressing. Ordinary Greeks have been upset by the way the media has presented their fiscal woes and resulting strikes and demonstrations, giving the false impression that Greece is on its knees. **Jain Cook**, long-time Director of Studies for a company in Patras that owns 10 schools, reported that except at their main school which caters primarily to university students from other towns, the numbers of students did not drop in 2010, and indeed at seven of the schools the numbers of students increased substantially.

Despite some contraction in recent years, thousands of private language schools – the term *Kentra xenon glosson* is gradually replacing the term *frontisteria* – continue to supplement the language education of most children aged 6–16. A few years ago the state school system lowered the age when students began to learn English so parents want very young children to 'get ahead of the game' and have a good grounding in English before they start their state school lessons. An increasing number of older students are also enrolling, because many jobs require proof of advanced attainment in English, not just the basic secondary school level.

Greek language schools are often run by local entrepreneurs and because they are limited to three or four classrooms are often housed in buildings which were not purpose-built as schools. Secondary school pupils in Greece are obliged to study 15 subjects, all of which they must pass before being allowed to proceed to the next year. In most areas the teaching of English in state schools is considered inadequate so that the vast majority of pupils also attend *frontisteria*, and it is not uncommon for a 15 year old to have two or three hours of lessons a day (in other subjects as well as English) in one or more private establishments to supplement the state schooling. Despite this gruelling timetable, the students are usually motivated and generally participate enthusiastically in their lessons, reaching a very high level of proficiency by age 16.

English language teaching in Greece has been described as an exam industry, and there is fierce competition among the international exam bodies. At one time Cambridge First Certificate and Cambridge Proficiency examinations ruled the roost only to be replaced a few years ago by University of Michigan exams. Recently, there has been intense competition between the London Tests of English and the English Speaking Board exams, eating into Michigan's share of the market. These are administered by two rival associations of language schools, PALSO and EUROPALSO. A newcomer has just arrived on the scene in Greece, the City & Guilds, which is aggressively marketing their exams. In fact, there are now 15 exams to choose from, all administered by different examining boards, and the terminology can be confusing. A certificate in one of these exams earns points to help the applicant get on the waiting list for a job in the civil service or in a state school. Some teachers and students still refer to the exams by exam board names such as First Certificate and Proficiency (Cambridge), Michigan and Michigan Proficiency, Edexcel, etc. A new structure for language learning and assessment has been laid down by the European Union (called the Common European Framework of Reference for Languages) which has been gradually gaining acceptance in Greece. B2 denotes someone who can function in English as an 'Independent User' and C2 denotes the highest level 'Mastery' of English.

PROSPECTS FOR TEACHERS

The employment situation for teachers is undeniably more difficult than it was in the boom years when schools were opening left, right and centre. Many schools throughout Greece shut down at the beginning of the academic year in 2009 and more are expected to shut in the future. The decrease in student numbers is partly due to the drop in the birth rate, which is now feeding through the system, and partly due to the fiscal crisis.

Yet prospects for EU nationals with a university degree and a TEFL qualification are far from hopeless, particularly outside Athens. A fairly recent development is that ESP classes are booming in Greece and institutions organising company classes are always on the lookout for professional, highly trained teachers.

A qualification is becoming essential, though not necessarily experience. The government stipulates that in order to obtain a teacher's licence, English teachers must have at least a BA in English Language and literature or education, so that all but the most dodgy schools will expect to see a degree certificate. Having a TEFL qualification, as always, will make the job hunt easier. Given the size of the ELT market in Greece, it is surprising that so few training centres offer the CELTA or the Trinity TESOL certificate in Greece. The main teacher training organisations in Greece tend to concentrate on training Greek speakers to become English teachers, though Anglo-Hellenic in Corinth and Via Lingua in Crete run courses mainly attended by native English speakers. The main ELT training organisations in Greece are listed below:

Anglo-Hellenic, PO Box 263, 201 00 Corinth (train@anglo-hellenic.com; www.anglo-hellenic. com). TEFL International Certificate course (www.teflcorinth.com) held monthly (see Directory of Training Courses).

CELT, 77 Akademias St, 10678 Athens (210 330 2406/201 330 1455 info@celt.edu.gr; www. celt.edu.gr). Offers CELTA and range of other courses.

Study Space, D Gounari 21, 54622 Thessaloniki (2310 269697; www.studyspace.gr). Cambridge-approved centre that specialises in CELTYL because the local market mainly comprises 7–16 year olds but also offers CELTA package which includes a promise to graduates of employment in their partner schools in Thessaloniki and throughout northern Greece.

Via Lingua Crete, Chrysanthou Episkopou 48, Chania, Crete 73133 (28210 57438; crete@ vialingua.org).

Americans and other non-EU nationals will find it difficult to find a school willing to hire them, purely because of immigration difficulties. The government can impose stiff penalties on employers who break the rules, and few, at least in the major cities, will risk it, as **Tim Leffel** found out: '*We had planned on teaching in Greece, but as Americans, we were not exactly welcomed with open arms in Athens; they told us to try the countryside.*' Tim moved on to Turkey instead.

A further complicating factor is the high number of Greek emigrés to North America and Australia who have returned (or whose children have returned) to Greece. In many cases, they are virtually native English speakers of English but are favoured because of their ancestry. Of course there will always be schools prepared to hire Americans and others if well qualified, such as the Hellenic American Union, which has one of the largest programmes in adult EFL in Athens.

One reason why EU nationals with basic qualifications can expect to land a job in Greece is that wages are not high enough to attract a great many highly qualified EFL teachers. Greece tends to be a country where people get their first English teaching job for the experience and then move to more lucrative countries. Also, few schools place any emphasis on staff development or provide in-house training, so serious teachers tend to move on quickly. The majority of advertised jobs are in towns and cities in mainland Greece. Athens has such a large expatriate community that most of the large central schools at the elite end of the market are able to hire well qualified staff locally. But the competition will not be so keen in Edessa, Larissa, Preveza or any of numerous towns of which the tourist to Greece is unlikely to have heard.

FINDING A JOB

IN ADVANCE

Unless you elect to register with one of the recruitment agencies (that deal primarily with Certificate-qualified teachers), it may not be worthwhile trying to find a job in advance, since so much in Greece is accomplished by word of mouth. Getting a list of language schools from outside Greece is not easy. A considerable proportion of *frontisteria* belong to the Pan-Hellenic Federation of Language School Owners (PALSO Headquarters, 2 Lykavitou St/Akademias St, 106 71 Kolonaki, Athens; 210 364 0792). There are local branches of PALSO all over Greece though they are unlikely to offer much help to job-seeking teachers until they are looking on the spot. Note that the Athens association of language school owners has recently split from PALSO and now calls itself EUROPALSO (Akademias 98–100, Athens 10677; 210 3830 752; www.europalso.gr). EUROPALSO consists of more than 2,500 schools in the Athens area and it keeps a file of applications submitted by teachers who visit in person and school owners often look for teaching staff there. PALSO-Chania has a separate web presence at www.palso-chania.gr (Partheniou Kelaidi 72, Chania 73100; 28210 92622) while the Heraklion branch is at www.palsoher.gr and only in Greek (2810 322002).

An alternative association of language schools is QLS (Quality in Language Services), which aspires to be a Panhellenic Association of Accredited Language Schools. Overseeing its 20 member schools, the main office is in Volos (Aristotelous 53, Volos 38333; qls@qls.gr; www.qls.gr) with secondary offices in Athens (Evrinomis 73, Zografou, Athens 15771) and Thessaloniki (Tsimiski 104, Thessaloniki 54622). The prestigious European language school association EAQUALS has six accredited member schools in Greece (see www.eaquals.org/schools/members_print.asp).

The internet is not as useful for the job-seeker in Greece unless you can read the Greek alphabet. Some of the main Greek internet service providers maintain lists of language schools; try http://dir.forthnet.gr/1651–0-en.html and the Hellenic search engine www.robby.gr for language schools and foreign language education listings in English.

Most schools do their hiring for the following academic year between May and July. Obviously the major chains of schools offer the most opportunities, and it is worth sending your CV in the spring to organisations such as the Stratigakis Group, which has about a hundred schools in northern Greece (2310 264263; www.stratigakis.gr). Another major group is The Scholars Group (www.the-scholars.gr).

Fortunately there are several active recruitment agencies that specialise in Greece with offices in Greece and/or Britain. These recruitment agencies are looking for people with at least a bachelor's degree and normally a TEFL qualification and/or experience (depending on the client school's requirements). All client employers provide accommodation. The following undertake to match teachers (with EU nationality) with language schools and do not charge teachers a fee: Anglo-Hellenic Teacher Recruitment (see entry), Cambridge Teachers Recruitment (with entry) and Hyphen, based in Thessaloniki (www.hyphen.gr), which posts 'Jobs Sought' advertisements from ELT professionals on their careers page (hr@hyphen.gr).

When discussing your future post with an agency, don't be lulled into a false sense of security. It is wise to check contractual details for yourself and verify verbal promises. Check to see whether you are entitled to any compensation if the employer breaks the contract and similarly whether you will have to compensate the school if you leave early. Find out if there will be any other native English speaking teachers in the area, and ask about the possibility of contacting your predecessor in the job.

After graduating from the TEFL Corinth certificate course, **Jerry Melinn** (aged 56) began working in Katsianos School of Foreign Languages in Athens and has been teaching there ever since, though he plans to move to another *frontisterion* for September 2010:

Like all schools in Greece it's exam-oriented but I was aware of this before I started teaching so the system was no surprise to me. Everyone works very hard, including the students, and the school has a very high pass rate in all the exams, Cambridge and Michigan, Lower and Proficiency. The pay and conditions are the same as most schools beginning at €700 a month with accommodation provided and all bills paid as well as IKA (health insurance), which I thought was very good.

I have read some horror stories on the internet about teaching in Greece but my experience has been great. The TEFL course in Corinth prepared me well for teaching. I have learned so much, made many new friends and grown very attached to the school and especially the students. I have nothing but admiration for them as they come to lessons twice a week after Greek school and the vast majority are well-behaved and good-humoured.

Phil Tompkins graduated from the Corinth course in 2010 and is looking forward to his first TEFL post on the small island of Kea in the Cyclades. His 'interview' with the Director of the Kea school simply involved catching a bus to Athens and meeting her for an informal chat over coffee at a street café. Jerry and Phil are not the only more mature candidates who have trained in Corinth and found work straight afterwards.

IAN PARR has been working since January 2010 at a chain of three language schools in a suburb of Athens called Vyronas:

This has been my first job as an EFL teacher, having previously worked as a laboratory scientist in England for ten years. I decided I wanted a new challenge and to travel so in Nov/Dec 2009 completed the TEFL International course at Corinth. I first heard about this school in Athens through a contact I made on a Living in Greece website. I rang the school and spoke to the owner who asked me to come to Athens for an interview the same week. I met the school owner who was friendly and who checked my degree and teaching certificates, asked me a few questions about myself and told me that she expects her teachers to act professionally at all times whilst at the school. She then told me she would have work for me from January until the end of the school year in June, around 20 hours a week and that she would pay me €10 an hour. On returning to Greece after the Christmas holidays I soon found a small apartment to rent in the centre of Athens.

As is usual, the Greek teachers teach the younger children and also teach grammar to the older students. Native teachers teach everything except grammar. This is common in Greece apparently and is a little frustrating as teaching grammar was a challenge I was looking forward to. Altogether my hours only added up to 12 hours a week which was disappointing considering I'd been promised 20. Over the months I have worked extra hours covering classes, doing mock speaking tests and giving extra classes close to the exams. The biggest difficulty has been surviving financially in what is an expensive city. Eventually it has gotten easier as I now have a private lesson and do some editing work for a local English man who owns a publishing company. I have been offered a full-time contract to work at the same school for next year and will take it as I have enjoyed my time here and want to learn more of the culture and language here in Greece.

ON THE SPOT

So many *frontisteria* rely on agents to find teachers for them, that it can be difficult to walk into a job. After gaining a lot of on-the-ground experience of Greece, **Jane McNally** from County Derry in Ireland concluded that knocking on school doors can be discouraging, a view corroborated by **Jain Cook**:

> There do not seem to be as many vacancies for teachers as there used to be in the Peloponnese. I have interviewed about 15 British teachers in the past few weeks, all of whom have stressed the difficulty of finding work in this area. They were all personable, smartly dressed, well qualified and experienced, but as yet have received no definite job offers.

The majority of schools have filled all their vacancies by July, so September is usually too late for prospective teachers to be looking for work. One of the best times to look is January. Greece is far less attractive in mid-winter than in summer, and many foreign teachers do not return to their posts after Christmas. Finding work in the summer is virtually impossible; most English language summer courses in resorts or on the islands are staffed by people who have taught for an academic year. **Will Brady** is one of the co-founders of Atlantis Books on the island of Santorini (www.atlantisbooks.org). He picked up a teaching job on the island:

> It was just an opportunistic thing. I knew that I needed to earn some money so having recently got a TEFL qualification I thought I'd try my hand at a bit of TEFL teaching. I wandered around Fira and asked if there were any language schools, discovered that I was facing one, and walked in. I met a very strange man, who was the manager (the owner didn't speak English). This guy had studied psychology in England. I think he took a liking to me because I was English. I asked if I could do some work for them and he more or less told me straight away that I could, but kept things on very vague terms. Whilst I was back in England to arrange a few things, I negotiated with him over the phone. Then when I got back to the island I just went in and started. There was no interview whatsoever.

Although Will had enquired about working legally, he concluded that advice from the Greek Embassy in London '*seemed to lead to no certain conclusions about what was the correct protocol.*' He ended up working under the table, an arrangement that suited both himself and the school owner, and was paid a wage equivalent to the British minimum. Work was part-time, teaching (or assisting in the classroom) about 2–3 hours a day, 3–4 times a week. The language school had never hired a native English speaker before and all the Greek teachers would defer to Will on grammatical points, something he found 'quite strange', because he was considerably younger.

Cassandra Filio worked in Ioannina, in the north-western part of Greece, where the school and officials were not very concerned with her (non-legal) work status: '*Had I tried to get a work permit there would have been quite a lot of wait, paperwork and headaches.*' However, despite not having a contract that was legally binding (a risk), Cassandra did have an agreement that she would teach for a year and re-evaluate the situation towards the end of the year. Her employer found and paid for her apartment, a block away from the school in a nice part of town, and the wages were enough to live on, but did not stretch to foreign travel.

Although **Jamie Masters** knew that October was not prime time for job-hunting, that is when he arrived in Heraklion to look for work:

> I advertised (in Greek) in the Cretan newspapers, no joy. I lowered my sights and started knocking on doors of frontisteria. I was put onto some guy who ran an English-language bookshop and went to see him. Turned out he was a lynch-pin in the frontisterion business and in fact I got my first job through him. Simultaneously I went to the PALSO office and was given a list of schools which were looking for people. The list, it turned out, was pretty much out of date. But I had insisted on leaving my name with them (they certainly didn't offer) and that's how I found my second job.

The Lexis chain of bookshops throughout mainland Greece and some of the islands can be a useful place to enquire, since they are usually very well informed about who needs teaching staff or who wants a private teacher.

Once you arrange an interview, be sure to dress well and to amass as many educational diplomas as you can. This will create the right aura of respectability in which to impress the potential employer with your conscientiousness and amiability. Decisions are often taken more according to whether you hit it off with the interviewer than on your qualifications and experience. Jamie Masters found that no one cared a fig about his PhD in Latin.

Check the adverts in the English language weekly *Athens News* (www.athensnews.gr) where *frontisteria* very occasionally advertise but where you are more likely to see a listing for an informal arrangement: many Greek families are looking for live-in or part-time tutors for their children. You could also try placing your own advertisement in the situations wanted column. Another major paper worth checking is *Ta Nea* (www.greeknews-tanea.com).

When you elicit interest from a language school owner or a family, take your time over agreeing terms. Greece is not a country in which it pays to rush, and negotiations can be carried out in a leisurely and civilised fashion. On the other hand, do not come to an agreement with an employer without clarifying wages and schedules precisely. Make sure you read your contract very carefully so that you are familiar with what you should be entitled to. Anglo-Hellenic provides a detailed four-page contract in Greek and English, a sample of which is available on its website (http://anglo-hellenic.com/teachers/contract.htm).

FREELANCE TEACHING

Private lessons are not as easy to find as they were. Established EFL teachers might now have three or four private pupils when before they had as many as 15. This is partly because of the falling birth rate in Greece and also because the middle classes have less disposable income and prefer to send their children to the local *kentro xenon glosson* or to someone they know locally who has passed the B2 level examination and who charges much less than a native English speaker, sometimes as little as €2–€3. This is a huge contrast with the going rate for qualified private tutors of €25 per hour for B2 tuition, and €30 per hour for C2, probably more in Athens.

Private tutoring jobs seem to materialise either from the language schools (whose directors seldom seem to mind their teachers earning on the side) or from conversations in a café-bar. It is a good idea to pin your card up at private schools, local shops and so on.

Trading English lessons for board and lodging is a common form of freelance teaching in Athens and elsewhere. Sometimes contracted teachers are offered free accommodation in exchange for tutoring their boss's children. In Athens, the rich suburbs of Kifissia and Kolonaki are full of families who can afford to provide private English lessons for their offspring. The suburbs of Pangrati and Filothei are also well-heeled. It is also possible to start up private classes for children, provided you have decent accommodation in a prosperous residential area, though this will usually be too expensive if your only source of income is private teaching. **Leah White** solved her accommodation problem in Athens by approaching managers of blocks of flats to see whether they could arrange for her to have a rent-free flat in exchange for teaching their children.

REGULATIONS

English teachers must first obtain a teacher's licence and then a residence permit (which is also a work permit) and the bureaucratic procedures involved can be stressful, even with a supportive employer. The two documents needed for a teacher's licence used to be a health certificate and a degree certificate. The Ministry of Education considers a BA or higher degree in English Literature or a degree in Education a sufficient qualification, though a TEFL certificate strengthens your application of course. You must have your degree certificate officially translated and notarised, either before you leave home (which is usually cheaper) or in Greece. The health certificate can be obtained only in Greece, and involves a chest X-ray and in some cases a blood or stool test.

In 2007 it was proposed that native English speakers would have to take a Greek Proficiency exam to prove they are fluent in Greek. But in the face of opposition from the EU, this proposal has not been enforced (see http://anglo-hellenic.blogspot.com/2009/01/greek-language-requirements.html).

If teachers work illegally, they will not be paying IKA (national health insurance) so will not be eligible for unemployment benefits, bonuses, pension, etc. Teachers are advised to contact the Greek Ministry of National Education/Department of Private Education which issues the teaching licence: Andrea Papandreou 37, Marousi 15180; 210 344 2505/6/8 (www.ypepth.gr/en_ec_page 1537.htm).

English speakers of Greek ancestry find it much easier to obtain a teacher's licence and are generally more attractive prospects, as explained by **Jain Cook**:

Australian, Canadian, South African and American Greeks are classed as native speakers because English is their first language, but most have a Greek passport which makes it all much simpler for them. As Director of Studies at the Koutsantonis School, I have interviewed dozens of such teachers. Although many have no teaching experience or qualifications, they have already obtained a teacher's licence and therefore school owners are more than willing to consider them. A Greek national's teaching licence is for life, whereas a foreigner has to renew it every year. This is another advantage for the school owner.

The paperwork is supposed to be getting simpler, but I haven't seen any signs of it myself. I've been here for 19 years now, and it took many years before I was issued with a five-year residence permit. Until now I have been doing all the running around for the paperwork every year. The authorities are supposed to be abolishing this practice for EU citizens, but if you ring any police station, they will tell you that you still need one.

When the teacher's licence arrives from Athens, the teacher must take it along with his or her passport, photos and a lot of patience to the police station to apply for a residence permit, which should come through in about a month. The health certificate and residence permit must be renewed annually, though if you protest loudly enough you can usually get away with just having a chest X-ray. You will, however, have to take your IKA book (see below) to renew your residence permit and a form from your employer which shows the length of your term of employment. The first residence permit is normally valid for just six months, subsequent ones for one to three years. Keep photocopies of all forms.

Frontisteria usually tend to leave all the bureaucratic legwork to the teachers. Employers will take on the necessary transactions only if they are convinced that a candidate will be an asset to their school. Non-EU teachers often find that the Ministry of Education delays and then turns down their applications for a teacher's licence. Officially applicants must obtain a letter of hire from a language school which must be sent to an address outside Greece. The teacher takes the letter to the nearest Greek consulate and applies for a work permit; the procedures take at least two months.

It is mandatory for Greek employers to register full-time employees with the Greek national health insurance scheme (IKA) and pay employer contributions which amount to more than 30% of the salary (increased in the wake of Greece's financial catastrophe in 2010); the employee's contribution is 16–20% and should be deducted from the salary at source. Be sure to find out ahead of time whether the salary quoted is before or after the IKA deduction. You should go with your employer to the local IKA office in order to apply for an IKA book 60 days after starting to pay contributions;

thereafter you are entitled to free medical treatment and reduced cost prescriptions on production of the book. The custom of claiming unemployment benefit over the summer when teachers on nine-month contracts are not paid is likely to come to an end under the new belt-tightening dispensation. Very few teachers declare their private earnings for tax purposes. Income tax is paid annually and it is up to the teacher to register with the tax office.

CONDITIONS OF WORK

Standards vary enormously among employers. Although there is specific legislation which is meant to regulate the operation of language schools, this is seldom enforced. The way to recognise a good *frontisterion* is by its exam results and by its ability to retain staff.

In general the large chains are better, probably for no other reason than that they have a longer history of employing native English speakers. You also have some back-up if you have been hired through a mediating agency. Some of the small one-man or one-woman schools are cowboy outfits run by barely qualified entrepreneurs who have had little contact with the English language; their teaching techniques involve shouting (usually in Greek) at their students and getting them to recite English irregular verbs parrot fashion. In fact this kind of school is on the decline, and standards have been rising.

Wages are determined by the central government. The minimum hourly rate of pay for 2009/2010 is €8.81 gross, which has remained unchanged for more than two years and is unlikely to rise any time soon. Deductions of 16%–20% cover national insurance contributions, leaving a net hourly wage of €7–€7.50, though this increases if the teacher is married, has children, a master's degree, and for each year of teaching experience. It can be a combination of all or some of these, putting the minimum hourly rate up to €12 per hour. Although the hourly rates are very low compared to those paid in other European countries, jobs bring a range of statutory benefits, e.g. holiday pay and bonuses as described below (assuming these survive the swingeing cuts ahead). Teachers should be paid an extra hour's wage for marking for every 10 hours of teaching, though some employers try to evade this. Until recently, the basic salary was augmented by compulsory bonuses at Christmas, Easter and summer. However at the time of writing in May 2010, bonuses for all workers are being scrapped as part of the government's austerity measures.

The teaching year has been shrinking, so that an increasing number of schools now start their courses at the beginning of October and finish at the end of May. So some schools offer eight-month contracts rather than the nine months that used to be standard. Teachers should always check beforehand the date up to which they will be paid. Native English speakers are often employed to teach exam classes that actually finish earlier than the end of May. For example, classes for Michigan exams in 2010 finished on 7 May, just before the ECCE and the ECPE exams. Teachers should check that they will be paid until the end of the month if they are not going to continue at least a few hours a week doing oral work with their students. Schools have been known to break the contract by paying off teachers as soon as their classes have taken the exams.

The majority of employers allow two paid fortnight holidays at Christmas and Easter (remember that the Greek Easter is usually later than elsewhere) and have been paying compulsory generous bonuses calculated according to the number of days worked. It remains to be seen whether these will continue. If you have queries about the collective labour agreement, contact the Greek Labour Office (OAED) at Ethnikis Antistaseos 8, 17346 Alimos (210 998 9000).

Employers who have suffered from staff desertions in the past may hold back some of your monthly pay as a bond (*kratisi*) against an early departure. The number of hours of teaching available from an average *frontisterion* is also decreasing, which of course means lower earnings. According to Jain Cook, the average working week is now just 12 hours and it is unusual for new teachers to get more than that. This means that the school does not have to pay IKA. Teachers with so few hours are forced either to work at more than one school (which school owners are not keen on) or to take on private students. Split shifts are now very uncommon except in technical colleges or universities. Almost all teaching at *frontisteria* takes place between 5pm and 10pm.

It is not unusual to be expected to teach in two or more 'satellite' sites of the main school in villages up to 10 miles away. Local bus services are generally good and cheap but you could find yourself spending an inordinate amount of (unpaid) time in transit and standing around at bus stops.

> **All areas have a local workers' office, where you can go if you are in dispute with your employer or fear that you are being ripped off.**

PUPILS

Most native English speakers are employed to teach advanced classes, usually the two years leading to Cambridge exams. Because of the Greek style of education, pupils may not show much initiative and will expect to be tested frequently on what they have been taught. **Andrew Boyle** found the prevailing methodology of 'sit 'em down, shut 'em up and give 'em lots of homework' was moderately successful.

Another problem is that there is a great deal of pressure to assign pass marks just to retain the students' custom. Some school owners are so profit-motivated, they have euros for eyeballs. Students expect to be told the answers and bosses want their teachers to be lenient with the marking so that the students all pass and parents will re-enrol them.

Will Brady, teaching on the island of Santorini, found the pupils quite challenging, particularly the girls:

> *The job was littered with problems because the kids, for a start, were pretty uninterested. They were the offspring of hotel owners on the island, for the most part, whose only reason for having their kids learn English was so that they could be of use in the family business when the tourists came in summer. They had a level of MTV English but that was about it. They weren't motivated to learn and it was quite difficult to get them interested in the subject. I had a particular problem with a class of 15–16-year-old girls who were quite difficult to discipline. For some lessons I was alone and they took advantage of the fact that I didn't speak Greek. They were not even bothering to whisper, but talking openly to each other, and playing footsie with me under the table, and it was very difficult to know how to handle that. The manager took me aside and told me in no uncertain terms that I should not respond to any of the advances. Thankfully, I hadn't entertained the idea.*

ACCOMMODATION

Since most schools provide a flat or at least help in finding a flat, teachers are often not too concerned about their living arrangements. Placements arranged by the recruitment agencies offer free accommodation in addition to the full salary. It is definitely worth checking in advance about furnishings. Flats are sometimes quite spartan but some of the better ones are comfortably furnished and may have a washing machine and television in addition to the essentials. However, some flats, especially in Athens, are unfurnished which is a serious nuisance for someone on an eight-month contract.

Utility bills come every two months, and winters in Greece can be surprisingly cold. Even in a small flat, the electricity bill will run to hundreds of euros. Water bills are very cheap, however. Before taking over accommodation, try to find out if the bills have been paid. Changing the name is such a major hassle (involving tax returns, etc.) and unfortunately it is not uncommon for tenants to move on without paying their bills and the new tenant becomes liable. Non-payment of electricity and phone bills (but not water bills) will result in disconnection, and no final reminders are sent out.

LEISURE TIME

Teachers in Athens should have no trouble constructing a social life. The visitors' site www.breath takingathens.com contains details of clubs and events of interest to expats. Outside Athens, the social order is still fairly conservative. A further problem is the enormous language barrier in a country where it will take some time to learn how to read the alphabet. Watching Greek television is a good way to learn the language plus Greek lessons are run free of charge in many locations. **Cassandra**, based in the north of Greece, found that '*teaching was a bit more difficult and isolating than I expected, but once I was used to the lifestyle I enjoyed it… with hindsight I would have enrolled in Greek lessons sooner and tried to get out and meet more people.*'

Most teachers find the vast majority of Greek people to be honest, friendly and helpful and are seldom disappointed with the hospitality they receive. As anyone who has visited Greece knows, the country has countless other attractions, not least the very convivial tavernas. Eating out is no longer the bargain it once was. With the increase in VAT, many goods and services have risen in price, and even wine which used to be exempt is about to be taxed. Travel, particularly ferry travel, is affordable and a pure delight out of season. Despite all the hassles, most people enjoy a year in Greece.

LIST OF EMPLOYERS

ANGLO-HELLENIC TEACHER RECRUITMENT

PO Box 263, 201 00 Corinth

jobs@anglo-hellenic.com

www.anglo-hellenic.com

NUMBER OF TEACHERS: About 80 vacancies every year in a wide choice of locations.

PREFERENCE OF NATIONALITY: British.

QUALIFICATIONS: University graduates with a TEFL certificate.

CONDITIONS OF EMPLOYMENT: Most vacancies are in September, several in January and a few throughout the year.

SALARY: 9-month contracts pay the going rate of about €900 per month plus bonuses and 4 weeks' paid holiday.

FACILITIES/SUPPORT: Accommodation in a furnished flat. A four-page contract will be provided by agency (specimen copy available beforehand). Anglo-Hellenic also take care of the bureaucratic essentials, and encourage meetings and exchange visits of their teachers and provide interactive web-based facilities for information, opinion and social chat. TEFL certificate courses (120 hours) are run every month, with shorter professional development courses also being offered throughout the year.

RECRUITMENT: Interviews are conducted in London, Athens or Corinth, throughout the summer.

BETSIS LANGUAGE SCHOOLS

Thivon 109, 18542 Piraeus

+30 210 4920871

Second site: Pyrgou 31, 18542 Piraeus

+30 210 4923475

abetsis@otenet.gr; abetsis@hol.gr; lmamas@yahoo.com

NUMBER OF TEACHERS: 15–20.

PREFERENCE OF NATIONALITY: British and Irish.

QUALIFICATIONS: Bachelor's degree and Cambridge exams.

CONDITIONS OF EMPLOYMENT: 8 month contracts. 18–24 hours per week. Also opportunities for teachers to work at the publishing company, Andrew Betsis ELT, specialising in ELT exam books. Positions are available in the editorial and marketing departments.

SALARY: €9,000–€10,000 per year.

FACILITIES/SUPPORT: School helps teachers find rental accommodation and with the bureaucracy involved in applying for a work permit.

CONTACT: Lawrence Mamas, Director of Studies

Anglo-Hellenic

Established in 1997, over the past 15 years Anglo-Hellenic has become synonymous with English teaching in Greece. Anglo-Hellenic Director **Peter Beech** moved to Greece to take up his first teaching post as a young graduate in 1987, and 10 years later inaugurated Anglo-Hellenic to fill the need for a reliable service linking schools and teachers. It was the search for native-speaker teachers to staff his own school in Corinth that led to the realization that there was no dependable agency to provide that service. Over the next few years, Anglo-Hellenic quickly expanded to the point where it was organising placements for around a hundred teachers each year, and to date has placed well over a thousand native-speaker teachers in jobs in Greece.

Having established a network of clients throughout the country, Anglo-Hellenic used its influence to spearhead improvements in conditions for teachers - one result of this is that it is now standard practice for schools to provide rent-free accommodation for their teachers. Anglo-Hellenic has also been at the forefront of the movement to protect the rights of English teachers in Greece, most recently in organising opposition to proposals that would require English teachers to be proficient in the Greek language.

In addition to teacher recruitment, Anglo-Hellenic also offers a range of teacher training courses. The TEFL international certificate course, run every month in Corinth, is a four-week course designed primarily for native-speakers of English intending to work in Greece. Providing extensive observed teaching practice with Greek students, children and adults, this course is the most effective preparation for teaching in Greece. Anglo-Hellenic also organises seminars and training courses for schools throughout Greece, as well as participating actively in conferences both in Greece and internationally.

WESTERN EUROPE

GREECE

CAMBRIDGE TEACHERS RECRUITMENT
17 Metron St, 143 42 Athens
UK contact address of main interviewer during the summer: Andrew MacLeod-Smith, 53 Green Acres, Parkhill, Croydon CRO 5UX
macleod_smith_andrew@hotmail.com

NUMBER OF TEACHERS: 30–40 per year.
PREFERENCE OF NATIONALITY: British or EU.
QUALIFICATIONS: Degree and TEFL certificate, a friendly personality and conscientious attitude.
CONDITIONS OF EMPLOYMENT: Contracts usually between September and May, although some summer work. Usual hours are Monday to Friday between 4pm and 10pm (25 hours per week).
SALARY: Roughly €600–€1,000 net per month plus flat, bonuses, holiday pay and pension contributions.
FACILITIES/SUPPORT: Accommodation is provided (not necessarily free) plus health insurance and pension. Holiday pay is given at Christmas and Easter. Applicants can expect to receive plenty of information about working in Greece.
RECRUITMENT: Comprehensive interviews are conducted between mid-June and the end of August. Interviews are held in hotels in central London.

CP STUDIES
6 Trizinia Str, N Kifissia, 14564 Athens
210 622 52441

NUMBER OF TEACHERS: 1.
PREFERENCE OF NATIONALITY: British.
QUALIFICATIONS: Talented teachers.
CONDITIONS OF EMPLOYMENT: Usual hours of teaching are 4–10pm.
SALARY: Negotiable.
FACILITIES/SUPPORT: Advice given on finding accommodation.
CONTACT: Christine Petridou, Owner.

185

NUMBER OF TEACHERS: Out of staff of 35 in 10 schools, only about 2 are British.

PREFERENCE OF NATIONALITY: Native English speakers with Greek ancestry.

QUALIFICATIONS: University degree. Preferably a teaching qualification and some experience.

CONDITIONS OF EMPLOYMENT: 8 month contracts. 12–18 teaching hours per week, evenings only, Monday–Friday.

SALARY: From legal minimum of €9 gross according to qualifications and experience.

FACILITIES/SUPPORT: School owner will help with search for an apartment and might be able to lend furniture.

RECRUITMENT: Generally teachers leave their CVs in person and are called back for interview when a vacancy occurs. Very occasional interviews held in UK.

CONTACT: Jain Cook, Director of Studies (cookj@otenet.gr).

NUMBER OF TEACHERS: 10.

PREFERENCE OF NATIONALITY: Britain.

QUALIFICATIONS: University degree and TEFL qualification.

CONDITIONS OF EMPLOYMENT: Most teachers stay 2–3 years. 18–25 hours per week.

SALARY: €700–€1,000 per month, less 16% deductions.

FACILITIES/SUPPORT: Assistance given in finding accommodation. School assists with residence permit after teacher provides a verified copy of his/her degree; official translation can be done in Heraklion.

RECRUITMENT: Via newspaper adverts, personal contact and PALSO Association. Telephone interviews.

CONTACT: Irene Lambraki, School Director.

NUMBER OF TEACHERS: 3–5 native English speakers.

PREFERENCE OF NATIONALITY: EU nationals.

QUALIFICATIONS: University degree, TEFLA or CELTYL or CELTA and EFL teaching experience.

CONDITIONS OF EMPLOYMENT: Standard contract 8 months. 24–26 hours per week.

SALARY: €800 to €1,000 according to qualifications. 17% deductions for tax and social security.

FACILITIES/SUPPORT: Assistance finding accommodation and obtaining a legal status/teaching permit.

RECRUITMENT: Via detailed CV, interview, model lesson (with lesson plan). Interviews are carried out in Thessaloniki every May and June.

CONTACT: Harry J. Nikolaides, School Director.

Branches in Pireaus, Nikea and Glyfada.

NUMBER OF TEACHERS: 45.

PREFERENCE OF NATIONALITY: British. Majority are Greek-Americans or Greek. Must possess a valid visa.

QUALIFICATIONS: Minimum age 21. Bachelor's or master's degree and teacher training.

CONDITIONS OF EMPLOYMENT: 1–3 year contracts to teach at least 4 hours a day. Hours extend late into the evening.

SALARY: Approx. €850 net; €382 deductions.

FACILITIES/SUPPORT: No help with accommodation.

RECRUITMENT: Interviewees teach a demo lesson. Successful candidates must then complete the in-service training programme and sign a probationary 3-month contract.

CONTACT: Ino Panayotou, Director of Studies.

ITALY

English language schools are thriving throughout Italy and opportunities for qualified native English speaker teachers are very good, especially in towns and cities which cannot boast leaning towers, gondolas or coliseums. Small towns in Sicily and Sardinia, in the Dolomites and along the Adriatic have more than their fair share of private language schools and institutes, all catering to Italians who have failed to learn English in the state system. (English teaching in Italian schools is generally acknowledged to be inadequate.)

PROSPECTS FOR TEACHERS

A complete range of language schools can be found in Italy, as the *Yellow Pages* will confirm. At the elite end of the market, there are the 44 schools which belong to AISLI, the Associazione Italiana Scuole di Lingue (www.aisli.com). Prospective teachers should apply directly to the schools and not to AISLI.

Very strict regulations mean that only ultra-respectable schools can become AISLI members so there are thousands of good schools outside the association. AISLI schools normally expect their teachers to have advanced qualifications and in return offer attractive remuneration packages and conditions of employment.

At the other end of the spectrum, there is a host of schools which some might describe as cowboy operations, though these are decreasing in number. The CELTA is widely recognised and respected in Italy (unlike in France, for instance) as are other certificates. The days of finding work without a qualification are all but over. US qualifications are less well known for the simple reason that work permits are very difficult for non-EU citizens to obtain. There are so many job-seekers with TEFL training that qualifications are necessary in order to compete with all those native English speakers so keen to live, work and teach in Italy. A healthy number of schools wanted their job vacancies to be registered in this book and can be seen advertising on the main ELT websites and relevant journals. Private language schools also cater to Italians who need Business English for work or to those who are interested in improving on their general conversation skills (one-on-one) in English for travel and tourism.

Strict employment regulations and red tape in Italy make small companies reluctant to offer full-time contracts. A few schools offer a British contract (i.e. one that is not subject to Italian legislation) in which the wages are lower than on an Italian contract but the benefits better and the red tape much less (see entries for *Alpha Beta Piccadilly* and *Caledonian Communications* for example). Compulsory contributions for social security and expensive perks make hiring a permanent member of staff very costly so most of the jobs available are eight- or nine-month contracts, October to May. The majority of English teachers in Italy work on contract with no long-term job security, which is acceptable for those who want to spend only one or two years in the country. A lot of teaching work in Italy is paid under the table. Contracts shouldn't be expected at the start though they are more likely to be given by private language schools in smaller out of the way places. Many English teachers in the main cities work for more than one private language school and also do freelance teaching on the side.

A useful starting place for information on training and teaching English in Italy is www.teachingenglishinitaly.com, a website maintained by **Sheila Corwin**, an American resident in Florence who has been working and living as an English language teacher and teacher trainer in Italy (on and off) since 2002. Her website includes affordable online options in basic TEFL certification and allows registration for onsite courses in TEFL/TESOL/CELTA and a Teaching Practice (TP) programme in Florence and other cities in Italy is also available (sheila@teachingenglishinitaly.com).

FINDING A JOB

IN ADVANCE

There is no single compendium of the hundreds of language school addresses in Italy. The relevant *Yellow Pages* (*Pagine Gialle*) are user friendly; go to www.paginegialle.it and choose the handy English version of the site. Typing in 'English language school' produced 645 entries in 2010. The search engine allows you to search by city or more generally by region.

International language school groups such as Benedict Schools, Linguarama, Berlitz and inlingua are major providers of English language teaching in Italy. International House has 13 affiliated schools throughout the country. Wall Street Institute now has more than 90 centres in Italy – nearly twice as many as two years ago – and actively recruits native English speakers. Vacancies are posted at www.wallstreet.it/lavora-con-noi/attuali-offerte-dimpiego.html; in most cases applications should be sent directly to the school, whereas other recruitment is done by head office (staff@wallstreet.it).

Several Italian-based chains of language schools account for a large number of teaching jobs. Many operate as independent franchises. For example you can get contact details for all 175+ British Institutes on their website www.britishinstitutes.it (click on *Sedi*) or contact the personnel office at personale@britishinstitutes.it.

Other chains include the British Schools Group (www.britishschool.com) with more than 60 member schools, which carry out a lot of their recruitment through Saxoncourt International in London (020 7491 1918). Most language schools in Italy seem to incorporate the word British, English, Oxford or Cambridge randomly combined with Centre, School or Institute, which can result in confusion.

American citizens have a lot of problems finding work in Italy, largely because it is so difficult to obtain a work permit. However, a solution suggested by **Carla Valentine**, an English teacher in Venice, is to try working for one of the Department of Defense US army schools on the military bases in Italy. Under these circumstances, work permits are processed in the USA.

ON THE SPOT

The online *Yellow Pages* is probably still the best source of possible employers. Italians like face-to-face contact and, according to **Sheila Corwin**, Director of teachingenglishinitaly.com, stopping by a school to meet the director often works better than blindly sending out resumés through snail or electronic mail. When **Bruce Nairne** and **Sue Ratcliffe** went job-hunting in Italy a few years ago, they relied on the *Yellow Pages* as a source of potential employers:

> *Rather unimaginatively we packed our bags and made for Italy in the middle of the summer holidays when there was no teaching work at all. Nevertheless we utilised the Yellow Pages while we were in Sicily and proceeded to make 30 speculative applications, specifying our status as graduates who had completed a short course in TEFL. By the end of September we had received four job offers without so much as an interview.*

Unfortunately, the jobs in Bari which they chose to accept never materialised and so they once again resorted to the *Yellow Pages*, this time in Milan railway station, where they managed to secure the interest of three or four establishments for part-time work.

Often a few hours teaching can gradually be built up into a full-time job by those willing to say 'Yes'. If you're there when they need you, you can usually get something. Most find that the longer they stay, the more hours they get, though there is still no job security working this way.

ALEX NEUMAN, a globetrotting journalist, describes how she set about finding teaching work in the town of Bergamo where she and her partner had decided to spend a year or two:

The first step these days is to go online. I quickly found three or four English schools in Bergamo: Shenker, Wall Street, Inlingua and two small local firms run by individuals. I decided I should also look in Milan since it is only 45 minutes by train from Bergamo.

This is where you quickly realise this is not like job hunting in your own country and in your own language. Few Italians answer e-mails from strangers. You have to pick up the phone – a challenge when your language is rusty but as these were English schools most had an English speaking receptionist. Then I discovered the vagaries of the private teaching system which basically is out to make as much money as possible while paying as little as possible to teachers and expecting infinite flexibility on the teacher's part and no flexibility on the school's part!

You will need patience and a sense of humour at this stage. I quickly got an interview with Wall Street Institute and Shenker and was accepted at Shenker. Being accepted is not a problem it's actually getting onto the payroll and teaching that takes time. It was three months before I got on a two week training course where I was promised €150 a week. In fact I received this money in December – two months after I'd done the course and five months after the initial interview. So it is best to have plenty of spare cash to see you through the first six months of finding work.

Shenker was good for me because I had no formal teaching qualification and it is based around a system so all your lesson plans are provided, you simply turn up and teach the system. For this you will be paid about €13.50 an hour before tax. I get about 15 hours work a week, although they promised 20. But as I started working for them during the financial crisis their student numbers were considerably down.

They do offer 30 hour-a-week contracts but at a much reduced rate of pay. This will suit some people as it means you can stay in the country if you have a work contract. However, the pay is truly abysmal and you have to do the 30 hours a week, which can often involve split shifts including working till 8.30pm every evening and Saturday mornings. Plus these contracts only run from September to July so you don't get paid in August.

The upside to teaching is that the Italians working in the schools are great on the whole. Everyone knows that the system is bad and tries to help each other through it. The students are also great and if you have a class you get to know, teaching can be really fun. It's a good way to get to know people and the Italians are by and large extremely friendly and always willing to help you out if they can. It also gives you a sense of belonging and really getting involved.

Melanie Drake has had much better luck in Bari, as she reported in 2010:

Italy has been a very positive experience for the most part, though living in the south without knowing the language can be quite problematic! It is really pretty easy to get work in Italy once TEFL-qualified, as the English level here is low (in the south especially). Money isn't fantastic but it balances out as life is fairly cheap, particularly if like me, you can walk to work. Often accommodation is included with the contracts offered too. Ironically I am earning half of what I got in London, though here I can save fairly easily as my outgoings are halved. It works out pretty well.

Scouring adverts in English language newspapers has worked for some. The fortnightly publication *Wanted in Rome* (www.wantedinrome.com) is very useful (particularly in the spring) and also the

Italian-language classified ads paper *Porta Portese*. (If you happen to see a request for 'mothers only', this means that they are looking for someone whose mother tongue is English not a female with small children.) Other publications with useful classifieds include *The Florentine* and *Easy Milano*.

FREELANCE TEACHING

Another possibility is to set up as a freelance tutor, though a knowledge of Italian is even more of an asset here than it is for jobs in schools. A participant on a *Guardian* web forum on ELT careers wrote in an encouraging vein for older job-seekers (April 2010):

> *I'm a career changer in my mid-50s and have had no problems here in Italy. I don't teach in language schools but contract direct with local state schools, libraries and private students, but that is based on having had means of support until I developed the requisite contacts.*

Alex Neuman is another teacher in middle life who has found Italy and Bergamo in particular a welcoming place. She has been supplementing her hours at local academies with private students:

> *Italians are desperate to speak English so getting private students isn't that hard. The best students I have got are through word of mouth. A very friendly neighbour is always recommending me to friends and colleagues and I have managed to find myself three or four that keep me busy. I got my very first student by putting up a notice on the university notice board in Bergamo but have never had to do more than that. When writing an ad for private students you must always use the words 'mother-tongue speaker' – even though 'native English speaker' is more correct English! Rates for private students vary between €15 and €25 an hour.*

You can post notices in supermarkets, tobacconists, primary and secondary schools, etc. In Rome, the noticeboard at International House's training centre (Accademia Britannica, Viale Manzoni 22, 00185 Rome) displays requests for teachers. Also in Rome, check out the noticeboards at English language bookshops such as the Lion Bookshop in Via dei Greci and the Economy Bookshop on Via Torino, or frequent the right pubs such as Ned Kelly's near Palazzo Valdassini and Miscellanea near the Pantheon. The noticeboard at the English language Paperback Exchange in Florence can also be explored.

Most cities have an *Informagiovani* or Youth Information Centre, for example the one at Vicolo Santa Maria Maggiore 1 in Florence, which may be able to supply information about teaching work or where to search. Listings of private language schools are often kept and provided on request by local tourist offices in Italy. University students looking for private tuition might consult university noticeboards such as the one at the Citta Universitaria in Rome, main campus of the Sapienza University of Rome.

Porta Portese is also a good forum in which to advertise your availability to offer English lessons in Rome; adverts placed by women should not betray their gender and meetings with prospective clients should not take place in private homes. It cost **Dustie Hickey** about £15 to advertise in four editions of the free paper in Rimini. As long as you have access to some premises, you can try to arrange both individual and group lessons. Whatever way you decide to look for work, remember that life grinds to a halt in August, just as in France. Competition is keenest in Florence and Venice which are both saturated, so new arrivals should head elsewhere including Rome. **Peter Penn** recommends Trieste, where he was offered two jobs with no experience.

> *Freelance teaching can be very lucrative and you can expect to make around €20 an hour, which is still undercutting most of the language schools (which charge around €26 per hour and take over half themselves).*

Universities throughout Italy employ foreigners as *lettori* (readers/lecturers), who teach English as well as other subjects such as business and science in English. For decades they have been locked in a dispute with Italian universities over pay and conditions, since they are assigned to a low employment grade and paid less than their Italian counterparts. There are probably around 1,000 *lettori* on yearly contracts (maximum three years) earning about the same as EFL teachers in private institutes.

SUMMER WORK

Paid work is available at a number of summer camps offering English instruction, a good opportunity for young people to spend a summer in Italy and learn more about teaching English to young learners. This opportunity is open to non-European nationalities, since the work period is so short. Some teacher training is often provided by the schools and companies that run these camp programmes. Some of these teaching programmes are listed on the website www.teachingenglishinitaly.com. Most of these companies pay about €200 a week (less for city day camps). Successful summer teachers are often offered contracts for the academic year.

See entries at the end of this chapter for ACLE, Lingue Senza Frontiere (also based in San Remo, but unrelated) and International House in Campobasso. Other summer employers include:

Kid's World (s.charlesworth@kidsworld.it; www.kidsworld.it). Runs residential summer camps from June to August, located 3 hours from Rome. Applicants should be dynamic, out-going and have experience working with children. Wages, board, lodging and training offered to successful applicants.

Berlitz Italy (louise.thorne@berlitz.it or summercamps@berlitz.it; www.berlitz.it). Candidates must be native English speakers and experienced with children to work at camp in Tuscany. 2-week minimum stay in June/July.

Kids in the World (danila.monaco@kidsintheworld.it; www.kidsintheworld.it). This company takes on motivated young actors, teachers, musicians and artists to join a team that operates English language weeks at summer centres in Capena, Rignano Flaminio and Riano. Programme operates in June, July and September. Staff must be native English speakers (or have passed a Cambridge Advanced or Proficiency exam) and have some experience teaching children. Training provided.

Smile, Modena (www.smilemodena.com) employs summer tutors to mount English language productions with groups of children. Summer staff are chosen after auditioning, including in London in October.

Scotia Personnel, 6045 Cherry St, Halifax, Nova Scotia B3H 2K4, Canada (902 422 1455; info@scotia-personnel-ltd.com; www.scotia-personnel-ltd.com/teaching_english_Italy.htm). This North American agency runs an organised scheme whereby young North Americans are recruited to work on language and sports camps in Italy in exchange for pocket money.

REGULATIONS

The bureaucratic procedures for EU nationals are fairly straightforward and teachers don't need a work permit or a residence permit, although the latter can be helpful for long-stayers. To obtain one teachers must take their passport and other papers (including a declaration of residence/consular declaration from your country's consulate in Italy) to the local *Questura* (police department) to obtain a *permesso di soggiorno* (residence permit).

PHILIP LEE from New Zealand wanted to spend his summers working in Europe. After a successful camp job in Switzerland, his attention turned to Italy. Although he didn't have direct experience of teaching English as a foreign language, he had worked with children and given tuition and revision classes. Here he describes the highs and lows of the job:

I searched online for work over the summer in Italy. There were a lot of random jobs that didn't really lead to anything and a lot of misleading job adverts. However I found some English teaching websites that were credible and I applied. After completing a written application on my background and experience in teaching, working with children and art/drama/games/sport and providing references, I was hired by Lingua Senza Frontieres. I taught English through various indoor and outdoor activities. About 90% of my time was spent playing a game/sport or completing an activity that was explained and conducted in English and there was very limited traditional 'classroom' teaching. The focus was to do as much as possible in English, including the instructions for each activity. Depending on the children's age and their familiarity with English, it was possible by using simpler words, shorter sentences and demonstrating my instructions at the same time. Teaching was very physical: I spent most of my day - about five hours of teaching and two of supervision – standing. Because a lot of the children were not very familiar/comfortable with English I had to be very energetic, positive and supportive throughout the day to keep them encouraged.

Lunch was up to two hours long and we were always treated to a good and big Italian lunch. Most schools were happy to cater to special diets as long as they were given prior notice. I stayed with the most hospitable and generous families, most of whom lived by the seaside. While living with the host families, who often had children in the camp as well, I was given my own room and sometimes my own bathroom. The families were very accommodating and understood that non-Italians did do some things differently, such as eating more than one biscuit for breakfast. They also understood that I wanted to experience as much of Italy as possible and took me out on numerous occasions. We went to vineyards, restaurants, farms, relatives' houses, shops, the beach, holiday homes, bars and clubs with the older host brothers and sisters, the pool, concerts and neighbouring towns and cities. They were also quite happy when I went out to socialise at night.

The wages are not high, however I considered the English camp as a working holiday and was not aiming to leave with many savings. The biggest problem was the language difficulties with the children and at the schools. This was because it was uncommon for any of the tutors to speak much Italian. Any tutor who spoke Italian was instructed not to make this known so that the children would not take advantage of it. The difficulty in communication made our job harder, but arguably it gave the children a better learning experience. The training sessions that the camp organisation provides are really vital and it would have been a great benefit if I had written down all the ideas for games and activities for future reference.

There were a few behavioural problems with some children but we were not expected to deal with these. Each camp had a local Italian teacher in charge of the camp and we would tell her of any problems. If she did not handle it, we could inform our employer who would communicate directly with the school.

Altogether it was a great opportunity to meet people from all over the world as well as Italians, to spend time in Italy not as a tourist, and incredible fun working with children, as all day is spent playing games or doing activities.

As mentioned above, non-EU citizens have very little chance of getting their papers in order unless they are dual nationals or receive a firm offer of a job while they are still in their home country. According to the Italian Embassy in Washington, language teachers from the USA need a visa for *lavoro subordinato*. To qualify they must first obtain from their employer in Italy an authorisation to work issued by the Ministry of Labour or a Provincial Office of Labour (*Servizio politiche del lavoro*) plus an authorisation from the local *Questura*. The originals of these plus a passport and one photo must be sent to the applicant's nearest embassy or consulate. These procedures can take up to a year to complete and as **Carla Valentine**, an English teacher in Venice points out, 'no school director in his right mind is going to bother going through that process when there are plenty of British teachers here who can work without visa red tape'. It is for this reason that so many Americans and other non-EU citizens work in Italy without work visas. However, there are two legal alternatives for US citizens. The first is to go to Italy as a student, which allows you to work for up to 20 hours a week (enough to live on). This is the route that Carla took:

> *Getting a student visa is very easy. I paid $500 to enrol for a year at Instituto Venezia to learn Italian. With a letter of enrolment from the school I was able to get a student visa from the Italian Consulate in Boston for one year (whether or not I attend class is irrelevant, although obviously I do).*

The second option is to become an independent contractor. This involves getting a tax code number (*partita IVA*) from the local town government which you have to do once you are earning more than €5,000. To get this number, you need a *codice fiscale* (similar to a social security number), which is available from the local town hall upon presentation of a passport or may also be obtainable online from the Agenzia delle Entrate (Revenue Agency). With this number it is possible to obtain the *partita IVA* from the municipal authorities, though it will probably be necessary to use the services of an accountant. With these numbers you can find work and get paid, even though technically without a *permesso di soggiorno* you are still an illegal immigrant. Australians and New Zealanders can take advantage of working holiday schemes, which allow a 12-month stay, although holders are not meant to work for more than three months.

Tax is a further headache for long-stay teachers. As soon as you sort out the work documents, you should obtain a tax number (*codice fiscale*). The rate of income tax (*Ritenuta d'Acconto*) is usually about 23% in addition to social security deductions of 8–9%.

CONDITIONS OF WORK

A typical salary for a full-time timetable would be about €1,200 net per month (roughly £1,000) though novice teachers sometimes earn less than €1,000. Staff on a *contratto di collaborazione* are paid by the hour, normally ranging from €12 to €18 net. Always find out if pay scales are quoted net or gross, since the two figures are so different. Take-home pay is not as high as might have been expected because of the high cost of compulsory national insurance, social security and pension contributions. Salaries tend to be substantially higher in northern Italy than in the south to compensate for the much higher cost of living. Business English, as always, can be very lucrative. Intensive Business English, based in Milan (see list of employers) offers a gross salary of between €1,700 and €3,250. However, some teachers in Rome, Milan, Bologna, etc. have had to reconcile themselves to spending up to half their salaries on rent. Even for Italians, salaries are low when compared with the cost of living.

Only professional teachers will benefit from the industry-wide agreement or *Contratto Collettivo Nazionale del Lavoro* (CCNL), which sets a high salary for a regulation 100-hour working month. Because of the high costs of legal employment, there is a lot of dubious practice in Italy and prospective teachers should try to talk to an ex-teacher before committing themselves, especially if offered a job before arrival. **Rhys Sage** was disappointed at the discrepancy between what he had been promised by a language institute in Chivasso near Torino and what he found when he arrived:

> *They had given a glowing description of the locality and of the cost of living, of the flat they were offering and of the high wages. Upon arrival, it transpired that the wages were minimal, the prices quite high and the flat shoddy. The toilet didn't work and neither did the heating. The school also wanted a sizeable deposit in advance for the first month and would then deduct from my salary for the rent. When I discovered the extent to which I'd been told a tissue of lies, I regretted going to Chivasso and left. In the end my Italian trip turned into a holiday.*

Few teachers complain about their students. Even when pupils attend English classes for social reasons (as many do in small towns with little nightlife) or are generally unmotivated, they are usually good-natured, hospitable and talkative in class. In contrast to Greece, many language school directors are British rather than local.

LEISURE TIME

Italian culture and lifestyle do not need to have their praises sung here. A large number of teachers who have gone out on short-term contracts never come back – probably a higher proportion than in any other country. While rents are high, eating out is fairly cheap and public transport is quite affordable. Women teachers should be prepared to cope with some Mediterranean machismo, particularly in the south, and may have to contend with unwanted male attention.

> *Compared to many languages, Italian is easy to learn, though courses are expensive. It may be possible to swap English lessons for Italian ones, which might lead to further freelance teaching.*

LIST OF EMPLOYERS

ALPHA BETA PICCADILLY
via Talvera/Talfergasse 1a 39100 Bolzano/Bozen
📞 +39 0471 978600
📧 marsh-hunn@alphabeta.it
💻 www.alphabeta.it

NUMBER OF TEACHERS: 10–15.
PREFERENCE OF NATIONALITY: Must have EU passport.
QUALIFICATIONS: Minimum CELTA or equivalent. DELTA plus at least 2–3 years TEFL experience preferred.
CONDITIONS OF EMPLOYMENT: 9-month contract with 18–22 contact hours per week.
SALARY: Around £1,530–£1,650 per month gross based on a British contract, depending on qualifications and experience. Standard UK income tax and social security deductions are made.

FACILITIES/SUPPORT: School has 2 flats available for teachers to share. Assistance given with work permits however these are relatively straightforward.
RECRUITMENT: Usually via www.tefl.com. Interviews are essential and are occasionally held in the UK.
CONTACT: Peter Marsh-Hunn, Director of Studies, English.

A.C.L.E. – SUMMER & CITY CAMPS
Via Roma 54, San Remo 18038
📞 0184 506070
📧 info@acle.org
💻 www.acle.org

NUMBER OF TEACHERS: 400+ for both day camps and residential camps.

PREFERENCE OF NATIONALITY: Native English speakers between 19 and 30 years of age.

QUALIFICATIONS: Minimum age 19. Must have experience working with children and the ability to teach English through the use of theatre and outdoor activities. A fun-loving personality and genuine interest in children, high moral standards and a flexible attitude to work required, preferably with some experience of living and travelling abroad.

CONDITIONS OF EMPLOYMENT: Camps start in June and run until September. Minimum of 3 weeks commitment required. The average tutor works for 4 weeks or more.

SALARY: €225 (city camp)/€275 (summer camp) per week, plus full board and accommodation. Transport between camps provided plus bonus.

FACILITIES/SUPPORT: Intensive 5/6-day introductory TEFL-TP (Teaching English to Foreign Learners through Theatre and Play) course provided for fee of €150 usually deducted from wages.

RECRUITMENT: Application online at www.acle.org.

ANDERSON HOUSE - QFG

Via Bergamo 25, 24035 Curno (BERGAMO)

✆ 035 46 30 74

✉ info@andersonhouse.it

🖥 www.andersonhouse.it, www.cambridge exams.it

AH is one of the founder members of QFG (Quality First Group, www.qfg.com) a network of 40 schools specialising in corporate language training. It is a leading centre for language testing and certifications (CAMBRIDGE, BULATS, TOEIC and TOEFL) and a translation company and is currently starting to promote management training courses such as Intercultural Awareness, TIP, DPI both for companies and trainer-training. Anderson House is a founder member of SIETAR Italia (www.sietar-italia.org).

NUMBER OF TEACHERS: 5 full-time, 5 part-time for English. 10 part-time for other languages.

PREFERENCE OF NATIONALITY: British and Irish. European passport essential.

QUALIFICATIONS: Degree plus CELTA (minimum grade B) TESOL, DELTA or CertIBET (Trinity's Certificate in International Business Training) and minimum 2 years' experience.

CONDITIONS OF EMPLOYMENT: Minimum age 25. Couples with car a bonus. Contracts from October to June (8/9 months) or from January for 5 months. All contracts renewable. To work 25 hours per week, 8am–10pm (one period of the day free). Some Saturday morning work; some summer work (June, July, September).

SALARY: €1,200 net for qualified teachers with 2 years' experience. Salary negotiable for those with more experience.

FACILITIES/SUPPORT: Italian lessons at cost. 90% is company work (general and business) both on and offsite. School has 3 small company cars and helps teachers with accommodation. Excellent facilities, staff resource centre, free internet access.

RECRUITMENT: via www.tefl.com and direct application.

CONTACT: Peter Anderson, Director and Owner.

ASSOCIAZIONE ITALO BRITANNICA

Via XX Settembre 2/37, 16121 Genoa

✆ +39 010 591605

✉ mzacco@italobritannica.it

🖥 www.italobritanncia.it

NUMBER OF TEACHERS: Approximately 15.

PREFERENCE OF NATIONALITY: None.

QUALIFICATIONS: Degree and CELTA or equivalent.

CONDITIONS OF EMPLOYMENT: Teachers are freelancers with approximately 12–15 hours work per week.

SALARY: €14 per hour net, VAT is paid by the school.

FACILITIES/SUPPORT: Help may be given to find accommodation.

RECRUITMENT: Interviews may be held in London but preferably in Genoa.

CONTACT: Marina Zacco, Director.

BENEDICT SCHOOL

C. so Alberto Pio 68, 41012 Carpi (MO)

✆ 059 695921

✉ info@benedict-carpi.it

🖥 www.benedict-carpi.it/job.asp

NUMBER OF TEACHERS: 10.

PREFERENCE OF NATIONALITY: British or American.

QUALIFICATIONS: Minimum TEFL (CELTA or equivalent certification).

CONDITIONS OF EMPLOYMENT: Mid-September until mid-July. Minimum 90 hours per month guaranteed (average 120 hours). 80% of work is with companies; 20% with private students.

SALARY: To be discussed at interview.

FACILITIES/SUPPORT: Accommodation provided by school. Assist non-EU and EU teachers with permits.

RECRUITMENT: Internet and recruitment agency.

BRITISH INSTITUTES – NEW SCHOOL

Via de Ambrosis 21, 15067 Novi Ligure (AL)

0143 2987

noviligure@britishinstitutes.it

www.newschool.it

NUMBER OF TEACHERS: 8.

PREFERENCE OF NATIONALITY: British, American.

QUALIFICATIONS: TEFL Diploma/degree plus 1 year's experience.

CONDITIONS OF EMPLOYMENT: 9 months, renewable. Average of 25 hours per week.

SALARY: €11 per hour net.

RECRUITMENT: Via www.tefl.com.

CONTACT: Daniela Oddone, Director.

BRITISH LANGUAGE SERVICES/LINGUAVIVA

Via C. De Cristoforis 15, 20124 Milan

+39 02 659 6401

segreteria@linguaviva.net

www.linguaviva.net/job.htm

NUMBER OF TEACHERS: 20–25.

PREFERENCE OF NATIONALITY: British and Irish (EU only).

QUALIFICATIONS: Minimum CELTA or equivalent, degree plus some experience. Must be dynamic.

CONDITIONS OF EMPLOYMENT: October to June/July. 15–25 hours per week.

SALARY: Freelance based plus benefits.

FACILITIES/SUPPORT: Teachers can stay in a residence sharing with another teacher for the first month or the whole period.

RECRUITMENT: Adverts followed by personal interviews in Milan or London. Send full CV with photo and e-mail addresses of 2 referees.

BRITISH s.r.l.

Via XX Settembre 12, 16121 Genoa

010 593591

britishsrl@libero.it or britishgenova@libero.it

www.britishgenova.it

NUMBER OF TEACHERS: 12.

PREFERENCE OF NATIONALITY: EU, American, Australian and Canadian.

QUALIFICATIONS: Bachelor's degree plus CELTA and some experience.

CONDITIONS OF EMPLOYMENT: 25+ hours per week between mid-September and mid-June.

SALARY: Variable according to hours worked.

FACILITIES/SUPPORT: Assistance given with accommodation, teaching materials and course programming.

RECRUITMENT: Interviews essential, usually take place in Italy or by phone.

CALEDONIAN COMMUNICATIONS

Viale Vigliani 55, 20148 Milan

02 4802 0486/1086

info@caledonian.it

www.caledonian.it.

NUMBER OF TEACHERS: 15–35, depending on time of year.

PREFERENCE OF NATIONALITY: EU citizens or others with permits already. British nationals can be hired on UK contract and given help to find accommodation. First 2 weeks are provided free and in some cases up to 1 month.

QUALIFICATIONS: Degree (preferably in a business subject) followed by TEFL qualification.

CONDITIONS OF EMPLOYMENT: 4–12 months, renewable. 40 hours per week, split up into maximum 30 contact hours and the rest didactic and travelling to clients.

SALARY: Choice of UK (if you are British) or Italian contract. UK contract pays between £725 and £1,100 monthly depending on age and experience, plus benefits including tax-free daily living allowance of £10, one return flight to UK per year, 2 days paid leave for every month worked plus Italian public holidays and statutory sick pay. To qualify you must have a UK bank account. Italian contract starts at €1,800 per month with no benefits or accommodation. Deductions on UK contract vary according to amount earned, can be tax-free initially. Deductions on Italian contract: 24%–39%.

RECRUITMENT: Word of mouth, newspapers, magazines, internet and CVs sent on spec.

CONTACT: Maria McCarthy, Managing Director (maria@caledonian.it).

CLM-BELL

Via Pozzo 30, 38100 Trento

0461 981733

clm-bell@clm-bell.it

www.clm-bell.it

NUMBER OF TEACHERS: 25 approximately.

PREFERENCE OF NATIONALITY: Native English speakers.

QUALIFICATIONS: Minimum 2 years' experience with CELTA/DELTA qualification.

CONDITIONS OF EMPLOYMENT: 9-month contracts. To work 22 hours per week, can be extended.

SALARY: From £900 to £1,100 per month.

FACILITIES/SUPPORT: Shared or single subsidised accommodation on a limited basis. Help provided with work permits.

RECRUITMENT: Via TEFL.com or direct applications. Interview required.

CONTACT: Ivana Ferrari, Centre Manager.

DARBY SCHOOL OF LANGUAGES – ROME – MILAN
Via Mosca 51, Villino 14, 00142 Rome
℃ 06 51962205
✉ darby@darbyschool.it
🖥 www.darbyschool.it
Also: Via Concordia, 6 San Donato Milanese-Milano
Skype: 'darby school of languages rome'

NUMBER OF TEACHERS: 40–50.

PREFERENCE OF NATIONALITY: None, but must be native English speaker.

QUALIFICATIONS: TEFL certificate CELTA.

CONDITIONS OF EMPLOYMENT: Freelance. Teachers for both Roma and Milan can choose their hours which usually are an average of 20–25 hours per week. More hours available if wanted.

SALARY: The average salary of about €1,400 is sufficient and more to live on in Italy.

FACILITIES/SUPPORT: New teachers are helped to find accommodation.

RECRUITMENT: Relevant CVs and interviews.

CONTACT: Gilda Darby.

ENGLISH ACADEMY Sas
Via Carlo Zucchi 64, 41100 Modena
✉ callan@englishacademy.it
🖥 www.englishacademy.it/insegnanti.php

QUALIFICATIONS: No special teaching certification necessary as teachers are trained in the Callan Method.

CONDITIONS OF EMPLOYMENT: No lesson preparation necessary; no homework to be set or corrected; all lessons last 50 minutes; small groups of mainly adults (maximum 6 per group).

FACILITIES/SUPPORT: Full training given. Assistance given with finding accommodation.

CONTACT: Mr M T Di Salvo, Director of Studies.

THE ENGLISH CAMP COMPANY LLC
Via Della Madonna Delle Grazie, Santa Maria Delgi Angeli, Assisi (PG) 06081
℃ +39 075 8041 402
✉ info@theenglishcampcompany.com
🖥 www.theenglishcampcompany.com

NUMBER OF TEACHERS: 8–15.

PREFERENCE OF NATIONALITY: None.

QUALIFICATIONS: Previous teaching experience or experience working at summer camps with children.

CONDITIONS OF EMPLOYMENT: 2 month contract. Working hours 9am–5pm.

SALARY: €175 per week.

FACILITIES/SUPPORT: All teachers are housed with host families.

CONTACT: Ashleigh McLean and Nathanial Poerio, Founders and Directors.

THE ENGLISH CONVERSATION CLUB
Via XX Settembre 26/09, 16121 Genova
℃ +39 010540964
✉ enquiry@thetrainingcompany.org
🖥 www.thetrainingcompany.org

NUMBER OF TEACHERS: 12.

PREFERENCE OF NATIONALITY: None.

QUALIFICATIONS: CELTA/DELTA or equivalent. Online certificates are not acceptable.

CONDITIONS OF EMPLOYMENT: 10-month contract. 100 working hours per month.

SALARY: €1,100–€1,300 per month net.

FACILITIES/SUPPORT: Assistance given to find accommodation prior to arrival.

RECRUITMENT: Usually via the internet. Interviews are essential and can be carried out over the phone or occasionally in the UK.

CONTACT: Stephen Murrell, Director.

IIK ANCONA SCUOLA DI LINGUE
Scalo Vittorio Emanuele II, 1, 60121 Ancona
℃ 071 206610
✉ info@iik.it
🖥 www.iik.it

NUMBER OF TEACHERS: 5–6.

PREFERENCE OF NATIONALITY: British preferred; EU nationals.

QUALIFICATIONS: Minimum 3 years' teaching experience and TEFL/TESOL certificate. (Taster weekend courses and distance learning courses without observed and assessed teaching practice will not be considered.)

CONDITIONS OF EMPLOYMENT: Generally from September until end of June. Guaranteed minimum 25 hours per week. Teaching takes place between 8.45am and 9pm.

SALARY: €10 net per hour.

FACILITIES/SUPPORT: Assistance given with finding accommodation but teacher responsible for paying rent. School advises EU teachers on getting residence permit, fiscal code and enrolling in health services.

RECRUITMENT: Direct contact and www.tefl.com.

CONTACT: Maria Margherita Gargiulo, Director of Studies.

INTENSIVE BUSINESS ENGLISH

Via Colautti, 1 20125 Milan

☎ 02 69002017

✉ info@ibeschool.com

🖥 www.ibeschool.com

NUMBER OF TEACHERS: 40.

PREFERENCE OF NATIONALITY: British, Irish, Australian, New Zealander.

QUALIFICATIONS: Minimum 3 years' experience and relevant certificate/qualification.

CONDITIONS OF EMPLOYMENT: 12-month contract. Usual hours are 9am–7pm, Monday to Friday.

SALARY: Between €1,700 and €3,250 gross depending on type of contract and experience. 20–30% deductions for taxes.

FACILITIES/SUPPORT: Accommodation in flats owned by the school at very low rates.

RECRUITMENT: By the internet, advertising in local magazines and through the teacher network in Milan. Interviews essential.

CONTACT: Gordon Doyle, Director of Studies.

INTERNATIONAL CLUB

P.le A. Moro, 6, 20034 Giussano (MB)

☎ +39 0362 354057

✉ info@internationalclub.it

🖥 www.internationalclub.it

NUMBER OF TEACHERS: 35.

PREFERENCE OF NATIONALITY: British, Irish, or any other native English speaker in possession of EU citizenship.

QUALIFICATIONS: For adult classes, CELTA/TESOL or any other TEFL qualification. At least 1 year's experience with teaching groups at all levels. For children's classes, any qualification for teaching children (not necessarily as an EFL teacher) and experience with teaching children. Must have a driving licence.

CONDITIONS OF EMPLOYMENT: Standard contract is 9 months or longer. Permanent teachers welcome. Sometimes teachers are employed shorter term and summer contracts from June to July are offered. Teachers work average of 25 hours per week.

SALARY: €12 net per hour/€1,200 net per month.

FACILITIES/SUPPORT: Accommodation in flats owned by the school at very low rates.

RECRUITMENT: By direct contact or recruitment agencies. Interviews can be carried out on the phone or by internet. Occasionally interviews arranged in the UK or USA during the summer.

CONTACT: Mary Sposari, Director of Studies.

INTERNATIONAL HOUSE (CAMPOBASSO) ITALY

Via Zurlo 5, 86100 Campobasso

☎ 0874 481321

✉ mary@ihcampobasso.it

NUMBER OF TEACHERS: 20 for summer camp in Italy.

PREFERENCE OF NATIONALITY: British/American.

QUALIFICATIONS: CELTA qualification and experience teaching children and teenagers essential.

CONDITIONS OF EMPLOYMENT: Contract 2/4 or 6 weeks from end of June to August. 6 hours teaching per day. Pupils aged 8–16.

SALARY: Approximately €650 per shift.

FACILITIES/SUPPORT: Accommodation and all meals provided.

RECRUITMENT: Direct application.

CONTACT: Mary Ricciardi.

INTERNATIONAL HOUSE (PALERMO)

Via Quintino Sella 70, 90139 Palermo

☎ 091 584954

✉ ihpa1@ihpalermo.it

🖥 www.ihpalermo.it

NUMBER OF TEACHERS: 8 plus 1 Director of Studies and 1 Children Coordinator.

PREFERENCE OF NATIONALITY: British; others considered (only European passport).

QUALIFICATIONS: Degree and CELTA (minimum grade 'B'). School interested in career teachers only.

CONDITIONS OF EMPLOYMENT: 8-month contracts. 25 hours per week, usually 1pm–9.30pm.

SALARY: From €1,200 plus increments.

FACILITIES/SUPPORT: Assistance with finding accommodation (rent €350–€400 per month). Weekly seminars and workshops. School will subsidise in-service diploma course by distance learning for suitable candidates. Italian survival lessons. CELTA courses offered in June every year.

RECRUITMENT: Via IH London or directly. Interviews essential.

INTFLEX SRL – BRITISH LECCO
Via F.lli Cairoli 9 (Isolago), 23900 Lecco
0341 369383
info@intflex.com
www.britishlecco.it

NUMBER OF TEACHERS: 12.

PREFERENCE OF NATIONALITY: European.

QUALIFICATIONS: TEFL or TESOL diploma.

CONDITIONS OF EMPLOYMENT: October to May, 25 hours per week.

SALARY: Varies with experience.

FACILITIES/SUPPORT: Flats available for teachers' use.

RECRUITMENT: Via internet (www.tefl.com, etc.).

LANGUAGES INTERNATIONAL SRL
Via Macaggi 23/13, 16121 Genoa
+39 010 595 8889
robertson@languagesinternational.it
www.languagesinternational.it

NUMBER OF TEACHERS: 35–70 (depending on the time of year) in 3 schools around Italy.

PREFERENCE OF NATIONALITY: Native English speakers.

QUALIFICATIONS: Minimum 2 years' teaching experience, university degree and TEFL/TESOL certificate.

CONDITIONS OF EMPLOYMENT: Between 24 and 34 working hours per week, depending on which city the teacher is based in and their flexibility.

FACILITIES/SUPPORT: Assistance is given with accommodation, i.e. appointments to visit rooms are set up.

RECRUITMENT: Usually via the internet or word of mouth. Interviews are carried out over the phone if the candidate is not in Rome, Milan or Genoa.

CONTACT: Millica Robertson, Director of Studies.

LINGUE SENZA FRONTIERE
Corso Inglesi 172, 18038 – Sanremo (IM)
+39 0184 533661
Christina@linguesenzafrontiere.org
www.lingasenzafrontiere.org

NUMBER OF TEACHERS: Approximately 150 per summer.

PREFERENCE OF NATIONALITY: Native English speaker.

QUALIFICATIONS: TEFL certificate or equivalent and/or relevant experience. Must have a genuine interest in working with children. Italian is not required but is useful.

CONDITIONS OF EMPLOYMENT: 2-week contract plus a free 4-day training course, which is compulsory. Working hours are 8.45am–4.15pm, Monday to Friday.

SALARY: €450 net per 2-week camp.

FACILITIES/SUPPORT: Accommodation is provided from beginning to end of contract. During the training period accommodation is in shared rooms, then with an Italian host family during the camp.

CONTACT: Christina Niknejad, Tutor Coordinator.

LIVING LANGUAGES SCHOOL
Via Magna Grecia 2, 89100 Reggio Calabria
Also: via Madonna, 21 Gallico, 89100 Reggio Calabria
info@livinglanguages.it
www.livinglanguages.it

NUMBER OF TEACHERS: 8.

PREFERENCE OF NATIONALITY: Native English speakers.

QUALIFICATIONS: TEFL, CELTA.

CONDITIONS OF EMPLOYMENT: 9-month renewable contracts. British contract. Teaching hours 3pm–9pm, Monday to Friday.

SALARY: Approx. €826 (net) per month for an inexperienced teacher.

FACILITIES/SUPPORT: Help given with accommodation.

RECRUITMENT: Via adverts. Interviews sometimes carried out in UK.

LONDON SCHOOL
Corso Rosmini, 66, 38068 Rovereto (TN)
info@londonschoolroverto.it
www.londonschoolroverto.it

NUMBER OF TEACHERS: 4–5.

PREFERENCE OF NATIONALITY: British.

QUALIFICATIONS: Degree, and excellent command of English language. Pronunciation and grammar must be perfect. Teachers who also speak Italian are preferred. For summer work, training or experience in teaching young learners is preferred, e.g. online TESOL plus TEYL course (via www.teachingenglishinitaly.com).

CONDITIONS OF EMPLOYMENT: 1-year contract which may be renewed. 20–25 working hours per week. Summer vacancies are also available at children's courses held between mid-June and mid-August at the BluHotel in Folgaria in the mountains of northern Italy. Summer teachers work between 2 and 9 weeks.

SALARY: €12–€15 per hour. Summer teachers earn €300 (net) a week in addition to full board and hotel accommodation; wages are paid at the end of the contract.

FACILITIES/SUPPORT: help is given to find accommodation. Work permits are taken care of by the school's accountant.

RECRUITMENT: References, detailed CV and interviews essential.

CONTACT: Gordana Marjanovic, Owner.

LORD BYRON COLLEGE
Via Sparano 102, 70121 Bari
080 523 2686
johncredico@lordbyroncollege.com
www.lordbyroncollege.com

One of the largest independent language schools in Italy, with 38 years' experience and an annual attendance of 1,500 students of all levels and ages. Authorised by the Italian Ministry of Education and member of EAQUALS (European Association for Quality Language Services).

NUMBER OF TEACHERS: 30 full-time, 30 part-time.

PREFERENCE OF NATIONALITY: British; Canadian, American and Australian applicants can be considered only if they have dual European citizenship.

QUALIFICATIONS: Degree, TEFL qualification, at least 1 year's teaching experience and knowledge of a foreign language.

CONDITIONS OF EMPLOYMENT: UK contracts for 8 months from October to June or 5 months from January, renewable. National insurance and pension coverage. 27.5 hours per week including paid training and development hours. Students of all ages and levels. Salary and conditions: starting salary from €900 net per month. Paid orientation week. 5 weeks' paid holiday.

FACILITIES/SUPPORT: Free in-house DELTA course for teachers with minimum 1,200 hours' teaching experience. Teacher training and development programme for all teaching staff. Large self-access centre with video club, cinema, large TEFL resource centre and library and staff internet access. Participation in school's film dubbing and voiceover programme. Free Italian course. Assistance finding accommodation.

RECRUITMENT: Online application form in the Teaching Opportunities section of the website can be submitted by e-mail or post with full CV, recent photograph, names and e-mail addresses of two teaching-related references, copies of degree, TEFL qualification and EU passport. Interviews and hiring in June for October start and in December for January.

CONTACT: John Credico, Director of Studies (johncredico@lordbyroncollege.com).

MAC LANGUAGE SCHOOL
Via Alessandro Cruto,8 00146 Roma
+39 0683664460
hr@maclanguage.biz
www.maclanguage.biz

NUMBER OF TEACHERS: 57.

PREFERENCE OF NATIONALITY: None if native English speaker.

QUALIFICATIONS: 3 years' experience or certified teachers.

CONDITIONS OF EMPLOYMENT: 4–8 hours per day.

FACILITIES/SUPPORT: None.

RECRUITMENT: Internet, newspapers, other. Interviews essential. Sometimes phone interviews can be arranged.

CONTACT: Carmen Lora, Director of Studies.

MADRELINGUA SCHOOL OF ENGLISH
Via San Giorgio, 6–40121 Bologna
051 267 822
info@madrelinguabologna.com
www.madrelinguabologna.com

NUMBER OF TEACHERS: Around 10.

PREFERENCE OF NATIONALITY: None, but must be eligible to work legally in Italy.

QUALIFICATIONS: Degree plus CELTA (or equivalent) essential, YL qualification and/or DELTA preferred. The school contributes to course fees for staff wishing to do the DELTA or CELTYL.

CONDITIONS OF EMPLOYMENT: Academic year is October to June. Teachers work evenings and Saturday mornings. Some permanent positions available.

SALARY: Depending on experience but above average for the local market. Minimum €20 an hour gross. Taxes are around 20%.

FACILITIES/SUPPORT: The school can arrange a 'homestay' on a temporary basis. English teachers may take subsidised Italian language courses.

RECRUITMENT: Speculative CVs.

CONTACT: Daniel Stephens, Director.

NUMBER OF TEACHERS: 15–20.
PREFERENCE OF NATIONALITY: EU only.
QUALIFICATIONS: Degree in early children/early years education or psychology.
CONDITIONS OF EMPLOYMENT: 10 months. 36 hours per week.
SALARY: €1,000–€1,300 net per month.
FACILITIES/SUPPORT: No help with accommodation or visas.
RECRUITMENT: Interviews essential, can be by phone or Skype.
CONTACT: Antonella Manuli, Head of Recruitment.

NUMBER OF TEACHERS: 10.
PREFERENCE OF NATIONALITY: European passport, native English speaker.
QUALIFICATIONS: CELTA plus 2 years' experience.
CONDITIONS OF EMPLOYMENT: 8-month contracts, October to May; 25 hours per week.
SALARY: Approx €1,000 (net).
FACILITIES/SUPPORT: Accommodation provided. Help given with obtaining all necessary documents. Training available.
CONTACT: Massimo Sponsiello.

NUMBER OF TEACHERS: 20–30 for 13 schools in northeast Italy; most are independent franchises (60–70 teachers employed altogether).
PREFERENCE OF NATIONALITY: British.

QUALIFICATIONS: Degree, TEFL and knowledge of Italian needed. Candidates must be holders of an EU passport.
CONDITIONS OF EMPLOYMENT: 9-month contracts or longer, 22 hours per week.
SALARY: Varies according to hours and length of contract. Tax deductions of about 23% give minimum health and welfare cover.
FACILITIES/SUPPORT: Accommodation at teacher's own expense, but school will help to find it.
RECRUITMENT: Interviews in London from mid-May or in Italy.
CONTACT: Philip Panter, Administrator.

NUMBER OF TEACHERS: 7.
PREFERENCE OF NATIONALITY: Native English speakers with an EU passport.
QUALIFICATIONS: Preferably 2 years' experience but not essential. However, a degree and CELTA or TESOL certificate are required.
CONDITIONS OF EMPLOYMENT: Usually 8 months, October to the end of May. 4-month contracts also offered (January to May).
SALARY: €1,100 guaranteed base salary per month.
FACILITIES/SUPPORT: Modern school offering training to become an official Cambridge ESOL oral examiner. Perks include internet, a large range of resources and a return flight to the UK at the end of the contract term and holidays are fully paid. The school will also help teachers find fully furnished accommodation, arrange tax file numbers and medical visits.
RECRUITMENT: Direct. Telephone interviews possible.
CONTACT: Teresa Matteucci, quagi@quagi.org.

NUMBER OF TEACHERS: 10.
PREFERENCE OF NATIONALITY: British (work contracts for non-Europeans much more difficult to arrange).
QUALIFICATIONS: Degree plus Trinity or Cambridge certificate, plus 1 year's experience. Basic knowledge of Italian preferable.

CONDITIONS OF EMPLOYMENT: Mid-September to mid-June. Hours between 3pm and 9pm.

SALARY: Approximately £850 per month (depending on experience).

FACILITIES/SUPPORT: Accommodation arranged and paid for and school car available.

RECRUITMENT: Through www.tefl.com.

CONTACT: Carolyn Davies, Director of Studies.

WALL STREET INSTITUTE – LUCKY LION SCHOOL SRL
Via Libertà 191 c/d/e, Palermo
+39 91 9865100
palermo@wallstreet.it
www.wallstreet.it

NUMBER OF TEACHERS: 4.

PREFERENCE OF NATIONALITY: None.

QUALIFICATIONS: Native English speakers with CELTA or equivalent.

CONDITIONS OF EMPLOYMENT: Contracts are generally less than 1 year but are renewable. Approximately 25 hours per week depending on the time of year.

FACILITIES/SUPPORT: Help provided to find private accommodation.

RECRUITMENT: Face-to-face interview and demonstration lesson essential.

CONTACT: Jacqueline Louise Scott, Service Manager.

WINDSOR SCHOOL OF ENGLISH
Via Molino delle Lime 4/F, 10064 Pinerolo (TO)
0348 3914155
windsor@vds.it
www.windsorpinerolo.it

NUMBER OF TEACHERS: 6–9.

PREFERENCE OF NATIONALITY: British or EU applicants only.

QUALIFICATIONS: Minimum Certificate in TEFL, experience of teaching Military English.

CONDITIONS OF EMPLOYMENT: 9–10 months (October to June).

SALARY: About €1,000 net per month.

CONTACT: Sandro Vazon Colla, Director.

PORTUGAL

As one of the weaker economies in the Eurozone, Portugal has been struggling with the recession. Although its situation is not nearly as dire as that of Greece, unemployment is high: in 2010 it hit a record 11% in the northern region around Porto which has traditionally been the country's economic powerhouse. This means that there is less disposable income around for English courses, though plenty of leisure time if one in five under-24s does not have a job.

Yet plenty of opportunities persist especially in the teaching of young learners. Relations between Portugal and Britain have always been warm and a preference for British teachers remains strong. Most schools cater for anyone over the age of 7, so you should be prepared to teach children. The Portuguese government has been pushing for English to be taught from first grade and as a result parents are eager to start their children very young in private English classes. The enrolment for children's courses has gone up and a number of schools serve a student body that is 90% under the age of 17. Schools often find it hard to recruit teachers who have experience of teaching children and a basic knowledge of Portuguese, which is useful when teaching young children.

In fact, some schools organise courses in nursery/primary schools for children from the age of 3, sometimes as part of the Ministry of Education's 'Teaching and Understanding of the first level of basic English' programme. For example the Windsor School in Ovar, south of Porto, offers courses to 'toddlers' (www.windsorschool.ws/careerops.htm).The vast majority of British tourists flock to the Algarve along the southern coast of Portugal, which means that many Portuguese in the south who aspire to work in the tourist industry want to learn English. Schools such as the Wall Street Institute in Faro and the Centro de Línguas in Lagos cater for just that market. But the demand for English teachers is greatest in the north and central Portugal. Jobs crop up in historic centres such as Coimbra, Braga and Viseu and in small seaside towns like Aveiro and Póvoa do Varzim. These can be a very welcome destination for teachers burned out from teaching in big cities, first-time teachers who want to avoid the rat race, or teachers who simply want to secure a good wage and accommodation. The British Council (www.britishcouncil.org/portugal) has English language centres in Coimbra, Greater Lisbon and Porto, and recruits teachers with a degree, TEFL certificate and two years post-TEFL qualification EFL teaching experience (see www.britishcouncil.org/portugal-ensinar-informacao-professores.htm for information about teachers who are locally engaged rather than hired through the Council's Teacher Recruitment department in London).

FINDING A JOB

Most teachers in Portugal have either answered adverts or are working for one of the large chains. International House (www.international-house.com) has 11 affiliated schools in Portugal. Wall Street Institute (www.wsi-pt) is well represented with 33 centres.

About three-quarters of all IH students in Portugal are children, so expertise with young learners is a definite asset and IH in Lisbon and Porto offer the specialist Cambridge training courses in teaching young learners. IH and the British Council, among others, also offer 'courses to help professionals', so expertise in law/finance and business should also prove helpful when trying to secure a job.

Outside the cities where there have traditionally been large expatriate communities, schools cannot depend on English speakers just showing up and so must recruit well in advance of the academic year (late September to the end of June). The Bristol School Group (see entry) offers the only possibility of which we have heard for working in the Azores, so if you want to work in the most isolated islands in the Atlantic Ocean – more than 1,000km west of Portugal – this is your chance. Small groups of schools, say six schools in a single region, is the norm in Portugal. A number of the schools listed in the directory at the end of this chapter belong to such mini-chains. One of the most well-established is the Cambridge Schools group which every year imports up to 100 teachers.

A company that specialises in teaching children aged 3–13 is Fun Languages/Kids Club (www. kidsclub.pt) with dozens of clubs throughout the country. It is possible to submit an online application form, which is circulated round all the clubs and any with vacancies will make contact.

Many schools are small family-run establishments with fewer than 10 teachers, so sending off a lot of speculative applications is unlikely to succeed. As is true anywhere, you might be lucky and find something on the spot. The Cambridge CELTA is widely requested by schools and can be obtained at IH in Lisbon.

REGULATIONS

The red tape for EU nationals working in Portugal is refreshingly painless. All that is required (as throughout the EU) is to obtain a residence permit (*Autorizacao de Residencia*) after an initial 3-month stay by taking documents to show proof of accommodation, health insurance and means of support. If you are employed, you must show that you have been registered in the social security system and are not being paid less than the Portuguese minimum wage. These must be presented to the local authorities, i.e. any office of the Serviço de Estrangeiros e Fronteiras (SEF) or Aliens Office (regional addresses are given at www.sef.pt).

Non-EU residents will have a much more difficult time trying to work in Portugal, as **Rachel Beebe**, an American, discovered recently:

> *I was not able to obtain a work visa of any kind: I found that this is very difficult for Americans living and working in Portugal. I had to work using recibos verdes ('green receipts'), which are intended for use by temporary workers in the country. This situation prevented me from securing a contract with my school; a contract would have allowed me a more permanent position as well as vacation time and other benefits. To get a work visa, you need a work contract in hand. While my school offered me a letter of their intent to employ me, you are required to have a legal contract when applying for the visa, which can then take upwards of a year (or more) to process. In the meantime, you are only allowed to stay in the country on a 'temporary stay visa,' which will allow you to stay up to nine months from the time of your arrival in Portugal. Needless to say, this period of time will expire before you are able to obtain a work visa. After the nine months, you would be expected to leave the Schengen area (which includes most Western European countries, with the notable exception of the UK) for an equal period of time. Ostensibly, this would prevent most would-be American teachers from being able to teach long-term in Portugal. You could always try to secure a contract twelve months in advance of your planned arrival date, but I have never heard of a school hiring more than five or six months before the start date. In my case, I managed to get my hands on a book of green receipts and taught for a few months using those. However, many government offices will give you conflicting information, and I was only able to get the receipts with the help and direction of a friend who was able to tell me exactly where to go and what to say to whom.*

The other alternative is to seek employment with schools that may prefer American speakers: any school with 'American' in the title is probably a good bet. Try the American School of Languages (Av. Duque de Loule, 22–1°, 1050 090, Lisbon; 21 314 6000; www.americanschooloflanguages. com) or CAA (Centro Anglo-Americano in Chaves and Vila Real (www.caaenglish.com). The latter is a family-run school that prefers to hire EU citizens because they are cheaper, although they'd make an exception for qualified candidates (who rarely apply).

Since most teachers working for nine months are working on a freelance basis, they are responsible for paying their own taxes and contributions. There are seven income tax brackets ranging from 10.5% to 42% and an array of tax deductions, credits and special benefits. Tax laws and regulations are frequently subject to change, so it is best to check with the relevant authorities (Direcção-Geral dos Impostos, dsdsitarp@dgci.min-financas.pt).

CONDITIONS OF WORK

The consensus seems to be that wages are low, but the cost of living, at least outside the major cities, is reasonable. Imported consumer goods are taxed and expensive and the cost of domestic fuel and tolls on roads and bridges are high, but local produce such as olive oil, fruit, vegetables and wine are still relatively inexpensive. Public transport is quite cheap, as well as eating out. Working conditions are generally relaxed and students are generally helpful, as Rachel Beebe discovered:

Most students had a good attitude and tried very hard to speak the language. I spoke virtually no Portuguese in encounters or classes, and the students made every effort to use what they were learning to communicate with me.

The normal salary range is €700–€1,000 net per month. Full-time contract workers are entitled to an extra month's pay after 12 months, which is partly why most teachers are employed on 9/10 month contracts. Some schools pay lower rates but subsidise or pay for flights and accommodation. Several provide free Portuguese lessons. Teachers being paid on an hourly basis should expect to earn €10–€17, but they will of course not be eligible for the 13th month bonus or paid holidays. Rates per hour can sink as low as €6.50, which isn't enough to live on unless you can also secure free accommodation. If you are living in an urban centre, then you'll also need to factor in any unpaid travel time to find out how much you are 'really' getting paid.

LIST OF EMPLOYERS

AMERICAN SCHOOL OF LANGUAGES

22 - 1° Avenida Duque de Loulé, 1050 090 Lisbon

+351 21 314 6000/+351 96 790 7035

admin.asl@mail.telepac.pt

www.americanschooloflanguages.com

NUMBER OF TEACHERS: 5–10.

PREFERENCE OF NATIONALITY: EU citizenship is a plus but not essential.

QUALIFICATIONS: University degree, TEFL training course (preferably CELTA), EFL experience with adults preferable but not essential.

CONDITIONS OF EMPLOYMENT: Contract runs from October to June with some summer work an option. Contract is renewable for the next academic year, 21–24 working hours per week.

SALARY: €1,200–€1,600 per month with adjustments for inflation and opportunities for advancement.

FACILITIES/SUPPORT: Some assistance given to find accommodation, i.e. help making phone calls to prospective landlords, etc.

RECRUITMENT: Interviews in Lisbon are essential.

CONTACT: Suzanna Tavares, Director of Courses.

BRISTOL SCHOOLS GROUP

Bristol School – Instituto de Línguas da Maia, Trav. Dr. Carlos Pires Felgueiras, 12–3°, 4470 158 Maia

22 948 8803

bsmaia@bristolschool.pt

www.bristolschool.pt

Comprises a group of 9 small schools: 4 in Oporto area, 2 in the Azores and 3 inland (Castelo Branco, Fundão and Colvilha). Addresses on website.

NUMBER OF TEACHERS: 25.

PREFERENCE OF NATIONALITY: British only (couples preferred).

QUALIFICATIONS: Bachelor's degree and TEFL qualification. 1 year's experience essential.

CONDITIONS OF EMPLOYMENT: Minimum period of work 15 September to 30 June, 25 hours per week. Pupils aged from 8 to Proficiency level.

SALARY: Basic salary plus Christmas bonus and end-of-contract bonuses plus tax rebate. Legal contract of work.

FACILITIES/SUPPORT: Assistance with accommodation given. No training.

RECRUITMENT: Direct application preferred.

CAMBRIDGE SCHOOL
Avenida da Liberdade 173, 1250 141 Lisbon
- 21 312 4600
- info@cambridge.pt
- www.cambridge.pt

Portugal's largest private language school with 5 centres in Lisbon and one each in Porto, Coimbra and Funchal (Madeira).

NUMBER OF TEACHERS: 90–110.

PREFERENCE OF NATIONALITY: EU citizens or in possession of an EU work permit.

QUALIFICATIONS: Bachelor's degree plus CELTA, Trinity CertTESOL or an equivalent EFL qualification. Online qualifications are not acceptable. EFL experience preferred, however, newly qualified applicants may be successful.

CONDITIONS OF EMPLOYMENT: Initial contracts for 9 months from 1 October to 30 June. All contracts are for full-time positions (22 50-minute lessons a week).

COMPENSATION: In a typical month, most starting teachers (2010) will average between €1,200 and €1,300 after deductions and extras. Two bonus salaries paid per year (Christmas and summer). One month's paid summer holiday. All staff currently receive a monthly meal subsidy of €138. In addition to joining the Portuguese National Health scheme, the school employs its own medical officers. Salaries are adjusted at the beginning of October.

FACILITIES/SUPPORT: All schools have 2–3 senior staff.

RECRUITMENT: Adverts on tefl.com. Applicants should send CV, recent photograph, contact telephone number and copies of degree and EFL certificate. Interviews are usually held in London in May and possibly mid-summer depending on requirements. Visitors to Portugal can be interviewed in Lisbon by prior arrangement.

CONTACT: Jeffrey Kapke, Pedagogical Director, or Richard Nicholas, General Director of Studies.

CENTRO DE INGLES DE FAMALICAO
Edificio dos Correios, n° 116 – 4° Dto, Rua S. Joao de Deus, 4760 V.N. de Famalicao
- centroinglesfam@gmail.com

NUMBER OF TEACHERS: 4.

PREFERENCE OF NATIONALITY: EU nationals.

QUALIFICATIONS: Degree and CELTA (or equivalent) essential; experience an advantage but not essential.

CONDITIONS OF EMPLOYMENT: 9-month renewable contracts. 24 contact hours per week.

SALARY: At least €948 per month (net).

FACILITIES/SUPPORT: Fully furnished flat near school provided rent-free, sharing with other teacher(s). Help given with work permit procedures. Lessons are regularly observed and feedback given.

RECRUITMENT: Via adverts on the internet (www.tefl.com). Interviews essential, normally in London at the end of July.

CONTACT: David Mills, Director of Studies.

CIAL – CENTRO DE LINGUAS
Avenida Republica 14–2, 1050 191 Lisbon
- 213 533 733; mobile 918 500 300
- linguas.estrangeiras@cial.pt
- www.cial.pt

NUMBER OF TEACHERS: 15–17.

PREFERENCE OF NATIONALITY: EU nationals.

QUALIFICATIONS: University degree, CELTA, EFL teaching experience to adults (minimum 2 years); Business English teaching experience.

CONDITIONS OF EMPLOYMENT: Contracts October to June. Early morning, lunch-time and evening teaching hours.

SALARY: Depends on work agreement. Possibility of full-time, part-time or hourly basis. Monthly performance evaluation bonus paid as well as free Portuguese lessons and free health insurance as fringe benefits.

FACILITIES/SUPPORT: Family accommodation can be arranged for first 4 weeks if requested.

RECRUITMENT: Pre-selection through detailed CV; personal interviews compulsory.

CONTACT: Isabel Coimbra, Director (isabelcoimbra@cial.pt).

ENGLISH LANGUAGE CENTRE Cascais
Rua da Palmeira 5, 1A/B, Cascais
- 214830716/916060170
- caroline.darling@elc-cascais.com
- www.elc-cascais.com

NUMBER OF TEACHERS: 9.

PREFERENCE OF NATIONALITY: UK.

QUALIFICATIONS: CELTA and 1 year experience.

CONDITIONS OF EMPLOYMENT: 10-month renewable contract. 15–18 hours per week.

SALARY: €850 per month (for teaching a basic 15 hours per week).

FACILITIES/SUPPORT: Recruitment locally; pedagogical support – regular training workshops.

RECRUITMENT: Through tefl.com/local adverts. Face-to-face interviews essential.

CONTACT: Caroline Darling, Director.

ENGLISH SCHOOL ÉVORA

Praça da Muralha, 12 – 1° esq. 7005 248 Évora

✆ 266743231/938512574

✉ englishschoolevora@gmail.com

🖥 www.englishschoolevora.com

NUMBER OF TEACHERS: 3.

PREFERENCE OF NATIONALITY: EU nationals, native English speakers.

QUALIFICATIONS: Degree, TEFL qualification, minimum 2 years' experience.

CONDITIONS OF EMPLOYMENT: 9-month renewable contract, 23 hours plus possible overtime.

FACILITIES/SUPPORT: Some assistance with finding accommodation.

RECRUITMENT: Through the internet. Interviews are often by phone.

CONTACT: Michael W. Lewis, Director.

ILC CENTRO INTERACTIVO DE LINGUAS

Rua Mouzinho de Albuqerque 56 1° Esq., 2440 Leiria

✆ +351 244 765307

✉ Sergio.g@il-c.com.pt

🖥 www.il-c.com.pt

NUMBER OF TEACHERS: 12.

PREFERENCE OF NATIONALITY: None.

QUALIFICATIONS: Degree.

CONDITIONS OF EMPLOYMENT: Standard contract is 10 months with 25 working hours per week.

SALARY: €12 per hour.

RECRUITMENT: Interviews carried out in Portugal.

CONTACT: Sergio Gomes, Director.

INSTITUTO DE LINGUAS DE S. JOAO DA MADEIRA

Rua Durbalino Laranjeira S/N, 3700 – 108 S. João da Madeira

✆ 256 833906

✉ institutodelinguas@hotmail.com or institutodelinguas@gmail.com

NUMBER OF TEACHERS: 14 working in schools/companies outside the Institute; 5 working at the Institute.

PREFERENCE OF NATIONALITY: British.

QUALIFICATIONS: DELTA/COTE plus 2 years' experience.

CONDITIONS OF EMPLOYMENT: 9 month contracts from mid-September.

SALARY: Dependent on qualifications.

FACILITIES/SUPPORT: No help given with accommodation, work permits; training sessions, workshops, seminars at the British Council Oporto.

RECRUITMENT: Interview essential.

CONTACT: Helena Borges, Director.

INTERLEARNING CENTRE

56 Rua Capitão Mouzinho de Albuquerque, Edifício Alice, 1° andar, Leiria

✆ +351 244 830950

✉ leiria@il-c.com.pt

🖥 www.il-c.com.pt

NUMBER OF TEACHERS: 11.

PREFERENCE OF NATIONALITY: None.

QUALIFICATIONS: TEFL certificate plus some prior teaching experience is preferable.

CONDITIONS OF EMPLOYMENT: Contract runs from mid-September to end of June with 4 teaching hours per day.

FACILITIES/SUPPORT: Assistance can be given with finding accommodation and applying for work permits.

RECRUITMENT: Spontaneous CVs and interviews.

CONTACT: Linda Martins, Director of Studies.

INTERNATIONAL HOUSE (PORTO)

Porto: Rua Marechal Saldanha 145–1°, 4150 655 Porto

✆ 22 617 7641

✉ info@ihporto.org

🖥 www.ihporto.org

Matosinhos: Leça da Palmeira, Rua Oliveira Lessa 350, 4450 Matosinhos

✆ 22 995 9087

✉ business@ihporto.org

NUMBER OF TEACHERS: 10.

PREFERENCE OF NATIONALITY: British, Canadian, Australian, New Zealander and American.

QUALIFICATIONS: CELTA/Trinity.

CONDITIONS OF EMPLOYMENT: 1-year contracts, 22 hours per week, pupils aged from 7.

SALARY: Depending on qualifications and experience.

FACILITIES/SUPPORT: Assistance with accommodation. Portuguese lessons available. Training provided.

RECRUITMENT: Direct application.

CONTACT: Shawn Severson, Business Services Manager.

INTERNATIONAL LANGUAGE SCHOOL

Av. Republica Guiné-Bissau, 26 A, 2900 588 Setubal

C +351 26 522 7934

@ ils@netcabo.pt

NUMBER OF TEACHERS: 6.

PREFERENCE OF NATIONALITY: Native English speakers.

QUALIFICATIONS: CELTA or equivalent, 1 year's experience or more.

CONDITIONS OF EMPLOYMENT: October–July, 25 teaching hours per week.

SALARY: Approximately €1,300 per month (gross).

FACILITIES/SUPPORT: Accommodation provided.

RECRUITMENT: Via www.tefl.com. Interviews can be conducted by phone.

CONTACT: Tanya Garcia, Director.

LANGUAGE PROJECT – INSTITUTO DE LINGUAS

Rua de Camões Lt 15, Quinta Nova de S Roque, 2670 Loures

C +351 219 823084

@ lproject@sapo.pt

💻 www.language-project.com

NUMBER OF TEACHERS: 3.

PREFERENCE OF NATIONALITY: None.

QUALIFICATIONS: CELTA or equivalent, relevant degree and 2 years' experience including with young learners.

CONDITIONS OF EMPLOYMENT: Contract is 9 months (1 academic year) with 22–24 contact hours per week.

SALARY: €1,200 gross per month.

FACILITIES/SUPPORT: Assistance given with finding accommodation if necessary.

RECRUITMENT: Usually via adverts in schools, word of mouth or local websites. Interviews are essential either face-to-face or via Skype.

CONTACT: Niki Joseph, Director of Studies.

THE NEW INSTITUTE OF LANGUAGES

Avenida das Tulipas, N° 20B, 1495 159, Miraflores, Lisbon

C 21 412 0929 or 21 943 5238

@ nilportugal@gmail.com

NUMBER OF TEACHERS: 9 /10 English teachers for three schools in and around Lisbon.

PREFERENCE OF NATIONALITY: British preferred.

QUALIFICATIONS: Experienced and inexperienced graduates who have successfully completed a recognised TEFL course.

CONDITIONS OF EMPLOYMENT: 9-month (October–June) contract that is renewable, 22 contract hours per week (Monday–Friday).

SALARY: Depends on experience.

FACILITIES/SUPPORT: Secretarial and administrative help in finding and renting accommodation. The school can act as guarantor for rentals. Week-long orientation course end of September to aid teachers in the classroom.

RECRUITMENT: Website advertising followed by possibility of London interviews in June/July and September

CONTACT: Nicholas Rudall, Director of Studies.

OXFORD SCHOOL

Lisbon: Rua D. Estefania, 165–1°, 1000 154 Lisbon

C 21 354 6586/796 6660

@ info2@oxford-school.pt/Zildamaro@oxford-school.pt

Cacém: Av. Bons Amigos, 37–1° Dto, 2735 077 Cacém

C 21 914 6343

💻 www.oxford-school.pt

Member of AEPLE and ELITE (Excellent Language Institutions Teaching in Europe).

NUMBER OF TEACHERS: About 40 employed at two branches in Lisbon and one in Cacém; 6 new hires per year.

PREFERENCE OF NATIONALITY: British.

QUALIFICATIONS: Minimum TEFL course (e.g. CELTA), qualifications and some experience.

CONDITIONS OF EMPLOYMENT: October–June. Hours mainly 1pm–3pm and 5pm–9pm.

SALARY: Minimum €17 per 1 teaching hour or €1,400 per month for 20 teaching hours per week. Deductions for taxes and social security approx 15%.

FACILITIES/SUPPORT: Help given with finding a shared flat.

RECRUITMENT: Direct application. Interviews essential in Lisbon or London.

CONTACT: Zilda Amaro, Manager.

POMBALINGUA ESCOLA DE INGLES

Rua de Ansiao, 29, 3100 474 Pombal

236 214 319

info@pombalingua.com

www.pombalingua.com

QUALIFICATIONS: Experience preferred but not essential.

CONDITIONS OF EMPLOYMENT: 9-month renewable contracts available, usually contracted on a freelance basis, to work 18 hours per week.

SALARY: €12 per hour.

CONTACT: Paul A. Araújo, Headmaster/Director.

ROYAL SCHOOL OF LANGUAGES – ESCOLAS DE LINGUAS, LDA

Rua José Rabumba 2, 3810 125 Aveiro

+351 234 429 156 or 234 425 104

rsl@royalschooloflanguages.pt

www.royalschooloflanguages.pt

Schools also in Porto, Agueda, Guarda, Ovar, Viseu, Ilhavo and Albergaria-a-Velha. Languages taught: English, French, German, Italian, Spanish and Portuguese.

NUMBER OF TEACHERS: 30–35 in the whole group.

PREFERENCE OF NATIONALITY: British, Australian, Canadian and American.

QUALIFICATIONS: University degree plus TEFL/TESOL certificate.

CONDITIONS OF EMPLOYMENT: 9 month contracts. 25–27 teaching hours per week.

FACILITIES/SUPPORT: Assistance with accommodation and working papers.

RECRUITMENT: Via CVs or interviews, which sometimes take place in UK.

SPEAKWELL ESCOLA DE LINGUAS

Head office: Praça Mário Azevedo Gomes, N 421, 2775 240 Parede

21 456 1771

speakwell@speakwell.pt

www.speakwell.pt

NUMBER OF TEACHERS: 10 full-time and 20 part-time.

PREFERENCE OF NATIONALITY: None, but must be native English speakers.

QUALIFICATIONS: TEFL certificate, preferably plus some business experience, or experience teaching children.

CONDITIONS OF EMPLOYMENT: Can guarantee full-time hours October to June. School opening times are weekdays and Saturday morning. Business trainers and qualified school teachers also required.

SALARY: Above the average hourly rate for Portugal.

FACILITIES/SUPPORT: Nothing formally, but will help people to find accommodation through contacts, etc.

RECRUITMENT: Internet, local advertising, word-of-mouth.

YORK SCHOOL, LISBOA

Travessa de Santa Quitéria 34B, 1250-212 Lisbon

+351 213 869142

info@yorkschool-lisboa.com

www.yorkschool-lisboa.com

NUMBER OF TEACHERS: 6.

PREFERENCE OF NATIONALITY: British.

QUALIFICATIONS: CELTA.

CONDITIONS OF EMPLOYMENT: Standard contract is 1 year with 6 working hours per day.

SALARY: Variable.

RECRUITMENT: Interviews are not essential.

CONTACT: Andrew Basto, Director of Studies.

SCANDINAVIA

Certain similarities exist in ELT throughout Scandinavia. The standard of English teaching in state schools is uniformly high, as anyone who has met a Dane or a Swede travelling abroad will know. Yet many ordinary Scandinavians aspire to fluency so keep up their English by attending evening classes, if only for social reasons. Sweden, Denmark and Norway have excellent facilities for such people, which are variations on the theme of 'folk university', a state-subsidised system of adult education. Classes at such institutions are the ideal setting for enthusiastic amateur teachers.

But as elsewhere in Europe the greatest demand for the English language comes from the business community, particularly in Finland. Enthusiastic amateurs tend to be less in demand in this setting than mature professionals. Yet Scandinavia is not a very popular destination for such teachers, despite its unspoilt countryside, efficient public transport and liberal society. So there is scope for most kinds of teacher to work in Scandinavia.

Since Finland and Sweden are EU members, red tape is straightforward for EU teachers. But even in Norway, whose people voted by a referendum not to join, the formalities are straightforward for EU nationals and language institutes employ foreign teachers. Billington Recruitment Consultants (www.billingtonuk.com) provides a recruitment consultancy to employers in Scandinavia, especially those looking to hire teachers of Business English with some professional work experience.

Denmark

There is little recruitment of English teachers outside Denmark, apart from the Cambridge Institute Foundation, which is Denmark's largest EFL institution with 26 branches and specialises in Business English. The Danish government has tightened up the immigration laws making it virtually impossible for non-Europeans to get working permits. Many schools expect their teachers to speak Danish, and there seems to be almost enough fully bilingual candidates resident in Denmark to satisfy this requirement. It is worthwhile for any native English speaker with an appropriate background who is staying in Denmark to enquire about part-time openings.

Like Scandinavians generally, Danes are enthusiastic self-improvers which means that evening classes in English (and hundreds of other things) are very popular. These are purely recreational and are meant to be fun and informal (*hygge* in Danish). Folkehøjskoler (folk high schools) offer residential courses of varying lengths where working conditions are generally so favourable that there is very little turnover of teaching staff. The tradition of voluntary organisations including trade unions running courses is still strong in Denmark. It might be worth tracking down one of the voluntary organisations which run evening classes countrywide such as the Danish equivalent of Workers' Education, Arbejdernes Oplysnings Forbund or AOF (www.aof.dk). Addresses of the Danish Folkeuniversitet can be found on its website at www.folkeuniversitetet.dk.

Wages in Denmark are set by law and teaching English is no exception. The minimum is kr170, and that is what most new arrivals earn. However, once you're established you can expect to earn £25 an hour teaching in the state sector (which is much better funded and resourced than its UK counterpart). Denmark has among the highest taxes in the world, i.e. over 50% until you acquire a tax card (*frikort*) whereupon the rate drops and only earnings over a certain limit are taxed.

Finland

Although Finland's second language is Swedish, English runs a close second (or third). Finns are admirably energetic and industrious in learning foreign languages, possibly because their own language is so impenetrable (belonging to the Finno-Ugric group of languages along with Hungarian and

Estonian). English is taught in every kind of educational institution from trade and technology colleges to universities, in commercial colleges (*Kauppaloulu*) and in Civic and Workers' Institutes. Private language schools flourish too and traditionally have not been too fussy about the paper qualifications of their native English speaker teachers. They seldom teach straight English courses but tailor-make courses for clients, e.g. 'English for presentation skills', so they are not looking for young first-timers to teach their wealthy corporate clients. Still, some private schools (such as Berlitz) may take on native English speakers without a teaching qualification.

Children start their primary education at age 7, and many children between the ages of 3 and 7 are sent to private kindergartens, many of which are English (as well as German, American, etc.) These sometimes welcome a native English speaker with experience of teaching children. (The only skill which concerned one of these nurseries-cum-kindergartens looking to hire a young British graduate was singing.) Local teachers all have an MA degree since this is the minimum requirement. Provision of English is so good in state schools that there is little scope for picking up slack from disgruntled school leavers who feel they can't speak enough English. Neither is there a demand from an immigrant population since there are few foreigners or refugees in Finland compared with Denmark or Sweden.

FINDING A JOB

Finnbrit is the new name of the long established Federation of Finnish-British Societies, with an emphasis on language courses; its head office is at Fredrikinkatu 20 A 9, 00120 Helsinki (9 687 70 230; www.finnbrit.fi). It takes on a few native English speakers, mostly experienced teachers, for their teaching operation.

Another big player in the provision of English language teaching is Richard Lewis Communications (RLC) with offices throughout Finland and Sweden as well as England (see entry). RLC draws most of its students from senior management in both the public and private sector, and also provides cross-cultural training. Of course not all the teaching takes place in the capital. There is a significant demand for freelance teachers for business in Turku, Oulu and other cities.

Teachers without European nationality will still encounter serious problems. American university students and recent graduates (within two years) over 21 can apply to the American-Scandinavian Foundation (58 Park Avenue, New York, NY 10016; 212 879 9779; training@amscan.org; www. amscan.org/work.html) for work permits to cover a self-arranged internship. At one time there was a well-developed programme of teaching placements in Finland but that has all but disappeared. It might still be worth asking ASF about TEFOL positions in Finland for the academic year, from the end of August until the end of May.

The Nordic School based in St Petersburg (7 812 303 86 96; lena1909@mail.ru; www.nordicschool.ru/eng) and with an office in Moscow mounts an ambitious series of children's summer schools at 11 different colleges in Finland (several of them Christian establishments) plus one in Sweden, for Russian children aged 7–17 learning English (age range varies among camps). Eighty native English speakers from the USA, Canada, Australia and New Zealand as well as the EU were recruited in 2010 to implement an intensive programme of conversation lessons, for 24 fortnight-long camps. Teachers are given free transport from St Petersburg to Finland, accommodation and meals plus a wage of €400–€500 at the end of each camp, and also offered transport to another location for those working at consecutive camps. The programme continues to expand and soon they will have camps in the three other seasons as well as summer.

CONDITIONS OF WORK

Freelance arrangements have largely replaced contracts. A teaching unit of 45 minutes is the norm, with less evening work than elsewhere. Wages are high, but so is the cost of living. Some schools compress the teaching into four days a week, leaving plenty of time for weekend exploration of the country.

Taxes are high and are usually the responsibility of the teacher, whereas contributions should be paid by the employer; social security and unemployment insurance deductions will amount to at least 6% of the salary. Note that there is virtually no possibility of accepting payment 'under the table'. The system is highly controlled and everybody pays his or her taxes.

The Finnish Embassy in London's website (www.finemb.org.uk) has limited information about living and working in Finland. Helsinki has about 35 museums and art galleries plus a high density of sports facilities, ice rinks, etc. The long dark winters are relieved by a wide choice of cheerful restaurants, cafés, bars and clubs in the cities, and saunas almost everywhere.

Norway

The trend in Norwegian EFL is similar to that in Denmark, and most schools rely on a pool of native English speakers already resident in Norway. The instructional supervisor for Berlitz Norway says that he finds it next to impossible to recruit teachers from abroad because '*they don't have a place to stay, a bank account, a work permit, can't attend interviews or training 'next week'. On top of this I have so many applicants who have all of these things in place and are in the Oslo area*'. Most jobs are for part-time work and of course do not offer accommodation. At least things are easier from an immigration point of view than they used to be. Although Norway is not a member of the EU, it does allow the free reciprocity of labour so that EU nationals are allowed to work in Norway without a work permit. Immigration restrictions on non-EU teachers remain stringent.

The *Yellow Pages* for Norway are available online at www.gulesider.no, though typing in *Sprakin-stitut* produced only two results. As throughout Scandinavia, the Folkuniversity of Norway plays an important role in language tuition and hires native English speakers, mostly on an occasional basis for evening classes (www.folkeuniversitetet.no/site/Spraakkurs). There are branches in 300 Norwegian municipalities with fairly major teaching operations in Stavanger, Skien, Kristiansand and Hamar. Berlitz (see entry) hires native English speakers with no TEFL background provided they are graduates and successfully complete the Berlitz Instructor Training.

The basic hourly wage is about kr160, though this can double for high-level business teaching. Expect to lose about a third in deductions.

Casual opportunities may crop up in unpredictable places. **David Moor** was simply intending to spend a month on holiday skiing in Norway, but then he saw an advert in a local supermarket for a native English teacher and jumped at the chance:

> *A teacher put me up and fed me. I'd intended to stay in the hostel or a cheap hotel, but was finding Norway expensive. I was just working for keep, teaching three days a week, so I had lots of spare time. I had a fantastic time, much better than a normal holiday.*

Sweden

For many years the EFL market has been in a slow but inexorable decline, as standards of English among school leavers have improved. The Folkuniversity of Sweden has a long-established scheme (since 1955) by which British and other native English speakers may be placed for nine months (one academic year) in a network of adult education centres throughout the country, but they no longer have a policy of actively recruiting applicants from abroad. They take on new staff who are already resident in Sweden and even then, the work is part-time, at least initially (+46 8 679 29 50; www. folkuniversitetet.se).Originally the teaching at the Folkuniversity consisted of evening classes called a 'Study Circle', an informal conversation session. Circumstances have changed, however, and the range of pupils can be very varied from unemployed people to business executives, as well as people who want to prepare for Cambridge examinations or IELTS. People who need English at work are in the majority these days.

FINDING A JOB

Advertisements seldom appear in the educational press. Teachers with a solid ELT background might try the main state universities which put on English courses or the language schools listed in the *Yellow Pages* of Stockholm, Malmö, Gothenburg, Orebro and Uppsala. **Charlotte Rosen** decided to do a TEFL course in London before going to Sweden to be with her Swedish fiancé:

> *I had visited Sweden several times before going to Gothenburg to work. After I'd been in Sweden for about six weeks, I looked through the Yellow Pages for language schools and sent off my CV in English, which wasn't a problem because everyone speaks English really well. I was offered several interviews, including by the British Institute. Many of them said they were interested but the terms only start in September and January so you have to time your applications quite carefully.*

Another possibility is to try some of the private schools in Sweden (not fee paying, as in Britain), particularly if you are interested in staying in Sweden longer term. The Swedish school system has changed dramatically over the last years and private schools (*friskolor* – free schools) are now plentiful. There are a few English schools within the state system but most of them are independent. Internationella Engelska Skolan (www.engelska.se) is one of Sweden's leading independent schools, founded by an American, and branches are opening all over the country. The website has detailed information about teacher recruitment which applies primarily to certified subject teachers. The schools follow the Swedish curriculum, are authorised by Skolverket and are free for the students.

Cathryn Lock, who has a Swedish fiancé and a degree from an English university, started working at a secondary school a couple of years ago. She found the job through the national employment service Arbetsförmedlingen (www.ams.se), sent in a letter of application and was interviewed by the Headmaster. Cathryn has since gone on to pass a teacher exam in Sweden and she believes that it is quite possible to get a job if you come from the UK.

Although a business background will stand you in good stead, some of the private language schools accept certification, or even just a degree. The British Institute sometimes has vacancies for teachers with the CELTA. Making a breakthrough as a freelancer is difficult without a knowledge of the language, or the Swedish labour market and a functioning network of contacts.

CONDITIONS OF WORK

Teachers must pay tax in Sweden on a scale that varies according to the municipality. Swedish income tax is notoriously high, and the FU estimates that teachers lose about 30% in deductions. However, the upside of paying lots of tax is that Sweden is famous for the quality of its public services, its generous childcare and sick-day policies, and its efficient and moderately priced public transport system. Although Swedes groan about tax, they do not often express frustration that their money is 'wasted'. Constructing a lively social life can be a challenge. **Ann Hunter** points out that it can be difficult to make Swedish friends:

> *The only Swedes you meet regularly are your pupils and the professional relationship can make it awkward to socialise, though after your first term you can get to know ex-pupils quite well. Learning Swedish, if it is possible, is a good way to meet people, though your fellow students are foreigners of course.*

Andrew Boyle had mixed feeling about Sweden and Swedish people:

> *Sweden is a pleasant place to live, if a little dull at times. It is a generally liberal place, although the increasingly multicultural nature of society is causing Swedes to have to face up to their own prejudices. The students are generally of a high level and although initially quiet not unfriendly and even chatty after they know you a little better.*

Still, once you meet one outgoing Swede you'll find yourself quickly drawn into a group, which manages to avoid the horrific cost of dining out/drinks by sticking to meals and parties in people's homes, trips to free galleries and museums and various meetings of social clubs/interest groups. There are also of course cheaper places to eat out, which you'll discover once you're able to find your way around. Stockholm has a great vibe, although the stylishness of its inhabitants can sometimes be intimidating. Gothenburg has a younger feel, and is the city of choice for hip young Scandinavians (and other nationalities since the Swedish government is remarkably supportive of promising artists).

Outside the major cities, especially further north, you have to be independent and comfortable with your own company for long periods to enjoy Sweden. During the seven months of the winter the locals either hibernate or devote all their leisure to skiing. Anyone who enjoys outdoor activities will probably enjoy a stint in Sweden, especially ramblers and hill-walkers, who take advantage of the *Allemannsrätt,* the law which guarantees free access to the countryside for everyone. Island hopping around the (car free) Stockholm archipelago with a tent is an excellent and cheap way to enjoy nature, eat far too many cinnamon buns and lie around in the sun. Summers are usually very warm, certainly more so than in Britain, which is why so many Swedes have an enviable golden tan.

LIST OF EMPLOYERS

DENMARK

BERLITZ LANGUAGE SERVICES SCANDINAVIA
Vimmelskaftet 42 A, 1161 Copenhagen K
- +45 33 69 25 39
  mobile +45 22 96 71 96
- lucinda.duncan@berlitz.dk
- www.berlitz.dk

NUMBER OF TEACHERS: Varies for openings in Norway, Finland, Sweden and Denmark.
PREFERENCE OF NATIONALITY: None.
QUALIFICATIONS: Minimum bachelor's degree and/or business-related work experience.
CONDITIONS OF EMPLOYMENT: Freelance basis and mostly part-time. All new trainers must attend compulsory one-week Berlitz training course. Timetable changes from week to week; most teaching takes place in mornings and evenings.
FACILITIES/SUPPORT: No assistance with accommodation given.
CONTACT: Lucinda Duncan, Nordic Manager of Instruction.

CAMBRIDGE INSTITUTE FOUNDATION
Vimmelskaftet 48, 1161 Copenhagen K
- 3313 3302
- info@cambridgeinstitute.dk
- www.cambridgeinstitute.dk

NUMBER OF TEACHERS: 26 in various schools in the Greater Copenhagen area.

PREFERENCE OF NATIONALITY: British, Irish.

QUALIFICATIONS: Bachelor's degree, TEFL qualification and at least 1 year's TEFL experience abroad.

CONDITIONS OF EMPLOYMENT: 7 month renewable contracts (October to May). Minimum 20 hours per week, students aged 18–70.

SALARY: Approximately £25 per teaching hour.

FACILITIES/SUPPORT: Assistance with accommodation. Training given.

RECRUITMENT: Through adverts in UK newspapers.

SANWES SPROGINSTITUT APS
Kokholm 1, 6000 Kolding
- 7551 7410
- sanwes@sanwes.dk
- www.sanwes.dk

Also branches at Horsensvej 39C, 7100 Vejle (7572 4610), and Fredericia Uddannelsescenter, Mosegardsvez, 7000 Fredericia (7594 1411).

NUMBER OF TEACHERS: 20–22.

PREFERENCE OF NATIONALITY: British, American, Australian.

QUALIFICATIONS: Should have some business background, be open-minded, cheerful and have lots of initiative.

CONDITIONS OF EMPLOYMENT: Freelance; preferred minimum period 6 months. daytime hours; total number depends on clients.

SALARY: Approximately kr172 (about £20) per hour.

FACILITIES/SUPPORT: No assistance with accommodation. Pre-service training from other teacher. Help given with work permits.

RECRUITMENT: Local interviews.

FINLAND

AAC GLOBAL
Ludviginkatu 6–8, 00130 Helsinki
- 9 4766 7800
- recruitment@aacglobal.com
- www.2.aacglobal.com

NUMBER OF TEACHERS: With growing operations in Sweden, Denmark and Russia, the company has over 300 trainers (80 native English speakers) and a total of eight offices in Finland, including Helsinki, Tampere, Turku, Jyväskylä, Kouvola, Vaasa and Oulu. It trains over 20,000 professionals yearly.

PREFERENCE OF NATIONALITY: British, American and Canadian.

QUALIFICATIONS: University degree plus CELTA/TEFL or equivalent or degree plus business background; teaching experience preferred. Driving licence is an asset.

CONDITIONS OF EMPLOYMENT: Trainers expected to deliver an interesting range of challenging language courses with a multicultural perspective.

FACILITIES/SUPPORT: Possibility of one-way airfare being paid. Induction training provided and a system of head trainers to support the trainers in each language.

RECRUITMENT: Direct application (see careers page of website), newspaper ads and recruitment websites.

MARK RICHARDS BUSINESS ENGLISH OY
Kaisaniemenkatu 4 A, 00100 Helsinki
- +358 9 612 40362
- office@mrbe.net
- www.mrbe.net

NUMBER OF TEACHERS: 7

PREFERENCE OF NATIONALITY: British, Australian or American.

QUALIFICATIONS: Degree plus CELTA or equivalent or PGCE.

CONDITIONS OF EMPLOYMENT: Teachers are freelance.

SALARY: €22–€28 per 45 minutes. Tax rate starts at 20% plus pension contribution of 4.5%.

RECRUITMENT: Interview is essential.

CONTACT: Mark Burton, Managing Director.

RICHARD LEWIS COMMUNICATIONS
Länsituulentie 10, 02100 Espoo, Helsinki
- 9 4157 4700
- info.finland@rlcglobal.com
- www.crossculture.com

Offices also in Turku, Tampere, Oulu, Jyväskylä and Kuopio (contacts on website); and in the UK: Riversdown House, Warnford, Southampton, Hampshire SO32 3LH.

RLC has a network of offices worldwide, especially Scandinavia, specialising in cross-cultural and communication skills training and language teaching.

PREFERENCE OF NATIONALITY: British or American.

QUALIFICATIONS: University degree and TEFL preferred.

CONDITIONS OF EMPLOYMENT: Freelance work only.

FACILITIES/SUPPORT: Assistance with finding accommodation. New teachers are given thorough training in RLC's methods and cross-cultural tools/courses.

RECRUITMENT: Apply online.

NORWAY

BERLITZ A/S
Akersgate 16, 0158 Oslo
22 33 10 30
teaching@berlitz.no
www.berlitz.no

NUMBER OF TEACHERS: Varies.

PREFERENCE OF NATIONALITY: None. Non-Europeans must obtain a contract after the compulsory 1-week Berlitz training course and take it to the *Ligningskontoret* to have three-month tourist visa extended.

QUALIFICATIONS: Minimum Bachelor's degree and/or business-related work experience. Must be energetic, outgoing, creative and open to web-based instruction.

CONDITIONS OF EMPLOYMENT: Freelance basis and mostly part-time. Timetable changes from week to week; most teaching takes place in mornings and evenings.

FACILITIES/SUPPORT: No assistance with accommodation given.

FOLKEUNIVERSITETET/FRIUNDERVISNINGEN OSLO
Torggata 7 (P.B. 496 Sentrum), 0105 Oslo
22 47 60 00
info@fuoslo.no
www.fuoslo.no.

NUMBER OF TEACHERS: 2 full-time, 8–12 part-time.

PREFERENCE OF NATIONALITY: None, but must be native English speaker.

QUALIFICATIONS: TEFL experience and/or qualification(s) (min. CELTA or equivalent).

CONDITIONS OF EMPLOYMENT: No contracts. Non-EEA residents will need a work permit. Students aged 18–65.

SALARY: Varies according to course (270–300 Norwegian krone per 45 min. lesson).

FACILITIES/SUPPORT: No assistance with accommodation, monthly teacher development workshops. Possibility of working at other centres around Norway.

RECRUITMENT: Local interviews only.

CONTACT: Wayne Kelly.

POLARIS INSTITUTE AS
Kristian Augustgate 13, 0164 Oslo
22 11 52 00
polaris@polaris.institute.no
www.polaris.institute.no

NUMBER OF TEACHERS: 12.

QUALIFICATIONS: Native English speakers with education in business, pedagogy or psychology and teaching experience.

CONDITIONS OF EMPLOYMENT: Standard contract is 2 years.

CONTACT: Richard Stephenson.

SWEDEN

RICHARD LEWIS COMMUNICATIONS
Riversdown House, Warnford, Hampshire SO32 3LH, UK
info@crossculture.com
www.crossculture.com

NUMBER OF TEACHERS: 40.

PREFERENCE OF NATIONALITY: Must be native English speakers.

QUALIFICATIONS: An EFL qualification, teaching experience in Business English and some personal business experience would be an advantage.

CONDITIONS OF EMPLOYMENT: Various locations in Europe, mainly UK, Finland, Sweden and Germany. Full-time and freelance positions available.

SALARY: Depends on location and experience.

FACILITIES/SUPPORT: Varies depending on location.

RECRUITMENT: Send CV to info@crossculture.com, with a covering letter.

CONTACT: David Lewis (david.lewis@rlcglobal.com).

SPAIN

Despite having been hit harder by the global recession than some other European countries, Spain continues to offer opportunities for native English teachers. Major companies in every sector from transport to fashion employ English teachers to improve their staff's English skills; language schools continue to attend to the massive demand from students and young adults just out of university keen to improve their CVs, and from parents who continue to send their young children and teenagers to English classes and summer camps, to help them pass school exams and eventually cope with a job market that often demands fluency in English.

There is a national push to introduce English early; it is compulsory in state schools from the age of eight, and in some regions they are trying to start even earlier (each *Comunidad Autonoma* is responsible for taking decisions about education). In conjunction with the Spanish Ministry of Education and Science, the British Council, has been recruiting experienced EFL teachers to work in primary schools (www.britishcouncil.org/spain-education-bilingual-project.htm). This trend has filtered through to private language providers, some of which offer courses to very young children.

Thousands of foreigners teach English in language schools (*academias*), from the Basque north (where there is a surprisingly strong concentration) to the Balearic and Canary Islands, as well as Madrid and Barcelona. The entries for language schools occupy many pages of the Madrid *Yellow Pages* and more than 800 listings in the online *Yellow Pages*. Almost every back street in every Spanish town has an *Academia de Ingles*. *Academias* are privately run and unregulated by the *Ministerio de Educación*.

Spain has always been a popular destination for EFL teachers. Who can fail to be attracted to the climate, scenery, history and culture? And yet, many new arrivals in Spain soon realise that Spain and the Spanish people of their imagination bear little resemblance to what they find, at least in the major cities. Economic expansion and increased prosperity has brought about a dynamic, fast-paced society, while traditional stereotypes of flamenco and bull-fighting are completely out of context in the centre and north, where Basques and Catalans have their own culture and language and consider themselves more European.

In some places, the ELT business has become cut-throat with academy owners doing their best to squeeze out every last euro of profit, which can lead to poor working conditions. High inflation and rising costs mean that a teacher's salary does not go all that far, although it is still possible to have a three-course meal with wine for less than €10, and even cheaper outside the big cities: if you ask for a *caña* (small glass of beer) or a glass of *tinto* in Granada you're given decent portions of several tapas for free. A travel pass for 10 journeys in Madrid's metro and bus system costs €9. Teaching wages rarely allow more than a tolerably comfortable lifestyle, and certainly do not allow you to save. These are points to bear in mind when visions of paella and beaches dance before your eyes.

PROSPECTS FOR TEACHERS

The days are gone when any native English speaker of English without a TEFL background could reasonably expect to be hired by a language academy. Almost all self-respecting schools these days require a solid TEFL certificate and shorter or distance learning courses are frowned upon. Many schools in some major cities echo the discouraging comments made by the director of a well-established school in Barcelona who said that he has found that there is a large supply of well-qualified native English speakers on hand so that his school cannot possibly reply to all the CVs from abroad that they receive as well. However, despite this trend, schools report that the number of applications from candidates with a recognised TEFL certificate has increased simply because so many more centres in the UK and worldwide are churning them out. At least one director is not terribly impressed by the standard of applicants and wonders why certificate courses continue to concentrate on teaching adults when increasingly it is children and adolescents who are the main market. In the case of his school the number of adults has remained static in recent years whereas the number of young learners has doubled. Another problem he has encountered more than once is being let down by selected candidates late in the day so that he has to do rushed telephone interviews to fill the posts.

Opportunities for untrained graduates have all but disappeared in what can be loosely described as 'respectable' schools, though there are still more opportunistic language academy directors who might be prepared to hire someone without qualifications, particularly part-time. A number of schools fall into this category. To take a random example, the expatriate director of a well-established school in Alicante estimated that of the 20 or so schools in town, only four operate within the law (i.e. keep their books in order, pay social security contributions for their staff, etc.)

Many Britons and Irish people with or without TEFL qualifications set off for Spain to look for work on spec, preferably in early September, visiting, calling in and faxing across their CVs once they get there. Many employers do much of their recruitment locally, and at the last minute, which is one Spanish habit that hasn't changed. A very high percentage of schools depend on word-of-mouth and local walk-ins for their staff requirements, or advertise heavily in the local press. Anyone with some experience and/or a qualification should find it fairly easy to land a job this way. With a knowledge of Spanish, you can also fill one of the many vacancies for teachers of children, or low-level adult classes, but speaking Spanish is not a must for most jobs. The usual process is to put together a timetable from various sources and be reconciled to the fact that some or all of your employers in your first year will exploit you to some degree. Those who stay on for a second or further years can become more choosy.

The situation for Americans has become almost impossible if they want to work legally (see section on Regulations below).

Companies such as ModLang in Zaragoza (www.modlang.es) cunningly interweave sport and language learning by running intensive English and sports summer courses for children aged 5–18. For these, native English speakers are recruited in large numbers before mid-April, to teach the language and coach sports and/or supervise swimming. Other companies to try include Red Leaf (www.redleaf.es), Eurobridge International (www.eurobridge.net) and TECS (see entry).

FINDING A JOB

Because schools run the whole gamut from prestigious to cowboy, every method of job-hunting works at some level. Many independent language schools are run by expatriate Britons and Irish people, and a few of these will offer guidance and support for newer teachers as well as opportunities for further professional development.

IN ADVANCE

Candidates who know that they want to teach in Spain should consider doing their TEFL training with an organisation with strong Spanish links such as Oxford TEFL in London with schools in Barcelona and Cadiz (see Training chapter, Trinity College TESOL courses). Better still, do your training in Spain, which will allow you to get to know the country, and the specific needs of the students, to take advantage of the job guidance of trainers that know the local job market well, as well as being on the spot for job vacancies. This option is often even cheaper than staying in the UK, given the lower cost of living and the fact that many centres offer a package that includes low-priced accommodation. International House has centres in Barcelona and Madrid offering the CELTA course, as does CLIC in Seville.

For a listing of English language schools in Spain, the most complete source is the *Yellow Pages* which can be accessed on the internet (www.paginas-amarillas.es) – you simply type in 'Academias de Idiomas' and the city or town of interest. You can find a list of members of FECEI, the national

Locations: **Barcelona** - **Cadiz** - **London** - **Prague**

OxfordTefl
teacher training

tesol@oxfordtefl.com - **www.oxfordtefl.com**

Teach English Abroad

- Teach and Travel **worldwide.**
- Experience **new cultures.**
- Learn **new languages.**
- Life-time **job finding assistance** worldwide.
- **Highly qualified and experienced** tutors.
- Courses **every month.**
- Internationally recognised and externally **validated by Trinity College London.**
- **Accommodation** finding service included in your fees.

Trinity Certificate in TESOL
Teaching English to Speakers of Other Languages

In **just 4 weeks** you can become TEFL (TESOL) certified and receive job guidance and assistance to begin teaching English as a foreign language worldwide.

ANDY HEATH describes how he made good use of the Spanish TEFL Jobs Fair in 2009:

Fresh out of my CELTA course and with very little idea of what to do next, I was lucky enough to hear about the Spainwise Recruitment Fair, a kind of one-stop shop for TEFL jobs across the country. The only problem was I had already booked a return ticket home. Attending the fair would involve travelling to and from Spain twice in a month, difficult on a teacher's salary, almost out of reach of an unemployed one. I was serious about teaching, though, and equally serious about finding a good place to do it. I'd heard all the scare stories about exploitation, fly-by-night schools and shady operators. The chance to meet dozens of potential employers face to face and size them up while they did the same to me seemed too good to pass up.

A month later, as I mulled over three job offers, each in a different province of Spain and each from someone I was sure I would enjoy working with, I knew I'd made the right decision. The school I chose, Academia Blue Door in Cordoba, eased me through all the red tape and helped me with accommodation, as all the schools involved in Spainwise had offered to do. The job itself involved longer hours than you would ever teach without a break in England, but I appreciated the way that teaching in the evenings left mornings and afternoons free to sleep or enjoy life in a new city. A ten o'clock finish coincides with when most Spaniards finish their dinner and start thinking about which bar to visit afterwards, so you don't miss much nightlife.

federation of language schools (*Federación Española de Centros de Enseñanza de Idiomas*) on the Spainwise website (www.spainwise.net). Also on the Spainwise site you will find details of the annual Spanish TEFL Jobs Fair held in late May, which acts as a showcase for FECEI schools. For further details, contact Aidan O'Toole (info@spainwise.net).

FECEI is concerned with maintaining high standards, so its members are committed to providing a high quality of teaching and fair working conditions for teachers. FECEI schools represent the elite end of the market and are usually looking for well-qualified teachers. However, FECEI represents only a fraction of the thousands of language schools that exist, and there are many quality language institutions that are not members of FECEI.

Successful candidates from Teacher Training Madrid (see entry in Directory of Training Courses Worldwide; www.ttmadrid.com) are guaranteed an interview with Training Express, one of the largest teaching agencies in Madrid (jobs@trainingexpress.es; www.trainingexpress.es), which also offers teaching by telephone.

British or Irish nationals with a TEFL qualification or PGCE might want to make use of a recruitment agency, whether a general one or one which specialises in Spain such as EES Madrid (see entry). The owner Richard Harrison has been interviewing, assessing and recommending teachers to client schools since 1986, charges no fee to teachers and can advise and help with both short-term and long-term accommodation in Madrid. He suggests that candidates with just a degree and TEFL qualification should come to Spain in early September and contact his agency on arrival since he is at his busiest through September and well into October trying to satisfy requests for teachers from client schools all over Spain. However, schools continue to request teachers throughout the academic year and for summer intensive and residential courses and applications are welcome at any time. Richard Harrison also runs a small English-speaking theatre company based in Madrid called Moving Parts (richardinmadrid@gmail.com), which tours Spain throughout the academic year and offers paid work to young teachers with performance ability, especially those applying in pairs. Speculative applications are welcome at any time.

ON THE SPOT

Most teaching jobs in Spain are found on the spot. Interlang Business Language Centre in Madrid (address below) is hardly unusual in stipulating that they meet all candidates in person before hiring so do all their interviewing in Madrid only. With increasing competition from candidates with solid TEFL qualifications it is more and more difficult for the under-qualified to succeed. The best time to look is between the end of the summer holidays and the start of term which falls in the first two weeks of October, although you can find jobs in late October too. Since a considerable number of teachers do not return to their jobs after the Christmas break and schools are often left in the lurch, early January may also be possible. Try outlying towns and suburbs if work is scarce in the city centres. In Madrid there are usually at least part-time jobs going most months of the academic year, though after Easter demand dies down. Many schools shut over the summer, but there is some work to be had in those that remain open, since most of their teachers disappear over the summer too, as well as teaching kids in a number of English summer camps dotted around the country.

Once in Spain, the local press is very useful, for example newspapers such as the twice-weekly *Cambalache* in Seville, the *Vanguardia* on Sunday and the daily *Segundamano*. In *El Pais* look in the classified section of the salmon-coloured supplement Negocios, under 'Idiomas', and in *Segundamano* under 'Ofertas de Empleo – Profesores'. The classified advert papers *Cambalache* and *Segundamano* are also good for flat hunting, as is the webpage www.loquo.com (which can be viewed in English).

In Madrid (www.in-madrid.com) and *Madrid Insider* (www.madridinsider.com) are good for just about anything. *In Madrid* also allows you to post free 'job wanted' adverts online and in its print edition.

The website www.madridteacher.com is a comprehensive source of information about teaching opportunities in Madrid (specifically), and also in the rest of Spain. It is run by a group of freelance teachers who teach in small and mid-sized companies, academies, schools and with private students in Madrid. The Expatriate Café website (www.expatriatecafe.com/index.php?option=weblinks&Itemid =4&topid=7) contains useful information about language schools, as well as TEFL training, certification and ESL.

You can visit the regional British Council offices, which maintain lists of language schools in their region (which partially duplicates FECEI lists) apart from Madrid which does not keep a register of schools.

Local magazines may advertise the possibility of *intercambio* which means an exchange of English for Spanish or Catalan conversation practice – a great way to meet locals. Some Irish pubs not only offer the opportunity to meet other expats but often organise weekly intercambio nights, which will be listed in the English-speaking press. English language bookshops sometimes have a noticeboard with relevant notices, as do the EOIs (*Escuelas Oficial de Idiomas*) in major cities (these are enormous state-sponsored official language schools with up to 10,000 students).

After finishing A levels, **Sam James** and **Sophie Ellison** decided to spend their gap year in Barcelona if possible. After acquiring their Trinity certificates in their destination city, they did the rounds of the language schools:

> *Though tedious, this did work and we doubt we would have found work any other way. Job availability didn't seem that high in Barcelona when we were looking in October and we both accepted our only job offers. (Our age may have put off some employers.) Most schools seem to have recruited in September, so October was a bit of a lean month. I got my job by covering a class at two hours notice for a teacher who had called in sick. When this teacher decided to leave Barcelona, I was interviewed and offered her classes on a permanent basis. I got the job permanently about a fortnight after handing out CVs. Sophie was asked to her first interview after about three weeks of job-hunting. She was selected but then had to wait for several more weeks while her contract was finalised.*

Conventional wisdom says that the beginning of summer is the worst time to travel out to Spain to look for work since schools will be closed and their owners unobtainable. However, **Sam James** handed round his CV again in May (when his hours were cut) and was given some encouragement. He thinks that because so few teachers look for work just six weeks before the end of the academic year, employers are sometimes in need of replacements and this might well be a way for teachers to get ahead of the queue for September jobs. With so many no-frills cheap flights on the market, it might be worth a gamble.

When knocking on doors, bear in mind that most language academies will be closed between 2pm and 4pm when directors are invariably away from their desks. Try to leave a CV with a contact telephone number (most *pensions* won't mind). It is a very good idea to buy a mobile or at least an inexpensive local SIM card with a local number for your own phone. A serious director will probe into claims of experience and will soon weed out any bogus stories. Other directors are just checking to see that you are a reasonable proposition or at least not a complete dud.

A more probable scenario for the untrained is that they will elicit some mild interest from one or two schools and will be told that they may be contacted right at the beginning of term and offered a few hours of teaching. The academies do not know how many classes they will offer and how many teachers they will need until students finish signing up in October. It can become a war of nerves; anyone who is willing and can afford to stay on has an increasingly good chance of becoming established.

The great cities of Madrid and Barcelona act as magnets to thousands of hopeful teachers. **Sam James** blamed his lack of job security and bitty hours on Barcelona's popularity, '*the result of the great supply of willing teachers here keeping working conditions down and making it hard to exert any leverage on an employer when one is so easily replaced*'. For this reason other towns may answer your requirements better. There are language academies all along the north coast and a door-to-door job hunt in September might pay off. This is the time when tourists are departing so accommodation may be available at a reasonable rent on a nine-month lease.

LIVE-IN POSITIONS

If you want a base from which to look for work and some contact with the kinds of Spaniards who are eager to learn English, you might like to consider a live-in position with a family who wants an

MICHELLE MANION from Australia enjoyed taking part in an exchange programme. Several American organisations including InterExchange in New York (www.interexchange.org) and AIDE (www.aideabroad.org) arrange Teach in Spain programmes whereby fee-paying young Americans (mainly women) live with a family in exchange for speaking English and providing 15 hours of tutoring a week for 1–3 months; fees are from $700 to $1,800. Michelle says:

I would recommend live-in tutoring to anyone in my situation, i.e. anyone who wants to live in Spain but not as an au pair and is not entitled to a work permit. I was placed with a family with two boys aged 11 and 14. In the morning I went off for my Spanish lesson and then gave a lesson to the boys in turn. Spanish boys are notorious for being spoilt and impossible to control, but also for possessing wonderful personalities and great senses of humour. Carlos and César were typically Spanish and always managed to be both delightful and infuriating. Anyone interested in undertaking this venture should try to ascertain the children's level of English before arriving in Spain and to bring textbooks, magazines and children's books to work with, since English books are difficult to find in Spain. Also, when you arrive in Spain try to make as many friends and take up every opportunity you're given as this is the best way to learn Spanish.

English tutor for their children or a voluntary position as an English assistant on summer language/ sports camps. Further details may be sought from Relaciones Culturales, the youth exchange organisation at Calle Ferraz 82, 28008 Madrid (91 541 71 03; www.clubrci.es), which places native English speakers with Spanish families who want to practise their English in exchange for providing room and board; the placement fee is €150 for stays of up to three months, €350 for a year.

FREELANCE TEACHING

As usual, private tutoring can pay better than contract teaching because there is no middle man. **Stuart Britton** easily found private pupils to supplement his school income in a small town in the untouristy north of Las Palmas de Gran Canaria. However when his employer found out, he was told to drop them or risk being sacked, even over the summer when the school was closed and Stuart had no other source of income. He resented this so much that he advises not bothering with small schools, and simply concentrating on obtaining private students.

As always, it is difficult to start up without contacts and a good knowledge of the language; and when you do get started it is difficult to earn a stable income due to the frequency with which pupils cancel. The problem is particularly acute in May when undergraduates and school pupils concentrate on preparing for exams and other activities fall by the wayside. Spaniards are fond of taking off the days between a mid-week fiesta and the weekend known as *puente*, meaning bridge.

Getting private lessons is a marketing exercise and you will have to explore all the avenues which seem appropriate to your circumstances. Obviously you can advertise on noticeboards at universities, EOIs, community centres (*centros cívicos*), public libraries, corner shops and wherever you think there is a market. Major stores are a good bet, for example Jumbo and Al Campo in Madrid. A neat notice in Spanish along the lines of '*Profesora Nativa da clases particulares a domicilio*' might elicit a favourable response. Send notices to local state schools asking them to pin it up broadcasting your willingness to ensure the children's linguistic future. Compile a list of addresses of professionals (e.g. lawyers, architects, etc.) as they may need English for their work and have the wherewithal to pay for it. Try export businesses, distribution companies, perhaps even travel agencies. Make the acquaintance of language teachers who will know of openings.

> *Because private classes can be so much better paid than institute teaching, they are much in demand, including by contract teachers, most of whom are engaged in some private tutoring. The ideal is to arrange a school contract with no more than 15 or 20 hours and supplement this with private classes, which are lucrative though unstable.*

REGULATIONS

All EU citizens planning to live in Spain for more than three months are obliged to register in person at the Foreigners' Office (*Oficina de Extranjeros*) in the province of residence or at a designated police station. You will be issued with a Residence Certificate stating your name, address, nationality, identity number and date of registration. The number on your resident card is your NIE (*Número de Identidad/Identificación de Extranjero*), an identification number necessary for filing taxes, establishing a business, opening a bank account (not necessary for foreign accounts), and for almost any other form. Once you start work, your employer should apply for a social security number on your behalf; if you are self-employed, this is your responsibility.

Many long-stay foreigners engage a specialist lawyer called a *gestoria* to assist negotiating the bureaucracy, especially if they are buying property. Further details are contained in the Living in Spain notes on the British Embassy in Spain site (http://ukinspain.fco.gov.uk) or from the website Spain Expat (www.spainexpat.com), which is full of useful information about living and working in Spain.

The immigration situation for people from outside Europe is very difficult indeed. Most of the schools that once hired North Americans now refuse to tackle the lengthy procedures involved in obtaining work permits. Berlitz cautions, '*unfortunately, the European Union (EU), of which Spain is a part, seldom issues work permits to non-EU citizens unless they are married to an EU national*'. Americans with Irish or Italian ancestry often prefer to chase the papers that will get them an EU passport.

This pessimistic view of the chances for Americans and Canadians was voiced by so many schools that it seems almost superfluous to describe the procedures. Briefly, you need to submit a slightly dizzying array of documents to the *Subdelegación del Gobierno* in the city you are trying to move to and work in, including, but not restricted to, an official job offer form, original official company fiscal identity document, and official certification that the job on offer has already been advertised in the official Provincial Unemployment Office and that no suitable European candidate has applied. Then you need to make an appointment with the Spanish Consulate serving your official home address (in country of origin) in order to process all the documentation that they require for a work visa, including, among others, a formal job offer from an employer in Spain, a recent medical certificate, *antecedents penales* (police certificate of good character), notarised degree certificate and seven passport photographs. Once your home country's Spanish consulate has processed your work visa, you have to fetch it in person. It cannot be handed to anyone other than you. Then you can return to Spain and finalise applications for a work/residence permit. According to Institut Nord-America (www.ien.es) in Barcelona, which has a vested interest in employing people with a North American accent, visa processing takes 12–16 months. They go on to stipulate that they prefer, '*applicants with Spanish/European work permit/citizenship*', for obvious reasons.

None of this means that there aren't any Americans or other nationalities teaching in Spain without permits. According to **Jon Loop**, many post-Hemingway Americans go to Spain for a year to learn Spanish and 'find themselves man' (or maybe even find themselves a man). The teacher-training schools in major cities are full of American as well as British trainees, and Americans, Australians and New Zealanders also find work, not just teaching private classes but through numerous intrepid academies who hire them off-contract and send them off to teach in companies rather than on school premises. Anyone who works on a tourist visa will have to renew it every three months by leaving the country.

Social security (*seguridad social*) contributions are between 4% and 7% of earnings, typically 6.4%. Tax residents will need to pay income taxes in Spain and are generally defined as those who live in Spain for more than 183 days in each calendar year. However, www.spainexpat.com suggests that in many cases you only need to file a tax return in Spain when you make more than €22,000 per year; unlikely if you are a language teacher. Spain and Britain have a double taxation treaty: for more information follow the links from www.hmrc.gov.uk/cnr/form_spain.htm. Under EU legislation, language schools must give contracts and make contributions for all staff, whether full-time or part-time. In practice, this does not always happen. After a few months of teaching for one academy, Jon Loop asked for a contract and was given a special 11-hour contract (though at the time he was teaching 20 hours a week). Contracts for fewer than 12 hours a week do not require more than minimal social security contributions. **Joanna Mudie** from the Midlands describes the situation which results from this:

> *There's a great deal of uncertainty and insecurity about all aspects of work: hours, days, rates of pay, insurance, etc. Contracts (if you're lucky enough to get one) are a load of rubbish because employers put down far fewer hours on paper to avoid paying so much insurance, and also to protect themselves if business dwindles. My advice is, forget your English sense of honesty and obeying the law. 'When in Rome…' Relax and simply don't worry about the legalities. It usually seems to work out okay, and if not, well, it's a nice life in the sun.*

Schools that sidestep the regulations to maximise profits and who do not pay contributions to cover their employees' social security might well be the ones willing to employ non-Europeans and pay cash in hand.

CONDITIONS OF WORK

Salaries are not high in Spain and have not increased significantly over the past decade. A further problem for teachers in Madrid and Barcelona is that there is not much difference between salaries in the big cities where the cost of living has escalated enormously and salaries in the small towns. The minimum net salary is about €900 per month, though most schools offer €1,000–€1,150 after deductions for 25 hours of teaching a week. A standard hourly wage would start at €14, although some pay their starter teachers more. The very best paid hourly wages are paid to registered freelancers sent out to firms. Spanish TEFL is no different from TEFL in other countries in that there are lots of employers offering low pay, long hours and exploitative conditions. For example, teachers have discovered that pay has been deducted when they have been unavoidably absent or that their bonuses have been withheld with no explanation. Sam James was taken aback when his hours were drastically cut by his employer in Barcelona with no notice. The simple explanation was that Sam was working without a contract, which would have guaranteed a certain number of hours. He advises get-

BARRY O'LEARY wrote from Seville in his third year of teaching there. In his first year he worked for a slightly disorganised and crafty academy where there was no mention of a contract, classes started at 8am and staggered throughout the day until 10pm and it was difficult to predict how much you would earn from month to month because of all the unpaid festivals in Spain. Luckily in his second year, after mingling with the other ex-pat teachers, he was able to land himself a job with a more professional establishment. He now works fixed hours from 4pm until 10pm, Monday to Thursday, leaving the mornings free, and there are excellent ongoing training sessions on Friday mornings. The language school is one of the most successful in Seville with 12 academies scattered throughout the city and it takes care of its teachers, offering fixed contracts for long-term prospects:

The students, who are often passionate and keen to learn English, range in age from six to sixty so there is never a dull moment. Classes have a maximum of twelve, all material is provided and there is scope to move away from the syllabus now and then. A lot of extra work is necessary in February and June when the exams take place but it's worth the agony.

Life in Seville is fun and varied, with an abundance of festivals including the religious Semana Santa and the livelier Feria. The city is a great place to live and a base for exploring Andalucía. Evenings can be spent in the many bars enjoying tapas, watching flamenco or Sevillanas (a local dance) or just mingling with the locals. Seville is generally safe and with the year-round blue skies, it's a great place to brush up on your Spanish and experience a different way of life.

ting a contract if at all possible, even on a lower rate of pay, since contracts bring security, a reliable income and holiday pay (which he knows because his girlfriend Sophie had one).

Sophia Brown worked in a school in Barcelona and objected to the terrible timetable (always late evenings), the lack of organisation and the low hourly rate. She also didn't really like the city, although her American friend, Dylan, is still working at the school and at last report was hoping to be trained as a tester, which is much more lucrative.

As always, you can gain an idea of an employer's integrity by talking to other teachers as well as by using your intuition at the interview. Asking lots of questions is a good idea since then you can find out your pay and maximum hours so that you will be in a stronger position to argue should your employer try to mess you around. But realistically, most new arrivals feel exploited at least in some respects in their first year. **Laura Phibbs** was spared the possibility of being exploited, since her promised job evaporated overnight:

> *The Madrid school director rang me to inform me that I had got the job and I was to start nine days later. When, as instructed, I rang to confirm the arrival time of my plane, I was told that there was no job for me after all since the school had gone bankrupt. I think what really made me angry was that I had rung him rather than the other way round. He did not even say sorry or sound in the least remorseful.*

It is possible that the bankruptcy was just an excuse in the face of insufficient pupils. Some schools tend to work their teachers very hard, expecting them to teach around 30 hours. Considering that preparation and travelling is extra, this can result in a gruelling schedule. The ideal full-time timetable is 24–26 teaching hours a week. **Dennis Bricault** refers to the notoriously uncongenial timetable of most EFL teachers (and not just in Spain) as a 'bookend schedule', whereby you might have to teach between 8am and 10am, then again through the evening. According to Spanish law, workers are not entitled to paid holiday until they have been working for 12 months, hence the near-universality of nine-month contracts. Most teachers find it impossible to save enough in nine months to fund themselves abroad for the rest of the year. Most pay agreements also already include the bonuses (*pagas extraordinarias*) which have already been pro-rated, of which there are two or three a year. Legal schools will pay *finiquito* (holiday pay) at the end of a contract which should be equivalent to the pay for two and a half days of every month worked, based on your base (not full) salary.

If the terms of a contract are being breached and the employer does not respond to the teacher's reminders, recourse can be taken by means of a *denuncia*, which involves informing the authorities (either in person or via a union, such as the *Commissiones Obreros*) that your school is not complying with, for example, tax and social security rules or fire regulations. The *denuncia* can effectively close a school if it is taken seriously and if the school does not have the proverbial friends in high places. In fact the procedure is complicated and time-consuming but the mere mention of it might improve your working conditions.

The experience of teaching at a summer camp is entirely different. The pay is fairly good (say, €800 for a four-week stint plus free board and accommodation, rising to €1,200, including accommodation, if you're particularly fortunate) though some organisations offer little more than accommodation, meals and pocket money. **Glen Williams** describes his summer job at a summer language camp in Izarra in the Basque Country:

> *The children learned English for three hours in the morning with one half hour break (but not for the teacher on morning snack duty trying to fight off the hordes from ripping apart the bocadillos). Then we had another three or four hours of duties ranging from sports and/or arts to shop/bank duty. For many of us, inexperienced with dealing with groups of kids, there were a few problems of discipline. It was the kids' holiday and they quickly cottoned on that we English teachers in general were a bunch of hippie types.*

PUPILS

For reasons which remain obscure, Spaniards have the reputation for being somewhat challenged at learning languages. This is more tolerable in adults who are motivated, but often hard-going with children (unless you are especially fond of kids). This was one of **David Bourne**'s biggest problems and one which he thinks is underestimated, especially as a high proportion of English teaching in some academies is with children and teenagers

> *I have found that a lot of the younger students only come here because their parents have sent them in order to improve their exam results. The children themselves would much rather be outside playing football. There are days when you spend most of the lesson trying (unsuccessfully in my case) to keep them quiet. This is especially true on Fridays. I have found it very hard work trying to inject life into a class of bored ten year olds, particularly when the course books provided are equally uninspiring.*

In such cases it might be a good idea to change your aim, from teaching them English to entertaining them (and paying your rent). If students don't want to learn, you will only break your heart trying to achieve the impossible.

Adults are usually an easier proposition, willing to listen and think and with a good sense of humour. In general the Spanish will welcome opportunities to speak animatedly in class and express their opinions. A good knowledge of Spanish is helpful if not essential when teaching junior classes as **Peter Saliba**, director of a language school in Malaga, explains:

> *We need teachers with a fluent command of Spanish, not the typical grasp of elementary phrases which may get them by in a social context. On a limited two or three hour per week teaching timetable, there simply is not time for cumbersome English explanations of English grammar and vocabulary. It is worse still with young learners and teens, who will 'run riot' or at the very least run circles round non-Castilian speaking teachers.*

Needless to say, Spaniards are a nation of talkers. If things seem to be going awry in your classes, for example students turning up late or being inattentive, don't hesitate to make your feelings known, just as Spaniards do.

ACCOMMODATION

Rents usually swallow up at least a quarter of a teacher's income, more in the big cities and much more if you don't share. In small towns, it is not uncommon for schools to arrange accommodation for their teachers at least for an initial period. Many Spanish students want to live with English students so check language school, EOI, and university noticeboards for flat shares, especially in the Facultad de Filologia, which includes the Department of English. Some teachers even arrange to share a flat rent-free in exchange for English lessons.

When renting a flat expect to pay a month's rent in advance, plus one or two months' rent as deposit. Since your first pay cheque may not arrive until November, you should arrive with as much as £1,000 to tide you over. Try to avoid using an *inmobiliaria* (property agency) which will charge a further month's rent (at least). Be aware of the agencies or associations with seedy premises that charge you a fee before showing you anything. You will quickly distinguish their ads from private ones in the classifieds. In Madrid and Barcelona many people use the free ads paper *Segundamano*; if you do decide to compete for a flat listed in this paper, get up early since most flats are gone by 8am. When **Barry O'Leary** was looking for a two-bedroomed apartment to rent in central Seville, he advertised in Spanish on the university noticeboard site http://sevilla.campusanuncios.com. It is easier flat hunting in July and August, than in September/October or February.

LEISURE TIME

Once you acquire some Spanish, it is very easy to meet people, since Spaniards are so friendly, relaxed and willing to invite newcomers out with them. Of course there is also a strong fraternity of EFL teachers almost everywhere. With luck you will end up socialising with both groups in bars, at parties, *romerías* (pilgrimages), *fiestas*, etc.

If you're looking for traditional Spanish culture, don't go to Madrid, and certainly don't look for it in Barcelona which is not Spanish at all but Catalan. Seville, Granada and Valencia are lovely Spanish cities. While teaching in Andalucia, **Joanna Mudie** appreciated the chance to learn about the traditional but still very much alive dances of Spain, e.g. Sevillanas, Malagueras and Pasadoble.

Deryn Collins is clearly enjoying a good quality of life while teaching at the Academia Blue Door in Córdoba, as she reported in 2010:

Living in Spain gives me freedom. I never have to get up with an alarm; I have my mornings free to enjoy my hobbies and attend classes myself, and go for lazy breakfasts with friends before work. Then I get another time for myself after my day's work is done. I can go to the cinema at midnight, meet friends for tapas and a beer, go to the pub quiz, dance my socks off or listen to some live blues in a dark and smoky dive. At weekends I get out into the country, or explore the rest of the province around Cordoba...

Teaching in Spain has provided me with an easy and relaxed lifestyle with more job satisfaction than I've found in any other field. Remember never mind how brilliant or grotty the job is, nor how great or awful the pay, nor how marvellous the working conditions are or aren't, you will not be happy in Spain (or anywhere else) unless you come with the right attitude. Come with a desire to integrate into the culture, to learn the language and to develop both on a professional and personal level.

Glen Williams describes his spare time activities in Madrid, a city with an enormous variety of nightlife where he was clearly enjoying himself to the full:

Madrid is a crazy place. We usually stay out all night at the weekend drinking and boogying. During the gaps in my timetable (10–2 and 4–7) I pretend to study Spanish (I'm no natural) and just wander the back streets. I suppose I should try to be more cultural and learn to play an instrument, write poetry or look at paintings, but I never get myself in gear. I think most people teach English in Spain as a means to live in Spain and learn the Spanish language and culture. But there is a real problem that you end up living in an English enclave, teaching English all day and socialising with English teachers. You have to make a big effort to get out of this rut. I am lucky to live with Spanish people (who do not want to practise their English!).

A few schools offer free or subsidised Spanish lessons as a perk to teachers. Otherwise investigate the government-run *Escuela Oficial de Idiomas*.

If the idea of teaching in Spain appeals at all, it is almost always a rewarding and memorable way for people with limited work experience to finance themselves as they travel and live abroad for a spell.

LIST OF EMPLOYERS

ACADEMIA BLUE DOOR

C/Alhaken II, 6, 14008 Cordoba

957 491535; recruitment@bluedoorspain.com

www.bluedoorspain.com

NUMBER OF TEACHERS: 12.

QUALIFICATIONS: Native speakers of English with university degree and TEFL qualifications.

CONDITIONS OF EMPLOYMENT: Student groups no larger than 6. Contracts are from the end of September to the end of June.

SALARY: School offers a competitive package with salary above national pay agreements plus full national health and social security cover.

RECRUITMENT: Blue Door is a member of ACEIA and FECEI, and recruits at the Spainwise annual recruitment fair in May (www.spainwise.net).

CONTACT: Aidan O'Toole, Director (+34 692 613687).

ACADEMIA BRITANICA International House Cordoba

C/Rodriguez Sanchez, 15,14003 Cordoba

957 470350

info-cordoba@acabri.com

www.acabri.com

NUMBER OF TEACHERS: 20

PREFERENCE OF NATIONALITY: EU passport holders who can get residence permits easily.

QUALIFICATIONS: A or B in CELTA plus minimum 1 year's experience, especially in teaching younger learners.

CONDITIONS OF EMPLOYMENT: 9-month contracts, mid-September to mid-June, 22–25 hours per week.

SALARY: Monthly average around €1,600 gross (2009/10). Average 12% tax; 6.5% social security deductions.

FACILITIES/SUPPORT: Help with finding accommodation. Residence permits are applied for by the school and the teacher is accompanied to the permits office soon after arrival.

RECRUITMENT: Through IH recruitment system, or locally. Interviews in the UK for teachers recruited through IH World.

ASTEX SERVICIOS LINGUISTICOS

C/Hermanos Bécquer 7–6°, 28006 Madrid

91 590 3474

selem@astex.es/dwarner@astex.es

www.astex.es

NUMBER OF TEACHERS: ASTEX employs around 300 ESL teachers at any one time, and usually hires 30 new teachers each September/October, with vacancies needing to be filled throughout the year.

QUALIFICATIONS: Require CELTA or equivalent and minimum 2 years' EFL teaching experience.

PREFERENCE OF NATIONALITY: Native English speakers.

CONDITIONS OF EMPLOYMENT: 9-months contract/20–25 hours per week.

SALARY: Contracted teachers earn €17–€17.50 gross; freelancers earn €23–24 gross.

FACILITIES/SUPPORT: Teachers' room: library, computers (free internet) and printer. Free workshops for teachers.

RECRUITMENT: Interview required.

BAKER STREET INTERNATIONAL

Calle Sangre, 7–13, 46002, Valencia

963 516 312

valencia@bkstreet.com

www.bkstreet.com

NUMBER OF TEACHERS: 25–35.

PREFERENCE OF NATIONALITY: British, Irish.

QUALIFICATIONS: University degree, TEFL certificate and experience with children.

CONDITIONS OF EMPLOYMENT: Usually 4–8 weeks full-time in the summer camps. Students are usually 11–16 years of age with lower English abilities.

SALARY: Net salary approximately €1,200 per month, accommodation included.

FACILITIES/SUPPORT: Accommodation is always offered but no travel allowance. Teachers are expected to hit the ground running, to 'muck in' and to come willing to use their own material and share it with other staff. Resources are available but internet and photocopiers are not always reliable, especially over the summer.

RECRUITMENT: Telephone interviews are possible so it is not necessary for applicant to be in Spain for the recruitment process to take place.

CONTACT: Joshua C Goldblatt, Director.

BRITISH SCHOOL

Plaza Ponent, 5–2nd floor, 43001 Tarragona

british@bstarragona.com

www.bstarragona.com

NUMBER OF TEACHERS: 5.

PREFERENCE OF NATIONALITY: Native English speakers with EU passport.

QUALIFICATIONS: University degree, CELTA or Trinity EFL teaching qualification and minimum 1 year's experience teaching English abroad.

CONDITIONS OF EMPLOYMENT: October to June, 21 class hours per week.

SALARY: Gross salary €1,067 per month for 21 class hours a week; new-year bonus €245 and end-of-contract holiday pay €536 and travel expenses €211.

FACILITIES/SUPPORT: First week's accommodation paid in hotel; school video and book libraries.

RECRUITMENT: Internet with telephone interview.

CONTACT: Bernard Tingle, Director.

BVRNS ACADEMY

Kalebarria 44–46 bajo, Durango, 48200 Vizcaya

 946 203 668

 info@bvrnsacademy.com

NUMBER OF TEACHERS: 5.

PREFERENCE OF NATIONALITY: British, native English speakers; also bilingual French-English.

QUALIFICATIONS: Degree, TEFL qualification and experience. Teachers should be cheerful, lively, genuinely interested in teaching and enjoy working with both children and adults. Some knowledge of Spanish preferable.

CONDITIONS OF EMPLOYMENT: Standard 9-month contract. Students vary from young children to mature adults. Courses are grouped according to their level and age and take place mainly in the afternoon and evening (some in the morning). Maximum 8 in a class. Number of teaching hours around 25.

SALARY: €1,400 per month for academic year (2010/11). Bonus at Christmas of €200 and at the end of the course €400 on successful completion of contract.

FACILITIES/SUPPORT: Shared furnished room in a flat available for rent of about €270 monthly plus bills.

RECRUITMENT: Telephone interview required.

CONTACT: Ana Lopez, Director.

CALEDONIA SCHOOL OF ENGLISH

Avenida Del Quinto Centenario, Edificio Mirasol 3, local 2, 11540 Sanlúcar de Barrameda (Cádiz)

 956 380097

 caledon@arrakis.es

 www.caledoniaschool.es

NUMBER OF TEACHERS: 6.

PREFERENCE OF NATIONALITY: Native of UK or Ireland.

QUALIFICATIONS: University graduate, preferably in Spanish or Modern Languages. Need recognised TEFL qualification or PGCE, 1–2 years' experience in TEFL or minimum 150-hour TEFL course for newly-qualified graduates.

CONDITIONS OF EMPLOYMENT: Contracts 9.5 months or indefinite, 21–24 hours per week. Full health and social security coverage.

SALARY: Highly competitive on a national scale.

FACILITIES/SUPPORT: Assistance finding accommodation.

RECRUITMENT: Interview held at school essential.

CONTACT: Iain Cunningham.

CAMBRIDGE ENGLISH STUDIES

Avenida de Arteijo 8–1°, 15004 A Coruña

 981 160 216

 camcor@arrakis.es

NUMBER OF TEACHERS: 12 teachers, 8 in Coruña and 4 in Ferrol.

QUALIFICATIONS: Teachers must be EU nationals and hold a recognised TESOL qualification (e.g. CELTA/Trinity College London /RELSA).

CONDITIONS OF EMPLOYMENT: Contracts run from mid-September to end June, teaching 25 hours per week.

SALARY: Basic net salary is €1,000 per month plus increments for experience and qualifications. Taxes and social security paid by the school.

RECRUITMENT: Interviews required, but telephone interview is acceptable.

CONTACT: Nick Shaw, Director.

CAMBRIDGE HOUSE

C/Lopez de Hoyos, 95 1°A, 28002 Madrid

 91 519 4603/64 795 0087

 teachers@cambridge-house.com

 www.cambridge-house.com

NUMBER OF TEACHERS: 25.

PREFERENCE OF NATIONALITY: British or Irish teachers. In the case of non-EU teachers, they must already have their working papers.

QUALIFICATIONS: University degree, EFL certificate and at least some teaching experience.

CONDITIONS OF EMPLOYMENT: The average length of contract is 9 months but summer work is available to teachers who want to stay on. Contact hours are between 22 and 26 hours with 3 hours paid preparation.

FACILITIES/SUPPORT: Advice offered on accommodation and help in all matters of social security and residency application. Workshops and staff meetings are held regularly to inform teachers of any extra courses available.

RECRUITMENT: Applications are received by e-mail and acknowledged immediately. CVs are kept on file for future vacancies that crop up.

CONTACT: Penny Rollinson, Director of Studies.

CAMBRIDGE SCHOOL
Placa Manel Montanya 4, 08400 Granollers, Barcelona
93 870 2001
admin@cambridgeschool.com
www.cambridgeschool.com

NUMBER OF TEACHERS: 65

PREFERENCE OF NATIONALITY: Native English Speakers who can legally work in Spain, i.e. EU members or non-EU members with a work permit.

QUALIFICATIONS: At least CELTA or equivalent.

CONDITIONS OF EMPLOYMENT: Contract length September to June or possibly July, 20 contact teaching hours per week.

SALARY: Average salary is €1,300 a month for 20 contact hours per week.

FACILITIES/SUPPORT: Assistance with accommodation, weekly seminars and workshops are part of the job, school library, teachers room and extensive teachers materials available.

RECRUITMENT: Teachers should send their CV to admin@cambridgeschool.com and will be interviewed either face to face or by phone.

CONTACT: Alistair Jones, Director.

CENTRO EDIMBURGO IDIOMAS
Edificio Edimburgo, Plaza Niña, 21003 Huelva
959 263821/26382/959 250168
info@centroedimburgo.com or
centroedimburgo@hotmail.com
www.centroedimburgo.com

NUMBER OF TEACHERS: 20.

PREFERENCE OF NATIONALITY: Must be EU national or hold work permit for Spain.

QUALIFICATIONS: Degree, CELTA plus 1 year's experience. Must speak conversational Spanish.

FACILITIES/SUPPORT: School helps find flats.

RECRUITMENT: Recent photograph and 2 references must be sent with application. Interviews essential.

CONTACT: Erica Buchanan, Coordinator of Studies.

CIC
Via Augusta 205, 08021 Barcelona
93 200 1133
idiomes@iccic.edu
www.iccic.edu

NUMBER OF TEACHERS: 80.

PREFERENCE OF NATIONALITY: Mix of native English speaking and teachers with 'native competence' from all around the world.

QUALIFICATIONS: Cambridge/Trinity certificate and 1 year's experience.

CONDITIONS OF EMPLOYMENT: Most new teachers are given a temporary 9-month contract running from October to June.

SALARY: Discussed during interview.

FACILITIES/SUPPORT: In-house training and professional development if funded by school.

RECRUITMENT: CVs via internet, all suitable candidates are interviewed.

EES MADRID (ENGLISH EDUCATIONAL SERVICES)
Calle Alcalá, 20–2°, 28014 Madrid
+34 91 531 4783/+34 91 532 9734
richardinmadrid@gmail.com
www.eesmadrid.es.tl

NUMBER OF TEACHERS: 100–120 across Spain per year.

PREFERENCE OF NATIONALITY: EU passport holders.

QUALIFICATIONS: Degree level education and CELTA/TESOL certificate/PGCE, etc.

CONDITIONS OF EMPLOYMENT: 9-month contract from September to June. Alternatively, 1–2 month contracts available in summer (July and sometimes August). Working hours are between 4pm and 9.30pm.

FACILITIES/SUPPORT: Assistance given with finding accommodation.

RECRUITMENT: Interviews are essential and are usually held in Madrid but occasionally in the UK.

CONTACT: Richard Harrison, Director.

EIDE SCHOOL OF ENGLISH

Genaro Oraa 6, Santurce 48980

94 493 7005

eide@eide.es

www.eide.es

NUMBER OF TEACHERS: 2.

QUALIFICATIONS: Bachelor's degree and some teaching experience.

CONDITIONS OF EMPLOYMENT: 9-month contract; 15 hours per week in the evenings.

SALARY: €12 per hour plus bonus for holidays at the end of contract; 8% tax and social security deduction.

FACILITIES/SUPPORT: Help finding accommodation.

RECRUITMENT: Interview essential.

CONTACT: Marisol Largo, Director.

EL CENTRO DE INGLES

C/Calderos 7, 23740 Andújar (Jaén)

dirección@elcentrodeingles.es

NUMBER OF TEACHERS: 2–3 new teachers required every year for September start.

QUALIFICATIONS: CELTA/Trinity and 2 years' experience, especially valued if with children.

CONDITIONS OF EMPLOYMENT: To work until June of the following year (contract renewable). Teachers work 21 contact hours per week (34 hours with preparation, meetings and teacher training). Usually there are no morning classes.

FACILITIES/SUPPORT: Help with accommodation, paper-work, settling in, induction.

RECRUITMENT: Via internet (www.tefl.com or www.spainwise.net). Interview required in Spain or England.

CONTACT: Julie Hetherington, Director.

ENGLISH 1

Marqués del Nervión 116, 41005 Seville

+34 95 464 20 98

info@english1sevilla.com

www.english1sevilla.com

NUMBER OF TEACHERS: 6.

QUALIFICATIONS: Degree and TEFL certificate (or diploma) and experience, especially with young learners preferred.

CONDITIONS OF EMPLOYMENT: 23 contact hours per week, Monday to Thursday only, teaching children, teenagers and adults. Nine-month contract from October to June.

SALARY: Starting salary €1,100 gross plus extra payments for Cambridge exam preparation classes.

FACILITIES/SUPPORT: In-house training and great support in a very friendly and harmonious working atmosphere. Lots of assistance in finding accommodation.

CONTACT: Jennifer Fricker.

THE ENGLISH CENTRE

Calle Nuñez de Balboa 17, Bajo Derecha, 28001 Madrid

91 577 91 22

empresas@theenglishcentre.org or julia@centroingles.net

NUMBER OF TEACHERS: Approximately 60 teachers.

PREFERENCE OF NATIONALITY: British and Irish. Other nationalities employed only if they already have residence and work papers.

QUALIFICATIONS: CELTA qualification or equivalent and preferably at least 1 year's experience.

CONDITIONS OF EMPLOYMENT: Part-time and full-time contracts offered from September/October to June. Paid holidays during contract. Classes mainly in companies in central Madrid and own school.

FACILITIES/SUPPORT: Help provided with getting NIE and social security numbers. Formal workshops are held from time to time and a team of 4 offers constant support to help teachers with their classes. Extensive teacher resources are available including a library of EFL books, audiovisual materials and internet access. Informal help sometimes given with finding flat-share, etc.

RECRUITMENT: Teachers are recruited through the internet, and by contacts through present and past teachers. Interview required.

CONTACT: Julia Hoare.

THE ENGLISH COLLEGE

Carrer Empedrat 4, 03203 Elche, Alicante

+34 965458401

englishcoll@terra.es

NUMBER OF TEACHERS: 3–5.

QUALIFICATIONS: University degree, TEFL qualification and 1–2 years' experience of similar kind of teaching. Some knowledge of Spanish desirable but not essential.

CONDITIONS OF EMPLOYMENT: 9-month contract (renewable), 29 hours per week.

SALARY: €1,250 per month (gross).

FACILITIES/SUPPORT: School will assist in finding accommodation.

CONTACT: Mark Harper, Director.

ESIC IDIOMAS

Sancho el Fuerte 38, Bajo, 31011 Pamplona

✆ 948 173011

🖰 idiomas.pam@esic.es

💻 www.esicidiomas.com

NUMBER OF TEACHERS: 28 (some part-time).

PREFERENCE OF NATIONALITY: Native English speakers.

QUALIFICATIONS: Recognised TEFL qualification and relevant experience.

CONDITIONS OF EMPLOYMENT: 9-month contract; 24 hours per week.

SALARY: €1,240–€1,320 depending on experience; €18 per hour self-employed.

FACILITIES/SUPPORT: Help is given to find accommodation and paperwork necessary to work in Pamplona. An initial induction course, with accompanying handouts, is given and various training and information sessions are given throughout the academic year.

RECRUITMENT: Sometimes interviewed by phone.

CONTACT: Fay Williams, Coordinator (fay.williams@esic.es).

EUROSCHOOLS

Plaza de la Independencia, Regueiro 2, 36211 Vigo

✆ 986 291748

🖰 euroschools@moriartys.com

NUMBER OF TEACHERS: 15.

PREFERENCE OF NATIONALITY: Must be EU.

QUALIFICATIONS: Good degree preferably in English, Spanish or modern languages, TEFL qualification, some experience preferred. Must have knowledge of Spanish and outgoing, friendly personality.

SALARY: Competitive plus allowances are paid for university degree and TEFL teaching qualifications in proportion to qualifications.

FACILITIES/SUPPORT: Assistance given with finding accommodation. Holiday entitlement is 2+ weeks at Christmas, 1 week at Easter, 2 days at *Carnaval*. Access to internet and school computer network available to teachers.

RECRUITMENT: Good references needed.

CONTACT: John Moriarty, Managing Director.

IDIOMASTER LANGUAGE CENTRES

C/Juan Rico 8, Apartado de Correos 591, 14900 Lucena (Cordoba)

✆ 957 591678

🖰 idiomaster@terra.es

💻 www.idiomaster.net

NUMBER OF TEACHERS: 9.

QUALIFICATIONS: University degree, CELTA and at least 1 year's experience, preferably with children.

SALARY: Minimum monthly gross salary €1,250 plus end of contract bonus of 2.5 days salary per month worked. Full social security and national health insurance cover.

FACILITIES/SUPPORT: Ongoing internal teacher training and support plus external teaching conferences and courses. Digital classrooms with interactive whiteboards. Help with finding accommodation. Preparation centre for the Cambridge suite of exams. A registered Trinity College, London examination centre and member of ACEIA and FECEI.

CONTACT: Alan McDyre, Director.

INLINGUA SANTANDER

Avenida de Pontejos 5, 39005 Santander

✆ 942 278465

🖰 inlingua.santander@inlingua.com

💻 www.inlinguasantander.com

NUMBER OF TEACHERS: 10.

PREFERENCE OF NATIONALITY: EU native English speakers or having a work permit for Spain.

QUALIFICATIONS: TEFL certificate and/or teaching experience, university degree.

CONDITIONS OF EMPLOYMENT: Contract for academic year or summer, full-time contract: up to 26 teaching hours a week.

SALARY: Minimum €1,008 net.

FACILITIES/SUPPORT: Assistance with accommodation, inlingua Method course, workshops, school library.

RECRUITMENT: Via internet, interview by phone.

CONTACT: Ingrid Antons, Director.

INSTITUTE OF MODERN LANGUAGES

Puerta Real 1, 18009 Granada

✆ 958 225536

🖰 director@imlgranada.com

NUMBER OF TEACHERS: 20

PREFERENCE OF NATIONALITY: British, other native English speakers.

QUALIFICATIONS: University degree, TEFL qualification and relevant experience.

CONDITIONS OF EMPLOYMENT: Contract for the academic year, contract for part-time work, national insurance, social security.

FACILITIES/SUPPORT: Good resources, Examination Centre for University of Cambridge ESOL Examinations in Granada, Almería and Málaga.

RECRUITMENT: EFL teachers are recruited from among the best qualified in Granada at the time. Initial short-list drawn up by director of studies from available CVs, then school owner carries out second interviews of short-listed candidates.

CONTACT: Jonathan Baum.

INTERLANG
C/Velázquez, 117, 1ª, Madrid
91 5158422
formacion@interlang.es
www.interlang.es

NUMBER OF TEACHERS: 70.

PREFERENCE OF NATIONALITY: None but must have permission to work in EU if non-EU citizen.

QUALIFICATIONS: CELTA plus 2 years' TEFL experience and some business experience.

CONDITIONS OF EMPLOYMENT: Standard 9-month contract, working 8.30am–11am/1pm–6pm.

SALARY: €18 per hour gross on contract, €23 per hour gross for registered freelancers. Tax deductions vary, but for freelancers there's a 7% deduction for the first two years and then 15%.

RECRUITMENT: Via the internet: the school has a permanent page on www.madridteacher.com. A face-to-face interview in Madrid is essential.

CONTACT: Sean O'Malley, Director of Studies.

LANCASTER COLLEGE RIVAS
Avda. Jose Hierro, 92 – Local 24, 28529 Vacimadrid, Madrid
+34 914998930
yes.school@lancastercollege.pt
www.lancastercollege.pt

NUMBER OF TEACHERS: 8.

PREFERENCE OF NATIONALITY: None.

QUALIFICATIONS: TEFL certificate or equivalent with 1–2 years' experience.

CONDITIONS OF EMPLOYMENT: Standard contract is 8 months with 24–26 working hours per week.

SALARY: €1,100 per month for 26 hours per week.

RECRUITMENT: Via the internet. Interviews in Madrid are essential.

CONTACT: Michael Brandao, School Director.

THE LANGUAGE CLUB
C/Rosalia de Castro 63, 08025 Barcelona
gillian@thelanguageclub.org
www.thelanguageclub.org

Teachers hired for business and academic full-immersion courses for all ages, taught on school premises or in-company.

LINC, ENGLISH FOR LIVING
c/Polavieja 13, 41004 Seville
+34 954 500 459
sevilla@linc.es
www.linc.es

NUMBER OF TEACHERS: 15–20.

PREFERENCE OF NATIONALITY: Must be an EU passport holder and native English speaker.

QUALIFICATIONS: Degree plus EFL qualification (CELTA or Trinity) and 1 year's teaching experience. Some knowledge of Spanish helpful.

CONDITIONS OF EMPLOYMENT: Standard contract is 9 months from October to June. Full and part-time contracts available. Full-time is 24 contact hours per week.

SALARY: €1,200 per month for full-time contracts.

FACILITIES/SUPPORT: Help is given with finding accommodation, particularly if the teacher can't speak Spanish.

RECRUITMENT: Interviews held via Skype or phone.

CONTACT: Mick Lawson, Director of Studies.

MCGINTY SCHOOL OF ENGLISH
Avda, Cabo de Gata, 82, 04007 Almeria
director@mcgintyschool.com
www.mcgintyschool.com

NUMBER OF TEACHERS: 10.

PREFERENCE OF NATIONALITY: None.

QUALIFICATIONS: Minimum CELTA or PGCE, preferably language graduate with 2 years' teaching experience.

CONDITIONS OF EMPLOYMENT: 1-year contract with the possibility to renew. Working hours between 4pm and 9.30pm, Monday–Friday.

SALARY: Starting full-time salary is €1,150 net per month but may increase depending on experience and qualifications.
FACILITIES/SUPPORT: Assistance provided with finding accommodation and applying for work permits.
RECRUITMENT: Usually via internet and newspaper advertising. Interviews are essential and can be conducted in Spain, the UK or over the phone.
CONTACT: Angus McGinty, Director.

MAUCAL SL
Pol. Argualas Nave 35, 50012 Zaragoza
℡ 976 350 205
✉ maucal@maucal.com
🖥 www.maucal.com

NUMBER OF TEACHERS: Approximately 4.
QUALIFICATIONS: EFL qualification and bachelor's degree (with honours) preferable.
CONDITIONS OF EMPLOYMENT: Contracts of 9–10 months; from 12 to 34 hours a week.
SALARY: Depends on hours a week.
RECRUITMENT: Application via www.tefl.com or CV. Interview essential.
CONTACT: Natalia Alastuey.

MERIT SCHOOL
Campo Florido 54–56, 2a, 08027 Barcelona
℡ 93 243 15 24
✉ dos@meritschool.com
🖥 www.meritschool.com

NUMBER OF TEACHERS: 40–50.
PREFERENCE OF NATIONALITY: Native English speakers. Must have EU passport or current work permit for Spain.
QUALIFICATIONS: University degree, TEFL certificate, 1–2 years' experience. Classroom experience with young learners or teenagers an advantage.
CONDITIONS OF EMPLOYMENT: Most contracts run from October to June with the possibility of extension into July for summer courses. Number of teaching hours varies – part-time and full-time teachers are sought.
SALARY: €15–€18 per hour. Travelling fee for off-site classes.
FACILITIES/SUPPORT: Three departments: Campo Florido campus (Young Learners, Teenagers, Adults), UPC campus (University students and staff) and in-company depart-ment (Business and General English for adults off site in companies) Regular in-house workshops, financial assistance to attend external training events, good library of teaching resources, peer observation scheme, regular observations and feedback by senior staff. Spanish classes.
RECRUITMENT: Mostly local (internet sites like www.loquo.com) but sometimes on international sites like www.tefl.com. Applications from interested teachers are always welcome. Face-to-face interview required. Best time to apply is late May to July or September.
CONTACT: Michael Terry, Director of Studies.

PUEBLO INGLES
Madrid
℡ 91 391 3400
✉ anglos@puebloingles.com
🖥 www.puebloingles.com or www.morethan english.com/anglos/index.asp

Informal exchange of English conversation for 8 days in various holiday resorts in Spain, which are 'stocked' with native English speakers and Spanish clients who want to improve their English. Participants receive free room and board, and transport from Madrid.

SPEAK ENGLISH SCHOOL
Cimadevilla 17 Ent F, 33003 Oviedo, Asturias
✉ speakschool@hotmail.com
🖥 www.speakschool.com

PREFERENCE OF NATIONALITY: British.
QUALIFICATIONS: TEFL certificate and a minimum of 2 years' experience.
CONDITIONS OF EMPLOYMENT: 9-month contracts, to work 25 hours per week.
SALARY: Net salary of €1,000 per month plus end of contract bonus.
FACILITIES/SUPPORT: The school can help with finding accommodation.
RECRUITMENT: Interviews essential, but can be carried out in the UK. Sometimes, telephone interviews can be arranged.
CONTACT: Mick Gordon, Director.

TECS (The Educational Consortium of Spain)
The English Centre, Apdo. Correos 85, 11500 El Puerto de Santa María, Cadiz
℡ 956 853000
✉ tecscamp@tecs.es
🖥 www.tecs.es (commercial) and www.tecs.es/ employment (employment site with online application)

NUMBER OF TEACHERS: 15–20 teachers required throughout the year. More than 130 staff employed in summer (40–50 teachers, 50–60 monitors and 20–30 management and support staff) at two residential camps in southern Spain, close to Cadiz in Andalucia.

QUALIFICATIONS: Employees must be team players who are young at heart and full of energy, with a mature and responsible personality.

CONDITIONS OF EMPLOYMENT: Minimum 1 month.

SALARY: Free board and lodging.

RECRUITMENT: Online.

CONTACT: Douglas Haines, Summer Camp Recruitment.

TENIDIOMAS

C/Caracuel 15, 11402 Jerez de la Frontera (Cadiz)

info@tenidiomas.com

NUMBER OF TEACHERS: 6.

PREFERENCE OF NATIONALITY: British.

QUALIFICATIONS: TEFL certificate and university degree.

CONDITIONS OF EMPLOYMENT: 9-month contract, 22 teaching hours per week.

FACILITIES/SUPPORT: Monthly workshops run by DOS.

RECRUITMENT: Usually recruit new teachers via internet, telephone interview required.

CONTACT: Gerry Rylance, Director.

TRAINING EXPRESS S.L.

Plaza del Cordón N° 1, 28008 Madrid

+34 91 521 1554

rebecca@trainingexpress.es or jobs@training express.es

www.trainingexpress.es

Madrid-based language consultancy.

NUMBER OF TEACHERS: 200.

PREFERENCE OF NATIONALITY: None.

QUALIFICATIONS: Minimum 2 years' experience plus TEFL.

CONDITIONS OF EMPLOYMENT: 9-month contracts, 80 hours per month constitutes full-time schedule.

SALARY: €900–€1,200 per month gross. Standard deductions of about 6%.

FACILITIES/SUPPORT: Assistance given with accommodation through a relocation agency. Help given with obtaining the necessary permits, including liaising with local state ministry.

RECRUITMENT: Via international websites such as www.tefl. com and local sources. Interview required.

CONTACT: Rebecca Webb, Executive Director.

VAUGHANTOWN

Avda. General Perón 38, Edificio Master's I, 2ª Planta 28020 Madrid

91 748 5950

anglos@vaughantown.com

www.vaughantown.com

Intensive 6-day cultural exchange programme or 'talk-a-thon', from a Sunday to a Friday, held almost every week year round. 15 Spaniards and 17 English speakers are put together in a relaxed environment, accommodation in 4-star hotels in Spain, to re-create an English-speaking village. The programme is based on both one-to-one sessions and group activities, as well as excursions, parties and walks in the countryside.

SALARY: None but free food and accommodation, and transport from Madrid.

SWITZERLAND

The status of English is steadily rising in Switzerland. Partly in response to parental pressure, some cantons (including Zurich) decided in 2001 to teach English rather than French as the first-choice second language, to the consternation of many Swiss. According to the Superintendent of Education in Zurich, the decision was taken because children and young people are far more motivated to learn English than any other language and he believes that this should be the starting point for success in teaching. English will become compulsory throughout the curriculum in all Swiss schools by 2010, which will involve massive retraining of Swiss teachers and possibly more demand for foreign teachers of English.

Yet prospects are gloomy for people who fancy the idea of teaching the gnomes of Zürich or their counterparts in other parts of Switzerland, unless they are ultra-qualified. Although immigration regulations are not as restrictive as they once were (see next section), Switzerland will not suddenly be welcoming an army of foreign language teachers. Teachers may also like to consider whether they wish to face the barrage of regulations that are part and parcel of living in Switzerland, from attempting to open a bank account without possessing a small fortune, to falling foul of strict rubbish disposal regulations.

The Swiss economy remains solid, but is not as invincible as it was once considered to be, as the director of a *Sprachschule* in Basel explained:

As a small language school in a country and region which has been experiencing severe withdrawal symptoms (from full employment, job and financial security), it is unlikely that we will be recruiting staff from outside Switzerland, especially as there is a large reservoir of potential candidates here in the Basel region and work permits for staff from outside Switzerland are now a rarity.

This was corroborated in 2010 by **Estelle Bieri** of the chain of Migros Club Schools (www.ecole-club.ch):

In order to teach English, we require teachers to be either native speakers or to have a C2 level of English, preferably with a good Cambridge Proficiency pass. Teachers must have a B residence permit. In addition, they require a qualification in teaching English as a foreign language to adults, for example a CELTA or equivalent, or higher. This is valid for any Swiss school which is Eduqua validated (Eduqua is an independent body for quality control). Many of our teachers have university qualifications. Teaching experience is welcome, particularly with regard to teaching certain levels and types of classes (ESP, etc.).

There are nine Wall Street Institutes and the same number of Bénédict Schools in Switzerland; a list of addresses is available at www.wallstreetinstitute.ch and www.benedict-international.com. One of the biggest Wall Street schools is the one in Lausanne at Rue du Simplon 34, 1006 Lausanne (21 614 66 14; wsi.lausanne@wallst.ch). If you are hired by a Swiss language school, wages are high, ranging from SFr30 to SFr60 for a 50-minute lesson.

Private tutoring is a possibility for those who lack a permit as the American world traveller and free spirit **Danny Jacobson** discovered when he was living with his Swiss girlfriend in Bern:

A Swiss friend advised me to apply at one of the English schools but I didn't think it would work without a permit. So I just made my own flyer and put it up around town and the next thing I knew I had a bunch of people calling me up to help with proofreading seminar papers/assignments and to give private lessons. I figured I'd go for quantity and low-ball the market, charging only CHF20 per hour. But I found a few adverts for people looking for teachers and with those, I went with their offered price, which was much more.

A qualified teacher can charge about CHF80 an hour in the cities, so even CHF40 might be considered a bargain.

The English Teaching Association in Switzerland (www.e-tas.ch) operates a jobs board with a few vacancies, mainly for part-time trainers for business. The newsgroup http://groups.yahoo.com/group/swissenglish is aimed at EFL teachers already in Switzerland, not those enquiring about job opportunities.

REGULATIONS

No permit is needed for EU nationals who stay for less than three months. If they want to stay beyond that, e.g. to continue job-hunting or to do a seasonal job, they must apply for an L permit (short-term residence permit). The L-EC/EFTA permit (*Kurzaufenhalter/Autorisation de Courte Durée*) is issued for periods of work lasting less than 12 months and can be renewed once for a further year. EU nationals simply need to take their passport and contract of employment to the local cantonal office. L-permits are no longer tied to a particular job or canton.

If the contract of employment is going to extend beyond two years, it is possible to apply for a B-permit, valid for between one and five years. Note that until 2011, Switzerland will continue to impose quotas on the number of permits granted for foreigners who want to stay longer than four months. However, slowly, the Swiss are opening to the outside world. In a popular vote held in February 2009, nearly 60% of the Swiss people voted in favour of the continuation of the agreement on the free movement of persons. Detailed information about the regulations is published by the Federal Office of Migration (www.bfm.admin.ch). Detailed information in English is sometimes available from the cantonal authorities, for example downloadable brochures about living and working in Zurich are available at welcome.zh.ch. The canton of Zurich also allows foreigners to apply for a work permit online via their WorkPermits gateway, which shortens the application time. The searchable forum www.englishforum.ch can also be helpful on technical matters.

As a result of Switzerland moving towards integration with Europe, non-EU citizens will now find it harder to gain legal access to Switzerland's English-teaching market unless they apply in special categories like spouse or trainee. If a non-European does find an employer willing to sponsor their application, the applicant will have to collect the documents from the Swiss embassy in his or her home country.

VACATION WORK

More possibilities for teaching English exist at summer camps than in city language institutes, as can be seen from the programmes listed in the directory below. There are a number of international schools in Switzerland, some of which run English language and sports summer schools. The Swiss Federation of Private Schools produces a list of summer schools in Switzerland held at its member schools, indicating which ones teach English. This is available at www.swiss-schools.ch. Watch for occasional ads or, if you are in Switzerland, make local enquiries.

In addition to the organisations with entries below, the following organisations offer summer language courses between June and September and may need teachers or monitors (or some combination of the two):

Aiglon College Summer School, 1885 Chesières (24 496 6128; www.aiglon.ch).
Collège Alpin Beau Soleil, Holiday Language Camp, Avenue Centrale, CH-1884 Villars-sur-Ollon (www.beausoleil/ch).

PHILIP LEE from New Zealand spent his summers during university working at English language summer camps on the continent including one summer with Village Camps (see entry). The application for the position of counsellor involved a formal application and phone interview, plus he had to complete a basic first aid/CPR course (CPR etc) at his own expense. This opportunity is open to non-European nationals as Philip reported in 2010:

There wasn't much of a visa problem as most tutors from outside the EU (US/Canada/Australia/NZ) had a three-month tourist visa I believe. I never encountered any problems in relation to my visa and working and even when I was working in Switzerland, where I expected more regulation and controls, there wasn't a problem at all. I worked in Switzerland for a two-week camp. But there were people who stayed there for up to 12 weeks working without problems.

I was paid cash in hand for the Swiss camps. I think payment was always a bit of concern for people working in this line of work for the first time, in the sense that there were no 'employment rights', but at the organisations I worked with, payment was always managed very professionally.

ESL (Ecole Suisse de Langues), Grand-Rue 42, CP 1206, 1820 Montreux (21 621 88 88; www.esl-schools.org/en/language-courses/summer-camps/informations/jobs/index.htm). Summer programmes in Leysin, Montreux, Ascona and Zug.

Institut Le Rosey, Camp d'Eté, CH-1180 Rolle (21 822 5500; summercamp@rosey.ch; www.roseysummercamps.ch). Qualified or experienced EFL teachers over 20 for co-educational summer camps with sports coaching on Lake Geneva. Teachers must be capable of carrying out boarding school duties.

Institut Monte Rosa, 57 Avenue de Chillon, CH-1820 Montreux-Territet (21 965 4545; info@monterosa.ch; www.monterosa.ch).

Leysin American School in Switzerland, CH-1854 Leysin (24 493 37 7 www.las.ch/summer/staffhome.html). Contact the Director of Summer Programs.

St George's School in Switzerland, 1815 Clarens/Montreux (www.st-georges.ch).

Surval Mont-Fleuri, Route de Glion 56, CH-1820 Montreux 1 (www.surval.ch).

TASIS (The American School in Switzerland), Summer Language Programs, Via Collina d'Oro, 6926 Montagnola-Lugano (91 960 5151 http://switzerland.tasis.com). Employ Americans among others in Lugano.

LIST OF EMPLOYERS

BERLITZ SCHOOL OF LANGUAGES AG

Gerbergasse 4, 4051 Basel

61 226 90 40

www.berlitz.ch, https://secure.berlitz.eu/
Berlitz_CH/en/basle/job_vacancies

NUMBER OF TEACHERS: 15.

PREFERENCE OF NATIONALITY: Must have work permit.

QUALIFICATIONS: Bachelor's degree or professional experience, e.g. business, banking. Berlitz is looking for motivated and enthusiastic employees who can openly engage with others, have a love of language and culture, and a positive disposition. Must have teaching skills and be a communicative person.

CONDITIONS OF EMPLOYMENT: No limit on contract length. Flexible hours of work. Pupils are adults whose average age is between 30 and 40.

SALARY: SFr22.50 per 40-minute lesson plus 10–20% supplements for some programmes.

FACILITIES/SUPPORT: No assistance with accommodation. Training provided.

RECRUITMENT: Through adverts. Local interviews essential.

THE CAMBRIDGE INSTITUTE

Silk Street 6, 8001 Zurich

44 221 12 12

zuerich@cambridge.ch

www.cambridge.ch

PREFERENCE OF NATIONALITY: Native English speaker who is already resident in Zurich.

QUALIFICATIONS: English teaching certificate or diploma (e.g. CELTA or equivalent). The candidate must have already obtained the required permits to live and work in Switzerland.

CONTACT: Keith Daborn, Director of Studies.

HAUT-LAC INTERNATIONAL CENTRE

1669 Les Sciernes

26 928 42 00

info@haut-lac.com or jobs@haut-lac.com

www.myswisscamp.com

NUMBER OF TEACHERS: Teachers/monitors needed for summer, spring, autumn and winter language camps for adolescents.

PREFERENCE OF NATIONALITY: Native English speakers, preferably with EU passport.

QUALIFICATIONS: TEFL CELTA or equivalent plus it is useful to have experience in sports, drama, art or games organisation.

CONDITIONS OF EMPLOYMENT: Summer camp (mid-June to end of August); winter ski camp (end of December to early April); spring camp (early April to early May) and autumn camp (late September to mid-October).

FACILITIES/SUPPORT: Full board and lodging provided in single, twin or three-bedded rooms. Help given with travel expenses. Free laundry facilities and use of sports equipment.

RECRUITMENT: Send for an application form to jobs@ haut-lac.com.

CONTACT: Mark Gallagher (mark@haut-lac.com).

INLINGUA - BASEL

Dufourstrasse 50, 4052 Basel

41 61 278 99 33

Christian.ruetti@inlingua.com

www.inlingua.com

NUMBER OF TEACHERS: 20–25.

PREFERENCE OF NATIONALITY: Must be an EU citizen.

QUALIFICATIONS: University degree is essential. If the degree is not a teaching degree then CELTA or equivalent is also required (online courses are not accepted).

CONDITIONS OF EMPLOYMENT: Generally open-ended contracts but a two-year minimum commitment is expected. Lessons are held from 7am to 9pm and the teachers' work load depends on their availability.

SALARY: Starting full-time salary is approximately CHF 6,200.

FACILITIES/SUPPORT: All paperwork for work permits is handled by the school.

RECRUITMENT: Usually via ETAS (English Teachers' Association of Switzerland), advertising online or, most commonly, spontaneous applications. Interviews are essential. First round is conducted via telephone followed by two rounds of personal interviews at the school.

CONTACT: Christian Rüttu, Personnel and Office Manager.

TLC – THE LANGUAGE COMPANY

Bahnhofstarsse 44, 5400 Baden

41 56 205 51 78

info@tlcsprachschule.ch

www.tlcsprachschule.ch

NUMBER OF TEACHERS: 25.

PREFERENCE OF NATIONALITY: Native English speakers.

QUALIFICATIONS: Minimum CELTA plus experience teaching English to adults. Some business experience is preferable.

CONDITIONS OF EMPLOYMENT: Open-ended contract. Classes start at 8am and finish at 9.30pm. If the teacher is flexible in terms of location and time they can work up to 26 hours per week.

SALARY: SFr58–SFr70 depending on qualifications, experience and range of teaching.

RECRUITMENT: Usually through ETAS (English Teachers' Association of Switzerland), adverts on websites such as www.jobs.ch or through word of mouth. Interviews are essential. Preliminary interview can be done by phone and successful candidate will need to take a trial lesson in Switzerland.

CONTACT: Daniela Ziegler, HR Manager.

VILLAGE CAMPS

Personnel Office, Centre Village Camps, CH1854 Leysin

 +41 24 494 2353 camps

personnel@villagecamps.com

www.villagecamps.com/personnel

Language summer camp at Leysin near Lake Geneva in French-speaking Switzerland (also in York, England).

PREFERENCE OF NATIONALITY: European, North American, Australian, New Zealand passport holders may apply.

QUALIFICATIONS: Applicants must be at least 21 years of age, possess a recognised qualification in language teaching (minimum 4 weeks) and be a native English speaker of the language of instruction. A second language is desirable and experience in sports, creative and/or outdoor activities is essential. A valid first aid and cardiopulmonary resuscitation (CPR) certificate is required while at camp.

CONDITIONS OF EMPLOYMENT: Employment periods vary from 3 to 8 weeks between June and August.

SALARY: Room and board, accident and liability insurance and a weekly allowance provided.

RECRUITMENT: Starts in January. There is no deadline to submit applications, but positions are limited. Interviews are by telephone. For information on dates, locations, and positions available and to apply directly online, visit www.villagecamps.com.

CENTRAL AND EASTERN EUROPE

The transition to a market economy throughout the vast area of Eastern and Central Europe has resulted in a huge demand for professional assistance at all levels, especially when it comes to improving the skills of communication. The dramatic changes which have taken place in the former Communist Bloc since 1989 mean that in every hotel lobby, office boardroom and government ministry from Silesia to Siberia, deals are being struck, export partnerships forged and academic alliances developed between East and West. The eastern Europeans benefiting from this new commerce tend to be the ones who have acquired the English language.

While Russia and many of its former satellites have continued to wrestle with their political and economic demons, the more stable Central European states of Hungary, Poland, the Czech Republic, Slovakia, the Baltic States and most recently, Bulgaria and Romania, have been welcomed into the European fold by acceding to the EU.

In some quarters of Central Europe there has been a noticeable backlash against what has been seen as a selling out to the West, especially in the major capitals, which are now swarming with foreigners. School directors are now perfectly aware of the English-speaking foreigner who masquerades as a teacher but really intends to indulge in cheap beer and clubs. They are suspicious of anyone projecting this hidden agenda, disliking the fact that so many foreigners used the region as an extended party venue early on.

Yet despite having moved past making 'Western' synonymous with 'desirable', the majority of Central European people are still remarkably welcoming to British and American ELT teachers. On most street corners, private language schools employ native English speaking teachers. Working in Central and Eastern Europe may not seem as attractive as it did just after the 'revolution', but thousands of Britons and Americans continue to fall under the spell of famous destinations such as Prague, Budapest, Kraków, as well as many other beautiful towns in Slovakia and Bulgaria. Even those who find themselves in the less prepossessing industrial cities usually come away beguiled by Central European charm.

Even if ordinary people no longer see English as an automatic passport to higher wages and a better life, they have not stopped wanting to learn it. The English language teaching industry in those countries has grown up, and is now much more likely to hire teachers with proven experience or an appropriate qualification. Massive amounts of money have been invested in Poland, Hungary and the former Czechoslovakia in retraining local teachers for the teaching of English in state schools and these programmes have been largely successful. Thousands of young people from Central Europe move to English-speaking countries to earn some money and improve their English. Yet, demand continues for native English speakers in state schools, private language schools and universities, often for those with a sophisticated understanding of linguistic methodology.

Opportunities persist. While the wealthy elite can afford to pay for extra tuition in English (and other subjects), most citizens must endure fairly small education budgets in their local schools, particularly in countries such as the Slovak Republic where local teachers hardly earn enough to live on. It is worth bearing these issues in mind when considering where to head to teach EFL, as emphasised by **Steve Anderson** from Minneapolis who spent two years teaching in Hungary, the first in a well-resourced urban school, the second in an impoverished rural one but which he found much more fulfilling.

The explosion in the number of training centres for TEFL/TESL teachers in all English-speaking countries means that the pool of certified available teachers is fairly large. Teachers who can claim to specialise either in teaching Young Learners or in teaching Business English are especially attractive since both these areas of ELT are buoyant. Tourism training colleges in Hungary, the Czech & Slovak

Republic and the Baltics are especially keen on encouraging conversational English, while some schools in Poland are offering practical conversation classes which teach pupils to fill in English forms and rent a flat. Failing that, the easiest way to become more employable is to acquire a TEFL qualification which could prove especially useful (and incidentally cheaper) if obtained in Eastern Europe. For example International House in Prague, Budapest, Bratislava, Katowice and Wroclaw all offer the CELTA course while ITC Prague offers a TESOL certificate (see the Directory of Training Courses) as do many others.

North Americans may find that the accession of some of the former Eastern bloc countries to the EU has resulted in immigration regulations favouring English teachers from Britain and Ireland. Note that former Yugoslav republics (i.e. Slovenia, Croatia and Macedonia) are included in the chapter 'The Rest of Europe' following this section, though some placement organisations mentioned here include them as part of Central and Eastern Europe.

One of the first language teaching organisations to break into Eastern Europe has continued to be one of the most active and energetic in the region, International House. IH-affiliated schools are flourishing in Belarus, Lithuania, Ukraine, Poland, Romania and the Republic of Slovakia. The affiliation agreement with all IH schools states that the schools can employ only teachers who have passed the CELTA course. Similarly the British Council is often in need of suitable candidates to fill vacancies in its teaching centres in Bulgaria, Romania, Ukraine, etc.

Local salaries can seem absurdly low when translated into a hard currency. Some schools pay what is usually a generous salary by local standards but which can leave little after paying for food and accommodation. It is difficult to generalise but a typical package would include a monthly net salary of £400–£600 in addition to free accommodation and possibly some other perks such as a travel stipend. The best paid jobs are for firms which teach in-company courses, especially in Poland, though they are unlikely to offer accommodation.

A host of private language schools which are either independent or part of larger language teaching organisations are represented in Eastern and Central Europe. Most of the Central European schools listed in the directory are well established and offer above-average working conditions. Some mainstream schools in the stable democracies have delegated to specialist recruiters the task of finding teachers. But in the more volatile climate of Russia and former Soviet republics (which are several years behind the Central European nations), locally managed schools come and go, and tend to choose their teachers from the pool of native English speakers on the spot, who also come and go. Intrepid travellers visiting the Central Asian Republics with no intention to work are still often invited to stay a while and do some English teaching, as was happening in off-the-beaten-track towns in Poland and the former Czechoslovakia 15 years ago.

> *One interesting option for those who do not wish to commit themselves for a full academic year is to work at one of the many language summer camps which are offered to young people, usually in scenic locations from Lake Balaton in Hungary to Lake Baikal in Siberia.*

CONDITIONS OF WORK

The financial rewards of working in the old Russian Empire are usually so negligible that trained/experienced teachers cannot be enticed to teach there unless they have an independent interest in living in that part of the world or are supported by a voluntary organisation such as the Soros Foundation. Even the large language chains which offer reasonable working conditions (e.g. flat provided, plenty of support) do not pay high enough wages to allow ordinary EL teachers to save any money. Russia itself can offer reasonable wages, particularly now that the economy is performing well, but the cost of living can be very high in Moscow and St Petersburg and inflation continues to be a problem.

Volunteering programmes arrange for eager volunteers in search of a cultural experience to spend time in this part of the world, provided they don't mind being out-of-pocket at the end of a short stint of teaching. The role of native speaking volunteers is to conduct practical English classes (i.e. conversation classes) to supplement grammar taught by local school staff.

Most of the Central European cities and larger towns have sprouted Western-style supermarkets and other consumerist outlets, often to the disgruntlement of the older generations who have a fondness for their local shops. Living in these cities begins to feel not so very different from living in France or Italy, particularly with the influx of international companies. Smaller towns and rural areas can still be a very different proposition (until you come across expats who have bought property on the cheap in Bulgaria (etc).

However, the entry of these countries into Europe, with its capitalist ideals, has been attended by problems and pitfalls such as an absence of co-ordinated educational policies (or political infighting on the topic) and the possibility of shoddy or exploitative working conditions for teachers, not to mention price rises, unemployment and an increase in crime. Similarly, locals worry about the 'Westernisation' of their countries, the unfortunate influx of English-speaking tourists determined to get very drunk or buy up prime local property, and the exodus of young people to wealthier countries.

The bubble of opportunism about EU integration has probably burst for just about all concerned; although the upside of this for qualified native English speaking teachers is that the market is more stable, realistic and developed.

FINDING A JOB

A range of vacancies in Central and Eastern Europe, particularly in Poland, continue to be advertised in the educational press or on the internet, which is fast usurping the role of recruitment agencies. As has been stressed elsewhere, the possibility of creating your own job in this region still exists. Much of what takes place happens by chance, and protocol is often given a back seat to friendly encounters. Obtaining work often comes down to the right (or wrong) hairstyle or whether you've got any Polish/Lithuanian/Slovak/Azerbaijani ancestry. Looking professional, being persistent and asking as many questions as you answer, rather than sitting back on your heels, usually pays off. EU teachers will have an advantage in securing 'on the spot' jobs in private language schools, although public school jobs may involve more red tape, particularly in the case of Hungary.

If you want to arrange a position through a mediating organisation, here are the main ones in the UK which continue to recruit teachers for more than one country in the region. (Organisations that deal only with one country are included in the relevant chapter.) In addition to IH, the major chains have some franchise schools in the region, chief among them EF English First, which sends many teachers to Russia and elsewhere, and Language Link with affiliated schools in Russia and Central Asia (www.languagelink.co.uk). ITC International TEFL Certificate in Prague 1 (www.itc-training.com) offers TEFL training with lifetime job guidance included (though they no longer claim to be able to guarantee immediate employment in Eastern Europe as they once did).

Sharing One Language (SOL), 2 Bridge Chambers, The Strand, Barnstaple, Devon EX31 1HB; (01271 327319; info@sol.org.uk/ sol@sol.org.uk; www.sol.org.uk). Non-profit-making organisation which annually recruits teachers with a degree (ideally in Education or Languages) plus at least an introductory TEFL/TESOL certificate to teach in schools in the state sector in some Eastern and Central European countries, especially Hungary, Slovakia and Romania. All posts include local salary and free independent housing thus giving enough to live reasonably. The teacher's only expense is the cost of getting there and back. The website provides contact details for country coordinators in Hungary, Poland, Slovakia, Bulgaria, Serbia and Romania.

Projects Abroad, Aldsworth Parade, Goring, Sussex BN12 4TX (01903 708300; info@projects-abroad.co.uk; www.projects-abroad.co.uk). Recruits volunteers to work as English language teaching assistants for the summer or during the academic year in 25 countries worldwide. No TEFL background required. Packages cost from £895 and include placement, accomodation, 3 meals a days. Full medical and travel insurance and 24 hour staff support.

FOR NORTH AMERICANS

Several US organisations are actively involved in teacher recruitment for the region.

Bridges for Education (www.bridges4edu.org). Recruits and trains volunteer teachers to spend July on an international peace camp in Belarus. Volunteers are given basic ESL training before departure. Participants pay their airfare and programme administration fee of about $1,000.

Central European Teaching Program (CETP) (www.cetp.info). Places approximately 65 native speakers of English in Hungary (see chapter) with plans to expand into the Czech Republic.

Peace Corps, 1111 20th St NW, Washington DC 20526 (toll-free +1 800 424 8580; www.peacecorps.gov). Provides volunteer teachers on 27-month contracts to many countries in Eastern Europe, with the largest numbers in Ukraine, Bulgaria, Kyrgyz Republic and Romania. Must be US citizen, over 18 and in good health. All expenses, including airfare and health insurance, are covered. Recruits people to teach at both secondary and university level and to become involved with teacher training and curriculum development.

The rest of this chapter is organised by country. Bulgaria, Czech Republic, Slovak Republic, Hungary, Poland and Romania are followed by Russia and its former satellite states (the Baltic states, Ukraine and the Central Asian Republics).

BULGARIA

Since Bulgaria joined the EU in 2007 it has attracted more EU tourists as well as property specula-tors and foreign businesses. The demand for English teachers is substantial, although the market has moved on a long way from the excitable years following the post-1989 transition to a market economy. Those without a degree or teaching qualification are much less likely to secure a position than they once were. Schools will usually expect to see at least a degree and teaching certificate, and some want relevant experience as well.

FINDING A JOB

The Sofia-based non-profit organisation Teachers for Central and Eastern Europe, 21 V 5 Rakovski Boulevard, Dimitrovgrad 6400 (707 276 4571 USA; +359 391 2 47 87 in Bulgaria; tfcee@usa. net; www.tfcee.8m.com) is active in Bulgaria. Since 1993 TFCEE has been recruiting native English speaking teachers for English-medium secondary schools, schools of natural sciences or universities in cities of over 50,000 for an academic year (mid-September to late June). TFCEE also recruits na-tive English speakers for a summer programme which operates in July and August. A TEFL certificate is recommended and teaching experience is an advantage.

The weekly teaching load with TFCEE is 18/19 40-minute classes per week. The monthly salary in Bulgarian leva is equivalent to €200 (higher than that of a Bulgarian teacher), in addition to free furnished accommodation, 60 days of paid holiday, paid sick leave, free Bulgarian language instruc-tion, internet, free healthcare and free multiple-entry visa and work permit. A €60 application fee is required when applying to this programme.

The British Council in Sofia has a thriving English centre, which offers courses for young learners, adults and businessmen and women; to enquire about any forthcoming teaching vacancies email learnenglish@britishcouncil.bg.

American teachers with at least a master's degree could try the AUBG, a private American-style liberal arts university located in Blagoevgrad (www.aubg.bg). All classes are in English and the uni-versity's English Language Institute prepares future AUBG applicants for the TOEFL and SAT ex-ams, as well as teaching courses every semester to absolute beginners and intermediate students. Outside the official education system a reasonable number of language institutes and educational establishments are on the look out for well-presented, confident candidates.

One of the first private schools to be established after the revolution of 1990 was the AVO-3 School of English with two schools in Sofia (www.avo-3.com) affiliated to Bell Worldwide. It runs CELTA courses (see entry in the Directory of Training Courses) and employs native English speaking staff who must have a degree, TEFL certificate and at least three months of teaching experience.

The English Academy has two centres in Plovdiv and Varna (www.englishacademybg.com), whilst the Real English School (www.realenglishschool.eu), run by Vicky and Collin Williams, is based in the beautiful old town of Veliko Turnovo (see entries below). The Real English School sends teachers to work at the local private high school, which also employs a few native teachers of their own.

Many companies run in-house English language training, and jobs with them tend to be well paid and stable.

REGULATIONS

Bulgaria's accession into the EU has made it easier for teachers in terms of red tape. EU nationals only need a letter from their employer in order to get permission to stay for one year. It's a little time consuming, but basically unproblematic, and is done at the local police station. US citizens, on the other hand, need a visa obtained from the Bulgarian Embassy. For this reason the Real English School, among others, only employs EU citizens or non-EU citizens who have a right to stay for some other reason (e.g. marriage to a Bulgarian). The English Academy, however, will consider employing US citizens who are responsible for their own visas, although some assistance is given with paperwork.

LEISURE TIME

Vicky Williams, co-director of the Real English School based in Veliko Turnovo, finds that living in Bulgaria is never dull:

> *As for living and working in BG, it is a country which is changing rapidly. There are still plenty of vestiges of communism around in terms of architecture, cars, bureaucracy and lack of choice in shops, etc., but on the other hand there is a huge amount of building going on and many people now do have a lot of money. It's a fascinating place to live in at the moment – it is a country of contrasts. There are American style malls springing up everywhere, full of designer clothes shops that are frequented by people who drive 25 year old Ladas.*

The average salary has been steadily rising and is now about 600 leva in Sofia, more than twice what it was two years ago. Outside the cities, wages are much lower and living conditions can be primitive, for example in the countryside you still see peasants with donkeys and carts and stooped old ladies lugging branches of trees home to burn for firewood. Yet in town the place is packed with bars, nightclubs, casinos, Ray-Banned teenagers and flashy 4 × 4s parked all over the (crumbling) pavements.

LIST OF EMPLOYERS

ENGLISH ACADEMY PLOVDIV

28 Gladstone Street, Plovdiv 4000

 +359 32 623 457

 plovdiv@englishacademybg.com

 www.englishacademybg.com

NUMBER OF TEACHERS: 4.

PREFERENCE OF NATIONALITY: Only native English speakers.

QUALIFICATIONS: First degree and recognised teaching certificate such as the Cambridge CELTA.

CONDITIONS OF EMPLOYMENT: 3, 6 and 12-month contracts. Full-time: Tuesday to Friday, 5.40pm–9.40pm

and Saturday 9am–1pm and 2pm–6pm. Part-time: less than 24 hours per week within the same time frame.

SALARY: 15 Bulgarian Leva per hour, 10% flat rate tax.

FACILITIES/SUPPORT: Arranges with local agents for accommodation viewings and assists with translation. Non-EU citizens are responsible for their own visas although assistance is given by the school.

RECRUITMENT: Telephone and/or in person interviews.

CONTACT: Mark A Faulkner, Director of Studies (markfaulkner@englishacademybg.com).

ENGLISH ACADEMY VARNA

48 Preslav Str, Nezavisimost Square, Varna 9000

☎ +359 52 622351

✉ varna@englishacademybg.com

💻 www.englishacademybg.com or www.varnaschool.com

NUMBER OF TEACHERS: 14.

PREFERENCE OF NATIONALITY: Only native English speakers.

QUALIFICATIONS: Degree in any subject and teaching certificate are essential, 2 years' experience preferred. Must be friendly and outgoing.

CONDITIONS OF EMPLOYMENT: 6 or 12-month contracts, 24 teaching hours a week, 5 days a week (Monday to Friday or Tuesday to Saturday, although a lot of teaching takes place at weekends).

SALARY: 20 leva per hour (approximately €10), more for technical/non-standard teaching. 10% flat rate tax.

RECRUITMENT: Through the internet (mainly www.tefl.com). Interviews essential, either by telephone or face-to-face. Non-EU citizens are responsible for their own visas, but assistance given with the relevant paperwork.

CONTACT: Mark Mctaggart, Director of Studies.

THE REAL ENGLISH SCHOOL

21 Hadji Dimitar Street, Veliko Turnovo 5000

☎ 62 605 749/ 886 171753

✉ information@realenglishschool.eu

💻 www.realenglishschool.eu

NUMBER OF TEACHERS: 6.

PREFERENCE OF NATIONALITY: Must have EU passport, native English speakers only.

QUALIFICATIONS: CELTA or equivalent, prefer minimum 1 year's experience. Without CELTA, must have BA/MA in English or PGCE plus 2 years' TEFL experience. Experience teaching any exam courses (FCE, CAE, CPE, TOEFL, SAT, IELTS, ILEC) will be an advantage. The school teaches General and Business English (students are aged from 8 to adult).

CONDITIONS OF EMPLOYMENT: 1-year standard contract. 24 contact hours a week.

SALARY: 1,000 Bulgarian Levs per month (net).

FACILITIES/SUPPORT: Free Bulgarian lessons. Assistance with locating accommodation and registering with the police, etc.

RECRUITMENT: Through tefl.com, eslbase.com, and local hire. Interviews are essential, and can be by phone. Very occasionally interviews are required.

CZECH REPUBLIC

The proliferation of TEFL qualified teachers has allowed language schools to become far more discerning, especially in Prague. Language institutes generally do not accept online TEFL certificates, and adhere to the international standard of looking for teachers who have had at least 106 class hours in a four-week on-site programme, with at least six hours of observed teaching practice. Smaller Czech towns including some rather uninspiring places in the steel-producing heart of the country and the Moravian capital Brno offer interested teachers more scope for employment than the tourist-clogged capital. **Katie Boland** of the Boland School highlights the problems of working in the country's stunning capital:

> *Living and working conditions change dramatically as soon as you leave the capital, especially in terms of the TEFL market. Prague offers low pay, dreadful hours, split shifts and cut-throat competition between language schools that leads to a lot of job insecurity for teachers. However, the rest of the country is a delight, offering the opportunity to earn some decent money and enjoy a wonderful teaching experience. I would advise people to look around a bit before jumping into a position.*

Teaching private lessons is the most lucrative but the most difficult to fix up for new arrivals. Private lessons now go as high as 300 crowns an hour for businesses, but most earn the teacher about 200 crowns. A good way to attract pupils initially is to charge at the lower end of the scale but to teach in groups of three or four.

FINDING A JOB

Most schools express no preference for nationality, and prefer a mixture of accents. Americans are still in the ascendancy (it has been estimated that there are between 20,000 and 30,000 in Prague alone), but Canadians, Britons, etc. are all welcome. Australians are generally well received partly because of the large number of Czechs (about 20,000) who emigrated to Australia, though they will encounter more visa difficulties than teachers from Britain, Ireland or the USA. The Czech Republic's entry into the EU also gives Britons a red-tape advantage. It is interesting to note that no schools in the list below stipulate that they hire only EU nationals.

STATE SCHOOLS

Qualified teachers are recruited to teach in Czech primary and secondary schools, usually on a one-year contract with low-cost or free accommodation and a salary of 15,000–25,000 Czech crowns net per month. The centralised contact is the Academic Information Agency (AIA) in Prague (see entry). AIA is part of the Ministry of Education, and distributes its literature through Czech Embassies abroad. Almost since the Velvet Revolution of 1991, the AIA has assisted native English speakers interested in teaching English at primary and secondary state schools. Far fewer schools turn to the AIA nowadays for help with filling posts. At the time of writing, only one vocational and technical secondary school was publicising a vacancy for the 2010/2011 academic year. Any positions that are registered with the AIA are likely to be in smaller towns and certainly not Prague. The school year runs for 10 months from 1 September to 30 June, though some vacancies occur in January between semesters. Although the minimum requirement is a BA/MA in English/Applied Linguistics, additional teaching qualifications (TEFL or PGCE) and experience give an applicant priority.

Applications should be submitted before the end of April. The AIA simply acts as a go-between, circulating CVs and applications to state schools that have requested a teacher. Schools then contact applicants directly to discuss contractual details. **Brian Farrelly** spent a very successful year teaching in state schools:

> *I taught in two state schools in the Czech Republic and had a really great time in both. I felt really privileged to teach the students there. In my first job in a 'gymnazium' secondary school in a small town called Sedlcany, south of Prague, the staff and students made me tremendously welcome. I also greatly enjoyed the freedom to teach as I saw fit, although I felt initially very daunted by the lack of guidance regarding what I should be doing with the students. My next job was found by the AIA in Prague. After visiting, I was offered a number of schools and I chose another gymnazium in another small town called Jevicko, north of Brno.*

The growth of a free market economy means that the role of voluntary organisations has diminished, and in fact SOL (see introduction to Eastern Europe) has dropped the Czech Republic from its list of destination countries as of 2010. Although CETP is more active in Hungary (see chapter), it is about to expand into the Czech Republic to place volunteer EFL teachers in small Czech towns (not Prague).

PRIVATE INSTITUTES

A wide range of well-established schools offers high standards of instruction. The main international chains of language schools such as Berlitz have large established operations in the country. Most teachers are recruited locally, often through their TEFL training centre, such as Prague School (www. tefl.cz) or via noticeboards, for example at the British Council and English language bookshops.

It is not difficult to find contact details for English language institutes in Prague and elsewhere. The most established schools which are externally vetted and their quality standards monitored belong to the Asociace Jazykovych Skol CR (AJSCR) or Czech Association of Language Schools (Kolodějská 8/3077, 100 00 Prague 10; +420 602193978; http://ajscr.cz); its site links to its 16 members. Expats.cz lists scores of language schools and www.eslbase.com/schools/czech provides links to more than 150 language teaching companies. Also the *Yellow Pages* (Zlaté Stránky) is an excellent source of addresses under the heading *Jazykove skoly* as is the Business Directory of the *Prague Post* (http://bol.praguepost.com/english).

Of the institute websites that are available in English, a surprising number provide teacher vacancy information and often online application forms, so it is worth doing a lot of googling in anticipation of a job-hunt. Among the Prague schools that indicate ongoing recruitment needs are:

English Link s.r.o, Prague – www.englishlink.cz/en/vacancies.html
London Institute – www.londoninstitute.cz/job-opportunities
James Cook – www.jamescooklanguages.cz
Glossa Škola jazyků – jobs@glossa.cz; http://glossa.cz
    In Brno try:
ILC International House – www.ilcbrno.cz
Jazyková Skola PARK – www.jspark.cz/en/teach-in-the-park

Even though most schools in Prague claim to receive plenty of CVs on spec from which to fill any vacancies that arise, their willingness to describe their recruitment procedures online indicates that the demand for teachers is still very strong. Anyone who is well qualified or experienced should have few difficulties in finding a job on the spot, particularly if they are lucky with their timing. The market in Brno is booming too, with more than 80 language schools listed as operating in the country's second largest city (many will be one person outfits), catering to a population of just over 400,000. Most people wait until they arrive in Prague before trying to find teaching work, which is what **Linda Harrison** did:

> *The best time to apply is before June. I arrived in September which was too late, but if you persevere there are jobs around. A lot of teaching work here seems to be in companies. Schools employ you to go into offices, etc. to teach English (though not usually Business English). After a short job hunt, I was hired by a company called Languages at Work which paid well and provided food and travel vouchers as well as helping with accommodation.*

Languages at Work has since morphed several times and is now the Spěváček Education Centre (see entry). People end up teaching in Prague via the most circuitous routes as **Anne Morris** from the USA describes:

> *Although I'm near retirement age, I'm still a free spirit and am living in Prague now more or less by chance. I ran into an American couple at a jam-packed event in Old Town Square on a visit to Prague two years ago who said they were teaching English here. I've always loved this city so I asked how one would get a job like that and they scratched out a website on the back of an envelope (TEFL Worldwide). I lost them in the crowd but on return to the US came across the envelope in a coat pocket and decided to check it out – and now here I am teaching English. Just wish I'd made this discovery much earlier in my life!*

Outside of Prague, chances are reasonable of finding jobs in the private sector all year round, with the greatest selection available in late August through to November and in January/February. Those without qualifications or experience will find it very difficult. Unlike state schools, private schools in Prague do not offer accommodation, and will give preference when hiring to anyone who is already resident.

If you are stuck for a job during the summer months, then a good option is to work in a summer camp until the school year starts. There are a number of good summer camp options available, particularly teaching children, as well as intensive one-week courses for adults at holiday resorts. Children's camps do not generally pay very well, but food and accommodation are included, and many teachers use the camps as an opportunity to get to know a bit more of the country before going back to their city jobs in September. One to try is run by Grant Language School in České Budějovice (www.grant-langschool.com).

There are a few advertisements for teaching jobs in the local English press, primarily the *Prague Post* (www.praguepost.com); the classifieds can be read online. At the time of writing there were more English teachers offering private lessons than jobs offered. It is very cheap to place your own advert of 25 words or less by contacting classifieds@praguepost.com. It may be worth advertising your speciality as an English tutor (e.g. marketing, law, etc.) ahead of time. **Kathy Panton** suggests enlisting the help of a Czech friend:

> *A better way to find work is to get someone to translate 'Native speaker will tutor English to intermediate or advanced students, and send it to a newspaper like MF Dnes or Annoncé.*

REGULATIONS

Since accession, EU nationals no longer have to apply for a visa or work permit. However, those who stay for more than 30 days are required to register with the Alien and Border Police by filling in an application form and presenting a copy of their contract. Other foreigners who want to stay more than

90 days must apply for a long-stay Czech visa before arrival in the country. This requires gathering a raft of documents including a work permit issued by the employer, proof of accommodation, police certificate, etc. all presented in the original or a notarised copy. The work permit is valid for one year and only for the teaching position at the school for which it has been issued. An extension must be applied for at the local Employment Office at least six weeks before the expiry date.

Many non-EU teachers enter the Czech Republic as tourists (valid for three months) then cross a border to renew their tourist status or ask their employer to sort out the paperwork and then apply for the visa at the Czech embassy in Vienna or other neighbouring capitals. Those who hail from outside the EU must also ensure that their employer obtains a work permit from the local employment office (*Urad práce*). They will need a signed form from you plus a photocopy of your passport (valid for at least three months longer than the intended stay) and the originals or notarised copies of your education certificates.

All of this is quite a palaver and (realistically) takes about four months. The necessity of conforming with these procedures puts some candidates off. In Prague many schools simply hire teachers without worrying about the legal issues – a luxury they can afford due to the over-supply of teachers in the city. Outside the capital however, schools are more cooperative. Indeed several schools in Brno will actually take their teachers to the embassy to submit the paperwork and then take them again the following month to pick up the visa.

The Czech Republic has working holiday agreements with New Zealand and Canada which allows young people aged 18–30/35 who meet the acceptance criteria, to reside in the Czech Republic for up to 12 months (www.mzv.cz/ottawa and www.mzv.cz/sydney).

CONDITIONS OF WORK

People teaching at private institutes in Prague where there is a definite glut of foreign teachers, attracted by the cultural chic of the city, have been called the 'sweat shop labourers' of the TEFL world because of the low wages employers can get away with paying. Salaries in the capital are sometimes lower than in smaller cities such as Brno, even though the cost of living is higher.

Working conditions in state schools are generally better than in private schools, though opportunities are far fewer than they used to be. The guaranteed salary at state schools, even if you're sick or there is a holiday, is a definite advantage. If you are lucky enough to be teaching mostly final year students, your working hours in the exam month of June will be minimal, even though the teaching day at a state school might start at 8am. This counts as a lie-in compared with teaching in private companies, which is often underway by 7am or 7.30am. And of course in state schools there is no evening or weekend work.

The monthly wage range in state schools of 15,000–25,000 crowns gross is catching up with wages in the private sector. Subsidised accommodation can make the package seem even more attractive. If you are on your own, for accommodation expect to spend between a fifth and a quarter of your earnings on simple accommodation. Hourly fees start at roughly 200 crowns net, though a more usual wage is 230–250 crowns. A full-time salary should be adequate to live on by local standards but will not allow you to save anything, unless you take on lots of private tutoring.

In Brno, wages nearly match those of Prague, but you should expect a few thousand less in smaller cities such as Olomouc, Xlin, Hradec Kralove, etc. However, outside the Czech Republic's major cities the cost of living drops dramatically and many teachers in smaller cities and towns find that they are able to save much more despite actually earning a lower monthly salary.

The majority of private language school clients are adults who are available for lessons after work, so most teaching takes place between 4pm and 8pm, Monday to Thursday. Some schools do specialise in teaching children, for which a basic knowledge of the Czech language, or a TEFL

Do not plan on living on your income for several months at least. Schools usually only give you a few classes to start out. Also you are not paid when classes are cancelled for one reason or another or school is on vacation (I found this out the hard way in February when classes stopped during winter break) and there are a lot of initial expenses involved in housing, agency fees, health insurance, phone, internet, etc. so best to have a bit of a stash to fall back on.

One reward has been the opportunity to, if not totally assimilate, be a part of the native culture to some extent. An example was last night when I attended my high school's prom or 'ball' as they call it. Such fun to compare this universal ritual to a US prom! For starters, it was held in a palatial hall by any standards – not a crepe paper decorated basketball court as I remember high school dances and, heaven forbid, alcohol was served! A definite no-no in the US. And of course the kids outdid themselves with originality of style and sophistication. Really fun to be an onlooker.

qualification which includes some training in teaching children is essential. One to try is a British company Wattsenglish with children's schools in Prague, Liberec, Usti nad Labem, Teplice, Karlovy Vary, Sokolov, Pardubice, Olomouc, Ostrava and Mlada Boleslav (www.wattsenglish.com/teachers-wanted.php).

Accommodation in Prague is more plentiful than it used to be. If you have a friend to translate for you, you can try the accommodation listings in *Annoncé*, the Prague free ads paper, or craigslist in English (http://prague.craigslist.cz). Most employers are prepared to help newcomers to find accommodation, usually a room in a small shared flat or university hostel. In the rest of the country there is less competition for affordable accommodation. However, those moving to Brno or Zlin will find that the real-estate agents have taken over the market, so those without local support will find themselves having to pay one month's rent to the agent as a finder's fee. On the other hand, agents do offer the advantage of providing a wide selection of furnished flats covering a range of budgets and in a variety of neighbourhoods. Many people place an advert in the local *Inzert Expres* or other classifieds magazine, looking for accommodation. Many Czech students welcome the opportunity to share a flat with a native English speaker in order to practise their English for free.

Students are reported to be 'a delight to teach, alert, intelligent, fun-loving, keen and interested'. Many English teachers avail themselves of the excellent resource centres run by the British Council in Prague and Brno. The British Council's teaching centre in centre of Prague has very occasional openings for teachers who are TEFL certified with two years' relevant experience. One of the strongest motivations among secondary school (*gymnazium*) students to learn English is the prospect of the 'Maturity' (school-leaver's) exam. At the beginning of the year they are given 25 topics (e.g. the British Royal Family, the influence of the media) and at the end of the year they must talk in English about one topic (chosen at random) for 15 minutes. This is a very good incentive for class participation.

LEISURE TIME

The cost of living in Prague continues to creep up, though most things are still affordable in other towns. For example a decent midday meal at a Brno restaurant (soup, main course and beer) will cost 80–90 crowns, whilst Brno rents are around 6,000 minimum a month. Due to the fact that the

Czech crown has appreciated rapidly against the dollar/pound/euro, everything has become a lot more expensive when recalculated to other currencies.

Prague has a vibrant nightlife with clubs and cafés, cinema, opera, poetry and dance. There is so much expat culture, that a new arrival serious about getting into Czech culture will encounter difficulty. There is also something of a backlash among Czechs against Western 'good-for-nothings', who spend Czech currency as if it was *Monopoly* money. In Prague theft is a serious problem, though walking the streets is still safe. In small towns, however, English teachers are still likely to be treated as honoured guests with many offers of hospitality and invitations, for example to join skiing trips (which are very cheap), as **Hannah Bullock** from Oxford discovered in her year out between school and university in the town of Strakonice:

I've got some great Czech friends here. A colleague of mine has been very kind (as I've found most Czechs are) and has been like a mentor-cum-grandpa to me, taking me to visit castles, nearby towns, beautiful little villages and to walk in the mountains which border Germany. Most of this would have been very difficult without a car (the trains go very infrequently and at unsociable hours). I've spent many weekends in Prague since it's only one and a half hours by bus. I had to do double takes on hearing English spoken and seeing the Guardian being passed round the bars. Now instead of seeing Prague as the opening to Central Europe with its old-fashioned trams and cobbled streets as I did when I first arrived in September, I now think of it as the door back to Westernisation.

One final tip: if you play a musical instrument, take it with you since it's a great way to make local friends.

LIST OF EMPLOYERS

A SCHOOL
Obliní trh 2, Brno 602 00
recepce@aschool.cz
www.aschool.cz

NUMBER OF TEACHERS: 5.
PREFERENCE OF NATIONALITY: None.
QUALIFICATIONS: CELTA or TEFL.
CONDITIONS OF EMPLOYMENT: 1-year renewable contract. Working hours can be between 7am and 9pm, Monday to Friday.
FACILITIES/SUPPORT: Assistance provided with finding accommodation if necessary. Applications for work permits are coordinated on behalf of the teacher.
RECRUITMENT: Interviews and a demo lesson are essential. If necessary, the interview can be carried out via Skype.
CONTACT: Michaela Hromková, Director of Studies.

ACADEMIC INFORMATION AGENCY (AIA)
Centre for International Service, Ministry of
Education Youth & Sports (Dum zahranicních sluzeb MSMT), Na Porici 1035/4, 110 00 Prague 1
222 850 504
aia@dzs.cz
www.dzs.cz/scripts/detail.asp?id=599

NUMBER OF TEACHERS: Teachers needed for state primary and secondary schools throughout the Czech Republic though numbers have been decreasing over the years.
PREFERENCE OF NATIONALITY: Native English speakers from UK, Canada, USA, Australia.
QUALIFICATIONS: Professional teachers are preferred for teaching at primary and secondary schools. All candidates are required to have a college or university-level degree, preferably in English or in a related field. Additional

qualification in teaching English as a foreign language (e.g. CELTA) is necessary for applicants who are graduates of courses in non-related subjects. Previous experience in teaching English in a classroom setting is greatly welcomed. High motivation is expected.

CONDITIONS OF EMPLOYMENT: 10-month contracts, 1 September to 30 June, 24 hours per week.

SALARY: 15,000–25,000 Czech crowns per month (before taxes and compulsory social insurance deductions).

FACILITIES/SUPPORT: Accommodation provided by schools (free or subsidised). Non-EU citizens – work and residence permits organised before arrival.

RECRUITMENT: Interested applicants register their availability with AIA, which circulates details to schools looking for a teacher. Actual vacancies with contact details are posted at www.dzs.cz/scripts/detail.asp?id=612.

CONTACT: Karla Benesová.

AKCENT INTERNATIONAL HOUSE PRAGUE
Bitovská 3, 140 00 Prague 4
2 6126 16 38/ 6126 16 75
info@akcent.cz
www.akcent.cz

NUMBER OF TEACHERS: 100.

PREFERENCE OF NATIONALITY: None (need to comply with Czech immigration laws).

QUALIFICATIONS: Degree plus CELTA or equivalent (minimum).

CONDITIONS OF EMPLOYMENT: 10 or 12 months from September/October. Approximately 21 contact hours per week. Mostly teaching General English to adults, though some YL teaching. Teaching both on-site and in-company.

SALARY: 10,000–19,000 crowns (before tax) per month plus accommodation and other benefits.

FACILITIES/SUPPORT: Health insurance covered and 25 days paid holidays per calendar year. Contribution made to cost of travelling to Prague. Offers CELTA/DELTA courses plus courses in teaching Young Learners and Business English.

RECRUITMENT: helena.linkova@akcent.cz.

THE BRITISH SCHOOL
Tynska 21, 110 00 Prague 1
2 24808 243
britishschool@britishschool.cz
www.britishschool.cz

NUMBER OF TEACHERS: 15–20.

PREFERENCE OF NATIONALITY: English-speaking country including Commonwealth countries.

QUALIFICATIONS: Certificate TEFLA (Trinity or Cambridge) and degree. Some experience teaching teenagers or adults.

CONDITIONS OF EMPLOYMENT: Teaching adults September/October to June. 21 hours per week, in Prague or Pilsen. Part-time work also available.

SALARY: 21,000 crowns per month (fixed salary). Compulsory deductions about 4,000 crowns. Part-time work also available.

FACILITIES/SUPPORT: Can guarantee furnished flat accommodation to be shared with another teacher and health insurance. Computer access and books. EU citizens can be employed immediately. For non-EU teachers, assistance with work permit application and visas provided; such teachers should bring their TEFL certificate, birth certificate, photos, passport and degree certificate.

RECRUITMENT: Send a CV with dates and a detailed covering letter to the above address – followed by interview in Prague or (rarely) by telephone.

CONTACT: David Camidge, Principal.

BRNO ENGLISH CENTRE
Starobrnenska 16/18, 602 00 Brno
+420 54121 2262
hooper@brnoenglishcentre.cz
www.brnoenglishcentre.cz

NUMBER OF TEACHERS: 16.

PREFERENCE OF NATIONALITY: Native English speakers.

QUALIFICATIONS: A university degree plus an internationally recognised TEFL/TESOL qualification (not online), together with a minimum of 1 year teaching with a similar institution.

CONDITIONS OF EMPLOYMENT: Standard contract is from September to May (9 months). 18–20 hours of teaching per week, plus preparation, training and meetings.

SALARY: Around 24,000 crowns per month. The average teacher would take home about 18,000–19,000 crowns.

FACILITIES/SUPPORT: Centre finds affordable accommodation, pays the fees associated with this and advances the first month's rent. Work permits are generally not a major problem. It is more problematic gaining the residence permit needed for non-EU citizens, although the centre provides assistance.

RECRUITMENT: Normally by direct application. The centre does not go through agencies or intermediaries. Interviews are essential and can, in theory, be carried out in the UK or else by phone.

CONTACT: Simon Hooper, Director.

THE CALEDONIAN SCHOOL
Vltavská 24, Prague 5
☎ 2 57 313 650
✉ jobs@caledonianschool.com
🖥 www.caledonianschool.com

NUMBER OF TEACHERS: 300+ in various locations in Prague and in schools around the Czech Republic (also in Slovakia).
PREFERENCE OF NATIONALITY: None.
QUALIFICATIONS: Bachelor's degree plus Trinity CertTESOL or CELTA or equivalent, eg the Caledonian TEFL certificate.
CONDITIONS OF EMPLOYMENT: 10-month contracts from mid-September to end of June plus possible summer teaching. 20–26 45-minute lessons. School teaches adults and young adults, in-school and in-company.
SALARY: Approx 18,000 crowns per month for qualified teachers. Free local transport pass. Free visa assistance for non-EU citizens. Free healthcare plan. Free Czech lessons. Spanish, German, Italian and French with 50% discount.
FACILITIES/SUPPORT: School arranges and pays for flats for teachers who teach in out-of-Prague sites. Regular teacher development workshops held, usually twice a month. Library has over 3,000 EFL titles, photocopiers and internet access for teachers. Social events at the Caledonian café for staff.
RECRUITMENT: Via jobs@caledonianschool.com. School hires year round.
CONTACT: Dan Casey, Personnel and Placement Coordinator.

DAVID'S AGENCY
Dr. Veseleho 1042, 763 26 Luhacovice
☎ +420 603 346 618
✉ davidsagency@hotmail.com

NUMBER OF TEACHERS: 2 in Zlin and Luhacovice spa town.
PREFERENCE OF NATIONALITY: British or other native English speakers.
QUALIFICATIONS: University degree and TEFL.
CONDITIONS OF EMPLOYMENT: 10-month contracts, 8am–noon and 1pm–4.30pm.
SALARY: 24,000 crowns (gross) less about 25% for tax, health insurance and social benefits.
FACILITIES/SUPPORT: Accommodation arranged for 5,000 crowns per month. Assistance with work visa process. Training given in Czech language and culture.

RECRUITMENT: Via email. Early application encouraged to allow visa processing time. Interviews are held in Britain in the summer.
CONTACT: David Catto, Director (davidsagency@hotmail.com).

HAMPSON CS
Vaclava Klementa 601, 293 01 Mlada Boleslav
☎ +420 326 732 732
✉ hampson@hampson.cz
🖥 www.hampson.cz

NUMBER OF TEACHERS: 4.
QUALIFICATIONS: Native English speakers.
CONDITIONS OF EMPLOYMENT: Contracts last for 1 school year. To work 20–27 hours per week.
SALARY: On application.
FACILITIES/SUPPORT: Teachers provided with apartment and help given with accommodation.
RECRUITMENT: Apply to the above address.

THE PHILADELPHIA ACADEMY s.r.o.
T.G.M. 916/111, 293 01 Mladá Boleslav
☎ 326 733 386
✉ philadelphia@dragon.cz
🖥 www.philadel.com

NUMBER OF TEACHERS: Approx. 40 in total (around 5 native teachers).
PREFERENCE OF NATIONALITY: None (though visas for Canadian and Australian citizens are problematic).
QUALIFICATIONS: BA/MA in English plus TEFL/TESOL/CELTA.
CONDITIONS OF EMPLOYMENT: 1 school year at least. About 25 hours per week (20 guaranteed – more is possible).
SALARY: 200 crowns per hour. Deductions depend on agreement.
FACILITIES/SUPPORT: Fully furnished flat with satellite dish, DVD player etc. located 15 minutes walking distance from the school building – paid for by school, except for utilities.
RECRUITMENT: Internet advertising. Interviews essential.
CONTACT: Dana Zbíralová, Owner.

POLYGLOT SPOL S.R.O.
Mečislavova 8, 140 00 Prague 4
☎ +420 241 740 566
✉ skola.praha@polyglot.cz
🖥 www.polyglot.cz

NUMBER OF TEACHERS: Approximately 50 for 7 branches throughout Prague.

PREFERENCE OF NATIONALITY: None.

QUALIFICATIONS: CELTA/TEFL or other certification of at least 120 hours of training plus experience.

CONDITIONS OF EMPLOYMENT: Between 7 and 20 hours teaching per week depending on whether the employee teaches in the morning or afternoon.

SALARY: 200–300 crowns per hour.

RECRUITMENT: Interviews are not always essential.

CONTACT: Jana Havickova, Branch Manager.

SPEVACEK EDUCATION CENTRE
Namesti Miru 15, 120 00 Prague 2

✆ 222 517 869

✉ centrum@spevacek.info

🖥 www.spevacek.info

Member of Czech Association of Language Schools (www.ajscr.cz). ISO 9001.

NUMBER OF TEACHERS: 150.

PREFERENCE OF NATIONALITY: Must be a native English or Czech/Slovak speaker, EU nationals preferred.

QUALIFICATIONS: Minimum requirements are university degree and a recognised TEFL certificate. Formal EFL teaching experience is valued and rewarded. Professionalism, reliability, enthusiasm and smart appearance expected.

CONDITIONS OF EMPLOYMENT: 10-month renewable contracts. 80 teaching units per month (more if requested). Teaching adults only, mainly in-company General and Business English, small groups and individuals. Teaching kindergarten children, teenagers or (optional) public courses in a sister school.

SALARY: Approx. 22,000 crowns (gross) per month plus performance bonus and contract completion bonus.

FACILITIES/SUPPORT: Accommodation assistance, full assistance with visas, free internet access, well stocked library in the city centre. Full academic support. Rich social life.

RECRUITMENT: School recruits year-round but main recruiting month is August. Resumés/CVs and cover letter welcomed by e-mail with 'Recruitment' in subject line. Interviews conducted in Prague or via Skype.

CONTACT: Martin Hejhal, DOS (martin.hejhal@spevacek. info).

STATE LANGUAGE SCHOOL BRNO
Jazykováškola s právem státní jazykové zkoušky, Kotlářská 9, 611 49 Brno

✉ kucerova@sjs-brno.cz

🖥 www.sjs-brno.cz

NUMBER OF TEACHERS: 5.

PREFERENCE OF NATIONALITY: British.

QUALIFICATIONS: Must have TEFL qualification.

CONDITIONS OF EMPLOYMENT: 1 academic year (September to June). Approximately 20 hours per week.

SALARY: About 17,000 Czech crowns per month.

FACILITIES/SUPPORT: Assistance with finding accommodation, full help with work permits and training available at staff meetings.

RECRUITMENT: Liaise with other schools.

CONTACT: Iveta Kučerová, Deputy Head.

VISTA WELCOME
Konevova 210, 130 00 Prague 3

✉ vista@iol.cz

🖥 www.vista-welcome.cz.

NUMBER OF TEACHERS: 6 native speakers. 32 Czech teachers.

PREFERENCE OF NATIONALITY: British, Canadian, American.

QUALIFICATIONS: TEFL certificate and/or proven ELS teaching experience. Mature teachers preferred, though enthusiasm important. School does not want to hire people who are just looking for a way to see the world. Experience in teaching business English a plus.

CONDITIONS OF EMPLOYMENT: 1-year contract minimum. Teaching hours vary. Full-time teachers guaranteed at least 20 lessons (45 minutes each) per week. Courses aimed at firms and organisations looking for in-house courses. Teachers often work for more than one school to get enough teaching hours.

SALARY: 230 crowns per hour plus medical and social insurance; or 320 crowns without insurance.

FACILITIES/SUPPORT: No accommodation provided though advice may be given to new arrivals.

RECRUITMENT: Adverts in the local English-language newspaper for expats (*Prague Post*), the internet and via other schools in Prague.

CONTACT: Ela Stružková, Principal.

SLOVAK REPUBLIC

The republic of the Slovaks has been somewhat neglected not only by tourists but by teachers as well. As one language school director put it a couple of years ago:

> *Many teachers head for Prague, which is why Slovakia stands aside of the main flow of the teachers. That's a pity as Prague is crowded with British and Americans while there's a lack of the teachers here in Slovakia.*

Another wrote from a small Slovakian town, '*It would be wonderful if through your book more native speakers come to Slovakia*'. The density of private language schools in the capital Bratislava and in the other main cities such as Banska Bystrika makes an on-the-ground job-hunt promising.

IH Bratislava (Námestie SNP 14, 811 06 Bratislava; 2 52 96 26 75; jurbanova@ihbratislava.sk; www.ihbratislava.sk) is one of the largest private language schools in the Slovak Republic with over 40 teachers based in Bratislava and other towns around the Slovak Republic. They are looking for teachers with a TEFL certificate such as CELTA, Trinity CertTESOL, IHC etc. Teaching experience and business work experience are an advantage, but not essential.

Once considered a backward part of Europe, huge resources have been poured into the country's development including into increasing access to English instruction. The European Social Fund has targeted groups who need English and provided subsidised or even free courses for people working in education or the civil service. As a result a substantial demand exists for native English teachers, although the wages are fairly low so many teachers tend to take on private students and/or economise. The salary range for teachers is €450–€500 net, €600–€800 gross. Many schools pay by the lesson which should be around €12, though the ones that provide free accommodation of course offer a lower wage, e.g. from €6. The flat rate of tax in Slovakia is 19%.

Dana Piffkova, a young Slovak, explains that it is very important to speak English if you want to secure a good job. She works for an international company where all communication and paperwork are in English. She thinks that knowing English is more important now than it was a few years ago, and that although Slovaks are taught English twice a week at high school from the first grade onwards, university language courses are 'rare or very short'. Dana took extra tuition from a local English teacher to help her become fluent (although she'll insist that she isn't). In-company training is also in demand, as attested by the success of International House, which caters to the business market.

University students often leave Slovakia to work abroad during the summer (many in English-speaking countries). Although students can learn English by immersion, many will wish to be reasonably fluent so they can land a decent job in the first place.

It used to be a level playing field for English-speaking foreigners wanting to teach in Slovakia, but now EU citizens have a clear advantage, needing only to confirm residency for tax purposes. Registration can be done at the local police station. For candidates from outside the EU, the Slovak visa process is expensive and time-consuming. The main costs are getting a criminal record check from the teacher's home country (cost varies) and the visa fee of €170. Documents may need to be officially translated, and the applicant may need to submit a medical certificate, evidence of accommodation and so on. A blood test must be carried out within a couple of weeks of arriving as a pre-requisite for a residence permit. Most employers guide their teachers through the process but not many will cover the cost.

As well as the British Council at Panská 17 in Bratislava (info@britishcouncil.sk), there are six British Centres around the country with libraries and facilities of interest to English teachers. As always, much has moved online so that the Council in Slovakia offers lesson plans and materials to support English teachers and organises workshops and events.

The only English language newspaper is the weekly *Slovak Spectator* published on Mondays. Occasionally the classified column carries an advert of interest to people looking for teaching work.

You might also consider advertising your availability to give private tuition (www.spectator.sme.sk). Although wages can be low, prices for food and meals out are not expensive, though they crept up when Slovakia joined the euro in 2009. Accommodation in Bratislava is about twice as expensive as in small towns in central Slovakia.

Budapest, Vienna and Prague are all within easy reach. Slovakia also offers good conditions for mountain walking along thousands of miles of hiking routes up to an altitude of 2,500m and for mountain cycling.

GEOFF NUNNEY is enjoying Slovakia so much that he has stayed on for a second year in 2010 at Vages School (see listing below):

It's thanks to your book that I found Slovakia. I teach at two local schools and two businesses here in Nitra. The people here are great and were incredibly supportive when I lost both parents last year and also when I returned to England for treatment for a chronic health problem.

During the school's opening hours (7am–8pm) I teach kids, teenagers and adult conversation classes. The school provides good teaching resources, internet, copying and up-to-date text books. The recruitment processes were very thorough, consisting of a face-to-face interview with the headteacher, who was very informative, approachable and asked relevant questions.

The best thing you need in Slovakia is a sense of humour. I have been in school plays, and they are a very friendly nation of people. Their standard of English is very good, and they are great fun to teach. For example last Friday, a student stopped me and said, 'Geoff, the walls have ears' to demonstrate his mastery of an English idiom. Oh yes, I am even dating a Slovak teacher, who asked me out – very forward people the Slovaks – she stole my business card, rang my mobile, and we had a night out at the Irish Pub in Nitra. So things are definitely looking up.

Teaching wages in Slovakia allow you to cover the basic cost of living, but not much else. You can survive, pay the bills, but don't expect to save a lot. Although wages aren't great here, the locals and the scenery and the supportive staff make up for it. I speak a little Slovak, and if you immerse yourself, you will get the rewards. I love it out here, and it has stunning mountains and walking country. I would describe it all as a Slovak adventure!

LIST OF EMPLOYERS

ACADEMIA ISTROPOLITANA NOVA
Prostredna 47/A, 900 21 Svaty Jur
2 4497 0449
ruth@ainova.sk
www.ainova.sk

NUMBER OF TEACHERS: 6.
PREFERENCE OF NATIONALITY: UK citizens.
QUALIFICATIONS: University graduates preferably with pedagogical degree or holders of CELTA, TEFL or other internationally recognised certificate.

CONDITIONS OF EMPLOYMENT: 1-year contract, 80 teaching hours per month.
SALARY: By agreement.
FACILITIES/SUPPORT: Assistance giving in finding accommodation but teachers pay rent.
RECRUITMENT: Personal recommendation and ELT training centres. Phone interviews possible.
CONTACT: Ruth Zorvan, Head of Professional Communication and Language Programmes.

AKADEMIA VZDELAVANIA – ACADEMY OF EDUCATION

Gorkého 10, 81517 Bratislava

+421 2–5441 0033

pbrooks@aveducation.sk

www.aveducation.sk

NUMBER OF TEACHERS: Approximately 20 full-time posts in branches throughout Slovakia but mainly in Bratislava.

PREFERENCE OF NATIONALITY: Native English speaker holding an EU passport.

QUALIFICATIONS: CELTA or TESOL qualification (or recognised equivalent) and degree. Energy, enthusiasm and an interest in people required. Must be willing to teach a range of classes, including teenagers or young learners.

CONDITIONS OF EMPLOYMENT: 1 academic year (mid-September to end of June). Teachers' contracts are for a maximum of 22.5 contact hours per week.

SALARY: Net monthly salaries in Bratislava are as follows: €465 for a new teacher with less than 1 year's experience, €488 for a new teacher with minimum 1 year's experience.

FACILITIES/SUPPORT: Accommodation provided, work and residence permits arranged and paid for, health insurance, travel passes, luncheon vouchers, and contribution to air fares. Academic and pastoral support, regular seminars and workshops; orientation for new teachers.

CONTACT: Philip Brooks, Director of Studies.

THE CALEDONIAN SCHOOL

Vltavská 24, Prague 5

2 57 313 650

jobs@caledonianschool.com

www.caledonianschool.com

Teachers hired for schools in Slovakia as well as the Czech Republic – see entry in chapter on Czech Republic.

THE ENGLISH CLUB

Pri Suchom mlyne 36, 811 04 Bratislava

+421 904 415 490

oravecmartin@ba.telecom.sk

www.theenglishclub.sk

NUMBER OF TEACHERS: 1–3.

PREFERENCE OF NATIONALITY: British.

QUALIFICATIONS: University degree plus TEFL/TESL/CELTA and 1 year's experience.

CONDITIONS OF EMPLOYMENT: 10-month contract from September to June. Working hours between 7am and 9.45pm, 30 hours per week.

SALARY: From €6 per 45 minutes.

FACILITIES/SUPPORT: Shared flat with wifi is available. All necessary paperwork for work permits is completed by the school.

RECRUITMENT: Usually via the internet. Interviews are essential.

CONTACT: Martin Oravec, Director.

EUROTREND 21

Namestie slobody 16, 81332 Bratislava

info@eurotrend21.sk

www.eurotrend21.sk

NUMBER OF TEACHERS: 4.

PREFERENCE OF NATIONALITY: None.

QUALIFICATIONS: Minimum university degree, TEFL certificate and experience.

CONDITIONS OF EMPLOYMENT: Minimum contract 6 months. Hours available mornings, afternoons and evenings.

SALARY: Dependent on experience. Starts at €12 per 45-minute lesson.

RECRUITMENT: Interviews are essential and are carried out on-site.

CONTACT: Magda Nagyova, Director.

HARMONY SCHOOL

26 Kapitulska, 91701 Trnava

marketing@harmonyschool.sk

www.harmonyschool.sk

NUMBER OF TEACHERS: 2.

PREFERENCE OF NATIONALITY: EU citizens.

QUALIFICATIONS: CELTA/DELTA or equivalent.

CONDITIONS OF EMPLOYMENT: 1-year contract with 30 teaching hours and 10 admin hours per week.

SALARY: €1,000–1,500.

FACILITIES/SUPPORT: Assistance given with finding accommodation.

RECRUITMENT: Interviews are essential.

CONTACT: Jana Chynoradska, Managing Principal.

INŠTITÚT EURÓPSKYCH JAZYKOV

J. Borodača 2, 071 01 Michalovce

907 448 408

institute.ej@gmail.com

www.institut.sk

NUMBER OF TEACHERS: Rolling vacancies.

QUALIFICATIONS: Must be university graduate. School is looking for professionalism, strong educational background, experience, personality, and communication and people skills.

Teachers should be patient, enthusiastic, good team players, with a sense of humour.

CONDITIONS OF EMPLOYMENT: Semesters start mid-September, early January and early April. 90-minute lessons. Many clients are graduates and civil servants, since the European Social Fund pays for free English courses for these categories.

FACILITIES/SUPPORT: Accommodation provided and help given with settling into local area.

CONTACT: Petra Gondkovicova, Owner/Manager.

IVEGA LEARNING CENTRE
Moldavska 8, 04011 Kosice
55 642 7864 or mobile 905 212 417
gtroskoo@orange-mail.sk
www.ivega.sk

NUMBER OF TEACHERS: 2.

PREFERENCE OF NATIONALITY: None.

QUALIFICATIONS: Minimum TEFL/TESL or CELTA certificate plus teaching experience.

CONDITIONS OF EMPLOYMENT: At least 1 academic year, approximately 20 hours of teaching per week.

SALARY: €600–€700 gross salary.

FACILITIES/SUPPORT: The school takes care of all necessary arrangements for residence and work permits and will assist teachers to find accommodation. Work permits not necessary for EU citizens.

RECRUITMENT: Applicants should send CVs and letters of reference by mail. Short-listed candidates will be invited to interview, although interviews are not essential.

CONTACT: Gabriela Troskoova, headteacher and owner.

JAZYKOVÁ ŠKOLA START
Kriva 18, 040 01 Kosice
+421 915 846 728
recruitment@jazykova.sk
www.jazykova.sk/jobs.php

NUMBER OF TEACHERS: 6.

PREFERENCE OF NATIONALITY: Native English speakers, mainly British, American, Australian.

QUALIFICATIONS: TEFL or previous experience is an advantage. Apart from being a native speaker, the only condition a candidate absolutely must fulfil is they must have a university degree (in any subject).

CONDITIONS OF EMPLOYMENT: 1 academic year, extendable to a permanent contract. Usual hours are 3pm–8pm with some morning lessons.

SALARY: By negotiation. About €800 per month in term time, or €500 per month out of term. Luncheon vouchers provided.

FACILITIES/SUPPORT: School finds accommodation for teachers. School assists logistically but not financially with visas (e.g. €170).

RECRUITMENT: Via the internet. Also, a number of teachers come to Slovakia because they are in a relationship with a local and their partners make the initial contact in response to advertising. Interviews are carried out by phone or Skype. In the case of teachers already in Slovakia they are carried out in person.

CONTACT: Richard Swales, Director.

S-CLUB
Vojenska 30, 934 01 Levice
36 631 3224
info@sclub.sk
www.sclub.sk

NUMBER OF TEACHERS: 8.

PREFERENCE OF NATIONALITY: British, Irish.

QUALIFICATIONS: TEFL/TESOL and some experience.

CONDITIONS OF EMPLOYMENT: Academic year (September to the end of June), 25 teaching units of 45 minutes per week in the afternoons.

SALARY: €7 per lesson.

FACILITIES/SUPPORT: A furnished flat is provided free by the school. No special permits needed for EU citizens.

RECRUITMENT: Via the internet. First contact by email. Telephone interviews.

VAGeS
Hodzova 25, 94901 Nitra
37 652 4098
vages@vages.sk
www.vages.sk

NUMBER OF TEACHERS: 1.

PREFERENCE OF NATIONALITY: British, American.

QUALIFICATIONS: TEFL or university student preparing for a career in TEFL.

CONDITIONS OF EMPLOYMENT: 1 year (renewable), 20 lessons (45 minutes) per week.

SALARY: €8 per lesson, less 19% tax.

FACILITIES/SUPPORT: Room in the university students' hostel is paid for by the school.

RECRUITMENT: Through the local university, AIESEC programme, personal contacts and through sister city programme in the USA.

CONTACT: Elena Vargicova, Head Teacher/Owner.

HUNGARY

English is compulsory for all Hungarian students who wish to apply for college or university entrance, and university students in both the Arts and Sciences must take courses in English. The Hungarian education system has much to be proud of, not least the efficacy with which it retrained its Russian teachers as English teachers after the return to democracy in 1989. The network of bilingual second-ary schools (*gimnazia*) has produced a large number of graduates with a sophisticated knowledge of English. In cities and even some small towns, bilingual schools now operate at the elementary level as well. From first grade onwards, students study basic subjects in English and Hungarian. The vast majority of private language schools are owned and run by Hungarians rather than expats. Even though the calibre of Hungarian teachers is very high, some schools still seem keen to employ native English teachers.

The invasion of foreigners in Budapest was never as overwhelming as it was (and is) in Prague, but still Budapest has a glut of teachers, among them some who have fled over-crowded Prague. The opportunities that do exist now are mostly in the provinces. Even in the more remote parts of the country, formal academic qualifications are important. It is a legal requirement that the bilingual schools employ a native English speaker as lector. Most *gimnazia* liaise with the Fulbright Commission or the *Central European Teaching Program* and take on Americans, though Britons are also eligible.

Teachers are poorly paid in Hungary, aside from in the top-notch private schools. Rents in Budapest are high and take a major proportion of a teacher's salary; some schools help by subsidis-ing accommodation, or it may be possible to arrange accommodation in return for English lessons. Teachers through the Central European Teaching Program (see entry) have housing and utilities provided. Low as the salaries may seem, native English speakers can console themselves with the thought that they are usually better paid than Hungarian university lecturers.

FINDING A JOB

Very few jobs in Hungary are advertised in the UK and only one or two UK sending organisations (no-tably Sharing One Language; www.sol.org.uk) include Hungary in their list of destinations. A handful of teaching companies publish information for job-seekers on their sites, for example Arkhé Stúdió Nyelviskola in suburban Budapest (1 216 9061; www.arkhestudio.hu), Cambridge Schools with two branches in the capital (670 369 2001; www.cambridge.hu), M-Prospect (www.m-prospect.hu) and Berlitz (6 70 336 5475; www.berlitz.hu). In the USA, recruitment of conversational English teachers and sometimes of other academic subjects as well takes place via the Central European Teaching Program. The programme offers 'cultural immersion through teaching' and is open to anyone with a university degree, preferably some experience of TEFL and overseas teaching/study experience and a willingness to pay the programme fee. CETP liaises with the relevant government department in Hungary to place teachers in state schools as well as in some parochial schools throughout the country. Hungary has a network of Dual Language Grammar Schools in which English is the medium of instruction for some subjects.

AFTER ARRIVAL

The British Council in Budapest (www.britishcouncil.org/hungary.htm) closed its teaching opera-tions and its library in 2007. However, it continues to contribute to the professional development of teachers by organising courses and workshops with partner organisations across the country and by promoting online resources. Its partner libraries' GatewayUK information points house English language teaching and learning collections that members can borrow and host events for those interested in British culture and learning English. Partner libraries are located in Budapest, Bekescsaba, Debrecen, Eger, Gyor, Kecskemet, Szeged, Szekszard, Szolnok, Tatabanya and Veszprem. The British Council employs well-qualified native English speaking teachers to supervise exams.

A useful resource for native English speaking teachers is the 'Book of Lists' from the *Budapest Business Journal* which contains about 40 addresses of private language institutes. Try to find it in a library because the 2010 edition costs €95 to buy.

Of interest to Americans is the Regional English Language Office located in the Public Diplomacy section of the US Embassy (Szabadság tér 7, 1054 Budapest; 1 475 4565; relomail@usembassy. hu). The Regional office does not run its own English teaching programme but provides some assistance to Hungarian teacher training programmes by providing access to English language materials. A small lending/resource collection of professional ELT materials is available to professionals in the field in the Information Resource Center in the Embassy's Public Affairs section. Note that this office arranges the summer camp for young people on Lake Balaton, Teaching Tolerance Through English (see entry).

PRIVATE SCHOOLS

While it has become increasingly difficult for foreigners to find teaching jobs in Hungarian state schools, private institutes have mushroomed, primarily to meet the needs of the business community and also for children whose parents are keen for them to supplement the English teaching at state schools. It is estimated that there are over 100 private language schools in Budapest alone and 300 around the country, both very fluid numbers since schools open and close so quickly. Many private schools use native English speakers as live commercials for the schools, though nowadays they want to advertise the qualifications of their teachers too.

Anyone with a recognised TEFL Certificate and experience of the business world has a good chance of finding at least some hourly teaching after arrival in Budapest or elsewhere. British and American accents are both in demand. International House offers one-year contracts for qualified teachers of both adults and children and (according to a former teacher) has 'a wonderful social and professional atmosphere'.

To find the less-well-established schools on the spot, keep your eyes open for the flyers posted in the main shopping streets or check out the English language weeklies. To find out what new institutes have opened or expanded, look at Hungarian papers such as *Magyar Nemzet* or the free ads paper *Hirdetes* (www.hirdetes.ws) to see if any courses in *Angol* are being advertised at *Nyelviskola* (language schools).

Private tutoring provides one way of supplementing a meagre salary. Freelance teachers may find a developing market for their linguistic expertise in companies. Many executives need English for business as Hungary seeks to integrate with the economies of the West and attract foreign investors. The Department of Commerce, for example, employs teachers to train bankers, traders and top electrical engineers. Many professionals need English as part of their work and are both able and prepared to pay for it.

Another option is the Budapest-based agency SELTI founded in 2007, which provides English language training by native English speaking teachers to client companies and schools such as H-Net Language Center on the Pest side of the city.

REGULATIONS

Since Hungary's accession to the EU in 2004, EU nationals no longer require a residence permit and immigration procedures have been much simplified. However before the 93rd day of their stay, they should report their presence to their nearest regional Office of Immigration and Nationality. The office will issue a registration certificate, which permits indefinite stays. EU nationals working full-time in Hungary are subject to the same social security and pension obligations as Hungarians. Employees must make payments into the National Health Insurance Fund and into a pension fund.

Non-EU citizens must arrange work permits and residence permits before leaving their country of residence. A foreign employee cannot be legally paid until she or he has a work permit (which costs $120). This fee has been waived for those applying to teach through the Central European Teaching Program. Those nationals who require a work permit must find a Hungarian employer who is entitled to apply for a work permit from the relevant Regional Employment Office. General information in English is available on the website of the Hungarian Ministry of Foreign Affairs (www.kulugyminiszterium.hu).

CONDITIONS OF WORK

Salaries vary, but teachers at private institutes tend to earn from 200,000 forints a month. It is essential to find out whether pay is net or gross since Hungarians lose more than a quarter of their already meagre wages on tax and contributions. It is also important to check whether your employer is taking out insurance on your behalf: an insurance mix-up turned **Ellen Parham**'s 'satisfactory' high-school salary into something worse than meagre.

American graduate and CETP participant **Genevieve Pierce**, found that teaching teenagers in a state school could be challenging:

> *They are totally uninterested in learning, don't complete their homework, and lack any opinion or viewpoint. This is a result of the political situation in Hungary and the low salaries. I am sure my students overhear their parents complain about money and politics constantly which has to drain the students' hope for a future. I think they feel trapped in Hungary. One student even said, 'Why should I do my homework when I'm going to live in Hungary and be a shop clerk like my mother?'*

On a more positive note, Genevieve found that going to class with a topic that everyone could talk about and allowing lessons to evolve was a more successful teaching strategy than following a strict lesson plan. In general students in the rural areas of eastern Hungary are better behaved than their counterparts in Budapest, though their level of English will be lower. This kind of problem won't arise if you are teaching in the business community. Freelance teachers can ask from 3,000 forints per lesson.

LEISURE TIME

The Opera House in Budapest is one of the most beautiful in the world, the Széchenyi thermal baths are the perfect place to unwind graciously and the coffee houses are ideal for watching the world go by. It is easy to make a strong argument for living in Budapest, but there are downsides, as long-stay American teacher **Ellen Parham** explains:

Everything is convenient for me here in Budapest, but some of the others in the CETP programme who are teaching in smaller towns are treated like celebrities and everyone knows them. Living in a big city is hindering my ability to speak Hungarian, too. Everyone speaks English and I am never forced to speak Hungarian.

Being made to speak this notoriously difficult language, however, can be a mixed blessing, as **Genevieve Pierce** discovered while living in a quaint city on the Romanian border:

Teaching in a place where you don't speak the language is difficult because you feel like a child. I seriously need a babysitter if I'm going to do anything of grave importance (i.e. visit the doctor, purchase a bicycle, arrange a postage delivery). Though, with all that said, teaching abroad has been the best experience of my life. I love to see students' faces when they finally realise what I'm talking about. I have enjoyed all the school functions such as dances, initiation ceremonies, and graduation. The best part has been learning about another culture, understanding their way of life. It's like nothing I could learn from a book.

LIST OF EMPLOYERS

AMEROPA LANGUAGE SCHOOL
Móricz Zs. Körtér 14, 1117 Budapest
- +36 1 209 5243
- nyelviskola@ameropa.hu
- www.ameropa.hu

NUMBER OF TEACHERS: 60.
PREFERENCE OF NATIONALITY: None.
QUALIFICATIONS: Minimum bachelor's degree and teacher training (TEFL, CELTA or equivalent).
CONDITIONS OF EMPLOYMENT: Ongoing contracts, usually between 6 and 24 months with 10–20 working hours per week.
SALARY: Competitive.
FACILITIES/SUPPORT: Assistance given with work permits.
RECRUITMENT: Interview and demonstration lesson are essential.
CONTACT: Balázs Szegedi, Managing Director.

CENTRAL EUROPEAN TEACHING PROGRAM
3800 NE, 72nd Avenue, Portland, Oregon 97213, USA
- 503 287 4977
- mary@cetp.info or hajni@cetp.info
- www.cetp.info

NUMBER OF TEACHERS: 65+.
PREFERENCE OF NATIONALITY: Native English speakers: USA, Canada, Australia, New Zealand, and native English speaking European.
QUALIFICATIONS: Minimum bachelor's degree. Those with no teaching certificate must be willing to undertake an online TEFL certificate. Retired people welcome.
CONDITIONS OF EMPLOYMENT: Standard contract 1 school year, although teachers can be placed for 1 semester. To teach 22 hours per week.
SALARY: $500–$600 per month after taxes.
FACILITIES/SUPPORT: All teachers receive a furnished apartment with utilities paid. Apartments range from a small studio to a spacious 1 or 2 bedroom flat. All are equipped with TV and washing machine, among other amenities. CETP provides teachers with all necessary documents for residence visas. A several-day long orientation is provided in Budapest prior to the start of the school term. A Hungarian director oversees CETP teachers throughout the year.
RECRUITMENT: Via word of mouth, the internet and university placement offices.
CONTACT: Mary Rose, Director.

INTER-EX CENTRE

4/a Budaörsi Str. 1118 Budapest

✆ 1 361 0248

🖱 interex@hu.inter.net

🖥 www.interexcentrum.hu

NUMBER OF TEACHERS: 1–2.

PREFERENCE OF NATIONALITY: None.

QUALIFICATIONS: Any TEFL qualification and Cambridge CELS language exams.

CONDITIONS OF EMPLOYMENT: 20 hours per week, open-ended contract.

SALARY: 200,000–300,000 forints per month.

FACILITIES/SUPPORT: Possibility of some assistance with accommodation.

RECRUITMENT: Candidates must be interviewed in Hungary or occasionally UK.

CONTACT: George Gallo, Director.

INTERNATIONAL HOUSE BUDAPEST

Language School & Teacher Training Institute, Vermezo út 4, 1012 Budapest

✆ +36 1 212 4010, ext 47

🖱 dos@ih.hu

🖥 www.ih.hu

NUMBER OF TEACHERS: 40.

QUALIFICATIONS: Minimum Cambridge CELTA.

CONDITIONS OF EMPLOYMENT: Contracts are for 25 contact hours per week including in-company teaching young learners, explan prep, groups, one-to-one and special projects.

SALARY: 198,000 forints per month (net).

FACILITIES/SUPPORT: Assistance given with finding accommodation. In-service teacher development.

RECRUITMENT: Through direct application. Interviews essential, conducted if necessary by telephone or Skype.

CONTACT: Stuart Willats Director of Studies.

IH Budapest

I chose to do my CELTA at IH Budapest because I had heard about its fantastic reputation as a teacher training centre, and it exceeded all my expectations. I had taught for a year before the CELTA and the course really helped me to develop as a teacher, both inside the classroom and out.

Claire, now teaching in Malaysia

Doing the course in Budapest in particular was enjoyable because the school has so much training experience and the city is so central for travelling to other cities in Central Europe.

Sophie, now teaching in Budapest

What made the course special for me was the great atmosphere created by the trainers and staff at the school. The trainers were always supportive and enthusiastic. The CELTA course was very hard work but immensely rewarding.

Jill, now teaching in Morocco

The staff and other teachers at IH Budapest were friendly and helpful, and the trainers were excellent. The school is a short tram ride from the city centre, so when you have a spare moment, you can get out there and explore one of the most exciting cities in the new Europe.

Paul, now teaching in Australia

KARINTHY FRIGYES GIMNAZIUM
Thököly ucta 7, Pestlorinc, 1183 Budapest
📞 1 291 2072
✉ ba@karinthy.hu
💻 www.karinthy.hu

NUMBER OF TEACHERS: About 100.
PREFERENCE OF NATIONALITY: Native English speakers.
QUALIFICATIONS: MA in English (preferred) or teaching English. BA in English or teaching English, or in any subject plus teaching certificate for English as a foreign language.
CONDITIONS OF EMPLOYMENT: 1–2 year contracts, 22 lessons a week.
SALARY: National salary plus all costs of accommodation in a pleasant, fully furnished and equipped flat near the school. 10% taxes and social security deduction.
FACILITIES/SUPPORT: Assistance with work permits; authorised copies of degrees and/or certificates are needed by the end of June.
RECRUITMENT: Application directly through agencies and foundations. Interviews preferred and conducted via Skype, web cam or telephone.
CONTACT: Dr Anikó Bognár, Deputy Head.

KATEDRA LANGUAGE SCHOOL
Anker köz 1–3, 1061 Budapest
📞 +36 1 700 0137
✉ info@katedra.hu
💻 www.katedra.hu

NUMBER OF TEACHERS: 15.
PREFERENCE OF NATIONALITY: Native English speakers.
QUALIFICATIONS: CELTA, DELTA or equivalent.
CONDITIONS OF EMPLOYMENT: Standard contract is 6 –12 months, 12–16 45-minute lessons per week.
SALARY: From 2,750 to 3,250 forints per lesson.
FACILITIES/SUPPORT: Assistance given with applying for work permits.
RECRUITMENT: Interview and mock lesson in Budapest is essential.
CONTACT: Ildikó Tóth (tothildiko@katedra.hu), Director of Studies.

LIVING LANGUAGE SEMINAR
Eló Nyelvek Szemináriuma, Fejér György u. 8–10, 1053 Budapest
📞 +36 1 317 9644
✉ elonyelv@t-online.hu
💻 www.elonyelvek.hu

NUMBER OF TEACHERS: 3–5 native English teachers
PREFERENCE OF NATIONALITY: British, American, Canadian.
QUALIFICATIONS: A great deal of ESL teaching experience, registered City & Guilds, Local State Examinations centre. Preparation for City & Guilds, Cambridge and local ITK-Origó exams, TOEFL iBT, business English.
CONDITIONS OF EMPLOYMENT: Contracts from 3 months. Negotiable hours. Mainly teaching adults (aged 16–40).
SALARY: High by local standards.
FACILITIES/SUPPORT: No assistance with accommodation at present.
RECRUITMENT: Through adverts. Interviews required.
CONTACT: Paul Biró.

MANHATTAN LANGUAGE SCHOOL
Örs vezér tér 25/C, 1106 Budapest
📞 +36 1 431 8630
✉ info@manhattannyelvstudio.hu
💻 www.manhattannyelvstudio.hu

NUMBER OF TEACHERS: 8–10 depending on the term.
PREFERENCE OF NATIONALITY: None.
QUALIFICATIONS: Teaching qualification (preferably CELTA or equivalent) and some teaching experience.
CONDITIONS OF EMPLOYMENT: Teachers work on free-lance basis. Working hours depend on the type of course that is taught, e.g. company courses can start as early as 7am or in-house courses can finish after 8pm.
SALARY: €7–€11 per hour depending on the level taught and location of the course.
RECRUITMENT: Face-to-face interview although on rare occasions a phone interview may suffice. Candidates must also conduct a mock lesson.
CONTACT: Zsuza Orzoi (orzoi@manhattannyelvstudio.hu), Director of Studies.

SELTI INTERNATIONAL

Kacsa utca 10 I1, Budapest 1027

✆ 1 785 7743

✎ vacancies@selti-international.com; info@
selti-hungary.com

💻 www.selti-hungary.com

Specialist provider to client schools and private companies of language teaching by native English teachers.

PREFERENCE OF NATIONALITY: Native English speakers including American, British, Canadian, Australian and New Zealander.

QUALIFICATIONS: Some background in tertiary/higher education and TEFL qualification needed, since company motto is to deliver quality and experience.

CONDITIONS OF EMPLOYMENT: 6–12-month contracts. 20 contact hours per week plus preparation and travel time.

FACILITIES/SUPPORT: Accommodation is provided in the package. Also, assistance with work permits.

RECRUITMENT: Rolling recruitment from online advertising. Interviews are essential but can be carried out by telephone.

CONTACT: Ryan Peden, Managing Director (ryan.peden@selti-international.com)/Phillip Spear, Assistant Manager (phillip.spear@selti-international.com).

'TEACHING TOLERANCE THROUGH ENGLISH' SUMMER CAMP

Camp Location: Kalória Kht. Gyermeküdüló, Úszó u. 5, 8638 Balatonlelle

✆ +36 85 700 610 +36 1 475 4328

✎ relomail@usembassy.hu

💻 http://teentolerance5.pbworks.com

PREFERENCE OF NATIONALITY: Native English speakers.

QUALIFICATIONS: University graduate over the age of 21.

CONDITIONS OF EMPLOYMENT: Camp counsellors are required for the Teaching Tolerance through English summer camp in July–August. Counsellors are responsible for organising sports, arts, leisure and cultural activities as well as teaching English.

SALARY: Modest stipend.

FACILITIES/SUPPORT: Full board accommodation is provided.

RECRUITMENT: Main recruitment drive from April to May.

CONTACT: Gergo Santha (santhaG@state.gov).

TUDOMANY NYELVISKOLA

Tavasz u.3, 1033 Budapest

✎ info@tudomanynyelviskola.hu

💻 www.tudomanynyelviskola.hu

Sister school is Európai Nyelvek Stúdiója at Tavasz ut 2 (www.europainyelvek.hu).

NUMBER OF TEACHERS: 10–15.

PREFERENCE OF NATIONALITY: British and American.

QUALIFICATIONS: TEFL/TESL preferred.

CONDITIONS OF EMPLOYMENT: 10-month contracts, hours vary.

FACILITIES/SUPPORT: Assistance with accommodation not usually given. Training sometimes available. Affiliated with ELT training centre Via Lingua Budapest (see Training listings).

RECRUITMENT: Local interviews essential.

CONTACT: Zsuzsanna Tölgyesi, Director of Studies (zsuzsa@tudomanynyelviskola.hu or dos@tudomanynyelviskola.hu).

VOCATIONAL ACADEMY

Teleki u 18, 9022 Györ

✆ +36 96 512010; +36 30 868 2620

✎ nagyotto@vocational.hu

💻 www.vocational.hu

NUMBER OF TEACHERS: 34.

PREFERENCE OF NATIONALITY: British, American, Canadian.

QUALIFICATIONS: TEFL and/or a master's degree. University degree needed, preferably in economics.

CONDITIONS OF EMPLOYMENT: Minimum 1 year. Hours of teaching 7.30am–4.30pm.

SALARY: €580 per month plus 4 weeks' paid holiday per year and extra benefits (e.g. flat, cheap meals, etc.). Deductions amount to about €65.

FACILITIES/SUPPORT: Student residence or block of flats owned by school, or employer helps teacher find other rental accommodation. School provides work and residence permit provided teacher passes medical test and has relevant documents and certificates to hand.

RECRUITMENT: Advertising. Face-to-face interview not essential.

CONTACT: Paul Rogerson, Principal (paul.rogerson@ihh.hu) or Tamás Vaniss, School Director (forlang@t-e-mail.hu).

POLAND

Prospects for English teachers in Poland, western Poland in particular, remain reasonable, even if the seemingly insatiable demand for English teachers that has characterised the past 15 years is now a thing of the past. Poles are still keen to learn English, but with the explosion of cheap flights to and from Poland and the opening of borders, millions of Poles simply get on a plane and come to Britain or Ireland, mainly to work but sometimes to sign up for English language courses.

This is gradually having a knock-on effect on the quality of Polish English teachers working in their home country, although the reverence for 'native speakerhood' still runs very high. A famous Polish poet described (in perfect English) how his teenage daughter and her friends largely communicate in English, or at least a form of English picked up from TV shows and pop songs, and that some of the older generation are worried that Poland is becoming swamped by the English language and Western culture.

For now, certain types of English classes, largely taught by native English speakers are still popular; according to one director of studies: 'realistic' conversation classes teach Poles how to rent a flat or order a drink, while others teach students how to fill in forms (good luck to them).

Major cities such as Warsaw, Wroclaw, Krakow, Poznan and Gdańsk are possible destinations, especially for people with experience of preparing for Cambridge exams or those looking for in-company work. The smaller towns, for example in Silesia in southern Poland are more promising destinations, where the competition for jobs will be less intense and you may still receive preferential 'foreigner' treatment if you gain a dependable reputation as a teacher. Foreign teachers usually find their students friendly, open and keen to learn more about the world. Discussion classes are likely to be informed and lively, with students well up to date on developments and very well motivated to practise their English. In some companies, promotion depends on the level of English achieved, which spurs students from the business world to be especially committed. On the other hand, if the company is paying for an employee's lessons, there may be little incentive to attend regularly or with enthusiasm.

FINDING A JOB

Interested teachers should not expect to be snapped up unless they have at least a TEFL certificate and some sort of teaching experience. International House has a big presence in Poland with schools in Bielsko-Biala, Bydgoszcz, Katowice, Kielce, Koszalin, Opole, Torun and Wroclaw, some of which are listed in the directory. The Bell Educational Trust has an Associate Network of schools in Bydgoszcz, Gdańsk, Gdynia, Sopot, Szczecin, Warsaw, Poznan and Krakow. These high profile ELT organisations are founding members of PASE, the Polish Association for Standards in English which promotes ethical practices in the private sector. PASE has 43 member schools, 19 in Warsaw, which are linked from www.pase.pl. PASE members employ almost exclusively teachers with a recognised teaching qualification. Schools approved by the Polish Ministry of Education insist that their teachers have a university degree and a teaching qualification.

ON THE SPOT

Semesters begin on 1 October and 15 February, and the best time to arrive is a month beforehand. After arrival, try to establish some contacts, possibly by visiting the English department at the university. Although some school directors state a preference for British or American accents, many are neutral provided you are a native English speaker.

Private language schools can be found everywhere, catering for all kinds of English. The Warsaw *Yellow Pages* carries several pages under the heading *Jezykowe Kursy, Szkolenia*. Alternatively you can trawl databases such as www.ang.pl/szkoly_jezykowe.php. The very busy British Council in Warsaw (near Central station) and the smaller partner offices and libraries in other cities may be able to assist personal callers.

While some institutes have high standards in those they hire, others are looking more for personality, as a rather jaundiced poster on an online forum complained in 2010 (www.polishforums.com/work-study-43/ih-school-krakow-19621):

> It's a sad fact that the English teaching market in Poland is driven by price not quality. School owners want bright and bouncy 21 year olds straight off a degree, ideally with a CELTA, who are going to entertain the customers and not have an opinion on teaching. They'll complain that 'natives are unreliable' when these 21 year olds stay in the pub till 2 in the morning on a weekday but it's a fair trade at the end of the day because they won't start demanding better standards like a more experienced teacher would (e.g. Being paid. On time. As agreed).

If you base yourself in Warsaw and wish to advertise your availability for private English tuition, try placing a notice just to the right of the main gate of Warsaw University or in one of the main dailies, *Gazeta Wyborcza* or *Zycie Warszawy*. Job ads are published every Monday in the *Gazeta* and can be checked online at www.praca.gazeta.pl. A further idea is to visit Irlandzki Pub 3 at ul. Miodowa 3 near the castle which many English speakers use as their watering-hole.

Freelancing is very popular, and there has been a huge increase in demand for tailor-made one-to-one courses. When **Kathy Cooper** was based in the small town of Raciborz in Silesia she worked for three language schools over seven years and also freelanced on the side. She found that once her name was established around town, she had a waiting list of willing students. Banks are likely clients and often pay very well by Polish standards. Kathy also taught corporate clients (signed through the school), including '*food/chocolate, cement, power plants, furniture, steel, industrial cleaning and sanitation, automotive, banking, industrial equipment, manufacturing, legal profession, doctors, and hotel industry. Yes, I am in Poland, land of opportunity for teachers*'.

Competent freelancers ask for 40 zloty an hour. As usual private students can be unreliable so try to get them to pay for, say, a month's lessons in advance. For this work, teachers should have enough ELT awareness to be able to devise their own syllabus. They will also have to put up with early or late hours (8am/9pm) and the inevitable cancelled lessons as business execs reschedule due to important meetings. Kathy Cooper got around this problem simply by calling another business client who wanted to make up lost hours.

ACADEMIC INSTITUTES

NKJOs are teacher training colleges specialising in training teachers of foreign languages. NKJOs are sometimes willing to hire qualified, experienced teachers. Virtually every institute of higher education (universities, medical academies, technical universities, economics academies, art schools, etc.) has a Studium Jazykow Obcych (Foreign Language Department) which is where the students who aren't language majors fulfil their foreign language requirements. The learners are less advanced and possibly less motivated in English than at the NKJOs, and they may be prepared to accept less well qualified native English speaker assistants while offering the attractions of an academic setting.

Jobs attached to universities usually offer stability and a light workload, say 12–15 classroom hours a week during the two 15-week semesters. The salary is paid over 12 months and includes full health insurance, housing perks and discounts on train travel. Bear in mind that if you are tutoring some of them privately, this income will vanish over the summer vacation.

HOLIDAY LANGUAGE CAMPS

Private language teaching organisations run short-term holiday courses in summer and sometimes winter, requiring English native speakers. ESCS (see entry) hires teachers for language schools in southern Poland and summer language camps at the Polish seaside. Pay is 25–30 zloties an hour, 2,200 zloties a month. American **Alicia Wszelaki** was full of praise for ESCS after spending a year immersing herself in Polish culture in the southern town of Myslenice. Similarly **Will Gardner** greatly enjoyed his summer job with ESCS which he had fixed up from England in the spring:

> *I spent one month working for ESCS at their summer camp on Poland's Baltic Coast. The camps were well organised and great fun. As an experienced teacher who has worked in several different countries for a range of schools, I would just like to say what a pleasure it was to work with such a well organised group of people and for a school that completely lived up to its promises. The school supplied a wide range of resources to assist teachers, although a lot of emphasis was placed on originality. The focus was always on communication and fun. The camp facilities were perfect for the situation. Food and accommodation were supplied and the weather was beautiful. Although the students were attending lessons daily, a holiday atmosphere prevailed over all activities.*

To take one example RCKU (Regional Centre for Continuing Education) in Pulawy was advertising vacancies in 2010 for two summer camps lasting three weeks in which English tutors were offered accommodation, food, pocket money of €100 and a five-day trip around Poland after the camp, but not international travel (camp.pulawy@gmail.com). American young people might be interested in volunteering to work at one of the many English language immersion camps run by the Kosciuszko Foundation's Teaching English in Poland Program (www.thekf.org/kf/programs/summer/teaching_english_in_poland). The three-week English language camp takes place at a boarding school in Tczew near the Baltic Sea.

Another company advertising for summer teachers in 2010 was the Lewis School (www.lewis-school.co.uk/jobs.htm), which was looking for teachers for Kampinos near Warsaw.

REGULATIONS

Poland's requirements for EU teachers are broadly in line with the rest of Europe. They no longer need to apply for a work permit, however teachers wishing to stay for more than three months must obtain a residence card from the regional governor of their chosen city/town. Applicants will need to justify their stay in Poland and confirm that they have sources of income (e.g. a statement from a bank account). Employers should assist with the documentation and the necessary translation of official documents into Polish.

Non-EU nationals who want to stay for more than 90 days and for less than a year will have to jump through the usual hoops prior to departure from their home country. The required documents must be presented in person to a Polish Consulate: a valid work permit certificate issued by the Office of Wojewoda in Poland or a promissory work permit from your Polish employer, your passport, two photos, a completed application form and the current fee for a work visa. In order for your employer to obtain permission to employ a foreign teacher, he or she will have to submit originals or notarised copies of your degree diploma and TEFL certificate (if applicable) with official translations.

After arrival with the visa, you will need to obtain a work permit. Most schools will assist with the documentation but may not bear the financial cost. When the initial visa expires (after three months), it is possible to apply for a residency card from inside Poland which will be valid for two years. Most employers who take on foreign teachers are well aware of the procedures which, according to one, could fill a book on their own. English language teachers planning to work in Poland at universities or colleges can submit a Certificate of Employment issued by the president of the hiring institution instead of a work permit certificate. The Polish Embassy in Washington can provide further details (www.polandembassy.org).

CONDITIONS OF WORK

Generally speaking, private language schools in Poland offer reasonable working conditions. Instead of hearing complaints from teachers of employers, it tends to be more often the other way round, as the Director of Studies of a private language school makes clear:

> *My boss, who has been employing British native speakers for seven years and who has proved to be a very patient person, could provide you with some hair-raising stories of teachers signing their contracts and withdrawing at the very last minute (having probably found a more lucrative job in Japan), teachers returning a couple of days late after the Christmas break without presenting any adequate excuse (or not returning at all), not to mention the state of flats and equipment which, after being used for nine months, is often left in a wrecked condition.*

Wages are much higher than they used to be, but the cost of living has crept up too. Wages that look low on paper may come with free accommodation. Accommodation does not present as major a problem as it did in the early days because most employers either offer staff accommodation or will assist in a flat hunt. The terms of service are seldom exploitative. It is not uncommon for overtime to be paid to teachers for hours worked in excess of the contracted number (typically 24) and for transport perks to be offered.

ERICA JOLLY and **PAUL ROBINSON** describe the situation in Gdansk:

> *The big schools in and around Gdansk all seem similar. They are well equipped but don't pay that well. Class sizes are around 12–15 students and hours are usually a minimum of 18 teaching hours per week. The director in charge of teaching is an experienced EFL teacher and teacher-trainer herself, and is always available to help and advise. My only criticism is the propensity towards paperwork: each teacher is obliged to complete forms after each lesson giving details of everything covered, comments, etc.*

The current average net salary in the private sector starts at about 2,100 zloties (£400) per month and may include accommodation at that level. Until recently, few foreigners in their first two years were asked to pay income tax, though a deduction was made for social security. However, now that Poland is in the EU, the Polish tax authorities are becoming increasingly tough on language schools, and so it is unwise to work 'black' and run the risk of being asked to pay unpaid tax even after you have returned to the UK.

HEIDI ROTHWELL-WALKER enjoyed company teaching, which was a contrast with the basic adult education she had been doing in Britain:

I was expected to work any time from 7am to 6pm. Sometimes the early hours (especially in the long winter) can get you down, but you will be rewarded financially for starting at 7am. There was a lot of travelling and waiting at bus stops, but working conditions in the companies were excellent. Not every company gave you access to a white board, overhead projector or cassette player but they could be made available upon request.

Once you are working either in the public or private sector, you may be approached with various proposals, from 'verifying' English translations of scientific research papers or restaurant menus, to coaching actors and singers preparing for English performances and doing dubbing or voice-overs for films and TV.

KATHY COOPER is an American grandmother who suddenly decided to live in Europe. Immediately after obtaining a Trinity certificate in TESOL in the UK, she was offered a job in southern Poland and has fallen in love with her life there, the chemical-free foods, the teaching and the culture. She began her Polish teaching career in the town of Opole, where she was thrown in at the deep end. With time, she was able to refine her teaching schedule:

Teaching varies from school to school, and from classroom to classroom. Starting out, I was thrown immediately into a range of beginning children to executive business and British Council exam classes. It was either to be my death or destiny. I now specialise in only executive business and exam classes. Periodically I embark on a student who wants to attend either high school or university in America whence I teach TOEFL exams for both. SLEP (Secondary Level English Proficiency) testing is the new format for high school entrance in America, it is part of the TOEFL system. I can proudly relate that my last student attending a foremost university in the States has just been asked to return, and on scholarship, to obtain her MA in Graphic Design. She was their first Pole of several thousand foreign students. Teachers are a mix of English speaking nationalities; I have worked with all, including other Americans. It is most common you will tandem teach with Polish teachers. In my case, again, I have some executives and advanced students that require only native speakers because of their language level. Facilities vary; I've been lucky to have had beautifully renovated and comfortable buildings and classrooms. It's not always the norm. Depending on the age of the company, depends on your resource library. I am with a young school now, and we are stocking year by year.

Despite a considerable amount of disorganisation at many schools, no one complains of a lack of hospitality from the Poles. Once they get to know the teacher, students will offer whatever services they can from mending shoes to giving large quantities of home-preserved fruit or splendidly arranged floral displays. **Marta Eleniak** especially enjoyed her experience teaching children:

> *Teaching in the primary school was really enjoyable as the little kids make you feel so appreciated by giving you flowers, drawing pictures for you and performing songs, poems or dances for you. They always wanted to continue after the bell had gone. One class was so keen that they invited themselves for a lesson even though it was my break.*

All of this makes a refreshing contrast with the lot of the EFL teacher in many other parts of the world. Poles even seem to have the ability to crack jokes in English when their English is very elementary, so lessons are not usually dull. On the whole they are also very well-motivated and hard-working, including adolescents.

LEISURE TIME

Poland offers no shortage of sights to see, pubs to visit, museums, theatres and parks to enjoy. Films are usually in English with Polish subtitles. Travelling is fairly cheap and easy. The transport system in Warsaw and some other cities looks complicated at first glance but is in fact straightforward. People in shops and so on can seem rude and abrupt, though this should not be taken personally.

Kathy Cooper has fallen for the food, '*Poland yields the most amazing hams, kielbasas and bacon that have ever melted in my mouth. Add the dense and daily purchased homemade breads that taste like my grandmother's, the variety of local and international cheeses, harvests of the freshest chemical-free fruits and vegetables that can be found, plus ice creams, baked goods, and phenomenal yogurts abound. Need I say more?'*... although she does go on to say that the Western plague of hypermarkets is starting to lead to the closure of traditional small shops.

Heidi Rothwell-Walker is convinced that she made the right decision when she chose to work for a school in Poland rather than at one of the other schools around the world that offered her a job:

> *The language is difficult, comprising such wonderful names as, 'Sczcyrk,' a tiny ski village, but it can make for a good atmosphere in the classroom as you struggle with Polish pronunciation whilst your students try to get their tongues round English words.*

> *Poland can seem a bit of a backwater, but it's a tremendous experience. It'll change your thinking completely and you'll either love it (like 98% of people) or hate it, but you must try it. I have just renewed my contract for another year because I have been very impressed by them and am very happy here.*

LIST OF EMPLOYERS

AMBER ENGLISH COURSES
ul. Langiewicza 22b, 35–085 Rzeszów
+48 17 853 47 11
suecallow@op.pl
www.amberenglishcourses.pl

NUMBER OF TEACHERS: 3 per year.
PREFERENCE OF NATIONALITY: British.

QUALIFICATIONS: Experienced, qualified ESOL. Minimum 140-hour course (not online); experience of Cambridge Exams at all levels, main suite and business would be an advantage. Experience of teaching young learners: 7–11, 12–15, teenagers 16+ and adults, all levels of ability. Teaching Business English and English for specific purposes. Successful candidates should have 'personality' and the desire to teach those in their care.

CONDITIONS OF EMPLOYMENT: September to June, contract hours: 20, 45-minute lessons per week. Opportunity for 10+ extra hours, proofreading, organising extra activities for young learners (kid's club) and adult recreational workshops.

SALARY: 45–70 zloty per 45 minutes (gross). Less deductions of 19% for tax and medical insurance, on average 300 zloty per month.

FACILITIES/SUPPORT: Assistance with finding accommodation near the school and contribution of half the monthly rent. Teacher pays own utility bills, internet, etc.

RECRUITMENT: Via TEFL recruitment sites. Face-to-face interviews not necessary.

CONTACT: Sue Callow, Owner.

ANGLOSCHOOL
ul. Klaudyny 12, 01–684 Warsaw
klaudyny@angloschool.com.pl
www.angloschool.com.pl

NUMBER OF TEACHERS: 10–12 native English speakers in 6 centres in Warsaw.

QUALIFICATIONS: CELTA or equivalent and a university degree. Teaching experience preferred.

CONDITIONS OF EMPLOYMENT: 9-month contract from mid-September, up to 28 hours per week teaching 3pm–8.30pm Monday to Friday. Some morning classes 8.30am–10am.

SALARY: Competitive. School pays taxes and social security (45%).

FACILITIES/SUPPORT: Accommodation is provided by the school in the form of two or three roomed shared flats or single rooms in a house. Accommodation includes all necessary facilities, i.e. furniture, a phone, cable TV, a washing machine, kitchen with necessary equipment. Initial training course and ongoing workshops.

RECRUITMENT: Cooperates with schools running CELTA, TEFL courses, which provide a job placement service. Advertising in newspapers, internet (www.tefl.com) and recruitment agencies. Direct application with CV welcomed.

ANGOL SCHOOL
Srodkowa 13, Konstancin, 05–510 Jeziorna
+48 668001075
angolschool@gmail.com or chris@angolschool.com
www.angolschool.com

NUMBER OF TEACHERS: 5 for school that opened in 2009.

QUALIFICATIONS: Minimum 1 year of TEFL experience, preferably in the Callan Method, though school is introducing the Direct Method as well.

CONDITIONS OF EMPLOYMENT: To teach conversational English, Business English, young learners English, mature preparation and professional English, in various homes and businesses around Warsaw.

CONTACT: Christopher Bradbury.

BRITISH CENTRE S.C – ENGLISH LANGUAGE COURSES
Dabrowskiego 8/6, 42–200 Czestochowa
office@britishcentre.pl
www.britishcentre.pl

NUMBER OF TEACHERS: 2.

PREFERENCE OF NATIONALITY: British.

QUALIFICATIONS: CELTA and experience with preparing students for Cambridge ESOL exams.

CONDITIONS OF EMPLOYMENT: 1-year contract with between 15 and 20 lessons per week.

SALARY: 35 Zloty per lesson (45 minutes). 26–25 Zloty after tax and social security deductions.

FACILITIES/SUPPORT: Room provided in English teacher's house.

CONTACT: Hanryka Rabenda. Co-owner.

ELS-BELL SCHOOL OF ENGLISH
Al. Niepodleglosci 792/2, 81–805 Sopot
recruitment@bellschools.pl

In association with Bell Educational Trust of Cambridge.

NUMBER OF TEACHERS: 90 for centres in Gdansk, Gdynia, Bydgoszcz, Sopot, Szczecin and Warsaw. Other Bell affiliates are Program Bell in Poznan, and Gama Bell in Krakow.

PREFERENCE OF NATIONALITY: British and Irish. Non-EU considered with relevant experience.

QUALIFICATIONS: CELTA or Trinity TESOL plus university degree. Experience preferred.

CONDITIONS OF EMPLOYMENT: September to June, up to 24 lessons a week (45 minutes each). Annual workload is 680 hours. Also run summer camps for young learners (aged 9–17).

SALARY: 2,400–2,800 Zloty net, plus end-of-contract bonus of 1,000 Zloty. Warsaw wages are higher: 3,000–3,600 Zloty.

FACILITIES/SUPPORT: Accommodation found. Cost of obtaining work permits is reimbursed by school. Health insurance taken out. In-house teacher development programme. Warsaw centre also runs CELTA and DELTA courses.

RECRUITMENT: Ads on internet. Interviews necessary, usually by phone.

CONTACT: Chris Bogner.

ENGLISH LANGUAGE CENTRE 'RIGHT NOW'

Pszczynska 17, 44–240 Zory, Silesia

(C) +48 32 434 2929

info@rightnow.com.pl

www.rightnow.pl

NUMBER OF TEACHERS: 2–3.

PREFERENCE OF NATIONALITY: EU passport holder.

QUALIFICATIONS: TESOL certificate or equivalent, and at least 1 year's teaching experience to speakers of other languages.

CONDITIONS OF EMPLOYMENT: 9–10 months September to mid-June. 12 90-minute lessons per week.

SALARY: About 2,000 zloty per month after deductions and taxes.

FACILITIES/SUPPORT: Free accommodation in a two-person flat within walking distance of the school.

RECRUITMENT: Internet ads followed by interviews in person or by telephone.

CONTACT: Rafal Zurkowski, Owner/Manager.

ENGLISH SCHOOL OF COMMUNICATION SKILLS (ESCS)

Ul. Krakowska 47/5, 33–100 Tarnow

personnel@escs.pl

www.escs.pl

NUMBER OF TEACHERS: 20 for 2 schools in southern Poland (Tarnow and Katowice). Also hold summer courses/camps at Polish seaside.

PREFERENCE OF NATIONALITY: Native English speakers.

QUALIFICATIONS: Degree level of education plus TEFL methodology certificate or ESCS's own training course offered in February and August.

CONDITIONS OF EMPLOYMENT: 1-year contracts, 20 hours per week. 600 teaching hours per school year (October to June) plus 36 project hours. Teaching all ages (6–60). Pre-selected course books, standardised texts and many extracurricular activities for students (baseball, drama club, video club, etc.)

SALARY: Hourly rate; base salary 2,200 zloties per month; varies according to experience and qualifications.

FACILITIES/SUPPORT: Seminars and workshops held. Teacher resource centre includes videos, cassettes and supplementary material. Photocopying and computers on-site.

RECRUITMENT: Via universities. Interviews held whenever possible. Applications should be sent to the Personnel Department.

CONTACT: Renata Bogucka-Wisniewska, ESCS Personnel Dept.

ENGLISH UNLIMITED

ul. Podmlynska 10, 80–855 Gdansk

work@eu.com.pl

www.eu.com.pl

NUMBER OF TEACHERS: 4 for 4 centres around the Tri-City (Gdansk, Gdynia and Sopot). Also possibility of teaching at the Teacher Training College in Gdansk.

PREFERENCE OF NATIONALITY: None; must be native English speakers (EU citizens preferred).

QUALIFICATIONS: Bachelor's or master's degree and Cambridge certificate or diploma plus experience of overseas teaching.

CONDITIONS OF EMPLOYMENT: 9-month contracts from September. Varied hours of teaching. Courses offered in ESP (e.g. Business English).

SALARY: About £350 per month (net).

FACILITIES/SUPPORT: Help given with arranging accommodation. Training provided.

RECRUITMENT: Adverts on internet. Interviews essential.

CONTACT: Kamila Anflink, Director of Studies.

GLOBAL VILLAGE

Al. Legionów 42, 25–035 Kielce

office@gv.edu.pl

www.gv.edu.pl

NUMBER OF TEACHERS: 7.

PREFERENCE OF NATIONALITY: EU nationals preferred.

QUALIFICATIONS: Bachelor's or master's plus a CELTA, DELTA or TEFL certificate.

CONDITIONS OF EMPLOYMENT: Standard contract length 1 academic year, to work 3pm–8pm, Monday to Friday.

SALARY: Competitive.

FACILITIES/SUPPORT: The school organises accommodation.

CONTACT: Urszula Szczepanczyk, Director.

GREENWICH SCHOOL OF ENGLISH

ul. Gdanska 2, 01–633 Warsaw

rekrutacja@greenwich.edu.pl

www.greenwich.edu.pl

NUMBER OF TEACHERS: 20 full-time, 10 part-time for 4 branches in Warsaw and 1 in Gdansk (58 305 70 89; telc@greenwich.edu.pl).

PREFERENCE OF NATIONALITY: British or any other native English speaker.

QUALIFICATIONS: Minimum bachelor's or master's degree and teaching certificate and experience preferred. Willing to consider enthusiastic people who like working with students, are creative, open-minded and good team players.

CONDITIONS OF EMPLOYMENT: One school year contract, e.g. 30 September to 30 June. Guaranteed minimum 80 hours per month plus up to 15 hours overtime. Full sick and holiday pay.

SALARY: Approx. £470–£600 basic per month (net guaranteed) depending on experience, qualifications and ability. Plus end of contract bonus.

FACILITIES/SUPPORT: Accommodation found by school, normally in shared flats. Rent is approximately £160 per calendar month. Fully-paid work visa. Regular programme of seminars.

RECRUITMENT: Interviews essential and held in various locations in the UK in July or by phone where necessary.

INTERNATIONAL HOUSE – WROCLAW
Ul. Leszczynskiego 3, 50–078 Wroclaw
biurowroc@ih.com.pl
www.ih.com.pl

NUMBER OF TEACHERS: 12.

PREFERENCE OF NATIONALITY: EU passport holders, but non-EU passport holders may also be considered.

QUALIFICATIONS: Minimum CELTA or Trinity certificate. One year's experience or CELTA Pass 'A' or 'B' preferred.

CONDITIONS OF EMPLOYMENT: 9 month standard contract, 21 contact hours per week.

SALARY: 2,600–3,400 zloties per month net (in first year) depending on qualifications and experience.

FACILITIES/SUPPORT: The school helps new teachers find suitable accommodation on arrival.

RECRUITMENT: Via IH Human Resources in London or direct at wrocdos@ih.com.pl. Interviews are carried out by IH Human Resources in London or else directly in Wroclaw in person or by phone.

CONTACT: John Fowler, Director of Studies.

INTERNATIONAL LANGUAGE CENTERS (ILC)
Al. Slowackiego 56/8, 30–018 Kraków
+48 12 429 67 88 / 606 997 990
info@ibes.pl or info@learnpolish.net
www.ibes.pl, www.learnpolish.net

NUMBER OF TEACHERS: Variable, according to need.

PREFERENCE OF NATIONALITY: American, British, Irish, Australian, New Zealander, South African.

QUALIFICATIONS: No university qualifications necessary, although teaching experience with the Callan Method is useful, as is other teaching experience. Generally only hire with minimum of 1 year's experience or TEFL certificate. Other useful skills include an ability to multi-task, clear projecting voice, and an ability to remain active and engaging throughout the lesson.

CONDITIONS OF EMPLOYMENT: Full-time load is 20 hours per week. with a possibility of working up to 25 depending on school needs. Part-time work available.

SALARY: Commensurate with experience and qualifications.

FACILITIES/SUPPORT: Accommodation listings supplied and assistance with translation. In-house training required upon arrival, free for teachers. Training courses conducted for those who wish to obtain Callan certification for use elsewhere, although these courses are paid for by recipient. Teachers are supplied with necessary documents and translations to obtain residency, usually after 3 months.

CONTACT: Joanna Krolikowska-Rajchman, Director of Studies.

LEKTOR SZKOLA JEZYKOW OBCYCH
ul. Olawska 25, 50–123 Wroclaw
rmyszkowski@lektor.com.pl or metodyk@lektor.com.pl.

NUMBER OF TEACHERS: 70.

PREFERENCE OF NATIONALITY: British, Irish, American, Canadian, Australian.

QUALIFICATIONS: Certificate in TEFL required (CELTA, DELTA or equivalent).

CONDITIONS OF EMPLOYMENT: Contracts for one or more years, 20–25 lessons per week. Our students are young adults.

SALARY: From 55 zloties per hour.

FACILITIES/SUPPORT: Assistance with finding accommodation and obtaining work permit if necessary.

RECRUITMENT: Personal interviews essential.

CONTACT: Roman Myszkowski.

LINGUA NOVA
ul. Wspólna 41, p.II, 00519 Warsaw
+48 22 584 10 10/37; Mobile +48 668 041 650
Kursy@linguanova.com.pl
www.linguanova.com.pl

NUMBER OF TEACHERS: 16.

PREFERENCE OF NATIONALITY: British, American, New Zealander, Australian or Canadian.

QUALIFICATIONS: Bachelor's or master's degree, CELTA/DELTA or similar qualifications of teaching ESL.

CONDITIONS OF EMPLOYMENT: 1-year contract with working hours between 7am and 8pm.

SALARY: 45 Zloty per 45-minute lesson.

FACILITIES/SUPPORT: Assistance is given with finding accommodation and applying for work permits.

RECRUITMENT: Usually via online advertising. Interviews are essential and can be carried out by phone.

CONTACT: Marta Migala, Senior Teacher and Methodology Supervisor (m.migala@linguanova.com.pl).

MULTISCHOOL SZKOLA JEZYKOW OBCYCH

Ul. Olawska 5, 01–494 Warsaw

(phone) 22 638 23 39; Mobile 604 97 33 49

(email) biuro@multischool.pl

(web) www.multischool.pl

NUMBER OF TEACHERS: 70–80 in 7 branches in Warsaw.

QUALIFICATIONS: TEFL course, higher education; experience not necessary.

CONDITIONS OF EMPLOYMENT: 12 months. Teaching hours 8am–3pm and 3pm–8pm.

SALARY: $1,000 a month average, varies according to timetable. Less 10% for deductions.

FACILITIES/SUPPORT: Help given in finding a flat to rent and in obtaining a work permit.

RECRUITMENT: Prefer to interview candidates but can rely on CVs, letters of motivation and telephone conversations.

UNIVERSITY OF LODZ

English Language Centre, Lindleya 8, 91–131 Lodz

(phone) 42 66 55 755; 42 66 55 760

(email) magda.matz@elc.pl

(web) www.elc.pl

NUMBER OF TEACHERS: 20.

PREFERENCE OF NATIONALITY: British preferred.

QUALIFICATIONS: CELTA, DELTA or equivalent teaching qualification. Candidates with higher education preferred.

CONDITIONS OF EMPLOYMENT: October to mid-June. Lessons take place 3pm–8.30pm and Saturday mornings 10am–1pm.

SALARY: Approximately €13 per hour before tax. Minimal deductions for social security.

FACILITIES/SUPPORT: Help to arrange accommodation and hope in the future to offer accommodation.

RECRUITMENT: After initial contact, applicants are sent questionnaire with some methodological questions, referees are contacted and then a phone interview.

CONTACT: Magdalena Matz, Director of Studies.

YORK SCHOOL OF ENGLISH

ul. Mackiewicza 12, 31–213 Krakow

(phone) +48 12 415 1818

(email) info@york.edu.pl

(web) www.york.edu.pl.

PASE (www.pase.pl) and Quality English (www.quality-english.com) recognised school, City & Guilds and LCCI approved examination centre.

NUMBER OF TEACHERS: 30, including approximately 10 full-time native English speakers.

PREFERENCE OF NATIONALITY: British and Irish, also American, Canadian or Australian (EU visa holders).

QUALIFICATIONS: BA/MA (preferably in English or Linguistics). TEFL certificate (CELTA/Trinity or equivalents). ELT experience, references.

CONDITIONS OF EMPLOYMENT: Minimum 1-year contract (September to June). 28 hours per week. Excellent working conditions.

SALARY: Monthly average salary 3,000 zl gross depending on qualifications and experiences.

FACILITIES/SUPPORT: Help given with accommodation. Bonuses. Professional development, regular workshops and conferences.

RECRUITMENT: Tefl.com.

CONTACT: Ewa Krupska, Director of Studies (e.krupska@york.edu.pl).

ROMANIA

English was barely taught before the downfall of Ceaucescu in 1989 and the collapse of communism and there are few private language schools in Romania at present, though with Romania's admission to the EU in January 2007 and increased investment from Brussels, this is changing. Romania's economy has been slow to develop, but strong consumption and investment expansion is resulting in a steady growth of the gross domestic product (GDP).

The Ministry of Education in Bucharest does not recruit EFL teachers directly, though it co-operates with the British Council to improve standards of local teachers and place volunteers. The British Council (www.britishcouncil.org/romania) has been very active in promoting English in Romania at all levels and runs its own Teaching Centre in Bucharest at Calea Dorobantilor 14 (21 307 9650; teachingcentre@britishcouncil.ro). Further along the same street in the capital is the expanding Cambridge School at number 39 (www.cambridgeschool.ro), which was advertising for experienced teachers in 2010. In the last few years the government has made a foreign language exam compulsory for graduating from school and university.

Despite the demand for native English speakers, however, the government doesn't always make it easy for foreign teachers to work in Romania. The American organisation Central European Teaching Program used to supply teachers to schools, particularly in the Hungarian-speaking areas of Transylvania, but decided to pull out a couple of years ago. It found that the government would reassign its teachers to locations such as Bucharest, regardless of promises made to CETP.

The vast majority of English teaching is carried out by Romanian teachers, who seem to do a splendid job judging from the extremely high pass rate their pupils achieve in the Cambridge exams. Teenagers are also motivated to learn English, at least according to one young person, because of the desire to live and work abroad.

QUEST Romania (www.quest.ro) is the Romanian Association for Quality Language Services, which operates as a quality control system on the basis of an inspection scheme. Its website seems to have stagnated somewhat and it is not known how reliable the members' contact details are. The Language Centre members of QUEST employ well-qualified teachers (most of them Romanian) and operate as private language schools registered as non-governmental organisations (NGOs) and recognised by the Ministry of Education. For example, the Access Language Centre in Cluj-Napoca (www.access.rom) is such an NGO supported by the British Council.

Under the heading *Limbi Straine – Cursuri* in the *Golden Pages* there are over 700 addresses around the country though these are unlikely to employ a native English speaker.

The arrival of Western investment and companies such as McDonald's and Hilton Hotels is creating more demand for commercial English though not necessarily the prosperity to pay for it. Romanian language schools find it next-to-impossible to attract native English speaker teachers because they simply can't afford to pay them.

As the director of one QUEST member school wrote:

> *While we would welcome having native English teachers on our staff (we do occasionally receive enquiries from interested people), it is true that given how small our school is (approximately 400 students a year altogether) we cannot afford spending too much on employing them. For the moment, we only employ highly qualified local teachers on part-time contracts. I do not want to mislead people before we reach a more secure position and financial situation, in a very unstable country, economically speaking.*

Many years ago, **Minna Graber** arrived in Romania to celebrate the New Year and has been besotted with the country ever since:

We went straight into a Carpathian village at the top of a mountain complete with gypsy fiddlers and not an internal combustion engine for miles around. I fell for the place hook, line and sinker and haven't been able to kick the habit. I wanted to teach in the northeast of the country and so contacted the British Council in Iaşi who in turn referred me to SOL. I met the director Grenville Yeo at a café and we talked for a long time about the challenges, rewards and requirements. In the end the job offer was with one of the best schools in Bucharest where the students all go on to university, (and a significant minority are these days applying for British University places. I work for 18 teaching periods a week. I am not supposed to teach grammar which at least in my school is seen as the Romanian English language teachers' prerogative partly, I fear, because they assume native speakers are not capable of this. This is despite the fact that I am fully trained to do so.

The wages sound terrible – 1,100 Lei a month after deductions for tax and National Insurance. The other teachers have to pay for accommodation out of this so in comparison I have a big advantage (the school's parents' association provides and pays for my very simple small studio flat and for the running costs). I am very good at living frugally but find that I still have to take on a couple of private students to make ends meet. The rest of the staff work long hours, giving these private lessons.

According to Minna, native speakers of English can command a high fee for giving private tuition. She charges around 60 Lei an hour ($17). If you work in a private kindergarten, as she did at one point, you can charge even more. Despite her modest earnings, she is far from discontent with her lifestyle:

I go to all the best concerts, have private lessons in Romanian, attend martial arts classes and choir every week and travel a lot. I am even able to put a little by at the end of the month. My students are all completely delightful. I love teaching them. They are respectful and talented. I do have to mother them a little over matters such as getting work in on time. Occasionally they, and occasionally their parents, try to exert pressure on me over marks. If a form tutor asks my help in rescuing a student who has problems or who might otherwise get expelled I always do so, otherwise I resist changing marks.

As for leisure time, many a Saturday has been spent haring up the mountains with Bucharest's enormous and enthusiastic mountain club. As a result of my wanderings over the mountains in the summer I made friends with some traditional shepherds and peasant farmers and am always welcome to visit. The times spent with these friends in the countryside are like a journey back into a far distant past. Of course, for all of this a command of the Romanian language is essential.

Nobody knows anything about Romania and the upside of this is that it is very tourist-free area and you enjoy status as a visitor from the outside world. People are interested and welcoming largely because there are so few visitors. Catch it whilst it still lasts.

A few British charities have recruited volunteers for summer language camps in the past, though British-Romanian Connections in Liverpool says that it will not be sending anyone to Piatra Neamt in the summer of 2010; check its Facebook group where they say that 'Romania 2011 is still very much on the cards'. DAD International UK-Romania (+40 788 473523; www.dad.ro) was recently advertising for summer volunteer teachers and offering an expenses-paid three or four weeks in various parts of Romania including Transylvania, Moldavia and the Black Sea (flights excluded).

Since the accession of Romania to the EU, red tape for Europeans has become simpler. Any teacher wishing to stay for longer than 120 days should apply for a temporary resident permit, preferably in their home country: American citizens are not required to obtain Romanian visas for stays up to 90 days within 6 months.

LIST OF EMPLOYERS

PROFESSIONAL LANGUAGE CENTRE
197 1 Decembrie 1918, St. Targu-Mures 4300
+40 365401212
acotoara@rdslink.ro
www.professionalcentre.ro

NUMBER OF TEACHERS: 1.

QUALIFICATIONS: Bachelor's degree or equivalent.

CONDITIONS OF EMPLOYMENT: 1-year contract. To work 4pm–8pm, 5 days a week.

SALARY: $7 per hour. Taxes and social security paid by the school.

FACILITIES/SUPPORT: Assistance with finding accommodation and acquiring work permits.

RECRUITMENT: Interview required.

CONTACT: Angela Cotoara, Director.

WORDLAND INTERNATIONAL LANGUAGE AND BUSINESS TRAINING CENTRE
14, Constantin Sandu Aldea St., 1st floor, 012063 Bucharest 1
office@wordland.ro
www.wordland.ro

NUMBER OF TEACHERS: 3.

PREFERENCE OF NATIONALITY: Native English speakers.

QUALIFICATIONS: University degree in linguistics and teaching. Past experience teaching EFL, particularly to adults in business-orientated environments.

CONDITIONS OF EMPLOYMENT: After a 3-month trial period the teacher is offered an open-ended contract. Working hours between 9am and 6pm with 1-hour lunch break.

FACILITIES/SUPPORT: Salary includes transport, phone, meal tickets and training. Assistance given with finding accommodation and applying for work permits.

RECRUITMENT: Candidates are invited for an interview and practical teaching test in Bucharest.

CONTACT: Viviana Ball, Managing Director.

RUSSIA

It seems that you can't pick up a paper these days without reading one alarming headline or another about organised crime in Moscow or repression. A report published by the watchdog organisation Freedom House in 2010 ranked Russia 175th out of 196 countries on a scale of global press freedom. But this is hardly the full story and there are still plenty of opportunities for native English teachers who wish to experience this vast and diverse country safely.

Russian business suffered with the rest of the world during the 2009 recession, and language schools have noticed a decline in corporate clients. However, some have reported that the shortfall has been made up by employees themselves who believe that in a tough job market, a knowledge of English is even more worth the time and money in acquiring.

Russians are still basically conservative and concerned by the need for good education, but there is a constant shortage of Russian English teachers in state schools so private language schools continue to be popular. The large chains such as Language Link, BKC-International House and EF English First are constantly recruiting teachers for their schools. Rather than employ an underqualified native English teacher, most language schools would rather turn to home-grown English teachers for whom teaching English is a profession and not simply a one to two year pastime. Russian English teachers are also far cheaper and do not require visa support and other costly add-on benefits such as accommodation, health care and travel allowances.

However, exceptions are made for qualified candidates, e.g. native English teachers with a CELTA or Trinity College TESOL certificate. Most schools will also accept applicants who hold TEFL certificates obtained on credible 100+ hour training courses with teaching practice. If you do not hold a certificate but have gained valuable experience teaching General English, Business English and/or international examination courses (IELTS, FCE, CAE and their like) and you have taught both adults and children, you should have little difficulty finding a job teaching English in Russia.

Robert Jensky, who kindly provided most of the information for this chapter, is convinced that high standards are essential:

> *I have personally seen many unqualified teachers fail because they did not fully realise the difference between speaking English and teaching English. Although Russians can vary in temperament and personality, they share a respect for education. Russians who under communism did not have to pay for education have come to accept the fact that it is now necessary to do so. There is little debate among Russians as to the significance of the English language both domestically and globally. Their only concern is that they get their full money's worth from each and every lesson. Russian students are demanding and place high expectations on their teachers, and so do the companies which employ them (including those that hire EFL teachers illegally). Given these circumstances, it is strongly recommended that any teacher coming to Russia has with him or her a good grammar book, a dictionary and a concise guide to TEFL methodology.*

Many young Russians are already fairly competent in the language and want to become more conversant with Western culture, not just for its own sake but to enhance their career prospects. Jobs in international firms are often advertised only in English. Russians young and not-so-young who want to work in advertising, banking, computing and so on need to speak English and therefore are drawn to the intensive English courses advertised all over the Moscow metro and on lamp-posts.

There are also plenty of jobs tutoring and looking after young children, as affluent parents hope to give their children a head start by showing off at the same time. This sector seems to be expanding, with several companies and individuals posting adverts in newspapers/websites such as www.expat. ru. Kindergartens and specialist companies that offer tutors, nannies and governesses for children have also realised that native English speakers '*create a good image for your company*', according to **Sveta Kotwani**, Director of Little Angels Kindergarten in Moscow (see List of Employers). Two other specialist agencies are Gouverneur International (www.gouvernior.ru) and Bonne International with offices in London and Moscow (www.bonne-int.com). Both take on native English speakers for a number of vacancies, mainly in and around Moscow. ESL-qualified native candidates are needed to tutor children aged 4 to 10 years. MsPoppins (495 744 0651; www.mspoppins.com) also advertises for native English tutors for children aged from 4 to 12.

FINDING A JOB

Finding a vacancy in Russia shouldn't be too difficult. Russia is, after all, the largest country on earth, spanning 11 time zones. You only need to decide where in Russia you'd like to settle down to teaching English. As a rule, salaries can drop the further you go from Moscow. A lower salary, however, is usually more than made up for by the lower costs of living found in many of the big away-from-Moscow cities of Russia; and a lower cost of living usually means a higher standard of living. Likewise, you're more likely to experience real Russia and real Russians.

Rob Jensky cautions against focusing your job hunt entirely around salary and perks:

For newly qualified teachers, academic support can mean the difference between success and failure as a teacher. And speaking of success as a teacher, having tons of personality is imperative. Students want to like their teachers and the way to gain their affection is by truly liking them back. Teachers who like their students will spend the time needed to prepare for their lessons adequately and this is where the value of proper academic support cannot be underestimated. The availability of a good Director of Studies and other experienced teaching staff who can help you with lesson preparation is a benefit that cannot be counted in terms of dollars and cents or pounds and pence.

Teachers who are capable of performing in a variety of EFL classroom settings (Young Learners, adults, General, Business English, examination preparation) are in the greatest demand. Likewise, teachers who are prepared to be flexible with regard to teaching schedules will find a far greater number of employment opportunities. This is especially true in the great metropolitan areas where the number of both business and one-to-one clients is on the rise, many of whom want to be taught before or after the working day.

The three most popular websites used by Russian employers looking to hire English teachers are: www.TEFL.com, www.ESLcafe.com and www.teachabroad.com. When writing to potential employers in Russia make sure that the company has the right to invite and employ teachers in Russia (see visa section for details), check whether the salary is net or gross and ask if accommodation is free/included. Some companies such as the Samantha School of English in Moscow (www.samantha.ru) have a UK recruiter who can interview prospective candidates in the UK.

An estimated 900 tertiary institutes offer English courses, and many employ one or two highly educated native speakers to assist. Most universities and polytechnics offer free or subsidised accommodation and a civilised timetable but usually can't pay more than a couple of dollars an hour.

Some of the main language chains recruit abroad, including Language Link and EF English First, which recruits large numbers for 27 language schools in Russia on reasonable terms with return flight, medical insurance and visa costs included. Many foreign teachers prefer the security of working for a Western-owned company. Even if the wages are not brilliant, the support and fringe benefits usually make up for it. Language Link (www.jobs.languagelink.ru) offers an array of different employment opportunities designed to fit the needs of most EFL applicants from qualified to unqualified willing to be interns or volunteers. In addition to jobs for qualified EFL teachers, Language Link also recruits for its teacher internship, work-study and volunteer programmes. For details visit www.languagelink.ru.

Barry Robinson spent a number of years in Moscow working the EFL circuit and has provided a snapshot of the main employers. He admits that his opinions are totally subjective and are meant purely as a guide:

EFL in Moscow can often be more rewarding financially on a freelance basis, but for those who prefer to tie in with an all-inclusive contract, here is some info on what's on offer. BKC have an excellent reputation for teacher development and you get loads of professional support. They always pay on time and for work finished, and they are a decent company who will always look good on your CV. The same applies to Language Link who are friendly, fair, very supportive and will find you a flat. EF English First probably offer the best contract. They allow teachers to find their own flat (and pay for temporary accommodation during house-hunting) and their schools are always well-equipped. They insist that you stick to the EF book so there isn't much room for teacher development.

A thriving English language press has established itself in Moscow and St Petersburg. Check adverts in the *Moscow Times* and the *St Petersburg Times* (www.sptimes.ru). Look out also for the free ads paper *Iz Ruk v Ruki* in about 15 towns in Russia and check the online messageboards community for English speakers living in Moscow on www.expat.ru, which at the time of writing carried lots of adverts for native English speaker teachers.

Since 1992 the Serendipity Russian-English Program has been sending Americans to work at the American Home in Vladimir Russia, a city 200km east of Moscow. Not only do they teach English but also deliver lectures on American culture. Contracts last 8–9 months (renewable) starting in mid-August. The annual deadline for applications is 15 March. The project is located at the American Home (Ulitsa Letneperevozinskaya 3, 600000 Vladimir) though the programme is administered from the USA (www.serendipity-russia.com).

Jim Clost from Canada did not have a TEFL certificate when he went to Russia but he had studied the language at university and so joined a voluntary teaching scheme organised by a local travel agency:

I was required to work between four and six hours a day, only conversation and listening. Accommodation and meals were provided with a local family (normally one of the students) however no wages were paid as the position was voluntary. I met wonderful students, kids and adults and made friends that I go back to see regularly. The pupils were in general quite shy but some were ready to speak up and chat with me right away. Once we got to know one another conversation flowed more freely. Many of my students were quite eager to have me in their home for dinner. This is normal in Russian society where meeting with foreigners on a personal basis is a rarity. In my free time, I skated, swam, visited friends for tea and dinner, walked and talked.

Students of Russian should investigate the programme run by the Pro-Ba Centre in St Petersburg where four or eight weeks of intensive study of Russian is followed by a period of work in schools, kindergartens or summer camps (www.studyrussian.spb.ru). Fees are from €2,750 for two months to €3,750 for four months.

The youth exchange company CCUSA (www.ccusa.com) runs a Summer Camp Russia Programme whereby teacher/counsellors from the UK and USA are placed on youth camps in Russia lasting four or eight weeks between mid-June and mid-August. Participants must be between the ages of 18 and 35, have experience of working with children and/or abroad, and have an interest in learning about the Russian language and culture. Camps are widely scattered from Lake Baikal in Siberia to the shores of the Black Sea. The programme fee of £795 includes round-trip travel from London to Moscow, visa, travel, insurance, orientations on arrival and room and board.

Australian **PAUL JONES** spent the summer in Russia:

I worked as a counsellor in a summer camp near the city of Perm. When I first arrived, my heart sank because it looked like a gulag (for which the area around Perm is famous!). But you soon forget the physical conditions, mostly anyway. If I didn't like the food at the start, I definitely learnt to like it by the end and now reminisce about the worst of it! My job, as with American summer camps for kids, was to help lead a group of up to 30 children for their 3 weeks stay at the camp. Because I did not speak the language, I was placed with two other leaders so my services weren't really necessary. However, this region of Russia doesn't exactly get many international visitors so the role I played at camp sometimes felt more like being a rock star! The types of activities the kids did ranged from football, basketball and swimming (the colour of the pool was scary) to singing, dancing and crafts. But while I tried as best I could to lead my group of kids in their daily activities, every single kid in the camp wants a piece of you because you're the foreigner! So a lot of the job is to just be there and share a different culture with the kids (and their parents sometimes), other Russian counsellors and the Camp Director. I found that a few words in Russian go a long way to bridging the culture gap. And if possible take some souvenirs for the kids. Even a pack of cards with the British flag on them provides 52 little gifts.

CONDITIONS OF WORK

The unregulated housing market makes it difficult for foreign teachers to find independent accommodation. Furthermore rents in Moscow and St Petersburg are staggering relative to the quality on offer. Company-provided accommodation is easily a $600–$900 add-on benefit. Of course, as you leave the bright lights of Moscow and St Petersburg, rental costs come down. Employers normally arrange accommodation for their teachers in small shared flats. As single flats are much more expensive, your employer is unlikely to cover the extra cost of providing you with this luxury. Teachers might also lodge with landladies, of whom there is no shortage considering how many widows are trying to make ends meet on vanishingly small pensions.

Russians generally take a far more laid back attitude to work than their counterparts in Western society. This sometimes results in standards of efficiency and service that are somewhat lower than people generally expect in the UK or the USA. As Robert Jensky puts it: '*Whereas in America everything should be done 10 minutes ago and in the UK it should be done right now, in Russia it probably won't get done until the end of the working day (or week)*'. This is particularly true of those working in administrative and official capacities who are often slow, unhelpful and inconsistent, but is less so in some of the larger chains of language schools where a high level of professionalism prevails. Teachers need to be flexible in their approach to the working world in Russia and be prepared to compromise and adapt to an unfamiliar working environment.

A cultural difference which many newcomers find difficult to accept is the apparent unfriendliness of the Russian people. However, the cold face of Russian officialdom could not be in starker contrast to the warmth that will greet you when you get to know Russians better. **Elizabeth Bearman**, a teacher in Moscow, goes some way to unravelling the mystery of the cold Russian exterior:

The Russian man in the street does not smile unless he is happy, he does not engage complete strangers in meaningless conversation and he does not suffer fools gladly. There is a Russian proverb that perhaps sums it up: 'Only a fool smiles all the time'. However, while Russians can appear rude and unfriendly, when you get to know them they are considerate, helpful, generous and well ... friendly. The Russian concept of friendship is much deeper and less superficial than elsewhere.

With a serious shortage of teaching aids in many places, resourcefulness will be necessary. Not surprisingly, the younger generation seems more willing to embrace new communicative teaching methods than the older one, according to the director of the Sunny Plus English School in Moscow (www.sunnyplus.ru) which has a constant need for native English speaker teachers:

Adults cause headaches. They get upset with grammar. Many of them can't easily accept modern methods of teaching. The progress is very slow. For many weeks they can't understand a teacher. They demand changing him. Their pronunciation is terrible, but during classes they keep silent.

However, **Joanna Graham**, a teacher trainer at BKC Moscow (affiliated to International House), has had quite a different experience of teaching adults in Russia:

The students here are great, and one of the main reasons I have stayed at this school for so long. English lessons are not cheap (about a quarter of most people's monthly wage) and because more companies require it to communicate with overseas clients, etc. adult students tend to be very motivated. They want to learn and, for most of the classes I have taught, the more homework I give them the better (I've actually been told off by students for not giving them enough!)

Don't be fooled into believing that just because you choose to work for a chain school, you are going to be working in either a large school or one staffed by native English speaking teachers. Many major chains operate small teaching operations in far-flung locations. Proximity to good healthcare cannot be taken for granted, and could be an issue for people with medical conditions. If proximity to cultural and recreational outlets such as theatres, cinemas, museums, parks, circuses and other tourist attractions is important to you psychologically, then be sure to investigate locations prior to accepting a job.

REGULATIONS

Legalising your status as a teacher has always been fraught with difficulties, particularly for the companies that employ foreigners. Most had mastered the system until they were hit with a bombshell at the end of 2009. For a long time foreign language schools had enjoyed an exemption from the rule that they had to be registered employers who were obliged to obtain work permits from the Federal Migration Service. They simply had to be licensed with permission to invite foreigners. Overnight this special status was revoked or at least the law was applied differently and language school employers were told that they would need work permits for all their staff. To read a news article entitled 'Moscow language schools in visa limbo' from 2010, just Google it in connection with the *Moscow News*.

Some teachers work on multiple entry business visas, though it is not legal to do so. Foreigners entering the country on one-year multiple entry business visas may remain on Russian soil for a maximum of three months before having to leave Russian territory for at least three months; in other words, they may remain in Russia for only three months during any six-month period. To obtain a work visa, you need a visa sponsor. If you have accepted a teaching job with an organisation which has the right to obtain work permits, be prepared to wait for weeks and even months while the wheels of the Russian bureaucracy grind around.

Although some Russian sources state that an HIV test is not required for issuance of a visa, you will undoubtedly be required to submit proof of being HIV-negative. Specialist visa agencies may be able to advise such as Real Russia (www.realrussia.co.uk). To access a forum on English teaching and visas look at www.visarus.co.uk, which is a community of ESL teachers in Russia.

Teachers travelling to Russia will be required to fill in and submit a migration card along with their passport and visa when arriving at passport control. One copy is retained by the border guard and the other is returned to you with a stamp on it. Be sure that you get back your half and that it is stamped because this will be necessary for your proper registration in Russia.

LIST OF EMPLOYERS

BENEDICT SCHOOL

4 Admiraltejskaya Nabereznaya, St Petersburg 190000

- 825 7574/3
- benedict-adm@peterlink.ru
- www.benedict.spb.ru

The biggest English Language school in St Petersburg and North-West Russia.

NUMBER OF TEACHERS: 18–20 for St Petersburg and the surrounding cities.

PREFERENCE OF NATIONALITY: British, American, Canadian, Australian.

QUALIFICATIONS: TEFL qualification preferred. Benedict school offers its own intensive 4-week training courses 4 times a year (in cooperation with Via Lingua).

CONDITIONS OF EMPLOYMENT: 3–12 months. 15–25 hours per week.

SALARY: $1,000–$1,500 per month.

FACILITIES/SUPPORT: Visa support and help with accommodation given. Library and resource centre.

CONTACT: Natalya Rostovtseva, Director.

BIG BEN LANGUAGE SCHOOL

Office 203, 2 Komsomolskaya Street, Ufa, 450003

- +7 347 293 2075
- bigbenschool@yandex.ru
- www.bigbenschool.ru

NUMBER OF TEACHERS: 2–3.

PREFERENCE OF NATIONALITY: British or Canadian.

QUALIFICATIONS: CELTA.

CONDITIONS OF EMPLOYMENT: 12-month contract with 30 academic hours per week.

SALARY: $1000–$1500 per month including travel and healthcare.

FACILITIES: Furnished flat is provided for each teacher and the school will assist with visas and work permits.

RECRUITMENT: Usually via internet advertisements. Interviews are essential and usually conducted via telephone but occasionally in the UK in the summer.

CONTACT: Martyn Judd, Academic Director.

BKC – INTERNATIONAL HOUSE Moscow

Starovagankovsky Pereulok 15, office 32, 119019 Moscow

- 495 737 5225
- recruit@bkc.ru or recr@bkc-ih.com
- www.bkcih-moscow.com

NUMBER OF TEACHERS: Approximately 200 contract and hourly paid teachers in Moscow, 50 teachers in the Moscow region.

PREFERENCE OF NATIONALITY: None.

QUALIFICATIONS: CELTA, Trinity TESOL, DELTA, BA/MA/PhD in TESOL/Applied Linguistics.

SALARY: $800–$1,450 net depending on qualifications and experience, plus end of the contract bonus.

FACILITIES/SUPPORT: The school provides visa support, shared accommodation (rent and all utilities except long-distance phone calls paid by BKC), airfare allowance, healthcare, paid holidays and up to 90% discount for Russian classes. Great opportunities for professional development – an active in-house training programme, consisting of regular monthly training seminars and different workshops. Currently also offers DELTA and IHCYL (International House Certificate in Teaching Young Learners) training.

CONDITIONS OF EMPLOYMENT: 3, 6 or 9-month contracts; 30 or 24 teaching periods (1 lesson = 45 min) per week. Typical timetable includes some teens' or children's classes as well as adult classes. Business English, conversational and exam classes also offered.

RECRUITMENT: All year round.

CONTACT: Nadya Maximova or Nastya Eremkina, Recruitment Managers.

NUMBER OF TEACHERS: About 40 for 30 schools
(19 including 1 business school in Moscow, 2 in Vladivostok,
3 in St Petersburg, 1 in Stavropol, Rostov, Tyumen, 2 Nizhny
Novgorod, Novosibirsk, Almatievsk, Yuzhno Sakhalinsk
and Tver).

PREFERENCE OF NATIONALITY: British, North American,
Australian, New Zealander, Irish.

QUALIFICATIONS: CELTA/TESOL/EF TEFL certificate
plus a university degree, minimum 1 year ESL teaching
experience.

CONDITIONS OF EMPLOYMENT: 9-month or 12-month
renewable contracts. Schools open 9am–9pm, Monday
to Friday, and 9am–6pm, Saturday. 24 contact hours
per week.
Modern classrooms all fitted with computers and LCD
screens with online supplementary materials. Support with
finding accommodation. Visas arranged. Paid holidays. Flights
paid. Orientation upon arrival and ongoing training. Medical
insurance provided.

CONTACT: Svetlana Shulzhik (Svetlana.shulzhik@ef.com),
Polina Vasilieva (polina.vasilieva@ef.com).

NUMBER OF TEACHERS: 3.

PREFERENCE OF NATIONALITY: British or American.

CONDITIONS OF EMPLOYMENT: One year contract with
working hours between 9am and 3pm or 3pm and 9pm,
Monday to Saturday.

SALARY: $10–$15 per hour net.

FACILITIES/SUPPORT: Hostel accommodation is provided
or help finding other accommodation is given. The school will
also assist with work permits.

RECRUITMENT: Interviews via Skype are essential.

CONTACT: Elena Doroshenko, Principal.

NUMBER OF TEACHERS: 26.

PREFERENCE OF NATIONALITY: British, Irish, Australian,
New Zealander, Canadian, American.

QUALIFICATIONS: Minimum CELTA or equivalent, plus ideally 2 years' experience.

CONDITIONS OF EMPLOYMENT: 12-month standard
contract, 26 academic hours per week.

FACILITIES/SUPPORT: A housing manager helps to
accommodate all teachers based on what they would like.
Centre organises a work visa invitation, then when the
teacher is in Russia, organises all the necessary documents
to make sure the teacher is fully registered and has all
correct documentation.

RECRUITMENT: Through TEFL websites. Telephone
interviews are essential. If possible the school tries to set up
face-to-face interviews in London.

NUMBER OF TEACHERS: 10.

PREFERENCE OF NATIONALITY: British, American or
Canadian.

QUALIFICATIONS: 3 years or more EFL teaching experience
or EFL certificate.

CONDITIONS OF EMPLOYMENT: 1-year contract.

SALARY: $20 per hour.

FACILITIES/SUPPORT: Assistance is given with renting a flat
and applying for work permits and visas.

RECRUITMENT: Usually via the internet.

CONTACT: George Agababyan, Head of Education.

NUMBER OF TEACHERS: 200 for 40 schools throughout
Russia (Moscow, Moscow Region, St Petersburg, St

Petersburg Region, Obninsk, Samara, Ufa, Krasnoyarsk, Rostov na Donu, Zelenograd, etc.)

PREFERENCE OF NATIONALITY: British, American, Canadian, Australian, New Zealander and South African.

QUALIFICATIONS: CELTA or Trinity Certificate/Diploma (or equivalents) required. Candidates without a 100-hour TEFL qualification may enter Language Link's Teacher Internship Programme. Openings also available to those without experience or qualifications as volunteers or summer camp staff.

CONDITIONS OF EMPLOYMENT: 6, 9 or 12-month contracts, 25 teaching hours per week, usually 4 hours a day, 5 days a week. Adult classes, children's classes and in-company. Also runs a number of English language summer camps near major cities (camps@languagelink.ru) starting the beginning of June.

FACILITIES/SUPPORT: All teachers provided with free accommodation in 2-room flat (for 2 teachers). Paid medical services and full visa/work permission support. Academic support.

RECRUITMENT: Application is online. Minimum 2 professional references. Telephone interviews are compulsory unless carried out by Language Link in London.

CONTACT: Robert Jensky, Director.

LITTLE ANGELS KINDERGARTEN
St Novocheremushkinskaya no 49, Office 12, Moscow
litang@mail.ru
www.littleangels.ru

NUMBER OF TEACHERS: 5.

PREFERENCE OF NATIONALITY: British, Canadian or Australian.

QUALIFICATIONS: A strong background in early childhood education and a TEFL qualification. Also he/she should have experience of teaching.

CONDITIONS OF EMPLOYMENT: Standard 1-year contract, usual hours are 9am–5pm.

SALARY: Depends on qualification and experience but at least $1,500. If the employee has a work permit from Little Angels, 13% of the tax is deducted from their salary.

FACILITIES/SUPPORT: No help with accommodation or work permit at the moment. Usually, teachers already have a work permit from a company or agency.

RECRUITMENT: By interview, filling in a questionnaire and taking a class. Interviews are essential.

CONTACT: Sveta Kotwani, Director.

OXFORD ENGLISH ACADEMY
Chapaevskaya St., 227, Samara 443001
+7 846 972 1452
info@oxfordenglishacademy.ru
www.oxfordenglishacadmey.ru

NUMBER OF TEACHERS: 10–12.

PREFERENCE OF NATIONALITY: None.

QUALIFICATIONS: Minimum 2 years' experience plus CELTA or other TEFL qualification and bachelor's degree.

CONDITIONS OF EMPLOYMENT: 12-month contract, 30 working hours per week.

SALARY: 300 roubles per hour net.

FACILITIES/SUPPORT: Flats are provided for teachers and assistance given with applying for work permits.

RECRUITMENT: Usually via word of mouth. Interviews are essential.

CONTACT: Richard Corrigan, Director of Studies.

PRAKTIKA
18/7 Bolshaya Posadaskay U1, St Petersburg 197046
+7 921 9376593
office@flpractice.com
www.flpractice.com

NUMBER OF TEACHERS: 20.

PREFERENCE OF NATIONALITY: British or American.

QUALIFICATIONS: DELTA, CELTA or equivalent.

CONDITIONS OF EMPLOYMENT: 6-month contract with average workload between 20 and 30 hours per week.

SALARY: $1,000 per month is the starting point for 20 hours per week contract.

RECRUITMENT: Usually via local advertising and word of mouth. Interviews are essential.

CONTACT: Gleb Evzikov, Director of Studies.

SUNHILL SCHOOL
Bankovskaya Street 6a, Solnechnogorsk, Moscow region 141500.
495 726 9617 (September to May); 962 973 7271 (summer)
www.sunhillschool.ru

NUMBER OF TEACHERS: 4 for schools in Solnechnogorsk and Mendeleeva.

PREFERENCE OF NATIONALITY: British, Irish, American, Canadian, Australian, New Zealander.

QUALIFICATIONS: Degree holder. Previous teaching experience preferred, e.g. 1 year's EFL teaching abroad. Enthusiasm and desire to work essential.

CONDITIONS OF EMPLOYMENT: 9-month contracts from September. 24 teaching hours per week plus 2 hours on standby.

SALARY: From $1,000 a month, 23 days paid holiday per year.

FACILITIES/SUPPORT: Free shared accommodation provided by school, close to work. Flight compensation and end-of-contract bonus from $50 per month. Visa fees paid at consulate plus HIV test. Healthcare and insurance provided. Free internet.

RECRUITMENT: Telephone interview.

CONTACT: Natalia Kruglova, Director.

WINDSOR ENGLISH LANGUAGE SCHOOL
Office 7004, 16–1 Olympiysky Prospect,
Moscow 129090, and 7 Komsomolsky Prospect,
Moscow 119146
495 225 35 07
job@windsor.ru
www.windsor.ru/eng

NUMBER OF TEACHERS: Vacancies almost all year round, especially for people experienced with IELTS preparation.

PREFERENCE OF NATIONALITY: British, Canadian, Irish, American, Australian and New Zealander.

QUALIFICATIONS: Bachelor's degree or higher and a TEFL certificate (CELTA, Trinity College TESOL, etc.).

CONDITIONS OF EMPLOYMENT: 9 or 12-month contracts. Summer openings in Siberia (Abakan in the Republic of Khakasia).

SALARY: Starting salary 3,000 roubles, no deductions.

FACILITIES/SUPPORT: The school provides good quality accommodation and fully assists teachers with obtaining work visas.

RECRUITMENT: Interviews are absolutely essential, usually done by telephone.

CONTACT: Helen Ruseva, Recruitment Manager.

THE BALTICS

Arguably the most Westernised part of the old Russian Empire, the Baltic countries of Lithuania, Latvia and Estonia all became fully fledged members of the EU on 1 May, 2004. This has significantly eased the bureaucracy for EU passport holders, while other citizens will need to apply for a work permit which can take six months. For this reason and due to extra costs, most schools strongly prefer to employ EU citizens. A number of budget airlines as well as national carriers operate to the region (e.g. Ryanair to Kaunas and Riga) and ticket prices can be remarkably low.

Latvia and Lithuania

Of the three Baltic states, Latvia has been slowest to embrace change, although its beautiful capital, Riga, has become a mecca for a certain type of British tourist (at the lager lout end of the spectrum). English is increasingly necessary for anyone working in the hospitality sector, although there are still relatively few commercial language schools and these vary widely in quality. Perhaps because of this shortage, it is quite easy for teachers to pick up private students.

Qualified ELT teachers should make contact with the Latvian Association of Teachers of English (LATE) in Riga (www.late.lv).

Even voluntary opportunities are few and far between. One of the few volunteer and gap year agencies that deals with Latvia is Changing Worlds. **Karen Rich** decided in her 30s to get some TEFL training and do something completely different from her career as airline cabin crew. The country that took her fancy was Latvia, so she made contact with Changing Worlds (www.changingworlds.co.uk), paid the programme fee (currently £2,345 for three months) and ended up enjoying herself enough to extend her three-month stay to a full year:

> *It's truly been a life-changing year for me. I changed careers, I moved to the small town of Tukums where I'm the only English person and I've travelled to many new and exciting countries including Russia, Lithuania and Estonia. I hadn't expected to have so many students and classes. I had to call a halt at around 50 students and working weeks of 40 hours. I felt so proud that students who had been shy and reserved at the beginning of the year were relaxed and able to chat to me quite openly at the end. However, loneliness was a problem. All my colleagues in the school were Latvian and had their own families, so it was difficult to mix with the local people as the culture was different and it's not acceptable for a single woman to sit in a café and drink coffee. I noticed that the people didn't laugh much.*

Two Latvian language schools that may be able to offer decent facilities are the Language Centre International House Riga-Satva (www.ihriga.lv) and ILS Riga (www.ilseurope.com), both of which can help with visas, flat-finding and teaching support.

The market in Lithuania seems to have shrunk over the past year or two with EF English First scaling back and the ILS franchise up for sale. The only vacancies being advertised at the time of writing were for English for Academic Purposes at a private Christian university in Klaidepa (www.lcc. lt) affiliated to the heavy-duty proselytising City Church.

Estonia

Estonia is arguably the most progressive of the three Baltic countries, and the British Council in Tallinn has a list headed 'Major Language Schools in Estonia' with a couple of dozen addresses of universities and private language schools. The demand for native English speaker teachers is not very high as illustrated by the language institute in Tallinn that communicated with this book to say that it already has plenty of native speaking English teachers in its database with few vacancies.

LIST OF EMPLOYERS

AMERICAN ENGLISH SCHOOL
Naugarduko 4, 01141 Vilnius, Lithuania
2 79 1011
egle@ames.lt or vilnius@ames.lt
www.ames.lt

NUMBER OF TEACHERS: 40.

PREFERENCE OF NATIONALITY: None.

QUALIFICATIONS: TEFL certificate required.

CONDITIONS OF EMPLOYMENT: 5 days per week (mornings and afternoons). Other conditions negotiable. Students are teenagers, adults and corporate clients, private and public sector.

SALARY: $9–$12 per contact hour.

FACILITIES/SUPPORT: Initial in-house training provided; continuous in-house training and teacher support provided.

RECRUITMENT: Demo class to be taught after the interview.

CONTACT: Egle Kesyliene, Director.

INTERNATIONAL LANGUAGE SERVICES
Roosikrantsi 8B, 10119 Tallinn, Estonia
627 7171
info@ilstallinn.com www.ilstallinn.com

NUMBER OF TEACHERS: 12–15.

PREFERENCE OF NATIONALITY: Native English speakers, non-EU teachers (native speakers) also welcome.

QUALIFICATIONS: Minimum CELTA or Trinity certificate; experience preferred.

CONDITIONS OF EMPLOYMENT: 10-month or 22-month contracts, 96–120 45-minute lessons per month.

SALARY: About €700–€900 per month after deductions.

FACILITIES/SUPPORT: Travel allowance, all procedures for work permits handled by school. Regular seminars and teacher development programme leading to LCCI Further Certificate in Teaching Business English. Sponsorship for the Trinity DipTESOL by distance for teachers on longer contracts.

RECRUITMENT: Internet and TEFL/TESOL press. Phone interviews.

CONTACT: Phil Marsdale, Director phil@ilstallinn.com.

UKRAINE

The vast republic of the Ukraine's EFL market is still in its infancy, although demand is increasing as citizens realise that they may be able to double their earning power by learning English and open up opportunities for their children by sending them to private tutors. This increase in demand has not been met by an influx of native English teachers, partly because the government appears to have no centralised recruitment policy for foreign teachers and partly because wages can be very low and conditions primitive. Computers and televisions may be in short supply outside the major cities, while books can be out of date. Students are trying to make the transition from Soviet-style language learning techniques to the more fluid, communicative methods favoured these days.

Teaching in the Ukraine can be a very rewarding experience, especially as one of the biggest problems encountered by Ukrainians studying English is the lack of contact with native speakers, as **Sara Coleman** discovered when she went as a paying volunteer to teach in the country's capital, Kiev:

> *The main concern of Ukrainian English teachers and pupils alike was pronunciation. There are very few exchange programmes for students or teachers and it is almost impossible to receive a visa to visit England even if they could afford it. As I was one of the few English people to have visited the school I was in great demand. I never took over one class for a long time, as they wanted me to go around as many classes as possible, to give everybody the chance to hear a real native speaker!*

Many native English speaking teachers in the Ukraine remark on the enthusiastic reception that they receive from pupils. Many of the younger pupils express an adoration for the teachers, which can at first be quite overwhelming, and prospective teachers should be prepared for an abundance of invitations to students' homes in order to meet their families. Although this can initially be a little unnerving, most teachers find that the generous hospitality of people so poor is one of the things that makes teaching in the Ukraine such a worthwhile experience.

Teachers must be prepared to accept a modest standard of living, though it is gradually improving. **Sara Coleman** describes what she found a few years ago:

> *I was fairly shocked by the country's poverty and I had to endure difficult living conditions. I was staying in a small apartment in a tower block in Kiev's suburbs. Whilst my host family were very hospitable and tried to make me as comfortable as possible, the flat would regularly run out of water and conditions were very cramped. The lift regularly broke down and the fact that most of the lights on the stairwell were broken made the long climb to the eighth floor fairly daunting.*

For professional opportunities, well-qualified candidates can try the British Council in Kiev (www.britishcouncil.org/ukraine), which has a teaching centre and can also supply a list of about 35 English language institutes that provide exam preparation (www.britishcouncil.org/ukraine-exams-schools-list.pdf). International House has a strong presence in the country and its schools in Kharviv and Odessa hire foreign teachers through www.ihworld.com/recruitment, in addition to IH Kyiv and IH Lviv with entries below.

Pay has risen in the local currency; however, the exchange rate means that, in dollar terms, starting salaries have gone down to $700. Most private language institutes will pay in the region of $10-$15 per hour. Good schools will add on perks such as contributions to flight, accommodation and visas. US nationals must obtain the IM-1 visa, for which they will need a labour authorisation form (*dozvil na pratsevlashtuvannia*) from their employer.

A new departure for Ukraine is the arrival of English language summer camps. This huge country has many beautiful landscapes for hosting such camps, from the Carpathian mountains to the

Crimea. A company advertising for summer staff on tefl.com in the spring of 2010 was Dec Camp Ltd (info@dec-camp.com) with offices in Kiev and a camp on the shores of the Black Sea.

Valuable information about teaching in the Ukraine may be found at www.tryukraine.com/work/english.shtml, a site maintained by an expat teacher who will post CVs on his site for a fee (e.g. $20 for one month).

LIST OF EMPLOYERS

INTERNATIONAL HOUSE – KYIV
7 Vandy Vasilevskoy Street, Kyiv 03055
- 44 238 98 70
- dos@ih.kiev.ua or info@ih.kiev.ua
- www.ih.kiev.ua/en/vacancies

NUMBER OF TEACHERS: 27–30.
PREFERENCE OF NATIONALITY: Native English speakers.
QUALIFICATIONS: Minimum TEFL/CELTA certificate.
CONDITIONS OF EMPLOYMENT: 1-year contracts. Teach up to 25 hours per week.
SALARY: $1,000–$1,500 a month based on experience, paid in Ukrainian currency.
FACILITIES/SUPPORT: The school provides the teacher with a single room or shared apartment.
RECRUITMENT: Through IH London or locally.
CONTACT: Mark Alan Forehand, dos@ih.kiev.ua.

INTERNATIONAL HOUSE LVIV
3 Petrushevych Square, 79005 Lviv
- +38 032 22 55 190
- ihlviv@gmail.com
- www.ihlviv.com

NUMBER OF TEACHERS: 15.
PREFERENCE OF NATIONALITY: None, but should be native English speakers.
QUALIFICATIONS: CELTA/TESOL/IHC/Trinity certificate.
CONDITIONS OF EMPLOYMENT: 10 months plus 3 weeks' paid holidays. 24 teaching hours per week plus one meeting/seminar.

SALARY: From 5,200 hryvnias ($700 approximately) per month depending on experience.
FACILITIES/SUPPORT: US$400 of return ticket covered by the school. Furnished accommodation is provided for up to $200. The cost of the IM-1 visa is covered.
RECRUITMENT: Locally, via the internet and through IHWO recruitment services.
CONTACT: Marianna Ilyina, Director (marianna.ilyina@gmail.com).

LARISA SCHOOL OF LANGUAGE AND ADULT EDUCATION CENTRE
Sovietskaya and Shevchenko 63, Second Floor, Nikolaev
- +380 512 7171 96
- larisaschooloflanguages@gmail.com
- www.larisaschooloflanguages.com

NUMBER OF TEACHERS: 3.
PREFERENCE OF NATIONALITY: American, British or Canadian.
QUALIFICATIONS: TEFL/TESL.
CONDITIONS OF EMPLOYMENT: Minimum 6-month contract depending on the time of year. Usual working hours are Monday to Saturday, late afternoons and evenings.
FACILITIES/SUPPORT: Assistance is given with finding accommodation and applying for work permits.
RECRUITMENT: Usually via the internet. Interviews are essential and can be carried out through Skype.
CONTACT: Larisa Nemchenko, Director.

CENTRAL ASIAN REPUBLICS

With ever increasing frequency, the former Soviet republics are taking on their own national and regional identities due to geographic, cultural and economic factors. The number of treaty organisations that have emerged since the 'civilised divorce' of the former Soviet Union took place in 1991 is mind boggling. Whereas the Baltic States (Estonia, Lithuania and Latvia) desire few if any ties with Russia, other former Soviet republics especially those in north Central Asia (Kazakhstan, Kyrgyzstan, Tajikistan, Turkmenistan, and Uzbekistan) have joined with Russia (and China) to form a number of economic and security-related treaty organisations. In between these two extremes are the eastern European states (Belarus, Moldova and the Ukraine) and Caucasian States (Armenia, Azerbaijan and Georgia) which drift from one side to the other depending upon the nature of the area of cooperation. Prospective EFL teachers seeking to find employment in any of these countries or areas (exception being the Baltic States) would do well to investigate the prevailing influences affecting the particular country(ies) or area(s) in which they are interested at the time of their job search.

Though a decision concerning where to look for work will most likely depend upon a number of variables, prospective EFL teachers looking for teaching jobs in the former Soviet republics should give some thought as to whether they will be able to tolerate different attitudes to human rights, religious freedoms, etc. On the question of the religious flavour, not to say fervour, of the republic in question, as a general rule, the former western republics are mostly Eastern Orthodox Christian and the southern Central Asian Republics are Sunni Muslim, so there are noticeable differences between levels of tolerance in matters of sexual freedom, alcohol, dietary habits and even smoking.

Once an informed decision has been made to look for work in a former Soviet republic, the most obvious question is where to start. A search of the internet will yield only a few results. Though most TEFL job sites include these countries in their indexes, teachers will be disappointed to find few if any entries for many of the countries designated as former Soviet republics. Using search engines to turn up prospective TEFL work will likewise be disappointing. Compounding these difficulties is the fact that many established schools operating in the various countries of the former Soviet republics either don't have websites or are simply not found by the search engines. That said, a number of universities will be listed, which do employ at various times native English speaking teachers. Given the university nature of these jobs, they will no doubt be in either high demand or have teacher requirements above those held by the usual TEFL teacher. Unfortunately as attested to by internet experience, English teaching is still delivered by the state, for example the list of English language institutions sent by the British Council in the Uzbek capital Tashkent comprises only state universities and pedagogical institutes (i.e. teacher training colleges). University faculties often have their own international relations office which may have two or three vacancies for highly educated language assistants; try, for example, Pavlodar State University in Kazakhstan.

Another source of TEFL employment can be the NGOs operating in a number of former Soviet republic countries. In response to the increase in demand for English, the Peace Corps has sent a substantial number of volunteer English teachers to various nation states in recent years. Much of this demand has been spurred by the influx of businesses connected with the Caspian oil industry, which has particularly affected Kazakhstan, Uzbekistan, Turkmenistan and Azerbaijan. Opportunities with international companies exist for professional ELT teachers where the salaries are approaching those of the oil-rich states of the Middle East. A company called ETI (Language & Businesss Skills) operates in Georgia, Azerbaijan and Kazakhstan (www.eti.az) and may have jobs to teach oil company employees, NGO staff and others.

Georgia is forging ahead with efforts to enhance English proficiency in the country. In May of 2010, the co-founder of Footprints Recruiting (a Canadian teacher recruiter) met the Georgian Minister of Education in order to sign an undertaking to supply at least 500 English teachers. This was being hailed as a landmark step for the country of Georgia. Teachers are already employed by International House in Tbilisi, Georgia (www.ihtbilisi.ge). A Georgian language school that hosts intensive English summer courses for which it recruits native speaking teachers is the Caucasus Academic Centre in Tbilisi (www.cac.edu.ge).

Richard McGeough, a 28-year-old teacher from Britain, describes his stint working in the capital of Azerbaijan:

My primary motivation for coming to Baku was the salary my post offered, which was £15,000 a year. The students are highly motivated, well educated and almost embarrassingly hospitable and generous. I'm working in newly modernised premises now, but until recently we had to contend with alternately unheated and unventilated classrooms and regular power cuts in winter. Baku can be too quiet sometimes, although an acquaintance of mine who lived in Ashkhabad, Turkmenistan for two years says that Baku is like Paris compared to there. What Baku lacks in beauty it makes up for in interest. The centre of Baku – the Oil Town and the Old Town – is rustic and charming, and not at all what I'd expected of the old USSR. Having lived in Istanbul before, historical Baku was like a return to the 1950s before ugly modern apartment buildings were put up.

Chain schools such as Language Link and International House can also provide sources of TEFL employment. Language Link operates a teaching centre in Astana, Kazakhstan and may in future open others as long as the petro dollars flow. In Astana, Language Link trades under the name Incom Lingva and is located at Sary Arka.

Both International House and the Soros Foundation have also been active in opening up the region to English language learners. IH's partner in Almaty Kazakhstan is Interpress which does some of its own teacher hiring (recruitment@ih-almaty.com).

Belarus is another republic with various language teaching opportunities, for example at International House Minsk (www.ih.by) and SOL Minsk (www.so.by). Two Soros institutes which might have openings for people with an MA in TESOL are the English Language School in Bishkek, Kyrgyz Republic and the International Language Training Center in Chisinau, Moldova. Another US-oriented school in Chisinau is the American Language Center (http://alc.md), though it tends to hire only local staff. Few foreigners would be able to survive on the monthly stipend of $200 or thereabouts.

If salary is not a motivating factor in your search for TEFL employment in a former Soviet Republic, then **JOE SCARANGELLA**, employed by the London School in the Kyrgyz Republic, points out that there are benefits to be had:

For those interested in teaching in Kyrgyzstan, money will certainly NOT be a motivation. The vast majority, dare I say all of the work is located in the capital, Bishkek. With prices equivalent to those in Eastern Europe, it's difficult to save anything on the salary. But who cares?! With a landscape similar to Switzerland and a genuine hospitality extended by nearly everyone you meet, there is much more here than just money. Trips to the mountains are always breathtaking. And Bishkek has a unique multicultural population making people watching a national sport. Bishkek does wear the scars of its communist era. The architecture is drab and gray. The standard of living is lower than that of some of the other 'Stans'. Power cuts are frequent and hot water is unreliable. But things are on the rise. An increasing number of people have disposable income. This means that shopping, clubbing and general merriment are not just pipe dreams any more. People can now afford English lessons. All students (even the young ones) are highly motivated and remarkably knowledgeable about the world and current events. This makes things like in-class activities and conversation clubs almost a pleasurable experience.

In searching for a job, perhaps the best advice might be to limit your search to a couple of countries and thereafter do your research. A thorough understanding of the country, its culture and its regard for foreigners is absolutely essential. And be sure to check out the legality of any employment that you are thinking to engage in. As **William Kinsey** found out while working in Almaty, things are not always what they seem. '*Our school was raided by the police who demanded our visas and claimed incorrect registration. Our boss/owner was useless and two of my fellow teachers were brought to the police station and had their apartment raided. Further the boss asked us to lie on his behalf and say that we are not paid rather we are only English consultants not accepting salary. I can only speculate but I surmise it creates a tax escape for him.*' Given this, teachers are well advised to check with consulates rather than potential employers as to how legal working status is obtained. As laws change often, employers may not be lying to potential teachers, they may simply be out of date in their current thinking.

LIST OF EMPLOYERS

AZERBAIJAN

EF ENGLISH FIRST
Shafayat Mehdiyev 83 , AZ 1141, Baku
lala.talishli@ef.com
www.englishfirst.com

NUMBER OF TEACHERS: 1.
PREFERENCE OF NATIONALITY: British, North American, Australian, New Zealander.
QUALIFICATIONS: EFL/ESL certificate.
CONDITIONS OF EMPLOYMENT: 11-month contracts from September. Schools open 9am–9pm, Monday to Saturday, 24 contact hours per week. Mainly adults students.
SALARY: $2,000 per month.
FACILITIES/SUPPORT: Modern facilities, teacher library, computer laboratory, guidance and support of academic coordinator, flights paid on completion of contract, paid holiday, orientation and ongoing seminars and development. Assistance given with finding flat (not shared). Medical insurance and visa provided.
RECRUITMENT: Applications through English First (EF) teacher recruitment in offices worldwide.

KAZAKHSTAN

INTERPRESS-INTERNATIONAL HOUSE – ALMATY
InterPress-International House, 46 Mynbayev str,
Almaty 050057
+7 727 258 25 11/ +7 727 258 48 41
recruitment@ih-almaty.com
www.ih-almaty.com; www.ih.kz

NUMBER OF TEACHERS: About 60 foreign and local teachers employed, 35–40 new ones taken on each year.
PREFERENCE OF NATIONALITY: Native English speakers from UK, the USA, Ireland, Canada, Australia.
QUALIFICATIONS: Cambridge CELTA, IHC, Trinity TESOL, MA in TESOL as a minimum and at least 1 year of post-qualification teaching experience. Young learners qualification and experience in teaching for exam preparation (IELTS and TOEFL) is preferable.
CONDITIONS OF EMPLOYMENT: 9 or 12-month contract. Teaching load 120 hours (or 100 teaching hours) monthly plus 12 hours per month set aside for teachers' meetings, workshops and standby hours.
SALARY: 135,000–180,000 tenge net ($900–$1,200), depending on qualifications and experience. Bonus paid on completion of contract. Paid holidays. Teacher Training Fund for the purposes of professional development – 100,000 tenge per contract.
FACILITIES/SUPPORT: Free shared accommodation, all bills paid by the school (excluding long distance telephone calls, cable TV and Internet) or accommodation reimbursement. Airfare allowance. The school assists and covers the costs of a multiple entry 1-year work visa. Paid induction period on arrival. Healthcare and 24-hour hotline emergency assistance. Opportunities for promotion and transfer in one of the world's leading educational organisations.
RECRUITMENT: Direct applications to the school and through IHWO Recruitment Services (www.ihworld.com) and online advertising. Phone interviews essential.
CONTACT: Elena Vodolagina, Assistant to the Head of InterPress-IH Schools; Elmira Tursunkhanova, Recruitment Manager.

CONDITIONS OF EMPLOYMENT: Similar to Language Link Russia mentioned above.

CONTACT: Yelena Skarlat, Administrator.

KYRGYZSTAN

NUMBER OF TEACHERS: 8.

PREFERENCE OF NATIONALITY: American, British or Canadian native English speakers.

QUALIFICATIONS: CELTA and at least 1 year's teaching experience. Teachers without experience also would be considered.

CONDITIONS OF EMPLOYMENT: Minimum 6 months starting all year round. 22 hours per week, 5 hours per day, 4 days a week plus 1-hour interview with new students four times a month.

SALARY: From $650 to $800 a month with free accommodation and monthly cultural excursions within the country all year round.

FACILITIES/SUPPORT: Free room provided plus all accommodation expenses. Help given with work permits for which teachers must have CELTA certificate and two references from previous teaching jobs.

RECRUITMENT: Online application at: www.tlsbi.com/Tefl. htm. Teachers hired on basis of CV and references.

CONTACT: Kendje Aitikeeva, Director.

THE REST OF EUROPE

Outside the mainstream European nations, demand for native speakers of English obviously exists though immigration problems often occur. This chapter contains a miscellany of European opportunities in some quite obscure corners of the continent.

Albania

Information about teaching in this European country wedged between Greece, Macedonia, Serbia and Montenegro has not always been easy to find, but Albania is now fairly stable and offers some opportunities for teachers keen to escape the traditional EFL circuit. The number of paid teaching jobs is still limited by the country's poverty, but Albania is now signatory to a Stabilisation and Association Agreement with the EU, so there is hope that demand will increase if the country's economy slowly continues to grow.

English is certainly the favoured foreign language and is compulsory from the fifth grade through to university. Language schools have begun to open and most at least aspire to employ a native English speaking teacher, although few can currently afford it. The Language Schools in Albania Foundation (LSIA) is the largest non-profit private language tuition provider in Albania, founded in April 1994 by a group of Albanian university teachers and students. It currently enrols around 3,500 students in 15 locations across Albania and Macedonia, with the newest branches opening in Gramsh and Koplik (www.lsiaal.com/employment/employment.htm).

Out of 120 English teachers a handful are native English speakers. These schools have very limited funding and have started trying to recruit volunteer teachers to come to Albania to expose children from deprived backgrounds to English spoken by a native. Volunteers are likely to be offered local accommodation and LSIA will also assist with the red tape. **Blerina Gjonaj**, Head of the Overseas Department at LSIA, suggests that volunteering might lead to a paid job:

> *The demand for native English speakers is increasing every day, and the same can be said for paid employment, although that is not yet at the level that everybody wants. It is still easier to find a teaching job if you are a volunteer (maybe at the beginning), and then you can get involved as a paid employee. Albanian people are very interested in learning English. Language schools in Albania enrol children, mature students, adults and even parents of the students.*

Albania is still considered to be close enough to a developing country to have a contingent of 73 Peace Corps volunteers in place including a number who are teaching English at foreign language high schools and other institutes. **Margaret Sheridan** was a Peace Corps volunteer who says '*I had a terrific experience, teaching English in high school and to adults, then opening a TOEFL test site, the first in southern Albania, with a terrific Albanian colleague.*'

Other institutions that may be worth contacting are the Memorial International School of Tirana (Ish Shkolla Partise Rr. Dumes, Tirana; 4 223 7379; info@mistedu.net; www.mistedu.com) which currently employs one American, one Briton, and three Canadians. The school's minimum requirement is that teachers have some years of experience in their own fields, although the majority have completed university courses with components in education. The Abraham Lincoln Foundation offers English language courses for all levels and special English programmes for several professional institutions in Albania. It employs a few American teachers with English degrees at their three branches in Tirana: the main school is at Rruga Qemal Stafa, Nr. 184 (4 230880; info@lincoln.org.al; www.lincolnalbania.org).

Visa guidelines can be checked at the Embassy of the Republic of Albania in the UK or USA. If your stay is going to be less than 90 days, you do not need to apply for a visa in advance but you may be required to pay an entry tax of €10. You are not permitted to cross out of Albania and straight back in again to renew your tourist visa. If you intend to stay longer than 90 days, you must apply for a residency permit.

Living costs are very cheap by US and UK standards, though choice can be limited. One volunteer teacher complained that he had to travel five hours by bus to Tirana to buy ketchup. Albania has plenty of scenic attractions, including rugged mountains and a marvellous stretch of Adriatic coastline, blissfully free of package holiday tourists.

LIST OF EMPLOYERS

ABRAHAM LINCOLN PROFESSIONAL STUDIES CENTER
Rruga Qemal Stafa Nr. 184, Tirana; also at Rr
Ismail Qemali 21 and at Kompleksi Kika,
Rr Komuna e Parisit
📞 4 230880
📧 info@lincoln.org.al
🖥 www.lincolnalbania.org

NUMBER OF TEACHERS: Few native English speakers
for the three branches.
PREFERENCE OF NATIONALITY: American and others.
CONDITIONS OF EMPLOYMENT: Courses offered for all
levels and special English programmes for several professional institutions in Albania.
CONTACT: Edita Nikolli (enikolli@lincoln.org.al).

LSIA - LANGUAGE SCHOOLS IN ALBANIA
P.O.Box 1400, RR. Bardhyl NR.76/1, Tirana
📧 info.lsia@yahoo.com
🖥 www.lsiaal.com

New initiative to expose children in need to native English
speakers.
NUMBER OF TEACHERS: 6.
PREFERENCE OF NATIONALITY: None, but have to be
native English speakers.
QUALIFICATIONS: Master's degree in any specialisation,
job experience.
SALARY: Mainly volunteer positions so no salary.
FACILITIES/SUPPORT: School provides accommodation and
assists with work permit.
RECRUITMENT: Interviews are carried out depending on
the occasion. If the teacher is in Albania, then a face-to-face
interview will be possible.
CONTACT: Human Resources Division.

Andorra

Andorra lies in the heart of the Pyrenees between Spain and France, and can be seen as an extension of both countries, though it has its own elected government. It is too small to have many language schools, but the one listed here is a possibility (and you would be there over the skiing season).

LIST OF EMPLOYERS

CENTRE ANDORRA DE LLENGUES (CALL)

15 Carrer del Fener, Andorra-la-Vella

© 80 40 30

✆ centrandorra.lang@andorra.ad

💻 www.call.ad

NUMBER OF TEACHERS: 2.

PREFERENCE OF NATIONALITY: British, Irish and North Americans.

QUALIFICATIONS: BA in English or a foreign language plus TEFL qualification and 2–3 years' experience abroad most welcome. A good knowledge of Spanish and/or French can help. Non-smokers preferred.

CONDITIONS OF EMPLOYMENT: 9–10-month renewable contract which runs from October to June. 27 hours per week, 5 days a week. Teaching hours spread throughout the day. Teaching very young learners (6–7 years) and all other ages including professionals.

SALARY: €1,800 per month (plus overtime if any available).

FACILITIES/SUPPORT: Board and lodging available within walking distance costs from €500 per month. Work permit arranged and paid for by the school.

RECRUITMENT: Direct application with CV and photo by email.

CONTACT: Claude Benet.

Bosnia-Herzegovina

There are still few private language schools in Bosnia, and most operate as a small school. As usual you could check the list provided at www.eslbase.com/schools/bosnia which includes one larger company, Seal, with schools in Dvorovi, Brcko, Zvornik and Novi Sad (www.seal-rs.com).

LIST OF EMPLOYERS

NEW ACADEMY

Muharem Suljanovic Street, 79101 Prijedor

© 387 65 805 073 / 65 649 655

✆ new_academy@yahoo.com

PREFERENCE OF NATIONALITY: None.

QUALIFICATIONS: 2 years' TEFL experience.

CONDITIONS OF EMPLOYMENT: 1-year contract with working hours between 4pm and 10pm.

RECRUITMENT: Interviews are essential.

CONTACT: Zoran Beric, Principal.

Croatia

Building on its strong indigenous English teaching infrastructure, Croatia's private language schools flourish in Zagreb, Varazdin and Karlovac, as well as in other towns. For many schools, the idea of employing a native English speaker teacher is very attractive; particularly given Croatia's popularity as a British tourist destination, accessible by cheap flights. Teachers who go to work in Croatia are likely to find themselves being made welcome and treated well, certainly outside the usual tourist hot spots. Salaries are likely to be quoted in euros even though the national currency is still the kuna.

The market for private teaching is strong, however native English teachers need to be well qualified to secure a job. The Foreign Language School, Ziger, is fairly modest in size, with only one or
two native teachers, but they still ask for a degree, at least one year's experience, and a CELTA or
DELTA certificate.

Anyone wishing to work in Croatia must apply to the Embassy of the Republic of Croatia for a visa.
An application form must be completed by your employer and returned together with a passport, two
photographs and details of the job (e.g. a copy of your contract, length of employment, type of work,
location and full address of employer).

The British Council in Zagreb can offer informal assistance to prospective teachers and should be
able to put you in touch with the Association of Croatian Teachers of English (HUPE) which organises
teacher development activities but can't help foreign teachers to find jobs. The voluntary placement
organisation Sharing One Language (SOL) (see Central and Eastern Europe: Finding a job) sends a
few teachers to Croatia but posts are dependent on an unpredictable Ministry.

With its beautiful coastline and accessibility, Croatia has developed summer camps, some of
which teach English. The exchange company CCUSA sends volunteer teachers to Camp California
in Savudrija, almost on the Slovenia border, though counsellor-teachers here pay a programme fee
of £175 (www.ccusa.com) but get free room and board. **Geoff Nunney** wanted to find a summer
job in 2009 after the academic term finished at the language school in Slovakia where he had spent
the year. He got a job at Euroclub on Šolta, an island off the coast near Split (www.euroclub.hr), the
largest international youth camp on the Adriatic:

*I have a return invitation for this year, kids of all nationalities from 10 to 20. There's a big mixture of
teachers – I was known as the 'Crazy Teacher'. Lots of sports, lessons and a holiday atmosphere. I did
four weeks there, and the pay is enough to live on.*

LIST OF EMPLOYERS

FOREIGN LANGUAGE SCHOOL – ZIGER

S. Vraza 37, 42000 Varazdin

&#127; 42 330 385

&#127; irena.ziger@vz.htnet.hr

&#127; www.skola-ziger.hr

NUMBER OF TEACHERS: 1–2.
PREFERENCE OF NATIONALITY: British, American, Canadian.
QUALIFICATIONS: At least 1 year's experience, CELTA/
DELTA, university degree.

CONDITIONS OF EMPLOYMENT: Minimum 1-year
contract, teaching hours are usually late afternoon and
evenings.
FACILITIES/SUPPORT: Assistance with finding accommodation and work permit (school applies and translates
necessary documents).
RECRUITMENT: Via email contact. Interviews by
phone.
CONTACT: Irena Ziger, Principal.

Cyprus

A visitor to the Republic of Cyprus will be struck by the similarities with Greece – cuisine, architecture, landscapes and culture – but then be surprised at the relative prominence of English. Signs
are printed both in Greek and English, many (if not most) local people even outside the cities speak
some English, and the British influence can be noticed everywhere. Because of the longstanding

relationship between Cyprus and Britain, the English language is given much prominence in the state educational system. As a result the density of *frontisteria* is not as high as it is in Greece, though there are still a fair number of private institutes preparing children for external examinations.

Cyprus has a small population of about 862,000 people and therefore opportunities are not extensive. Also a large number of Cypriot students leave the island each year to study in the UK and USA, although there are still a number of afternoon language schools in the cities and towns.

To find an ELT job in Cyprus before you arrive is extremely difficult because very few of the ELT schools actually advertise on the internet and there is a sizeable expat community, from which native English teachers can be drawn. Some expats will also informally help Cypriot friends with their English over a glass of beer.

Sending speculative CVs is unlikely to succeed. It is more fruitful to visit schools in person and hand it in. Furthermore, state school jobs are extremely hard to come by for foreigners as you need at least a three-year degree in the relevant subject (e.g. English literature for teaching English) as well as a good knowledge of Greek. Therefore, most foreign teachers aim to find a job in a language school in the private sector, which will probably mean working in the afternoons or evenings, although some schools also have morning classes. One freelance opportunity might be to approach businessmen and women in the property sector, who have (or would like to have) English and American clients. You'd need a solid business background to succeed, and would be required to provide specialist vocabulary ('grouting', anyone?).

Since Cyprus has joined the European Union, visas are no longer a major hurdle. The country has also adopted the euro. If you wish to advertise your services as a tutor in the English language press of Greek Cyprus, contact the *Cyprus Mail* (www.cyprus-mail.com) though its Classified Jobs section isn't up to much, or *Cyprus Weekly* published on Fridays by Cyweekly (PO Box 24977, 1306 Nicosia; 22–666047; www.cyprusweekly.com.cy). Major English institutes include the Papantoniou Institute founded in 1999, (www.papantoniou-institute.com) which offers English at all levels.

Most schools offer a contract of 20–25 working hours a week for the academic year September to May/June. The hourly pay is above average for southern Europe, starting at about €12 per hour. As in Greece, there are usually two paid holidays during the academic year: two weeks over Christmas and two weeks for the Greek Orthodox Easter.

Most Cypriot schools have very good facilities, although they may be lagging behind somewhat in technology. Teacher support is readily available with regular free seminars organised by various publishers. In language classrooms, there is a wide range of levels for all ages. The majority of children enrol at language schools when they are about eight and finish around the age of 16, attending lessons twice a week. However, there is a growing demand for children as young as 4 to start learning English as a foreign language, so schools are introducing classes for younger children. A lesson can last from one to two hours for higher levels. Young students and adults are usually motivated and love interactive teaching. However, those teaching teenagers will need to be firm and to make lessons particularly interesting.

People move to Cyprus nowadays more for the lifestyle than for cheap living. The downside is that eating out etc. is not cheap; however, the improved infrastructure (like the very good motorways) makes life easier. Note there is no train service on the island. Over the next few years many marinas and golf courses are due to be built indicating that the island is going up-market as the government intends. If reunification with the Turkish north takes place on the island (a long way off but positive moves have been made) then the country could really flourish.

A decent studio apartment can be rented for about €350 per month. Eating out is not too ruinous at €17 per person. Public transport, on the other hand, is very sparse. By opening the English speaking newspapers, you will be able to find out what's on and where to meet new friends. If you want to find out more about life in Cyprus for ex-pats, visit www.cyprusliving.org and www.eastern-cyprus.com.

Turkish Cyprus

There are six private universities, four private schools and at least two language schools in the Turkish Republic of Northern Cyprus (TRNC). The main industry in Northern Cyprus is tourism, largely catering for an English-speaking clientele, so there is strong local demand to master the languages for employment purposes. However, it should be pointed out that the expatriate community numbers more than 4,000 so there is already a substantial pool of native English speakers on hand to fill any teacher vacancies that occur.

Malta

Although somewhat off the beaten track and although English is the first language of the tiny island, EFL is booming in Malta. A number of private language schools cater to groups coming from other Mediterranean countries on short courses in the spring, summer and at other times. Even the National Tourist Office of Malta distributes a leaflet 'Learning English in the Sun' or check the list of language schools on www.visitmalta.com (which devotes a whole section to 'language learning'). The Ministry of Education also publishes a list of 32 language schools that it has licensed plus a few that operate only in the summer (see www.education.gov.mt/edu/schools/english_language.htm). The interests of the most established schools are represented by FELTOM, the Federation of English Language Teaching Organisations Malta (+356 2131 0927; www.feltom.com); the site has good links to the 14 member schools and basic information about teaching on the island.

All EU nationals have the right to live and work in Malta, although it is necessary to obtain an EFL teaching permit from the EFL Monitoring Board of the Ministry of Education. In order to be eligible for the permit, a candidate must have an Advanced Level Certificate in English from a recognised institution, and have completed a TEFL course such as a CELTA. A 60-hour TEFL Induction Course is offered by the majority of FELTOM schools and also satisfies the government requirement. All teachers also need a clean police conduct certificate. Note that self-employed freelancers do not need to obtain a work permit.

Wages are paid hourly and are in the €8–€12 bracket, with a steady average of €10. Many professional teachers join MATEFL, the Malta Association of TEFL (www.matefl.com). Membership costs a modest €12. The NSTS English Language Institute (220 St. Paul St, Valletta VLT07; 2558 8000 http://nstsenglishlanguagemalta.com) markets its English courses in conjunction with sports holidays for young tourists to Malta. NSTS run weekly vacation courses from June to August, and it might be worth approaching them for a job, particularly if you are a water sports enthusiast. NSTS was keen to hire **Robert Mizzi** from Canada once it learned that he was half Maltese:

> *I was offered a job quite casually when NSTS found out I was volunteering conversational English in the main youth hostel in Valletta. Perhaps one reason they wanted to hire me was they knew the visa would not be a problem. However, I was surprised by how relaxed the offer was. It was just mentioned in passing rather than at an actual interview. I guess it is the Maltese way: once you are one of them, then everything is gravy.*

LIST OF EMPLOYERS

AM LANGUAGE STUDIO
299 Manwel Dimech Street, Sliema SLM1054
- 356 21324242
- info@amlanguage.com
- www.amlanguage.com

NUMBER OF TEACHERS: 3.
PREFERENCE OF NATIONALITY: British.
QUALIFICATIONS: CELTA or CertTESOL.
CONDITIONS OF EMPLOYMENT: Teachers are employed on a freelance basis and are required to work from July to August with 22.5–30 hours per week.
SALARY: €9.32 per hour.
FACILITIES/SUPPORT: As teachers are freelance they just have to register as self-employed with the local authorities and do not need to apply for a work permit.
RECRUITMENT: CV and telephone interview.
CONTACT: Larissa Jonk, Director of Studies.

ELANGUEST ENGLISH LANGUAGE SCHOOL
Keating House, Ross Street, St Julian's STJ 3243
- +356 21374 777
- info@elanguest.com
- www.elanguest.com

PREFERENCE OF NATIONALITY: British, Canadian and Australian.
QUALIFICATIONS: TEFL course plus A level in English. Applicants with CELTA or TESOL certificate are given preference.
CONDITIONS OF EMPLOYMENT: No contract, however applicants who can work all year round are given preference. Between 4.5 and 5.5 working hours per day.
FACILITIES/SUPPORT: Assistance given with work permits.
RECRUITMENT: CV and telephone interview.
CONTACT: Bernice Farrugia, Director of Studies.

GLOBAL VILLAGE ENGLISH CENTRE
St George's Street, St. Paul's Bay SPB 02
- 21 573417
- dos@gvmalta.com
- www.gvmalta.com

NUMBER OF TEACHERS: All staff are native speakers of English.

PREFERENCE OF NATIONALITY: None.
QUALIFICATIONS: Experience and TEFL qualification needed plus minimum 1 year's experience.
CONDITIONS OF EMPLOYMENT: Open-ended contracts. 15–20 hours per week in low season, 20+ hours per week in peak season.
SALARY: Varies according to experience and qualifications.
FACILITIES/SUPPORT: Advice given on rental accommodation in area.
RECRUITMENT: Mainly via teacher training courses run on-site. Interviews are essential and are usually carried out face-to-face with the Director of Studies and include analysis of lesson planning.
CONTACT: Judy Privitera, Director of Studies.

LAL MALTA
Matthew Pulis Street, Sliema
- +356 21 320381
- info@iels.com.mt
- www.lalgroup.com

NUMBER OF TEACHERS: 60.
PREFERENCE OF NATIONALITY: None.
QUALIFICATIONS: Minimum CELTA but no experience required.
CONDITIONS OF EMPLOYMENT: Open-ended contract with 15 or 22.5 working hours per week depending on preference and availability.
SALARY: €10.50 per hour.
FACILITIES/SUPPORT: Assistance given with work permits.
CONTACT: Angie Conti, Academic Manager.

SKYLARK SCHOOL OF ENGLISH
29, Victor Denaro Street, Msida MSD 1604
- +356 21 31 66 04
- pia@skylarkmalta.com / info@skylarkmalta.com
- www.skylarkmalta.com

NUMBER OF TEACHERS: 30 freelancers.
PREFERENCE OF NATIONALITY: EU citizenship preferred though willing to consider any CV as long as teachers are native English speakers.

QUALIFICATIONS: Minimum of a TEFL course and a high school level qualification in English Language (A level or equivalent). However, a CELTA/DELTA/TESOL certificate is preferable.

CONDITIONS OF EMPLOYMENT: Freelance basis only. Flexible timetable according to teacher's availability. Normally 15–30 class hours a week.

SALARY: €8–€12 per hour.

FACILITIES/SUPPORT: Non-local teachers are given assistance in finding housing as close to the school as possible and at the best rate possible.

RECRUITMENT: Face-to-face interview and on occasion class observation. Occasionally telephone interviews are conducted.

CONTACT: Pia Zammit, Director of Studies.

Serbia and Montenegro

With the short-lived union of Serbia and Montenegro breaking down in 2006, followed by Kosovo's declaration of independence from Serbia in 2008, the dissolution of the former Yugoslavia seems finally complete, with much underlying tension remaining.

The nascent ELT industry looks set to develop, perhaps rapidly, if the region remains stable. Possible leads include the Bejza Education Centre (Ul. Vuka Karadžića br.7 11000, Belgrade, Serbia; 11/328 14 49; www.bejza.edu.rs) and ELS Language School (www.els.rs).

In order to get a residence/work permit for Serbia, you must submit a contract of employment and a translated copy of your diploma. Further information on the regulations for entering and working in Serbia can be found at www.serbianembassy.org.uk.

As of 2010 the non-profit-making British organisation SOL (01271 327319; www.sol.org.uk) was working to set up volunteer placements at private schools in Serbia. After an exploratory trip, SOL's director was struck by the need: '*I have just been in Serbia and we are looking to the future there as a new destination. To see the catastrophic effect of our sanctions on the people and industry there makes me quite ashamed – yet reading our media, I fully supported the sanctions at the time as it seemed simply a political decision.*'

LIST OF EMPLOYERS

ELS LANGUAGE SCHOOL

Beogradska 70/I, 11000, Belgrade

📞 +381 11 30 86818; Mobile 63 77 92 951

✉ office@els.rs or els@sbb.rs

🖥 www.els.rs

NUMBER OF TEACHERS: 1–2.

PREFERENCE OF NATIONALITY: None.

QUALIFICATIONS: Bachelor's degree plus CELTA minimum. DELTA or MA in TESOL/Applied Linguistics and/or long standing experience preferred.

CONDITIONS OF EMPLOYMENT: Two 90-minute lessons per week in some cases.

FACILITIES/SUPPORT: Assistance may be available for accommodation, and work permits may be possible.

RECRUITMENT: Interviews arranged on basis of submitted CV.

OXFORD CENTAR

64 Rimiski trg, 81000 Podgorica, Montenegro

📞 +382 20 234 425

✉ oxford@t-com.me

🖥 www.oxfordcentar.com

NUMBER OF TEACHERS: 6.

PREFERENCE OF NATIONALITY: British, American, Australian, New Zealander, Canadian.

QUALIFICATIONS: 3–5 years practical experience.

CONDITIONS OF EMPLOYMENT: 4 or 9-month contract with 22 to 27 working hours per week.

SALARY: €750–850 per month plus flat allowance of €200 per month.

FACILITIES/SUPPORT: School pays for 2 nights in a hotel as teacher looks for accommodation. Assistance also given with applying for work permits.

RECRUITMENT: Usually via adverts on www.eslbase.com or www.tefl.com. Interviews are essential and can be via phone or Skype.

CONTACT: Dale Kiehl, Director of Studies.

Slovenia

As in Croatia, there are a good many private schools and many opportunities can be created by energetic native English speakers both as freelance teachers for institutes or as private tutors. Slovenia is a sophisticated little country with high standards of education and many well-qualified native teachers of English.

The English Studies Resource Centre at the British Council in Ljubljana has a list of private language schools throughout the country (see www.britishcouncil.org/slovenia-exams-list-of-language-schools.htm). The Council remains closely in touch with language schools and may be able to refer qualified candidates to possible employers, though the Ljubljana office is not open to the general public. The average hourly wage should be about €10.

As one of the countries that joined the EU in May 2004 and the Schengen Agreement in 2008, Slovenia now has fairly straightforward regulations for EU members. All EU nationals are able to work in Slovenia under the same conditions as Slovene citizens in their countries. However, teachers should obtain a temporary residence permit within three months of entering the country, and will need a valid passport whose expiry date exceeds by at least three months the intended period of stay, health insurance, sufficient means of subsistence and a legitimate purpose for their residence (like a job). The Embassy in London (10 Little College Street, London SW1P 3SH; 020 7222 5700) handles external applications for both British and Irish nationals; the average processing time is one month. Your school should report that you are working for them to the Employment Service of Slovenia, Zavod za zaposlovanje (Rozna dolino, Cesta IX/6, 1000 Ljubljana; 1 4790 900; www.ess.gov.si) within eight days of starting the job.

LIST OF EMPLOYERS

BERLITZ LANGUAGE CENTER
Gosposvetska 2, 1000 Ljubljana
+386 1 433 13 25
berlitz.ljubljana@berlitz.si
www.berlitz.si
Also: Svetozarevska 6, 2000 Maribor

NUMBER OF TEACHERS: 40.

PREFERENCE OF NATIONALITY: None.

QUALIFICATIONS: Sound educational background, good communication skills, professional attitude and appearance.

CONDITIONS OF EMPLOYMENT: Minimum 1 year. 4–8 teaching hours per day.

SALARY: €10+ per unit (40 minutes).

FACILITIES/SUPPORT: Try to assist teachers with accommodation. Compulsory training in Berlitz method. Regular support through observations and workshops.

RECRUITMENT: Adverts and personal recommendation. Interviews necessary in most cases, occasionally held abroad.

CONTACT: Luke Davis, Instructional Supervisor for Berlitz Slovenia.

NUMBER OF TEACHERS: 1–2.

PREFERENCE OF NATIONALITY: None.

QUALIFICATIONS: Experience essential. Teacher training course for TEFL required.

CONDITIONS OF EMPLOYMENT: School year from October to May. Minimum 30–40 lessons a month.

SALARY: Starting salary about €6.50 net per 45-minute lesson.

FACILITIES/SUPPORT: Help is given with finding accommodation but the rental charge is borne by the teacher.

RECRUITMENT: Contacts through the British Council.

CONTACT: Cilka Demsar, Director.

Located on the Adriatic not far from Trieste, Italy.

NUMBER OF TEACHERS: 15.

PREFERENCE OF NATIONALITY: England, Scotland, New Zealand, Australia.

QUALIFICATIONS: Bachelor's degree (hons) and TEFL certificate plus a year's teaching experience. Business background useful.

CONDITIONS OF EMPLOYMENT: Minimum 10 months September to June (preferably longer). Usual 24–26 hours contact time per week.

SALARY: About €13 per lesson. No tax or social security deductions.

FACILITIES/SUPPORT: The school finds accommodation for teachers and provides necessary documents for them.

RECRUITMENT: Email, internet.

NUMBER OF TEACHERS: 5.

PREFERENCE OF NATIONALITY: British.

QUALIFICATIONS: English teacher with a variety of TEFL experience (TEFL or CELTA certificate).

CONDITIONS OF EMPLOYMENT: Standard length of contract 1 year. 20–30 hours per week including morning, afternoon and evening lessons.

SALARY: €10 per hour (45 minutes of teaching).

FACILITIES/SUPPORT: Help is given with finding accommodation and acquiring the necessary permits.

RECRUITMENT: CV must be submitted. Successful applicants will be invited to attend an interview.

YURENA

Glavni Trg 11, 8000 Novo Mesto

7 337 2100

yurena@siol.net

www.yurena.si

NUMBER OF TEACHERS: 2–3.

PREFERENCE OF NATIONALITY: English.

QUALIFICATIONS: TEFL qualification.

CONDITIONS OF EMPLOYMENT: 1-year contracts. 25–30 hours per week.

SALARY: Approximately €1,000 per month.

FACILITIES/SUPPORT: Accommodation and help with work permits provided.

RECRUITMENT: Interviews essential.

CONTACT: Kati Golobic, Director.

MIDDLE EAST

Oil wealth has meant that many of the countries of the Middle East have long been able to afford to attract the best teachers with superior qualifications and extensive experience. Most employers can afford to hire only professionals and there are few opportunities for newcomers to the profession.

The main exception is Turkey where thousands of native English speaking teachers find work. Despite its adherence to Islam, Turkey does not fit comfortably into a chapter on the Middle East. But despite its aspirations to join the EU and its secular government, neither does it fit logically into a section on Europe. But whatever its geographical classification, Turkey is a very important country for EFL teachers, whatever their background, and is treated at length later in this chapter.

On the one hand, the wealthy countries of Saudi Arabia, Bahrain, Oman and the Gulf states generally employ teachers with top qualifications. On the other hand, countries such as Syria and Jordan may have more casual opportunities. Anyone interested in teaching English to the Palestinians scattered throughout the Arab World is likely to be working on a voluntary basis or for accommodation and a local stipend, rather than for expatriate salaries.

Despite the much publicised hostility to the West in the region, the demand for English has not disappeared. In the face of continuing enmity between Israelis and Palestinians, the taste for travel and employment in the Middle East has been quelled and some prospective teachers, especially from North America, have been put off by a perceived fear for their personal security. But panicky reactions may be out of place. Perhaps English language teachers can play a small part in diminishing the distrust and tension between the two cultures, bringing people together, allowing individuals on both sides to gain some understanding of the complexity of the world's problems.

Teachers who sign contracts in a strict Islamic country should be aware of what they are letting themselves in for. People usually spend a year or two teaching in Saudi Arabia to make some money, rather than because they enjoy the lifestyle (unless they are students of Arab culture). When the amount of money accumulating back home is the principal or only motivation, morale can degenerate. The situation can be especially discouraging for women. Yet not everyone is gasping to get home (or even to Bahrain) to freely available alcohol, etc. A high percentage of teachers are recruited locally from a stable expatriate community. Demand for native English teachers is increasing in Saudi Arabia, mainly due to the opening of new colleges and universities, both in the public and private sector, some of which employ scores of English language teachers and lecturers. Note that many of them accept only online applications, for example (to take just one) ALHOSN University in Abu Dhabi (www.alhosnu.ae/Site/JobOpenings.aspx). A useful list of institutes of higher education with, in some cases, links to current job vacancies can be found at www.university-directory.eu.

Middle Eastern language schools are also more likely to recruit non-native English speakers, specifically well-heeled teachers with pristine qualifications. **Ahad Shahbaz**, Director of Interlink Language Center, asks: '*If a non-native speaker is highly educated, has earned his credentials from the Harvards of ESL teacher training institutions, and has near-native and at times superior proficiency and eloquence in the language, should we not be hiring him or her?*'

FINDING A JOB

Unless you are more or less resident in the Middle East, it is essential in most cases to fix up a job in advance. Casual teaching is not a possibility in most countries for a number of reasons, including the difficulty of getting visas, the prohibitively high cost of staying without working and the whole tradition of hiring teachers. There are a few countries which can be entered on a tourist visa (i.e. Qatar, Yemen and the United Arab Emirates) if you want to inspect potential employers, but this would be an expensive exercise. Visa difficulties vary from country to country. In Jordan, for example, schools which would like to hire foreign teachers, are often put off by the cost of securing a work permit ($500 straight to the government and $150 in lawyers' fees) The American ESL Center, based in Jordan, (see list of organisations) employs foreigners as native English speakers.

Single women, no matter how highly qualified, are at a serious disadvantage when pursuing high-paying jobs in Saudi Arabia and other strict Islamic countries. The majority of adverts specify 'single status male' or, at best, 'teaching couples'. Another requirement often mentioned in job details which excludes many candidates is experience of the Middle East, in acknowledgment of the culture shock that many foreigners encounter in adapting to life under Islam.

Job adverts regularly appear on websites such as www.tefl.com and in journals such as the *International Employment Gazette*. The largest display ads in the British education press are quite often for Middle East vacancies, many placed by recruitment agencies on behalf of high-spending Saudi clients. It is always worth checking regional newspapers as well such as the *Khaleej Times* (www.khaleejtimes.com). The British Council has teaching centres in Bahrain (Manama), Lebanon (Beirut), Oman (Muscat), Qatar (Doha), Saudi Arabia (Riyadh, Jeddah and Dammam), Kuwait, Damascus in Syria and the United Arab Emirates (Abu Dhabi and Dubai). America-Mideast Educational & Training Services or Amideast is a private, nonprofit organisation with headquarters in Washington DC and provides English language and other professional training through its network of operations throughout the Middle East (and North Africa). Its website www.amideast.org carries lots of recruitment information.

The usual suspects are active in the region. International House has five schools in Saudi Arabia, one in Dubai, one in Iran, several in Lebanon and one in Oman. Berlitz has schools in Bahrain, Beirut, Oman, Qatar and UAE; the Regional Manager Leila Shehab may be able to advise on vacancies (+971 50 8131018; leila.shehab@berlitz.ae; www.berlitz.ae).

RECRUITMENT AGENCIES

In theory, being hired by an established recruitment agency in your own country should offer some protection against problems. However, this is not always the case. A couple of years ago an educational consultancy with an office in Toronto recruited a large number of EFL teachers to work for the United Arab Emirates military. When a dispute arose between client and recruiter, the teachers were the ones to suffer since they weren't paid promised salaries and their contracts were not honoured.

The mission society Interserve has salaried and other positions for ESL teachers at schools and universities in the Arab world (www.interserve.org.uk/Opportunities.aspx).

LEISURE TIME

The majority of teachers live in foreigners' compounds provided by their employers. Most of these are well provided with sports facilities such as tennis courts and swimming pools. In some locations, such as Jubail in Saudi Arabia, water sports are a popular diversion. Some have described expat life in the Middle East as a false paradise.

The principal pastimes are barbecues, reading out-of-date copies of the *International Herald Tribune*, playing with computers (which are cheaply available) and complaining about the terrific heat and the lack of alcohol (Saudi Arabia and Kuwait are completely dry states.) Others of course try to learn some Arabic and make local friends, always taking care not to offend against Islam. The constraints of living under Islam are well known. For example, in some countries anyone found drinking or smoking in a public place during the month of Ramadan could face a jail sentence, large fine and/or deportation.

LIST OF EMPLOYERS

BRITISH COUNCIL – MIDDLE EAST
Offices in Bahrain, Kuwait, Oman, Qatar, Saudi Arabia, Yemen and United Arab Emirates
🖰 www.britishcouncil.org/me-contact-us-job-opportunities.htm

NUMBER OF TEACHERS: Fluctuating vacancies across the region, but mostly in Saudi Arabia (teach@sa.britishcouncil.org).
PREFERENCE OF NATIONALITY: British.
QUALIFICATIONS: Minimum CELTA or equivalent plus 2 years' full-time ELT experience for hourly teaching, DELTA may be needed for more senior posts.
CONDITIONS OF EMPLOYMENT: Range of opportunities, e.g. hourly teaching in Riyadh.
FACILITIES/SUPPORT: Accommodation arranged plus medical insurance.
RECRUITMENT: Via British Council Recruitment Unit in London.

ELS LANGUAGE CENTERS – MIDDLE EAST
PO Box 3079, Abu Dhabi, United Arab Emirates
📞 2 6426640 1516
🖰 jobs@elsmea.com
🖥 www.elsmea.com

NUMBER OF TEACHERS: 30 full-time plus many part-time in 12 centres throughout the Middle East including Hawally

(Kuwait), Muscat, Salalah and Sohar (Oman), Jeddah, Riyadh and Dammam (Saudi Arabia), Dubai, Abu Dhabi, Al Ain and Fujairah (UAE) and Doha (Qatar).
PREFERENCE OF NATIONALITY: American, Canadian, British, New Zealander, Australian, though other nationalities are sometimes accepted.
QUALIFICATIONS: Preferred MA in TEFL/TESL and 2 years' experience with recognised TEFL certificate plus 3 years' experience. Minimum bachelor's degree plus TEFL plus experience.
CONDITIONS OF EMPLOYMENT: 1–2-year contracts; 30 contact hours plus 15 administrative hours per week for full-time teachers.
SALARY: Varies according to qualifications, experience and location. Some salaries are tax free and come with benefits such as housing, airfares and medical insurance.
FACILITIES/SUPPORT: Furnished accommodation provided, though teachers may choose to find their own within their housing allowance. Work and residence permits arranged in all countries, usually involving a medical examination and blood test and a notarised and attested copy of the teacher's degree and qualifications. Standard orientation for all new teachers and monthly workshops.
RECRUITMENT: Through TESOL USA and TESOL Arabia, and also via the internet. Telephone interviews sometimes sufficient. Face-to-face interviews arranged where possible.

THE AMERICAN ESL CENTER

PO Box 1240, Al Jubeiha, Amman, Jordan 11941

 6 534 1421

 admin@aeslc.com

 www.aeslc.com

NUMBER OF TEACHERS: 10.

PREFERENCE OF NATIONALITY: Native English speakers.

QUALIFICATIONS: ESL qualification and teaching experience.

CONDITIONS OF EMPLOYMENT: Standard 1-year contract, mostly teaching afternoons and evenings (usually 12pm–8:30pm).

SALARY: $1,000–$1,500 per month (average salary in Jordan is $600–$700). No deductions.

FACILITIES/SUPPORT: Assistance in locating accommodation near the centre. The company lawyer has offered a very low fee to process work permits for foreign employees. Cost of work permit $500 (paid to government). Cost of lawyer's fees is $150.

RECRUITMENT: Through internet/newspaper. 1 minute recording of the applicant's voice to be sent by email to determine language ability and accent.

CONTACT: Kara Murphy, Academic Director.

Afghanistan

This is the first time this book has included a section on this country where there is an overwhelming demand for English tuition. However, this information may not be of interest to anyone of a nervous disposition. **Tom Clark** from the USA taught here in 2008, and this information is largely based on his account (note that the situation may have changed since he was there). He concludes that Afghanistan is a great place '*for a journalist, spy or madman*'.

TOM CLARK, while teaching in Kuwait saw an advert on Dave's ESL Cafe which he followed up much later. It turned out that the American University in Kabul (the only private university in the country) was desperate to get teachers in place for a summer project funded by USAID. Since the programme was controlled by the US government, his visa was sorted out quickly. According to Tom, 'you could get a lot of stories about the funding and where it was going and how it got disbursed... It wasn't so much red tape as corruption, but that is everywhere in Afghanistan.' The job was teaching at the university prep programme plus he was doing extra work for the UN and a human rights organisation. Tom describes the job:

The contract with the university was the best I have had in the ESL world. It paid $5,000 a month with danger pay and other bonuses. It was better than Saudi. It offered holiday pay, housing, transportation, laptop, cell phone, we could fly on UN planes, etc. We stayed in a guesthouse with a beautiful garden, had security guards 24/7 and were fenced in, and we had electricity more than 4 hours a day. Our money went a long way, as the cost of living was so low there and the American dollar was welcome. Transferring money in and out was not easy, nor setting up bank accounts. Security was a problem, as we were not free to travel around or mix with the locals. If an aid worker was killed, we would be on lock down/house arrest for weeks at a time. Sometimes we wore bullet-proof vests, were always in the presence of security guards, had to be very careful associating with local people and would have to come up with colorful stories to get out and about into the 'field'.

The workplace was quite unorganised and a lot of people were disgruntled. We wanted to teach different subjects, but things were always censored there. My fellow teachers were of a higher caliber than I was used to. All had Masters in specialised areas and I had the feeling they all worked for organisations they did not mention on their CVs. They spoke multiple languages and seemed to have alternative agendas other than just teaching. Many of them had prior links to the State Department. It was an odd assortment at best.

The pupils were the cream of the crop. They were not from typical backgrounds, they were from high ranking military, intelligence and diplomatic families. Occupying our spare time was difficult since we always had to get permission to go anywhere, unless we hid under the radar. There were a handful of 'safe' establishments for foreigners, but after awhile you got bored with those and had to find a way to entertain yourself. If it were not for the money, it would be quite hard to stay and live there, unless you really liked reading books all the time.

Employment information about the university can be found at www.auaf.edu.af including about their internship programme open to graduates. In such an unstable setting as Kabul, things change fast and anyone who stays teaching for more than a year is likely to move up quickly. The British Council has a teaching centre in Kabul. Needless to say Afghanistan has a rich and complex history and the people are friendly, warm and wonderfully hospitable once you have gained their trust.

Bahrain

Bahrain is among the most liberal of the oil states, and one which attracts foreigners, including women because of its tolerance of women in the workplace. The British Council keeps a list of language schools and may be of assistance in referring a TEFL-qualified teacher to private clients, whether companies, individuals or secretarial colleges. Unlike in Saudi Arabia, it is possible to teach mixed classes of men and women.

ISRAEL

Because of the large number of English-speaking Jews who have settled in Israel from the USA, South Africa, etc. many native speakers of English are employed in the state education system and there is little active recruitment of foreign teachers. There are a number of private language schools, for example a number of Wall Street Institutes and Berlitz schools. The British Council maintains a presence in Israel and has teaching centres in Ramat-Gan (Tel Aviv), West Jerusalem and Nazareth, which recruit qualified EFL teachers mainly from the local English-speaking population.

TOM BALFOUR discovered there were openings in Israel, shortly after reacquainting himself with a girl he knew in Tel Aviv:

I sent emails with my CV to various English schools, mostly branches of the two big companies Berlitz and Wall Street Institute, explaining my situation – that I would be leaving Israel in a week to return to England for my summer job, but that I wanted to come back in September and teach English in Tel Aviv. Most of the schools simply sent me a reply saying 'get back to us when you return' but Wall Street Institute Tel Aviv invited me for an interview. In the interview I was asked various questions about teaching, and then the director pretended to be a low level student and asked me to explain various words to her. When she asked me what a model was, I said 'Naomi Campbell, Kate Moss' and then got up and did a pretend cat-walk round the room. Although I'm sure that my qualifications helped, I think that might be what got me the job: knowing how to keep explanations simple, and being prepared to look silly if it helped. She told me that if I came back I would be offered a contract.

I had heard (from this book in fact!) that with the high number of native English speaking immigrants in Israel there wasn't really a market for English teachers. I think, however, that my Trinity qualification and my planned work at the summer school made me stand out from the native candidates, some of whom were hoping for a job simply on the strength of being English speakers.

One difficulty that native English speakers may run into is getting a visa. You improve your chances by being in a relationship with an Israeli foreigner or Jewish foreigner.

Israel is an amazing country and Tel Aviv is a great, cosmopolitan city with a good beach and fantastic nightlife.

Palestinian Governed Areas

Education is all but impossible for many Palestinians and the situation is very difficult for teachers. Although the demand is there, the circumstances do not allow the vast majority of Palestinians to achieve their ambition. Like most international organisations, the British Council has withdrawn from the Palestinian Territories and its educational activities in Nablus, Ramallah, Gaza and East Jerusalem have been halted.

The charity UNIPAL (Universities' Trust for Educational Exchange with Palestinians – see entry) operates an educational and cultural exchange with Palestinian communities. The political situation has made it impossible for projects to continue in Gaza and even in the other Palestinian territories, so now its projects carry on only in Lebanon. Another charity which arranges for English tutors to spend the summer in Nablus or nearby refugee camps for Palestinians is Project Hope (see entry). Palestinian schools struggle on and anyone who supports their cause might be prepared to become a volunteer teacher. Senior people who can set up programmes would be especially welcome.

PROJECT HOPE (Humanitarian Opportunities for Peace and Education)

c/o One World Centre, 189 Princes Street, Dundee DD4 6DQ, UK

✆ recruiter@projecthope.ps

🖥 www.projecthope.ps

Offices also in Nablus and Toronto. Non-profit volunteer organisation that supports children denied access to basic services in Nablus om the northern West Bank and the nearby refugee camps of Balata and Askar.

NUMBER OF VOLUNTEER TEACHERS: 15–30.

PREFERENCE OF NATIONALITY: None.

QUALIFICATIONS: Teachers must have a TEFL qualification or teaching experience along with experience of working with groups of children and young people.

CONDITIONS OF EMPLOYMENT: 5 weeks to 1 year, 20–25 hours of teaching a week, with 2 full days off.

SALARY: None.

FACILITIES/SUPPORT: Accommodation provided in a shared apartment.

RECRUITMENT: Teachers fill in an application form and are then interviewed over the telephone (the recruiter calls the teacher).

CONTACT: Jenny, International Volunteer Recruiter.

Kuwait

Although teaching salaries are no longer in the stratosphere, as some were more than a decade ago, many organisations still seek to lure expat teachers with favourable terms. Educational standards are variable, as encountered by **B. P. Rawlins** in Kuwait:

> There are simply too many schools in Kuwait acting like pigs at a trough, all of them out there for the money. They dare not criticise any anti-social behaviour by pupils, parents or adult students for fear of losing fees in a competitive market. Professionalism is viewed with hostile suspicion in some quarters.

This negative view is not subscribed to by all who have spent time in the region. Many agree that English learners in Kuwait, as throughout the Arab world, can be a pleasure to teach because they are so eager to communicate, and so unhesitant to speak English in class.

As well as keeping an up-to-date list of the many international and English medium schools in Kuwait, the British Council (PO Box 345, Safat 13004; 2252 0067; info@kw.britishcouncil.org) employs teachers year round and for July/August summer courses.

LIST OF EMPLOYERS

AMIDEAST

Mail: PO Box 44818, Hawalli 32063, Kuwait.

Physical Address: Block 3, Corner of Fourth St and Yousef Al-Qanaie St, Building 15, Salmiya

📞 +965 2575 0670

✆ kuwait@amideast.org

🖥 www.amideast.org

NUMBER OF TEACHERS: All part-time.

PREFERENCE OF NATIONALITY: North American.

AMIDEAST emphasises American style English.

QUALIFICATIONS: BA/BEd and MA in TESL is essential. 5 years of teaching experience is required.

CONDITIONS OF EMPLOYMENT: Hired as independent contractors. Contracts are usually 6 weeks long and renewable according to demand. Average 2 hours a day, 3 days a week; generally evenings.

SALARY: Depends on qualifications and experience.

RECRUITMENT: Newspaper ads and referrals.

CONTACT: Maureen Aldakheel, Country Director.

TQ LOGISTICS SERVICES W.L.L. (TQLS)

PO Box 4697, Safat 13047

 +965 22322030

 recruitment@tqls.com.kw

www.tqls.com.kw

Company has taken on the role of Education and Training for IPETQ (Institute For Private Education & Training).

NUMBER OF TEACHERS: About 90.

PREFERENCE OF NATIONALITY: British, Irish, American, Canadian, Australian.

QUALIFICATIONS: English language instructors ideally need a degree in an English or related subject from a recognised university, EFL teaching qualification such as CELTA/ DELTA or TEFL, minimum of 5 years' teaching experience with adult students, experience in teaching ESP and CALL experience.

CONDITIONS OF EMPLOYMENT: Open contract. Hours vary according to project requirements; split shifts are common. 6 weeks' paid leave per year plus standard insurance.

RECRUITMENT: Directly to recruitment@tqls.com.kw or through the Human Resources Department of TQ Education and Training (Garden Court Pavillions, Lockington Hall, Main Street, Lockington, Derby DE74 2SJ; 01509 678442; hr@ tq.com).

CONTACT: Ziad Moussa, Administration Manager.

Lebanon

Lebanon has traditionally been an important commercial hub for the Middle East, although the major military campaign launched by Israel in 2006 set back the progress of an otherwise forward-thinking, artistic and entrepreneurial country. There continues to be heavy UN presence in the south and many foreign embassies advise against non-essential travel to the area.

Most teaching jobs in Lebanon are found in Beirut. Locals are generally open-minded and many speak three languages: English, French and Arabic. Male and female teachers will find it relatively easy to adjust (compared to the major culture shock experienced in other Middle East destinations), although the pace of life is slower and more conservative outside Beirut.

Finding an English teaching job in Lebanon can be difficult as there is a local pool of qualified teachers. A few schools advertise abroad and recruit on teaching websites, but most do not. If you cannot find a posting, search online; find the contact information of any school and then start sending off your CV. Most full curriculum schools are English or French, with the other language plus Arabic taught as second languages, although English continues to gain ground over French, to the chagrin of the French. The popularity of English is increasing due to its status as the international language of business and also to a strong tradition of Lebanese emigration to the USA and Australia.

However, even schools that do not use English as the medium of instruction employ English teachers. The website www.schoolnet.edu.lb has links to some private schools around Lebanon; www.lebweb.com is an on line directory for everything from banks to schools in Lebanon and the classified section of www.dailystar.com.lb carries occasional teaching vacancies (but check daily). For info about teaching English to adults try the American Lebanese Language Center (see entry) or the British Council (www.britishcouncil.org/lebanon). It's perhaps also worth trying the Lebanese American University (PO Box 13–5053, Chouran, Beirut 1102 2801; www.lau.edu.lb). While the demand for teachers exists, the wages can be low unless you are lucky enough to be hired by a large and foreign-operated school or university. The minimum wage is about $300 per month and local teachers earn about $600 per month as a starting salary. Foreign teachers can expect to earn about $800–$1500 a month, depending on credentials, experience and how the contract is negotiated. Contact hours are often high and teachers may be assigned additional tasks. Lebanon has 20 official holidays.

A few larger schools offer on-site housing and those that do not will help teachers find decent accommodation. Finding a flat from abroad is difficult, although some English websites and newspapers list private and shared accommodation.

RED TAPE

Schools will manage your work visa, but expect this to take time. Teachers generally arrive at the airport on a tourist visa. After arrival, the school begins processing work papers, which may take between two weeks and more than two months. Lebanon is a developing country, paperwork is not always straightforward and government offices are not easy to negotiate (if they ever are). Note that teachers from the UK and USA are sometimes preferred simply because their visas are half the price of Canadians and Australians. However, **Shelley Beyak-Tarabichi**, who works for International House in Beirut, provides words of reassurance: '*Canucks and Aussies still get hired!*' Shelley is originally from Canada and has provided most of the information for this chapter.

Increasingly it will be worthwhile investigating possibilities in this tiny but fascinating country. While accompanying her husband on a short-term contract in Lebanon, **Anne Cleaver** (an early-retired teacher) easily found work (albeit voluntary) at a new Special Needs Centre just outside Beirut:

> *Even during my short period there, I was tentatively offered a full-time post at a neighbouring school and even an opening in Abu Dhabi. There is a real eagerness to learn English in Lebanon. I found Lebanese educationalists, parents and children most welcoming and enthusiastic. Being a British teacher there made me feel more valued, I regret to say, than back in the UK.*

Good education is extremely important and costly in Lebanon and families pay large sums to ensure their child attends a distinguished school and also invest in tutoring outside of school. Children are expected to study hard inside and outside of school, as government tests are difficult.

A very different experience would be to teach in the Palestinian refugee camps. As mentioned the charity UNIPAL (Universities' Trust for Educational Exchange with Palestinians) operates a summer volunteer teaching programme for teenagers in Palestinian refugee camps located in Lebanon. Volunteers must be native English speakers, based in the UK and at least 20 years old. Previous work with children is essential, and previous teaching experience preferred. TEFL/TESL qualifications are an advantage, but not necessary. The approximate cost of the programme is £500 to cover airfare and insurance.

LEISURE

Shelley Beyak-Tarabichi has come to appreciate life in Lebanon:

> *Lebanese hospitality is renowned, the food is fantastic (healthy and vegetarian-friendly) and the weather is comfortable. You can swim at a beach resort in the summer, ski in the winter and hike all year round. There are gyms, malls, outdoor groups, concerts, art schools and mountain resorts along with traditional Arabic cafés, monasteries, mosques and historical sites dating back thousands, if not millions, of years. While the political situation in Lebanon is termed unstable, it is not evident on a day-to-day level as one would expect.*

LIST OF EMPLOYERS

ALLC IH BEIRUT

American Lebanese Language Center – International House Beirut, PO Box 55463, Confidence Center, 7th Floor, Sin el Fil, Beirut

- 1 500978/1 489166, 1 485475
- recruitment@allcs.edu.lb
- www.allcs.edu.lb.

NUMBER OF TEACHERS: Varies, most locally hired. Also for branches in Dbayeh, Jounieh, Byblos and Zahle.

PREFERENCE OF NATIONALITY: American, British.

QUALIFICATIONS: CELTA certified, 2+ years' experience. Business English experience essential.

CONDITIONS OF EMPLOYMENT: 12-month standard contract. 26 contact hours per week, split shift between 11am and 9:30pm.

SALARY: $900–$1,200, depending on experience and qualifications. No deductions.

FACILITIES/SUPPORT: Will assist in finding suitable accommodation ready on arrival and at teacher's expense. All work permit paperwork is done by the centre.

RECRUITMENT: Normally through IH recruitment page, unsolicited applications and emails. Interviews are essential, usually carried out via telephone.

CONTACT: Elaine Kniveton, Director of Studies (elainek@allcs.edu.lb) or Lorianne Uminski, HR Manager (lorianneu@allcs.edu.lb).

UNIPAL

BCM Unipal, London WC1N 3XX, UK

- info@unipal.org.uk
- www.unipal.org.uk

NUMBER OF TEACHERS: 30.

PREFERENCE OF NATIONALITY: Native English speakers.

QUALIFICATIONS: Experience with children or teaching. TEFL a bonus.

CONDITIONS OF EMPLOYMENT: 5-week contracts, 5 hours a day in July/August.

SALARY: None – volunteers pay £500 for flight, accommodation, food, insurance, etc.

FACILITIES/SUPPORT: Accommodation and training provided.

RECRUITMENT: Through application form and interview in March, which is essential.

CONTACT: Brenda Hayward, Director.

Oman

According to experienced American teacher **Tom Clark**, who has worked in Egypt, Syria, Turkey, Kuwait and Saudi, Oman where he taught last year is '*the best in the Middle East for being friendly and open and laid back*'. Tom thinks Oman is experiencing a sort of boom now in tourism and employment and is growing and developing very fast. He feels that it is at its best now and as more luxury hotels are built and local residents moved from the beaches, it will become a different country, so urges people to go now. Technical colleges such as the Salalah College of Technology where Tom worked – alongside 59 other ESL teachers – are hiring in a big way in anticipation of the Sultan making announcements that will benefit teachers.

Since the 1970s Oman has had to import the majority of its skilled labour including teachers. Teachers of English are employed from Sudan, Sri Lanka, India and North Africa which means that there is a much broader mix of accents than usual. Positions for native English speakers from the UK etc. become available each year with the British Council and Amideast in Muscat, and the major employers of Western teachers are the Ministry of Higher Education, Sultan Qaboos University and CfBT. CfBT Education Services LLC, Oman, supplies expertise in Education and Training for various public and private sector clients including the Ministry of Education, the Ministry of Higher Education and Petroleum Development Oman (PDO). With more than 26 years experience in-country, CfBT LLC maintains a project office in Muscat and has expanded operations to the Gulf Region. Further details are available at www.cfbtoman.com or www.cfbt.com.

Despite an expanding EFL market, there's no room at all for visiting job-seekers, since a tight hold is kept on tourist visas. It will make it much easier to land a job if you have an MA in TESOL or Applied Linguistics (or at least be enrolled in a distance learning ELT Master's degree) with at least three years' experience, preferably at university level. IH Muscat (Polyglot Institute) in Oman asks for teachers with a BA (English major), CELTA or Trinity TESOL, plus 3–5 years EFL experience post-CELTA. If the first degree is a BSc, the approving body require 5 years' experience post-CELTA. The main recruiting season begins in March just prior to the annual TESOL Arabia conference.

Exactly why an MA in TESOL should be necessary is not very clear, at least not to **Sandeha Lynch** who provided some of the information in this section. His wry description of students in higher education could apply equally to students throughout the Middle East:

> *Unfortunately there is a widespread idea that experts in linguistics and the like have what it takes to teach English. It can come as a bit of a shock, therefore, for teachers who have studied phonics, syllabus design, methodology and socio-linguistics to discover that they are teaching 'Headway Elementary' units 1 to 5 to groups of up to 40 students per class. Not exactly what the MA prepares you for. One could say that the school-leavers who come to the colleges and higher institutes are ill-prepared.*

On the other hand Tom Clark found his students to be polite and really engaged with their studies. This is not life in the fast lane of academic endeavour but something of an academic lay-by. If you choose to work in one of the colleges of higher education, you may find that the concept of rigorous academic standards is imperfectly understood, and therefore rarely applied.

The quality of life is favourable. Tom Clark was put up in a guest house until he could find something on his own. They were presented with a choice of places from villas in the mountains to plantations in the woods, luxury apartments in the suburbs to places on the beach. It is possible to acquire a drinking licence for the five bars in town. Other recreations include scuba diving, boating, desert camping Bedouin-style, picnicking in the mountain valleys, camel racing or just haring around in a 4WD. The countryside and coasts are stunning and if you can handle the heat and at times the humidity, mountain walking is popular. Just try not to get bored with these activities. There are no others, unless you happen to live near Muscat where you can indulge in wandering around glossy shopping malls, watching Hindi movies and eating sushi.

LIST OF EMPLOYERS

AMIDEAST OMAN
11 Fahoud Street, Al Qurum (Opposite Qurum Park), PO Box 798, PC 116, Mina Al Fahal, Muscat
(phone) +968 2456 1727
(email) oman@amideast.org
(web) www.amideast.org

NUMBER OF TEACHERS: 5 full-time EFL instructors for on- and off-site assignments.

PREFERENCE OF NATIONALITY: Americans and other native English speakers.

QUALIFICATIONS: Bachelor's degree plus recognised international certificate in TEFL/TESL and a minimum of 2 years' successful experience teaching English to non-native speakers.

CONDITIONS OF EMPLOYMENT: General English classes for children, teenagers and adults held between 8am and 9pm. Business English and other ESP courses conducted for public and private sector organisations. 40-hour work week, including 24 contact hours.

SALARY: Commensurate with qualifications and experience.

FACILITIES/SUPPORT: AMIDEAST will offer assistance in locating affordable housing. All visa related fees and procurement will be managed by AMIDEAST upon arrival.

RECRUITMENT: Via www.amideast.org plus regional and international TEFL conferences.

CONTACT: Russell Barczyk, English Language Program Manager (rbarczyk@amideast.org).

CfBT EDUCATION SERVICES
PO Box 2278, PC 112 Sultanate of Oman
244 85290
gen@cfbtoman.com

NUMBER OF TEACHERS: About 12 in British Training Institute in Muscat; about 40 in projects with Ministries of Education and Higher Education.

PREFERENCE OF NATIONALITY: British, North American, Australian, New Zealander.

QUALIFICATIONS: Usually DELTA.

CONDITIONS OF EMPLOYMENT: 1-year renewable. Up to 25 teaching hours a week.

SALARY: Approximately £16,000 per annum. Tax-free.

FACILITIES/SUPPORT: Free accommodation or accommodation allowance; work permit; annual return flight.

RECRUITMENT: Normally through advertisements on internet (tefl.com, edufind.com), agents abroad; CfBT database and www.cfbt.com.

CONTACT: Tim Eyres, Country Manager.

SUR UNIVERSITY COLLEGE
PO Box 400, Postal Code 411, Sur, Oman
job@suc.edu.om
www.suc.edu.om

PREFERENCE OF NATIONALITY: Native English speakers.

QUALIFICATIONS: Bachelor's or master's degree, TEFL certificate plus minimum 5 years' overseas teaching experience with intensive EAP course experience.

CONDITIONS OF EMPLOYMENT: 1-year renewable. 25 hours per week. To teach on foundation course for Omani students who want to study business and IT at university.

SALARY: Tax-free. 40 days paid summer holiday.

FACILITIES/SUPPORT: Free furnished accommodation and assistance with work permit. Transport provided plus medical insurance, utilities allowance and bonus.

Qatar

The tiny traditional emirate of Qatar is surrounded by Saudi Arabia, Bahrain, the United Arab Emirates and Iran, and has a stable ELT industry. Sweeping reforms a few years ago by the Emir of the state, Sheikh Hamad bin Khalifa Al-Thani, promoted English over Arabic as the medium of instruction in the state school curriculum, while trying to balance respect for the heritage and conservative nature of Qatar's people.

As a country high in natural gas and oil reserves, Qatar has a per capita income that exceeds some of the leading industrial countries of Western Europe, and as such offers some enticing expatriate packages to teachers. After completing a Master of Education in Canada, **Arshiya-Nageen Ahmed** went to Qatar to teach and to research education practice in the Middle East:

I was actively looking for careers related to my field while volunteering to gain additional experience. After receiving three job offers I had to decide my best option. The interview procedures were long, however, I got the job in Qatar and have been working ever since. Students are hesitant to speak English at times since they do not want to make mistakes. Thus the best way is to build good student-teacher rapport so that the students become comfortable in an English language environment. I was already aware that students would find some difficulty in adjusting to a foreign accent but from their feedback, they seem at ease in understanding a Canadian accent. Furthermore, it is important to encourage students to speak English with their peers so that they stay in practice.

The main teaching opportunities are to be found in the state schools and post-secondary education institutes. There are also opportunities for in-company development of business English for those with the appropriate qualifications. The British Council has an office in Doha (93 Al Sadd Street, PO Box 2992, Doha; general.enquiries@qa.britishcouncil.org) offering eight-week English courses to adults and children and possible advice on finding teaching work. It offers the CELTA course in the autumn (8,000 Qatari rials).

There are also possibilities within private language institutes: Inlingua Qatar is partnered with Score Plus (careers@score-plus.com), which claims to be looking more for 'intra-preneurs' than teaching employees.

LIST OF EMPLOYERS

QATAR AERONAUTICAL COLLEGE
PO Box 4050, Doha
📞 440 8813
✉ qataraerocol@qatar.net.qa or doha.hr@gmail.com

NUMBER OF TEACHERS: 30–35.
PREFERENCE OF NATIONALITY: Native English speakers.
QUALIFICATIONS: Bachelor's degree, CELTA, DELTA, TEFL certificate or master's plus minimum 3 years' experience.

CONDITIONS OF EMPLOYMENT: Length of contract ranges 6 months to 1 year. Working hours are 7am–2pm.
SALARY: $3,000–$3,400 per month.
FACILITIES/SUPPORT: Furnished accommodation, government health card and assistance with work permits provided.
RECRUITMENT: Interviews required, usually carried out in the UK.
CONTACT: Head of English Language Teaching or Human Resources.

Saudi Arabia

Recruitment of English teachers is booming and the recruitment websites are full of advertised vacancies. Whereas in the 1990s, employers had very high standards and expected their teachers to have many years of experience, now there are some teachers in the kingdom who don't even have a university degree. Part of the problem is that the country is so wealthy that many from the elite classes know that they will never have to work for a living and do not particularly value education. The teaching is not always very serious and there is an expectation that everyone will 'pass' no matter what. The days of fabulously high salaries are also over, and rising violence against foreigners has acted as a further disincentive. But expatriate packages are still very attractive, with substantial salaries, free airfares and accommodation plus generous holidays and other perks.

Teaching in a naval academy or petrochemical company while living in a teetotal expatriate ghetto is not many people's idea of fun, especially after a request for an exit visa has been denied. The rare woman who gets a job as a teacher (at a women's college) may live to regret it when she finds that she is prohibited by law from driving a car and must not appear in public without being covered from head to foot.

Bell Worldwide has almost constant adverts for qualified staff for Saudi Arabia (ksu.recruitment@bell-worldwide.com). A few specialist ELT recruiters such as Footprints Recruiting deal with Saudi employers (www.footprintsrecruiting.com/teaching-in-saudi-arabia) whereas the Canada-based agency Teachaway.com offers jobs to certified teachers in a private school in Jeddah. Creative English is a company in Cardiff which recruits for the giant oil and gas company Aramco (+44 7790

479238; creative_english@hotmail.com). They warn that mobilisation to Saudi Arabia takes three to four months from the interview.

A dedicated website www.teachsaudi.com carries a searchable database of jobs. A sprinkling of companies advertise in the UK educational press, including Arabian Careers Ltd., with a London office (www.arabiancareers.com) and TQ Education and Training in Derbyshire (www.tq.com).

TOM CLARK has also taught in Saudi Arabia. He describes the interview process in the UK with a large group of recruiters who rush the applicants through like cattle and then make them wait around all day to hear the outcome as an 'awful experience':

Saudi is by far the oddest place to get paperwork done. The embassy people are not friendly and really try your patience. Every day they told me to come back, which meant I was paying for a hotel and paying for taxis and food, etc. waiting for nothing. Yet the company told me the visa was all ready and signed by the Ministry.

I have worked in Saudi on three separate occasions, with Aramco, M-Trading and most recently with the Bin Laden Group. The contract means nothing, as everything is done by favours and who you know. Accommodation is normally in a compound, some of which have pretty high security with maybe three different check points, jeeps with machine guns, barricades, etc. The job in Jeddah put us up in a hotel though where there was no security at all.

I hate to be negative about any place, but Saudi is not an easy place. Depending on where you are, you could be in a very conservative place where shops close for two hours every prayer time. You need to keep covered and to be careful about what you say about most topics, but especially religion, politics and even history. There is no drinking and forget talking to the opposite sex. It is a very regimented lifestyle and you need some pretty tough skin to stay there. The religious police are everywhere and as a foreigner in the kingdom you are always being watched by someone. I had an all-women's class which by law had to be in a separate building. The students could see me on a screen, but I couldn't see them. An official was present to censor my lesson and shut down the power if I got off topic, even talking about how some battles were fought and won.

Depending on where you are, it is pretty slim pickings to find things to do in your spare time. Even to go around the country is not easy without proof of being Muslim. To the best of my knowledge there is only one cinema in Riyadh for mothers and children only. Jeddah offers some variety with the beaches and old town and more liberal culture. If you are going to be anywhere try to be in Jeddah.

Professional teachers tempted by the money should bear in mind the drawbacks, as **Philip Dray** did:

I decided against Saudi Arabia. The money was most appealing, but I couldn't think myself into a situation where there was no nightlife and limited contact with women. A year may seem short when you say it fast, but you could get very depressed in a situation like that. Money is nearly everything but it can't buy you peace of mind. So I opted for a job at a school for boys in the UAE which, from the description, sounds sociable, inviting and accessible.

After Philip's arrival at the Oasis Residence in Dubai, he was well pleased with his decision, since living conditions in his luxury apartment complex, complete with pool, steam room, squash court and gym, were just as lavish as he would have been given in Saudi. **Rachid Taouil** was pleased with his job with WSI Saudi Arabia and with the country, largely because WSI were very welcoming and helped him with red tape:

> *Many teachers are like me and are offshore hires. They are professional and very friendly. I had the pleasure of attending some of their classes whilst receiving my induction. They helped me understand the requirements of the students and their needs. The students on the other hand were two types; private students urged by the need to learn English to forward their studies and company students urged by the necessity and the requirements of their job to learn English.*

Morris Jensen working for Elite Training (see entry) points to the good things about Saudi Arabia including the hospitality, ease of finding lucrative private work, excellent sports facilities, shopping and accessibility of places of interest in the Middle East. He also acknowledges the problems, such as the religious and cultural clashes which arise in the classroom and the frustrating bureaucracy.

Visas are not granted to people over the age of 55. Among the documents required for a work permit are a medical certificate notarised by the Foreign and Commonwealth Office in London, an authorisation from the Saudi Ministry of Foreign Affairs, copies of diplomas, a contract of employment and accompanying letter from the sponsoring company. The fee of 50 riyals payable before leaving your home country is only the beginning. Your passport is held by your sponsoring employer while you carry around an official copy as identification, at least until you are issued with an *iqama* (resident visa). Every time you want to leave the country you must request an exit and re-entry visa which is given at the discretion of your employer. Some foreign workers have reported having to pay a very substantial sum for an exit visa.

LIST OF EMPLOYERS

ELITE TRAINING PROGRAMS CENTER
PO Box 11015, Gulf Building, Jubail Industrial City 31961
☏ 3 347 7060/1/3
✉ training@etpc.com.sa
🖥 www.etpc.com.sa

NUMBER OF TEACHERS: 5 for Jubail and Yanbu City.
PREFERENCE OF NATIONALITY: Male UK passport holders only.
QUALIFICATIONS: Minimum CELTA or equivalent plus 3–5 years' experience (preferably 1 abroad). Also require 2 technically trained teachers (male only) who also have an EFL background.
CONDITIONS OF EMPLOYMENT: Contracts from 6 weeks to 1 year (usually the latter). 25 contact hours per week plus 15 hours admin.
SALARY: $3,000–$3,500 per month plus Western-style accommodation, transport and related expenses.
FACILITIES/SUPPORT: Free furnished single accommodation. Work permits obtained. Free medical insurance.
RECRUITMENT: Personal recommendation and via the internet (www.eslcafe.com and www.tefl.net).
CONTACT: Ali Mowlana, Consultant (Marketing & Operations).

EUROPEAN CENTRE, AL RAJHI CO. FOR HRD
PO Box 60617, Riyadh 11555
☏ +966 505363109
✉ euro3@al-rajhi4hrd.com
🖥 www.theeuropeancentre.com

NUMBER OF TEACHERS: 20–40 in various cities across Saudi Arabia
PREFERENCE OF NATIONALITY: British, American, Irish, Canadian, New Zealander, South African.
QUALIFICATIONS: Bachelor's degree in a language related field as a minimum plus a teaching certificate with at least 1 year of previous experience.
CONDITIONS OF EMPLOYMENT: Standard 12-month contract, 7:45am–4:00pm, 5 days per week. Average load of 27 contact hours per week.
SALARY: As of February 2010 the range is from 8,400 SAR gross to 10,900 SAR gross with additional 3,600 SAR or 7,200 SAR per month overtime available in certain locations. Salary scales undergo periodic review.
FACILITIES/SUPPORT: Free, fully furnished accommodation and transport allowance provided. Company provides valid work visas and residence permits (*iqamas*) at company cost and medical cards (*Tawuniya*) for private medical cover with £80 approx of the annual fee paid by the employee.

The company also refers candidates at point of hire to a visa broker who does all the necessary paperwork for visa processing. The company covers the broker and visa medical charges, as well as the cost of the actual visa. Prepaid flights are provided. British management. Centre uses labs, tactile learning and simulator facilities, plus Adobe format materials for projectors and smart boards. On-the-job training provided.

RECRUITMENT: In person or by telephone. CV with scanned copies of qualifications and a photo should be sent by email. A comprehensive pdf information pack is usually sent out to a candidate within 48 hours of receipt of a suitable application. Candidates may apply at any time of year.

CONTACT: Aidan Chalk, Managing Director.

INTERLINK LANGUAGE CENTER
Al Yamamah College, PO Box 45180, Riyadh 11512
yamamah@interlink.edu
www.interlink.edu

NUMBER OF TEACHERS: About 50, 80–85% of whom are native English speakers.

PREFERENCE OF NATIONALITY: The centre doesn't base its selection on whether teachers are native or non-native; rather on their philosophical orientation, linguistic and cross-cultural competence, past experience, and many other attributes determined through 'dialoguing', questionnaires, and final interviews.

QUALIFICATIONS: MA in TESL, at least three years of teaching experience, and good cross-cultural background, either working or living in another culture.

CONDITIONS OF EMPLOYMENT: Minimum 2-year contract, longer preferred. 20–25 hours per week.

SALARY: $35,000–$40,000, tax-free.

FACILITIES/SUPPORT: Free housing, medical insurance and transportation.

RECRUITMENT: Resumés collected through multiple websites. Interviews are essential and can be organised by conference call.

CONTACT: Ahad Shahbaz, President.

JUBAIL UNIVERSITY COLLEGE
English Prep Year Programme, PO Box 10074, Jubail Industrial City 31961
+966 3 342 9000 ext 1008
ucjjobs@gmail.com
www.ucj.edu.sa

NUMBER OF TEACHERS: 25+.

PREFERENCE OF NATIONALITY: British, Irish, American, Canadian, South African, Australian, New Zealander.

QUALIFICATIONS: BA in English, Linguistics or TESOL; or bachelor's degree in any discipline from an internationally recognised Anglophone university plus a CELTA/Trinity TESOL certificate. All teachers must have at least 2 years' of full-time ESL/EFL/EAP/ESP teaching experience at university/college level and be a native English speaker, or have near-native competency.

CONDITIONS OF EMPLOYMENT: Initially 2-year contracts, renewable annually thereafter. 40 hours per week (20 contact teaching hours, 10 prep hours, 10 office hours).

SALARY: Varies depending on qualifications and experience. Salary is tax-free.

FACILITIES/SUPPORT: Free furnished accommodation provided. Full details are supplied to teachers when salary offer accepted on how to get medical clearance and visa application.

RECRUITMENT: Web-based advertising. Interviews conducted by Skype or telephone.

CONTACT: Mike Creed, Academic Recruiting Officer.

KING FAHD UNIVERSITY OF PETROLEUM & MINERALS
Preparatory English Program, College of Applied and Supporting Studies, Box 5026, Dhahran 31261
recruite@kfupm.edu.sa
www.kfupm.edu.sa

NUMBER OF TEACHERS: 90 (further 24 teachers are employed in the University English Program).

PREFERENCE OF NATIONALITY: American, Australian, British, Canadian, Irish, New Zealander.

QUALIFICATIONS: Master's degree or full-time postgraduate diploma in TESOL/Applied Linguistics, or Cambridge DELTA, plus minimum 4 years' overseas experience. Cambridge CELTA or equivalent may be acceptable with particularly relevant experience.

CONDITIONS OF EMPLOYMENT: Male, native speakers of English. 2-year contracts starting September and February. 20 hour teaching week Sat–Wed. Pupils aged 18–20.

SALARY: 124,000–180,000 SAR ($30,000–$42,000).

FACILITIES/SUPPORT: On-campus furnished accommodation with all services available for married or single status. Annual airfares. Local education. Contract completion bonus.

RECRUITMENT: Send cover letter and CV by email to recruite@kfupm.edu.sa. Video conference interviews are required.

CONTACT: Jeffrey Gibbons, Director of the Preparatory English Program.

THE KNOWLEDGE ACADEMY OF LEARNING

P.O Box 63440, Hofuf 31982

✆ 3 5811131

✉ mosharyhol@hotmail.com

NUMBER OF TEACHERS: 10.

PREFERENCE OF NATIONALITY: UK.

QUALIFICATIONS: BA (preferably in English) and a DELTA or CELTA.

CONDITIONS OF EMPLOYMENT: Contracts are 2 years renewable, although the target is long-term employment, 5 years +; 6 hours teaching a day.

SALARY: Based on qualification and experience.

FACILITIES/SUPPORT: Furnished family housing. Processing of work permit all done by academy.

RECRUITMENT: Through contacts. Interviews sometimes take place in the UK or USA.

CONTACT: Moshary AlHolaibi, MD.

SKYLINE GLOBAL SOLUTIONS

10 Cannon Hill Lane, Phoenixville, Pennsylvania 19460, USA

✆ 610 230 0296

🖥 www.skylinetechsolutions.com

NUMBER OF TEACHERS: 50+ for positions in Saudi Arabia.

PREFERENCE OF NATIONALITY: American, British, Canadian and South African.

QUALIFICATIONS: Bachelor's degree. 1–2 years of teaching experience preferred.

CONDITIONS OF EMPLOYMENT: 1-year contract, 25 contact teaching hours, total of 40 working hours per week.

SALARY: Tax-free salary of $36,000 per year.

FACILITIES/SUPPORT: Furnished shared accommodation provided. Recruiter manages the visa process and works with local partners to get visas processed.

RECRUITMENT: Print media and internet. Interviews are essential and are conducted in the US.

CONTACT: Esllam Elghamry, International Recruitment Specialist.

Syria

The opportunities in neighbouring Syria have almost completely closed down since an incident in October 2008 which Syria considered a terrorist act of aggression on the part of the USA. In response to a bomb blast in Damascus, American helicopters landed in the eastern border village of Sukariyya and eight Syrians were killed. This prompted massive anti-American demonstrations and the closure of American-linked educational institutes including the Cultural Center, the American Language Center (ALC) and the Damascus Community School (DCS). For the time being Syria is probably off-limits to aspiring English teachers especially Americans.

Staff at the small British Council offices in Damascus and Aleppo may be willing to advise individual enquirers. However, the British Council cautions that:

Teachers wishing to teach here should make sure of their positions before arrival. They should obtain sponsorship from the prospective employer for residence purposes and have an agreed written contract.

To enter Syria, you must have an entrance visa from the Syrian embassy in your country. If your passport contains an Israeli stamp, you will be refused entry. If you are planning to travel to Jordan or Lebanon and return to Syria, apply for a double or multiple entry visa for Syria, which are difficult to obtain after arrival.

United Arab Emirates

STEPH FUCCIO, after a few years of English teaching in Asia, (who blogs at http://eflgoddess.blogspot.com) decided to move to a different part of the world with her husband in March 2010. The huge diversity of nationalities that makes up the population of the oil-wealthy Emirates means that English is the lingua franca, and almost everyone is eager to improve his or her knowledge of the language.

Somehow we have magically ended up in the Middle East, which is amazing. We are working for Abu Dhabi University in the United Arab Emirates which is most famous for Dubai, another city in the country, although Abu Dhabi is its capital. Most advertised jobs in the UAE, as throughout the Gulf, say that they require at least a master's degree. Instead of that I have about 5 years of EFL teaching experience covering everything from Toefl-iBT, academic, Business and General English classes. When we applied to universities and similar in Oman and the UAE, most places did cite the lack of an MA as the reason our applications were not moved forward. Having said that, our current employers also said they required a master's and hired us both anyway.

This is the first place I've lived where the British Council does not pay the highest English teaching wage, although they have a nice location on the island and still offer their high standard of organisation and good professional development. The rule of thumb for getting on here, much like Italy and some other countries I've been in, is it depends on who you know, no matter what your experience and education are. 'Wasta' is key here: it's who you know, your connections, that get things done, including internet service, speeding tickets and teaching jobs.

The pace in the classroom, much like the pace of life here in general, is slower than most Western institutes. Adult students expect a lot of personal attention (not to be confused with correction) but usually this dedication is not expected of them in return, i.e. they rarely will do any work outside of class, and sometimes will come up with amazing reasons not to do work even in class. Overall, they are good humoured. Although their sense of humour is different from mine, there is always an intersection of silliness that is available. They will always be late for class and want many breaks. They will usually have their 3–4 cell phones on the seat next to them, ready to take a call at the first ring. Emiratis are very well taken care of by their government. Although 80% of the population of the UAE is comprised of foreign nationals, it is the Emiratis who get the best jobs with the highest salaries and best benefits.

I wish I could make it sound more glamorous and inviting. The weather is great for the region, the low humidity is a relief after living in South East Asia. The food is amazing. The money is spoiling and the lifestyle isn't as strict as in neighbouring Saudi and Bahrain. But this isn't for the faint at heart or first timer.

Once again, the financial rewards are the principal attraction and make the red tape hassles bearable. The lowest jobs pay about 10–11,000 Dirhams (nearly US$3,000) per month plus free housing. The cost of living is surprisingly inexpensive, so most people can save a lot of money. Abu Dhabi and Dubai look very Western and familiar, though these similarities are only skin deep. Other potential good employers include VETI (Vocational & Educational Training Institute) in Abu Dhabi (www.veti.ac.ae) and Higher Colleges of Technology (see entry).

LIST OF EMPLOYERS

BERLITZ LANGUAGE CENTER
PO Box 41720, Abu Dhabi
🕾 2 667 2287
berlitz@emirates.net.ae
www.berlitz.ae/career.php

Centres also in Dubai (PO Box 71453, Dubai; 4 344 0034; berlitz2@emirates.net.ae; and PO Box 71453, Sharjah; 6 572 1115; berlitz3@emirates.net.ae).

NUMBER OF TEACHERS: 45.

PREFERENCE OF NATIONALITY: None.

QUALIFICATIONS: University graduates with teaching diplomas. CELTA/TEFL. For candidates with non-education or teaching university degrees, a CELTA or TEFL certificate is essential. All instructors need to undergo and successfully complete training in the Berlitz Method of instruction.

CONDITIONS OF EMPLOYMENT: Minimum contract is 1 year. Usual hours are Sunday to Thursday, between 7.30am and 9:30pm, Saturdays between 9am and 1:30pm. A weekly schedule is provided by the Centre Director specifying working days and hours.

FACILITIES/SUPPORT: Accommodation is provided in a shared teachers' apartment. A work visa and labour card are issued to new candidates on full time contracts. Original degrees/diplomas and a reference describing the candidate's experience is necessary, with attestation from the UAE Embassy or Ministry of Foreign Affairs in country of origin, plus copy of passport and passport photos.

RECRUITMENT: Through email applications, referrals and adverts in newspapers or websites. Interviews are important; for international applicants phone interviews are carried out.

CONTACT: Manal Mahshi, Director, Abu Dhabi; Reem Shehab, Director, Dubai; Sereen Masri, Director, Sharjah.

HIGHER COLLEGES OF TECHNOLOGY
http://recruit.hct.ac.ae

NUMBER OF TEACHERS: Up to 450 English faculty teachers involved in teaching ESL in 16 colleges throughout the UAE.

PREFERENCE OF NATIONALITY: None.

QUALIFICATIONS: English Faculty minimum requirements are master's degree in TEFL (preferred) or bachelor's degree and TEFL diploma; 3 years' teaching experience (tertiary preferred); practical teaching qualification (CELTA, DELTA or PGCE); knowledge of contemporary teaching practices and computer-assisted learning.

CONDITIONS OF EMPLOYMENT: Teaching year is from September to June. To teach 20 classes a week (Sunday to Thursday).

SALARY: Tax-free income. Salary based on experience and education. Annual rises are given upon receiving positive performance evaluations.

FACILITIES/SUPPORT: Visa arranged by HCT. Singles and families welcome. Unfurnished accommodation and a furniture allowance, excellent benefit package offered – details provided upon request or to short-listed candidates.

RECRUITMENT: Online HCT application required. Interviews can be conducted via video teleconference.

Yemen

Many people consider Yemen to be the most beautiful and interesting of all Middle Eastern states. According to a recent article in the *Yemen Times,* more than a hundred ESL schools are now operating in Sana'a alone. The US Embassy-backed YALI (Yemen-American Language Institute, www.yali.org.ye) has the lion's share of the market but other professional schools are competing well. Amideast and the British Council both recruit English teachers. MALI (see entry) is broadening its appeal by offering business, IT and tourism training alongside ESL courses. Teaching salaries at the respectable institutes allow a good lifestyle since the cost of living is so low. A few years ago, **Mary Hall** worked for an aid agency in Yemen and became familiar with the teaching scene:

> *There are more and more places teaching English here. The main ones recruit mostly qualified teachers from England or the US. Some others hire any old bod who turns up and don't pay very well. I had a lodger who was teaching at one place for a pittance as the boss took money out of her wages to pay for her lodgings, even after she moved in with me. I think she was getting a couple of dollars an hour. This is something you sort of get used to. It can be very cheap living here, with rent about $50 a month or less if you're not fussy.*

Although Yemen has attracted a growing number of tourists, rebels trying to force concessions from the authorities have kidnapped foreigners, Al-Qaida is active and in April 2010 a suicide bomber carried out an unsuccessful attempt on the life of the British Ambassador.

LIST OF EMPLOYERS

AMIDEAST YEMEN
Box 6009, 162 Miswat Street, Khormaksar, Aden, Yemen
- aden@amideast.org
Sana'a: Box 15508, Off Algiers St., Sana'a
- 1 400279/80/81
- sanaa@amideast.org
- www.yemenjobs.org

NUMBER OF TEACHERS: 4–8 for Sana'a and Aden with outreach operations in Mukalla/Sheher and Taiz.

PREFERENCE OF NATIONALITY: American mainly though other native English speaking nationalities accepted.

QUALIFICATIONS: Degree plus TESOL/CELTA certification and minimal teaching experience. Suitable for part-time and entry-level teachers.

CONDITIONS OF EMPLOYMENT: 1-year contracts. 6-week sessions with 1 week off between. 2–4 or 4–6 hours teaching per day, 5 days per week.

SALARY: $9–$15 per instructional hour.

FACILITIES/SUPPORT: Furnished housing or monthly housing allowance provided.

RECRUITMENT: Internet and word of mouth. Most recruitment now via dedicated website yemenjobs.org on which applicants can upload their documents. Interviews can be by phone/email.

CONTACT: Nafisa Bin Tayeh, Academic Coordinator (nbintayeh@amideast.org).

MODERN AMERICAN LANGUAGE INSTITUTE (MALI)
44 Djibouti St, Hadda, PO Box 11727, Sana'a
- 1 441036
- mazen.luqman@mali-training.net
- www.mali-training.net

NUMBER OF TEACHERS: 60 for 3 branches in Sana'a, Aden and Taiz.

PREFERENCE OF NATIONALITY: British, Canadian, American, Australian, New Zealander, South African.

QUALIFICATIONS: University degree and relevant ESL certification. Teaching experience preferred. Should be enthusiastic, motivated and willing to adapt to a different culture.

CONDITIONS OF EMPLOYMENT: 1-year contracts. 26 hours per week teaching time.

SALARY: $1,500–$2,000 per term (5 weeks) depending on qualifications and experience.

FACILITIES/SUPPORT: Single room in an apartment (shared among three) provided free. Return airfare, Arabic classes and visa provided.

RECRUITMENT: Send CV and recent photo to Mazen Luqman (mazen.luqman@mali-training.net). Phone interview can be arranged with shortlisted candidates.

CONTACT: Mazen Luqman, Founder & Director; Julie Manning, General Manager.

TURKEY

The ELT industry in Turkey still absorbs an enormous number of globe-trotting English teachers although schools in Istanbul have been cutting back on pay, free accommodation and holidays, while increasing their teachers' workload. By describing the problems which many have encountered on short teaching contracts in Turkey, it is to be hoped that readers can guard against them. Every single one of the teachers who has complained about employers breaking their promises, run-down accommodation, sexual harassment and so on, has concluded by saying that Turkish people are wonderful and the country fascinating.

PROSPECTS FOR TEACHERS

Turkey's ambition to join the EU, together with a remarkable expansion in tourism at the beginning of the 21st century, means that Turkey's prosperous classes are more eager than ever to learn English. It also means that they may have the money to pay for it because 'pre-accession assistance' from the EU is worth many millions of euros. The boom in English is not confined to private language schools (*dershane*) which have proliferated in the three main cities of Istanbul, Ankara and Izmir. In order to prepare students for an English language engineering, commerce, tourism or arts course, many secondary schools hire native speaker teachers. Hundreds of private secondary schools (*lises*) consider as one of their main priorities the teaching of the English language. Similarly at the tertiary level, some universities, both private and public, use English as the medium of instruction.

Turkey is a good choice of destination for fledgling teachers of any nationality. Not only are there a great many jobs, but a number of schools still offer a package which includes free accommodation and free airfares (London-Istanbul) on completion of a contract. Virtually all of these employers want to see a university degree and a TEFL Certificate of some kind, preferably the Cambridge CELTA or equivalent. Both a degree and a specialist qualification are required by the Turkish Ministry of Education before it will approve a work permit (see Regulations below).

The bias in favour of British English over American is not particularly strong. Many schools claim to have no preference and yet because they advertise in the UK press and are more familiar with British qualifications, there is a preponderance of British teachers. Also, the requirement that work visas be applied for in the country of origin makes matters more difficult for teachers from the USA, Australia, etc.

FINDING A JOB

IN ADVANCE

The British Council offices in Istanbul, Izmir and Ankara have lists of private language schools, primary schools and high schools and run a wide range of teacher training courses including Drama for English Language Teachers as well as the usual suspects.

There is also a Job File where local institutions advertise for TEFL teachers. International recruitment agencies rarely have contacts in Turkey. English-medium universities employ considerable numbers of language instructors, such as Bilkent in Ankara (see entry) and Istanbul Sehir University (www.sehir.edu.tr). Occasional job alerts are emailed to people who subscribe to the ITI Job List (http://jobs.iti-istanbul.com) managed by the International Training Institute in Levent, Istanbul which offers the CELTA and other TEFL training courses. EF, Dilko English, English Time, Bilge Adam (www.bilgeadam.com), the Turco-British Association and the City of London College (www.clc-turkiye.com) are all well established In Istanbul.

Quite a few ads for Turkish schools appear on the main TEFL job sites and the educational press in the spring and through the summer. One site with a good selection of Turkish vacancies is http://youcanteachenglish.com. Many ads specify that they are looking to hire teachers already in Turkey. If you are considering accepting a job with an advertiser, consider asking for the name and telephone number of a previous teacher for an informal reference before accepting. An even better indication is if they have been able to keep their teachers for two or more years. If the school is reluctant to provide this kind of information, be suspicious. It may also be worth phoning the British Council office in the relevant city, since they keep a file of complaints about language schools.

The Hocam Benim Educational Consultancy (www.hocambenim.com) matches experienced teachers with clients looking for individual or group tuition, from children to professionals. Demand outstrips supply so registered teachers in Istanbul have a good chance of being assigned courses (534 849 20 11).

ON THE SPOT

Although not the capital, Istanbul is the commercial, financial and cultural centre of Turkey, so this is where most of the EFL teaching goes on. On the negative side, there may be more competition from other teachers here and also in Izmir than in Ankara or less obvious cities. **Daniel Eldridge** from Seattle spent four months teaching in Istanbul:

> *The English teaching scene in Istanbul is absolutely huge and insane. Without the necessary charisma and connections (and confidence, maybe) I stayed on the bottom rung. I also had no TEFL certification which seemed to be important to some and not to others.*

Given the huge demand for native speaker teachers, Turkey is one country where scouting out possibilities on the ground can pay off, rather than signing a contract at a school you have never seen. After **Bruce Lawson** had a terrible experience with a private language teaching organisation in Istanbul ('*their contract was a fiction that Tolstoy would have been proud of*'), he concluded that he could have earned half as much again if he had been hired by a school which hired its teachers in Turkey.

Tim Leffel and **Donna Marcus** from New Jersey were amazed by the contrast between job-hunting in Greece (where Americans encounter visa problems even when they have a Cambridge Certificate as Tim and Donna had) and Turkey:

> *There's a huge demand for teachers (any nationality really) in Istanbul. We lined up work on our second day of interviews. We interviewed at three schools and all of them offered us positions. We chose one in Bakirköy because there were two jobs available in the same place and we were allowed to wear anything within reason (no ties, no new clothes to buy). They were satisfied that we could only commit ourselves for four months. We did see a lot of applicants turned away, even when there was a need for new teachers, because they lacked TEFL credentials.*

Fewer and fewer schools are willing to employ people with no formal TEFL background.

FREELANCE TEACHING

The standard Ministry of Education contract prohibits private teaching outside the bounds of the signed contract. In fact, unless you are blatantly pinching students from the institution that employs you, most employers turn a blind eye. University English departments might be a place to look for private pupils. The top rate of pay goes up to £20 an hour.

In Istanbul there is a flourishing English Spoken Café where Turkish language learners can meet up with native speakers informally (though with their dictionaries at the ready). Join the Facebook group to find out where and when events are being held.

REGULATIONS

It is necessary to apply for a visa before arrival in Turkey as the Vice Consul at the Turkish Consulate General in London clearly explains:

> *Anyone who intends to work in Turkey has to obtain a work visa before departing for Turkey. Otherwise, he/she will not be permitted to take up employment in the country, unless he/she chooses to work illegally.*

The application by the candidate in his or her own country must happen simultaneously with the employer in Turkey submitting an application to the Department for Work Permits for Foreigners, part of the Ministry of Labour and Social Security. It is not unknown for a hopeful teacher to proceed with the visa application while the employer does not carry out his side of the bargain, in which case the effort and money will be wasted. The current work permit fee for Britons is £235. Employers may be willing to pay this expense but it is not usual.

Teachers are required to submit their degree and ELT certificate. These have to be translated into Turkish by an official Turkish translator and then notarised. The Turkish employer needs to send permission from the Ministry of Education that he or she is authorised to employ foreign teachers, among other documents. Once these have arrived, the teacher takes them with the original contract of employment and completed forms in person to the Consulate to apply for a work visa, preferably eight weeks before the proposed departure. Clarification may be requested from the Office of Labour and Social Security Attaché in London (0207 581 5988; www.turkishconsulate.org.uk/en/work_visa.asp).

The regulations allow you to leave and re-enter the country without having to pay again for a visa, as long as your work and residence permits are still valid. If you stay in Turkey longer term (i.e. longer than the tourist visa) you are meant to obtain a residence visa as well.

The complications involved in obtaining a work visa have created a rise in language teachers who are working on just a tourist visa. In fact the majority of transitory language teachers opt for this route and as a result are forced to make a trip to either the border or the immigration office every three months, in order to renew their tourist visa. On entry make sure you get a multiple entry visa which allows you to enter and exit the country more than once within a one-year period and you can stay in Turkey for three months each time. The tourist visa fee payable at the border is £10 in sterling or $20 for US citizens. Normally people cross the border to Greece, though a trip to Northern Cyprus is more pleasant. If you do this too many times the border officials will become suspicious. If you have overstayed, you become liable for a hefty exit fine of about $250.

Before agreeing to work on a tourist visa, teachers should negotiate financial help or at least a subsidy for their border run. Schools are often willing to do this as it is still cheaper for them than arranging a work visa. All salaries in Turkey are quoted net of deductions which amount to about 25% for contributions and tax. If the school makes social security contributions on your behalf, you will have medical cover from your first day of work. The scheme pays all your doctor's bills and 80% of prescriptions. Once again it is prudent to confirm that your employer keeps any promises he or she makes. More than one teacher has realised at a critical moment that, despite assurances, insurance premiums have not been paid by the school.

A complication for people who intend to teach English in a *lise* or secondary school is that the Ministry of Education insists that teachers of English have a university degree in English, Linguistics or related degree and preferably a PGCE or a BEd with English as a main subject. **Barry Wade**'s degree in philosophy with a minor in English was deemed inadequate to teach English at an Istanbul secondary school, despite what he had been told by an agent in England, and he was fobbed off with having to work for less money at a private language school instead.

CONDITIONS OF WORK

The normal deal is a one-year contract with airfare out and back from London, free or subsidised shared accommodation and a monthly salary in Turkish lira equivalent to $1,000 or more in private language schools, more in primary and secondary schools. The major player English First pays 2,400–3,000 Turkish lira (£1,000–£1,300) per month which includes a rent subsidy. Hourly employment used to be fairly unusual in Turkey, but increasingly employers are finding it more profitable to pay by the hour, especially during low seasons when the number of teaching hours decreases dramatically.

Over the years many employers have come in for criticism with words such as 'cowboy', 'unprofessional' and 'untrustworthy' being bandied about by disappointed teachers. Browsing the web will eventually bring you to sites which name and shame schools that sack their teachers to save money, slash wages, fail to honour contracts, withhold certificates to prevent staff from leaving prematurely and so on. It is not always easy to establish how current some of this information is.

A clearly disgruntled teacher calling himself 'Whistleblower Istanbul' made contact in 2010 with a depressing catalogue of woes:

> Schools offer long hours, i.e. over 30 contact hours. You will have to prepare lessons on top of that, another 15 hours, plus any travel time between sites. Pay is okay to live on but not to save anything. Holiday entitlements are poor: 1 or 2 weeks if you are lucky on a 12-month contract. Usually only 1 day off a week. Teaching in mornings and evenings with a large gap in the middle makes it a long day. Teaching all weekend. Some institutes are professional, some not. Accommodation is sub-standard. Most employ illegal workers in terms of qualifications, TEFL, degree, work/visa requirements. Students can pass exams if they pay enough money! I've just returned from Istanbul. Never again.

Although one individual's personal experience is not always a good basis for generalising, there has been a lot of duplication in the litany of complaints made about language schools in Turkey which focus on contracts being ignored, late payment of wages, assigning inflated marks to students to keep or attract custom, and so on. It may be a mistake to expect Western attitudes towards employees to prevail. In Turkey the manager is the boss and in many cases does not feel it incumbent on him or her to work efficiently or to look out for the welfare of their staff. Nevertheless, some people in the ELT business believe that the situation is gradually improving, among them a director of studies at a major Istanbul school:

> I have worked for approximately four years in Turkey, in Istanbul and in a small remote town in the south. Prospective teachers always hear many horror stories about working in Turkey and to an extent they are well founded. In the past, schools and employers openly abused teachers' rights. But this is definitely changing. There are many good, up-and-coming organisations which can be trusted. Teachers should ask around, be careful about contracts and conditions, and not agree to the first job they are offered without checking out the school, its size, reputation, etc.

Yet it seems that there are still many dodgy operators and swashbuckling and unscrupulous employers. So it is important to remember that some teachers have a marvellous time, as **Raza Griffiths** had at the first school he worked for, which was in the town of Ordu on the Black Sea coast:

> It would be no exaggeration to say that as a native English person in a region of Turkey unused to foreigners, I enjoyed celebrity status, with lots of inquiring eyes and lots of invitations to dinner.

Although the town did not exactly have a thriving cultural life as we would understand it, this was more than compensated for by the sociableness of the people and their deep desire for communication. Because it was a private school, money was not in short supply and the facilities were excellent with computers, etc. The free furnished flat I was given was large and very comfortable, and there was a free school minibus service that took teachers to the school. On either side of the school there were hazelnut gardens, behind there were mountains and in front the Black Sea, all quite idyllic, especially in summer. The other teachers (all Turkish) were very welcoming from day one, despite the fact that I was less experienced and was getting four times their salary. I could live very comfortably on my salary and still have a lot left over for spending on holidays and clothes.

Contracts are usually for 9, 10 or 11 months; some offer 3-month summer contracts, for example with the Southampton-based Lewis School of English which runs English language camps for children in Bodrum (www.lewis-school.co.uk/jobs). If you want to stay longer than a year you are normally paid over the summer holidays. Do not put too much faith in your contract. **Rabindra Roy** described his as a '*worthless and contradictory piece of paper*'. Private language schools will expect you to work the usual unsocial hours and may chop and change your timetable at short notice, while *lises* offer daytime working hours plus (sometimes onerous) extra-curricular duties such as marking tests, attending school ceremonies, etc.

The standard holiday allowance for teachers is four weeks. At inferior schools, national holidays must be taken out of this annual leave, including Muslim holidays such as Seker Bayrami, usually celebrated at the end of Ramadan and Kurban Bayrami. The former last three days, the latter four days, and it is customary to make the bridge to a full week. Christmas is not observed much and you may be offered very little time off, especially in smaller schools where the majority of the staff is Turkish. Big chains of schools, where native English speakers are in the majority in the staff-room, tend to close for a week or a bit more. Most things can usually be negotiated in Turkey, be it the price of a carpet, or the terms of a contract. One English teacher with extensive experience of teaching in Istanbul suggests shopping around carefully before accepting a job. (Ideally before choosing you'd meet someone like him to give you the current lowdown):

I worked at four different schools in Istanbul. You'll want a school that's professional (with good resources, support and teacher development), offers a good package (salary, accommodation, holiday entitlement) and has a reasonable timetable (i.e. no split shifts and non-consecutive days off). Make sure your 24 contact hours are 24 50-minute lessons and not 32 45-minute lessons. Take a broad view of 'professionalism'. At one school, the conditions were fine but some practices illegal. At another school they provided workshops and observations but one of the managers gossiped (truthfully or not) about former teachers. One school provided a teacher with a fake university degree (economics 1st class).

THE PUPILS

The major schools are well equipped with TVs, videos, language labs and course materials. But better than the back-up facilities is the enthusiasm of the pupils who are usually motivated, conscientious and well-behaved, and enjoy group discussions. Teachers should not, however, expect too much interaction between teacher and pupil, as **Tara Dermot**, a teacher in Istanbul describes:

Walk into a classroom in Turkey and you are likely to find every kind of student that you would find all over the world: the eager, the shy, the lazy, the clever one... What sets Turkish students significantly apart in my experience is their passivity. Turks grow up in an incredibly teacher-centred learning environment so that is what they are expecting. Having them participate in a far more student-centred, communicative course can therefore be frustrating, but given time and perseverance they will soon see the benefits and the fun to be had.

'*Willing if unimaginative*' was one teacher's description of her students. One undesirable aspect of Turkish education is that many *lises* (high schools) are too strongly oriented to exam preparation and university entrance. On the whole, however, the friendly openness of young Turks may cause a foreign teacher to forget that Turkey is still an Islamic country where dress is conservative and where only a small percentage of women of university age actually attend (around 14%). Teachers are still regarded as important figures in society and as such are expected to dress fairly conservatively.

Student behaviour differs radically depending on what kind of institution you teach in. Private secondary schools tend to be populated with spoiled and immature kids who do not always respect their teachers. **Joan Smith** found this hard to stomach at the private school in Kayseri where she taught:

> *Turkish parents indulge their children something rotten. Rich spoilted students abound in my classroom and discipline goes out the window. Foreign teachers are regarded as inferior and are given even less respect than the Turkish teachers.*

Joan did not think that she should have to tolerate some of the innuendos her male students were getting away with, but had little hope of justice if they and their friends denied her allegations.

DICK BIRD and others' experiences have been very different. Dick, a veteran EFL teacher, taught in Turkey a long time ago but his description of his pupils is still apt:

> *I have found women students defer to a far higher level of male chauvinism than would be acceptable anywhere in the West. Turkish women also seem to have exceptionally quiet voices and I can't help feeling that this irritating characteristic is somehow related to their role in society – a case of being seen but not heard until you are very very close perhaps? Sometimes my students know too much grammar to be able to express themselves freely. As their own language is radically different to Indo-European languages they have a lot of difficulty adapting to the sentence structure of English: they regard relative clauses as a perversion and are baffled, if not mildly outraged, by the cavalier way English seems to use any tense it fancies to refer to future actions but is puritanically strict about how one may describe present and past events. Another difficulty Turks have is that we EFL teachers like to use a lot of words in our meta-language (i.e. language about language e.g. adjective, verb) which do not have cognates in Turkish as they do in other European languages, for example a teacher may inform their students that 'will' expresses probability, not intention; this will be readily understood by an elementary level Spaniard but is total gibberish to a Turk (as I suspect it is to a great many native speakers of English).*

Dick's analysis of Turkish EFL students ends with a light-hearted description of their irrepressible energy and enthusiasm:

> *Whenever the class is asked a question they would fain prostrate themselves at their teacher's feet were it not that years of instilled discipline keep them penned by invisible bonds within the confines of their desks until the ringing of the bell, whereat pandemonium breaks loose as a thousand berserk adolescents fling themselves across the (highly polished) corridor floors and down the (marble) steps headlong into the playground. (This phenomenon may help to explain why fire drills are not a regular feature of Turkish school life.)*

Paul Gallantry, at one time Director of Studies at Dilko English in Bakirköy, agrees that Turkish students are fun to teach but identifies a few of the problems he has encountered:

> *They have several major problems with English, especially mastering the definite article, the third person singular and the present perfect, none of which exists in Turkish. On the whole, their pronunciation is good, but they do have difficulty with words that have three consonants back to back. (My own surname Gallantry inevitably gets pronounced 'Galilantiree') If I have to be critical of my students, it is that they neither listen to, nor read, instructions; five minutes into an exercise there is always someone asking 'What am I supposed to do?'. Also a recurring problem is that some students merely come to a language school in order to use it as a social club. They're more interested in meeting someone of the opposite sex than learning English, and this can have a demoralising effect in class.*

ACCOMMODATION

If accommodation is provided as part of your contract, it may be located close to the school in a modern flat which you will have to share with another teacher or it may be some way away, possibly in an undesirable neighbourhood. Fortunately not many teachers are assigned accommodation as gruesome as **Philip Dray**'s in Izmir:

> *Cockroaches, centipedes, noisy neighbours, a filthy shower room and a fitted kitchen circa 1920, I was slowly adjusting to it all. But one day, while I was having a shower, I saw a rat looking at me from the ventilation shaft and I knew that my patience had run out. I asked for a new flat but they said they couldn't get a new one before May. So, reluctantly (as there were some very nice people at the school) I had to leave.*

If the school doesn't provide a flat they will certainly help you find one and act as go-between with the landlord. Most provide some kind of rent subsidy, since rents in Turkey are high relative to the cost of living. The situation in over-crowded Istanbul is especially tight. It is usual to bargain over the rent as if you were buying a second-hand car. Flats are advertised through *Hurriyet* newspaper, or there are estate agencies called *emlak* but these tend to charge a month's rent. Foreigners are usually considered an attractive proposition as they tend to be undemanding tenants.

In Istanbul, the nicest flats are along the Bosphorus where the air is clean, the views stunning and a lot of the buildings are older properties with a lot of character; this is why they have been snapped up by well-heeled diplomats and multinationals. The Asian side of the city might have less charm but it also has less pollution and many people prefer it.

Flats in Istanbul do not offer standards such as those in Europe or other Western countries, but things appear to have improved somewhat in recent years, and the horror stories of cockroaches, and freezing window-less rooms have been replaced with less drastic reports of leakages, small rooms, old facilities and untidy flatmates. **Ian McArthur**'s school was in a suburb on the Asian side, but he chose to stay in a cheap hotel in Sultanahmet, partly for the social life:

> *I had to commute (from Europe to Asia in fact) for an hour in the morning and evening, but the marvellous views of the sunrise over the domes and minarets from the Bosphorus ferry whilst sipping a much-needed glass of strong sweet tea, made the early rise worth it.*

LEISURE TIME

Even if you are earning a salary at the lower end of the scale, you should be able to afford quite a good life, especially if you eat a lot of bread, drink local wines and use public transport. Basic meals and food, transport, hotels and cinemas (most films are subtitled rather than dubbed) are still very reasonable, especially away from the seaside and Istanbul. With the benefit of hindsight, a former teacher decided the hassles weren't so bad after all:

Recognise why you are in Turkey – for the experience – and try to enjoy that. You have a chance to live in a fascinating city for a year on the basis of a one-month certificate. You may live near Taksim and let's be honest, could you afford to live a stone's throw from the equivalent in London or New York? Don't fall into the trap of mixing only with EFL teachers. Broaden your horizons and don't spend all your time in ex-pat bars with a clique of English teachers. Socialising all the time with the same teachers can lead to a climate of moaning. Constructive criticism/advice is fine but too many teachers become bitter and vengeful. Most Turks are OK. If you want to make Turkish friends, get involved in sport or something where you'll see the same people regularly.

Dick Bird points out the advantages of living in Ankara:

It's safer than any European capital (except maybe Reykjavik) and although it may not hum at night, there are enough clubs etc. to keep you going for a year, plus very cheap classical concerts and cinemas. And the air pollution is not as bad as it was.

Travel in Turkey is wonderfully affordable. The efficiency, comfort and low cost of Turkish bus travel put the coach services of most other countries to shame (though not their safety record). There is very little crime in Turkey. Women will have to learn to handle pestering, which is usually best ignored. Paul Gallantry tries to put the problem into perspective:

While Turkey is generally an exceptionally safe place, women teachers can expect a certain amount of harassment from a minority of Turkish men, who seem to believe that all foreign females are prostitutes. This attitude leaves a lot of teachers with a thoroughly negative attitude towards Turkey and Turkish people as a whole, which is unfair.

Turkey generally is a great place to live and work. It's a fascinating country, full of contradictions, as befits a land that is the bridge between East and West.

LIST OF EMPLOYERS

BEST ENGLISH
Bayindir (2) Sokak No. 53, 06650 Kizilay, Ankara
312 417 1819/417 2536
management@bestenglish.com.tr
www.bestenglish.com.tr

NUMBER OF TEACHERS: 30 native English speakers.
PREFERENCE OF NATIONALITY: None.

QUALIFICATIONS: First degree plus CELTA or equivalent plus minimum 2 years' experience.
CONDITIONS OF EMPLOYMENT: 1-year renewable contracts. Teaching load is 25 hours per week. Variable hours between 9am and 9pm, 7 days a week, with 2 days off a week. Students mostly young adults.
SALARY: Varies according to qualifications and experience.
FACILITIES/SUPPORT: Shared accommodation provided. Health insurance. One way airfare paid on completion of

1 year, plus 3 weeks' paid leave; return airfare and 4 weeks' paid leave if teacher renews contract. In-house training.

RECRUITMENT: Adverts and online application via website.

CONTACT: Mustafa Kutlay Yavuz, Director of Studies (mkyavuz@bestenglish.com.tr).

BILKENT UNIVERSITY SCHOOL OF ENGLISH LANGUAGE
06800 Bilkent, Ankara
- +90 312 290 5401
- intrec@bilkent.edu.tr
- www.bilkent.edu.tr/~busel

Privately funded English-medium university.

NUMBER OF TEACHERS: EFL/EAP instructors are regularly recruited.

PREFERENCE OF NATIONALITY: Native English speakers only; Australian, Canadian, British, American.

QUALIFICATIONS: Must be degree holder, preferably BEd or language degree, but teaching experience not required.

CONDITIONS OF EMPLOYMENT: Contracts from August to June, 15 contact hours per week.

SALARY: Salary paid half in dollars and half in Turkish lira ($760 per month net plus 1,100 Turkish lira).

FACILITIES/SUPPORT: Free accommodation on/off campus, private health insurance, airfare and baggage allowance, residence permit, work visa, etc. Good facilities and opportunities for career advancement, e.g. to study for an MA in Management in Education or DELTA on scholarship. Offers possibility to teachers of studying for the CELTA on full scholarship.

RECRUITMENT: Via agents, adverts or directly via www.bilkent.edu.tr/~busel/interrec/index.html.

CONTACT: Isik Cotton, International Employment Coordinator.

CAGDIL ENGLISH LANGUAGE CENTRE
Altiparmak Cd. 2, Otel Sk, I. Uluca Ismerkezi, 16050 Bursa
- 224 220 4482/224 222 22 52
- cagdil@cagdil.com
- www.cagdil.com

PREFERENCE OF NATIONALITY: British.

QUALIFICATIONS: University degree plus TEFL certificate.

FACILITIES/SUPPORT: Rent-free shared furnished flat available. Turkish classes. Opportunity to work as oral examiner for Cambridge ESOL examinations.

RECRUITMENT: Through advertising and direct.

DIALOGUE LANGUAGE SCHOOLS
Akdeniz Cad. no. 69, Fatih, Istanbul
- 212 621 70 62
- fatih@dialogueokul.com

Branch office: Istayon Cad. Yakut Sk No. 8, Bakirkoy, Istanbul
- 212 570 30 60
- bakirkoy@dialogueokul.com

Branch office: Halitaga Cad. Vahapbey Sk. No. 18, Kadikoy, Istanbul
- 216 550 13 17
- kadikoy@dialogueokul.com
- www.dialogueokul.com

NUMBER OF TEACHERS: 30 in 3 branches in Istanbul.

PREFERENCE OF NATIONALITY: British, American, Canadian, Australian and New Zealander.

QUALIFICATIONS: Native English speaking teachers with a clear non-regional accent, who have completed university education, have communicative abilities and desire to teach, are available for at least a year and have a teaching certificate or experience.

CONDITIONS OF EMPLOYMENT: 12 months for full-time teachers; shorter periods for part-time teachers. Variable hours with classes 6 days a week in daytime and evenings.

FACILITIES/SUPPORT: Full-time teachers are given rent allowance to find their own accommodation. No help with work permits.

RECRUITMENT: Interviews essential.

EF INSTITUTE – BAKIRKOY BRANCH
Zeytinlik Mah, Fisekhane Cad, Atakoy Palas Apt No:56, D: 1–2, Bakirkoy, Istanbul
- +90 212 571 6424

NUMBER OF TEACHERS: 8.

CONDITIONS OF EMPLOYMENT: As for EF Levent branch (entry below).

CONTACT: Michael Cassidy (Director of Studies) mcassidy@efdilokulu.com.

EF INSTITUTE – BURSA BRANCH
Doğanbey cad. Berk iş hani No:13 Kat:4 Osmangazi, Bursa
- 224 2 212 212

NUMBER OF TEACHERS: 8.

PREFERENCE OF NATIONALITY: Must be a native English speaker or a Turk.

QUALIFICATIONS: Degree plus CELTA/TESOL minimum. 1 year+ post-CELTA teaching experience desirable.

CONDITIONS OF EMPLOYMENT: 9 or 12-month contracts. About 120 hours teaching a month. 1 week paid holiday plus national holidays (10 days).

SALARY: 1,800–2,000 Turkish lira monthly (about $1,500), depending on experience, including accommodation allowance of 400 Turkish lira. Full private health and life insurance.

FACILITIES/SUPPORT: Assistance given in finding accommodation, usually shared with other teachers. Teachers pay their own rent. Active in-house teacher development programme, teachers required to attend 2 workshops per month. Free Turkish lessons. Financial and academic support for teachers taking DELTA. School has computer room, internet access and excellent resources/facilities. School organises work and residence permits. Registered centre for IBT TOEFL test.

RECRUITMENT: Internet, direct application. Interviews essential but can be by telephone/Skype.

CONTACT: Carol Kesim (carol.kesim@yahoo.com).

EF INSTITUTE – LEVENT BRANCH
Aydin Sok. F Blok No. 12 1, Levent, Istanbul
C +90 212 282 90 64

NUMBER OF TEACHERS: 15.

PREFERENCE OF NATIONALITY: Must be native speaker or Turk.

QUALIFICATIONS: Degree plus CELTA/TESOL minimum. 1 year+ post-CELTA teaching experience desirable.

CONDITIONS OF EMPLOYMENT: 9, 10, or 12-month contracts based on a 5 day working week with 2 consecutive days off and 30 contact hours teaching per week. Half-time and three-quarter contracts are also available. Paid holiday, number of days depending on the length of the contract, plus state and religious holidays.

SALARY: 2,400–3,000 Turkish lira monthly, depending on experience and qualifications, including accommodation allowance of 500 Turkish lira. Relocation allowance of up $750. Full private health and life insurance.

FACILITIES/SUPPORT: As above.

RECRUITMENT: Internet, direct application. Interviews essential but can be by telephone/Skype.

CONTACT: Dean Monfort (Director of Studies), (dmonfort@efdilokulu.com).

EF INSTITUTE – SUADIYE BRANCH
Kazim Ozalp Sok. 15/4 Saskinbakkal, Kadikoy 34740, Istanbul
C +90 216 385 84 31/+90 302 72 50

NUMBER OF TEACHERS: 18.

CONDITIONS OF EMPLOYMENT: As above.

CONTACT: Deirdre Costello (Director of Studies) dos@efdilokulu.com or Zeynep Gunduzyeli zgunduzyeli@efdilokulu.com.

ENGLISH WEST
Cumhuriyet Bulvari, No 36 Kapani Ishani Kat 3, Konak, Izmir (Pier Karsisi, Konak-Izmir)
C 232 489 4747
🖱 info@englishwest.com

NUMBER OF TEACHERS: 3.

PREFERENCE OF NATIONALITY: English, Scottish, American and Australian.

QUALIFICATIONS: Schools licensed by the Ministry of Education require teachers to have at least a 2-year university/college degree, however, a 4-year bachelor's degree is preferred. Those with a 2-year degree or bachelor's degree in a non-relevant field require a TEFL/TESOL certificate. This can be obtained online (preferably TEFL/TESL certification module and a special grammar module). Outgoing personality needed, with the ability to work in a team. The Callan Method of teaching English requires a sense of urgency, the use of miming and gesticulation, and the presentation of a clear accent with excellent pronunciation skills.

CONDITIONS OF EMPLOYMENT: 1-year contract, renewable for a second year, 20–25 hours per week.

SALARY: Salary is calculated either on hourly or salary-package basis. This varies by school and location, and will be discussed with candidate. All teaching positions have a 6-month probationary period with an increase in pay provided after successfully competing the probationary period.

FACILITIES/SUPPORT: Free accommodation for at least a month. Once teacher finds own accommodation, accommodation allowance of 250 Turkish lira is paid. Help with work permits and expense met. Intensive 1-week teachers training programme via the Callan Method given at time of hire and before starting teaching.

RECRUITMENT: Via eslcafe.com and others.

CONTACT: Koray Altan M.Sc. (Manager) and Bradley Brandt (Education Group Coordinator).

GENCTUR

Istiklal Cad. No.212, Aznavur Pasaji, Kat: 5, 80080 Galatasaray, Istanbul

212 244 62 30

workcamps@genctur.com or workcamps.in@genctur.com

www.genctur.com

NUMBER OF TEACHERS: 10.

PREFERENCE OF NATIONALITY: Native (or good) English speakers.

QUALIFICATIONS: Experience with children, workcamp or teaching experience is preferred.

CONDITIONS OF EMPLOYMENT: Volunteering for teaching English to children aged 12–17 at summer camps for 2 weeks, through outdoor activities, games and songs.

SALARY: Free board and lodging.

RECRUITMENT: Only through partner voluntary organisations abroad (e.g. IVS GB, Thorn House, 5 Rose Street, Edinburgh EH2 2PR; 0131 243 2745; info@ivsgb.org; www.ivsgb.org).

ICEP (INTERNATIONAL CULTURAL EXCHANGE PROGRAMS)

81 Oxford Street, London W1D 2EU, UK

020 7580 3106

uk@icepworld.co.uk

www.icep.org.tr/English/teach.asp

London office of Turkish exchange organisation with offices in Ankara (312 418 44 60) and Istanbul.

NUMBER OF TEACHERS: Varying number for positions at language school, English-medium university, private company or with host family where you will teach English to the family members.

PREFERENCE OF NATIONALITY: British and others.

QUALIFICATIONS: TEFL qualification e.g. CELTA, Trinity CertTESOL or DELTA required. Experience in teaching university level preferred.

CONDITIONS OF EMPLOYMENT: 5-day work week, 27 teaching hours per week plus 3 curriculum hours.

SALARY: Typically $500 per month. Possibility of better paying positions.

FACILITIES/SUPPORT: Accommodation, medical insurance and meals are provided.

CONTACT: Celemet Yener, Branch Manager.

INKUR ENGLISH LANGUAGE INSTITUTE

Ankara Cad. No: 8 izmit, Kocaeli

262 321 53 25

inkur@inkur.com

www.inkur.com or www.inkur.org

NUMBER OF TEACHERS: 3–8.

PREFERENCE OF NATIONALITY: EU and OECD countries are preferred (easier visa procedure).

QUALIFICATIONS: Minimum qualifications are a bachelor's degree and TEFL/TESOL certificate.

CONDITIONS OF EMPLOYMENT: 9-month contracts, 28 teaching hours per week.

SALARY: Between $500–$700 per month.

FACILITIES/SUPPORT: Free accommodation available. School applies for the work permit with teachers' academic document copies.

RECRUITMENT: Face-to-face and/or telephone interviews, sometimes carried out in the UK or USA.

CONTACT: N. Gökçiçek Doğan, Owner and Director.

KENT SCHOOL OF ENGLISH – ISTANBUL

Address: Kirtasiyeci Sokak No.1, 34714 Kadiköy, Istanbul

216 347 2791 / 347 2792

info@kentenglish.com

For job applications:

dos@kentenglish.com

www.kentenglish.com.

www.tefl-turkey.com

NUMBER OF TEACHERS: 12+.

PREFERENCE OF NATIONALITY: Native speakers of English from the USA, the UK, Canada and Australia.

QUALIFICATIONS: Bachelor's degree and TEFL certificate required. Priority given to teaching experience.

CONDITIONS OF EMPLOYMENT: 8, 10 or 12-month contracts. Weekend, weekday and evening classes in and away from school premises (in-company training programmes). Weekly teaching hours 25 +.

SALARY: Average $1,400 per month.

FACILITIES/SUPPORT: Work and residency permits arranged. Some training provided. Paid vacation. Health insurance. Intensive CTEFL course (Via Lingua) available for those without a teaching certificate.

RECRUITMENT: Local interviews, telephone, fax, mail.

SDM LANGUAGE SCHOOL AND EDUCATION AGENCY
Halaskargazi Caddesi No: 336/1 Kat:3–4, Sisli, Istanbul
☎ +90 212 233 02 49; business mobile +90 533 224 37 16
✆ akin@sdm.com.tr
🖳 www.sdm.com.tr

PREFERENCE OF NATIONALITY: Native English speakers.

QUALIFICATIONS: University graduate and experience of teaching adults.

CONDITIONS OF EMPLOYMENT: 6-day working week (with Fridays off). Working hours between 10am and 10pm. To teach mainly professionals.

FACILITIES/SUPPORT: Assistance with work permit given.

CONTACT: Akin Isik.

TURCO-BRITISH ASSOCIATION
Bestekar Sokak No. 32, Kavaklidere, 06680 Ankara
☎ 312 419 18 44
✆ admin@tba.org.tr
🖳 www.tba.org.tr

NUMBER OF TEACHERS: 20–30.

PREFERENCE OF NATIONALITY: British.

QUALIFICATIONS: Degree plus EFL qualification. Experience desirable.

CONDITIONS OF EMPLOYMENT: 2 years, 27 contact hours per week (45 minutes each lesson).

FACILITIES/SUPPORT: Shared, fully furnished accommodation, paid utilities, close proximity to school (about a 5-minute walk). Assistance with travel costs at the beginning and end of a 2-year contract. Residence and work permit procedures undertaken and costs met. 4 weeks paid annual leave, Christmas holiday, national Turkish holidays. Settling-in bonus, national social security covered.

RECRUITMENT: Via the *Guardian*, internet and locally.

CONTACT: Ozlem Fraser, Administrative Co-ordinator.

UKLA ACADEMY LANGUAGE SCHOOL
Dikkaldirim MH. Zübeyde Hn Cd. 15/A Demir Apt 16090 Osmangazi – Bursa
☎ +90 224 232 1440
✆ english@ukla.com.tr
🖳 www.ukla.com.tr

NUMBER OF TEACHERS: 15–20 per year.

PREFERENCE OF NATIONALITY: Must be native speakers as this is government policy for foreign English teacher employment.

QUALIFICATIONS: Bachelor's degree and CELTA or equivalent certification. Relevant experience is an advantage.

CONDITIONS OF EMPLOYMENT: One year contract with 20–30 teaching hours per week.

FACILITIES/SUPPORT: Fully furnished shared housing close to the school is offered to teachers. Assistance is given with applying for work permits.

RECRUITMENT: Process involves an application essay, lesson plan and a final interview carried out over the phone.

CONTACT: Canan Aktung, Director of Studies.

Contradictions abound in a continent as complex as Africa, and one of them pertains to the attitude to the English language. On the one hand the emergent nations of Africa want to distance themselves from their colonial past. Hence the renaming of Leopoldville, Salisbury and Upper Volta to become Kinshasa, Harare and Burkina Faso. On the other hand, they are eager to develop and participate in the world economy and so need to communicate in English.

What makes much of Africa different from Latin America and Asia (vis-à-vis English teaching) is that English is the medium of instruction in state schools in many ex-colonies of Britain including Ghana, Nigeria, Kenya, Zambia, Zimbabwe and Malawi. As in the Indian subcontinent, the majority of English teachers in these countries are locals. But there is still some demand for native English speakers in the secondary schools of those countries. The only countries in which there is any significant scope for working in a private language school or institute are the Mediterranean countries of Morocco, Tunisia and Egypt.

The drive towards English extends to most parts of the continent. VSO supports ELT programmes in Rwanda and Ethiopia, among others. More than a decade ago, newly independent Namibia decided to make English its official language to replace the hated Afrikaans. A demand for hundreds of native English speakers, mainly at the advanced teacher-trainer level, was created overnight, which organisations such as the Department for International Development and VSO attempted to supply. Across southern Africa, the dominant language of business and commerce and the language of university textbooks is English, leaving Portuguese-speaking Mozambique out in the cold. which is why there are so many EFL teachers posted there by Skillshare Africa and VSO.

To balance the picture, it must be said that in some countries (such as Zambia, Nigeria, Sudan) the demand for English teachers has fallen off in favour of science, maths, technology and other languages. Even in ex-colonies of France (Morocco, Tunisia, Senegal, Mali, etc.) and of Portugal (Mozambique), English is a sought-after commodity. World traveller **Bradwell Jackson** discovered paid on-the-spot teaching opportunities in Mali, Mauritania and Senegal. The British Council has nine Teaching Centres in Africa, including in Francophone Cameroon (Yaoundé the capital and Douala), Eritrea (Asmara) and Mauritius. Some other British Council offices have an English Language Officer (ELO) who may be willing to advise on local opportunities (or the lack thereof). The Council is active in North Africa particularly in Tunisia where it has a large teaching centre (87 Avenue Mohamed V, 1002 Tunis Belvédère, Tunisia; 71 84 85 88; info@tn.britishcouncil.org; www.britishcouncil.org/tunisia.htm).

Political instability has beleaguered a few of the countries where English is in demand, such as Algeria (which is currently too dangerous for expat teachers to consider) and Liberia from which scores of American teachers had to be evacuated some years ago. The situation in Zimbabwe has deteriorated to such an extent that most foreign teaching and voluntary programmes have ceased operations. The situation in Kenya is relatively calm at present, although the 2008 violence was a salutary warning that even African countries that seem stable and desirable (at least to holiday makers) can be politically volatile. The situation is different in North Africa where there is relatively more stability and prosperity.

PROSPECTS FOR TEACHERS

Few language schools exist in most African countries and even fewer can afford to employ expatriate teachers. The British Council maintains offices in most African countries and their assessment of the prospects for teachers tallies with that sent by the Information Manager of the British Council in Mbabane, Swaziland:

The English language is taught from a very early stage in Swaziland. As a result there are no institutes which specifically teach it. However, you may want to consider the university and colleges as institutions which teach English, even though it is at an advanced level.

Because a high proportion of teaching opportunities in Africa is in secondary schools rather than private language institutes, a teaching certificate is often a prerequisite. Missionary societies have played a dominant role in Africa's modern history, so many teachers are recruited through religious organisations, asking for a Christian commitment even for secular jobs. Apart from work with aid or missionary agencies, there are quite a few opportunities for students and people in their gap year to teach in Africa. Students and other travellers have also stumbled upon chances to teach on an informal basis.

FINDING A JOB

Many organisations including a range of gap year agencies send people to Africa to teach English. These postings are normally regarded as 'voluntary' since if wages are paid at all they will be on a local scale though they often come with free housing. In some cases a substantial placement fee must be paid. See the chapter 'Finding a job' in Part I of this book for further details of the general agencies that send students such as **Sarah Johnson** from Cardiff to Zanzibar to teach English and geography at a rural secondary school. Once she started work Sarah discovered that:

The expectations which Zanzibari children have from school are worlds away from those of British school children. They expect to spend most of their lessons copying from the blackboard, so will at first be completely nonplussed if asked to think things through by themselves or to use their imagination. I found that the ongoing dilemma for me of teaching in Zanzibar was whether to teach at a low level which the majority of the class would be able to understand, or teach the syllabus to the top one or two students so that they would be able to attempt exam questions, but leaving the rest of the class behind. Teaching was a very interesting and eye-opening experience. I believe that both the Zanzibari teachers and I benefitted from a cultural exchange of ideas and ways of life.

Networks like Couchsurfing (www.couchsurfing.com) have hosts registered all over Africa, who might be interested in exchanging hospitality for English lessons. **Bradwell Jackson** stayed with a couch-surfing host in Bamako, Mali, for two months:

He is a wealthy man who lives in a nice house, and I get all my meals, internet, my laundry, and a few other odds and ends done for free. I teach him two hours every day, which leaves me lots of time to explore Bamako and do whatever else I like.

Just one word of caution about internet offers: if you see a job advertised that looks too good to be true: $4,000 a month, say, for teaching in a relatively poor country such as Nigeria, then caution is advised. Although thankfully rare, scams aimed at 'greedy' foreigners can be sophisticated and seemingly plausible.

PLACEMENT ORGANISATIONS

Africa, Asia & Americas Venture, 10 Market Place, Devizes, Wiltshire SN10 1HT (01380 729009; av@aventure.co.uk; www.aventure.co.uk). Offers students and recent graduates (aged 18–24) the chance to spend 4–5 months teaching a wide variety of subjects, especially English and sports in Africa (Uganda, Kenya, Tanzania and Malawi). The 2010 participation fee is £3,125 for 4–5 months plus airfares.

Africatrust Networks, www.africatrust.org.uk. 3 or 6 month placements in Cameroon, Ghana (for English speaking volunteers), and Morocco (for French/Arabic speaking volunteers). Programme includes (not exclusively) teaching English in schools, rural community centres, urban computer centres and in orphanages/institutions for the disabled. London interviews throughout the year for departures mainly in January and September.

MondoChallenge (www.mondochallenge.co.uk). Volunteer teachers including year-out students, career breakers and others are sent to projects in three African countries: Tanzania (60 volunteers for projects in Longido, Arusha and Moshi), Gambia and Senegal. Fee of £2,140 for 3 months. Board and lodging in local family homes is included.

Peace Corps, 1111 20th St NW, Washington DC 20526 (+1 800 424 8580 (toll-free)). Volunteers teach on 27-month assignments in more than 25 African countries, ranging from Morocco to South Africa. Must be US citizen, over 18 and in good health. All expenses, including airfare and health insurance, are covered.

Projects Abroad, Aldsworth Parade, Goring, Sussex BN12 4TX (01903 708300; info@projects-abroad.co.uk; www.projects-abroad.co.uk.) Work placements in schools in Ethiopia, Ghana, Morocco, Senegal and South Africa.

Project Trust, Hebridean Centre, Ballyhough, Isle of Coll, Argyll PA78 6TE (01879 230444; info@projecttrust.org.uk; www.projecttrust.org.uk). Sends school leavers (aged 17–19) to teach (often other subjects as well as English) in schools across Africa including Namibia, Uganda, Botswana, Senegal and Swaziland. Participants must fund-raise to cover part of the cost of their 12-month placement, at present £4,660.

Skillshare International, 126 New Walk, Leicester LE1 7JA (0116 254 1862; www.skillshare.org). Registered charity that recruits volunteer teachers to work for two years in southern Africa (Lesotho, Botswana, Mozambique, Swaziland, Namibia, Kenya, Tanzania, Uganda and South Africa). Pay approximately £500 per month plus flights, accommodation, insurance, etc.

Travellers (www.travellersworldwide.com). Teaching placements (English, Maths, Drama, etc.) and Sports Coaching placements in Ghana, Kenya, South Africa and Zambia.

VAE Teachers Kenya, Bell Lane Cottage, Pudleston, Nr. Leominster, Herefordshire HR6 0RE; 01568 750329; vaekenya@googlemail.com; www.vaekenya.co.uk. 3-month or preferably 6-month gap year placements teaching in rural schools in the central highlands of Kenya. Inclusive fee of about £3,350. (No vacancies until 2012.)

Village Education Project (Kilimanjaro), c/o Katy Allen, Mint Cottage, Prospect Road, Sevenoaks, Kent TN13 3UA (01732 743000; project@kiliproject.org; www.kiliproject.org). 6–9-month attachments to village primary schools in the district of Marangu in Tanzania for about eight participants a year, both gap year students and people taking career breaks. Training is given in the UK for two weeks before departure. The cost to the volunteers for participating in the project is about £3,250.

Village-to-Village, Bradford (enquiries@village-to-village.org.uk; www.village-to-village.org.uk). Volunteers are sent to the Kilimanjaro region to assist on various projects including teaching English in primary schools and orphanages, teacher training as well as construction and sustainable agriculture projects. Typical 8-week placement requires a minimum donation of £1,450 (excluding international flights). The third and fourth months are charged at £300 each, and the following two months at £150 each. Accommodation is provided in volunteer centre or homestay.

Village Africa, Surrey (01242 250 901; www.villageafrica.org.uk). Current initiatives are to provide volunteers to teach English for 3 or more months in Yamba and Milingano, villages in the West Usambara Mountains of Tanzania, among other projects.

VSO, 317 Putney Bridge Road, London SW15 2PN (020 8780 7500, www.vsointernational. org). Leading international development charity sends teachers to Ethiopia, Mozambique, Tanzania, Eritrea and Rwanda. Placements are usually for one or two years, and all costs and accommodation are covered.

WorldTeach, Harvard University, Cambridge, Massachusetts 02138, USA (617 495 5527; www. worldteach.org). Nonprofit organisation that recruits volunteers to teach English in Namibia, Kenya, Rwanda and South Africa, among other countries around the world.

ON THE SPOT

The best chances of picking up language teaching work on the spot are in North Africa, in Egypt, Morocco or Tunisia (treated separately below). Language schools are thriving in South Africa staffed in large measure by English-speaking South Africans but also by foreigners. Tourists can enter South Africa on a tourist visa for three months, renewable for a further three (for a fee) at an office of the Department of Home Affairs.

If teachers (British as well as American) are prepared to travel to an African capital for an interview with one of the US State Department-sponsored English teaching centres in Africa (often attached to American embassies), they may be given some freelance opportunities. Virtually all hiring of teachers in these government-run language programmes takes place locally, so speculative applications from overseas are seldom welcome. This is how one American got her foot in the door and went on to become the director:

> *Work in an American Cultural Center is a great way to start off. I myself did it five years ago and am now running a programme. It allows a person to work in Africa but also provides up-to-date material which teachers in the national programmes are often forced to go without. Classes are small and the hours are not too heavy but can usually be increased depending on the capabilities of the teacher. We also do outside programmes in specialised institutions and thus give teachers experience in ESP (hotels, oil companies, Ministries). People with degrees in EFL are very much in demand.*

At the opposite end of the spectrum, grass roots voluntary organisations may have teaching positions. For example Ikando (www.ikando.org) is a volunteer and intern recruitment agency based in Accra which deals with education positions lasting up to eight weeks, as well as many others. Volunteers stay in the Ikando house in the centre of Accra and cover their living expenses (£87 per week after their initial fortnight at £481).

Till Bruckner is a veteran world traveller who has a decided preference for fixing up teaching and voluntary placements independently:

> *My advice to anyone who wants to volunteer in Africa (or anywhere else) is to go first and volunteer second. That way you can travel until you've found a place you genuinely like and where you think you might be able to make a difference. You can also check out the work and accommodation for yourself before you settle down. If you're willing to work for free, you don't need a nanny to tell you where to go. Just go.*

Opportunities crop up in very obscure corners of the continent. For example EU nationals are entitled to work in Réunion, a département of France between Madagascar and Mauritius. Apparently there is a market for freelance teachers; consider advertising in the papers *Quotidien* and *SIR*.

PROBLEMS AND REWARDS

If teachers in Finland and Chile suffer from culture shock, teachers in rural Africa often find themselves struggling to cope at all. Whether it is the hassle experienced by women teachers in Muslim North Africa or the loneliness of life in a rural West African village, problems proliferate. Anyone who has fixed up a contract should try to gather as much up-to-date information as possible before departure, preferably by attending some kind of orientation programme or briefing. Otherwise local customs can come as a shock. On a more basic level, you will need advice on how to cope with climatic extremes. Even Cairo can be unbearably hot in the summer (and surprisingly rainy and chilly in January/February).

One unexpected problem is being accorded too much respect, as **Mary Hall** describes:

> *A white person is considered to be the be-all and end-all of everyone's problems for whatever reason. It's quite difficult to live with this image. Stare and stare again, never a moment to yourself. I'd like to say the novelty wore off but it never did. Obviously adaptability has to be one of the main qualities. We had no running water, intermittent electricity and a lack of such niceties as cheese and chocolate.*

A certain amount of deprivation is almost inevitable; for example teachers, especially volunteers, can seldom afford to shop in the pricey expatriate stores and so will have to be content with the local diet, typically a staple cereal such as millet usually made into a kind of stodgy porridge, plus some cooked greens, tinned fish or meat and fruit. The cost of living in some African cities such as Libreville and Douala is in fact very high, and a teaching wage does not normally permit a luxurious lifestyle. **Peter Kent** taught in Tanzania and kept a journal throughout his stay:

> *Bit worried about the food situation, only seems to be tomatoes, onions and potatoes at the market so a pretty boring diet. Sijaona is, if I understand her right, going to show us where you can buy more exotic veg... Taught standard one (i.e. year 1) today for the first time since they started this term. There are 105 kids, 5 or 6 to a bench which fits 3 normally. Quite a sight really, 105 bright-eyed kids staring expectantly at you. Mrs Msigwa, their teacher, seems really nice, keen and capable. We may get somewhere between us. You get the impression that if you stuck with them for years to come they'd be speaking English.*

But of course volunteer teachers can't stick around that long and after less than a year it was time for Peter Kent to bid farewell to his school amidst present-giving, choir singing and emotional speeches.

Health is obviously a major concern to anyone headed for Africa. The fear of HIV-contaminated blood or needles in much of central Africa prompts many teachers to outfit themselves with a complete expat medical kit before leaving home (see Introduction). Malaria is rife and there is an alarming amount of mosquito resistance to the most common prophylactics, so this too must be sorted out with a tropical diseases expert before departure.

The visa situation differs from country to country of course but is often a headache. Whereas in Cameroon it is not really necessary to obtain a work permit, in Ethiopia it is much more problematic.

If all that Africa could offer was a contest with malaria and a diet of porridge, no one would consider teaching there. But anyone who has seen movies such as *Out of Africa, Gorillas in the Mist* or *The English Patient* can imagine how the continent holds people in thrall. A chance to see the African bush, to climb the famous peaks of Kilimanjaro or Kenya, to frequent the colourful markets, these are the pleasures of Africa which so many people who have worked there find addictive.

EGYPT

Despite past attacks on tourists by Islamic fundamentalists, there is anything but hostility to the English language in Egypt. Of Egyptians who want to learn English, a large percentage is from the business community, though there is also a demand among university students and school children. Many young Egyptians who aspire to work in their country's computing or tourist industry want to learn English. Students at computer training schools or at tourism training centres like the one in Luxor might be looking for some private tuition from a native speaker.

Check the online *Yellow Pages* in English at www.egyptyellowpages.com.eg; a search for 'Schools – Language' reveals nearly 200. At one end of the spectrum there are the two British Council Teaching Centres in Cairo (Agouza and Heliopolis) and the International Language Institute in Cairo affiliated to International House (www.arabicegypt.com). At the other there are plenty of dubious establishments. Whereas you will need a professional profile for the former, back street schools will be less fussy. The British Council in Cairo has a list of English medium schools in Cairo plus a short list of TEFL establishments, several of which are in the suburb of Dokki. The Council was recently hiring a number of new teachers itself because of growth in the numbers signing up for General English and Corporate courses.

The British Council at 192 El Nil Street, Agouza, Cairo is probably the first place to check for work. The minimum requirements are native English speaker status, UK passport, CELTA or equivalent and two years' post-qualification teaching experience. You can pick up an application form from the British Council reception or by email at teacherapplications@britishcouncil.org.eg. You will be invited for an interview and demonstration lesson (having sat in on another class beforehand). If they think you are suitable they'll take you on, which is more likely during the summer when the regular teachers tend to go away to escape the heat. During exam time there is also a need for paid invigilators. The British Council (as always) has a great library and is a good place to teach. There is another British Council in Heliopolis which is quite a way from the centre of town and therefore has its own social world. The El-Alsson School (PO Box 13, Embaba, 12411 Cairo; 2 388 8510; info@alsson. com; www.alsson.com) out near the Pyramids employs a number of expat teachers.

Dan Boothby has spent time in Cairo and found it almost alarmingly easy to find work:

I taught one-to-one lessons to several people and got about 5 hours a week work and charged £10 an hour. Frankly this was much more than I was worth but if you charge less than the market rate then it is felt that you are an amateur. I taught an isolated and lonely 5 year old, son of the Georgian Consul, where I was more a babysitter than a tutor. I felt so guilty about the fee I was charging that I spent an hour trying to get him to learn something. I didn't feel so guilty charging to tutor the Georgian Ambassador since he probably passed the bill onto his government.

I got a lot of students through friends that I made who were teaching at the international schools. The kids at these schools are often in need of extra tuition towards exam times when their parents realise that they've been mucking about all year and are close to failing. The problem is that the kids tend to be very uninterested and so it is difficult to make them concentrate. But I enjoyed one-to-ones. One could build up a large group of students and earn a decent wage but equally teach less hours and have more time – one of the reasons for getting out of England.

Cairo seems to be a city where work seeks out the casual teacher rather than the other way round. Taxi drivers and hotel staff may ask you, unprompted, if you are available to teach. Most of these are genuine offers but it is best (especially for women) to be cautious. Most job-seekers find that potential bosses are not as interested in their educational background and experience as in how much confidence they can project. It is not unknown for an interview to take place over a game of chess and plenty of glasses of tea so that your general demeanour can be assessed. Jobs seem to be available year-round, so there is no right or wrong time to arrive.

Language schools are not all located in central Cairo but also in the leafy prosperous residential areas such as Heliopolis, Maadi or Zamalek. For example the Al Bashaer Language School is behind the bakery in District 9, New Maadi (2 516 8245; info@albashaerschools.com; www.albashaer-schools.com). Teachers must have A levels and three years' teaching experience and are paid a monthly base salary of 1,000 Egyptian pounds in addition to free accommodation and a food allowance. The school's mission is to 'apply western methods of teaching with Islamic ideas and etiquette'.

Residential areas are also the best areas to look for private clients as **Ian McArthur** found:

> *In Cairo I sought to work as a private English tutor. I made a small poster, written in English and Arabic, with the help of my hotel owner. I drew the framework of a Union Jack at the top, got 100 photocopies and then meticulously coloured in the flags. The investment cost me £3. I put the posters up around Cairo, concentrating on affluent residential and business districts. I ended up teaching several Egyptian businessmen, who were difficult to teach since they hated being told what to do.*

A simpler way of advertising your availability to teach might be to place an advert in the expatriate monthly *Egypt Today* (www.egypttoday.com) or the fortnightly *Maadi Messenger* (www.maadimes-senger.info) published by the Maadi Women's Guild and distributed through expat haunts like English-speaking churches. Another publication to look out for is the *Middle East Times* (www. metimes.com). The American University, centrally located at the eastern end of Tahrir Square, is a good place to find work contacts though teaching for the AUC itself is difficult; only five candidates a month are granted an interview so they can afford to be highly selective. Also try the noticeboards at the Community Services Association (CSA No. 4, Road 21, Maadi, Cairo; 358 5284) where a range of adult education courses for expats is offered. In fact beginners and conversational English are taught on the premises. If you do decide to advertise your services as a freelance tutor, it might be a good idea to rent a post office box from a business centre (e.g. the IBA Center in Garden City).

According to **Dan Boothby**, the best places to meet other expats and find out about work opportunities are Deals Bar, restaurants in Zamalek, café-bars near the American University and the BCA (British Community Association) in Mohandiseen where you can only go as the guest of a member. Sunny Supermarket in Zamalek has a good noticeboard for jobs and flat shares.

STUDENTS

One former teacher describes his Egyptian pupils at a language institute in the northwest suburb of Sahafeyeen as 'rowdy and sometimes a little over-enthusiastic'. Having just obtained a Cambridge Certificate in London, he went to visit some friends in Cairo and was immediately offered a three-month summer contract where they were desperate for a teacher. He had to adapt his lessons to please both the ebullient Egyptian youths and a group of shy and industrious Somalis and describes his predicament with such a mixed class:

> *Different religions, different ways of thinking and (as I learnt in my first week at the school) different modes of dress must all be taken into consideration. One of the problems that English students in this area have difficulty with is hearing the difference between B and P. The exercise for this is to hold a piece of paper in front of the mouth and repeat the letters B and P. Since more air is exhaled during the sounding of the letter P than with B, the paper should fly up when P is said, and move only a little with B. The first time I made the students do this we went round the class, first Hamid the engineer from Alexandria, then Mona who was trying to get a job at the reception in the Hilton and then we came to Magda from Mogadishu (the capital of Somalia). All the Egyptians started to laugh – her whole face apart from her eyes was covered with a yashmak. I decided that this should not impede the exercise so if the yashmak moved it was a P, and not a B!*

Wages at the less prestigious schools will probably start at E£2,000 per month rising to E£4,500 (gross) at Heliopolis. Living expenses are cheap in Egypt and taxes low (5%-7%). The CELTA course offered by the British Council used to be one of the cheapest in the world, however, with the weak pound, the current fee of E£10,000 works out at an expensive £1,130.

Most teachers enter Egypt on a tourist visa and then ask their school to help them extend it. The tourist visa is valid for a maximum of three months. However, a business visa is issued for teachers to enter Egypt. This is valid for 6 months and schools will help to extend it. Work permits must be applied for from the Ministry of the Interior in Egypt, usually by your employer. UK citizens can find up-to-date visa information at www.egyptianconsulate.co.uk.

LIST OF EMPLOYERS

AMIDEAST EGYPT

Cairo Office: 23 Mossadak Street, Dokki-Giza, 12311 Cairo

📞 +20 2 19263/+20 2 333 20457

✉ egypt@amideast.org or akaram@amideast.org

🖥 www.amideast.org

Alexandria Office: 3 El Pharana Street, Alexandria

✉ alexandria@amideast.org

🖥 www.amideast.org

NUMBER OF TEACHERS: 15–22.

PREFERENCE OF NATIONALITY: North American, but all native English speakers are welcome to apply.

QUALIFICATIONS: Minimum CELTA or TESOL certification, and preferably 2 years of teaching adults.

CONDITIONS OF EMPLOYMENT: Local term-to-term hire agreements according to student numbers. 8–15 hours per week, 9 5-week sessions per year. Students are working adults and university students.

SALARY: US$5.50–$8 an hour (paid in local currency). Contracted teachers earn US$13, less 17.65% for tax and contributions.

FACILITIES/SUPPORT: Good teachers' resources, internet access, friendly working environment. Operates out of three historic mansions on the Mediterranean. No financial assistance with accommodation given, but temporary housing can be arranged at no cost. No assistance given with work permits.

RECRUITMENT: Pre-interview questions sent to applicants via email, and then a classroom demonstration.

CONTACT: David Godsted, Country Director; Ahmed Karam, English Language Programmes Senior Coordinator.

SUDAN

The long-established NGO, the Sudan Volunteer Programme, based in London and Khartoum (see entry), sends volunteers to help young Sudanese improve their English through contact with British volunteers. According to **Don Sloan**, writing in the most recent *SVP Newsletter*, English assignments include running discussion groups, providing support for teachers at universities, training for public servants, teacher-training course design, and developing course materials for English for legal purposes. Other volunteers have run General English courses and helped with English clubs, especially for pre-sessional and inter-sessional groups of university students. Some volunteers have recently produced and participated in radio programmes for learners of English and done editorial work for an English language newspaper, so there is plenty of scope for pursuing individual talents and interests.

This is all good news for a country in which the current government has shown little inclination to support the teaching of English as a second language and has instead promoted the Arabisation of the country's educational system. As a result, the general standard of English has sharply declined. However, English remains Sudan's second official language and is likely to be the official language of the South if, as widely expected, Southerners vote for secession in a 2011 referendum on self-determination. It also remains the language of instruction for medicine and engineering.

Some are worried about their personal security based on media coverage and FCO travel warnings. The director of the Sudan Volunteer Programme describes what he sees as the FCO bias:

> *We continue to be dogged by the negative and, I believe, misleadingly indiscriminate travel advice issued by the FCO which puts off potential volunteers, or more particularly their families. It stems it seems to me from the alarming experiences of embassy staff which induces them to put up ever higher fences to guard their premises and of course this siege mentality brings about an ever greater ignorance of the actual conditions. There was one threat to embassy security about 3 years ago and one murder of an American official in Khartoum in January 2008. There were otherwise no attacks in the recent years on foreigners in Khartoum or smaller northern towns. I do not belittle these outrages but they cannot be described as 'indiscriminate' as used in the FCO warning.*

Since the signing in 2005 of the Comprehensive Peace Agreement (CPA) between the Government of Sudan and factions in the South, volunteers have been posted in Juba for the first time. Travel to most parts of Sudan is much easier than it was and the rapid pace of development, since oil has come on stream, has brought about big changes – new roads, more cars, more shops, more building projects.

MARK TANNER, a New Zealand adventurer, found out about the Sudan Volunteer Programme by searching the web and was accepted onto the scheme:

While some volunteers were required to use the syllabus as a guide, I had a free rein over what I taught and how. This prompted me to ask the students to suggest topics that were of interest to them and allowed me freedom to encourage discussion about parts of the Sudanese culture I was interested in. The main objective was to provide the students with a native English speaker and get them used to conversation. We were encouraged to do less formal sessions called the English Club. For example we themed the cooking class as our university was all-female and cooking was something they considered important. Some classes stand out in my memory such as the one where we tried to teach the students to juggle. The classrooms could be quite hot and were equipped with blackboard and chalk, although we used teaching aids based on our own initiative.

The lodgings provided were basic, but by Sudanese standards good. The stipend was enough to subsist in Sudan, living like the Sudanese. As lovely as the Sudanese are, things are not as organised in the country as we would expect in the west. Yet it would be difficult to find more hospitable people than the Sudanese and there is never a shortage of offers for dinner or to visit a village, which provided a fantastic opportunity to experience the culture in a way many other NGO workers never saw.

There are many interesting things to see in Khartoum such as Nuba Wrestling, fish markets, Dervish dancing and museums. SVP has a deal with the Blue Nile Sailing Club which allows students to try their luck at sailing on the Nile. Many of the volunteers did other voluntary work for NGOs. I helped an NGO with marketing and to develop a website. My principal motivation for being in the Sudan was to paddle through Sudan on the Nile, and I spent a lot of my spare time trying to source permits for this.

One of the highlights for me was seeing the English of the students improve and the relationships develop from that. Teachers are greatly respected in the Sudan so volunteers are revered and treated with respect.

Not everyone is so positive about being placed by an agency, especially if their motives are strictly philanthropic. The placement that was fixed up for **Till Bruckner** in Sudan didn't live up to his expectations:

They'd told me at my interview in London that I'd be teaching international politics but when I arrived the local branch didn't know what I'd come for and wanted me to teach conversational English at a university in Khartoum. I figured that if I was going to teach English to kids from well-off families while living in a city of outstanding natural ugliness, I might as well go elsewhere and get paid for it. There'd be no problem finding work as an English teacher in Sudan. There's great demand and little supply as nobody (including most Sudanese) wants to live there. In a country with poverty on that scale, there's more useful things you can do with £500 than pay for a scheme to tutor English. If you want fun, go elsewhere; if you want to help, put the £500 in an Oxfam charity box.

However, that is just one point of view and many people have felt that their contribution as a volunteer teacher has not been futile, either from the point of view of broadening their own horizons or helping others.

LIST OF EMPLOYERS

ALENEA RECRUITING

29–30 Windmill Street, London W1T 2JL, UK

📞 020 7462 6481

✉ info@alenea.com

💻 www.alenearecruiting.com.

Recruiting for a training institute in Khartoum.

QUALIFICATIONS: Must have CELTA/Trinity plus experience teaching young learners.

CONDITIONS OF EMPLOYMENT: 9 or 12-month contracts. Hours in primary schools are from 8am to 2pm and from 9am to 9pm in EFL institutes.

SALARY: $1,300 net per month.

FACILITIES/SUPPORT: Flights, accommodation, visas and in-country travel are all provided.

RECRUITMENT: Applications accepted all year round.

SUDAN VOLUNTEER PROGRAMME

34 Estelle Road, London NW3 2JY, UK

📞 020 7485 8619;

✉ david@svp-uk.com

💻 www.svp-uk.com

UK registered charity which promotes English teaching among university students and other adults.

NUMBER OF TEACHERS: 10–20 at any time in and around Khartoum including Omdurman.

PREFERENCE OF NATIONALITY: None but should be native speakers of English and if not, they should be qualified English language teachers.

QUALIFICATIONS: TEFL certificate, experience of travelling in developing countries and some knowledge of Arabic are helpful but not obligatory. Volunteers must be in good health and have some university education.

CONDITIONS OF EMPLOYMENT: Preferred minimum 8 months to tie in with university semesters: October–January or January–May.

SALARY: SVP pays subsistence, accommodation and insurance beyond the initial 3 months. Volunteers must raise the cost of the airfare to Sudan (currently £485) plus £65 (towards the cost of the first 3 months' insurance).

FACILITIES/SUPPORT: Accommodation with self-catering facilities is arranged, usually at the university where you are teaching.

RECRUITMENT: Applications accepted year round. Two referees are also required. Prior to departure, medical check-up required plus selection interviews, orientation and briefings take place. Volunteers are required to write a report of their experiences and to advise new volunteers.

CONTACT: David Wolton.

KENYA

Kenya is another country with a chronic shortage of school teachers. Since 2003 when the government kept its promise to abolish school fees for primary schools, there has been a surge in student numbers. The worst shortages are in Western Province. English is the language of instruction in many Kenyan primary schools, so foreign teachers not knowing Swahili need not be an insuperable barrier. The Kenyan Ministry of Education restricts jobs in the state sector to those who have a university degree, teaching certification and at least one year of professional teaching experience. The few private language institutes that there are in Nairobi are not subject to this restriction. The British Council in Nairobi at Upperhill Road (20 283 6000; information@britishcouncil.or.ke) may be able to offer advice. One institute which carries information about year-round job openings on its website is The Language Center (PO Box 40661, Nairobi 00100; info@language-cntr.com); it hires native speakers with a degree and a recognised TEFL qualification.

According to the Kenyan High Commission in London (45 Portland Place, London W1B 1AS; 020 7636 2371), all non-Kenyan citizens who wish to work must be in possession of a work permit issued by the Principal Immigration Officer, Department of Immigration, PO Box 30191, Nairobi, before they can take up paid or unpaid work. The school should apply for work permits for the teachers even before they enter Kenya. Proof of professional qualifications is required. However, it is not certain that immigration regulations would be strictly enforced in the case of native English speakers looking for teaching work on the spot. Certainly in the past it was possible to fix up a teaching job by asking in the villages, preferably before terms begin in September, January and April. Be prepared to produce your CV and any diplomas and references on headed paper.

Also ascertain before accepting a post whether or not the school can afford to pay a salary, especially if it is a Harrambee school, i.e. non-government, self-help schools in rural areas. A cement or mud hut with a thatched or tin roof will usually be provided for the teacher's accommodation plus a local salary which would be just enough to live on provided you don't want to buy too much peanut butter or cornflakes in the city. Living conditions will be primitive, with no running water or electricity in the majority of cases. The Kenyan version of maize porridge is called *Ugali*. In Daisy Waugh's book *A Small Town in Africa* (no longer in print) she describes how when she arrived at the village of Isiolo (a few miles from Nairobi) where she had arranged to teach, she was told that they didn't need any teachers and there were no pupils. She patiently waited and five weeks into term, her class arrived.

People who choose to teach in Kenya do it for love not money. In the words of Ermon O. Kamara, PhD, former Director of the American Universities Preparation Institute in Nairobi:

> *Candidates must view being in Kenya as a holiday with pay. The cost of living and corresponding local salaries sound quite low to foreigners. Consequently they must think of the opportunities to enjoy Kenya's beaches, mountains and game parks as well as experiencing a new and interesting culture. During weekends and holidays, one can travel the breadth of Kenya. Also the proximity to other countries in East and Southern Africa permits a traveller to see a good deal of our continent.*

AVIF UK (Fair Mount, Hartwith Avenue, Summerbridge, North Yorkshire HG3 4HT; 0777 171 2012; volunteer@avif.org.uk; www.avif.org.uk) sends volunteers to help at children's summer schools in Kenya, including with teaching English. Volunteers pay only the price of the airfare plus subsistence costs to spend the month of August in Kenya. At the end of each programme, AVIF can advise volunteers on how to join a safari from a base camp in Oropile, Maasai Mara or to climb Kilimanjaro with an experienced guide.

LIST OF EMPLOYERS

THE LANGUAGE CENTER LTD
P.O Box 40661, 00100 Nairobi
+254 020 3869531, 3869532, 3870610, 3870612
tlc@language-cntr.com
www.language-cntr.com

NUMBER OF TEACHERS: Approximately 6.
PREFERENCE OF NATIONALITY: British, American.
QUALIFICATIONS: Minimum first degree plus CELTA, TESOL or any other recognised TEFL qualification.

CONDITIONS OF EMPLOYMENT: Standard length of contract is 2 years. Normal working hours 8.30am to 4pm.
SALARY: Around $8.50–$11 per hour for the first year plus medical insurance and gratuity.
FACILITIES/SUPPORT: Employer will handle the application process for work permits and pay half of the total expenses.
RECRUITMENT: Usually via internet or word of mouth. Interviews are essential and are conducted locally.
CONTACT: Agnes W. Ngugi, Managing Director.

MOROCCO

Although Morocco is a Francophone country, English is a requirement for entrance to university or high-ranking jobs, and there is increasing demand from the business communities of the main cities. Like so many African countries, Morocco has sought to improve the standards of education for its nationals so that almost all teaching jobs in schools and universities are now filled by Moroccans. But outside the state system there is a continuing demand for native English speakers.

The Moroccan Ministry of Labour stipulates that the maximum number of foreign staff in any organisation cannot exceed 50%. It also insists that all foreign teachers have at least a university degree before they can be eligible for a work permit. Work permits are obtained after arrival by applying for authorisation from the Ministère de l'Emploi, Quartier des Ministères, Rabat. You will need copies of your diplomas, birth certificate and so on. Although a knowledge of French is not a formal requirement, it is a great asset for anyone planning to spend time in Morocco.

A number of commercial language schools employ native English speakers. The hourly rate of pay at most schools is between $15 and $22 (equivalent in dirhams). The American Language Centers are located in the main cities of Morocco; see the website www.aca.org.ma for details. They are private institutes but are affiliated to and partially funded by the US State Department. Two are included in the list of employers. The Casablanca branch (http://casablanca.aca.org.ma/vacancies. asp) recruits native English speaker teachers from a number of courses including academic institutes in the USA such as the University of North Texas, which offers a graduate certificate in TESOL.

The workcamps movement is active in Morocco and some of these summer volunteer projects take place on English language camps for Moroccan adolescents (see CSM entry below).

LIST OF EMPLOYERS

AMERICAN LANGUAGE CENTER

1 Place de la Fraternité, Casablanca 20000

✆ +212 522 277765

✉ casa_dir@aca.org.ma

🖥 www.aca.org.ma or http://casablanca.aca. org.ma

NUMBER OF TEACHERS: 12–15 full-time teachers (mostly native speakers) plus about 40 part-time Moroccan teachers.

PREFERENCE OF NATIONALITY: North American, but British teachers are also welcome to apply.

QUALIFICATIONS: Bachelor's degree, TEFL Certification (CELTA preferred) and a minimum of 1 year EFL overseas teaching experience.

CONDITIONS OF EMPLOYMENT: A standard contract is for 12 months from 1 October to 30 September. 18 contact hours a week are standard for the Adult Program. However, some teachers have additional classes including young learners.

SALARY: Based on qualifications and experience. For example a bachelor's degree, certification and 3 years of TEFL experience would expect the equivalent of $22 per hour. There is also a tax-free housing allowance of up to 3,000 Dhs per month plus a 5,000 Dhs settling in

allowance which is also tax free. Taxes on salaries are relatively high (approximately 18% of the gross.) Complete medical insurance (80% reimbursable) is provided for all full-time teachers. A ticket to the teacher's residence in the USA (for North Americans) or UK (for British teachers) is provided if a teacher successfully completes 1 year at the Center. There is also an end of contract bonus.

RECRUITMENT: Send CVs with photo, scanned copies of original diplomas and 2 letters of recommendation. All paperwork necessary for teachers to obtain work permits is done by administration staff. New teachers have to bring a copy of their birth certificate and their original University diplomas and certificates.

CONTACT: David Neuses (casa_dir@aca.org.ma).

AMERICAN LANGUAGE CENTER, RABAT

4 Zankat Tanja, Rabat 10000

✆ 37 767103

✉ dir@alcrabat.org

NUMBER OF TEACHERS: 20 full-time and 25 part-time teachers.

PREFERENCE OF NATIONALITY: Applicants should be from a country where English is the first language.

QUALIFICATIONS: BA in Education, TESOL, or related field; knowledge of French or Arabic highly desirable. TEFL certification required.

CONDITIONS OF EMPLOYMENT: 1-year renewable contracts. 20–25 hours per week full time. Hours of work generally between 2pm and 9pm weekdays (Tuesday to Friday) and 9am and 5pm on Saturdays. Pupils aged from 7, mostly aged 14–35.

SALARY: Approximately $1,500 per month (gross) for October to July school year. Possibility of paid overtime. Paid sick leave and medical insurance provided as well as vacation allowance and round-trip airfare upon completing 2 years.

FACILITIES/SUPPORT: Free housing/homestay provided for 2 weeks while permanent accommodation is sought. Pre- and in-service training fully supported. Free access to high-speed internet, free language classes (French and Arabic) and other benefits.

RECRUITMENT: Through TESOL convention and some local hiring. Video conference interviews are also used.

CONTACT: Hal Ott, Director.

AMIDEAST

35 Rue Oukaimeden, Agdal, Rabat

℆ 37 67 50 75/81/82

Also: 3 Boulevard Al Massira Al Khadra, Maarif, Casablanca

℆ 22 25 93 93

🖱 knorris@amideast.org

💻 www.amideast.org/morocco

NUMBER OF TEACHERS: Approximately 35.

PREFERENCE OF NATIONALITY: Must be native English speakers.

QUALIFICATIONS: TEFL qualification.

CONDITIONS OF EMPLOYMENT: 1-year contracts, preferably with a view to extending. To work around 70–100 hours per month.

FACILITIES/SUPPORT: Settling-in allowance. Assistance with apartment search and work visas, which must be acquired within 3 months of arrival.

RECRUITMENT: CV and cover letter to knorris@amideast. org. Telephone interview required.

CONTACT: Kenn Norris, Director of Studies for Morocco.

BUSINESS AND PROFESSIONAL ENGLISH CENTRE (BPEC)

74, Rue Jean Jaurès, Casablanca

℆ +212 522 47 02 79

Branch office: Porte Verde, Imm N, 1 er etage, Mahaj Ryad, Hay Ryad, Rabat

℆ +212 537 57 07 57

🖱 info@bpec-english.com/ info-rabat@ bpec-english.com

💻 www.bpec-english.com

NUMBER OF TEACHERS: 4.

PREFERENCE OF NATIONALITY: British, American or Australian.

QUALIFICATIONS: Bachelor's or master's degree plus CELTA and minimum of 3 years' experience in teaching adults and young learners.

CONDITIONS OF EMPLOYMENT: 1-year renewable contract. Split shifts spread over the day between 8am and 9pm (no more then 4.5 hours teaching per day).

SALARY: 13,000 dirhams net.

FACILITIES/SUPPORT: Up to 1-week hotel accommodation provided then assistance will be given to find housing. Work permits are organised by the centre.

RECRUITMENT: Usually via www.tefl.com. Interviews are essential and can be carried out over the phone.

CONTACT: Riyad Mugawer, Managing Director, or Kaoutar Lasmak, Centre Manager, BPEC Rabat.

CHANTIERS SOCIAUX MAROCAINS (CSM – ICYE MOROCCO)

BP 456, Rabat

🖱 csm@wanadoo.net.ma or csm_morocco@ yahoo.fr

💻 www.csm.netsons.org

NUMBER OF TEACHERS: 40 volunteers in Rabat, Marrakech, Fez, Sale, Kenitra and Casablanca.

QUALIFICATIONS: Skills teaching children are required. French or Arabic an advantage. Independent attitude and the ability to work in difficult circumstances with little support.

CONDITIONS OF EMPLOYMENT: Voluntary work teaching English to Moroccan youths aged 15–18 from modest or poor families. Programmes run throughout the year and in the summer. Volunteers teach 25–30 students for 4 hours a day, Monday to Friday.

SALARY: Voluntary work. Volunteers pay approximately £580, covering return flights, insurance, induction and administration.

FACILITIES/SUPPORT: Local host families provide board and lodging. Pre-camp orientation at the beginning of July.

CONTACT: Raziq Abdeerazzak (Rabat) or Rachad Izzat at the above emails.

TUNISIA

Like its neighbour in the Maghreb, Tunisia is turning away from the language of its former colonial master. Although the young generation speaks fluent French because they have been taught it in school, many teenagers prefer English. Both Amideast (see entry) and the British Council Tunis Teaching Centre employ qualified native English speaker teachers. The latter runs a summer school in June and July with extra vacancies; teachers earn £1,800 for the whole period plus accommodation and flights.

ROGER MUSKER *found that people would be interested in paying you for lessons, even though you plan to be in the country for a relatively short time. He was in Tunisia for one winter:*

I decided to take a month off work as a kind of sabbatical and, if well planned, at no cost. I found all young people in Tunisia keen to practise and speak English whenever possible. I had one good contact in Sousse, who worked for the Tunisian Tourist Agency. I wrote to him from England and he replied that he could line up students on my arrival, which included himself and his ten-year-old daughter (who turned out to be my best student). At their house I was plied with extremely sweet tea and sticky cakes, which you are obliged to eat. Altogether I had eight keen fee-paying students including a blind telephone operator, a teacher of English on a revision course and students from the Bourguiba Institute at Sousse University, which claims to be the second oldest university in the world. For the latter it was necessary to get permission from the Ministry of Education via the headmaster.

Every day I tutored 8–10am and 5–7pm. The hourly rate was about £8, allowing me to cover basic costs while having a working holiday. Even without the contact and knowing Arabic, work is there for the asking. It just takes initiative. Go to any official institute, the tourism or municipal offices, demonstrate your availability and enthusiasm, give them your contact number and await replies.

The Bourguiba Institute in Tunis (47 Av. de la Liberté, 1002 Tunis; 71 832923; lblv@lblv.rnu.tn; www.lblv.rnu.tn) hires high-level teachers.

AMIDEAST TUNISIA
22 Rue Al Amine Al Abassi, B.P. 351, Cité Jardina
1002, Tunis
℡ 71 790 559/563, 841 488 or 842 523
✉ tunisia@amideast.org
🖥 www.amideast.org

NUMBER OF TEACHERS: 25 full or part-time independent contract TEFL/TESL teachers.

PREFERENCE OF NATIONALITY: Native speakers of English.

QUALIFICATIONS: Ideally a degree or accredited international certificate in TEFL/TESL. 2 years' successful experience of teaching English to non-native speakers would be a plus.

CONDITIONS OF EMPLOYMENT: 1 year. Half of return airfare from teacher's home reimbursed at end of contract. Classes for children, teenagers and adults held between 8.30am and 9pm. Courses also run for public and private sector organisations.

SALARY: US$12–$13.50 per hour depending on qualifications and experience.

FACILITIES/SUPPORT: School will on request try to identify a Tunisian family willing to house the new teacher for an initial period until they find accommodation (with help of school). During the 4 months that American and Canadian citizens are allowed to stay as tourists, the school handles arrangements for getting a work permit and visa. A 500-dinar travel grant is paid at the end of the 1-year contract.

RECRUITMENT: Via www.amideast.org plus regional and international TEFL conferences.

CONTACT: Lee Jennings, Country Director (ljennings@amideast.org).

BRITISH COUNCIL TUNISIA
87 Avenue Mohamed V, BP 96 Le Belvédère 1002 Tunis
☎ +216 71 84 85 88 (ext 1160)
✉ Sarah.Rolph@tn.britishcouncil.org
💻 www.britishcouncil.org.tn

QUALIFICATIONS: Minimum certificate in EFL (CELTA, Trinity or equivalent) plus two years' post-certificate teaching experience in EFL. Demonstrable ability to teach across the range of courses offered including adults and young learners. Experience of IELTS and Cambridge Exams desirable.

CONDITIONS OF EMPLOYMENT: 2-year full-time contracts. Also run summer school programme for which they need teachers for 8 weeks (June/July).

SALARY: Flights, baggage, medical insurance and pension contributions in addition to salary for full-time work. Salary for 2-month summer school is £1,800 plus flights, accommodation and medical insurance.

CONTACT: Sarah Rolph, Teaching Centre Manager.

ENGLISH CULTURAL CENTRE
Street of 7 November, immb El Itkan (Mez n°3) 3027 Sfax
☎ +216 74408949
✉ contact@englishculturalcentre.com
💻 www.englishculturalcenter.com/
www.english-tunisia.com

NUMBER OF TEACHERS: 4.

PREFERENCE OF NATIONALITY: British or American.

QUALIFICATIONS: 3 years' experience.

CONDITIONS OF EMPLOYMENT: 6 months or annual contract. Most classes are in the afternoon/evenings, 4pm–6pm and 6.30pm–8.30pm.

SALARY: 25 Tunisian dinars (£11) per 2 hour lesson.

FACILITIES/SUPPORT: Assistance given with applying for work permits.

RECRUITMENT: Interview is essential and can be conducted on the phone or Skype.

CONTACT: Agmed Zayani, Administrative Officer.

LIBYA

Libya is more like a Middle Eastern country and indeed tour operators trying to promote the country describe it as the 'new Jordan'. Colonel Gaddafi has been the country's absolute ruler since 1969. In recent years, there have been signals that the country is opening up, though the government's record on human rights remains unpredictable.

As a country in Northern Africa whose landscape is defined by the Sahara Desert, it is natural that Libya experiences water shortages. In most areas it receives only 400 mm of annual rainfall and this is as low as 40 mm in the southern regions. Lakes are few and far between and all are either brackish or salty. The government therefore constructed the so-called 'Great Manmade River' which transports water for irrigation and industrial use via the world's largest network of aqueducts and underground pipes. It reached Tripoil in 1996 and Gharyan in 2007.

Libya's wealth of course derives from its massive oil reserves which have attracted many international corporations. All of these run English teaching programmes, and pay their highly qualified teaching staff handsomely (e.g. £25,000 a year, potentially tax-free) to compensate for the privations of living in remote desert locations. The perks are generous too, with accommodation, food and flights often provided. Usually teachers are hired through specialist recruitment agencies such as Language Solutions International (crispin.tucker@langsols.com).

The British Council provides major English language programmes in Libya, primarily to corporate clients in the oil, gas and engineering sectors, and to a lesser degree in the tourist industry and government departments. They have been expanding their ELT operations in Benghazi and Sirte as well as Tripoli; go to www.britishcouncil.org/learning-teachingjobs.htm for current vacancies. Berlitz has also become active in the capital Tripoli (see entry). Note that 1-year visas will be granted to UK passport-holders only if they have no Israeli stamps.

BELL AWARDBRAND

Hillscross, Red Cross Lane, Cambridge CB2 2QU, UK

01223 275500

www.bell-worldwide.com/jobs

NUMBER OF TEACHERS: Numerous EDL opportunities to work in Libya, Saudi Arabia and other worldwide locations.

PREFERENCE OF NATIONALITY: Native English level speakers.

QUALIFICATIONS: A university degree, CELTA/Trinity TESOL or recognised equivalent plus previous EFL experience.

CONDITIONS OF EMPLOYMENT: Various short- and long-term contracts available as well as permanent positions, dependant on location.

SALARY: Competitive packages.

FACILITIES/SUPPORT: Great training and personal development opportunities.

RECRUITMENT: Applications accepted via website. Visa application may be required depending on location.

CONTACT: Recruitment Team.

BERLITZ LIBYA, LANGUAGE CENTRE AND INTERPRETATION

Tripoli, Orabi Basha St, Near the Merzan Mosque, PO Box 2694

+218 21 33 44 939

berlitz@berlitz.com.ly

www.berlitz.com.ly

NUMBER OF TEACHERS: 6.

PREFERENCE OF NATIONALITY: None.

QUALIFICATIONS: College/university degree and/or relevant work experience. Teaching qualifications are desired but not essential.

CONDITIONS OF EMPLOYMENT: 1-year minimum contract with 8 working hours per day.

SALARY: 1,750 Libyan dinars.

FACILITIES/SUPPORT: In addition to their salary, teachers are provided with local health insurance valued at 500 Libyan dinars. Accommodation is provided within the centre. Each teacher has a private room with shared kitchen, dining area and bathroom. Assistance is provided when applying for work permits.

RECRUITMENT: Usually via adverts on ESL websites. Interviews are essential.

CONTACT: Julia Crecan, Local Supervisor.

359

MAURITANIA

Mauritania is becoming a more popular overland route from Morocco to Senegal now that the tensions of the Western Sahara have cooled somewhat. The road from Nouadibou to Nouakchott is now paved, which makes travel considerably easier. When **Bradwell Jackson** visited he was surprised by how few Westerners he saw: '*It seems as though this country is up and coming as one of those unexplored gems that travellers haven't yet discovered.*'

Bradwell, who supplied all the information for this section, found a teaching job by a '*happy accident of fate*'. On striking up a conversation with a Westerner walking on the other side of the street, he asked her about English language schools, and was promptly taken to the front door of The English Language Centre:

> *I was lucky enough to speak with the owner right away. I was talking to her while she was busy doing some other things, so it was not a formal interview. I did not have to fill out an application, though she asked me to write a letter explaining why I wanted to work in Mauritania. She seemed very interested, and asked me to come back in a couple of days to do a mock class in front of her teachers. I was hired based on this.*

Bradwell's wages started at 50,000 ouguiyas ($180) a month and increased to 68,000 ($250) a month. He was told that a person hired from within the country is paid much less than a person hired from outside. Getting a work permit was refreshingly simple. The school simply took his passport to the employment office and paid for a 1-year work permit.

Bradwell found the students to be a joy to work with, because they were 'serious' and hungry to learn. Native English teachers could try Nouakchott English Center (B.P. 4473 ILOT P-29; 529 25 42; sagna@univ-nkc.mr). The Coordinator of the Center (which is affiliated to the Université de Nouakchott) hires 6–8 teachers, one or two of whom he would like to be native English speakers, although this would depend on the school's income. Teachers work four and half hours a week and are paid 1,500–2,500 ouguiyas per hour (about $5.50–$9/hour). British English is as popular as American English.

SENEGAL

The British Council has a flourishing teaching centre in Dakar (Rue AAB-68, Amitie Zone A et B, BP 6232; +221 869 2700; information@britishcouncil.sn) that hires well-qualified teachers. They will want to see your CV and certification, although Bradwell Jackson reports that they will consider hiring non-UK citizens and may leave you 'wriggle room' if you don't quite have the qualifications they officially require.

The British Senegalese Institute (Rue du 18 Juin BP: 35 Dakar; 822 28 70/40 23/77 8) is the oldest English teaching centre in the country. It does not require teachers to have a specific certificate or experience, although these are certainly desirable. The average hours per week are 15, and the pay is around 3,500 CFA per hour. Another possibility is the Centre Africain d'Etudes Superieres en Gestion (Boulevard du General De Gaulle, B.P. 3802, Dakar; 839 73 04 direct 839 74 39; moussa.dieng@cesag.sn). The school is located in a large, official complex and tends to cater for more affluent students. Bradwell Jackson spoke to Moussa Dieng, Chef du Departement Langues, who said that no specific certificate was required, just a good knowledge of the language. Moussa Dieng seemed to like the idea of hiring native English speakers.

The American Language Program in Senegal continues to recruit. Although Dakar is an interesting city of contrasts, Bradwell was not tempted to stay. He found the city sprawling and unwieldy, and a little too expensive.

OTHER AFRICAN COUNTRIES

CAMEROON

CAMEROON VISION TRUST

PO Box 1075, Limbe

9 58 02 92

camvisiontrust@yahoo.co.uk or rosembone@gmail.com

NUMBER OF TEACHERS: 15 per year.

PREFERENCE OF NATIONALITY: British or American.

QUALIFICATIONS: Basic TEFL qualification or higher.

CONDITIONS OF EMPLOYMENT: 2-year maximum contract, to work 15 hours per week.

SALARY: Voluntary work but hostel accommodation and a basic allowance are provided.

FACILITIES/SUPPORT: Assistance provided with work permits and visas.

RECRUITMENT: Interview required possibly in the UK and US.

CONTACT: Rosemary Olive Mbone Enie.

GHANA

VOLUNTEER GHANA

Volunteer Programmes Department, BUNAC, 16 Bowling Green Lane, London EC1R 0QH, UK

020 7251 3472

volunteer@bunac.org.uk

www.bunac.org

NUMBER OF TEACHERS: Varies each year.

QUALIFICATIONS: Applicants should be 18 or over. Previous classroom experience desirable.

CONDITIONS OF EMPLOYMENT: Placements available for 2 or 3 months. Travel time available during and/or after placement.

SALARY: Placements are unpaid and applicants are expected to take sufficient spending money with them (approx. £175 per month). Programme cost is £800 for 2 months, £900 for 3 months, plus flights (£600–£800), comprehensive insurance, etc.

FACILITIES/SUPPORT: Most stay in homestay accommodation, which gives applicants a chance to become fully immersed in Ghanaian culture. Back up support and advice provided by BUNAC in the UK and the host organisation, Student & Youth Travel Organisation (SYTO) in Ghana. Applications are accepted year-round. Group flights depart every month.

RECRUITMENT: Send a completed application form (downloadable from www.bunac.org), registration fee and any other documentation as specified to BUNAC's Volunteering Department at least 10 weeks before departure date. All applicants are invited to attend an interview as part of the application process.

MOZAMBIQUE

> **LYNDEN LANGUAGE SCHOOL**
> Av Zedequias Manganhela 267, JAT Building, 2nd Floor, Maputo
> 21 360494
> lynden@teledata.mz
> www.lynden.co.mz

NUMBER OF TEACHERS: 5.

PREFERENCE OF NATIONALITY: British, Australian, South African, etc.

QUALIFICATIONS: CELTA or Trinity plus 2 years' experience.

CONDITIONS OF EMPLOYMENT: 1 year, 25 hours per week.

SALARY: US$1,000; half paid in the local currency (meticals).

FACILITIES/SUPPORT: School finds and pays for accommodation. School applies to Ministry of Labour for work permit once teachers gather necessary documents.

RECRUITMENT: *EL Gazette* or internet. References checked by phone.

CONTACT: Denise Lord or Lynne Longley, Co-Directors.

SOUTH AFRICA

> **INTERLINK SCHOOL OF LANGUAGES**
> 28 Queens Road, Sea Point, Cape Town 8005
> 21 439 9834
> info@interlink.co.za
> www.interlink.co.za

NUMBER OF TEACHERS: 6.

PREFERENCE OF NATIONALITY: South Africans preferred but will consider native English speakers with permission to work in South Africa.

QUALIFICATIONS: Minimum CELTA with experience.

CONDITIONS OF EMPLOYMENT: Full-time contracts last for 1 year. Part-time contracts reviewed weekly according to demand.

SALARY: Varies according to experience and qualifications. Part-time salary R60 per hour.

RECRUITMENT: Interview required.

CONTACT: Luanne McCallum, Manager.

TANZANIA

> **AANG SERIAN ('HOUSE OF PEACE')**
> PO Box 19, Monduli
> +255 784 293671
> noonkodin@gmail.com or grosper@gmail.com
> www.serianuk.org.uk

NUMBER OF TEACHERS: 15–20 teaching assistants and qualified teachers in ESL and other subjects placed at Aang Serian Noonkodin Secondary School, in the rural Maasai village of Eluwai.

PREFERENCE OF NATIONALITY: All nationalities accepted. Non-native speakers of English should have IELTS 6.5 or above.

QUALIFICATIONS: Volunteers who want to be considered as independent class teachers of English should have the CELTA, TEFL or similar. Classroom assistants who work alongside a qualified Tanzanian teacher should ideally have completed a minimum of 1 year of undergraduate-level study in English, although school leavers with strong motivation and above-average qualifications will also be considered. Previous teaching experience in a school is strongly preferred, even if it is no more than a 2-week work experience placement. Maths and science teachers also needed.

CONDITIONS OF EMPLOYMENT: 2–3 months recommended for short-term volunteers though arrangements are flexible. Ideally 6–12 months from January or July for qualified teachers.

SALARY: Programme fee $420 includes a small donation to the school. Volunteers are also asked to cover their living costs, $40–$50 per week, plus are encouraged to carry out additional fundraising for the project.

FACILITIES/SUPPORT: Volunteers stay in a 3-bedroom staff house at the school (subject to availability) or in homestay. Some may camp during busy periods. Volunteers are also offered reduced rates for wildlife safaris, mountain-climbing expeditions, walking tours, short courses, academic lectures and visits to rural Chagga and Rangi communities, offered by a partner company in Arusha. Orientation is given on arrival plus Swahili tuition and optional drum and dance classes.

RECRUITMENT: Applications can be made online.

CONTACT: Gemma Enolengila, International Liaison (enolengila@yahoo.co.uk).

MONDOCHALLENGE LTD
Town Hall, Market Place, Newbury RG14 2QD, UK
📞 01635 45556
🖱 info@mondochallenge.co.uk
💻 www.mondochallenge.co.uk

UK-based organisation sending volunteers to work on community-based teaching and other projects in Africa and worldwide.

NUMBER OF TEACHERS: 60 volunteers for 12 teaching programmes in primary and secondary schools, and also in adult education in Longido, Arusha and Moshi in Tanzania, and also in Gambia and Senegal.

PREFERENCE OF NATIONALITY: All native English speakers.

QUALIFICATIONS: Preferred minimum age 22, though some gap year students accepted. Minimum qualification is A-level or equivalent in subjects to be taught. Must be able to cope with remote posting and to relate to people of other cultures.

CONDITIONS OF EMPLOYMENT: 6 weeks to 6 months with start dates throughout the year; average 3 months.

SALARY: Unpaid. Volunteers pay a programme fee from £600 for 1 month which includes board and lodging in local family homes.

CONTACT: Simon Palferman, Head of Operations.

UGANDA

SOFT POWER EDUCATION (SPE)
UK: 55 Guildhall St, Bury St Edmunds, Suffolk IP33 1QF
Uganda: PO Box 1493, Jinja
📞 256 774 162541
🖱 info@softpowereducation.com
💻 www.softpowereducation.com

British registered non-religious charity improving quality of life through education. Among numerous other projects, SPE offers TEFL courses for men and women in the community.

NUMBER OF TEACHERS: 1 or 2 at a time based at the Amagezi Education Centre.

QUALIFICATIONS: TEFL qualification and some experience preferable but not essential. Creativity and ability to work independently using one's own initiative essential.

CONDITIONS OF EMPLOYMENT: Minimum 3 months.

SALARY: None. Volunteers must cover their own living and travel expenses as well as a donation to the charity. Recommended amount is £75 a week.

FACILITIES/SUPPORT: Camping, dorms, private bandas or living within the local community. Guest houses in Jinja are also an option, but they are located some distance away from the Amagezi Education Centre so travel costs would be higher.

CONTACT: Sharon Webb, General Manager.

Although the English language is not a universal passport to employment, it can certainly be put to good use in many Asian countries where the demand for English teachers is substantial, even extraordinary as is the case with China, described as a 'black hole' for EFL teachers by a European director of studies.

Conditions and remuneration differ wildly between industrialised countries, such as Japan, Korea and Singapore with their Western-style economies, and developing countries, such as Nepal and Thailand, where both wages and the standard of living are lower. China combines rapidly industrialised cities with vast stretches of rural backwaters. A concerted job hunt in Asia will almost always turn up possibilities, and sometimes the difficulty comes in choosing among them. **Ross McKay** from Glasgow writes of his job hunt:

> *I was fifty and fed up for various reasons. So I wrote to about 500 institutions all over South East Asia. Whilst waiting for replies I did a distance TESOL course and College of Further Education teaching certificate. I got three offers, one in Hanoi, one in Bangkok and I chose Jakarta as I knew nothing about Indonesia. My colleagues come from all over the English-speaking world and often become great pals. But there are some head-cases. I guess one has to be a little crazy to live this life, and a few people crack up. The great thing about life in Indonesia is that every morning you wake up and have no idea what the heck is going to happen next.*

It may not be necessary to organise a mass mail-out in order to arrange a teaching stay in Asia. For American citizens and residents, both Princeton and Stanford universities have affiliated programmes which operate in various Asian countries and include TEFL teaching. VIA (Volunteers in Asia) has been providing international exchange opportunities since 1963. Each year VIA sends 30–40 volunteer English teachers to China, Vietnam, Indonesia, Thailand, Myanmar, Cambodia and Laos on short-term (summer) and longer term (1-year or 2-year) assignments. All programmes are open to college students or graduates over 18. Occasional exceptions can be made for people without a college degree. Applications are due in mid-February and the participation fee is between $1,500 and $3,000. Further information is available online at www.viaprograms.org (415 904 8033; info@viaprograms.org).

For information about the Princeton-affiliated programme, contact Princeton-in Asia, 194 Nassau Street, Suite 212, Princeton, NJ 08542 (609 258 3657 pia@princeton.edu; www.princeton.edu/~pia/). They currently place about 150 full-year fellows in 17 Asian countries: Cambodia, China and Hong Kong, East Timor, India, Indonesia, Japan, Kazakhstan, Laos, Malaysia, Mongolia, Nepal, Philippines, Singapore, South Korea, Taiwan, Thailand and Vietnam. Applications, available on their website, are welcomed from college graduates from all universities. Suitable candidates will be invited to a compulsory interview in January or February and a weekend's orientation in late May, both on the Princeton campus. Teachers on the programme must also complete a TEFL training weekend in Princeton in April and/or at least 20 hours of TEFL/TESL preparation in the form of a course or experience before their fellowship begins.

Recruitment organisations such as Saxoncourt (affiliated to Shane English Schools) and EF English First are very active in the region. Saxoncourt recruits for the 250-strong group of Shane English Schools in Japan, China, Taiwan and Vietnam. North American recruitment agencies such as Footprints (www.footprintsrecruiting.com) specialise in placing teachers in Asian countries. In the UK try the Anglo-Pacific (Asia) Consultancy in London (020 8452 7836). TEFLOne is a free placement service for native English speaking EFL teachers with the CertTESOL, CELTA or equivalent. Candidates are interviewed for positions starting every month in China. The package on offer is a monthly salary of RMB5,500+, end-of-contract bonus, paid return flight, free accommodation and welfare support (www.teflone.com).

In Hong Kong, Linda Yee Recruiting fills more vacancies in China and Taiwan than in Hong Kong (asiaconnections@gmail.com). The distance TEFL training course provider INTESOL is linked to HuntESL which is another active recruiter in the area (www.huntesl.com).

One issue that rears its ugly head from time to time is discrimination on the grounds of age and also race. For marketing reasons in Asia employers prefer their employees to look younger than 30 and many have complained that too much emphasis is placed on the photograph requested at the time of application. Racism is also a potential problem, as highlighted by a contributor to a *Guardian* TEFL forum in 2010:

> Myself and my girlfriend, both in our mid 20s and university graduates with good work experience, have been looking into TEFL in Asia for over a year now. We've gotten so far as getting interviews, but on several occasions we've been denied a job as my girlfriend is mixed race (Chinese/British). This hasn't been the explicit reason for not getting a job, of course, but it's been heavily implied. For instance, my girlfriend was asked whether she could dye her hair blond in order to be considered for a job in a school in Hong Kong.
>
> I think that racism in Asia is hushed over by many, especially recruiting companies and advisors. It's a serious issue and one that affects many people applying for work in China, Hong Kong, Korea and Japan especially. If you don't 'look' Western, you'll struggle significantly compared to your Caucasian brethren.

As one of the expert panellists sensibly replied, '*While some racism might be encountered, it doesn't mean the whole of Asia is inaccessible*'.

LIST OF EMPLOYERS

REACH TO TEACH
21 Everett Road Extension, Albany, New York
12205, USA
- 201 467 4612 (USA)/0203 286 9794
  (UK & Ireland)/2 8011 4516 (Australia)/9 889
  0557 (New Zealand)
- info@ReachToTeachRecruiting.com
- www.ReachToTeachRecruiting.com

Reach To Teach is one of the largest human resource companies for teachers in Asia and all services are free to teachers. See separate entries in chapters on China, Korea and Taiwan.

NUMBER OF TEACHERS: 300+ per year to work in Taiwan, Korea, China and Japan, with possibility of expanding into more countries.

PREFERENCE OF NATIONALITY: American, Canadian, British, South African, Australian, New Zealander and Irish.

QUALIFICATIONS: A positive, enthusiastic, dedicated and flexible attitude is the most important qualification. Teaching experience is a plus and some placements may require a TEFL qualification.

CONDITIONS OF EMPLOYMENT: All job placements are full-time positions and for 1 full year. Teaching schedules vary but are generally either mornings and afternoons or afternoons and evenings.

SALARY: Competitive packages that reflect the local market rate. Ability to save depends on lifestyle. Some job placements (especially Korea and China) offer free flights, free accommodation and bonuses.

FACILITIES/SUPPORT: Recruiter offers personal attention to every job placement. Through a partnership with a TEFL course provider, Reach To Teach can assist teachers in getting course discounts. All placements come with guidance on visas, flights, accommodation, etc. and workplace teacher training. All teachers have the option of continued support throughout year-long placement.

RECRUITMENT: Applications submitted via Reach To Teach website. Interviews conducted over phone or occasionally in person.

CONTACT: Richard Jones, Global Director of Recruiting (Richard@ReachToTeachRecruiting.com).

CHINA

Some commentators have predicted that the 21st century belongs to China. In order to fulfil this prediction, China wants to learn the language of the West in unprecedented numbers. The numbers are astronomical. For example, the government target for the Olympics was to have five million Beijing residents able to communicate in English which is more than a third of the city's metropolitan population.

In turn, native English speakers are heading to China in their thousands, barely bothering to look at teaching possibilities in Europe or even Japan. Cyberspace is a-buzz with new companies and organisations offering English language training from native English speakers. Western curiosity about this huge country, spurred on by a barrage of media stories, is rising exponentially.

Post 1978, one of China's first steps in its journey from collectivism to capitalism was to invite English language teachers to its institutes of higher education. More than three decades later thousands of native English speakers are teaching not only at schools and academic institutions around the country but in companies and (what would have been unthinkable not so long ago) private language institutes. Furthermore, the emerging middle class aspires to send its children for private tuition just as in the capitalist countries of Taiwan, Korea and Japan.

English is compulsory for school pupils from the age of 9. Although optional, English is now even taught from kindergarten. Many street and shop signs in the capital and other major cities are written in English as well as Chinese, though most Beijing citizens, especially the older generation, can say very little in English apart from 'McDonald's'. A great many students and teachers are very keen to improve their English to Cambridge Proficiency standard in the hope of being accepted to study overseas. Competition can be cut-throat although children from the wealthiest families may be less inspired, knowing that they'll be going abroad eventually, whether their English is fluent or not. But most are eager to learn, even if the style of learning to which they have become accustomed can be difficult for foreign teachers to adopt.

It is easy to forget, amid the well-reported stories of sprawling urban metropolises rising almost in the night, that about 80% of China's population still lives in the countryside. **Sam Meekings** was surprised to discover that although he headed off to Beijing every other weekend to stock up on Western foods and see the sights, most of his students had never left the small city of Hengshui; only 15 years previously it had all been farmland.

Writing in 2010, a teacher working in Shanghai summed up the contradictory experience:

> *'I feel like I am part of a developing educational system in an institution that puts great store by professional development. On the minus side, I feel like I have a life to build from scratch and a new culture to master – a task which can be challenging just as it can be daunting.'*

PROSPECTS FOR TEACHERS

'With just a university degree and a little determination anyone can find an opportunity to challenge themselves somewhere in twenty-first century China,' writes **Sam Meekings**, who taught in a state-run normal college before accepting an editing job with Oxford University Press in Shanghai (and is now a published novelist). A degree is normally a minimum requirement these days and any teaching experience is useful, but not so much importance is attached to TEFL qualifications and quite often references are not taken up. However, the better schools have recently started to become more stringent in their recruiting methods and foreigners cannot simply walk into more lucrative jobs in the same way that they did in the early days. Nevertheless, there are still many schools so desperate that they will employ anyone simply to have a 'token foreigner' and hence enhance their status.

Theoretically the Chinese government classifies teachers either as foreign experts (FEs) or foreign teachers (FTs). FEs are expected to have a master's degree in a relevant area (English, Linguistics, TEFL/TESOL, etc.) and some teaching experience at the tertiary level. FTs are normally under 25 and have only a university degree. In practice, most teachers are classified as 'FEs,' even if they only have a degree. Younger candidates including students on exchange schemes such as those run by gap year organisations, e.g. Lattitude and Project Trust, are usually placed in middle schools (public secondary schools, often boarding schools) or vocational schools. A large proportion of foreigners are employed in Beijing and (especially) Shanghai but there are many opportunities in the provinces as well, especially for FTs. The more remote the area or the more hostile the climate, the easier it will be to find a job. But there are also plenty of vacancies in comfortable cities such as Kunming and Dalian. Many vacancies for both FEs and FTs go unfilled. Specialist recruitment organisations are notified of more positions than they can find people to fill them.

Demand exists in the hundreds of universities, colleges, foreign language institutes, institutes of technology, teacher training colleges (called normal universities) and secondary schools, especially in the provinces. Normal universities often seem to be overlooked when FTs are assigned centrally, so they are a very promising bet for people applying directly or on the spot.

Sam Meekings taught at the normal university in Hengshui:

I lived on campus at the state-run normal college, sharing a kitchen and office with another foreign teacher. Though I was fresh out of university, I found myself teaching English literature to graduates who were often a couple of years older than me. This was initially challenging, only because, in common with teachers in most state schools, I was told that I must follow the syllabus. In practice, what this meant was not deviating from the textbook that all the students had been issued with.

Jessie Levene's first job was working for a company that hired teachers out to schools, which involved long hours (7am–5pm) and classes of 60 students. She prefers her second job, teaching at a university in Chengdu, '*I would highly recommend university teaching over working for a private company, even though the wages are much lower.*' She takes 14 classes a week of no more than 28 students. Classes last a manageable 40 minutes.

Applications can be made through the Chinese embassy in your country, through various placement organisations, recruitment agencies (which don't charge teachers a fee) and voluntary bodies, or by applying directly to institutions advertised on the internet and elsewhere.

Even ordinary secondary schools employ native English speakers; applications can be made through provincial education bureaux. Writing direct to the Foreign Affairs Office (*waiban*) of institutes of higher learning may lead to a job offer. Chinese institutes seem to attach more weight to the letter of application than to the curriculum vitae, but the CV should still be sent and should emphasise any work or experience in education. Also enclose a photo, a photocopy of the first page of your passport, a copy of any education certificates and two references. Jessie Levene notes that schools seem to prefer female teachers, particularly for younger students, and as a result, she was given more and more classes, despite an already full timetable.

It is becoming increasingly common for schools to offer a job to an applicant but not guarantee employment until they arrive at the school. This is the result of foreigners having abused the system in the past, accepting numerous jobs in order to keep their options open. Many schools have also introduced a probationary period of between two and 10 weeks. Although this may sound a bit daunting if you have already paid for flight tickets, it can work in the applicant's favour, as it allows time to ensure that the school is suitable for you. It is always best, wherever possible, to visit a school before signing a contract and talk to other FTs, to make sure that the school is everything it says it is and to examine the accommodation.

Some schools and private language institutes which do offer contracts to unseen candidates rely on long-distance phone calls or Skype. Any university graduate travelling in China should be able to arrange a teaching contract just by asking around at the many colleges in the towns and cities on his or her itinerary. Even when foreign travellers have not been looking for work, they have been approached and invited to teach English. The going rate in the big cities for private English tuition is £10–£15 an hour.

If you fix up a job at FT level on the spot, it may not be for an entire academic year and your pay may be calculated on an hourly basis.

FINDING A JOB

With the explosion in opportunities, the job-hunt is far more straightforward than it was a few years ago when most teacher applications were for state institutes and had to go through the Chinese Education Association for International Exchange or one of its 37 provincial offices. Nowadays CEAIE leaves recruitment to online companies such as www.chinajob.com (see below) and other private recruiters, foundations or China-linked companies eager to sign up native English speakers (with or without relevant experience) for an academic year.

Some of the tried and tested old schemes are still in place and still work. The British Council's Language Assistants Programme, in cooperation with the Chinese Education authorities places graduates in schools across China. TEFL training is provided on a two-week course in Shanghai which is paid for by the British Council. Participants receive free accommodation, and utilities and a flight back to the UK. Teaching experience and/or qualifications are not necessary. Details of the application procedure can be obtained from the Language Assistants Team at the British Council (10 Spring Gardens, London SW1A 2BN; 020 7389 4955; assistants@britishcouncil.org) or at www.britishcouncil.org/languageassistants-china.htm. The British Council accepts applications up until the end of February (non-refundable placement fee £48). Applications are screened and then interviews conducted in April for positions starting in August. The minimum requirement is a university degree, though a TEFL certificate and/or teaching experience, preferably abroad, improve your chances of acceptance. Opportunities are available in a large variety of cities throughout mainland China, though initial training takes place for all participants in Shanghai in August. Wages are not brilliant on this programme, i.e. 3,000–4,000 Renminbi (net) per month, but all teachers are provided with free accommodation.

The www.chinajob.com job fair is now in its tenth year and offers a great (and free) opportunity for teachers to look for 'on the spot' opportunities in educational institutions, language training organisations, and private and national companies. Job fairs take place annually in April in Beijing and Shanghai. For more information visit www.chinajob.com or the website of its partner, the State Administration of Foreign Experts Affairs (www.safea.gov.cn/english).

Some TEFL training courses offered in China also lead to jobs. Again chinajob.com is active and offers a seven-day training course to graduates which enables them to claim FE status. The course is offered in five of the major cities of China and costs 3,000 RMB; further details at http://tefl.chinajob.com. Another company offering a training course combined with job placement is affiliated to the American exchange agency Journey East (www.journeyeast.org). A similar programme with guaranteed job placement is run by US-China Education and Culture Exchange Center (www.teachinginchina.org).

Demand for qualified teachers is so high that any who advertise their services online may get an instantaneous response, as happened to a teacher writing from Shanghai in May 2010:

> *I put my CV on TEFL.com and the DoS of EF Academic Partnerships contacted me by email enquiring about my current location and availability. I replied that I was at home and currently seeking employment and asked for some more information. He promptly replied and we arranged an interview for the following Saturday morning.*

PRIVATE LANGUAGE TRAINING

Ever since the change in legislation allowing privatised companies to operate in the fields of media and education, a huge number of private language schools and training centres has opened. **Jane Pennington**, who taught for four years in China, carried out a little research and estimates that there are about 100 private language companies in Kunming, only about 15%–20% of which are officially licensed. These institutes are not allowed to invite FTs without a lot of red tape which is usually not worth their while. However, they are very eager to hire native English speakers on the spot, often people on a student visa at the university. Like private schools everywhere, a certain number of these are run by unscrupulous entrepreneurs interested only in profit. If considering working in the private sector, try to find out the degree of professionalism of the company that has expressed interest in hiring you, and talk to other foreigners working there, especially with regards to payment.

International ELT organisations such as EF English First or Wall Street Institute (see entries) are expanding quickly. **Yasmin Peiris** enjoyed working for the Wall Street Institute in Shenzhen, teaching different types of class 30 hours a week. Class sizes ranged from four to 15 people and the working environment was very good, '*with simple, modern classrooms and most teaching resources readily available*'.

> *The internet is a prolific source of possibilities and expanding all the time. According to a leading news agency, China has more people online than the USA. Any web search or a trawl of the major ELT job sites is bound to turn up plenty of contacts. Job China at www.jobchina.net, for example, publishes long lists of jobs, all dated and described. In the private sector, some large companies (e.g. hotel chains) have their own language training facilities for staff, especially if they are joint ventures with Western companies. Most recruitment of teachers by business and industry takes place locally, since they do not offer accommodation.*

PLACEMENT AGENCIES AND ORGANISATIONS

Many organisations recruit teachers from abroad for China. **Nina Capek** chose Buckland International Education Group (see entry below) to help organise her teaching job in China, and was full of praise for it:

> *Foreign teachers are not required to pay a fee to sign up with Buckland unlike some companies who charge a lot of money. They sorted out my work visa for me, they collected me from the airport and put all the new teachers up in a nice guest house for their first five days in the country. Pay was not as good as with some other companies, but the support and conditions made up for it and the wage was sufficient to live like a princess anyway. OK, some people lived like queens, but I wanted security.*

A number of North American organisations involved in teacher placements in China have entries in the listings at the end of this chapter including the Colorado China Council, Appalachians Abroad and the US-China Educational Exchange. WorldTeach, at the Center for International Development at Harvard University (79 John F Kennedy Street, Cambridge, Massachusetts 2138; 617 495 5527; www.worldteach.org), is a non-profit organisation that sends volunteers to teach in secondary schools in two provinces of China, Hunan and Yunnan, for a full academic year (August to July) or for the summer. Volunteers pay $1,000 for the year in Hunan, $2,500 for Yunnan and $3,990 for the summer in Hunan; all of these include flights from the USA.

CONDITIONS OF WORK

With the rise of the free market the once rigid distinctions between FTs and FEs has become blurred since many reward packages are now open to negotiation. But there is still a strong tendency to heap more perks on anyone with a higher degree. They are more likely to have their airfares or shipping costs reimbursed and they usually earn more than FTs. The general monthly salary range for most ordinary native English speaker teachers should start from RMB4,500 ($650/£450) but can rise in the private sector (especially in sophisticated Shanghai and Beijing) to well over double that. Note that the renminbi is a non-convertible currency and foreigners have to negotiate a clause in their contract to be able to convert a certain percentage (up to a maximum 70%). When **Bradwell Jackson** arrived in Tangshan, he assumed that since so many foreigners are working in China as English teachers, it must surely be straightforward to deposit earnings in a bank at home (in the USA in his case). After some research he discovered that the Bank of China will make deposits into US bank accounts, albeit for a significant fee, especially if you don't have an account with them.

Some people decide to change their money on the black market, known as the 'real bank'. Outside the major eastern cities you can live on RMB1,500 a month if your accommodation is provided, so it is important to be able to convert your saved renminbi into a foreign currency. However, those living in the major eastern cities are more likely to spend RMB3,000–5,000 per month, depending on their lifestyle. One highly qualified teacher in Shanghai estimated the cost of living in 2010 out of a salary of RMB10,500 per month: RMB2,000 for a flat (not shared), RMB500 to cover bills and RMB2,000–3,000 on food. Inflation is high in China so hanging out in expat bars and taking taxis is becoming more expensive. In Beijing, the automatic charge for a taxi is 10 renminbi, whereas in Tangshan (two hours east of the capital), it's only five.

Virtually all teachers working for educational establishments have their accommodation provided by the host institution, either in on-site residences or in a foreigners' hotel. In a very few cases a housing allowance will be offered in lieu to those teachers who want to choose their own flat. **Jessie Levene**'s first job provided a housing allowance; her current job at a university provides a free apartment, although she chooses not to live there, preferring somewhere that isn't full of foreigners.

The three or four week holiday over Chinese New Year should be paid as should vacation periods in state schools if you are contracted to continue teaching after it. Companies in the private sector may not offer payment during enforced breaks from teaching. **Paul Carey** identified the sudden six-week break from working and earning with little notice given by the employer as one of the low points of his experience with EF English First in Shanghai which was otherwise '*a worthwhile experience both personally and professionally*'. Many employers offer free internet access and some offer free Chinese lessons. **Michelle** from Ireland, who was employed by the Bond Institute in Guangdong (see entry), believes that the wages should be higher considering the amount of work she was asked to do. However, she appreciated being given the choice of an apartment in town or outside the city.

When you are first notified by your employer in China that you have a job, you should avoid the temptation to write back enthusiastically accepting it. Rather ask for more details such as your status, salary, timetable and other conditions. You could also ask for the names of any current foreign employees whom you can ask for inside information. What is agreed at this stage will set the terms of employment even though it is standard practice not to sign a contract until after two months' probation.

Although higher wages can be earned in the big cities of Beijing, Guangzhou and Shanghai, and also in any of the economic zones such as Hainan Island, life in Chinese cities has many drawbacks in terms of crowds and pollution. For quality of life, southwestern China is probably better than much of the east. Yunnan province has a particularly congenial climate. This area is also reputed to be less money-oriented than the east coast cities, which may have the drawback that it may be more difficult to find paying private students.

While teaching in a suburb of Shanghai, **Marybeth Hao** noticed many Chinese parents were more than willing to pay native English speaker tutors high fees to tutor their children outside school hours.

For her, one of the main rewards of teaching in Shanghai was to experience a culture in the midst of such dramatic and hurried changes.

FTs can be expected to teach anything from 15 to 30+ hours a week. A load of 20 hours is typical though this sounds lighter than it actually is because there are bound to be extra duties. Often there is a heavy load of marking not to mention marketing. Teachers in the private sector are routinely asked to attend student recruitment events, for example to hand out flyers or to appear at drop-in evenings whose main purpose is to rope in new clients. Some teachers are expected to staff an 'English corner' or English club, or deliver a weekly lecture on Western culture. **Jane Pennington** warns that you should be prepared to be the token foreigner at the many banquets you will be invited to when you first arrive and also be prepared to turn some of them down.

In cases where teachers are given a huge number of classes, the administration's main ambition is to maximise your exposure, which may have the effect of minimising your usefulness. On the whole

SAM MEEKINGS *describes how attendance at several Chinese banquets can lead to a succession of nasty hangovers:*

Every foreigner in China quickly becomes familiar with baijiu, *a sharp clear liquor with a cloying aftertaste, which is measured out into shot glasses in front of you at the start of a meal. Though beer is increasingly popular, no large event is complete without* baijiu. *At any large banquet, especially with officials or high-ranking teachers at the school or college, you will be encouraged to drink with them. Your glass will be topped up throughout the meal, and often many people will wish to toast you, meaning you must once again down your drink as a sign of mutual respect. This is why, by eight or nine in the evening, restaurants begin to clear out – many diners are too wasted to do anything but go home and sleep. It should be noted, however, that women are usually exempted from this custom, and though I would have liked to have been spared the attention (and the subsequent hangovers), my female colleagues were not impressed that they were simply expected to sit and slowly sip beer or Coca-Cola while all the men went through the intricate tradition of getting each other as drunk as possible. Similarly, while almost all the male teachers in the college were heavy smokers (one of the best gifts to present to someone is a box of cigarettes), women smoking was frowned upon. Though these attitudes cannot be found in big cosmopolitan cities, I am certain that they persist throughout the smaller towns that make up the bulk of this vast country.*

Michelle enjoyed her time in China, but she thinks that FTs should be given more advice on what is required of them before they start teaching. It is not unusual for the school to leave it up to the FTs to find out if any national exams are looming for which you should be helping the students to prepare. Hours of teaching are unpredictable and the teaching days can be very long. Students get up at 6am and work at night in supervised sessions. Michelle was asked to take classes at weekends, which left little time for travel. If you want to keep your weekends free for travel and relaxation, firmly decline teaching hours on Saturday and Sunday, and be aware that it is all too easy to over-commit yourself in the first few weeks.

On the other hand, you may find your colleagues and bosses bend over backwards to help and support you, as **Bradwell Jackson** reported last year:

I was offered a job with Aston in China on the basis of a telephone interview and I am very happy with this. Aston is good to me, and my co-workers scramble to help me whenever I have even a mild matter that needs attention. For example, when I told them I was looking for a kung-fu school, they took this as a very important issue and had many long discussions-cum-negotiations with each other in order to come up with the best option for me. I think it might be hard to convince a Westerner to come and stay in an out-of-the-way city like Tangshan.

Really, I'm living the life of Reilly here. I've got nothing to complain about. The school has given me a free apartment complete with cable TV, washing machine, toaster oven, microwave, and refrigerator. Whenever I'm hungry, I just mosey on down to the street vendors and get some proper Chinese food for a friendly budget price. Who can ask for more?

THE PUPILS

'Big noses' (foreigners) are normally treated with respect. In the early years of Western contact with China, English teachers outside the big cities found themselves lionised, unable to complete the simplest task in public without an enormous audience. There are not many corners of China these days into which foreigners, whether teachers or travellers, have not penetrated, although in Hengshui, three hours south of Beijing, **Sam Meekings** was amazed at the reaction he received from people in the town, who would stop and gape at him, as though they had seen 'dinosaurs or dragons'. **Yasmin Peiris**, based in Shenzhen, one of China's newest cities, agrees that the general attitude towards teachers is generally favourable, even though there is a language barrier. She chose to ask her students for advice on where to go at weekends and what to do (a foot massage, a little shopping and sampling tempting varieties of Chinese food were some of the suggestions).

As (censored) internet use continues to rise and more Chinese people come into contact with Westerners (in the ether or in person), it is unlikely that China's generally respectful attitude towards foreigners will continue unperturbed. **Bradwell Jackson** identified another interesting new trend in modern-day China from his experiences of teaching in a small city:

There is another interesting phenomenon in China, which is the syndrome of the 'Little Emperor'. Chinese children are well behaved, but they were even better behaved 10 or 20 years ago. With the advent of the one-child policy, some interesting changes took place. It seems that with just one child in the house, and especially if it's a boy, the child is much more likely to be spoiled and accommodated. Any English teacher here will probably get his/her small share of little brats who just can't understand why they can't do what they want.

I agree with the premise that a teacher has to be a bossy boots in order to establish the discipline straight off the bat. I certainly did this, maybe even a bit too much, so that now the (naughty) kids are just a tad bit resistant sometimes. The parents, on the other hand, are deliriously happy with me. They specifically love the fact that I'm strict with the kids.

Slowly, newer pedagogical methods are being accepted by students and administrators alike. A strange phenomenon has swept the country called 'Crazy English' pioneered by a charismatic former radio disc jockey Li Yang who holds huge rallies at which language learners are encouraged to put aside their diffidence and shout out English phrases. But this new boldness hasn't penetrated into many classrooms yet. Where in one place, techniques that smack of innovation are greeted with blank stares, in another, there can be lively class discussions.

Jessie Levene, reaching for some colourful similes identifies the lowpoint of her first teaching job was feeling like a 'robot' and a 'teaching monkey'. It seems that you may have to work fairly hard to introduce modern teaching techniques into the classroom, as from a very early age Chinese children are taught in a very traditional style, as **Nina Capek** found while teaching in a primary school:

The teaching style does take a bit of getting used to. The children are used to learning by rote and the general ethos is: whatever the teacher says, we copy. Teaching 'my name is...' to fifty-6-year-old children proved very entertaining as they all copied me and said 'My name is Nina'.

A teacher who started work at Shanghai Lixin University of Commerce in February 2010 was delighted with the standard of students:

> Their attitude has been excellent on the whole. I have only a couple of disruptive students, but they all seem to be very motivated to learn English and realise how important it can be to their future careers. I know little of their real expectations other than most are concerned more with fluency than complexity or accuracy.

At university, students expect to pass, as it has been difficult for them to get in while some have paid to get in or used connections (*guanxi*), which means they expect to sail through. Don't be surprised if just before exam time your students ply you with gifts, expensive meals and even offer money. Teachers who accept these offers may find that their students expect high marks even if they do not turn up to the exam!

ACCOMMODATION

Every university has either a purpose-built hostel or similar. These differ enormously from place to place, though on the whole the standard is more acceptable to people with Western tastes than it was a few years ago. In some places (such as Chengdu University of Science & Technology) the

SAM MEEKINGS like some other teachers, found that there is a demand for any English provided it is clearly enunciated. Imaginative interactive teaching methods can work as Sam discovered when he had to teach a 60-strong class of university students, whose homework left something to be desired.

> Each week I was supposed to go through the excerpts from Shakespeare or Dickens in the book, despite the fact that close to half of the class could barely communicate with me in English at all. Though the impulse was strong to follow the example of the Chinese teachers and teach only to the brighter students and hope the others kept quiet at the back, I soon found that it was much more enjoyable to try and work the material into games and activities that everyone could take part in. This took time, however, since some students were so used to either being ignored or simply learning by rote and repetition that they were too shy to speak up. This is a problem I have noticed even teaching in private school in bigger cities – students are often so heavily criticised for mistakes in their normal classes that they lack the confidence to risk answering a question or attempting to join a game or discussion in case they do something wrong. It sometimes feels as if you are not only in a different country but also in a different century. None of the students I taught had any real concept of exploring or questioning an idea. When I set some homework essays for my literature class or set debate topics for my English speaking class to try to engage with, I was invariably met with sixty identical responses. Students are taught to pass exams in China, to memorise the single correct response and then repeat it when instructed – there is no concept of coming up with your own ideas. My students were all adamant that there was always one right answer and that everything else could therefore be discounted as wrong. This meant most essays and debates were very, very short. Coupled with the fact that we were not allowed to fail any students (even if they could not write more than their name on the biannual exam papers we had to set), it quickly became clear that we would have to set aside most of our preconceptions about education. Yet when students do finally open up or try something new, there is no better feeling.

accommodation can be airy and comfortable. In other places it is decidedly spartan and in some cases downright depressing, especially if electricity and heat/air-conditioning are rationed. Find out ahead of time whether you will have internet access.

REGULATIONS

Most institutes will issue teachers with an invitation or letter of appointment and other documents to be taken to the Chinese Consulate or Embassy to apply for a visa before leaving their country. You will need a medical report completed on official Chinese forms. In most cases with a 'Visa Notification Form' or letter of invitation you will obtain a Business (F) visa valid for 60 days. This is often referred to as a Visitor Visa, as distinct from a Tourist (L) Visa. After arrival in China this can be converted to a long-stay (Z) work visa. Processing takes four to eight weeks.

Many people enter China on a tourist (L) visa (one to three months), sign a contract with an employer, collect the documentation, then leave the country (to Hong Kong or Macao) to apply for the Z visa. Some employers will even cover the costs. Make sure this happens before your visitor visa expires, which is calculated according to the date of entry to China rather than the expiry date of the visa. Otherwise you will be liable to a fine. Since the Olympics the authorities have become more prickly about residence and related documentation.

As always happens in countries that initially welcome a huge influx of English teachers, the government regulations gradually tighten up, and this is what has been happening in China in 2009/2010. It would be nice to provide a succinct summary of the visa rules, but that is not easy or even possible in a country as vast and diverse as China where rules are not enforced uniformly between regions or even municipalities. The toughest requirements for obtaining the Z visa are that candidates must have a degree plus TEFL plus two years' post-university teaching experience, as has been reported in Beijing and Shanghai. Elsewhere, the requirements seem not to be so tough, partly because schools that try to do things by the book are finding it difficult to recruit enough teachers. But the picture is not black and white and even within the most highly regulated regions, adverts can still be seen for teachers with minimal skills/qualifications. Any teacher considering answering an advert like this (e.g. for a no-degree-needed job) should find out in advance what visa the employer plans to get for them, Z or otherwise, and whether the school will provide them with basic employee benefits such as government health insurance.

The Z visa does not necessarily allow multiple entry so find out before you leave China. It is now compulsory to undergo a medical check-up in China. Everything has to be officially stamped. If you are found without the appropriate documents you will be harshly fined. For example, recently a teacher whose papers were mostly in order but hadn't got the resident's permit was fined RMB3,000 (more than half a month's wages). State institutes of education usually do everything by the book but you shouldn't expect the same of private language schools.

LEISURE TIME

Foreigners who teach in Beijing can lead a standard expatriate life if they want to, socialising at expat bars and clubs. Life in the provinces will be very different. You may still be one of the very few foreigners that the local people have ever seen and are bound to be the object of curious stares (which will be even more persistent if you happen to be a non-white person).

The main way of socialising in China is going to restaurants, because a large banquet shared by many people is only marginally more expensive than cooking for yourself. However, as most people go out to eat around 6pm–7pm, restaurants do not usually stay open later than 10pm. Students in state institutions can be restricted by a strict curfew, but when everything closes at 10pm, native English teachers start to realise why the students are not so bothered.

In smaller settlements, there may be no restaurants even to rival the Chinese take-away in your home town; but the locals will be far more interested in you and perhaps even teach you to cook your own Chinese food. If there are several foreigners, communal dining facilities (often segregated) will usually be provided. Glutinous rice, soy beans and cabbage are staples and fresh produce may be in short supply in winter. In Tangshan, **Bradwell Jackson** reports that he can have a 'killer meal' of dumplings, quick and right off the street, for only 2 yuan (yuan is an alternative word for renminbi). Learning Chinese is the ambition of many teachers and is a great asset especially outside cosmopolitan areas. Take a good teach-yourself book and CD/tapes, since these are difficult to obtain outside Beijing and Shanghai. Mastering Chinese characters is a daunting business, though the grammar is straightforward. Others prefer to study Tai Chi, Wushu or other exotic martial arts.

Despite China's rapid 'Westernisation' in economic terms, its cultural differences remain a challenge. A teacher summed it up in 2010: '*I found it quite difficult to understand the Chinese mentality and even the simplest of tasks seemed to take a lot longer than they really should, due mostly to cross cultural misinterpretation I would say.*'

Be prepared for noise and air pollution even in small towns, though it is usually possible to escape into the countryside by bicycle or bus. Some universities with large contingents of FTs organise group excursions for them from time to time. School and college vacations take place over Spring Festival in or around February, when the trains are very crowded and the weather is cold. Often the holiday dates are not known until the very last minute which makes it difficult to plan vacation travels.

Some cities such as Kunming have a good expat community to which the Chinese cater with Western-style cafés and restaurants. There are plenty of films to watch (all pirated) and a couple of galleries to visit. Much of the time you will be responsible for your own amusement, so take plenty of reading matter, including *Wild Swans*, an astonishing account of life in the Cultural Revolution or perhaps *Under Fishbone Clouds* by Sam Meekings quoted in this chapter, an interweaving of 20th-century Chinese history and folklore. **Jessie Levene** found lots to do in Chengdu: '*learn Chinese, take photos, enjoy the amazing Sichuan food, hang out with friends, go to bars...*'.

Bradwell Jackson would urge anybody to do TEFL in China:

> *My first impressions were that of a fascinating country with a splendid culture, and I wasn't even in a well-known city. The people are organised and respectful, and the food, of course, is a revelation. If you have just a little bit of travel experience to a non-Western country, you should be fine and have no worries at all. There is certainly no problem with safety. My school has been very good to me. You will find that most schools bend over backwards to get you here. All you need is a fair amount of teaching experience (and a college degree) and the whole new world of China awaits you.*

American **Ed Flok** is similarly enamoured of teaching in China and has just started his third year, this time at the North China University of Technology in Beijing:

> *Don't believe all the negative articles you read about China. Everywhere I taught (WECL-Qingdao and Yantai University) the people were awesome, and very polite, reaching out to make me their friend. I ate at personal dinner tables, swam in the Yellow Sea with students, ate at restaurants, went bike riding and socialised. The best of this experience was actually teaching the students English, and seeing how fast they learn. To this day I keep in contact with some of my first students. They really get attached to you as a role model, and want you as their friend.*

EF English First

I remember when I first started a career in teaching and was trying to make sense of all the terminology. I thought I was destined to drown in the number of acronyms used simply to define the industry: TEFL, TESOL, TESL, EFL, ESL and of course I also got these confused with some of the exams that use other, similar acronyms like TOEFL and TOEIC. Luckily, I managed to enrol in a teacher training course, rather than waste my money attending an exam prep class!

And of course, I did manage to eventually decipher these acronyms, although it was a rather anticlimactic moment when my trainer explained that Teaching English as a Foreign Language or as a Second Language was essentially the same thing.

This distinction didn't matter much to me again until later on in my career, when I began working in a language training school in China where TEFL was the buzz word. What was unique about this context, was it was also my first encounter with another popular term used widely in education: blended learning.

One huge advantage that ESL students have studying in an English-speaking country is their access to language outside the school. Students of English in China, for example, struggle to find enough opportunities to use and be exposed to language in the amount needed to make effective progress. However, having access to English learning tools on the Internet, combined with teacher-led classes, is one huge step to levelling the playing field.

Internet-based learning is still relatively new to China, but in major cities like Shanghai and Beijing it is becoming an increasingly popular way to study. It provides learners with a flexible, affordable, and interesting way to learn. And when combined with the advantages of face-to-face classroom learning, it is quite realistic to expect that English language learning in China will reach new heights.

William Dekker, National Academic Training Manager, EF English First

LIST OF EMPLOYERS

ALENEA RECRUITING
29–30 Windmill Street, London W1T 2JL, UK

☎ 020 7462 6481

✉ info@alenea.com

🖥 www.alenearecruiting.com

QUALIFICATIONS: Must have CELTA/Trinity plus some experience.

CONDITIONS OF EMPLOYMENT: 1-year contracts for client company that has 17 locations, mostly around Shanghai. 18 contact hours per week teaching both adults and children.

SALARY: RMB6,850–8,250 per month.

FACILITIES/SUPPORT: Accommodation will be found, however, the teacher must pay the rent (approximately 20% of salary). Flights will be reimbursed – half of the fare after 6 months and the rest after 12 months – and work permits are paid for.

CONTACT: Robin Summers.

AMITY FOUNDATION
71 Han Kou Road, Nanjing, Jiangsu 210008

☎ 25 83260836

🖥 www.amityfoundation.org

NUMBER OF TEACHERS: 40–50 plus more for 1-month summer programme.

PREFERENCE OF NATIONALITY: None, but must be native English speaker or have a high level of proficiency in English and language teaching experience.

QUALIFICATIONS: Minimum bachelor's degree (though a handful accepted without a degree for summer programme).

Teaching experience, a knowledge of Chinese or of living in Asia are useful but not essential. A Christian faith commitment is generally required, however, the 'mission' expected is to serve rather than to proselytise.

CONDITIONS OF EMPLOYMENT: Initial 2-year contract with possible year by year extensions to teach 12–16 in tertiary educational institutions in China, mostly small teacher training colleges in the western parts of China. Also SEP (Summer English Programme) for volunteers to provide oral English training to Chinese middle and primary school teachers of English in rural and minority areas, for 4 weeks from early July.

SALARY: Long-stay teachers receive $250 monthly plus RMB2,500. Expenses for travel, orientation, conferences and medical insurance are covered by the sponsoring agency. Summer volunteers pay fee of $1,200 to cover orientation, admin, etc.

FACILITIES/SUPPORT: Accommodation is usually provided in the form of an apartment on the school campus.

RECRUITMENT: Teachers are recruited primarily through church sending agencies, i.e. mission agencies of various denominations in a range of countries including the UK, Canada and the USA. See above website for contact details of these organisations. Interviews in person are expected and generally take place in the applicant's own country.

CONTACT: Ms. Ruhong Liu, Director, Education & International Exchange Division (liuruhong@amity.org.cn); SEP contact is Robert Ji, SEP Programme Coordinator (jixiaodong@amity.org.cn).

ANGLIA SCHOLARS EDUCATIONAL CONSULTANCY (ASEC)
24 Hampshire Terrace, Portsmouth, Hampshire PO1 2QF, UK
02392 826636
liuweidan@hotmail.com
www.angliascholars.co.uk/www.teach-in-china.co.uk

NUMBER OF TEACHERS: 10–15.

PREFERENCE OF NATIONALITY: British, American, Canadian and Australian.

QUALIFICATIONS: Bachelor's or master's degree, TEFL.

CONDITIONS OF EMPLOYMENT: One academic year, 20 hours per week.

SALARY: RMB5,000–RMB6,000. The first RMB5,000 are tax-free.

FACILITIES/SUPPORT: Free accommodation provided.

RECRUITMENT: Newspaper adverts. Interviews held in the UK.

CONTACT: Weidan Liu, Secretary.

APPALACHIANS ABROAD TEACH IN CHINA PROGRAM
Center for International Programs, Marshall University, One John Marshall Drive, Huntington, West Virginia 25755, USA
304 696 6265
gochina@marshall.edu
www.marshall.edu/gochina

NUMBER OF TEACHERS: 40–60 annually.

PREFERENCE OF NATIONALITY: American, Canadian and British.

QUALIFICATIONS: Bachelor's degree is essential; accepted ages range from new college graduates to early retirees.

CONDITIONS OF EMPLOYMENT: 10-month teaching contract from 1 September. Teaching 15–18 hours per week, at public and private primary and secondary schools and in institutes of higher education, mainly in Shanghai and Beijing but other areas as well.

SALARY: RMB5,000–14,000+ per month, up to 1 month paid winter school break and full international airfare paid on completion of teaching contract.

FACILITIES/SUPPORT: Accommodation provided free by hosting school. 5-day orientation in Shanghai in late August before arriving at Chinese host school.

RECRUITMENT: Internet adverts and phone interviews. Application deadline 31 March/15 April. Application fee is $100; job placement and administrative fee is $1,250 which includes 9 weeks of online China TEFL training and 5-day orientation in Shanghai, visa service, and 1-year travel accident insurance.

CONTACT: QingQing Zhao, Director of China Projects.

ASTON ENGLISH SCHOOLS
Dalian Head Office, Room 2003, Yue Xiu Mansion, No. 82 Xin Kai Road, Xi Gang Dist. Dalian, Liaoning Province 116011
+86 411 8376 9995
www.astonrecruiting.com

NUMBER OF TEACHERS: 200+ annually for about 50 schools all over China.

PREFERENCE OF NATIONALITY: American, Canadian, British, Irish, Australian, New Zealander and South African.

QUALIFICATIONS: University degree (any subject) and a TEFL certificate and/or TEFL experience. Candidates without a TEFL background can take a 1-week course in China which meets this requirement, at a cost of $110 (approximately RMB750), which is refunded after 3 months on the contract.

CONDITIONS OF EMPLOYMENT: Contract lengths of 6–7 weeks in summer or winter, 6 or 12 months starting mid-September of beginning of March, 7.5 or 13.5 months starting mid-January and mid-July. 15, 20 or 25 hours per week contracts.

SALARY: RMB6,200 for 25 hours, RMB5,000 for 20 hours and RMB4,000 for 15 hours per week. Varying end-of-contract bonuses of up RMB9,000 (approximately $1,150) based on hours and length of contract. Teachers pay for their own flights. Small tax deductions.

FACILITIES/SUPPORT: Contracts provide teachers with private bedrooms in a 2- or 3-bedroom Chinese-style apartment. Teachers must pay for utilities. Proper documents provided for work visas before arrival and residence permit after.

RECRUITMENT: Via all methods such as internet, phone and in-person interviews in China and the USA. Phone but not in-person interviews required. Recruiting representatives in USA, UK, Australia and New Zealand (see website or email for contact details). Teachers can meet recruitment staff in Seattle, Dalian or on-site at schools in China.

CONTACT: Michael Wisner, Head Recruiter in USA (503 320 3573; teachinchina@aol.com; Skype aesnewjersey).

BELL PARTNER SCHOOLS
Hillscross, Red Cross Lane, Cambridge CB2 2QX, UK
- 01223 275500
- www.bell-worldwide.com

NUMBER OF TEACHERS: Varying for 4 language training centres in Shanghai, Beijing, Ningbo and Macao.

PREFERENCE OF NATIONALITY: None, but must have native-like fluency.

QUALIFICATIONS: Bachelor's degree and CELTA and 1 year's experience, preferably in China.

CONDITIONS OF EMPLOYMENT: 1-year renewable contracts. Normally 20 contact hours per week over 5 days.

SALARY: Varies but example of job teaching corporate clients in Beijing of RMB102,000–150,000 gross per year. Approximately 12% deductions.

FACILITIES/SUPPORT: Flights for teachers recruited outside China. Accommodation or accommodation allowance provided. Work permit and visas arranged. End of contract payment. 6 weeks' paid holiday per year plus public holidays. Local medical insurance cover provided. Commitment to in-service training and continued professional development.

RECRUITMENT: Internet, newspapers, personal interview, telephone interview through Bell Worldwide in the UK.

BOND LANGUAGE INSTITUTE
Building No. 7, Song Mao Ge, Bai Yuan Xin Cun, Dong Qu, Shiqi, Zhongshan, Guangdong, 528403
- 86 760 88310963/88317181
- bond_ Institute@hotmail.com /bond_ Institute@yahoo.com.cn /zongcheng007@hotmail.com
- www.tefl-bond.com/www.bond-Institute.com

NUMBER OF TEACHERS: 100+.

PREFERENCE OF NATIONALITY: All major English-speaking countries.

QUALIFICATIONS: Preferably those with TEFL/TESOL certificates and college diploma and above.

CONDITIONS OF EMPLOYMENT: Usually a 6-month or 1-year contract. The maximum weekly workload is about 20 hours.

SALARY: RMB6,400+ ($970) less RMB125 for tax.

FACILITIES/SUPPORT: Complimentary accommodation; usually state-of-the-art fully-furnished apartment units equipped with major domestic and electric appliances. Nationally accredited and authorised to employ Western teachers and process work permits.

RECRUITMENT: By word of mouth and through partners throughout the world. Interviews are essential and are often carried out in the UK and in North America.

CONTACT: John Zhang or Maria Wang, Recruiting Officers.

BUCKLAND INTERNATIONAL EDUCATION GROUP
Dacunmen Villa District 555, Yangshuo, Guilin 541900
- 773 882 7555
- bucklandgroup@gmail.com
- www.bucklandgroup.org

NUMBER OF TEACHERS: 80+.

PREFERENCE OF NATIONALITY: Native English speakers – British, American, Canadian, Australian, Irish or New Zealander.

QUALIFICATIONS: Bachelor's degree or TESOL certificate preferable.

CONDITIONS OF EMPLOYMENT: 5 or 11-month renewable contracts available. 15 teaching hours per week from Monday to Friday.

SALARY: RMB4,500–6,500 after tax per month. Taxes paid by the school.

FACILITIES/SUPPORT: Free accommodation provided for all teachers. Fully furnished, private flats with at least 1 bedroom, living room, kitchen with full facilities, computer with internet access, air conditioning. Work visas provided for all teachers regardless of length of contract. Free training course which covers how to teach Chinese students.

RECRUITMENT: Usually via the internet (Dave's ESL Cafe). Interviews not essential.

CONTACT: Owen Buckland.

COLORADO CHINA COUNCIL
4556 Apple Way, Boulder, Colorado 80301, USA
303 443 1108
alice@asiacouncil.org
www.asiacouncil.org

NUMBER OF PARTICIPANTS: 20–35 per year in the year-long and the 3-week summer programmes. Participants are placed at universities throughout China, many of which CCC has worked with for nearly two decades.

PREFERENCE OF NATIONALITY: North American with no discernible regional accent.

QUALIFICATIONS: Minimum bachelor's or higher degree (all majors and professional backgrounds considered, though English, TEFL, linguistics, business, accounting, economics and engineering especially welcomes). Universities prefer that applicants have some teaching/public speaking/tutoring/ seminar presentation background. People with a master's degree or PhD are strongly encouraged to apply, as are couples. Must be under 65 at time of application and in excellent mental and physical health.

CONDITIONS OF EMPLOYMENT: Full academic year programme runs from September to June/July. Summer programme placements also available for 3 weeks in Nanjing to teach oral English to high school and college age students – a great way to get beyond the tourist trap and see China from the inside. Year-long programme: 16–20 hours per week; 3-week intensive TESL and Mandarin Training Institute in Shanghai in August for people on the year-long programme.

SALARY: Monthly stipend about RMB4,000–RMB11,000 per month depending on university, and academic or professional background, free housing in FTs' complex, medical benefits, most or all of round trip transportation costs reimbursed and 5–8 week paid vacation over Chinese New Year.

FACILITIES/SUPPORT: CCC provides full support if any problems or issues arise at any point. Most universities invite CCC's teachers to teach for a second year. Housing is adequate to excellent depending on city and university. CCC is the oldest, non-religious, China teaching, training and

placement organisation in the USA which accepts people from all over the country.

RECRUITMENT: Rolling application but after 1 February there is a late fee. Deadline for 3-week Nanjing summer Program is 1 March, or until all positions are filled. For fees, application and information please see the website.

CONTACT: Alice Renouf, Director.

EF ENGLISH FIRST
Teacher Recruitment Department, 666 Fuzhou Road, 1F Jingling Hai Building, Shanghai 200001
+86 21 6133 6047
efrecruitment@ef.com
www.englishfirst.com/trt/

NUMBER OF TEACHERS: 1,000 a year for more than 100 EFL schools in China.

PREFERENCE OF NATIONALITY: Native English speakers.

QUALIFICATIONS: University degree, internationally recognised TEFL certification and teaching experience.

CONDITIONS OF EMPLOYMENT: 12-month contracts. Teaching 21 (real) hours between 9am and 9pm, 5 days a week.

SALARY: Approx. $1,810 (RMB12,350) per month.

FACILITIES/SUPPORT: Shanghai, Beijing, Guangzhou and Shenzhen schools provide comprehensive benefits package including relocation assistance, flight allowance, health insurance, paid vacation, official working visa, Mandarin lessons, and ongoing training and professional development.

RECRUITMENT: Via EF's Online Recruitment Centre at www. englishfirst.com/trt or send resumé and qualification details to efrecruitment@ef.com.

GOLDEN APPLE CHILD EDUCATION (GROUP)
7 Xinguang Road, Gaoxin District, Chengdu, Sichuan 610041
28 85133381/15902804305
tranzchina@gmail.com or nigel@tranzchina. com
www.61bb.com/english/index.asp

NUMBER OF TEACHERS: 20–25.

PREFERENCE OF NATIONALITY: American, British, Canadian, Australian, New Zealander, Irish and South African.

QUALIFICATIONS: Minimum bachelor's degree in any subject and 2 years' post-graduation work experience in any field.

CONDITIONS OF EMPLOYMENT: Standard 1-year contract. 15–25 hours per week.

SALARY: RMB4,000–RMB9,000 per month depending on hours and experience. (ESL Teachers) RMB6,000–RMB20,000 per month, qualified kindergarten, primary, IB teachers/coordinators. Taxes are deducted from salaries over RMB4,800 per month.

FACILITIES/SUPPORT: School provides accommodation or a stipend towards housing, and a FE's licence and working 'Z' visa. The procedure requires teachers to sign a contract with the school and the government, and get a medical in their own country on the official Chinese embassy paperwork. The school then applies for a government invitation letter using the paperwork, which takes about a month or so to receive. An invitation letter to the teacher is then posted and teachers apply for a Z visa from the Chinese embassy.

RECRUITMENT: Through internet adverts, word of mouth.

CONTACT: Nigel Jones, Director of English Education.

HAINAN YUDA FOREIGN LANGUAGE ACADEMY
Cheng Zhong Cheng, Bldg. A, Guo Mao, First Floor, Haikou, Hainan 570125
- 898 6854 2687
- contact@yudafla.com; recruitment@yudafla.com
- http://yudafla.com/en

NUMBER OF TEACHERS: 7 for three branches in Haikou.

PREFERENCE OF NATIONALITY: American, Canadian, British and Australian.

QUALIFICATIONS: Minimum – bachelor's degree, master's degree preferred. Considerable preference given to career educators with former relevant teaching experience in country of origin.

CONDITIONS OF EMPLOYMENT: 12-month renewable contract.

Starting SALARY: RMB5,500–8,000 per month net, contingent on education and experience with automatic annual increments, plus up to RMB15,000 per annum in bonuses paid semi-annually.

FACILITIES/SUPPORT: High standard single and married couple accommodation (close to the school) provided with furnishings and a Western, coiled-spring mattress. All teaching materials provided.

RECRUITMENT: Email correspondence and telephone interview.

CONTACT: Miss Li, Principal.

INTERLINGUA SCHOOL
Guiyang: 79 Wenchangnanlu, Guiyang, Guizhou 550001
- 851 687 3852
Zunyi: Yangliu Street, Zunyi, Guizhou 563001
- 852 825 6850
- job@interlinguaschool.com
- www.interlinguaschool.com
- job@doesl.com
- www.doesl.com

NUMBER OF TEACHERS: 13.

PREFERENCE OF NATIONALITY: British, American, Canadian, Australian and New Zealander.

QUALIFICATIONS: Minimum bachelor's degree. ESL/EFL qualification and 2 years' teaching experience preferred.

CONDITIONS OF EMPLOYMENT: 1 year or longer. 16–26 hours per week.

SALARY: RMB4,200–RMB8,000 net, depending on qualifications. International trip allowance, end-of-contract bonus, healthcare and travelling allowance all paid.

FACILITIES/SUPPORT: Accommodation offered free of charge. School applies for work permit from the provincial education administration on arrival. Free Mandarin lessons.

CONTACT: Maosi Yan, Programme Director.

PEARSON LONGMAN SCHOOLS
655 Fuzhou Road, 17th Floor, Shanghai
- +86 21 6351 5923
- longmancareers.sh@pearson.com
- www.longmancareers.com

NUMBER OF TEACHERS: 50+.

PREFERENCE OF NATIONALITY: Native English speakers.

QUALIFICATIONS: Minimum bachelor's degree, TEFL and 2 years' teaching experience.

CONDITIONS OF EMPLOYMENT: One-year contract. Approximately 36 hours per week with a maximum of 20 teaching hours. Paid overtime available.

SALARY: RMB9,000–RMB 13,000 base plus paid overtime and year end bonus.

FACILITIES/SUPPORT: Assistance provided with finding accommodation and applying for work permit.

RECRUITMENT: Usually via the internet and recruitment agencies. Candidates are asked to write a lesson plan prior to interview (carried out by phone if the candidate is not local).

CONTACT: Tim Franta, Instructor.

For contacts in other countries, see entry at beginning of Asia chapter.

PREFERENCE OF NATIONALITY: British, American, Canadian, Australian and New Zealander, Irish, and South African.

QUALIFICATIONS: A full university degree (any discipline) is enough for most schools in the smaller cities or towns. Teachers in the bigger cities face much tougher requirements as the government will only issue work papers to those that have a TEFL qualification plus at least two years of work experience after leaving university (with one of those years being in a teaching or training-related field). Through a partnership with a TEFL course provider, Reach To Teach can assist teachers in getting course discounts.

CONDITIONS OF EMPLOYMENT: All job placements are full-time positions and for 1 year (and usually extendable). Teaching schedules vary but are generally either daytime, or afternoons and evenings.

SALARY: Depends on school, but commonly: reimbursed flights to and from China, free furnished apartment, salaries between RMB7,000 and RMB15,000 per month depending on qualifications and location.

FACILITIES/SUPPORT: China visa guidance, airport collection, teacher orientation, etc. are provided. Teachers have the option of continued support and contact with Reach To Teach throughout their year-long placement.

RECRUITMENT: Applications submitted via website. Interviews conducted over phone and occasionally in person.

CONTACT: Director of Recruiting – China.

NUMBER OF TEACHERS: 4–6.

PREFERENCE OF NATIONALITY: North American.

QUALIFICATIONS: College degree in English with a teaching credential.

CONDITIONS OF EMPLOYMENT: 1 year. Teaching hours 1pm–9pm.

SALARY: $1,000–$1,500 a month.

FACILITIES/SUPPORT: Fully furnished studio apartment for 1 is provided. Teachers can arrive on tourist visa and REC can organise visa upgrade after arrival.

RECRUITMENT: TESOL Conventions in North America. Otherwise via internet/email.

CONTACT: Robert H. Toomey, Director of Education.

NUMBER OF TEACHERS: 500 recruited for various schools on TOSIC (Teach or Study in China) programme.

PREFERENCE OF NATIONALITY: Canadian, American, British and Australian.

QUALIFICATIONS: Minimum bachelor's degree.

CONDITIONS OF EMPLOYMENT: Standard length of contract is 1 year. 20 hours per week.

SALARY: RMB3500+ net.

FACILITIES/SUPPORT: Free accommodation provided.

RECRUITMENT: Internet. Application can be made online.

CONTACT: Quartz Shi, Consultant.

NUMBER OF TEACHERS: 200–300.

PREFERENCE OF NATIONALITY: Native English speakers: British, American, Canadian, Australian and New Zealander.

QUALIFICATIONS: Minimum bachelor's degree and commitment to teaching.

CONDITIONS OF EMPLOYMENT: 6 months or 1 year. 15 hours per week.

SALARY: Varies.

FACILITIES/SUPPORT: Schools provide free housing and send candidates visa approval documents.

RECRUITMENT: Internet and newspaper ads. Interviews always conducted by phone.

USIT IRELAND

19/21 Aston Quay, Dublin 2, Ireland

☏ +353 1 602 1742

✉ volunteer@usit.ie

🖥 www.usit.ie

PREFERENCE OF NATIONALITY: None.

QUALIFICATIONS: Degree in any field.

CONDITIONS OF EMPLOYMENT: 5–12 months renewable contract. Between 4 and 6 hours per day.

SALARY: €5,500 to €12,960 per year.

FACILITIES/SUPPORT: Schools will organise accommodation for the teachers, free of charge. Otherwise, coordinator in China will assist with finding accommodation and obtaining work permits.

RECRUITMENT: Interviews essential and can be held using Skype.

CONTACT: Alan Byrne, Volunteer and Paid Teach Abroad Coordinator.

VET (VOLUNTEER ENGLISH TEACHERS) PROGRAM

No.78 Lane 1 Longyue Road, Yangshuo Guilin, Guangxi 541900

☏ +86 773 8811420

✉ vetchina.yangshuo@gmail.com

🖥 www.guilin-yangshuo.com/VET/index.html or www.vet-china.org.

Licensed charity set up in 2004 by retired Canadian professor living in Yangshuo.

NUMBER OF VOLUNTEERS: VET works in 4–5 rural primary schools and one orphanage, helping students in village schools improve their oral English and giving them an opportunity to meet foreigners, to improve their chances of getting out of poverty and finding employment in the tourist and service industry around Yangshuo.

PREFERENCE OF NATIONALITY: Anyone with a strong proficiency in English and an easily understood accent is acceptable.

QUALIFICATIONS: Minimum age 18, no maximum. Previous work with children aged 9–12 is desirable. Volunteers should be imaginative and creative, energetic, motivated, patient, with the ability to work independently and as a member of a team.

CONDITIONS OF WORK: 3+ months; shorter stays by arrangement.

SALARY: None. Volunteers must cover return airfare from the country of origin; a 3-month tourist visa (if a volunteer stays

longer VET will assist with a visa extension), spending money.

FACILITIES/SUPPORT: All volunteers have a 2-day orientation with a qualified teacher trainer and ongoing support from the VET team.

RECRUITMENT: Volunteers accepted throughout regular school year but not during exam or holiday periods; terms run September to mid-January and March to mid-June. Interviews are not required.

CONTACT: Laurie Mackenzie (Founder/Director) or Jennifer Jiang (Assistant Director).

VIP China TEFL Training Centre

1207E, Culture Tower, Renmin University of China, Zhongguancun Street 59, Haidian District, Beijing 100872

☏ +86 10 6251 4017

✉ lily511711@hotmail.com

🖥 www.vipchina.org.cn

NUMBER OF TEACHERS: Approximately 50 every semester.

QUALIFICATIONS: TEFL/TESOL certificate and a bachelor's degree or above. Volunteers and teaching interns do not need a degree. Aged between 20 and 55.

CONDITIONS OF EMPLOYMENT: 13 to 20 working hours per week.

SALARY: RMB4,000–RMB8,000 per month for an English expert, RMB2,000–RMB3,000 for a teaching intern and RMB500–2,000 monthly for a volunteer.

FACILITIES/SUPPORT: Free apartment or single room with shared kitchen is provided. Usually the water, electricity and gas are free of charge.

RECRUITMENT: Interviews are essential and can be carried out in the UK or USA.

CONTACT: Nancy.

WALL STEET ENGLISH

3f, Jin Mao Tower, 88 Century Avenue, Pudong, Shanghai 200121

☏ +86 21 5047 0629

✉ hywel_davies@wsi.com.cn

🖥 www.wsi.com.cn

NUMBER OF TEACHERS: Over 200.

PREFERENCE OF NATIONALITY: Must be native English speaker for visa requirements.

QUALIFICATIONS: Degree, CELTA or equivalent plus 2 years' post-graduation teaching experience.

CONDITIONS OF EMPLOYMENT: 1-year contract, with 2 options for working hours; 35 hours with 30 contact hours per week or 25 hours with 21 contact hours per week. All contracts include evening and weekend classes.

SALARY: Approximately $2,000 per month for 35 hour contract.

FACILITIES/SUPPORT: First week hotel accommodation is paid for. HR staff will help with accommodation thereafter as well as visa processing and general settling in. All visa costs are covered but teacher must pay rent and deposit for accommodation.

RECRUITMENT: Usually via online advertising and word of mouth. 2 rounds of interviews which can be conducted using Skype.

CONTACT: Hyw Davies, National Service Training Manager.

WECL ENGLISH COLLEGE QINGDAO

133 Fuzhou Road North, Building 4, Suite 302, Shibei District, Qingdao, Shandong Province
✆ +86 532 85699837
✉ fenglin616@hotmail.com
🖥 www.weclqd.com

NUMBER OF TEACHERS: 10.

PREFERENCE OF NATIONALITY: American or Canadian.

QUALIFICATIONS: At least 1 year's teaching experience.

CONDITIONS OF EMPLOYMENT: 1-year contracts. 20/24 hours per week.

SALARY: RMB4,000–RMB6,000 per month.

FACILITIES/SUPPORT: Free apartment. School will apply for a FE certificate and residence permit for the teachers once they provide a resumé, passport copy, diploma and certificate, medical report, 2-inch photo, reference letter, etc.

RECRUITMENT: Via internet agencies. Interviews are required.

CONTACT: Selina.

XI'AN JIAOTONG-LIVERPOOL UNIVERSITY ENGLISH LANGUAGE CENTRE

No.111 Ren'ai Road, Suzhou Dushu Lake Higher Education Town, Suzhou Industrial Park, Suzhou, Jiangsu 215123
✆ +86 512 88161300/1345
✉ elc.sec@xjtlu.edu.cn
🖥 www.xjtlu.edu.cn/depts/elc

NUMBER OF TEACHERS: 45.

PREFERENCE OF NATIONALITY: None.

QUALIFICATIONS: Tutors need a MA in TESOL/Applied Linguistics and assistant tutors need Cert. TESOL or equivalent.

CONDITIONS OF EMPLOYMENT: 1-year renewable contract. Office hours are between 9am and 5pm with 20 hours of teaching per week.

SALARY: RMB20,500 per month for a tutor position. Assistant tutor salaries range from RMB12,500 to RMB19,900.

FACILITIES/SUPPORT: Housing allowance of up to RMB3,000 per month and HR will assist with finding accommodation and applying for work permits.

RECRUITMENT: Usually via adverts on www.jobs.ac.uk and other websites. Applications are welcome all-year round but main recruitment drives are in March and May each year. Interviews and some pre-interview tasks are essential and can be carried out over the phone or internet.

CONTACT: Steve Jeaco, Director of the ELC.

XU BO ART AND CULTURE EXCHANGE

Room 2506, B Block, Lane 521, Wan Ping Road (South), Shanghai, 200032
✆ +86 21 54590999
🖥 www.xubo.org

NUMBER OF TEACHERS: 150 volunteers per year.

PREFERENCE OF NATIONALITY: None.

QUALIFICATIONS: None necessary.

CONDITIONS OF EMPLOYMENT: 1–3 months volunteer work. Between 10 and 15 lessons per week (40 minutes).

SALARY: None.

FACILITIES/SUPPORT: Accommodation is arranged. No working permits are needed.

RECRUITMENT: Via overseas volunteer organisations.

CONTACT: Jiong Duanmu.

Mongolia

NEW CHOICE MONGOLIAN VOLUNTEER ORGANIZATION

POB-159, Ulaanbaatar-210646 A

info@volunteer.org.mn

www.volunteer.org.mn

NUMBER OF TEACHERS: 5.

PREFERENCE OF NATIONALITY: None.

QUALIFICATIONS: Native speakers of English from UK, Ireland, USA or Australia with teaching skills.

CONDITIONS OF EMPLOYMENT: 12-week contracts. 4–6 hours per day; 20–30 hours per week.

SALARY: $100–$200 per month.

FACILITIES/SUPPORT: Accommodation provided with host families or in apartment. New Choice will apply for teacher's work permission and long-term visa.

CONTACT: Bayarjargal Damdindagva, Programme Director.

HONG KONG

Since the former British colony became the Hong Kong Special Administrative Region (HKSAR) of the People's Republic of China on 23 June 1997, '*everything has changed and nothing has changed*', or so the saying goes. Only international schools and specialist 'ESF' (English Schools Foundation) primary schools offer a curriculum using English as the medium of instruction (EMI), although it's more common in secondary schools. There is ongoing pressure to review the EMI/CMI situation and the issue has been much in the news in 2010. The situation is likely to change in the next academic year, when schools will be given more choice as to whether they switch to EMI. So, all in all, it's debatable as to whether English has seen a decline in Hong Kong as interest in Putonghua (simplified Mandarin Chinese) has increased, or vice versa. Certainly, many parents are still willing to spend vast sums on English courses for their children and there is a high demand for native English speakers willing to teach children from as young as 3 years. Many of these companies have proprietary learning systems and systematic phonics programmes.

To meet the demand for English teaching, the Hong Kong government employs hundreds of English speakers to teach in the state education system and in non-government schools too as part of the NET scheme (native English teacher) described below.

It is illegal to enter Hong Kong as a tourist and take up work so that those graduates who arrive on holiday and want to change their status are out of luck. However, it is possible to visit the city, find a teaching job and then apply for a work permit from a neighbouring country; Macao is the most convenient. The authorities will expect to see a university degree, relevant work experience and a corporate sponsor. Teachers who satisfy these requirements should have no difficulty obtaining a work permit. Anyone who manages to find an employer before arrival can seek sponsorship to obtain a work permit. This is a major undertaking for any employer so teachers should try to honour their commitments instead of flitting off to a better-paying school after a month or two.

FINDING A JOB

NET SCHEME

The NET scheme is administered by the Hong Kong Education Bureau (EDB), formerly the Education and Manpower Bureau (NET Administration Team, Room 1321, 13th Floor Wu Chung House, 213 Queen's Road East, Wan Chai; netrecruit@edb.gov.hk; www.edb.gov.hk/index. aspx?nodeID=262&langno=1). The website carries full details of the scheme and an application form. FTs known as 'NETs' can interview for any school with a vacancy and have some control over where they're placed. The NET community maintains an online 'blacklist' of schools to avoid. The reason the scheme is so popular is that salaries and benefits are generous.

Since the last edition of this book, the competition has become a lot keener for acceptance onto the scheme because there is no longer a shortage of applicants. Acceptance is easier if you have had teacher training, though the programme is open to university graduates of language-related subjects with a TEFL certificate. The salary range for primary NET is HK$19,835 (£1,760) to HK$40,290–38,265 (£3,570) per month and for secondary NET even higher, HK$22,985 (£2,000) to HK$48,400 (£4,300). Exact salaries are dependent on experience and qualifications. However, every NET whose home is outside Hong Kong gets a monthly cash housing allowance of HK$14,242 (£1,260) which really bumps up the salary. Also, there is a 15% gratuity on everything you earn, awarded at the end of the two-year contract, provided your conduct and performance have met with approval. Flights, medical allowance and baggage allowance are all additional perks.

Applications are usually accepted until mid-January and term begins around mid-August. After working in the private sector for the Chatteris Foundation (described below), **Tom Grundy** became a Netter and has posted lots of useful information about living and working in Hong Kong on his website (www.globalcitizen.co.uk/wp/hong-kong-job-hunting-links) and has provided information for this chapter. In comparing the two, Tom concludes:

> *The government NET programme is more highbrow and demanding but offers a better package and wage. However, you don't get the 'instant social circle' you would with an employer like Chatteris. NET is ideal should you decide to remain in HK and great if you already have a TEFL or PGCE qualification.*

He recommends the 'NET Survival Guide' at http://en.wikibooks.org/wiki/NET_Teacher_Survival_ Guide to answer any questions about the programme.

OTHER EMPLOYERS

Almost any English institute you locate on the internet will have a Recruitment or Careers page. One of the largest is the Chatteris Educational Foundation (see entry), which offers recent university graduates from English-speaking countries the opportunity to teach in Hong Kong. In 2009/10 this scheme, like the government scheme, became more difficult to enter, possibly because it is being scaled back or because the standard of applicant has risen.

Tom Grundy completed the nine-month programme before he became a Netter:

> *The wages were just enough to live on and save some for travel. I saved hard and was able to travel for three months around South East Asia afterwards, and even afforded two laptops. Chatteris has its problems and its 'charitable' status is questionable, but they support and train you. You'll be placed with another British, Canadian or American in a primary or secondary school, there'll be several dozen others who you'll train with and so you'll immediately have a big social network. Chatteris has also started a somewhat experimental 'college programme', though the more traditional school placements are a better option. With Chatteris, your emphasis will be on oral English with a 'non-formal' approach, i.e. games, crafts and other 'fun' activities.*

The basic wage of HK$13,000 hasn't risen much in the past couple of years and by about Christmas many CNETs (Chatteris Native-speaking English Tutors) conclude that their wages are exploitative. A further problem is the interference from the scheme management requiring constant paperwork, workshops and meetings which can upset the balance of the relationship with the school.

Ready to Learn (www.readytolearn.com.hk) employs about 30–40 teachers for a number of centres, although it is not interested in '*travellers seeing the world with a TEFL qualification or similar*'. They are looking for teachers who will commit longer term and take an interest in the company and its methods.

Dramatic English (see list of organisations) employs drama graduates on 10-month contracts, who are able to use their performance skills to help children learn English.

Demand is very strong for native English speakers to work in English-speaking kindergartens, for which a degree and a TEFL qualification are generally sufficient. English for Asia (www.englishforasia. com) in Kowloon is another major recruiter, though it can usually employ graduates of its own Trinity CertTESOL course (see Directory of Training Courses). Another reputable private language school which hires foreigners and also offers accredited TESOL certificates is Firstclass Intesol (http://in-tesol.firstclass.com.hk).

Both internet adverts and the more traditional print-based means of advertising jobs are still going strong. For example the bumper Saturday edition of the *South China Morning Post* might contain some useful leads; its classified section often carries teaching posts and can be consulted online at www.classifiedpost.com. *HK Magazine* is a weekly listings paper aimed at the ex-pat community which is available every Thursday evening from branches of Pacific Coffee and other 'ex-pat friendly' outlets. *BC Magazine* is a similar monthly publication. The online community http://jobs.asiaxpat.com carries many ads for teachers and the main resource for jobs in HK is www.jobsdb.com. The *Yellow Pages* are an alternative source of institute addresses. Landline calls and faxes within the city limits are free, so by phoning around you can easily get an idea of the possibilities. Although hiring is continuous, the summer months bring even more openings, while the Chinese New Year in January/February is a bad time.

Some companies specialise in recruiting and outsourcing teachers, saving schools the administrative burden of employing a foreigner. Elton Educational Services (www.eltoneducation.com) provides English courses and English teachers to Hong Kong kindergartens and primary schools.

Freelance teaching can prove lucrative although it's always a risk for non-permanent residents, as work visas forbid foreigners to work for anyone other than their named sponsor. An attractive advertisement strategically placed in the letter boxes of the ritzy apartment estates in Mid Levels, Jardine's Lookout and Causeway Bay suburbs or in busy supermarkets might winkle out some private students. It is also possible to pick up tutoring work where you visit a family's home and help their child with homework/English games. The standard payment is £20–£30 an hour. Summer schools, English drama organisations and language schools are also options in Hong Kong, but all foreign workers doing paid or voluntary work require a work visa, so make arrangements with an employer beforehand.

Although Hong Kong is famous for its big city smog and vivacity, there are quieter places and it is worth researching the exact place where you will be living and working. **J. W. Arble** worked at a secondary school in the New Territories in a suburban town 30 miles to the north of Hong Kong Island. *'I lived alone in a 12 by 16ft flat, 17 floors above a colossal shopping centre of six hundred stores, 30 restaurants and a single bookshop that mainly stocked self-help guides and comics. Everything shut at 10pm.'*

REGULATIONS

British citizens may visit the HKSAR without a visa for up to 180 days provided they can satisfy the immigration officer on arrival that they are entering as bona fide visitors with enough funds to cover the duration of their stay without working and, unless in transit to the Mainland of China or the region of Macau, hold onward or return tickets. USA citizens are given 90 days. The visa requirements are posted at www.immd.gov.hk/ehtml/hkvisas_4.htm. As already mentioned, visitors are not allowed to change their status after arrival.

Normally it will take about six weeks to process a visa application, assuming all accompanying documents are in order including the nomination of a local sponsor (usually the employer). Applicants should complete application form ID 990A and the employer should complete ID 990 B). The HKSAR Immigration Department is located on the 2nd Floor of Immigration Tower, 7 Gloucester Road, Wan Chai (2824 6111; enquiry@immd.gov.hk).

CONDITIONS OF WORK

If you do not have an official contract and are picking up some teaching at a private institute, you are likely to be paid on an hourly basis and not very well. Erratic hours are also a problem, as **Leslie Platt** found out:

My institute was very vague as to what hours I would be working. I would arrive in the afternoon as instructed only to be informed that no students had turned up but that I had better hang around for a few hours just in case one did. If none did, it meant I didn't get paid.

PUPILS

Hong Kong children are usually well behaved, eager and well mannered, even though so many are under huge pressure from exams, extra tuition, band practice, kung fu, lion dancing and extra sports. It can be just as important for teachers to help their pupils enjoy English and gain confidence, as to instil the finer points of English grammar. Hong Kong's British past can also lead to some interesting situations as **J. W. Arble** discovered:

It is traditional for Hong Kong students to adopt an English name alongside their Chinese ones. These too have, in fact, become family names, passed down with little variation and as a result I found myself surrounded by ghosts from the Edwardian era, Sibyls and Mabels and Ethels and Normans and even an Algernon. Other students chose their own English names: King Kong was the moniker of one five foot fourteen year old, School Bully was that of another, there was a Ferrari Vesper, an Ω – the student formerly known as Wong – and a Beckham, a fifteen year old covered in tattoos who literally slept through all my lessons undisturbed, who was rumoured to drive a minibus for the Triads. My favourite student name was Frozen Chicken Drumstick, belonging to a girl who had plucked it from a packet in the supermarket deep-freeze.

ACCOMMODATION

Hong Kong is Asia's most expensive city outside Japan and rents keep climbing. Serviced apartments, advertised in the *HK Magazine* and newspapers, are often a cheaper alternative. They are usually based in Jordan, Central, Wan Chai and Causeway Bay. The outlying islands such as Lamma and Lantau and the New Territories are still cheaper, often double the floor space for half the money. Even with HK's superb public transport system, the commute can be time-consuming, so living in Kowloon just north of Hong Kong island might be a happy medium. **Tom Grundy** suggests that the best deals are in old walk-up buildings without lifts where your money will buy comparatively more floor space. He goes on to recommend looking up flat shares on Asia Expat (the main expat community online – http://hongkong.asiaxpat.com), or Geo Expat (www.geoexpat.com) plus of course Facebook, Gumtree and similar.

Areas in Kowloon that are considered to be quite poor are becoming popular with foreigners, such as Sham Shui Po or Tai Kok Tsui, as they are cheaper and still on the MTR red line, which goes direct to Central on HK Island. A decent but standard shoebox-sized two-bedroom flat would set you back about HK$6,000 per month.

LEISURE TIME

Not surprisingly, culture shock is kept to a minimum in Hong Kong by the Western affluence and the lingering British bias. Hong Kong is famed as a shoppers' paradise in which the cheap food, clothing and travel help to alleviate the problem of expensive accommodation. **Tom Grundy** concludes that Hong Kong is an ideal place to live:

In Hong Kong, tax is low to non-existent, it's super clean, has a huge ex-pat community with lots of English clubs, activities, sports, events and the public transport is the world's best. It's very compact and all of Asia is on the doorstep (cheap flights and trains to China, Indonesia, Philippines, Thailand, Cambodia, Vietnam, Laos, etc). The territory has dozens of tropical beaches, temples, a mind-blowing metropolis at its heart, fantastic hiking and outdoor activities, 248 idyllic outlying islands, huge country parks (70% of HK's area is actually green) and everything's a good deal cheaper than home, what with China next door. It's an ideal balance of East and West, English is widely spoken and Western food and luxuries are available everywhere. Though Hong Kong is an aggressively consumerist, capitalist society, it is 'tempered' with Chinese tradition and Buddhist beliefs.

LIST OF EMPLOYERS

CHATTERIS EDUCATIONAL FOUNDATION
33 Sycamore Street, Tai Kok Tsui, Kowloon
- 2520 5736/ 2865 2815
- hr@chatteris.org.hk
- www.chatteris.org.hk

NUMBER OF TEACHERS: 50–60 CNETs per year.
PREFERENCE OF NATIONALITY: British, American, Canadian, Australian and New Zealander. Composition of CNETS in 2009/2010 was 36 Britons, 18 Americans and 2 Canadians.
QUALIFICATIONS: Bachelor's degree or higher qualification in any subject, no teaching experience necessary.
CONDITIONS OF EMPLOYMENT: 9-month contracts, 1 September–31 May (mandatory 2-week orientation begins mid-August). 8 hours per day with 1 hour lunch break, weekends free.
SALARY: HK$13,000.
FACILITIES/SUPPORT: Accommodation is provided free of charge by Chatteris during the first 2-week orientation period. During this time, flat-hunting workshops are provided to familiarise employees with the property system of Hong Kong. Chatteris office staff are also available for assistance with negotiation of rental agreements and any issues that may arise during this time. After acceptance into the programme comprehensive support is provided to applicants regarding the organisation and processing of work visa. Chatteris will request a number of documents such as original degree certificates, police clearance checks and references from accepted applicants in order for the visa to be processed.
RECRUITMENT: By word of mouth, seminars, online. Interviews are sometimes carried out in the UK/USA.
CONTACT: Grace Lee, Project Director.

DEBORAH INTERNATIONAL PRE-SCHOOL AND PLAY SCHOOL
G/F Shop 5–5B Site 9, Whampoa Garden, Kowloon
- 2994 8998
- deborah9admin@gmail.com

NUMBER OF TEACHERS: More than 60 for all schools; 8 kindergartens in HK and 2 in Shenzen, China.
PREFERENCE OF NATIONALITY: Canadian, Australian, British or American. Must be native English speakers.
QUALIFICATIONS: Any university degree or an early childhood certificate plus minimum 6 months' teaching experience.
CONDITIONS OF EMPLOYMENT: 2-year contract. School hours from 8.30am to 5pm Monday to Friday plus occasional Saturdays for special events. Must love children, since teaching children aged 2–6.
SALARY: HK$16,000 approx, depending on experience. Airfare, medical cover and 8–9 weeks approximately paid holiday provided.
FACILITIES/SUPPORT: Free shared accommodation per 2–3 teachers or HK$2,000 accommodation allowance.
RECRUITMENT: Via the internet, please send resumé/CV by email. Recruiting goes on year-round. Interviews not essential.
CONTACT: Ivy Chu or Ms Tam.

DRAMATIC ENGLISH
8/F, Breakthrough Centre, 191 Woosung Street, Jordan, Kowloon
- +852 2880 5080
- de@dramaticenglish.com
- www.dramaticenglish.org

NUMBER OF TEACHERS: Around 40 full-time.

PREFERENCE OF NATIONALITY: None but must be native English speakers.

QUALIFICATIONS: Company largely deals with recent Drama graduates. Candidates should have a degree in theatre/drama, or possibly some related field, backed up with performance experience. ESL qualification/experience is preferred, but not essential.

CONDITIONS OF EMPLOYMENT: Contracts run for 10 months with the option to extend for a further month. Teachers may also continue for another contract term. Working hours falling between 8.30am and 5 pm with confined 20 contact teaching hours/week, depending on school programmes and timetabling.

SALARY: $HK16,000 per month starting salary. Employees are required to pay their own taxes at the end of each financial year. There are tax-free thresholds, and due to the timing of contracts, first year employees end up paying little, if any tax.

FACILITIES/SUPPORT: A few company-owned housing options are available and also the option of temporary accommodation for new teachers. Local staff are happy to support teachers who experience communication problems with local real estate agents and/or property owners.

RECRUITMENT: Via direct contact with universities and some websites. Phone interviews are essential. The company very occasionally carries out interviews abroad.

CONTACT: Joan Lau, Human Resources Manager.

ENGLISH EXCEL SCHOOL OF ENGLISH
careers@english-excel.com
www.English-excel.com

British-owned and operated network of 8 schools around Hong Kong Island and Kowloon. The largest extra-curricular English school in Hong Kong.

QUALIFICATIONS: Degree and teaching certificate e.g. TEFL, CELTA. Applications from those without a teaching cert will be considered if they have demonstrated experience of working with children in other capacities. Classes are limited to 4 students per class and are highly interactive, so potential teachers need to be energetic and friendly.

CONDITIONS OF EMPLOYMENT: To teach students aged 3–16. Minimum contract duration is 12–14 months. Generous completion gratuities reflect the importance of the contract.

SALARY: Revealed to short-listed candidates.

FACILITIES/SUPPORT: Accommodation provided (about 90% accept this option). School applies for visas on behalf of the candidates before arrival in HK.

RECRUITMENT: Applications must include a cover letter and CV with photo. Recruitment is done via telephone interviews throughout the year.

CONTACT: Cheryl White, Owner.

HK INSTITUTE OF LANGUAGES
6/f Wellington Plaza, 56–58 Wellington Street, Central
+852 2526 8892
Christian.chasset@hklanguages.com
www.hklanguages.com

NUMBER OF TEACHERS: 5.

PREFERENCE OF NATIONALITY: British or American.

QUALIFICATIONS: University degree, CELTA or equivalent ESL teaching certificate plus state teaching certifications e.g. PGCE.

CONDITIONS OF EMPLOYMENT: 1-year renewable contract with 20–25 contact teaching hours per week.

SALARY: HK$20,000 per month.

FACILITIES/SUPPORT: Accommodation provided for the first week then assistance is given to find suitable permanent accommodation. Sponsorship offered for work permits and all paperwork is taken care of.

RECRUITMENT: Usually via advertisements on corporate and professional websites. Interviews are essential.

CONTACT: Christian Chasset, Director.

LINDA YEE RECRUITING
No 59 5/F Percival Street, Causeway Bay
+852 81911623
asiaconnections@gmail.com

NUMBER OF TEACHERS: Handful of teachers placed each year (in addition to China and Taiwan).

PREFERENCE OF NATIONALITY: None.

QUALIFICATIONS: Degree or diploma holder or non-degrees. Must be aged under 55.

CONDITIONS OF EMPLOYMENT: 1 year. 25 hours per week.

RECRUITMENT: Via partner recruiting offices.

CONTACT: Linda Yee.

PARAGON EDUCATION CENTRE

2/F, 111 Leighton Road, Causeway Bay

📞 +852 2838 1220

🖱 info@eparagon.com.hk

💻 www.eparagon.com.hk

PREFERENCE OF NATIONALITY: UK preferred, others considered.

QUALIFICATIONS: Degree holder, TEFL equivalent certification; preferably 3 years' teaching experience including one in Hong Kong; proficiency in second language a plus.

CONDITIONS OF WORK: permanent contract with 3 months' notice period, 5 days per week including Saturdays. Hours 9am–7pm, with 1.5-hour lunch breaks.

SALARY: Commensurate with experience.

FACILITIES/SUPPORT: Assistance offered in terms of advice and negotiations in renting accommodation. Sponsorship given for work permits which take around 6–8 weeks to be processed from date of application.

RECRUITMENT: Via tefl.com or local newspapers. 2 rounds of interviews are always conducted, held in Hong Kong or by phone.

CONTACT: Director of Human Resources.

WORD POWER ENGLISH LEARNING CENTER

North Point Branch: Shop 102–103, 1/F, Island Place, North Point

📞 2856 5232

🖱 manager@wordpower.edu.hk

💻 www.wordpower.edu.hk

NUMBER OF TEACHERS: 20.

PREFERENCE OF NATIONALITY: British, American, Australian and Canadian.

QUALIFICATIONS: 3 or 4-year full-time bachelor's degree plus TEFL/CELTA plus minimum 1 year teaching experience, preferably in Asia.

CONDITIONS OF EMPLOYMENT: 1-year contract. 110 contract hours per month.

SALARY: HK$20,000 per month (HK$240K per annum) subject to review after three-month assessment. A gratuity of HK$10,000 paid on satisfactory completion of 1-year contract.

FACILITIES/SUPPORT: Help finding an apartment provided, soft set up loan available to employees and also, visa sponsorship.

RECRUITMENT: Via internet with interviews in Hong Kong.

CONTACT: Clive Burns, Manager.

Macao

ENGLISH FOR ASIA LTD (MACAO BRANCH)

10E, Edificio Comercial Rodrigues, No. 599 Av. Praia Grande, Macao, SAR PRC

📞 +853 2870 5784

🖱 nathan@englishforasia.com

💻 www.englishforasia.com

NUMBER OF TEACHERS: 10–15 (at present).

PREFERENCE OF NATIONALITY: Native English speakers of any nationality.

QUALIFICATIONS: Minimum bachelor's degree and TESOL certificate (or other equivalent teaching certificate). Minimum of 2 years' experience preferred but not essential.

CONDITIONS OF EMPLOYMENT: 1-year rolling contracts (due to local labour laws). 27 teaching hours a week, plus an allocated 10 hours for preparation and admin work. Hours usually stretch over 6 days, with 1 full day off per week. Operational hours are 8am–9pm; teaching schedule can accommodate teacher's outside commitments.

SALARY: HK$18,000–$20,000 (depending on qualifications and experience). At current exchange rates, this is equivalent to £1,570–£1,750, about double the average wage in Macao. Deductions are made quarterly and are very low (approximately £45 per quarter).

FACILITIES/SUPPORT: Teacher trainer on hand to give on-the-job coaching and guidance. Reasonably priced temporary accommodation will be provided upon arrival until an employee finds a home in the territory. No housing allowance is given. Visa sponsorship is given; teachers provide a copy of their CV/resumé and original certificates for inspection. UK syllabus is followed. The process can take up to 3 months and teachers will be required to pay a fee of around £10 upon collection.

RECRUITMENT: Usually direct application for teachers already in the region. Interviews essential.

CONTACT: Nathan Fox, Centre Manager.

INDONESIA

Indonesia is the fourth most populous nation on earth. Since the president and vice-president were directly elected for the first time in 2004, the country has been reasonably stable and schools are attracting professional ELT teachers from abroad with benefits packages and reasonable salaries of more than 10 million rupiah (£750). The best jobs continue to crop up in the oil company cities. Although oil production has been declining, the industry is still crucial to the country's economy. The so-called 'native English speaker schools' with multiple branches in Jakarta and the other cities continue to deliver English courses to the millions of Indonesians who still want to learn the language. These organisations can still afford to hire trained foreign teachers and pay them about 10 times the local wage. EF English First is the biggest and most well-known chain of the franchised language schools, with schools in Jakarta as well as on Sumatra, Java, Sulawesi and Bali. Wall Street Institute has four branches in Jakarta including a plush branch on Jalan Jend. Sudirman, the capital's most prestigious thoroughfare. WSI (jobs@wallstreetinstitute.co.id) and Direct English, also on Jalan Sudirman, capture the market share by targeting office workers using a highly flexible schedule.

However, purely 'language' schools, as well as international schools, are feeling the heat from the burgeoning National Plus schools. According to the Sampoerna Foundation for improving education, there are now nearly 60 member schools of the Association of National Plus Schools (www.anpsonline.org). They tend to follow an international curriculum, often with some local content, and the medium of instruction is English, or a mix of Indonesian and English. They are favoured by middle-class Indonesians and expats who are not on oil company salaries and/or who don't get their children's education funded by their employer. Many schools tend to follow a religious path (usually Catholic), perhaps as a marketing tool that appeals to parents, and they tend to pay a little better than the language schools. They also tend to start lessons at 7am. Occasionally they advertise abroad, for example at the time of writing Prime One School (www.pos.sch.id) in Medan, North Sumatra, had posted an ad on tefl.com for two native English speaker teachers. Another source of work are the universities, although they don't always pay much more than small language schools.

FINDING A JOB

The CELTA is highly regarded in Indonesia and anyone who has acquired the certificate has a good chance of pre-arranging a job in Jakarta, Surabaya, Bandung or Yogyakarta (arguably the most interesting city in Indonesia). While some schools clearly favour either British or North American teachers, others express no preference, and there are also quite a few Australian and New Zealander EFL teachers in Indonesia. The government stipulates that teachers must be native English speakers from the UK, USA, Canada, Ireland, Australia or New Zealand in order to be awarded a work permit. Among the main schools in Indonesia it is standard to reimburse airfares and visa costs at the end of a successful contract. A number offer medical insurance and others offer free housing.

ON THE SPOT

More and more teachers are being hired on the spot, which suits the major schools, who then don't have to pay for airfares. Local recruits can negotiate shorter contracts, for example six months, unlike teachers recruited abroad who usually have to commit for 12 months. Most teaching jobs start in July or September/October. With a Cambridge or Trinity Certificate and university degree your chances of being offered a job are high. Unqualified applicants would have to be extremely well presented (since dress is very important in Jakarta), able to sell themselves in terms of experience and qualifications and prepared to commit themselves for a longish spell or to start with some part-time work in the hope of building it up. Caution is advised at the interview stage, because promises are not always kept or the full extent of deductions mentioned.

Local schools staffed by Indonesians abound, many willing to hire a native English speaker at local wages. Some can even arrange a work permit. However, there is no 'easy answer' for how prospective teachers should try and sell themselves, as **Ross McKay**, a long-term teacher in Jakarta, is keen to point out:

> *Each school has it own ethos. One place likes lots of chat but others are sober-sides who keep students' noses to the grindstone. I went to one interview and kept the class happy for an hour, only to be told that 'we're educators, not entertainers'. But another school didn't call me for interview because I'd stated that I took the job seriously and didn't go easy on students who habitually arrived late. Jam Karet, rubber-time, is a bad habit here, and you either adjust to it or get driven nuts.*

Travellers have stumbled across friendly little schools up rickety staircases throughout the islands of Indonesia, as the German round-the-world traveller **Gerhard Flaig** describes:

> *In Yogyakarta you can find language schools listed in the telephone book or you just walk through streets to look for them. Most of them are interested in having new teachers. I got an offering to teach German and also English since my English was better than some of the language school managers. All of them didn't bother about work permits. The wages aren't very high but it is fairly easy to cover the costs of board and lodging since the cost of living is very low.*

The Indonesian *Yellow Pages* is online at www.yellowpages.co.id and searchable in English under the heading 'Language Schools'. Opportunities exist not only in the large cities but in small towns too. **Tim Leffel** from New Jersey, USA, noticed a large number of English schools in the Javanese city of Solo, and others have recommended Denpasar (Bali). At local schools unused to employing native English speaker teachers, teaching materials may be in short supply. One of the problems faced by those who undertake casual work of this kind is that there is usually little chance of obtaining a work permit (see below). It is also difficult for freelance teachers to become legal unless they have a contact who knows people in power. The problem of visas doesn't arise if you teach English on a completely informal basis as **Stuart Tappin** did:

> *In Asia I managed to spend a lot of time living with people in return for teaching English. The more remote the towns are from tourist routes the better, for example Bali is no good. I spent a week in Palembang, Sumatra, living with an English teacher and his family. You teach and they give their (very good) hospitality.*

If you get stuck job-hunting in Jakarta, go to Jalan Jaksa, a small but lively street where many teachers hang out. They might be willing to pass on leads, and Romance Cafe-Bar is, according to **Ross McKay**, a pleasant place on a Saturday afternoon.

REGULATIONS

The work permit regulations are rigidly adhered to in Indonesia and all of the established language schools will apply for a visa permit on your behalf. Some even employ a dedicated visa coordinator. The embassy's 'General Information for Foreigners Wishing to Work in Indonesia' starts with the warning, '*Please be informed that it is not easy for foreigners to work and stay in Indonesia since Indonesia has very strict and complicated immigration/visa requirements and regulations, and the process can be very long*' (www.indonesianembassy.org.uk). The Indonesian government limits work permits to teachers holding passports from the six English-speaking countries as listed above.

If the job is arranged in plenty of time before you leave home, you may be sent a letter of sponsorship from your employer to take to the Indonesian embassy in London and, subject to current visa requirements, they will issue you with an Employment Visa valid for a maximum of 60 days, £35 non-refundable. Alternatively, you may apply for a one-year Temporary Stay visa (VITAS), which costs £100.

It is possible to enter Indonesia on a tourist visa and after being hired, have the school arrange the work permit but for this you will have to leave the country after supplying your CV, TEFL course and university degree certificates, photocopies of your passport and application forms. Anyone without the necessary professional qualifications is unlikely to be granted the visa. The application is sent to the Indonesian Ministry of Education, the Cabinet Secretariat and the Immigration/Manpower Departments. If and when the application is approved, the work permit will be valid for one employer only and will be revoked and the offending teacher deported if work is undertaken outside the terms of the contract.

After your work permit and temporary stay permit have been granted (with a maximum validity of one year), the documentation will then be sent to the nearest Indonesian Embassy (normally Singapore) where the teacher can have it stamped in his or her passport. These visa runs only take a couple of days and should be paid for by your employer, although some, such as Berlitz, consequently withhold 10% of your salary for the first six months, then reimburse the 10% monthly, starting in the seventh month, to ensure that teachers fulfil the year's visa.

> *It is possible to renew your tourist status by leaving the country every two months (e.g. flying to Singapore, or by ferry to Penang in Malaysia) but the authorities might become suspicious if you did this repeatedly. Anyone found working on a tourist visa will be deported and blacklisted from entering Indonesia in the future. Also, the employer would be in serious trouble.*

CONDITIONS OF WORK

Salaries paid by the 'native English speaker' schools can provide for a comfortable lifestyle including travel within Indonesia during the vacations. Most schools pay at least 8 million rupiah per month, after Indonesian tax of 10% (on earnings of up to Rp25 million) has been subtracted. However, the government has removed much of the subsidy on fuel prices, and this combined with other factors has caused prices to rise. As mentioned, reimbursement for airfares is commonplace, as described by **Bruce Clarke**, who worked for EF English First:

> *In addition to a decent starting salary, my school also agreed to reimburse me at the end of my contract for both the price of my plane ticket and my work visa. Basic living is relatively cheap. I spend about half my salary on Western luxuries like beer, CDs, movies, etc. I bank the rest so at the end of my year I expect to head home with a few thousand dollars saved. Most of the teachers I meet are in their early 20s, and are generally still at the 'let's party every night' stage of their lives. They complain about constantly being broke because they tend to go clubing two or three nights a week and waste a lot of money.*

Many schools offer generous help with accommodation, ranging from an interest-free loan to cover initial rent payments or deposits, to free housing complete with free telephone, electricity and maid service. This perk may be at the expense of free choice though, and it is worth considering if you mind where you live/who you live with. It is customary in the Jakarta housing market to be asked to pay the annual rent in a lump sum at the beginning of your tenancy, and so access to a loan from your employer is often essential. **Ross McKay** warns that housing contracts should not be undertaken lightly since one of his ex-colleagues who refused to pay a year's rent on a house he had occupied for two months ended up behind bars and subject to a huge payment of Rp20 million.

If you happen to work for a school which takes on outside contracts, you may have the occasional chance to work outside the school premises, possibly in a remote oil drilling location in Sumatra, for up to double pay. The majority of teachers, however, conduct lessons at their school through the usual peak hours of 3.30pm–8.30pm with some early morning starts as well. Many supplement their incomes with private pupils (provided their employer permits it). For example, Ross McKay was paid by a doctor to teach him while they drove into Jakarta in the morning, which boiled down to him being paid to be given a lift to work.

THE PUPILS

Outside the big cities, the standard of English is normally very low, with pupils having picked up a smattering from bad American television. Classes also tend to be large, with as many as 40 pupils, all expecting to learn grammar by the traditional rote methods. According to a VSO volunteer teaching in Western Java (as quoted in the *Times Educational Supplement*), '*If I want to do something interesting, the students complain that it isn't in the exam*'. As is the case elsewhere in the world, the average age of English learners is getting younger, so anyone with experience of teaching children or teenagers will be appreciated. **Andrew Whitmarsh**, a teacher for WSI in Jakarta, enjoyed being able to entice his students into university-style discussions:

> *As I look back over my experience, I would say that the best times have come during the classes when I almost forgot I was a teacher and they were my students, and instead felt like I was leading a discussion group back at university. At the other end of the scale there were certainly days that some classes felt repetitive, but I got through these by being sure to make creative and engaging social clubs to balance it all out.*

LEISURE TIME

Although Jakarta is a hot, dusty, overcrowded, polluted and poverty-stricken city, there is a great deal to see and do, and most teachers end up more than tolerating it. After quitting his job in information technology at age 37, **Bruce Clarke** obtained a TEFL certificate from Winfield College in Vancouver and immediately landed a one-year teaching contract with EF English First in Indonesia and concluded that Indonesia is 'okay', though not quite as glamorous as he had hoped. He liked his school and staff, but found Jakarta just another big, crowded city. On a happier note, a past Director of Studies at Executive English Programs (EEP) writes:

> *Jakarta has moved on in leaps and bounds in many ways since I first arrived in 1994. The traffic may be viler than ever, but while it still certainly isn't Hong Kong or Singapore food-wise, the variety of good quality, reasonably-priced restaurants is very impressive these days. Once you know your way around!*

Indonesia is a fascinating country and most visitors, whether short-term or long, agree that the Indonesian people are fantastic. Travel is cheap and unrestricted, and excursions are very rewarding in terms of scenery and culture. Travel by public transport can be time-consuming and limiting for weekend trips, so you might consider getting a motorcycle, although Jakarta's traffic problems make this too dangerous and unhealthy for many. Internal flights are also within the range of most teachers. **Ross McKay** recommends using Bluebird or Express taxis in Jakarta as the most dependable and to use air-conditioned buses (but not after midnight). He also advises newcomers to arrive with crisp, new notes since banks are loath to handle creased or tatty foreign currency.

Predictably the community of expatriate teachers participates in lots of joint activities such as football and tennis matches, chess tournaments, beach excursions, diving trips and parties. Most teachers have DVDs but occasionally go out to see an undubbed American film. The pleasant city of Bandung might prove an attractive alternative to Jakarta and offers a good quality lifestyle to teachers, with a good mixture of rural and city life. Since the completion of the new toll road from Jakarta to Bandung a journey time of two hours is possible. It's choked at the weekends, but fine during the week.

Speaking of weekends, **Andrew Whitmarsh** has no problem finding something to do, often with the help of his students:

This is one of the wildest and most wonderful countries I've worked in, so a lot of my time is spent getting out and seeing the city or jumping a train to check out the surrounding countryside. The traffic in Jakarta is tough to deal with and the air quality isn't great, but the opportunity for adventure and excitement is always just around the corner. Many of my students-turned-friends are great guides to the sights and always know the best nightclubs to visit, when the concerts are and where the best food is.

Bahasa Indonesian, almost identical to Malay, was imposed on the people of Indonesia after independence in 1949 and is one of the simplest languages to learn both in structure and pronunciation.

LIST OF EMPLOYERS

AIM FOR ENGLISH
Jalan Padang 5C, Manggarai, Jakarta
- 21 837 85 238
- ian@aimjakarta.com/info@aimjakarta.com
- www.aimjakarta.com

NUMBER OF TEACHERS: 10.
PREFERENCE OF NATIONALITY: British, American, Canadian, Australian, New Zealander and Indonesian (currently all are from UK, Australia and Indonesia).
QUALIFICATIONS: At least CELTA, and at least 2 years' experience (teaching adults, test preparation, Business English and academic English).
CONDITIONS OF EMPLOYMENT: 12-month contracts. 22 hours contact. 7 hrs in the office 5 days a week. Some evening work.
SALARY: 15 million Rupiah, equivalent to around US$1,600 per month.

FACILITIES/SUPPORT: Return tickets home, end of contract bonus, full health insurance. Ongoing career development. Work permits taken care of: outsourced to a reliable agent.
RECRUITMENT: Through online advertising, word of mouth. Interviews essential, and can be via web-meeting (via Skype/Yahoo messenger with webcam).
CONTACT: Ian Bishop, Managing Director.

BERLITZ LANGUAGE CENTRES
PT Berlitz, Hotel InterContinental MidPlaza Jakarta, Shopping Gallery R-26, Jl. Jendral Sudirman Kav. 10–11, Jakarta 10220
- 21 251 4589
- lincoln@biz.net.id or lincoln@berlitz.co.id

NUMBER OF TEACHERS: 10.
PREFERENCE OF NATIONALITY: British, American, Canadian, Australian and New Zealander.

QUALIFICATIONS: Degree minimum. TEFL certificate (CELTA or equivalent) and/or experience preferred but not essential.

CONDITIONS OF EMPLOYMENT: 12-month contracts. School hours: 7.30am–9pm, Monday to Friday; 7.30am to 3pm Saturday. Lessons scheduled as available between these hours.

SALARY: Approximately $1,000–$1,200 (net) depending on qualifications and experience.

FACILITIES/SUPPORT: Housing allowance paid and first month's housing arranged. Berlitz Instructor Training free of charge. Visa agent assists with permits and school bears the cost.

RECRUITMENT: Word-of-mouth, newspapers and via internet. Interviews by phone or held at nearby language centre.

CONTACT: Lincoln Taylor (Manager of Instruction) and Cora Ramschie (Instructional Supervisor).

EF ENGLISH FIRST

Indonesian Head Office, Wisma Tamara Lt. 4, Suite 402, Jl. Jend. Sudirman Kav. 24, Jakarta 12920

℡ 21 520 6477

✉ efrecruitment@ef.com

🖥 www.englishfirst.com/trt

NUMBER OF TEACHERS: More than 700 for 68 schools throughout Indonesia.

PREFERENCE OF NATIONALITY: British, Canadian, Australian, American or New Zealander only (due to work visa restrictions).

QUALIFICATIONS: TEFL/TESL certificate indicating 120 hours of class work, observations and evaluated practice teaching. Experience, bachelor's or master's degree and references may be submitted in lieu of the certificate.

CONDITIONS OF EMPLOYMENT: 12-month contracts. Usual hours are early afternoon until evening (1pm–9pm).

SALARY: Varies significantly between cities: 6–9 million Rupiah per month (no tax deduction).

FACILITIES/SUPPORT: Most schools provide shared housing free or a monthly housing allowance. Teachers preferring to live alone are given advice and help but bear the contractual responsibilities themselves. Schools provide and pay for necessary working papers. Orientation on arrival, ongoing training and development, medical insurance, paid holidays and completion bonus provided. All schools are well equipped with a variety of resources.

RECRUITMENT: Via EF's Online Recruitment Centre or approaching individual schools. Candidates are requested to register their details at www.teachenglishfirst.com.

EXECUTIVE ENGLISH PROGRAMS (EEP)

Jalan Ir. H. Juanda 130B, Bandung

℡ +62 22 250 3727

✉ dos@eepbdg.com

🖥 www.eepbdg.com

PREFERENCE OF NATIONALITY: British, American, Canadian, Australian and New Zealander.

QUALIFICATIONS: CELTA/Trinity certificate plus university degree and at least a year's experience preferred. EEP specialises in in-company training projects, for which oil and gas industry experience is a definite asset.

CONDITIONS OF EMPLOYMENT: 1-year contracts to work a maximum of 28 hours per week.

SALARY: Minimum 10,000,000 Rupiah per month for in-centre training. Increments for higher duties, in-company work and specialised training projects. Contract renewal bonus operates. Salary includes 20 days' paid holiday per year and limited medical coverage.

FACILITIES/SUPPORT: Will provide documentation and assist in finding accommodation.

RECRUITMENT: Through local newspapers (*The Jakarta Post*). Local interviews almost always necessary.

KELT SURABAYA (formerly International Language Programs)

Jalan Jawa 34, Surabaya 63105, Jatim

℡ 31 734 3535

✉ simonb@k-elt.com or jawa@k-elt.com

🖥 www.k-elt.com

NUMBER OF TEACHERS: 25 in 3 schools.

PREFERENCE OF NATIONALITY: Must be classified native English speaker (to satisfy work permit requirements) i.e. British, American, Canadian, Australian and New Zealander.

QUALIFICATIONS: Recognised EFL qualification required, e.g. CELTA or Trinity; short intro courses and online courses not acceptable.

CONDITIONS OF EMPLOYMENT: 1-year contracts, e.g. from July. 20 hours per week, teaching 5 days a week, between 2.30pm/3.45pm/5pm and 7pm/9.15pm. Pupils from age 4. 8 weeks holiday a year.

SALARY: Starting salary is 11,000,000 Rupiah (net) per month.

FACILITIES/SUPPORT: Accommodation provided including utilities and servants. Regular workshops held.

RECRUITMENT: Adverts on the internet. (tefl.com) Recruitment 4 times a year.

CONTACT: Simon Bradshaw, Coordinator of Studies (simonb@k-elt.com).

LONDON CITY INSTITUTE
Grand Wijaya Centre, Blok F, No 62 A, Jakarta Selatan 12160
☎ +62 21 72780106
📧 lci@londoncityinstitute.com
💻 www.londoncityinstitute.com

NUMBER OF TEACHERS: 3

PREFERENCE OF NATIONALITY: None.

QUALIFICATIONS: Accredited certificate such as TESOL or CELTA and experience teaching adults. Experience teaching in-company classes is preferred.

CONDITIONS OF EMPLOYMENT: Minimum 1-year contract with a maximum of 20 teaching hours per week.

SALARY: Starting salary is 10 million Rupiah per month plus bonus at the end of the contract. Taxes and social security are paid for.

FACILITIES/SUPPORT: Help given with finding accommodation and teachers are provided with all the necessary legal documents needed for a work visa.

RECRUITMENT: Usually via advertisements on websites such as www.eslbase.com and www.onestopenglish.com. Interviews are essential. If the candidate is outside the country telephone interviews can be arranged.

CONTACT: Richard Jackson, Academic Coordinator.

LPTM (LEMBAGA PROFESI TEKNIK DAN MANAJEMEN)
Jalan Tepi Kanal Baraya 9, Makassar 90153
☎ +62411313798
📧 lptm-mks@indo.net.id

LPTM Institute places volunteers on its emergency education programme for children of urban poor families (LPTM, Jalan Tepi Kanal Baraya 9, Makassar 90153). Opportunities are also available to teach school children or school teachers in urban or rural areas in the province and to exchange English conversation with young Indonesians in a cross-cultural exchange programme.

PREFERENCE OF NATIONALITY: Any speaker of English (native and non-native).

QUALIFICATIONS: Enthusiasm only. Minimum age 18, must be in good health, with travel and health insurance cover. More experienced candidates can become interns who teach more structured programmes and even help with curriculum development.

CONDITIONS OF EMPLOYMENT: Volunteers become partners in classes and in extracurricular activities and excursions. Minimum 2-hour sessions twice a week.

SALARY: None. Programme fee is $95 for registration and $650 per month to cover 3-day orientation, accommodation, two meals a day if staying with a family, plus local back-up.

FACILITIES/SUPPORT: Programme includes entitlement to 6-month visa rather than ordinary 1-month tourist visa. Many opportunities to visit local places of interest such as Toraja, Bantimurung, Malino and Tanjung Bira. After 1 month's stay, 1 week free time given for travel further afield, e.g. to Bali, Bunaken or Borobudur.

CONTACT: Baharuddin Abidin, Director.

THE BRITISH INSTITUTE (TBI)
Menara Kuningan, Unit F1, Jl. HR. Rasuna Said Blok X7 Kav. 5, Jakarta 12940
☎ +62 21 300 27988
📧 tbijakarta@tbi.co.id
📧 recruit@tbi.co.id
💻 www.tbi.co.id

TBI Jakarta is the only CELTA centre in Indonesia. Several other branches in Greater Jakarta plus Bandung, Medan, Surabaya, Semarang and Malang.

NUMBER OF TEACHERS: Currently 60. TBI has 14 schools across Indonesia.

QUALIFICATIONS: CELTA or equivalent plus university degree minimum. Previous English language teaching experience preferred. TBI schools require teachers with a keen interest in teaching a wide variety of classes.

PREFERENCE OF NATIONALITY: British, American, Canadian, Irish, Australian and New Zealander only (for visa reasons).

SALARY: Base salary varies based on relative cost of living and number of teaching hours per week (22–25). Monthly salary after tax ranges from 8,400,000 to 14,000,000 Rupiahs.

FACILITIES/SUPPORT: Free health insurance coverage, settling-in loan, work permits and documentation paid. Six weeks paid leave per annum. Professional development programme of workshops and observed teaching with feedback. Good career development prospects, including management positions.

RECRUITMENT: Local hire or distance. Local applicants must teach a demonstration lesson. Distance applicants must complete tasks and have a telephone interview.

CONTACT: Mr. David Bradbury, School Support & Projects Coordinator.

JAPAN

The glory days for English teachers in Japan may well be over. Of the five largest chains of language schools, three have filed for bankruptcy over the past two or three years, first Nova and then in April 2010 GEOS. These enormous groups of *eikaiwa* (conversation) schools had grown too big for their britches, and had developed some business practices that alienated their clientele. For this reason, as well as because of the general economic downturn, the number of new students registering at conversation schools is estimated to have fallen by more than one-third over the last year or so.

Observers predict that all of this will make it harder for the newly arrived job-seeker. After Nova collapsed in 2007 and now again with the demise of GEOS, many teachers are suddenly out of a job and searching around for any opening they can find. Several other major chains of commercial language schools continue to flourish but at least for now are not short of teacher applicants to fill their vacancies. Meanwhile many smaller independent schools are carrying on business as usual. Japanese people still want to learn English. They are obliged to study it in school and continue to swallow the idea that a knowledge of English will contribute to career success, so the demand will survive no matter what.

English language providers agree that their practices are going to have to change. One of the booming areas of the market is the teaching of English to preschool children. Also, successful schools are turning to new technologies and software solutions.

The basic monthly salary of 250,000 yen for full-time EFL teachers may not have risen in well over a decade, but it is worth nearly £2,000/$2,750, considerably more than can be earned in most other countries. Wages are of course meaningless without balancing them against the local cost of living which is notoriously high. People used to say that you can't expect to break even and begin to save before you've been in Japan for about a year, but the cost of living has stabilised and many teachers who live frugally do manage to save. Developments such as the increase in the number of '100 yen shops' (the equivalent of 'pound shops') have made it far easier to outfit an apartment or buy teaching materials at reasonable prices.

A university degree is a prerequisite for getting a teaching job, simply because it is a requirement for a work visa. However, despite the increase in competition for teaching jobs, there is still surprisingly little emphasis on TEFL qualifications. Image is of paramount importance to the Japanese and many employers are more concerned to find people who are lively and a touch glamorous than they are to find people with a background in teaching.

As long as your expectations are realistic, Japan should turn out to be a rewarding choice of destination. Native English speakers are hired in a surprising range of contexts: in-house language programmes in steel or electronics companies, state secondary schools, hot-house crammers, 'conversation lounges' where young people get together for an hour's guided conversation, vocational schools where English is a compulsory subject, 'ladies' classes' (quaintly so-called) where courses called 'English for Shopping' are actually offered, and also classes of children from as young as 2, since it has become a status symbol in Japan to send children of all ages to English classes. In fact, studying English for many Japanese is still more a social than an educational activity.

> *Culture shock grips most new arrivals to Japan. Incoming teachers are often so distracted by the mechanics of life in Japan and the cultural adjustments they have to make to survive that they devote too little energy to the business of teaching. On the other hand, anyone who has a genuine interest in Japan and who arrives reasonably well prepared may find that a year or two in Japan provides a wonderful experience.*

PROSPECTS FOR TEACHERS

Jobs teaching English in Japan can be looked for in a variety of establishments from kindergartens (increasingly popular) to universities (difficult to crack until you have been living in Japan for years).

Most private language schools in Japan are looking for native English speakers with a bachelor's degree (any nationality) and possibly some TEFL experience. Although only a minority are looking for professional qualifications in their teachers, there has been a noticeable increase in the number of qualified EFL teachers (especially from Australia) looking for work, and naturally schools prefer to take them over complete novices. In fact if you can prove that you have three years of full-time experience teaching ESL, that will be accepted even if you don't have a degree.

Old Japan-hand **Joseph Tame** reported on his blog that he was interviewed by an agency recruiting teachers, '*CELTA was once again highlighted by the interviewers as one of the main reasons they'd contacted me in the first place – it's good to know that it has an impact in the real world recruitment*'. Many schools have no set intake dates and serious applications are welcome at any time of the year, though most contracts begin in April and finish the following March (i.e. one year) which corresponds to the academic year.

The demand for Business English and (Test of English for International Communication Preparatory) courses is also considerable. Japanese workers who have paid employment insurance for over three years are eligible to take courses with accredited learning institutions and claim a portion of the cost back from the government. The growth in the demand for Business English is also due to companies expecting new recruits to be able to communicate in English in an increasingly global marketplace.

The favoured accent is certainly American and to a lesser extent Canadian. In fact, not many Japanese can distinguish a Scot from a Queenslander, or an Eastender from an Eastsider. What can be detected and is highly prized is clear speech. Slow precise diction together with a smart appearance and professional bearing are necessary to impress some potential employers. One way round this is that telephone teaching has just penetrated the language teaching market, for example English Telephone Club (www.aoki.com/job/etc) hires telephone tutors part-time.

FINDING A JOB

With the decrease in vacancies at a sub-professional level, it is more difficult for university graduates to find a job before arrival, though this is preferable because it means the employer will sort out visas and help with initial orientation and housing. The disadvantage is that the salary and working conditions will probably compare unfavourably with those of teachers who have negotiated their job after arrival; but most new recruits (*nama gaijin* or raw foreigners) conclude that the trade-off is a fair one. Of course the pool of foreign job-seekers already in Japan is large enough that the jobs offering good conditions tend to be snapped up quickly. Some organisations do not welcome speculative applications from outside Japan, and quite a few advertisements specify that they will consider only candidates who already have the right visa. One of the best ways of arranging a job in advance is to join the Japan Exchange and Teaching (JET) Programme, which is a prestigious government-sponsored programme that offers what many consider to be a 'dream job' for new graduates.

THE JET PROGRAMME

JET is an official Japanese government scheme aimed at improving foreign language teaching in schools and fostering good relations between the people of Japan and the 44 participating countries. The programme has been in existence since 1987 and is now responsible for placing more than 2,000 native English speakers of English for a minimum contract of one year in state junior and senior high schools throughout Japan, with an increasing number in rural areas. Many consider the emphasis to be more on cultural exchange than on English teaching.

The majority of participants are from the USA (contact details below). Britain annually recruits graduates to the programme – this year's intake was 150 compared with 200 in previous years – making it among the largest employer of new graduates after the UK government. Acceptance has become much more competitive and the prospects for people who become assistant language teachers (ALTs) in English on the JET Programme are excellent. Any UK national who is under 40 with a bachelor's degree and an interest in Japan is eligible to apply.

In the UK the scheme is administered by the JET Desk at the Embassy of Japan, 101–104 Piccadilly, London, W1J 7JT (020 7465 6668; info@jet-uk.org; www.jet-uk.org). Non-British applicants should contact the Japanese embassy in their country of origin for information and application forms. US applicants can obtain details from any of the 16 consulates in the USA or from the JET Office, Japanese Embassy, 2520 Massachusetts Avenue NW, Washington, DC 20008 (202 238 6772/3; jet@embjapan.org; www.us.emb-japan.go.jp/JET).

The timetable for applicants from the UK is as follows: application forms are available online from late September; the deadline for applications is the last Friday in November; interviews are held in January and February; an intensive two-day orientation for successful candidates is held in London and Edinburgh at the start of July and departures for Japan take place in late July/August.

Robert Mizzi from Canada worked hard on his application, which paid off since he was called to an interview:

> *The interview was probably the most difficult interview I have ever had. It was only 20 minutes, but a painful 20 minutes. Besides the usual 'Why' and 'Tell us about yourself' questions, I was asked to teach a lesson on the spot using dramatic techniques I would use in class. Stunned, I managed to get out of my seat and draw some pictures of the stars and moon on the board, taught them the meaning of those words and then proceeded to ask the interview team to stand up and learn a little dance to the song Twinkle twinkle little star. All I wanted to do was to create an impression and to stand out of the 300 people being interviewed. People remember you best when you are acting like a complete fool. When it is teaching English as a foreign language, the ability to act like a fool is one of the main requirements of the job. Getting Japanese men in suits up and dancing during a job interview with the prestigious JET programme was a half-crazed risk, but a successful one at that.*

Often government-run exchanges of this kind do not offer generous remuneration packages; however, pay and conditions on the JET scheme are excellent. In addition to a free return flight, JET participants receive 3,600,000 yen a year. This is the salary before income and inhabitant taxes have been paid (though some participants are exempt) and there are further social and medical insurance fees. The salary is standard for all JET participants. Contracts are with individual contracting organisations in Japan, so there can be discrepancies in working conditions. It is the luck of the draw that determines who goes where, although stated preferences will be taken into consideration. Pension regulations mean that JET teachers can reclaim money paid into the national insurance scheme as a lump sum equivalent to about one month's salary.

ALTs are theoretically expected to work a seven-hour day and quite often teachers are assigned an average of three classes a day, however, hours spent in the classroom will vary between placements. **Mark Elliot** feels that the JET programme is 'probably the best job in the world' and describes his situation:

> *I live on a wonderful island, three hours' ferry ride from Nagasaki, nearer Shanghai than Tokyo. There is lots more to the job than teaching. After all, the programme is just as much about meeting people and participating in cultural exchange as it is about teaching.*

All JET participants teach in partnership with a native Japanese teacher so those without significant teaching experience are not thrown in at the deep end. The degree of responsibility varies depending on the relationship built with the Japanese teacher with some ALTs effectively teaching the class in large part by themselves. Unfortunately this was not the case for **Charlotte Steggall** from Suffolk, who majored in Japanese and TESOL at university and is serious about pursuing TESOL at a master's level and as a career. She felt the ALT role to be of little actual value, but rather felt they were treated as '*singing, dancing white people to wheel out and show off in events in the town*'. This was not what she signed up for, yet she loved the students and so agreed to stay on for a second year (2009/2010):

What I do depends on which teacher I'm working with. Some ask me to do a 10-minute game in a lesson, some ask me to be a living tape recorder, some ask me to do full classes. Training Japanese teachers to work with ALTs is very hit and miss, and most have no idea what to do with us. What we do has little meaning to the kids, who see us and say 'yey! She's here today so we get to play games!' They would never ask us to do a lesson to prepare for a test, or anything else with responsibility. I love teaching. But we are here mainly to allow country kids to interact with us and to overcome racism for when they are older. When I try to help or do something more because I have passion, I am batted down again.

I have a lot of spare time at work. I study Japanese, read books, use the internet. After school, I earn more money and brush up my teaching skills by doing private lessons, which allows me to break free and try different teaching styles.

Other teachers are delighted with the easy timetable. As **Rabindra Roy** wrote from Shizuoka prefecture, '*I can think of very few jobs where a freshly qualified graduate with an irrelevant degree and no experience can walk straight into such a big salary for this little work*'. He also describes the programme as '*desperately well organised*'. But partly because of the variety in locations and schools and partly because Japan is such a weird and wonderful place, it is impossible to predict what life will be like, no matter how many orientations you attend. About two-thirds of JET participants renew for a second year, which indicates its success. A third of the second years stay for a third year, with five years being the maximum a candidate can stay. The programme offers a tremendous amount of support and even those who are placed in remote or rural areas are usually within striking distance of other JET participants. In retrospect, **Susannah Kerr** was not too sorry to have been turned down by JET because their teachers have little control over where they are sent and end up in small towns (however, she wouldn't have minded a JET salary).

IN ADVANCE

There are many other ways to fix up a job in Japan ahead of time, though these will usually require more initiative than signing on with JET. Some Japanese language schools have formed links with university careers departments, particularly in the USA and Canada, so anyone with a university connection should exploit it. Another possibility for Americans is to explore the Japanese-American Sister City Program which assists some native English speakers to find teaching jobs in the city twinned with theirs.

One or two language training organisations operate on a huge scale, with many branches and large numbers of staff. For instance Aeon (see entry) has four offices outside Japan: New York, Los Angeles, Toronto and Sydney (down from six a couple of years ago). They want to interview anyone with a university degree and a perfect command of English. Some chains have been described as factory English schools, where teachers are handed a course book and told not to deviate from the formula. They depend on a steady supply of fresh graduates who want the chance to spend a year or two in Japan. Often new recruits do not have much say in where they are sent and in their first year may be sent to the least desirable locations.

Shane English Schools confines its recruitment to the UK through its partner Saxoncourt. An energetic agency operating mainly online is TEFLOne Recruitment (www.teflone.com), which recruits qualified teachers for posts in Japan as well as other countries in the Far East. A major employer is iTTTi Japan which trades as Peppy Kids Club. The head office is in Nagoya but it has recruiting representatives in the UK, USA, Canada, Australia and New Zealand (see www.ittti.com). The company hires 350 native English speakers to work all over Japan, with the exception of central Tokyo and the Islands of Okinawa.

A steady trickle of adverts appear in newspapers, *EL Prospects*, *TESOL Placement e-Bulletin*, etc. placed by individual schools in Japan and agents. Quite often schools and groups of schools will appoint a foreign recruiter. Many schools have no need to advertise abroad since they receive so many speculative resumés (the American term for CV is used in Japan).

The internet is a valuable job search tool. Using any of the popular household search engines, type 'English Teaching in Japan' and dozens of job-related websites will appear. *O-Hayo-Sensei* (which means 'Good Morning Teacher') has pages of teaching positions across Japan at www.ohayosensei. com. Many ads specify that 'Candidates must currently reside in Japan'. *ELT News* (www.eltnews. com/jobs) lists ELT jobs around Japan and the online magazine carries news, classroom ideas, etc. for ELT teachers in Japan. It is a good idea to send your CV to the big employers before arrival, make some follow-up calls and hope to arrange some interviews in your first week. Professional teachers can make contact with JALT, the Japan Association for Language Teaching (www.jalt.org). JALT categorically cannot help with employment but it does run professional development activities through its local branches. Annual membership costs a hefty 40,000 yen.

ON THE SPOT

As has been mentioned, native English speakers with a bachelor's degree have a chance of landing a job as an English teacher on arrival in Japan. The crucial question is how long will it take. The murderous cost of living means that job-hunters spend hundreds of dollars or pounds very quickly while engaged in the time-consuming business of answering ads, sending round CVs, and going for interviews. If you're starting cold try to arrive on a weekend so you can buy the Monday edition of the English language *Japan Times*, which carries ads for English teachers. Note that ads often specify 'female' which usually indicates a job teaching young children. Male applicants for these posts may be expected to have prior experience of working with children.

Joseph Tame from Herefordshire arrived in Tokyo with two big advantages, a working holiday visa and a Japanese girlfriend with whom he could stay:

> *Having spent virtually all of my travel funds in my first 21 days in the city, I eventually decided to face the fact that I'd have to find a job, for a couple of months at least. What with all this talk of a global recession, I really didn't feel too positive. Furthermore I have virtually no experience teaching, have no teaching qualifications and indeed no university degree which all employers insist on. My first stop was the Japan Association for Working Holiday Makers. I was fortunate in that as I was being registered, a phone call came through from a private English school who were desperate for a teacher. Thirty minutes later I had a job paying £17 an hour. The catch was that it was only four hours per week, but that was my pocket money taken care of. I actually spent time surfing the web in an attempt to remember what pronouns and adjectives are; I only ever remember that a verb is a 'doing' word.*

Later he made good use of GaijinPot.com which remains a superb resource for jobs, accommodation and news for foreign residents in Japan. He also recommends www.findateacher.net for those wanting to teach English (or other languages); an alternative is www.findstudents.net. You simply enter the relevant information about what you teach, what area of Japan you teach in, how much you charge, etc. and the students will come to you. The free weekly English language magazine *Metropolis* (www.metropolis.co.jp) also has a good classifieds section which is worth checking for jobs, as is www.jobseekjapan.com. Another useful free publication is *Tokyo Notice Board* (www.tokyonoticeboard.co.jp). A typical advertisement randomly selected might read: We are seeking an energetic, gregarious and reliable job applicant who wishes to share their experience with Japanese Community. part time job (1,000–1,500 yen per hour free talk; 2,160 yen per hour for teaching a lesson) (3,000 yen for a dispatch lesson). A 'dispatch lesson' is a private lesson given at a company premises.

Few things could be more intimidating for the EFL teacher than to arrive at Narita International Airport with no job and limited resources. The longer the job-hunt takes, the faster the finances dwindle and the more nerve-racking and discouraging the situation becomes. One way to lessen the monumentality of the initial struggle would be to get out of Tokyo straightaway. Although there are more jobs in the capital, there is also more competition from other foreigners, to the point of saturation. Enterprising teachers who are willing to step off the conveyor belt which takes job-seekers from the airport to one of Tokyo's many '*gaijin* houses' (hostels for foreigners) may well encounter fewer setbacks. Osaka seems a good bet since it is within commuting distance of the whole Kansai area, including Kobe, which is 20 minutes away by train. In Osaka the cost of living is as much as a quarter less than it is in Tokyo. Another promising destination is Sapporo in the north, the fifth largest city in the country. **Ken Foye**, a reader of this book, chose to teach on Hokkaido, the northern island on which Sapporo is located:

I have been teaching here for a year and a half now and I would recommend Hokkaido to anyone, especially those who don't find living in a large urban metropolis very appealing. Here the people seem much friendlier than in Tokyo, the cost of living isn't as high, there's fresh air and the scenery is magnificent. And I probably would not have ended up here if not for your book.

Susannah Kerr was made redundant by Nova when it collapsed and swiftly began 'on the spot' job-hunting courtesy of websites such as www.gaijinpot.com. She considered a large employer, Gaba (http://careers.gaba.co.jp), which specialises in one-to-one teaching. According to Susannah, the advantage of working for Gaba is that you can choose your hours. The disadvantage is that earnings are dependent on your popularity as a teacher since students vote with their feet. Susannah was interviewed by a company called Balloon Kids, which employs up to 20 teachers and pays 250,000–300,000 yen per month. Instead of working from its own institute, the company hires rooms in (for example) suburban shopping malls, where 12–15 kids show up. The teacher would be expected to go to an office to pick up teaching materials and a key, and then let him/herself into the room, so there would be no contact with other teachers. They also withhold 10,000 yen per month to be paid at the end of the contract.

The six-month contract that Susannah eventually accepted was with M.L.S (www.mls-etd.co.jp/recruiting_e.html), a school that uses a proprietary Drama Method to teach English. With 36 branches in Tokyo and Yokohama, it is a small company by Japanese standards. Susannah was impressed with the efficacy of the method, and because the teachers were '*interesting, creative, often musical types, the children were often engaged and excited, and their spoken English really did improve. The teachers were always trying to use attention-grabbing games like charades*'.

TOKYO

One of the most often recommended places to start a job hunt in Tokyo is the Kimi Information Center (Oscar Building, 8th Floor, 2 42 3 Ikebukuro, Toshima-ku, Tokyo 171 0014; 3 3986 1604;

kimiinfo@kimiwillbe.com). Its website (www.kimiwillbe.com) carries teaching job adverts. Like so many postal addresses in Japan, it is difficult to find without a map (print one off from their website) or follow these detailed directions: from Ikebukuro station take the West Exit, walk straight past the McDonald's for one block and turn right when you see Marui Department Store. Go three blocks past Sumitomo Mitsui Bank. Kimi is on the right across from the Post Office.

The Kimi Center offers extensive services for foreigners such as internet café, photocopying, free guided tours with Japanese students as well as advising on cheap short and long-term accommodation, where tenants are not liable for key money. If you register with them online, you can receive information about new jobs daily. Their Teaching Job Search Register can be found at www.kimiwillbe.com/joboppo.htm. With this free service, Kimi can assist with searching for a suitable job and even setting up interviews.

Another useful source of guidance for new arrivals on a working holiday programme is the Japan Association for Working Holiday Makers (www.jawhm.or.jp) whose services are available to those with the appropriate visa (see section on Regulations below). **Joseph Tame** was a satisfied customer when he was on the programme:

> *My first stop was the JAWHM, one of whose offices was 20 minutes by bicycle from where I was staying. They were very helpful. After registering I had access to their lists of jobs. Essentially it's a job centre for foreigners. They also have the latest copies of all the relevant magazines and newspapers with sits vacant columns. They will advise on housing, etc.*

Registration now costs 1,000 yen, which is a very worthwhile investment. When looking for accommodation, try to pick up a list of gaijin houses from an information or tourist office and look for ones which charge a monthly rather than a nightly rent since these are the ones which attract long-term residents. Apple House (www.applehouse.ne.jp) is recommended for being affordable, friendly and in a good location; it advertises that it is a good place to meet language exchange partners from all over the world. A good place to look is Fontana (3 3382 0151; www.fontana-apt.co.jp) which provides an excellent service. Because it is so difficult to rent flats, some teachers continue living in gaijin houses after they find work. Many foreigners live and work in the Roppongi district of Tokyo which might therefore be a sensible place to base yourself.

A couple of years ago, **Susannah Kerr** rented a two-bedroom flat in a nice traditional Japanese neighbourhood of Kagurazaka for 160,000 yen a month, but when her flatmates moved on and she had to pay the rent by herself, she decided to move. Even when accompanied by a local, using a local rental agency proved impossible so she used an English-speaking rental agency to find a one-bedroom apartment for 80,000 yen in Okubo, a bustling 24-hour-a-day area known as Koreatown, with a mildly sleazy reputation but gradually improving. Foreign letting agencies offer the advantage of not insisting that you provide a local guarantor. The Sakura House agency, which caters for non-Japanese accommodation-seekers (www.sakura-house.com), has become a prominent feature of the accommodation landscape in Tokyo, but there are many others.

A free ads paper called *Tokyo Classifieds* is distributed in the Roppongi district on Fridays carrying job and accommodation ads. Even tourist offices such as the one at Hibuya station (exit A-3) have free noticeboards where private lessons may be sought or offered, as well as accommodation. **Amanda Searle** describes what she found in the newspapers when she was job-hunting:

> *Most companies give little idea in their adverts of the hours and salary, let alone the age and number of students or the textbooks used. They are not very willing to give that information over the phone, explaining that you will get the opportunity to ask questions if you are called for interview. I sent cover letters out with my resumé, explaining that I was looking only for full-time positions which offered visa sponsorship. I sent out about 20 applications and about ten companies contacted me and I went to eight interviews. I ended up being offered two full-time positions and three part-time ones.*

The initial phone call is very important and should be considered as a preliminary interview. Since you may be competing with as many as 100 people answering the same ad, you have to try to stand out over the phone. Speak slowly, clearly, and be very *genki*, which means bubbly and fun. You may be asked to fax your CV to them; the cover letter should be short and intelligent, and the CV should be brief and interesting, emphasising any teaching experience. Always carry a supply of professional looking business cards (*meishi*).

Demonstration lessons form an integral part of most job interviews in Japan, regardless of one's qualifications. Try to prepare yourself as much as possible if only because travelling to an interview in Tokyo is a major undertaking which can take up to three hours and cost a lot of money; it would be a shame to blow your chances because of a simple oversight. Dress as impeccably and conservatively as possible, and carry a respectable briefcase, since books are often judged by their covers in Japan. Inside you should have any education certificates you have earned, preferably the originals since schools have long since realised that a lot of forgeries are in circulation. Your resumé should not err on the side of modesty.

REGULATIONS

Britons, Irish, Canadians, Australians and New Zealanders (among a few other non-English speaking countries) are eligible to apply for a working holiday visa for Japan; details can be found at www. mofa.go.jp/j_info/visit/w_holiday/index.html. Applicants must be aged 18–30. The quota of working holiday visas for Britons has just been raised from 400 to 1000. Applicants must show that they have sufficient financial backing, i.e. savings of $2,000.

Some schools rely on a stream of Canadians, Australians and New Zealanders on working holiday visas which they must obtain in their home countries through the SWAP Japan Programme. SWAP allows students aged 18–30 to work for six months in the first instance but is extendable to 18 months. To qualify you must prove that you have $3,000 at your disposal.

For those ineligible for a working holiday visa, the key to obtaining a work visa for Japan is to have a Japanese sponsor. Documents which will help you to find a sponsor are the original or notarised copy of your bachelor's or other degree and resumé. As mentioned, three years of working full-time as an English teacher also make you eligible. Most teachers are sponsored by their employers, although on rare occasions it is possible for the sponsor to be a private citizen. Not all schools by any means are willing to sponsor their teachers, unless they are persuaded that they are an ongoing proposition.

If your visa is to be processed before arrival, you must have a definite job appointment in Japan. Your employer must apply to the Ministry of Justice in Tokyo for a Certificate of Eligibility which he or she then forwards to you. You must take this along with a photocopy of it, your passport, photograph and application form to any Consulate General of Japan. The regulations stipulate that anyone who works in Higher Education must have an MA in Education or TEFL. Sponsoring schools warn that the visa application process takes between three and five months.

The UK and US have a visa exemption arrangement with Japan (www.uk.emb-japan.go.jp/en/visa/visa-exempt.html). British citizens can stay for up to six months without a visa, US citizens can stay for up to 90 days. It is possible to enter Japan, look for work and then apply for a work visa. Those found to be overstaying as tourists can be deported. Furthermore, employers who are caught employing illegal aliens as well as the foreign workers themselves are subject to huge fines, and both parties risk imprisonment.

Finding an employer to sponsor you for a work visa is very important. A number of schools advertising for teachers state in their ads that they are willing to consider only those who already have a work visa. Although immigration laws are being tightened, the government is making it easier for foreigners to get working visas. Whereas previously it was necessary for the teacher to leave the country, at great personal expense, to change their visa status (the Korean Visa Tour), these days the teacher need only take their Certificate of Eligibility into the local immigration office, where the visa will be processed. However, those on a student visa still need to leave the country to complete the visa process. According to **Alan Suter** the cheapest way is to take a ferry from Kobe to Busan, Korea. The work visa is valid for 6 months, 12 months or 3 years. Renewal can be applied for in Japan.

When renewing, one of the most important requirements is a tax statement showing your previous year's earnings. It is difficult to obtain a new visa unless you can show that you have earned at least 250,000 yen per month. Cash-in-hand and part-time jobs may be lucrative but they do nothing to help your visa application. If you break your contract with your employer, you will have to find another sponsor willing to act as sponsor the following year.

You are permitted to work up to 20 hours a week on a cultural or student visa. Cultural visas are granted to foreigners interested in studying some aspect of traditional Japanese culture on a full-time basis. In this case you must find a teacher willing to sponsor you. Cultural visas are often granted for *shodo* (calligraphy), *taiko* (drumming), karate, aikido, ikebana (flower arranging) and *ochakai* (tea ceremony). At one time these study visas were liberally handed out but nowadays you must produce concrete evidence that you actually are studying.

Teachers usually have the basic rate of national income tax in Japan (6%–7%) withdrawn at source.

CONDITIONS OF WORK

Despite the high cost of living, most teachers seem to be able to save money without having to lead too frugal an existence. Some even save half their salary in their first year by avoiding eating out and going to the cinema. **Antoinette Sarpong** spent 2009/2010 teaching in Osaka and preferred to enjoy herself to saving:

> *I enjoyed Osaka's nightlife thoroughly. I also opted to save for travel, so I only put a small dent in my student loans. Having said that, I lived very comfortably and had a lot of friends who did save quite a bit of money because they stuck to a budget. Japan is an expensive country but it is possible to save heaps of money if you stick to a budget. I would also suggest living rurally, if you can – less temptation than the big cities.*

The longer you work in Japan the higher the salary and better working conditions you can command. Rank beginners outside Tokyo and Osaka can earn as little as 200,000 yen a month, but the steady average of 250,000 yen persists almost everywhere. Perks such as increments for higher qualifications, end-of-contract bonuses, free Japanese lessons and travel tickets, etc. are in fairly wide evidence, although it is always worth making sure that your contract mentions these perks. Teaching schedules can be exhausting. Cost-cutting is a big part of the new Japanese economy, with some supermarkets charging customers for shopping bags, banks closing branches, companies hiring temps rather than full-time employees to save on benefits, and rural municipalities merging for greater efficiency. Language schools are not exempt from this movement and the majority are filling teachers' schedules with bigger classes in an effort to reduce teacher numbers. Teachers are also increasingly asked to work 'outside their job description', helping out with advertising, student retention and the sale of study materials.

Timetables may be announced at the last minute, though it is more difficult to opt out in Japan than in other countries because of the dedication Japanese workers show to their firms. (At best a

Japanese worker gets 10 days' holiday a year and few take their full entitlement for fear of seeming lazy or disloyal to the company.) Some schools remain open all weekend and on public holidays too.

One of the advantages of working in state schools (as JET teachers do) is that they close for holidays, usually three weeks at Christmas and two weeks in August between semesters. Most schools offer one-week holidays (paid or unpaid or a combination of the two) at the beginning of May (the 'Golden Week') and in the middle of August ('O-bon vacation'). Holidays for those lucky enough to work in institutes of higher education are much more generous.

Private tutoring is still lucrative, paying between 3,000 and 6,000 yen an hour. **Susannah Kerr** managed to hold on to six hours of private teaching a week (teaching three children in one family) when Nova collapsed which netted her 18,000 yen, enough to eat. Occasionally you will meet someone who has been paid $100 just to have dinner with a language learner and converse in English, but these plums are few and far between.

THE PUPILS

The stereotype of the diligent Japanese pupil has becoming somewhat outmoded. The younger generation of Japanese is not always willing to play by the rules that their elders lay down, and there is increasing tension in schools which may manifest itself in (mildly) unruly behaviour. But mostly teachers find their students eager, attentive and willing to confer great respect on their teachers and in some out-of-the-way places even celebrity status. All teachers are expected to look the part and most schools will insist on proper dress (e.g. suits and dresses). But they do not want a formal approach to teaching.

Adults will have studied English at school for at least six years, and their knowledge of grammar is usually sound. They go to conversation schools in the expectation of meeting native English speaker teachers able to deliver creative and entertaining lessons. Yet some are crippled by diffidence or excessive anxiety about grammatical correctness. **Michael Frost** is one teacher who experienced a clash of cultures when trying to encourage discussion in his classroom:

> *It is very difficult for Japanese students to come out and express an individual opinion. The best tactic is to get them in pairs, so that together they can work something out. They are more productive and open in pairs, and it takes the pressure off them. Then get the pairs into fours, to express a mini-group opinion, then work for a total group agreement. The thing to avoid at all costs is to stroll into class, saying, 'OK, today we are going to discuss environmental issues. Tetsuya, you set the ball rolling: What do you think of pollution?' It will not work.*

It is a popular myth that Japanese students have good reading abilities in English and require only conversation practice. This was not the experience of **Nathan Edwards**, a diploma-qualified teacher from Canada:

> *I am currently teaching at the Tokyo YMCA College of English, a pioneer in English teaching in Japan, established in 1880. The fact is that both reading and speaking in English present major challenges even to students with years of English instruction in the Japanese school system. It is highly advisable for teachers to bring a good supply of realia with them (various English brochures, used tickets, maps, coins, etc.) and old lesson plans.*

Problems can arise in team teaching situations if your Japanese colleague has not attained a high enough level of English. While teaching in the JET programme, **Robert Mizzi** came to admire Japanese culture, but he did find some aspects of his job frustrating:

A lot of times I cannot introduce a game idea because, literally, it will take 20 minutes for the teacher to understand (never mind the students).

Amanda Moody worked in a small school in Nagoya, where she taught preschool-aged children using a mixture of the 'Gentle Revolution' and Rosetta Stone software:

My pupils were very smart and the children of successful Japanese. Some were the products of brain surgeons or music producers. Others were businessmen's kids. But most of them were reading and writing around the age of three. Their parents expected the world of both us and their children.

Amanda loved her students, but thought poorly of her employer, who fined teachers for 'infringements' such as 'smelled strange and suspicious acting: 500 yen fine'. Among the many strange aspects of Japanese culture is one which most foreigners find particularly disturbing. A native English speaker who happens to have non-Caucasian features will almost certainly be discriminated against.

ACCOMMODATION

It is not uncommon for teachers who are hired overseas to be given help with accommodation, which is a tremendously useful perk, even if the flat provided is small and over-priced, with poor insulation and a badly equipped kitchen. If you are on your own, you will be forced to use a foreigners' rental agency. Rental costs are likely to range from 40,000 yen to 70,000 yen per person per month (more in Tokyo, less in more distant prefectures). When you find a place through an agency, you will have to pay a commission of one month's rent and probably also a colossal deposit called 'key money' which can be as much as six month's rent in advance. Unlike rent deposits in the West you can't expect to recoup it all. The system of paying huge deposits has been coming under increasing pressure and large rental agencies are starting to reduce the amount that has to be paid up front to a more manageable one month's rent. 'LeoPalace', which has apartments all over Japan, now advertises 'zero down payment' for monthly apartments (apartments rented on a rotating monthly contract, often furnished), and only requires one or two months' rent for yearly leases. **Susannah Kerr** was lucky enough not to have to pay any key money, although she did pay a deposit of one month's rent. Well-established schools may be prepared to lend you the key money or (exceptionally) pay it outright.

There are great discrepancies in the accommodation assigned to JET teachers. While some get beautiful no-rent houses, others get one-room apartments with high rent. **Robert Mizzi** had no complaints about the rent, but he didn't get much for his money:

I have no oven, dryer, hot water, shower or heating. A lot of things I had to buy for the apartment and a lot of things I had to give up. (The thrill of having running water certainly is a luxury where I am.)

A further problem is the near total absence of furnished apartments because Japanese people do not like to use belongings that have been used by other people, which means you may have to go shopping for curtains and cookers on top of all your other expenses. Again, schools which normally hire foreign teachers may keep a stock of basic furnishings which they can lend to teachers. If all this sounds too much hassle, perhaps staying in a gaijin house long term is not such a bad idea.

Obviously it is to your advantage to live as close to your place of work as possible but, as noted above, many teachers are forced to spend a sizeable chunk of their earnings and a lot of time commuting. Ask your employer to pay for your travel, preferably in the form of a monthly travel pass which can be used for your leisure travel as well. If you're in Tokyo, bear in mind that city buses charge a flat fare of 200 yen.

LEISURE TIME

According to some veteran teachers, leisure time and how to spend it will be the least of your worries. Depending on your circumstances, you may be expected to participate in extra-curricular activities and social events which it would cause offence to decline – always a major concern in Japan. Although **Bryn Thomas** enjoyed the sushi which his school provided for teachers still at work at 9pm, he was less keen on the '*office parties when teachers were required to dress up in silly costumes and be nice to the students*'. Most teachers are happy to accept occasional invitations to socialise with their Japanese colleagues or pupils, even if it does mean an evening of speaking very very slowly and drinking heavily. Many teachers find the socialising with students fun if expensive. Knowing a gaijin is a considerable status symbol for many Japanese, many of whom are willing to pay good money just for you to go to their houses once a week and eat their food.

But it is not like that everywhere. A glut of Westerners in Tokyo means that your welcome may be less than enthusiastic. In fact non-Japanese are refused entrance to some Tokyo bars and restaurants. Many people head straight out of Tokyo for the more appealing city of Osaka. **Julie Fast** describes the contrast:

> *I am still enamoured of Osaka; it is like a village after Tokyo. I am constantly amazed at the trees we see everywhere. I never realised in Tokyo how much I hated being constantly surrounded by people. I never had personal space in Tokyo. No one does – which explains the distant, sour looks on most people's faces. What a difference in Osaka. Osaka people have the roughest reputation in all of Japan. From a Western point of view, they are the friendliest. I have been invited to houses for lunch, children say hello and people in shops actually talk to you. Which proves you can't judge a country by its largest city.*

All cities are expensive. Any entertainment which smacks of the West such as going out to a fashionable coffee house or a night club will be absurdly expensive. However, if you are content with more modest indigenous food and pastimes, you will be able to save money. A filling bowl of noodles and broth costs £3, though you may never take to the standard breakfast of boiled rice and a raw egg. Staying home to listen to Japanese language tapes or to read a good book (e.g. *Pictures from the Water Trade*, a personal account of life in Japan) costs nothing. Obviously the more settled you become, the more familiar you will be with the bargains and affordable amusements. For example, while the Tokyo superclubs impose a cover charge of up to 4,000 yen (£30), **Susannah Kerr** found much cheaper ones and in fact one where she got to know the DJs was free.

Finding your way around is nothing if not a challenge in a country where almost all road and public transport signs are incomprehensible. What use is an A–Z if you can't read the alphabet? Many feel that it is worth making an effort to master at least something of the written language. There are three alphabets in Japanese: kanji (ancient pictograms), hiragana and katakana (the characters used to spell loan words from English). **Amanda Searle** is just one teacher who feels that kana can be learned through independent study so that at least you will be able to read station names and menus. Learning some of the script not only impresses students and shows that you are making an effort to absorb some of the culture, it also helps you to survive. **Joseph Tame** signed up for Japanese lessons so he could get beyond 'large beer please' and 'I don't understand' to a variety of expressions to exclaim 'HOW MUCH?' in disbelief.

Japanese addresses are mind-bogglingly complicated too: the numbers refer to land subdivisions: prefecture, district, ward, then building. When in doubt (inevitable) ask a friendly informant for a chizu (map). It is also a good idea to get a Japanese person to write your destination in both kanji and transliterated into roma-ji (our alphabet). Japanese people will sometimes go to embarrassing lengths to help foreigners. This desire to help wedded to a reluctance to lose face means that they may offer advice and instructions based on very little information, so keep checking. Young people in jeans are the best bets. Outside the big cities the people are even more cordial. Wherever you go, you don't have to worry about crime.

Travel is expensive. For example the bullet train from Tokyo to Sendai, a couple of hundred miles north, costs about £82 one way. Yet the pace of a teacher's life in Tokyo or another big city can become so stressful that it is essential to get on a local train and see some of the countryside. Tour operators do sometimes have special deals on train fares. For example, JR East (which operates in Kanto in northern Japan) has an unlimited one day Saturday/Sunday ticket for 2,300 yen and a five-day ticket for just over £150, which includes bullet trains (Shinkansen). Shopping around for package tours is another good way to get to see Japan at the lowest possible price. For example, a two to three day hotel/transportation package, could end up costing significantly less.

The alienness of Japanese culture is one of the main fascinations of the place. It is foolish to become bogged down worrying about transgressing against mysterious customs. The JET literature, for example, may be unnecessarily intimidating in its pointing up of possible cultural faux pas. But in fact Japanese people are more tolerant of foreigners than many give them credit for. For example **Claire Wilkinson** felt quite overwhelmed after reading the JET literature. One of the many prohibitions mentioned is 'never blow your nose in public', and so the heavy cold with which she arrived made her even more miserable than it would have otherwise. But she soon discovered that the Japanese allow foreigners a great deal of latitude and that she could relax and be herself without causing grave offence. **Antoinette Sarpong** got better at her encounters with the local people after she realised that Japanese people do not like to say 'No' or directly express disagreement so she gradually learned to read between the lines and to interpret their subtle communication style.

The price you pay for the tolerance extended to your alien ways is that you will always be treated as an outsider, no matter how adept you become with chopsticks or at using Japanese phrases. For example, **Charlotte Steggall** is an accomplished baton twirler and would have liked to coach the team in her Japanese school hard to make them improve. But she was told that she could not take on this role for insurance reasons which she interprets as because she is not Japanese. She can attend practices as a guest but has to watch the teacher in charge who has no idea about the sport which she says is a 'crying shame'.

The expat scene is also not to everyone's taste, as **Antoinette Sarpong** from Canada described in 2010:

> One aspect of being here in Japan that was a little difficult was dating and body image. A conversation with a female mate from England the other day reminded me that it can be difficult for women first arriving in Japan, which is so patriarchal, and experience the highs and lows of the dating scene. However, for foreign men, it is often thought of as being much easier to meet women for relationships.

Japan is a fascinating country, but clearly not suitable for everyone: you will never be able to blend in or go incognito; it is very difficult to be 'accepted' by the Japanese. **Kristen Ghodsee** sums up the potential hazards:

> I have seen many foreigners leave Japan angry and full of hatred towards the Japanese because they were unable or unwilling to understand Japanese ways. Outside the metropolises, being pointed at, stared at and laughed at is commonplace. Be prepared to sacrifice all vestiges of privacy. You are fair game in Japan because you are different. You can make and save an incredible amount of money, but you must have an incredible amount of patience and self-confidence. The Japanese are wonderful, friendly people if you can get past the surface differences. If you're coming only to make the quick buck (as many do), and are not willing to be open-minded to a radically different culture, you will make yourself miserable and worsen the ever-worsening opinion the Japanese have of foreigners working in their country.

LIST OF EMPLOYERS

ACC ENGLISH SCHOOL

252 Genjishinmei-Cho, Hekinan-Shi, Aichi-Ken 447 0872

📞 +81 566 422 332

✉ info@acc-english.co.jp

💻 www.acc-english.co.jp

PREFERENCE OF NATIONALITY: Native English speakers for chain of schools in Aichi Prefecture (Nagoya, Anjo, Kariya, Handa, Hekinan, Nishio, Okazaki and Toyoake).

QUALIFICATIONS: University graduates. Teaching experience, basic Japanese language ability or TESOL training an advantage. Applicants must be prepared to teach all levels, from very young children to adults.

CONDITIONS OF EMPLOYMENT: 1 year full-time positions available to teach approximately 25 hours per week. Approximately 4 weeks of paid vacation. Part-time positions sometimes available.

FACILITIES/SUPPORT: One-week pre-service training provided. Subsidised furnished accommodation arranged (monthly rent is around 40,000 yen).

RECRUITMENT: Speculative applications should be emailed/posted to the above addresses with a photo of yourself in business attire.

AEON CORPORATION

222 Sepulveda Blvd., Suite # 2000, El Segundo, California 90245, USA

📞 310 662 4706

✉ aeonla@aeonet.com

💻 www.aeonet.com

One of the largest chains of English conversation schools in Japan with over 320 branches.

NUMBER OF TEACHERS: 800.

QUALIFICATIONS: Bachelor's degree in any subject and a perfect command of the English language.

CONDITIONS OF EMPLOYMENT: 12-month (renewable) contracts. 5-days a week. 38 hours/week work schedule.

SALARY: 270,000 yen per month.

FACILITIES/SUPPORT: Single occupancy apartment furnished to Japanese standards. Subsidised monthly rent of 55,000 yen. Accident and sickness insurance provided under Japan's Socialised Health Insurance plan. 3 weeks of paid vacation and paid training.

RECRUITMENT: 4 full-time recruiting offices outside Japan including 2 in the US (Los Angeles and New York), 1 in Toronto, Canada and 1 in Sydney, Australia. Group and personal interviews held on a regular basis in the USA, Canada and Australia and 2–3 times a year in London, UK and Auckland, New Zealand. Positions start every month. Rolling deadlines. Initial applicants should send résumé and minimum 500-word essay entitled 'Why I want to live and work in Japan'. For up-to-date information regarding recruiting trips and application instructions see www.aeonet.com.

ARK FOREIGN LANGUAGE ACADEMY

4519–4 Innoshima Takuma, Onomichi, Hiroshima 722–2324

📞 +81 845 22 8511

✉ contact@arkgaigo.com

💻 www.arkgaigo.com/jobs

NUMBER OF TEACHERS: 3.

PREFERENCE OF NATIONALITY: None.

QUALIFICATIONS: Degree.

CONDITIONS OF EMPLOYMENT: 1-year contract with 6 working hours per day.

SALARY: 200,000 yen per month.

FACILITIES/SUPPORT: Accommodation provided and sponsorship given for work visas.

RECRUITMENT: Interviews are essential.

CONTACT: Matt Winfield, Manager.

BERNARD ENGLISH SCHOOL OF JAPAN

Shamotto Tsukuba 2F, 4–2–7 Matsushiro, Tsukuba City, Ibaraki-ken 305–0035

📞 298 56 5093

✉ recruitment@bernard.co.jp

💻 www.bernard.co.jp

NUMBER OF TEACHERS: 15+.

PREFERENCE OF NATIONALITY: American, Australian, British, Canadian.

QUALIFICATIONS: Must have a four-year university degree (any field), TESOL-type qualifications are a plus, must have a valid driver's licence (either a Japanese or an international licence).

CONDITIONS OF EMPLOYMENT: 1–2 year contracts, renewable on mutual agreement. Contracts are a salary/

hourly hybrid. Full-time teachers average about 110 hours per month, spread over 44 weeks per year, with 8 weeks of school holidays spread throughout the year.

SALARY: First-year salaries for full-time work earn around 240,000 yen per month, depending on qualifications and experience. Monthly incentives are offered. Contract completion bonus of 60,000 yen.

FACILITIES/SUPPORT: Modern, fully equipped apartments are available through the company. Staff are free to choose other lodgings, if desired. Visa sponsorship can be provided. Company cars are available for lease. A vehicle is necessary for travel between schools. Weekly Japanese language classes available for all teachers free of charge.

RECRUITMENT: Usually takes about 2 months from initial contact. Telephone interviews will be conducted. References are also required.

CONTACT: Frank Pridgen, Foreign Staff Manager.

BERLITZ JAPAN

Shin Aoyama Bldg., East 16F, 1–1 Minami Aoyama 1-chome, Minato-ku, Tokyo 107–0062

🖳 http://teach.berlitz.co.jp

NUMBER OF TEACHERS: Over 1,200 for 63 locations, about half of which are in Greater Tokyo.

PREFERENCE OF NATIONALITY: None, must be native English speaker.

QUALIFICATIONS: Minimum university degree, business experience and/or teaching experience needed for some posts.

CONDITIONS OF EMPLOYMENT: Differ according to location. Some openings are just part-time (weekends and evenings), others offer 1-year contracts. Working hours vary but full-time normally around 27 hours per week.

SALARY: Starting salary of 250,000 yen, plus possibility of a contract completion bonus.

FACILITIES/SUPPORT: Will act as guarantor on accommodation for qualified employees. Visa assistance given in some cases but for part-time openings teacher must be already resident and in possession of a visa. All new hires must attend a 6-day Berlitz Instructor Qualification Programme (unpaid).

RECRUITMENT: Via the above website. Interviews are essential and are conducted in Japan or sometimes by telephone and Internet. Group interview sessions are organised at intervals.

CONTACT: Mark Richey, Manager.

CALIFORNIA LANGUAGE INSTITUTE

Yamaha Bldg 4F, Uomachi 1–1-1, Kokurakitaku, Kitakyushushi 802–0006

🖐 information@cli-kids.co.jp

🖳 www.cli-kids.co.jp

NUMBER OF TEACHERS: 50 for branches in various cities.

PREFERENCE OF NATIONALITY: None.

QUALIFICATIONS: None, but must like children.

CONDITIONS OF EMPLOYMENT: 12-month contract from September; 32.5 hours per week per 5-day working week.

SALARY: From 250,000 yen per month less income tax (7%).

FACILITIES/SUPPORT: Fully furnished single accommodation provided at rent of 67,500 yen. Work visa applications carried out through Japanese immigration.

RECRUITMENT: Interviews essential, available in UK. Adverts appear in the *Guardian* 2–4 weeks before interviews held in London (e.g. mid-April for early May interviews). CV and photo must be submitted in advance.

ECC FOREIGN LANGUAGE INSTITUTE

General Headquarters: 3rd Floor, ECC Honsha Building, 1 10 20 Higashi Tenma, Kita-ku, Osaka 530–0044

✆ 6 6352 3260

🖳 www.recruiting.ecc.co.jp (for job applicants)

Kanto Management Centre Head Office:
5th Floor, San Yamate Building, 7 11 10 Nishi-Shinjuku, Shinjuku-ku, Tokyo 160–0023

✆ 3 5330 1585

🖐 eastjinj@ecc.co.jp

Chubu Management Centre Head Office: Kanayama Building, 1 16 16 Kanayama, Naka-ku, Nagoya 460–0022

✆ 52 332 6165

🖐 nhr@ecc.co.jp

Kinki Management Centre Head Office: 8th Floor, ECC Honsha Building, 1 10 20 Higashi Tenma, Kita-ku, Osaka 530–0044

✆ 6 6352 0090

🖐 teaching@ecc.co.jp

NUMBER OF TEACHERS: 600+ at 155 schools throughout Japan.

PREFERENCE OF NATIONALITY: Citizens of countries in which English is the official language.

QUALIFICATIONS: Minimum bachelor's degree.

CONDITIONS OF EMPLOYMENT: 1-year contracts, ending yearly on 31 March; 29.5 total working hours per week, mostly evenings. To work 5 days a week with variable days off. Teachers work some Saturday or Sunday shifts. Opportunities for paid overtime are plentiful.

SALARY: From 252,000 yen per month.

FACILITIES/SUPPORT: Assistance with accommodation. Compulsory 50–70 hour pre-service training course over 2 weeks.

RECRUITMENT: Visit the website recruitment.ecc.co.jp for recruitment schedules. Main hiring period is January/February/March. *UK recruitment*: c/o A.I.L International Ltd, No. 36 Studio House, Delamare Road, Cheshunt, Hertfordshire EN8 9SH (01992 642677; ail.ine@btconnect.com). *Australia recruitment*: AMAC Recruitment, www.amacrecruitment.com.au (8 8131 0027; ECC@amacrecruitment.com.au). Canada and USA recruitment: ECC Canada Office, Suite 1801, Toronto Star Building, 1 Yonge Street, Toronto, Ontario M5E 1W7, recruitment.ecc.co.jp (416 703 3390; toronto@ecc.co.jp).

ENGLISH ACADEMY & HARVARD-KIDS ACADEMY
2-9-6 Ichibancho, Matsuyama 790–0001
℡ 89 931 8686
🖰 marinbu@post.harvard.edu
💻 www.e8686.jp

NUMBER OF TEACHERS: 7–9.

PREFERENCE OF NATIONALITY: None.

QUALIFICATIONS: Teachers with at least a 4-year degree. Some experience in teaching is also helpful although training is given. Native English speakers preferred. Experience with young children is preferred for Harvard-kids.

CONDITIONS OF EMPLOYMENT: 18-month contracts. Hours 12pm–9pm, Tuesday to Friday, 10am–6pm on Saturday.

SALARY: Starting at 250,000 yen per month. Income tax is withheld and different arrangements are made for social security or health insurance depending on the circumstances of the teacher.

FACILITIES/SUPPORT: Help in finding accommodation and loan in making initial deposit. Academy has two apartments which require only minimal deposits. Help to apply for Certificate of Prior Permission for a work visa and in visa renewal when the time comes.

RECRUITMENT: Advertise in publications in Japan and sometimes at Ohayo-Sensei. Telephone interviews.

CONTACT: K Marin Burch Tanaka (marinbu@post.harvard.edu).

THE ENGLISH VILLAGE
3F Soa Building, 3–5–8 Kinshi, Sumida,
Tokyo 130 0013
℡ 3 3624 3300
🖰 englishvillage@msg.biglobe.ne.jp
💻 www.englishvillage.gr.jp/jobs_e.html

NUMBER OF TEACHERS: 7 for branches in Kinshicho (area of Tokyo) and Funabashi in Chiba.

PREFERENCE OF NATIONALITY: British.

QUALIFICATIONS: Degree (any discipline) and CELTA qualification or equivalent. Valid visa essential.

CONDITIONS OF EMPLOYMENT: One year renewable. 30–50-minute lessons per week and sessions supervising free conversation room. School specialises in teaching British English to adult learners.

SALARY: 250,000 yen per month plus 200,000 yen completion bonus.

FACILITIES/SUPPORT: Subsidised accommodation is arranged. New teachers are given a period of thorough training before they start teaching, followed by in-service training.

RECRUITMENT: British press adverts. Interviews in the UK.

CONTACT: Neil Pearson, Principal.

INTERAC CO. LTD.
Fujibo Building 2F, 2 10 28 Fujimi, Chiyoda-ku,
Tokyo 102 0071
℡ 3 3234 7840
🖰 recruit@interac.co.jp
💻 www.interacnetwork.com

Non-governmental provider of Assistant Language Teachers in Japan.

NUMBER OF TEACHERS: Over 2,000 full-time employees throughout Japan.

PREFERENCE OF NATIONALITY: None, though majority are Australian, New Zealander, Canadian, American, British, Irish and Jamaican.

QUALIFICATIONS: Minimum university degree, 12 years' education in the medium of English (all subjects taught in English at school for at least 12 years) plus a passion for teaching and a strong desire to live in Japan and work in Japanese public schools. Japanese language skills and teaching qualifications preferred but not a necessity. Drivers licence and willingness to drive are an advantage.

CONDITIONS OF EMPLOYMENT: 12-month contracts from early April to late March. Up to 29.5 teaching hours per week, Monday to Friday 8am–5pm; 7 months contract available from late August to following year late March.

SALARY: Average monthly minimum of 230,000 yen; 10% deducted in tax.

FACILITIES/SUPPORT: Comprehensive orientation programme on arrival with follow-up training sessions. Company acts as guarantor for apartment contracts and visa sponsor. Private health insurance cover available. Free Japanese lessons available in some locations.

RECRUITMENT: Overseas recruitment offices located in Oxford, Provo and Toronto. Interviews conducted in other cities all year round. Check homepage for up-to-date information.

CONTACT: Denis Cusack, Recruitment Manager.

INTERNATIONAL EDUCATION CONSULTANTS

Shin Yokohama, IK Bldg. 604, 2 12 12 Shin Yokohama, Kohoku ku, Yokohama shi, 222–0003

📞 +81 45 308 6280

🖱 info@ieconsultants.co.jp

💻 www.ieconsultants.co.jp

NUMBER OF TEACHERS: 4.

PREFERENCE OF NATIONALITY: Native English speakers.

QUALIFICATIONS: University graduate.

CONDITIONS OF EMPLOYMENT: Part-time only. Lessons take place between 6am and 9pm.

SALARY: Hourly rate. Local taxes deducted at source.

FACILITIES/SUPPORT: No assistance with accommodation. Teachers should already be in Japan and have the proper visa.

RECRUITMENT: Word of mouth. Face-to-face interview required.

CONTACT: Ulrich Kulz, CEO.

JAMES ENGLISH SCHOOLS

Mitsui Sumitomo Bank Sendai Bldg. 9F, 2–2-6 Chuo, Aobaku-ku, Sendai, Miyagi

📞 22 267 4911

🖱 jesliaison@james.co.jp

💻 www.JesJapan.com

NUMBER OF TEACHERS: 70 for 15 branches in the Tohoku region of northern Japan.

PREFERENCE OF NATIONALITY: None.

QUALIFICATIONS: Bachelor's degree and TESOL.

CONDITIONS OF EMPLOYMENT: 1-year contract. Expect teachers to stay at least 2 years. 30 teaching hours per week (average).

SALARY: 250,000–290,000 yen per month.

FACILITIES/SUPPORT: Loan provided for initial settling in costs. Visa sponsorship. Training and regular professional development offered.

RECRUITMENT: Application process completed through website. Skype interviews.

CONTACT: Kathleen Sherba, Recruiting Manager.

JET PROGRAMME

JET Desk, Embassy of Japan, 101–104 Piccadilly, London W1J 7JT, UK

📞 020 7465 6668

🖱 info@jet-uk.org

💻 www.jet-uk.org

NUMBER OF TEACHERS: 150+ each year from UK going to educational institutions all over Japan.

PREFERENCE OF NATIONALITY: UK passport holders only.

QUALIFICATIONS: Must hold a bachelor's degree by the time of departure and be under 39 years of age. TEFL training or experience preferred but not essential.

CONDITIONS OF EMPLOYMENT: 12-month renewable contracts starting in August. Normal working hours are 35 hours per week, although teaching hours are between 15 and 20.

SALARY: Minimum salary is 3.6 million yen per year.

FACILITIES/SUPPORT: JET finds placement, organises visa and insurance, hosts 2-day pre-departure orientation day in London, beginners' TEFL training and basic Japanese language course, 2 day orientation in Tokyo, language books and return flights provided.

RECRUITMENT: Deadline for application is the last week in November. Interviews in following January/February with decisions given in April.

CONTACT: JET Desk.

KENT SCHOOL OF ENGLISH

Shoppers' Plaza 706, 1–4-1 Irfune, Urayasu-shi, Chiba Ken 279–0012

🖱 kentappli@aol.com

NUMBER OF TEACHERS: 8.

PREFERENCE OF NATIONALITY: None, but interviews held in London in July.

QUALIFICATIONS: Minimum university degree plus TEFL certificate plus 2 years' TEFL experience.

CONDITIONS OF EMPLOYMENT: 1-year contract.
23 contact hours per week. 6 weeks' paid holiday.
SALARY: From 260,000 yen per month plus outward flight.
FACILITIES/SUPPORT: Teachers' furnished flats available.
Some shared, some single. All deposits/key money/gratuities
paid, so teachers pay only the rent and utilities charges.
RECRUITMENT: Adverts in the *Guardian* and via the internet.
Interviews held in the UK in June. Once contract is signed,
permits are arranged and issued in mid-September.
CONTACT: Liz Fuse, Director of Studies.

RED ROOF ENGLISH SCHOOL
Okinawa Prefecture, Ginowan City, Samashita
157–1-102 (Kasa G2)
℅ 98 890 1228
✍ info@redroof.jp
🖥 www.redroof.jp

NUMBER OF TEACHERS: 3.
PREFERENCE OF NATIONALITY: None.
QUALIFICATIONS: University degree is essential for visa
sponsorship. Experience working with children is preferred.
CONDITIONS OF EMPLOYMENT: 1-year contract. Usual
teaching hours between 1pm and 9pm Monday to Friday or
Tuesday to Saturday.
SALARY: Starting from 185,000 yen to 225,000 yen per
month depending on expertise; 40,000 to 50,000 yen
deducted per month for rent and utilities.
FACILITIES/SUPPORT: Apartment with modest furnishings is
provided. Assistance is also given with setting up telephones
and banking etc.
RECRUITMENT: Usually through the internet or word of
mouth. Interviews are essential and can be held via web cam
or occasionally in Canada.
CONTACT: Ken Nakamura-Huber, Director.

SHANE ENGLISH SCHOOL JAPAN (SESJ)
🖥 www.saxoncourt.net/en/sesj.php

NUMBER OF TEACHERS: 360 for 185 schools in the
Greater Tokyo region.
PREFERENCE OF NATIONALITY: Native speakers of British
English.
QUALIFICATIONS: University degree required. CELTA or
Trinity CertTESOL preferred.
CONDITIONS OF EMPLOYMENT: 12-month renewable
contracts. Average 25 contact hours per week. Students from
age 2. 5–6 weeks' paid holiday.
SALARY: From 250,000 yen per month plus quarterly
bonuses and end of contract bonus.
FACILITIES/SUPPORT: Accommodation, visas and
health insurance arranged. Teaching English to
Young Learners training course and ongoing
training provided.
RECRUITMENT: Via Saxoncourt in London.
CONTACT: Ben Robinson, Recruitment Manager (ben.
robinson@saxoncourt.com).

VOLTA ASSOCIATES
Chiyoda Platform Square 1005, 3–21 Kanda
Hishikicho, Chiyoda-ku, Tokyo 101–0054
✍ info@volta-associates.com
🖥 www.volta-associates.com

NUMBER OF TEACHERS: 5.
PREFERENCE OF NATIONALITY: None.
QUALIFICATIONS: Bachelor degree with TESOL.
CONDITIONS OF EMPLOYMENT: 1-year contract.
4–6 lessons a day, 5 days a week.
SALARY: Approximately 230,00 yen.
FACILITIES/SUPPORT: Assistance given with finding accom-
modation (translating paperwork, finding estate agents etc).
TESOL course is provided.
RECRUITMENT: Usually via the internet. Interviews are
essential.
CONTACT: Bernard Oppong-Kusi, President and CEO.

KOREA

Anyone who has witnessed the early morning scramble by students and businessmen to get to their English lessons before the working day begins in Seoul might be surprised to learn that the motto for South Korea is 'Land of the Morning Calm'. Because Korea's economy is so heavily dependent on export, English is a very useful accomplishment for people in business. An English proficiency test must be passed by all aspiring university students which is why so many students of secondary school age study the language so feverishly. Both these groups have probably studied English for many years at school but need to practise conversation with native English speakers.

School and university vacations (July and January) often see a surge in student enrolment at private language institutes. The teaching of children is booming more than ever and there is a huge demand for English teachers to teach in schools where English is compulsory.

Unfortunately the language industry's bad reputation for shamelessly exploiting foreign teachers lingers on. Whatever the reasons, major language teaching organisations find themselves perennially short of native English speaker staff and job-hunting for graduates is generally a cinch. (Note that in the case of Korea, 'schools' normally refer to the state sector whereas 'institutes' mean private language academies run as businesses.)

The bias is strongly in favour of North Americans, especially Canadians, and there are still relatively few British TEFLers in Korea, though this might be slowly changing with the arrival of UK-based recruiters such as Flying Cows in Nottingham. The number of small to medium sized *hagwans* (private language institutes) in all Korean cities interested in hiring a few native English speakers is massive. Hiring from abroad is complicated and expensive, so the vast majority enlist the help of recruitment agents based in Seoul or abroad (or both). Identifying the good ones who are interested in more than collecting their commission is tricky. The fact that recruiters come and go indicates that some are just out to make a fast buck. When dealing either with *hagwan* owners or recruiters, ask to be put in touch with foreigners whom they have employed/recruited in the past for an informal reference. And find out how long a recruitment agent has been in business.

Of broader concern than the possible shark-like practices of potential employers is the looming proximity of North Korea. The torpedo-ing of a South Korean ship in March 2010 by the Democratic Republic has made the world twitchy about hostilities escalating. It also caused the currency (the won) to plummet. **William Naquin**, a well-qualified American who taught in Kyunggi-Do, sums up the politics as he saw them when he was there:

> *Korea is a divided country. We were quite nervous that war might break out here between the two Koreas. The situation in the north is universally reported to be extremely bad, with summary executions and food riots. Experts seem to think the North Korean regime will collapse at some point. This could be good for English teachers in Korea, and it could also be very, very bad. The North Koreans have nuclear missiles, nerve gas and chemical weapons, and are led by the most isolated, despotic lunatic and paranoid military strongmen in the world. Prospective teachers need to know that this is one of the most likely flashpoints for war on earth, and that coming here necessarily involves some degree of risk.*

For the curious, it is possible to visit the Demilitarized Zone (DMZ) between South and North Korea, however, it is not possible to enter the reclusive Democratic Republic from the south.

PROSPECTS FOR TEACHERS

There are hundreds of *hagwans* in Seoul the capital, Busan (Korea's second city, less than four hours south of Seoul) and in smaller cities. The majority of these are run as businesses, where profit is the primary or even sole *raison d'être*. ELT training is superfluous in the majority of cases. Native-speaker status and a bachelor's degree are usually sufficient to persuade the owner of an institute to hire an English speaker. Education is greatly respected in Korea and degrees generally matter far more to potential employers than specialist qualifications. For now, a bachelor's is sufficient and a master's (no matter in what field) counts heavily in one's favour. The vast majority of students have a low level of English so that TEFL qualifications are not deemed necessary.

If you wait until you get to Korea, it is exceedingly easy to fix up a job, but the visa is more difficult to arrange (see section on regulations below). **Peter Burnside** offers three brief tips to people considering going to teach in Korea: '*follow your heart, trust your instincts and take insane risks*'.

Bridge Recruitment for Korea

South Korea has emerged as the latest hotspot for teaching English as a foreign language. With an estimated 100,000 institutes offering English lessons and a government actively promoting English teaching in public schools, South Korea offers numerous work opportunities. The country is quickly becoming an electronic and technological giant, and the increasing international trade translates into a growing need for Business English. But the desire to learn English isn't limited to company executives - in fact, parents often enrol their children in private language schools from a very early age, sometimes as young as five years old! With almost everyone looking to learn English, students in Korea can range from corporate professionals to elementary school children.

Jason Featherhof taught English in Korea for five years. Here he talks about his experience.

I chose [to teach English in] Korea because it gave me the best opportunity to earn and save money, pay off student loans, and travel around East Asia. My BridgeTEFL certification allowed me to start at the highest level of the pay scale. Living and working here has been exciting because I have had the chance to experience festivals and holidays that are unique to Korea. A couple of my favorite things about Korea are the food and that when you befriend a Korean, you become a part of their family.

My schedule normally consists of four classes a day, starting at 8:30 and finishing at 4:30. A majority of my students enjoy coming to English Conversation class. Seeing the light above the student's head go on after explaining the lesson is always a great feeling.

I would recommend [teaching in Korea] if you are able to be independent and accept things that are not the norm in the West. If you get out and experience the whole country, learn the language - even if it is just the alphabet - and befriend not only foreigners but Koreans as well, you will enjoy your stay and may even want to stay for five years like me!

In addition to a decent salary, many teaching jobs in Korea offer benefits such as free housing, airfare reimbursement, and bonuses upon contract completion. Most teaching opportunities in Korea can be found in large cities, such as the capital, Seoul, in the north, and the metropolis of Busan on the southern coast.

For more information on teaching English in Korea, visit www.BridgeTEFL.com.

FINDING A JOB

IN ADVANCE

The Korean government administers an official teacher placement programme in imitation of JET in Japan. EPIK (English Program in Korea) is run by the Ministry of Education and administered through Korean embassies and consulates in the USA, Canada, Australia and the UK, placing about 2,000 foreign graduates in schools and education offices throughout the country. Private recruiters are also involved, such as www.tefljobplacement.com (part of Denver-based Bridge Linguatec) and Toronto-based Teach Away (www.teachaway.com); using these mediating agencies will make things easier but more expensive.

The annual salary offered on the EPIK programme is 1.8–2.5 million won per month (depending on qualifications) plus free furnished accommodation, visa sponsorship, 50% contribution to medical insurance and an end-of-contract bonus. An entrance and exit allowance covers airfares. The application deadline for starting in the autumn semester is mid-June, but documents can be submitted all year round in case of openings.

Details of the programme are available from the EPIK website (www.epik.go.kr) or by contacting the local Korea government representative, e.g. in the UK the Education Director, Korean Embassy, 60 Buckingham Gate, London SW1E 6AJ (020 7227 5547). Americans should contact any of the dozen Korean consulates in the USA. Other nationalities can contact the EPIK office in Korea (EPIK Office 301, 43 Ihwajang-gil, Jongno-gu, Seoul 110–810; 2 3668 1400/1; epik@korea.kr). Note that EPIK does not attract the same high praise that the JET Programme does, though it has been better organised in recent years.

A subsidiary government programme is called TALK (www.talk.go.kr), which is open to people with at least two years of university education. The teaching here takes place in after-school clubs, the commitment is shorter (6 months instead of a year) and the pay is lower (1.5 million won). Otherwise the internet is awash with job vacancies. Try for example Seoul-based www.eslpro.com and www.koreajoblink.com.

RECRUITMENT AGENCIES

Most private recruiters offer 1-year contracts to English speakers with a university or college diploma. Candidates with additional EFL/ESL qualifications and teaching experience should be able to negotiate higher monthly salaries than the standard 1.8–2.1 million won. Recruited teachers are asked to commit themselves to teach 120 hours a month which is a heavy load. Return airfares, free accommodation, paid holidays, contribution to medical insurance and completion bonus are all promised as a rule. Applicants who cannot be interviewed locally can do so by telephone or internet. Note that recruiters should not charge teachers any fee since they earn their commission from the schools and institutes. An agency in the UK called Flying Cows, formed in 2004, aims to be as honest as possible about the rewards and drawbacks of teaching in South Korea (see entry). TEFLOne Recruitment (www.teflone.com) recruits qualified teachers for posts in Korea as well as other countries in the Far East.

Here is a list of Korea-based recruiters active at the time of writing. The following list directs North American readers to recruiting contacts on their continent, all of whom are located in Canada.

Park English Recruitment Agency, Suite #402, 4th Floor Bomm Building, 124–7 Itaewon-dong Yongsan-gu, Seoul 140–858 (2 749 1140; www.parkenglish.com).
People Recruit, Busan – www.peoplerecruit.com.

SeoulESL Recruiting, 1014, LGSeochoECLAT, 1599–2 Seocho-dong, Seocho-gu, Seoul 137–727 (+82 2 585 7871; esl@seoulesl.com; www.seoulesl.com).

Think Outside, Woongjin Thinkbig Overseas Education Department 535–1, Moonbai-Ri, Gyoha-Eup, Paju-Shi, Gyeonggi-Do (31 9567326; www.thinkoutsiderecruiting.com).

The following Canadian agencies are willing to place more than just Canadians provide they meet the requirements:

Asia-Pacific Connections (APC), 1–4143 St-Laurent, Montreal, QC H2W 1Y7, Canada (514 842 4046; apply@asia-pacific-connections.com; www.asia-pacific-connections.com). Placed about 200 North American teachers in the past two years. Telephone interviews conducted globally or face-to-face if possible. Contact Kristopher Kinch, Director.

Canadian Connection Consulting Agency (see entry),

GMSC Recruiting (Vancouver office: toll-free +1 888 771 3350 or 778 786 2854; *Seattle office:* 425 949 7416; gmsc@gmsc-recruiting.com; www.gmsc-recruiting.com).

JC Canada Recruitment, Toronto (416 226 9787; jccakr@yahoo.com; www.iloveesl.com). Korean ESL job placement agency. Offices in Toronto and Seoul. Opportunities to teach English at Korean schools available throughout the year.

Korea Connections, 211–3030 Lincoln Ave, Coquitlam, BC V3B 6B4 (206 734 4863; admin@koreaconnections.net; www.koreaconnections.net). Recruit for EPIK among others.

Russell Recruiting, Vancouver (russell_recruiting@yahoo.ca; www.russellrecruiting.com). Caters to ESL teachers wishing to work in Korea. Agency made up of former and current teachers so all services provided are safe, secure and free for job applicants. Schools are inspected and recommended by the current teachers working in Asia.

Scotia Personnel, 6045 Cherry St, Halifax, NS B3H 2K4 (902 422 1455; info@scotia-personnel-ltd.com; www.scotia-personnel-ltd.com). Refers Canadians with university degree to teaching English in schools in South Korea. Employer provides airfare, accommodation, competitive salary and more.

Similar agencies are active in Australia and New Zealand. To identify just one: World English Service (53 Shetland St, Dunedin, New Zealand; 3 466 7980), whose website www.teachkoreanz.com contains 200 pages of hard information about working in Korea.

As mentioned above, it is usual to arrange a job without a face-to-face interview. One school suggests that would-be teachers send a cassette/CD of their voices or, even better, a video/DVD of them teaching a lesson, which would certainly be more memorable and impressive than simply sending a CV.

The internet is well equipped to keep track of the volatile English language market and many Korean employers rely exclusively on it. More than one webpage lists good and bad employers along with lots of horror stories. Dave's www.eslcafe.com devotes an entire section to feedback from Korea; check out the Black List and Grey List before taking a job.

Another possibility for anyone with an MA or advanced TEFL/TESL qualifications is to work for the language department of a Korean university (of which there are nearly 100). Universities probably offer the best paid and most stable employment. Serious teachers should enquire at their local Korean Consulate for addresses.

ON THE SPOT

Under new visa regulations (15 December 2007) any person who arrives in Korea to teach English must get their final visa processing completed in their own home country. This means that entering on a tourist visa for job-hunting is simply not possible, at least this is the official line. There are all kinds of interesting conversations happening in Korea as to whether this regulation is really necessary.

I taught at the only middle school in a small farming town, and the biggest problem I encountered was the extremely low English level of most of the students. Even simple directions were hard for me to give, so we had to spend some time learning simple instructions like 'Open your book to page 22' or 'Repeat after me'. The language barrier also made discipline more of a challenge for me. If the Korean teacher wasn't in the room at the time, I was pretty much limited to 'Stop that' 'No!' and 'Be quiet please'. I was mostly responsible for leading pronunciation and speaking exercises, along with conducting memory tests in which the students had to recite a passage from the text book. The teaching was mostly textbook based. The best feature of working in a state school as the only non-Korean teacher was the chance to be completely immersed in Korean culture in a way that would never be possible as a tourist. The wages at public schools in Korea are quite good and the pay of 1.8 million won per month was more than enough to cover expenses. Although I travelled quite a bit, including to Thailand and Mongolia, I still managed to save about C$10,000 over the year. The biggest reward of my experience in Korea was seeing the world from a different perspective. I was able to climb mountains, visit Buddhist temples, visit the border between North and South Korea, explore ancient palaces, and even eat a live octopus!

Every day there are adverts for teachers in the English language newspapers in Seoul, namely the *Korean Herald* and *Korea Times*. Often new arrivals stay in one of the popular *yogwons* (hostels) and hear on the grapevine about the English teaching scene.

REGULATIONS

For many years a number of Korean employers and agents asked English teachers to arrive on a tourist visa and do a Japan visa run. This is no longer allowed. Teachers must get their final visa processing completed in their home country if they are going to a *hagwon* job, although some exemptions exist for visa processing in a third country if you are going to a public school job. Anyone working without a visa risks fines and possible deportation. Similarly, the schools which hire freelance foreigners without permits can be closed down by the government. So, if at all possible, obtain a work visa (E2), which is available only to people with a 3- or 4-year bachelor's degree.

There are two formal stages of getting a visa for employment: you accept a contract and provide your required visa documents and signed contract to the employer, who files them into immigration to sponsor you. Immigration issues a visa issuance number, valid for 90 days and during this time you cannot apply for any other job or have your documents filed for any other employer unless your employer cancels this letter at the immigration office. In the case of working in a public school a letter of employment is issued, not an issuance number. Your employer informs you of the original visa issuance number (or posts your employment letter to you for public schools) and you take the number, your passport, your original degree, a copy of your university transcripts (courses and marks) in an unopened envelope, ID and the visa fee (£27.50 in the UK) to your nearest Korean consulate in your home country. The consulate officer will give you a short interview and then stamp your passport with an E2 visa stamp. You then enter Korea and present your passport to an immigration officer: finally, your visa becomes valid and you may commence work immediately.

The E2 visa is valid only for employment with the sponsoring employer which means that freelance teaching is not permitted under the terms of your work permit and can (and does) lead to fines and deportation. However, the extremely high rates of pay available for private lessons (40,000 won per hour is not uncommon) prove too much a temptation for the majority of teachers, including the normally law-abiding ones. Koreans who inform the authorities about illegal workers are rewarded, so working illegally is more risky than ever.

Teachers are liable to income tax from their first day of work. The rate of income tax for most teachers should be 3.3% so beware employers who try to hold back much more from earnings. Most teachers participate in the Korean National Medical Insurance Union; most employers pay half of the total leaving teachers to pay about 2% of earnings; total deductions will be less than 7%. The law permits foreigners to send up to two-thirds of their salary out of the country.

CONDITIONS OF WORK

Discontentment seems to be chronic among English teachers in Korea. So many American teachers have run amok of faulty contracts, that the US Embassy in Seoul issues a handbook offering guidance and tips for avoiding the pitfalls, which is currently being revised (check http://seoul.usembassy.gov/teach.html or visit the American Citizens Services Branch at 82 Sejongno Road, Jongno-gu, Seoul). Information about contracts in the Embassy's old edition is instructive:

> Foreign instructors in Korea occasionally have contract disputes with their employers. Many have observed that in Korea, a contract appears simply to be a rough working agreement, subject to change depending on the circumstances. Many Koreans do not view deviations from a contract as a breach of contract, and few Koreans would consider taking an employer to court over a contract dispute. Instead, Koreans tend to view contracts as always being flexible and subject to further negotiation. Culturally, the written contract is not the real contract; the unwritten or oral agreement one has with one's employer is the real contract. However, many employers will view a contract violation by a foreign worker as serious, and will renege on verbal promises if they feel they can. Any contract should be signed with these factors in mind.

Tim Leffel is one in a long line of American EFL teachers who came to the conclusion that '*nearly 100% of the* hagwan *owners are crooks or unbelievably inept – sometimes both and in Korea both oral and written contracts are a joke*'. He passes on the advice to carry a tape recorder to all interviews and meetings. By working for a big chain, he avoided most problems and was given a decent apartment, good wages and lots of support materials. He even got his post-contract bonus though he had to return to Korea six weeks after finishing work to insist on it. When there are conflicts over contracts, Tim advises teachers to choose their battles carefully and to remain civilised as long as possible.

The issue of severance pay is a sore point for many teachers. By law, anyone who completes a 52-week contract is entitled to one month's salary as severance pay. Employers have been known to make life quite unpleasant for their teachers near the end of their contracts, so that they're tempted to leave and forego the bonus. The opening remark in **Peter McGuire's** letter from Andong was '*You wouldn't believe how thrilled I am to be almost finished with a one-year contract here in Korea*'. He went on to say that he made it through to the end only because he is a very determined person and the stakes were high, since he was trying to clear debts at home in Wisconsin.

Bear in mind the quality of *hagwans* varies enormously. Some are run by sharks who may make promises at interview which they can't fulfil, and overfill classes to maximise profits. Many schools do not use recognised course books but rely on home-made materials of dubious usefulness. On

JONNY reported the following on a Guardian web forum on TEFL held in April 2010.

> Last year I worked in South Korea and it was the best year of my life. I have made friends all across the globe and loved every minute of my adventure in Busan, Korea's second largest city. It is a wonderful place and you can get to Seoul for a fun-filled weekend quite easily. The exchange rate is great and the free flights and accommodation allow for a high spending and saving lifestyle even though when the wage is measured against the pound it sounds fairly average.
>
> There are of course risks. But with Korea being a country unburdened by any large amount of crime and a love for Westerners, especially Brits, you are in good hands. Kids run around till midnight in the summer with no trouble. Old men drink soju all day and pass out on the benches at night; ajumas (old women) make you feel at home while joking about men and making harsh but delicious Korean treats. It's also wired up to the hilt with an extremely fast internet and a love for online gaming. Teaching can be challenging but it can also be a slacker's heaven, but I urge you to give it your all and you will feel better about yourself.
>
> Oh – and the beer is crap but you'll learn to love it.

the other hand, standards are rising in some schools and the experience of teachers in the private sectors is not all bad.

Another foreign teacher who was far from disappointed is **Patrick Edgington** from California who answered a recruiter's advert in a USA daily paper and was soon working for Ahil Foreign Language Institute in Ulsan (482–138 Seobudong Dong-Ku, Ulsan 682–036). While acknowledging that contracts in Korea guarantee nothing, he was lucky enough to find an honest employer who paid him on time and provided a 'cube' apartment above the institute building (which was acceptable, though cold in winter).

The financial gains are undeniably worthwhile, even if you have to work hard to earn them. Many graduates find themselves teaching in Korea primarily to pay off their student loans or other debts. The cost of living is very reasonable, the taxes negligible and so it is possible to save a significant sum while also enjoying life. The average teaching schedule in Korea is five or six hours a day, five days a week. Only *hagwans* catering to adult workers require very early morning starts. The majority of first-time teachers will find that their first lessons are after 10am or sometimes not until 2pm. Weekend work is less commonplace than in many other countries and when a contract does include Saturday teaching, the financial rewards are significant. The teaching load in universities is often lighter. The problem seems to be that *hagwans* realise that teachers come to Korea for no more than a year and therefore milk them for every working minute. **Kathy Panton**'s assessment is that the teacher is there to exploit Korea for money, so Koreans turn around and exploit teachers for labour. She topped the record quoted in a previous edition of this book by working 181 hours in a month including privates and excluding preparation.

The majority of Korean language learners are serious (some attend two-hour classes three or four times a week) and want to be taught systematically and energetically, though even those who have been studying for years often show precious little confidence in conversing. They also expect their teachers to direct the action and are not happy with a laid-back 'let's have a chit-chat' approach. Whereas **Judith Night** (a certified teacher) found her pupils in the public school system '*eager to learn and a joy to teach*', **Mark Vetare**, with no teaching background, found things very hard going, and concluded in the end that TEFL teaching was not for him:

The major drawback is teaching the sullen, bored, exhausted, precocious and Mok Dong spoiled children aged 14–16 – torture. (Mok Dong means upper mid class whatever that means.) They drain me of energy. What they want is a white monkey to entertain them and make them giggle. Trouble is they provide zero material to work from. No sports, no interests. Their stated hobbies are sleeping, TV and listening to music. Their parents want their kids to move up book by book as if that's a gauge of progress. 'Oh, you're in 10B, great.' Never mind that they still can't speak English.

ACCOMMODATION

Most schools that recruit teachers from abroad will sort out accommodation for their teachers. If you are looking for accommodation independently, be prepared (as in Japan) to be required to pay a large deposit ('key money'). This should be returned to you at the end of your tenancy, though as in Japan, disagreements can arise. If you don't hear about available flats from your school or other foreigners, check the English language newspaper or find an English-speaking rental agent.

LEISURE TIME

Visitors are often surprised to discover the richness and complexity of Korean history and culture, partly because Japanese culture is far better known. Despite being a bustling metropolis of more than 10 million, Seoul has preserved some of its cultural treasures. Assuming your teaching schedule permits, you should be able to explore the country and, if interested, study some aspect of Korean culture such as the martial art Tae Kwon Do. The country's area is small, the public transport good, though traffic congestion at weekends is a problem.

Teachers often find that their students are friendly. Anyone homesick for the West will gravitate to the area of Seoul called Itaewon, where fast food restaurants and discos are concentrated, not to mention a jazz club, a decent bookstore and other expatriate forms of entertainment. Teachers in the provinces will have to become accustomed to a very quiet life as **Judith Night** discovered:

Anyone interested in coming here to have a social life will be very disappointed. In fact, they had better be ready to deal with isolation, because most likely they will be the only foreigner in the town, and the people may never even have met any foreigners before. If I stay in Korea another year, I will choose to live in Seoul, due to missing a social life.

Although **William Naquin** was also working a long way from the bright lights, he fared a little better:

Insofar as spare time goes, many weekends are spent recovering from 40+ hours in the classroom. During periods when we aren't quite as busy we watch movies, work out at the primitive health club, go to Seoul and drink. Mountain climbing is big here and when the weather is nice our students take us along with them. Portable hobbies such as music, writing and reading are indispensable.

LIST OF EMPLOYERS

NUMBER OF TEACHERS: 60.

RECRUITMENT: Mostly via internet. Applicants already in Korea are interviewed in person. Overseas applicants are interviewed over the phone.

CONTACT: Alastair Middleton, Hiring Manager.

NUMBER OF TEACHERS: 300 per year.

PREFERENCE OF NATIONALITY: Canadian, American, British, Australian, New Zealander, and South African.

QUALIFICATIONS: Bachelor's degree in an English-related field, EFL qualification and teaching experience minimum.

CONDITIONS OF EMPLOYMENT: 1-year contract. To teach 22–30 hours per week.

SALARY: 1.8–2.5 million Korean won per month.

FACILITIES/SUPPORT: Accommodation is supplied and paid for (teachers pay utilities). Agency handles all visa applications, teachers must supply documentation including notarised copy of their degree, criminal record check, 2 reference letters, passport photos, university transcripts, and valid passport.

RECRUITMENT: Interview required.

CONTACT: Shane Finnie, Director.

One of the largest private language institutes in South Korea, with 120+ campuses teaching English to children.

PREFERENCE OF NATIONALITY: Canadian, American, British, Australian, New Zealander, Irish and South African.

QUALIFICATIONS: College graduates, with clean criminal records, from English speaking countries. Candidates ideally have previous experience working with children, although previous teaching experience is not a requirement. Employer is looking for a professional, patient, flexible and outgoing demeanour. A strong desire to teach children overseas is required.

CONDITIONS OF EMPLOYMENT: 12 months. 4–5 days a week. Usual hours are 4–10pm for learners aged 10–16, or 1–7pm for younger learners aged 5–10. Hourly teachers work 120 hours per month, with a guarantee of 96 hours per month.

SALARY: Varies according to previous teaching experience, level of education and other factors, including performance on the Aclipse interview and evaluation. Standard salary for a teacher who performs well on the Aclipse evaluation and has a strong resumé is 27,000 won ($22.50) per hour. Hourly teachers earn 2.2 million won per month for 96–120 hours, with paid overtime at an hourly rate. Teachers on a monthly salary are taxed at a rate of 7–8% on their monthly income by the Korean government. Teachers on an hourly salary are taxed at rate of 3%.

FACILITIES/SUPPORT: With the monthly salary, housing is paid for by the school and set up for the teacher, typically before they arrive. On the hourly salary, ChungDahm Learning helps their teachers find housing either before they arrive or upon arrival, assists with the Key Money (security deposit), and the teachers then pay rent directly to their landlord each month. Aclipse in the US assists candidates with obtaining the E2 visa. Teachers are responsible for obtaining the necessary visa documents, such as a state-wide criminal background check and original diploma, which the Aclipse office in Boston checks and forwards to ChungDahm in Korea. The visa code is then emailed to candidate who takes it to their nearest Korean consulate and gets visa stamped in passport.

RECRUITMENT: Online advertisements, social media, career fairs, and campus events/information sessions. Interviews are essential: initial interviews are typically done over the phone, with recruiters from the Boston office or by US recruiter Aclipse (www.aclipse.net) with offices in Boston and San Francisco as well as Seoul.

CONTACT: Rebecca McNeil, Marketing Manager at Aclipse (subsidiary of ChungDahm Learning/ChungDahm America).

NUMBER OF TEACHERS: Approximately 50 Western teachers in 16 franchises throughout Korea.

PREFERENCE OF NATIONALITY: None, but should be a native English speaker.

QUALIFICATIONS: Minimum 3 or 4-year bachelor's degree. Love of kids, mature interactive outlook.

CONDITIONS OF EMPLOYMENT: 12-month contract. Less than 30 hours' teaching. Return airfare, medical insurance, 10 days' vacation. End of contract bonus (1 month's salary).

SALARY: 2.2 million won per month.

FACILITIES/SUPPORT: Close to all amenities and the schools, free fully furnished, single or shared accommodation. Well-resourced schools, supportive work environment, job security.

RECRUITMENT: Via email and phone.

NUMBER OF TEACHERS: Over 1,300 for each Korean public school semester every February and August.

PREFERENCE OF NATIONALITY: Canadian, American, British, Australian, New Zealander, Irish and South African.

QUALIFICATIONS: Bachelor's degree in any field, between 21 and 55 years old, clean criminal record and must be in good physical and mental health.

CONDITIONS OF EMPLOYMENT: Contract length is always 1 year with the option to renew. Teachers must attend school from 8.30am to 4.30pm, Monday to Friday with 22 teaching hours per week. Overtime is paid plus 21–30 days' holiday. Pupils are elementary, middle or high school students.

SALARY: Between 2 million and 2.7 million won depending on qualifications and experience; 1 month's salary as severance pay upon completion of 1-year contract.

FACILITIES/SUPPORT: Teachers are paid a settlement allowance of 300,000 won upon arrival. The school provides furnished apartment rent-free but the teacher must pay for utilities. Married applicants can apply for couples' housing. A Korean co-teacher will sit in the class at all times to assist with translation and classroom management.

RECRUITMENT: Usually via online advertising. Interviews held over the phone.

CONTACT: Rod, Educational Consultant.

Agency so-named because it aims to provide a service 'without the bull'. Planning to extend into China in 2010/2011.

NUMBER OF TEACHERS: Up to 30 teachers placed per month in schools throughout South Korea.

PREFERENCE OF NATIONALITY: Mostly British although can also be Canadian, American, Irish, Australian, New Zealander, and South African.

QUALIFICATIONS: Minimum degree in any discipline. Experience of teaching or working with kids is a bonus. TEFL not necessary.

CONDITIONS OF EMPLOYMENT: 12-month contracts. 6 hours per day, with varying hours. Positions available in after-school academies and public schools.

SALARY: From 2.1 million won per month. Deductions made for health insurance and income tax.

FACILITIES/SUPPORT: School arranges and pays for the accommodation and flights. Assistance given for obtaining the relevant E2 visa. Support in all aspects of placement – contract negotiation, location advice, etc.

RECRUITMENT: Via ESL internet sites, university careers centres, media advertising and careers fairs. Applicants will be interviewed by an FC representative over the phone then by the school also by phone. FC staff have personal experience of teaching in Korea. Applicants are free to visit FC for one-to-one consultations.

CONTACT: Amanda McGillivray, Director/Senior Consultant.

NUMBER OF TEACHERS: Approximately 150 annually.

PREFERENCE OF NATIONALITY: None however, the Korean government only issues E2 visas to English teachers from UK, USA, Canada, Ireland, New Zealand, South Africa and Australia.

QUALIFICATIONS: Minimum bachelor's degree. BA in English, Education, Linguistics, TESOL or qualified teacher status is a plus though not mandatory. Clear spoken English and experience with working with young children.

CONDITIONS OF EMPLOYMENT: 1-year contract. Usual hours are 9am to 5pm Monday to Friday for public schools. Hours may be longer at private language institutes.

SALARY: Average basic salary is between 2 and 2.3 million won at franchised private schools and can be between 1.8 and 2.7 million won at public schools, depending on experience and qualifications.

FACILITIES/SUPPORT: Accommodation is provided by the schools. Usually the housing is single accommodation within walking distance of work. Sponsorship and assistance provided when applying for E2 visas and help is given with flight booking arrangements and airport pick up.

RECRUITMENT: Usually via word of mouth, university career centre and online advertising. Interviews are essential and can be held over the phone or Skype. Face-to-face interviews can be arranged internationally depending on where the consultants are located at that time. Interviews have also been arranged while visiting TESOL conventions and job fairs in USA, UK, Canada and Ireland.

CONTACT: Jamie Lee, HR Director.

REACH TO TEACH (SOUTH KOREA)
21 Everett Road Extension, Albany, New York 12205, USA
℡ +1 201 467 4612
✉ gillian@reachtoteachrecruiting.com
🖥 www.ReachToTeachRecruiting.com

Also has contacts in UK, Australia and New Zealand (see entry at beginning of Asia chapter).

NUMBER OF TEACHERS: 200+.

PREFERENCE OF NATIONALITY: Canadian, American, British, Australian, New Zealander, Irish and South African.

QUALIFICATIONS: Teaching experience is a plus, but not a requirement. Enthusiasm and enjoyment around children are musts. Teaching experience and/or a 100-hour TEFL qualification will often lead to a higher salary but are not essential.

CONDITIONS OF EMPLOYMENT: Public (EPIK, etc.) and private school positions. All job placements are full-time positions and for 1 year (and usually extendable). Schedules are generally either morning/afternoon (preschool or public elementary, middle or high school) or afternoon/evening (elementary school).

SALARY: 2–3 million won per month (from $1,650-$2,500) plus reimbursed flights to and from Korea.

FACILITIES/SUPPORT: Free housing always given in a furnished one-bedroom apartment or studio. Teachers pay a deposit which is reimbursed. Teachers are also helped with work permits from beginning to end. All teachers are welcome at various teacher social events and gatherings (often held in Seoul).

RECRUITMENT: Detailed telephone interviews are 100% essential. The company also carries out in-person interviews periodically in the USA and UK. Public school positions start twice a year (March and September) and the application process ideally needs to start 6 months in advance. Private school positions can be applied for year round and the time between application and arriving in Korea is often much quicker.

CONTACT: Gillian Benjamin, Director of Recruiting Korea (Gillian@reachtoteachrecruiting.com; skype gillian-reachtoteach).

USIT IRELAND
19/21 Aston Quay, Dublin 2, Ireland
℡ 1 602 1742
🖥 www.usit.ie

PREFERENCE OF NATIONALITY: None.

QUALIFICATIONS: Native English speaker (or can have level of English assessed). University degree required, which can be in any field.

CONDITIONS OF EMPLOYMENT: 12 months, possibly extendable. 4–6 hours per day.

SALARY: €18,000 a year (gross).

FACILITIES/SUPPORT: Some schools will organise accommodation for the teachers free of charge and in other cases the coordinator in Korea will assist them to find affordable accommodation. Help also given with visas.

RECRUITMENT: Prospective teachers apply online or come in person. Interviews essential and can be conducted in Dublin, occasionally elsewhere or via Skype.

CONTACT: Alan Byrne, Volunteer and Paid Teach Abroad Coordinator.

YBM EDUCATION ECC

YBM ECC Head Office, 56–16 Jongno 2ga, Jongno
Gu, 8th Floor, Seoul 110 772

2267 0532

eccmain@ybmsisa.co.kr

www.ybmecc.co.kr

NUMBER OF TEACHERS: 200 at 31 company-owned ECC
branches and about 450 at 74 franchise ECC schools that
are not placed by YBM Head Office. YBM/ELS schools are
for adults and offer slightly less advantageous terms of
employment (www.ybmhr.co.kr).

PREFERENCE OF NATIONALITY: Canadian, American,
British, Australian, New Zealander, and Irish.

QUALIFICATIONS: Minimum bachelor's degree, criminal
background check, academic transcripts. No teaching
experienced required but candidates must enjoy teaching
young children using curriculum provided (training
given).

CONDITIONS OF EMPLOYMENT: 12-month contracts.
Schedule 1: 9:30am–6pm. Schedule 2: 2pm–9pm.

SALARY: 2 million to 2.4 million won per month.

FACILITIES/SUPPORT: YBM provides rent-free, furnished
accommodation near the school plus prepaid airfare, medical, severance pay and pension compliance, guaranteed
contracts backed by the YBM Head Office, and assistance
with E2 visa.

RECRUITMENT: Job postings via internet, word of mouth
referrals from previous teachers. Every applicant undergoes
either a phone interview or a face-to-face interview if they
are in Korea.

CONTACT: Danny J. Kim, HR Manager, YBM Education ECC
Head Office.

YBM LANGUAGE INSTITUTES

7th Flr YBM Si/sa Annex Bldg, 56–16 Jongno 2-ga,
Jongno-gu, Seoul, 110–122

2 2003 1686

gregstapleton@ybmsisa.com, helenkim@
ybmsisa.com

www.ybmhr.co.kr

NUMBER OF TEACHERS: Between 200 and 250.

PREFERENCE OF NATIONALITY: Canadian, American,
British, Australian, New Zealander, and South African.

QUALIFICATIONS: Minimum bachelor's degree plus 1-year
formal teaching experience with adult learners. Candidates
with graduate degrees in applied linguistics or CELTA/TESOL
certification are preferred.

CONDITIONS OF EMPLOYMENT: 1-year renewable
contract, six 50-minute classes per day (30 hours
week).

SALARY: Depending upon academic qualifications and
teaching experience, salaries range from 2.1 million won
to 2.5 million won per month, plus 200,000 won housing
allowance.

FACILITIES/SUPPORT: Upon arrival teachers are provided
with accommodation in a motel near their school. Within the
first days the school's general affairs officer will show them
several apartments from which the teacher can choose.
The school then provides up to 10 million won in key money
(leasing) to secure the apartment.

RECRUITMENT: Primarily through web-based job postings,
followed by telephone/webcam interviews when candidates
are outside South Korea. Candidates applying from within
Korea must attend a face-to-face interview.

CONTACT: Helen Kim, National Recruiting Officer, YBM
Language Institutes.

INDIAN SUBCONTINENT

In contrast to Thailand and Indonesia with their strong demand for native English speaker teachers, other countries between Pakistan and the Philippines (with a few exceptions) are not easy places in which to find paid work as an English teacher. Poverty is the main reason why there is a very small market for expatriate teachers. Outside the relatively wealthy countries of Singapore, Malaysia and Brunei, there is no significant range of opportunities to earn money while teaching English. The largest growth area has been in Cambodia, Vietnam and Laos, where a number of joint venture and locally owned language schools employ native English speaker teachers.

Elsewhere, the demand may exist but the resources do not. Very few ordinary citizens in much of South Asia can dream of affording the luxury of English conversation classes. Few Westerners could manage on the wages earned by ordinary teachers in India, Nepal, Sri Lanka, Pakistan, etc. However, those foreigners prepared to finance themselves and volunteer their time can find eager students by asking around locally.

Mainstream voluntary organisations are active in the region, especially providing skilled volunteers to teachers' colleges and vocational colleges. Unskilled volunteers can be placed in the Indian sub-continent and beyond by the main commercial volunteer placement agencies like Travellers World-wide and i-to-i. Grassroots organisations are also active, especially those concerned with improving literacy in women and children. Plenty of commercial language teaching also goes on.

India

The emerging economy of India has some commentators predicting that together with China, its capacity and markets will overtake the West. The Indian economy is predicted to grow by an astonishing 8.5% in the financial year to March 2011. Even during the global financial crisis, growth was over 7%. High standards of education in the dominant class and an entrepreneurial spirit have helped India to flourish. English has been the medium of instruction in the elite schools and universities since India was a colony, and now is spreading to many ordinary middle class Indians who want to participate in the booming global economy. Much of the demand is met by English-speaking Indians rather than foreigners. For example, the British Council in Delhi that just two years ago looked to employ British English teachers now prefers Indian nationals.

Neveltheless, travelling English speakers have arranged to teach in the state sector, simply by entering a school and asking permission to sit in on an English class. Provided they do not expect a wage, some teaching role could probably be found for them. A volunteer from Derbyshire teaching in several village schools through VESL in Andhra Pradesh wrote that she and her teaching partner were in such demand that a busload of volunteers would find work. But it can be very challenging and discouraging. Facilities can be brutal with no teaching materials and no space. The majority of local English teachers, who have not really mastered the language, are very badly paid and can be transferred without appeal at any time; it is not too surprising to find that most are demoralised.

A number of organisations in the UK send volunteers to teach English in India in addition to VESL and Schoolhouse Volunteering with entries below, including the main gap year placement organisations. For example, Projects Abroad (01903 708300; www.projects-abroad.co.uk) arranges placements around Madurai in South India; fees start at £900 for two weeks up to £1,700 for three months. Postings are mainly to English-medium primary schools. New academies such as Valuepoint (see directory) cater to the insatiable demand in many Indian businesses to compete on an equal footing with the West. Just before **Raymond George** (age 62) started his official retirement from his job as a university physics lecturer, he noticed an advertisement on a college noticeboard for volunteer teachers with Travellers Worldwide. They were offering teaching placements in southern India, a region he was keen to see, so he enrolled for a two-month placement teaching spoken English in a primary school. This proved to be hugely rewarding, giving him a wonderful opportunity to experience life in a family and local community with enough spare time to travel to see the amazing temples of South India. Cross-Cultural Solutions with offices in the USA and UK (www.crossculturalsolutions. org) organises volunteer vacations in India. Volunteers work alongside grassroots organisations doing a range of tasks including English teaching. The programme fee is from about £1,500 excluding airfares. **Jenna Bonistalli** from New York City decided to use a windfall to fund six months off work to volunteer in India as a teacher:

Colleagues, friends and family were surprised upon hearing my decision to take off for half a year, especially when they learned my destination. The first three months were spent in the Himalayan hill town of Kalimpong in West Bengal. My boyfriend and I volunteered through HELP, the Himalayan Education Lifeline Programme (www.help-education.org), an organisation that places teachers in primary schools throughout Indian and Nepali Himalayan regions. We chose to go through them for a number of reasons, mainly location (we were both interested in going to this region mainly due to religious and cultural interest) and cost (their fees and donation requirements were VERY reasonable compared to some other outrageously high prices). This was after months of searching online, in books, on www.idealist.org and through recommendations. We had some choice in where we wanted to be placed and were able to read descriptions and see photos of the school and family, so this was helpful. There were no real requirements for being accepted, aside from an application form and references. Both of us had experience as educators in different capacities, so this made us more confident. Our experience in the Himalayas was unsurpassed – the setting, our students, the people we met, everything (aside from a bout of dysentery) was utterly amazing.

LIST OF EMPLOYERS

BRITISH COUNCIL NEW DELHI
17 Kastuba Gandhi Marg, New Delhi
℡ +91 11 2371 1401
🖥 www.britishcouncil.org/india

NUMBER OF TEACHERS: 16.
PREFERENCE OF NATIONALITY: Indian nationals preferred.
QUALIFICATIONS: Minimum CELTA qualification and 2 years' post-CELTA experience.
CONDITIONS OF EMPLOYMENT: Only hourly paid contracts are available at present.
SALARY: Starts at approximately Rs892 per hour for CELTA-qualified; Rs1,057 for DELTA qualified.
FACILITIES/SUPPORT: No help can be given with visas or accommodation.
RECRUITMENT: Interview required. May be conducted over the telephone.
CONTACT: June-Rose Davies, Deputy Teaching Centre Manager (11 2371 1401 ext 225).

BRITISH LINGUA
1/48, Lalita Park, Laxmi Nagar, Vikas Marg, Delhi 110092
℡ +91 11 32585879/+91 11 43026787
✉ britishlingua@yahoo.com
🖥 www.britishlingua.com

NUMBER OF TEACHERS: 2.
PREFERENCE OF NATIONALITY: None.
QUALIFICATIONS: University graduate.
CONDITIONS OF EMPLOYMENT: 1 year. 8 hours per day.
SALARY: Negotiable.
FACILITIES/SUPPORT: Assistance given with accommodation. No help with visas.
RECRUITMENT: Local interview necessary.
CONTACT: Birbal Jha, Managing Director.

MANJOORANS GROUP

Corporate Office: 3D, Metropalace, Opposite North Railway Station, Cochin, Kerala

Mobile 9446574292; (+91) 4812573071/481571771/4842396816

manjuran@sify.com; babu.manjuran@gmail.com

www.manjoorans.com/www.ieltslive.com

The group has more than 50 schools and 25,000 students undergoing School English Empowerment called 'Speak Perfect'.

NUMBER OF TEACHERS: 50 at various centres in South India.

PREFERENCE OF NATIONALITY: British, American, Australian, New Zealander, South African, Canadian.

QUALIFICATIONS: TEFL,TESOL,CELTA or just graduation.

CONDITIONS OF EMPLOYMENT: 6–12 months. Hours of teaching 9.30am–1pm and 2pm–4pm. To teach IELTS, TOEFL, conversational English.

SALARY: Rs10,000 plus accommodation.

FACILITIES/SUPPORT: Accommodation provided. Assistance given with sorting out visas.

RECRUITMENT: ELT websites. References needed. Interviews not essential.

CONTACT: Babu Manjooran, Director.

ROSE (Rural Organization for Social Elevation)

Social Awareness Centre, PO Kanda, Bageshwar, Uttarakhand 263631

jlverma_rosekanda@hotmail.com/ jlverma.rosekanda@gmail.com

www.rosekanda.org

PREFERENCE OF NATIONALITY: None.

QUALIFICATIONS: None required. Experience of teaching or living in a developing country useful. Flexibility, sense of humour and positive thinker.

CONDITIONS OF EMPLOYMENT: Grassroots development project which organises range of activities to help this rural community in the Himalayan foothills. Projects include teaching English in the KSS/ROSE office or the ABDIAL private English-medium primary school.

SALARY: None. Volunteers contribute to their living and food expenses as paying guests (about £5 or Rs600 per day). Also registration fee Rs3,500–Rs6,000.

FACILITIES/SUPPORT: Accommodation arranged in local homes as homestay. Hindi instruction. Cultural exchange available.

RECRUITMENT: Contact Bijon K Sinha and Richard Northridge, Cwm Harry Land Trust, Lower Cwm Harry, Tregynon, Powys SY16 3ES, Wales, UK; send a self-addressed envelope.

VALUEPOINT ACADEMY

2nd floor, Shankar House, 1 RMV Extension Makhri Circle, Bangalore 560080

+91 80 40793777

sales@valuepointacademy.com

www.valuepointacademy.com

PREFERENCE OF NATIONALITY: None.

CONDITIONS OF EMPLOYMENT: 1-year contract with maximum 8 working hours per day.

FACILITIES/SUPPORT: Assistance can be given with finding accommodation and applying for work permits.

RECRUITMENT: Interview and demonstration lesson.

CONTACT: Meenu Sood, Director.

Nepal

After a period of relative stability in Nepal, tensions are again rising between Maoist rebels and the government. The UN continues to play a key role in maintaining the peace between opposing factions, and at the time of writing (just after Maoist rebels had derailed a train in West Bengal in mid-2010, killing 76 passengers), the UN was expressing concern over the political situation in Nepal. So the moderates' hopes that Nepal's political problems would dissipate and the country be able to concentrate on improving the lives of its people are on hold once again. All the same, short-term volunteers and casual English teachers continue to stay on in Nepal, at least as long as their visa allows. Tourist visas (which can be purchased on arrival for $100 cash) are valid for 90 days (shorter stays for less money are also available) and can be extended for $2 a day thereafter, up to a maximum of five months normally.

A range of organisations makes it possible for self-funding volunteers to teach. Of course living expenses are very low by Western standards, though the fees charged by mediating or gap year organisations such as i-to-i and Africa, Asia & Americas Venture as well as by Nepali agencies (some listed below) can increase the cost significantly. If you want to avoid an agency fee, you can make direct contact with schools on arrival.

Relevant organisations in addition to the ones in the directory are listed below:

Cultural Destination Nepal, Kathmandu (www.volunteernepal.org.np). Volunteer Nepal, a service work programme. Fee of €249 for one month, €349 for two months.

KEEP (Kathmandu Environmental Education Project), Kathmandu (1 4216775/6; volunteer@info.com.np; www.keepnepal.org). KEEP is eager to recruit volunteers to help deliver English language training to Nepalis who work in the tourist industry in preparation for Nepal's Tourism Year 2011. KEEP also works in trekking villages, government schools and runs English language short courses in June/July and December/January. Volunteers will stay with a host family in order to adjust to Nepali culture (free of charge in some cases). The only fee charged is $50 administrative fee.

Alliance Nepal (Krishnatimi@gmail.com; www.volunteerworkinnepal.org). Prices from €200 for 2 weeks to €500 for 12 weeks.

Mondo Challenge, UK (www.mondochallenge.com.uk). Volunteers (mainly career breakers) are sent each year to placements in rural areas and in Kathmandu to teach mainly basic English to primary aged pupils. American and Australian volunteers accepted as well as British.

RCDP Nepal Volunteer, GPO Box: 8957, Tasindole Marg 95/48, Kalaniki 14, Kathmandu, Nepal (www.rcdpnepal.org). Paying volunteers work on various programmes lasting 2 weeks to 5 months, including teaching English. Volunteers stay with families in villages. Registration fee of $219 plus a weekly charge which goes down the longer you stay.

After **Melissa Evans**' placement in Kenya was cancelled at the last moment, her gap year agency, Adventure Alternative (www.adventurealternative.com), had to live up to their name and quickly find her an alternative adventure. They arranged for Melissa to fly a month later to Nepal where she taught in a school:

> *It was very, very rewarding, as the children really thrived off the teaching from a foreign teacher. I found the teaching a challenge as the children struggled with English, and also pronunciation. Sometimes, I found myself unable to understand the children and vice versa. However, familiarity over the three months allowed the language barrier to break down, and conversing with the children was easier by the end of my placement, as I had learned a little Nepali and they had grown used to my pronunciation. Before my gap year I had the ambition of being a teacher. However, after travelling for the first time my ambition changed, and now I aim to found an orphanage.*

Rachel Sedley spent six months between school and university as a volunteer teacher at the Siddartha School in Kathmandu, arranged through a UK gap organisation and conveys some of the flavour of the experience:

> *The sun is shining and the kids are running riot. New Baneshwar is a suburb of Kathmandu, very busy and polluted, but of course so friendly. I do get tired of being a novelty, especially when I'm swathed in my five metres of bright turquoise silk (we wear saris for teaching) but I'm really loving it here. Already after one month, the thought of leaving the kids and my simple lifestyle is terrible. I find it funny that as a Westerner I'm seen to represent infinite stores of knowledge and yet the servant girl is having to patiently teach me to wash my own clothes. And the general knowledge people have of the fundamentals of life makes me feel helpless and incapable. The children are so gorgeous (most of the time) and the Principal's family with whom I am living are lovely. It seems to me unnecessary to come to Nepal through an organisation. Everyone here is so keen to help.*

Rachel's main complaint about her situation was that she was teaching in a private school for privileged children when she had been led to believe that she would be contributing her time, labour and money to more needy children. While there, she met several people from various schools and orphanages who would love to have English volunteers.

LIST OF EMPLOYERS

HELP (HIMALAYAN EDUCATION LIFELINE PROGRAMME)
30 Kingsdown Park, Whitstable, Kent CT5 2DF, UK
- 01227 263055
- jim.coleman@help-education.org
- www.help-education.org

HELP enables young people from poor communities in Himalayan India (Sikkim, West Bengal, Ladakh and Himachal Pradesh) and Nepal (Kathmandu Valley, Pokhara and Chitwan) to improve their employment opportunities through education by providing financial and volunteer resources to their schools.

NUMBER OF PLACEMENTS: HELP supports some 25 schools in Nepal and the Indian Himalayas. Also a women's weaving cooperative in Pokhara.

QUALIFICATIONS: Ages 19/20–60+. Appropriate teaching experience and/or a basic TEFL qualification is essential. Volunteers should be mature and resourceful. Qualities needed include resilience and adaptability, an open mind and an interest in other cultures, good mental and physical health, plus tact and diplomacy. A love of and experience with children is vital.

CONDITIONS OF WORK: Minimum 2 months. Volunteers can stay for a maximum of 6 months (for visa reasons).

SALARY: None. Fee from £390 depending on volunteer's status and length of stay, including accommodation with host families or in school hostel.

FACILITIES/SUPPORT: Volunteers receive a briefing pack. Once in post, a local HELP representative is on hand to help with any problems.

RECRUITMENT: Applications accepted year round. Telephone interviews conducted after receipt of the online application form.

CONTACT: Jim Coleman, Executive Director.

HOPE AND HOME
Travel Program, PO Box 119, Kathmandu
- +977 1 443 90771 5393
- info@hopenhome.org/ US: hopenhome@gmail.com/ UK: aryal@hotmail.co.uk
- www.hopenhome.org

Community-oriented volunteer opportunities for international volunteers with homestay and cultural exchange.

NUMBER OF PLACEMENTS PER YEAR: 55–60 in the Kathmandu Valley, Pokhara, Chitwan and Nawalparasi areas of Nepal.

QUALIFICATIONS: Ages 18–35. All that is needed is a desire to help people.

CONDITIONS OF WORK: Volunteer opportunities lasting 2 weeks to 3 months are in the fields of teaching English, as well as community, health and environmental programme.

SALARY: None. Volunteer fees entirely fund programme and include homestay accommodation and food. From $400 for 2 weeks to $1,000 for 12 weeks plus registration fee of $200.

RECRUITMENT: Online applications accepted year round.

FACILITIES/SUPPORT: Language class, cultural information and project information provided.

CONTACT: Rabyn Aryal, Director; Binay Aryal (Director Europe – aryal@hotmail.co.uk).

INSIGHT NEPAL
PO Box 489, Pokhara, Kaski
- +977 61 530266
- insight@fewanet.com.np
- www.insightnepal.org.np

NUMBER OF TEACHERS: 60 volunteers accepted each year for development projects mainly in the Pokhara Valley.

PREFERENCE OF NATIONALITY: All.

QUALIFICATIONS: Minimum 'A' levels for UK volunteers, high school diploma for Americans. Age limits 18–65. Teaching or volunteering experience desirable but not necessary.

CONDITIONS OF EMPLOYMENT: Placements last 7 weeks or 3 months starting year round.

SALARY: None. Programme participation fee is $950 for 3 months, $690 for 7 weeks.

FACILITIES/SUPPORT: Accommodation and two meals a day provided, usually as homestay. 3-month programme includes pre-orientation training, placement in a primary or secondary school in Nepal to teach mainly English or in community development projects, a 1-week village or trekking excursion and 3 days in Chitwan National Park.

RECRUITMENT: Application forms, 3 photos and introductory letter should be sent 3 months in advance of proposed starting date.

VOLUNTEER NEPAL NATIONAL GROUP
Jhaukhel 4, Bhaktapur
☎ 1 661 3724
✎ info@volnepal.np.org or volunteer_
nepal2002@yahoo.com
🖳 www.volnepal.np.org/teaching_schools.php

Community-based non-profit organisation that coordinates local and international work camps to empower community self-help initiatives.

NUMBER OF PLACEMENTS PER YEAR: 100 in Kathmandu Valley near the historic city of Bhaktapur.

QUALIFICATIONS: Minimum age 18.

CONDITIONS OF WORK: Placements for volunteers in schools, colleges and universities, lasting 2 weeks to 5 months, starting mid-February or August. Volunteers usually spend 2–3 hours a day teaching English to children aged 6–13, plus help with sports, music, extra-curricular activities and other administrative and social welfare work.

RECRUITMENT: Application form, CV and references needed.

SALARY: None. Volnepal programme fees including pre-service training, language instruction, homestay and meals, trekking, rafting, jungle safari and volunteering, are from $350 for 2 weeks to $1,150 for 18 weeks.

CONTACT: Anish Neupane, Director.

Pakistan and Bangladesh

The need for English in Pakistan has been replaced in 2010 by the desperate need for more basic aid, following the catastrophic floods, water contamination and resulting disaster. It will be years before the infrastructure can be repaired and schools rebuilt. When that happens, once again schools should be willing to take on native English speaker teachers, but the problems will still pertain: lack of remuneration and difficulty with visas. Most opportunities are available only to teachers willing to finance themselves and to work on a three-month tourist visa. Security clearance and visa processing can take months, and is very difficult unless you have someone to push for you.

The British Council employs qualified teachers at its own teaching centre in Dhaka, who are recruited in London. The centre also employs a number of hourly paid teachers who are recruited locally but the demand for courses fluctuates so much that steady employment cannot be guaranteed. People who are established in Dhaka (such as spouses of expat managers, etc.) manage to earn reasonable part-time wages teaching private classes.

Far fewer gap placement agencies and other educational charities send volunteers to Bangladesh than to Nepal. Few private language schools exist in Pakistan. The British Council organises exams, but does not run teaching courses. The US counterpart is the Pakistan American Cultural Center (PACC) with several branches throughout the country. Security concerns are largely confined to places like the Swat Valley rather than the big cities. Demand for English is strong among the young not least because (sad to say) working in a Western call centre probably pays better than an engineering job.

Opportunities for native English teachers are probably there for the taking, tutoring businessmen, university students and children, if teachers are respectful and resourceful. While loitering in a secondhand bookshop in Scotland, **Hannah Adcock** fell into conversation with a Pakistani university professor who promptly offered food and board in exchange for working at his wife's private school for children near Karachi. Having a native English speaker is apparently a real status symbol for a school (something you wouldn't guess from reading the British/American press).

LIST OF EMPLOYERS

BANGLADESH WORK CAMPS ASSOCIATION (BWCA)
289/2 Workcamp Road, North Shajahanpur,
Dhaka 1217
℡ 2 935 8206/6814
✉ bwca@bangla.net
🖥 www.mybwca.org

BWCA organises workcamps and longer-term projects for volunteers in rural and urban areas of Bangladesh.

NUMBER OF TEACHERS: 5 per year (roughly equally divided male and female).

QUALIFICATIONS: Native English speakers aged 18–30.

CONDITIONS OF EMPLOYMENT: Volunteers work 30 hours per week on placements which last 2–6 months on the RYTP (Round the Year Programme). Work can include teaching and developing English speaking and writing to primary and secondary school teachers, as well as to students. For example, a 2010 project was in a Dhaka kindergarten.

SALARY: Voluntary work. Volunteers bear all expenses at a cost equivalent to $300 per month for the first 3 months and then $50 per month plus $2.50 a day for food. Homestay or other accommodation is provided.

Tibet

Tibet (known as Xizang province in Mandarin) in the far west of China, has fascinated people in the West for centuries and until 1986 was inaccessible to the outside world. On the highest plateau in the world and encompassing a large section of the Himalayan mountains, Tibet offers something quite different from the rest of China. While there is a certain appetite to communicate with the outside world and learn English, there is also anxiety about incursions into Tibetan culture. But with numbers of foreigners set to increase with the planned introduction of a luxury rail service (Beijing to Lhasa) demand to learn English is bound to increase.

Despite a decision taken some time ago to change the medium of instruction used in Tibetan schools in exile from English to Tibetan, there are plenty of volunteering opportunities in places such as Dharamsala in northern India. Try for example the LHA Charitable Trust (www.lhasocialwork.org). Note that opportunities to volunteer with the Tibetan community frequently emanate from Himalayan India and Nepal rather than Tibet itself.

Currently, there are almost no official positions for teachers in Tibet, due at least in part to the labyrinthine red tape involved in obtaining a work permit, and paranoia in official Chinese circles that foreigners will fill the heads of Tibetans with Western ideology. Most EFL teachers therefore enter Tibet as volunteers. Tibet covers a vast area of land, larger than Germany, France and Italy combined, yet it is still one of the poorest areas in the world.

The Chinese were quick to be seen providing aid to a remote part of eastern Tibet in April 2010 after an earthquake devastated the area. China has invested heavily in Tibet over the past eight years, and its economy has apparently maintained strong growth year on year (according to Chinese figures). However, anti-Chinese protests, harshly suppressed, rumble on and continue to keep the Autonomous (so-called) region politically fragile. Basic problems such as providing access to water and a shortage of doctors and qualified teachers takes time to remedy, as well as the political will to make sure that aid reaches Tibetans who need it most. Still, volunteering as an English teacher in Tibet can be a very rewarding experience as **Darin Wahl**, an intrepid traveller who spent some months volunteering as an English teacher in Tibet, discovered:

I worked with Tibetan children in an orphanage/special school. There were about 12–25 students in each class, many of whom had varying disabilities, but their attitudes and those of the other children made the hardships of Tibet (the cold, altitude sickness, the poverty) all worthwhile. Tibetans are not crippled by the stigmas that the Western world imposes on those with mental or physical disabilities, nor are they ashamed or made to feel so by society. The attitude was 'If you can talk you can sing; if you

LIZZI MIDDLETON's gap year was spent teaching English in a completely unexpected setting:

Not quite believing that I was embarking on what was to be the biggest adventure of my life so far, I arrived in Delhi and a few days later caught a 15-hour overnight bus to McLeodganj in north-west India, seat of the Tibetan government in exile and home of His Holiness the Dalai Lama. It was a further hour's hair raising bus journey down into the valley to my placement at the Jamyang Choeling Himalayan Institute for Buddhist women. The nunnery is in a very secluded area of the countryside, set in front of the stunning backdrop of the snow-capped foothills of the Himalayas. It was unbelievably picturesque and was a welcome relief after the madness of Delhi!

Finding out what we were meant to be doing, and where we were meant to be was our first major challenge. Tibetans are notoriously vague – we had been warned about this but it was vague on a level that I've never experienced vague before! This was one of the real cultural differences that I had to adapt to. Having just completed my A levels and the careful structuring of time that they had required, and coming from a family where we always let each other know where we are, life at Jamyang Choeling was quite a change. I had to learn to be very easy going, to not mind when a class just didn't turn up or when there was only half a class there.

My classes were loosely organised according to ability but to be honest that didn't mean much. Lessons were fun – I realised soon after I arrived that these women needed their hour with me to be educational but light-hearted. They get up at 5am every day and apart from an hour for lunch and an hour for dinner they don't stop until 10 or 11pm – they're studying Buddhism all day. My first few lessons were pretty diabolical as I tried to find my feet in a completely alien situation. I had no idea of how I was going to learn the names of 90 women, none of whom had any hair and who all wore exactly the same clothes!

So the teaching was the reason that I was there but there were lots of other things to be done at the nunnery too. Cooking for 90+ three times a day is no mean feat and so every day from 10am to noon I cut up vegetables with a small team of nuns. I found that it was a great time for the nuns to practise the English that they were sometimes too shy to use in front of each other in the classroom, and it was also an opportunity for me to learn some Tibetan and to listen to their stories – often of escape over the Himalayas from Tibet. I made some amazing friends. Together we had a huge amount of fun – riding on the roofs of local buses, swimming in the river, shopping for food for our leaving party, teaching each other national dances (I'm afraid we ended up opting to teach the Macarena), blowing up balloons, and a lot of the time just sitting and chatting about the similarities and most of all the differences between our lives, religions and cultures.

can walk you can dance', and they did. On top of this, the children were incredibly self-disciplined, they were interested and they were interesting.

It is possible to enquire about voluntary positions once in Lhasa. Darin was pointed in the direction of the Lhasa Jatson Chumig Welfare Special School, whose website www.jatsontibet.org carries some information about becoming a volunteer; enquiries should be sent to Tenzin Choedon, Assistant Director (jatson4@yahoo.com). Alternatively, you can do some online research before arriving. The website www.volunteertibet.org carries teaching vacancies for which you must send an email to receive further information. Most of the volunteer teaching positions are in Tibetan monasteries and nunneries in Himalayan India and Nepal. Volunteer organisations and NGOs that are active in Tibet may be able to place teachers in a school or orphanage and arrange a visa for the desired length of stay (visa extensions in Tibet are notoriously difficult to obtain and many applicants are lucky to get 10 days). Some organisations require TEFL qualifications, but the majority are happy to take on any native English speakers.

Specialist tour operators may be able to advise. For example, Tibetan Wild Yak Adventures publishes a little information about volunteering on a page of its website (www.tibetanwildyakadventures.com/teach_english.htm) including in orphanages in Tibet. It also links to a blog about teaching in Tibet (http://news.haverford.edu/blogs/tibet). Volunteer teaching positions often involve only 18–25 hours a week, leaving teachers free to earn a little spending money by offering private lessons, as **Darin Wahl** discovered:

> *There is no lack of opportunity for those interested in private tutoring. Even just putting up a sign will generate more than sufficient interest. The only problem is that few Tibetans have enough money to spend on luxuries such as schooling and it would be difficult to generate enough income to cover your living costs in Lhasa.*

Those looking for paid teaching work in a school will find that salaries are low (local Tibetan teachers receive a few dollars per day) and will have trouble staying on the right side of the law. Work permits are very hard to get, especially for American citizens. It seems that while foreigners can teach in Tibet, they can only do so in Lhasa. It might be worth trying to make contact with institutes of higher education, such as Tibet University where some foreigners study Tibetan (fsd@utibet.edu.cn), and the Tibet Academy of Social Sciences.

Schools in Lhasa may be prepared to take on the odd foreigner to teach without a work permit, but they generally do not advertise and tend to be slightly suspicious when approached. Public schools can be crowded, and the teaching difficult, with up to 50 students to a class. Generally the schools are clean and well run, but they struggle to provide the necessary resources. Teaching in Tibet promises to be an exciting and rewarding experience, as Darin Wahl puts it: '*Only a lucky few get to spend as much time here, to meet as many smiling faces and to be shown such kindness as teachers do.*'

Sri Lanka

In May 2009, the Sri Lankan government declared military victory over the Tamil Tigers, ending 26 years of civil war. Yet the FCO still advises against all travel to the Tamil-speaking northern provinces since there is a heavy military presence and many displaced people. This development has resulted in heightened nationalism and demonstrations outside the embassy of the old colonial masters, i.e. the UK. However, this has not stemmed the drive to introduce more English language education in the country, including in government-funded schools offering an English-medium stream. English is sometimes seen as a neutral choice between bitterly opposed Tamil and Sinhalese, and as in India, is used in some elite private schools.

The British Council at 49 Alfred House Gardens in Colombo (www.britishcouncil.org/srilanka) has offices with libraries and teaching centres in both Colombo and Kandy. The teaching centres offer classes to adults and young learners. Teachers need a minimum of two years' post-certificate experience to be considered. The Council runs part-time CELTA courses in Colombo April to June and October to December plus a full-time course in August, both costing £1,650. Originally called Volunteers for English in Sri Lanka, VESL has branched out to Thailand and India, but continues to send teachers to Sri Lanka. Also the Senahasa Trust based in London (www.senahasa.org) has been working in rural state schools in southern Sri Lanka since 2005 and recruits a few volunteer English teachers for the four schools the charity rebuilt after the Tsunami.

LIST OF EMPLOYERS

SCHOOLHOUSE VOLUNTEERING

Schoolhouse, Anderson Road, Ballater,
Aberdeenshire, Scotland AB35 5QW, UK

✆ 01339 756333

✎ info@school-english.com

🖥 www.schoolhousevolunteering.com

Schoolhouse Volunteering offers well-researched and well-supported English teaching volunteering opportunities in a range of formal and informal situations in Sri Lanka and India.

PREFERENCE OF NATIONALITY: Must be native or fluent English speaker. Ideally candidates can attend pre-placement training in Scotland.

QUALIFICATIONS: Teaching qualifications are not essential as there is a range of placements to match a range of skills and experience. However, newly qualified teachers seeking experience, those wishing to explore teaching with a view to training in the future, teachers seeking a refreshing sabbatical or holiday and retired teachers may be particularly interested. Volunteers must be good communicators, be enthusiastic and open to contributing to and learning from new and challenging experiences.

CONDITIONS OF EMPLOYMENT: Volunteer English teaching placements in government schools through the Ministry of Education in Colombo and other organisations in Sri Lanka and Tamil Nadu. Placements last 1 month to 1 year.

FACILITIES/SUPPORT: A free (optional) 2/3-day residential pre-departure training course is given at Schoolhouse premises in Scotland. The course aims to prepare volunteers and enable them to get the most out of their volunteer teaching experience, both in terms of contribution and self-development. Volunteers stay in campus accommodation, with selected host families or in a shared house or flat with other volunteers.

RECRUITMENT: Applications welcomed year round. After submitting the online application form (on the Schoolhouse site), Schoolhouse will develop a rapport with applicants to ensure an effective matching and good preparation.

Cost: £595 for one month (covers placement admin, training, airport pick-up, accommodation, most meals and ongoing support during placement).

CONTACTS: Alan and Cathy Low, Schoolhouse Volunteering.

VESL (VOLUNTEERS FOR EDUCATIONAL SUPPORT & LEARNING)

17 Silk Hill, Buxworth, High Peak, Derbyshire SK23 7TA, UK

✆ 0845 094 3727

✎ info@vesl.org or enquiries@vesl.org

🖥 www.vesl.org.

VESL is a charity registered in the UK (no. 1117908) and as an NGO in Sri Lanka and Thailand and sends volunteers to work on projects in Asia.

NUMBER OF TEACHERS: Up to 60 (including placements in India and Thailand as well).

QUALIFICATIONS: Minimum age 18, though most volunteers are older. Volunteers should be enthusiastic, motivated and up for a challenge. TEFL experience and some experience overseas are helpful but not a requirement.

CONDITIONS OF EMPLOYMENT: 4–6 week summer programmes in July and August and 3–6 month projects throughout the year. Some volunteers are also required to help run teacher workshop programmes in August each year. Volunteers and qualified teachers are sent to run English language summer schools in remote communities.

RECRUITMENT: Applications accepted throughout the year. All candidates must be able to attend a selection day and training weekend (dates and places in the UK to be notified).

SALARY: Voluntary work. All applicants pay a programme fee ranging from £900 for summer placement to £1,350 for 3 months, which covers cost of setting up the projects, training, orientation, insurance, accommodation, food, in-country travel and comprehensive back up and support. VESL is run mainly by volunteers so costs are kept to a minimum.

CONTACT: Tom Harrison, Programme Director.

MALAYSIA

For the many Malaysian students who aspire to go to university in the UK, USA or Australia, intensive English language tuition is an essential part of their training. The government has increased the profile of English as a medium of instruction in the state education system so the demand is set to increase. CfBT (Centre for British Teaching) has been in Malaysia for 28 years and is currently assisting the Malaysian Ministry of Education to improve the standard of English in schools. For details contact Chris Frankland, Senior Manager (Suite B-306, Block B, Phileo Damansara 1, No. 9 Jalan 16/11, Off Jalan Damansara, 46350 Petaling Jaya, Selangor; www.cfbt.com.my).

Positions include 32 District English Language Co-ordinators (DELCs) and 10 Project English Teachers (PETs). DELCs encourage and develop ELT in all aspects in target districts. DELCs work out of medium-sized provincial towns in Sabah, Sarawak and West Malaysia and liaise at district and schools levels, working closely with Heads, Heads of Departments and teachers. Applicants must have a degree, postgraduate qualification in ELT, a minimum of five years in ELT and a driving licence, since they will have the use of a project car. PETs teach in government residential schools for gifted students and provide native English speaker inputs for teachers and students, new ideas and approaches in the language classroom and encourage the use of English outside the language classroom. Applicants must have a degree, certificate in ELT and a minimum of two years' ELT experience. Benefits of a two-year package include a good local salary, return airfares, housing allowance, medical expenses and an end-of-contract bonus. The government issues work permits only to highly qualified applicants. People caught working on tourist visas can expect to be fined and deported.

Other education consultancies recruit teachers and senior trainers including the Kuala Lumpur-based Brighton Education Group (www.brightoneducation.org/recruitment.html). Recently it has linked up with the UK company Nord Anglia Education to supply qualified teachers to participate in TELL (Teaching English Language and Literacy), a new government initiative to be implemented in primary schools. A New Zealand company, Euroasia, also has a contract with a Malaysian partner to recruit teachers (www.euroasia.co.nz).

The British Council has teaching centres in Kuala Lumpur and Penang (www.britishcouncil.org/malaysia); the former offers the CELTA course part-time starting four times a year (price 8,000 ringgits). As an employer the British Council is highly regarded as long-time TEFLer **Steph Fuccio** from the USA reported after a stint of teaching in Kuala Lumpur at a different institute:

> *My husband and I moved to Malaysia right after we got married and worked for different branches of the same language school. After a lot of pondering and trying to make it work, we left after six months. While we were there the government switched from using English as the primary language in the schools back to Bahasa Malay. This switch apparently happens often, and with an unfortunate effect on the kids in the school system. Thus, there weren't as many jobs open to us as initially thought.*
>
> *The British Council was by far the best paying language school in town, pretty much doubling standard language school salaries, with more benefits to boot. We interviewed at many places and finally decided on another school because it offered set daytime hours, good pay (5,000 ringgits before tax), and they had locations near our apartment. Unfortunately, what we didn't bargain on was the materials that we were supposed to use, their own cut and paste versions of difficult grammar books, the method they wanted us to teach with (lecture, not communicative method) and just how penny pinching they were. My husband's school gave them a ream of paper each month for photocopies, my school had a copy tally. We were all 'talked to' monthly on lowering our copy numbers.*

Work permits must be obtained and can take up to three months. You will need to produce your degree and TEFL qualification certificates, university transcripts, reference letter from previous employer, medical report and passport photos. Also enquire about a minimum age stipulation. While Steph and her husband Evan were teaching in Malaysia, the government was issuing work permits only to people over 30. Also be sure to register at the tax office as soon as you start employment, and ensure your employer is taking taxes regularly from your pay. Otherwise you can be hit by a colossal bill when you leave, as happened to one of Steph's fellow teachers. Suddenly huge amounts were missing from his pay cheque with no itemisation, and they heard that this was not uncommon. The Erican Language Centre (see entry) offers teachers willing to relocate to various parts of Malaysia to teach children or adults an attractive package.

One aspect of life in Malaysia which can be difficult to accept is that racial Malays are accorded special privileges over other citizens of Chinese, Indian or tribal origins. For example, places at the universities are available exclusively to *bumiputeras* or 'bumis', which means literally 'sons of the soil', i.e. ethnic Malays. Otherwise Malaysia offers a pleasant multicultural environment and teachers usually experience less culture shock than they do in Thailand and Indonesia. Kuala Lumpur is a model of modernity and efficiency when compared with the neighbouring capitals of Jakarta and Bangkok.

LIST OF EMPLOYERS

ERICAN LANGUAGE CENTRE

C-19-4 Megan Avenue II, Jalan Yap Kwan Seng,
50450 Kuala Lumpur

C +60 3 2164 9999

hr@erican.edu.my

www.erican.edu.my

Language education and training company with 20+ centres across the peninsula.

NUMBER OF TEACHERS: 5 full-time.

PREFERENCE OF NATIONALITY: British, American, Canadian, Australian or New Zealander.

QUALIFICATIONS: Minimum bachelor's degree and a professional training certificate (CELTA, TESOL or equivalent).

CONDITIONS OF EMPLOYMENT: 12–24-month contracts to teach children and adults. Usual working hours (25 per week) between 9am and 5pm Monday to Friday.

SALARY: Approximately $1,200 per month plus monthly performance incentive, less 10% deductions for tax and social security.

FACILITIES/SUPPORT: Free shared room in teachers' hostel is normally available or the teacher will be subsidised by the centre (typically 500 ringgits per month) for private accommodation. The centre applies for work permits and covers all required visa charges. The visa application process may take 2–3 months.

RECRUITMENT: Usually via online advertisements. Interviews are essential and are normally via online video conferencing.

CONTACT: Ki Chong, Human Resources Manager.

SINGAPORE

Malaysia's tiny neighbour clinging to the tip of the Malay peninsula is a wealthy and Westernised city-state in which there is a considerable demand for qualified English teachers on minimum one-year contracts. Once a teacher does get established in a school, freelance teaching is widely available paying from S$30 an hour (over US$20).

The Foreign Recruitment Unit of the Ministry of Education in Singapore (MOE_FRU@moe.gov.sg) recruits foreign teachers in English language/English literature, as well as Geography, History and Economics, on one to three-year contracts in secondary schools and junior colleges (Grades 7 to 12). The scheme is very competitive, so only suitably qualified applicants should consider this option. Candidates should possess a relevant and very good degree preferably with teaching/higher qualifications and experience. Details and application form can be found at www.moe.gov.sg/careers/teach. Salaries for degree-holders start at S$2,550 (gross) plus an end-of-year bonus and airfares into/out of Singapore.

The British Council at 30 Napier Road has a teaching operation that hires qualified teachers locally especially for teaching young learners (and can also provide a list of approved language schools). Many are located in the ubiquitous shopping centres, especially along Orchard Road, for example Berlitz (501), Geos (Wellington Building, just off Orchard Road), Linguarama (220), Ikomo (350) and Goro (60b). Note that these are not complete postal addresses. The majority of commercial language centres are Chinese-owned with a high proportion of teachers from Australia.

Not strictly an ESL programme, native English speakers are being recruited to teach literacy skills to children with a company called I Can Read. As with the government scheme, candidates must have either a university teaching qualification or a degree in a humanities subject such as English literature, linguistics or psychology, in order to qualify for the Employment Pass. Two-year contracts start in July/August (www.icanreadsystem.com).

Singapore is not a recommended destination for the so-called 'teacher-traveller' who, without qualifications but with a smart pair of trousers, hopes to be able to impress a language school owner. Even people who have qualifications cannot count on walking into a job. However, persistent enquiries have resulted in the offer of hourly work. If you would like to go to Singapore to look for work you can apply online (www.mom.gov.sg) for the Employment Pass Eligibility Certificate (EPEC), which allows foreigners who are holders of selected university qualifications (their list includes most respectable universities) to stay in Singapore for up to one year to facilitate their job search. Generally, if you have been granted an EPEC by the Ministry of Manpower (MOM), you are likely to qualify for an Employment Pass upon securing employment.

Once you have a sponsoring employer, the prospective employer must contact the Singapore Immigration and Checkpoints Authority (10 Kallang Road, ICA Building, Singapore 208718; www.ica.gov.sg) for an application form and approval letter, or simply apply online. The process usually takes between six and eight weeks, and it is necessary to wait for the approval letter before travelling as you will be required to present it at Immigration Control in Changi Airport.

Some teachers have reported that they have quickly tired of Singapore, coming to see it as one giant shopping mall. So if shopping malls and a repressive regime (for example there are signs threatening to fine you $150 if you jaywalk or fail to flush the loo) leave you cold, Singapore is perhaps best avoided.

LIST OF EMPLOYERS

INLINGUA SCHOOL OF LANGUAGES

1 Grange Road, Orchard Building #04–01,
Singapore 239693

☎ +65 6737 6666

✉ info@inlingua.edu.sg

🖥 www.inlingua.edu.sg

NUMBER OF TEACHERS: 6 full-time English teachers
(40 teachers in total in 14 departments).

PREFERENCE OF NATIONALITY: Multinational team from
the UK, USA and Canada. Teachers from the UK preferred.

QUALIFICATIONS: Degree and teaching qualification
required (CELTA, CELTYL, TESOL or TEFL). Experience is not
necessary but candidates must be effective teachers who
can work well in a team.

CONDITIONS OF EMPLOYMENT: Standard 18-month
contract. 40 hours per week (8 hours per day maximum) on
school premises. This includes up to 25 hours of teaching
(30 lessons lasting 50 minutes each). Group lessons are
usually Monday to Friday 9am–1pm but trainers may also
have to teach until 9pm Monday to Friday and 8am–1pm
on Saturday.

SALARY: Starts at S$2,600 per month. After a 3-month
probationary period and satisfactory performance, salary
increases to S$2,900. After a further 3 months, salary
increases to S$3,000. End-of-contract bonus of 1–3 months
salary depending on performance. 18-month contracts taxed
at 3%. Teachers do not need to pay Central Provident Fund
contributions.

FACILITIES/SUPPORT: Temporary homestay accommodation can be arranged for at least 1 month. S$650 will be
deducted from salary. Teachers welcome to use staffroom
telephone and newspapers to secure their own accommodation.

RECRUITMENT: Please apply by email/fax/post by sending
2-page CV (not as email attachment). Interview and demonstration lesson in Singapore preferred but not essential.

CONTACT: Graham Sage.

MORRIS ALLEN STUDY CENTRES

#B1–27, Park Mall, 9 Penang Road, Singapore
238459

☎ +65 6334 2623

✉ principal@morris-allen.com.sg

🖥 www.morris-allen.com.sg

NUMBER OF TEACHERS: 40+.

PREFERENCE OF NATIONALITY: British, Australian, New
Zealand, Canadian, American and South African.

QUALIFICATIONS: Minimum 3 years' experience plus
degree in education; or bachelor's degree plus teacher
training specialising in English, primary or early childhood
education. Most teachers have classroom experience with
children whose mother tongue is English.

CONDITIONS OF EMPLOYMENT: 2 years (1 year is available, extensions welcome). 28 teaching hours per week
out of total working week of 35 hours. To teach Singapore
children aged 3 to 16 years, in an English-medium education
system.

SALARY: S$3,500 per month, tax free plus bonus of
S$3,000 at the end of 2-year contract.

FACILITIES/SUPPORT: S$700 per month per person
provided for accommodation expenses in first year,
S$900 second year, plus S$500 freight allowance.
Medical insurance provided. Two weeks initial hotel
accommodation and assistance given in finding an
apartment. Employer will submit visa applications.

RECRUITMENT: Adverts in foreign teachers' journals.
Face-to-face interview preferred; telephone interview
possible.

CONTACT: Peter Scarrott, Principal.

NYU LANGUAGE CENTRE

The Adelphi 04–35, 1 Coleman St, Singapore 179803

☎ 338 3533

✉ admin@nyu-online.com

NUMBER OF TEACHERS: 5.

PREFERENCE OF NATIONALITY: American, British.

QUALIFICATIONS: Degree with teaching experience in
English.

CONDITIONS OF EMPLOYMENT: 1-year contracts. Hours
9.30am–5.30pm, Monday to Friday.

SALARY: S$2,500–S$3,000.

FACILITIES/SUPPORT: Help given with work permits.

RECRUITMENT: Via advertisements or recommendation.

CONTACT: Nance Teo, Principal.

BRUNEI

Few people can locate Brunei Darussalam (Brunei, the Abode of Peace) on a map of the world, let alone anticipate that there is a steady demand for qualified English teachers there. This wealthy oil state on the north shore of Borneo can afford universal education for its population of less than 400,000. The Ministry of Education has been implementing a bilingual educational system which *'ensures the sovereignty of the Malay language while at the same time recognising the importance of the English language'*.

Brunei, mostly covered in luxuriant tropical rainforest, has a pollution free, healthy environment, few traffic jams and one of the lowest crime rates in the world. It provides a very pleasant place to live and work for those who like the outdoor lifestyle and don't crave a wide variety of nightlife. For watersports enthusiasts, the warm calm waters of the South China Sea provide an ideal environment for diving, sailing and power boating. Most expatriates join one of the many sports and social clubs which provide excellent facilities.

Brunei has a rich cultural heritage and still boasts the largest water village in the world in the capital, Bandar Seri Begawan. There are many opportunities to participate in colourful, cultural extravaganzas to mark national events such as the Sultan's birthday on 15 July and National Day on 23 February. In the rural areas there is an opportunity to see how the other indigenous groups celebrate their traditional harvest festivals. Although Brunei is a Malay Islamic monarchy, other religions are allowed to practise freely and Chinese New Year and Christmas Day are also national holidays, in addition to the numerous Islamic public holidays.

There are currently over 250 expatriate primary and secondary EFL teachers working in Brunei in state sector schools. CfBT Education Services (Locked Bag 50, MPC, Old Airport Road, Berakas BE3577, Brunei; hr@cfbt.org; www.cfbt.org) recruits suitably qualified and experienced individuals along guidelines set by the Brunei Ministry of Education. All teachers must have Qualified Teacher Status, e.g. PGCE or equivalent, plus a degree, a minimum three years' experience including EFL/ESL and be under 52 (primary) or 55 (secondary). The package currently includes tax-free salary, end-of-contract bonus, accommodation, flights, baggage allowance and other benefits. Contracts are usually for two years initially. A car driving licence is essential. CfBT also runs a range of courses for teachers and the public including Cambridge ICELT, General English and ESP, ICT and Malay. CfBT also administers IELTS. Borneo Outdoors is a division of CfBT in Brunei and runs Youth Enrichment and Environmental courses, GAP programmes and Professional Development programmes. They also cater to the corporate sector by providing Management Training/Team Building courses for clients in Brunei and Malaysia.

CfBT Education Trust

Top 30 UK charity CfBT Education Trust has been working in Brunei Darussalam, South East Asia for almost 25 years. Contracted to the Ministry of Education to assist its bilingual Malay-English language policy CfBT delivers English language services to primary and secondary schools throughout the Sultanate - reaching approximately 20,000 Bruneian children and young people every year. The work of its well-qualified and highly motivated teachers on this important and ambitious project has been shown to make a real difference to children and teachers and to the country as a whole. Since 2006 the number of O level credits amongst students in the Sultanate has more than doubled.

More than 200 CfBT teachers working across the Sultanate help CfBT to make this difference - particularly as Brunei embarks upon the ambitious Sistem Pendidikan Negara Abad Ke-21 - its National Education System for the 21st century.

Rob, 48, a British teacher working in Brunei for the past eight years explains what it's like teaching there:

> An average day starts at 7am and ends at about 12.30pm, usually with a 30-minute break at around 10am. At least two days a week my school work ends at about 1pm. On the other days I might be involved in extracurricular activities, extra classes or professional development activities in the afternoons.
>
> We have to complete a 'record book' of student work and lesson plans and in terms of the syllabus it is an interesting time as Brunei is currently implementing SPN 21, a new curriculum for the 21st century.
>
> The Bruneians are friendly, courteous and hospitable. The country is safe and relaxed and we enjoy a wonderful, healthy environment with a tropical climate and great opportunities for professional development - what more could you want?

Carol, 37, a CfBT teacher from Australia has been teaching in Brunei for four years. She adds:

> The pupils are respectful of their teachers and the schools are supportive places to work. If you are an adventurous and ambitious teacher looking for something different and professionally challenging I would certainly recommend teaching in Brunei. Located on the island of Borneo in the South China Sea, Brunei is a peaceful, highly attractive destination offering a wonderful cultural experience and high standard of living.

CfBT offers its teachers in Brunei competitive tax-free salaries, furnished accommodation, Cambridge ICELT, ESLM, ICT and Malay courses, annual travel allowances, subsidised private education for up to two children, and professional administrative, housing and welfare support.

If you are interested in taking up the challenge and joining Rob and Carol as a CfBT teacher in Brunei, helping support the Government's ambitious education vision and making a difference to the lives of learners across the Sultanate, email international@cfbt.com or visit http://careers.cfbt.com

VIETNAM

The commercial market supplying English language training is booming. Many of the local people wanting to learn English are doing so in order to be able to join a profession such as banking or to have a chance of acceptance at institutes of higher learning overseas. From Ho Chi Minh City (HCMC) in the south to Hanoi in the north, opportunities abound both for trained professionals and freshly certified CELTA/TESOL graduates.

Although Vietnam is still a one-party socialist republic (which still blocks Facebook), it bears all the trappings (complete with garish advertising hoardings and American pop music) of a capitalist society. ELT is a huge growth market and the number of schools in HCMC (the business capital) has grown more than eightfold in as many years. One of the reasons for this growth is the booming oil industry, which operates largely in English, as well as the growth of a young middle class, who invest in electronic goods, luxury items and English. Often these things can go together: Intel is investing $300 million in a new plant and test facility in HCMC and all employees will be expected to submit re-sumés and communicate in English. The British Council offers many different types of English course, from 'corporate training solutions' to 'English for study success'. Language Link Vietnam is rapidly expanding and is looking to employ 100 native English speakers (see entry). Base pay for university degree and CELTA qualifications starts at $15 per teaching hour, and rises to about $22. This should allow a comfortable lifestyle since the cost of living remains very low (for example, HCMC is much cheaper to live in than Bangkok), so Vietnam is a good country for those trying to save some money. The cost of living is higher in Hanoi than Saigon – the old name for HCMC is still in wide use – with rents and wages following suit. There is a two-tier system for utilities and travel in Vietnam, which means foreigners pay substantially more than locals for almost everything.

Prospective teachers in Vietnam should be aware that the country is becoming increasingly savvy about qualifications. A degree is often no longer seen as sufficient and EFL teaching qualifications are very desirable. This attitude is reflected in the fact that there are now five CELTA course providers in Vietnam including Language Link, Apollo Education and ILA Vietnam (see list of organisations).

Steph Fuccio had no trouble getting work in Hanoi with Language Link after doing the CELTA course:

> *Language Link is a great place to do a CELTA and start working. They have all the usual trappings of an EFL job such as unpredictable schedules, weekend work and so on. BUT, they do have a huge amount of resources, keen students and there is real opportunity to build up your teaching skills quickly. In my second year I taught English for Academic Purposes and Toefl-iBT along with my regular Business and General English classes.*

Often the best way to find work is simply to arrive in Hanoi or HCMC and look around. The British Council has offices in both Hanoi and HCMC and the latter office should be able to provide a list of language schools in the city with prestigious centres such as ACET (which specialises in academic English), RMIT, ILA, Apollo (affiliated to International House), AUSP and the British Council schools. RMIT in HCMC (employment@rmit.edu.vn) often advertises for qualified and experienced English language tutors to fill positions in HCMC and Hanoi. Another frequent advertiser is VUS Language Schools with a number of centres run by the Vietnam-USA Society around HCMC (stevebaker@vus-etsc.edu.vn; www.vus-etsc.edu.vn). Newly certified ESL teachers are welcome to apply.

There is a burgeoning ex-pat population and Korean, Japanese, Taiwanese and affluent Vietnamese parents are always on the look-out for private tutors. Opportunities also exist for consultancy work for those with master's qualifications or higher and relevant experience.

If you don't like cooking, the cities are wonderfully packed with good, cheap restaurants serving excellent healthy food and it is quite easy to get by on $5–$10 a day eating at Com Binh Dan or Bia

I have been living and teaching in Vietnam for almost five months now. I can honestly say that this has been the hardest, scariest, best and most rewarding months of my life. The people that I have met have been the nicest, friendliest people I have ever encountered, and I am continuously amazed at the generosity and hospitality of the Vietnamese people, especially my students.

On arrival I was continuously challenged by my surroundings. The first obvious problem I encountered was the language barrier. Simple things like ordering and paying for food, saying thank you or I'm sorry, it all got lost in translation. I took a crash course in learning Vietnamese – numbers, food, all the necessities for my daily needs. It turns out that I was capable of learning how to get by in a strange land. The more I explored Can Tho, the more I realised how fast English is becoming a second language for the locals.

My placement is as a volunteer English teacher at a university in Vietnam. I work about 20 hours a week in class, although with lesson preparation that's usually at least another ten hours a week. I also teach at a private English school at nights, which was my choice (I'm not contracted) and just a way to meet more students and make some extra cash. In most places in Vietnam (especially Saigon and Hanoi) you can find private schools to work at and as long as you are certified or have experience you can teach there. Most of the smaller cities, such as mine (Can Tho) love to have a foreign teacher and are more than willing to find a way to accommodate you.

It is amazing to watch a country develop right in front of your eyes. The Vietnam I am experiencing is not the same as it was even two years ago, and I am convinced it will not be the same in two years from now. This is truly a once in a lifetime experience, to call this amazing, thriving country home for a few months.

Hoi, the Vietnamese street side restaurants. Some of the very best food can be found at the smallest street stalls at ridiculously cheap prices. International restaurants and cafés are more expensive but still affordable for the average teacher.

Teachers are generally held in high regard and students will constantly be inviting you out especially on teachers' day. Exams are taking off in Vietnam and many students strive to obtain a good TOEFL score in the hope of going to America, while the Cambridge suite of exams and IELTS are popular with those wanting to take up scholarships to Australia and the UK.

Hanoi is smaller and more beautiful yet bustling and noisy whereas HCMC is a Bangkok in the making. This sophisticated, sprawling commercial centre boasts a skyline already dotted with fledgling skyscrapers. The main complaints thus are traffic, noise, pollution and street hassle. Vietnam is a developing country and although the wealth of the nouveau riche classes in the cities is very visible, the countryside is still desperately poor. Countryside and cities alike experience frequent power cuts and things in general don't always work as they are supposed to.

Travelling round the region is very affordable, and has become more so with the introduction of low-cost airlines such as Jetstar based at HCMC's new airport and Malaysia's AirAsia which has a few flights now from Hanoi and Saigon so that Kuala Lumpur can be used as a cheap hub to the region. In 2010 AirAsia purchased a one-third stake in VietJet to create VietJet AirAsia based in Hanoi, with plans to fly to HCMC and Da Nang. The *Reunification Express* is a train that runs the full-length of the country (over 1,300km). The cheapest fare for the Hanoi–Saigon trip is $24, though you will have to pay nearly three times that for an air-conditioned soft sleeper.

Bear in mind that what you see is not always what you get. Behind that charming Vietnamese smile is more often than not the intent to extract money. Of particular note are the numerous women in search of a foreign husband, a foreign passport and an airline ticket. Single men should beware. Internet access is widely available and improving although it is still unreliable, slow and censored. Government firewalls prohibit prying eyes from seeing anything they don't want you to see.

In order to get a work permit in Vietnam teachers need to bring with them from home the original copies of their university degree, TEFL certification and police clearance or criminal history certificate. Everything else can be taken care of in Vietnam with the help of an employer. The original or notarised documents are submitted to the immigration office with a medical report, and the work permit should be issued within about six weeks.

LIST OF EMPLOYERS

APOLLO EDUCATION & TRAINING (INTERNATIONAL HOUSE)
Hanoi: 176 Thai Ha Street, Dong Da District
4 3537 325167 Le Van Huu Street, Hai Ba Trung District, Hanoi/4 3943 205136 Phan Van Truong, Dich Vong Hau ward, Cau Giay District, Hanoi/4 3755 4733.
(Hanoi) personnel.hn@apolloedutrain.com
Ho Chi Minh City: 26 Phung Khac Khoan, District 1
8 3823 3597/3823 3596
personnel.hcm@apolloedutrain.com
Danang: 81 Quang Trung, Hai Chau District
5 11 3840 665
Haiphong: 484 Lach Tray Street, Ngo Quyen District
31 373 6996
www.apolloedutrain.com

Established in 1994, Apollo is affiliated to International House and offers training in English, professional development and overseas study consultancy as well as teacher training (Cambridge CELTA). Apollo also has an increasing number of younger learner and corporate classes in addition to partnership contracts with local schools.
NUMBER OF TEACHERS: Approximately 100 nationwide, more in the summer months.
PREFERENCE OF NATIONALITY: None, but must be native English speaker.
QUALIFICATIONS: Teachers must have a CELTA or equivalent (i.e. 100 hours minimum with at least 6–8 hours of observed classroom teaching practice). Vietnamese work permit regulations (for contracts longer than 3 months) stipulate that teachers must also have a degree.

CONDITIONS OF EMPLOYMENT: 1-year contract (some 3-month short-term contracts are available, particularly for the summer programme). Teaching hours are between 7.30am and 9.45 pm, Monday to Friday; 7.45am–8.15 pm, Saturday; 7.45am–6pm, Sunday.
SALARY: $1,360–$1,560 per month depending on qualifications and a competitive package including 20 days holiday, 9 days public holidays, contract completion bonus and re-signing bonus.
FACILITIES/SUPPORT: $550 contribution to medical insurance, sponsorship plus visa and internal work permit costs. For short-term contracts, accommodation is provided. For 1-year contracts teachers are placed in Apollo-rented accommodation or given agents' names and/or a Vietnamese member of staff can visit accommodation with the teacher to assist with translation and negotiation.
RECRUITMENT: Through ihworld.com, local adverts and internationally using posters, websites etc. Interviews are essential, and are occasionally carried out in the UK/USA.

ASIAN INSTITUTE OF TECHNOLOGY IN VIETNAM
Education Management Section, Building B3, University of Transport and Communications, Hanoi
4 37669493 ext. 120
hang@aitcv.ac.vn

NUMBER OF TEACHERS: 2.
PREFERENCE OF NATIONALITY: None.
QUALIFICATIONS: At least 5 years' experience and preferably a master's degree.
CONDITIONS OF EMPLOYMENT: Hours vary according to course availability.

SALARY: US$20 per hour (Diploma in TEFL/TESOL or TESOL Certificate), US$25 per hour (Master's in TEFL or TESOL).

FACILITIES/SUPPORT: Some assistance with finding accommodation. No assistance with work permit.

RECRUITMENT: Word-of-mouth. Interviews.

CONTACT: Nguyen Thu Le Hang.

ILA VIETNAM

402 Nguyen Thi Minh Khai St, Dist. 3,
Ho Chi Minh City

84 8 3838 6788

recruitment@ilavietnam.com

www.discovereltvietnam.com

NUMBER OF TEACHERS: 220+, with centres in Ho Chi Minh City, Danang, Vung Tau and Hanoi.

PREFERENCE OF NATIONALITY: Native English speakers.

QUALIFICATIONS: Minimum requirements are university degree (any discipline), CELTA or equivalent TEFL certifica-tion. Preference given to applicants who have experience with young learners or exam preparation classes.

CONDITIONS OF EMPLOYMENT: Standard 1-year contract. 25 hours per week.

FACILITIES/SUPPORT: School pays for the first week's accommodation at a guesthouse and then provides informa-tion and contact details for estate agents. Other teachers are always on the lookout for flatmates and there is an accom-modation board at the school. School oversees process for obtaining visa and work permit.

RECRUITMENT: Via the internet (tefl.com) and recruiters (e.g. Davidson Recruitment Services). Telephone interviews for overseas hires; in-person interviews for applicants in Vietnam. Applicants must send CV with covering letter, supporting documents, passport details and realistic start date. Local applicants must also provide visa details.

CONTACT: Shannon Hopkins and Suzanne Miller, Recruitment Executives.

ILA Vietnam

Whether you are a career-minded ELT professional or looking for a new challenge overseas, you will find few opportunities to match those offered by ILA Vietnam, Vietnam's leading English language training organisation with centres in HCMC, Hanoi, Da Nang and Vung Tau.

Why choose Vietnam?

Few countries can offer ELT teachers a lifestyle that compares to the one Vietnam offers. Vietnamese culture has a deep appreciation of learning and profound respect for teachers. The cost of living is low, and travel opportunities abound, meaning you can enjoy a fantastic standard of living while still saving money.

Why choose ILA Vietnam?

Our centres are designed, built and equipped to the highest standards, thus providing teachers, employees and students with an excellent study and work environment. We place a strong emphasis on academic quality and this is reflected in our approach to teacher recruitment, development, support and management.

ILA's support and development

ILA provides comprehensive academic support for both new and experienced teachers. Our teachers receive initial training before entering the classroom as well as regular, ongoing professional development activities.

ILA's Step career pathway

ILA offers a structured five-step career pathway and encourages teachers to progress into senior roles. Many of our management team started their career with ILA as teachers, and have gone on to become managers. ILA will support committed and enthusiastic teachers every step of the way.

" I started at ILA three years ago as a teacher in the Young Learners Department. I decided to do the DELTA in 2008 and found the pre-DELTA sessions offered by the school to be really useful and helpful. Since completing the course I have worked as an Academic Coordinator, an Assistant Academic Manager and am now a Teacher Trainer."

Briony Hewitt (Teacher Trainer)

ILA's teacher training courses

ILA Vietnam offers Cambridge teacher training courses (CELTA, YL Extension and DELTA) for teachers at different stages in their teaching career. The courses take place in one of its thriving training centres with world-class facilities, the most up-to-date resources, and a supportive learning environment.

" I find it hard to see how the support and resources offered by ILA could be bettered. Now that I'm teaching full time, I can see what an advantage it was to do this course, and I would recommend anyone interested in the CELTA to seriously consider doing the course at ILA."

William Brantingham (Teacher)

ILA Community Network

Even though teaching is a rewarding experience on its own, many of our teachers and staff at ILA get involved with orphanages, hospitals and shelters, through the ILA Community Network.

" I love that the ILA Community Network helps me to be involved in the community here. From teaching English to doctors and nurses at the cancer hospital to volunteering with the kids in the cancer ward, I know that I am helping out in a positive way."

Aimee Denham (Academic Coordinator)

If you would like further information about teaching in Vietnam, please visit our website (www.discovereltvietnam.com).

NUMBER OF TEACHERS: 100.

PREFERENCE OF NATIONALITY: Native English speakers.

QUALIFICATIONS: Bachelor's degree in any discipline plus 120-hour intensive teaching certificate.

CONDITIONS OF EMPLOYMENT: Minimum 1 year if hired from overseas, 6 months if already local. 70–100 contact hours per month.

SALARY: Hourly rate from $18 to $22; 70 hours minimum guaranteed after probationary period. Tax deductions 5%–30% on progressive scale.

FACILITIES/SUPPORT: Advice given on finding accommodation and assistance with obtaining work permit.

RECRUITMENT: Internet advertising and local press. Local interviews necessary.

CONTACT: Steve Cooper, Foreign Recruitment and Welfare Manager.

NUMBER OF TEACHERS: About 5 teachers of ESL for university posts in Vietnam to further Vietnam's educational development by increasing fluency of spoken English and to build bridges between people in Vietnam and the West, particularly the USA.

QUALIFICATIONS: Must be university graduate so most volunteers are over 21. Some experience and/or training in TESL needed, plus eagerness to live and work in Vietnam.

CONDITIONS OF EMPLOYMENT: Academic year September to June.

SALARY: Programme application fee US$50. Programme pays for airfare, health insurance and travel during Tet holiday. Host universities pay a cost-of-living salary and in most cases provide free housing, usually a room or suite in a campus guesthouse.

FACILITIES/SUPPORT: In-country orientation session provided, which covers cultural issues as well as practical matters for foreigners newly arrived in Vietnam.

RECRUITMENT: Deadline for applications is 1 April. Face-to-face interviews preferred but can be done by phone.

CONTACT: John Dippel, Executive Director.

PREFERENCE OF NATIONALITY: None.

QUALIFICATIONS: Degree in any field and 120-hour TESOL.

CONDITIONS OF EMPLOYMENT: 1-year renewable contract. Between 4 and 6 hours per day.

SALARY: €12,000 per year depending on qualifications.

FACILITIES/SUPPORT: Schools will organise accommodation for the teachers, free of charge. Otherwise, coordinator in Vietnam will assist with finding accommodation and obtaining work permits.

RECRUITMENT: Interviews essential and can be held using Skype.

CONTACT: Alan Byrne, Volunteer and Paid Teach Abroad Coordinator.

CAMBODIA

Cambodia is a relatively stable country, having emerged from the shadow of its tragic past. The ELT market has been wide open to private enterprise in Cambodia ever since the UN ceased to be in charge. Foreign ministries and government offices are all keen to sign up for private lessons as are the diplomatic corps and their families as well as the military. The British Council does not maintain an office in Phnom Penh. On a visit to Phnom Penh a few years ago, **Mark Vetare** was impressed by the demand for English teachers:

> *Just rent yourself a moto for the day and have a spin around Phnom Penh. There's virtually a school on every corner. Not all schools employ native speakers since many poor Khmer can't afford them. Pay and hours are the main problems for teachers. Time was when you could get four hours a day. Now you've got to stick around for the better times and more hours. Things are becoming more stringent in the 'real' schools. That being said, it's backpacker heaven: young men with long hair, good (but not necessarily native) English and no high level education still get jobs.*

Cambodia still operates on a dollar economy, so few wages are quoted in riels. Wages at the decent schools start at $15 an hour. Visa extensions are relatively easy to get and schools usually organise them for their teachers. Prospective teachers should arrive with extra passport photos and buy a Business B or Business E visa on arrival for $25.

One of the longest established schools is the Australian Centre for Education or ACE (see entry) which is flourishing and about to open a new school in the capital for 2011. There are many other commercial institutes such as ELT (www.elt.edu.kh), New World Institute (www.nwi.edu.kh) and Home of English International (www.homeofenglish.edu.kh), all in Phnom Penh. Opportunities can also be created in Kampong Som, Siem Reap and Batambang.

Volunteers can offer to teach at Savong's School, near Siem Reap, which was set up by Svay Savong to give children who can't afford tuition fees the chance to learn a language and improve their job prospects. The school's website (www.savong.com) advises: '*There's an informal tradition of taking the school such things as soccer balls, volleyballs or Frisbees as well as stationery – just ask Savong to see what he needs from the book store in Siem Reap and, if you're up to it, try a spot of teaching*'. On her gap year **Pascale Hunter** from Cambridge noticed a flyer for Savong's School up in her hostel and spent a short time teaching teenagers and younger children there. Although she found the experience interesting, she felt it was '*fairly commercial, with the kids clamouring for Western souvenirs*'. However, plenty of other volunteers have enjoyed their visit and are impressed by the dedication of the students.

Another organisation to try is Volunteer in Cambodia (www.volunteerincambodia.org), which re- cruits volunteers to teach at Conversation With Foreigners (CWF), a local conversational English school in Phnom Penh (No 247C, Street 271, Toul Pumbung II). Money raised by the programme goes towards the Cambodian Rural Development Team, a local organisation working to improve livelihoods in rural communities. Volunteers stay three months (there are specific group starting dates) and pay for their accommodation and meals, which currently costs $850 for three months. Teaching qualifi- cations/experience is an advantage, but not required. A sister organisation, CamTEFL, runs industry standard 120-hour TEFL courses in Phnom Penh (see training entry).

LIST OF EMPLOYERS

AUSTRALIAN CENTRE FOR EDUCATION

46, Street 214, Sangkat Boeung Raing, Khan Daun Penh, (PO Box 860), Phnom Penh, Cambodia

📞 23 724204

✉ info.phnompenh@idp.com or info@acecambodia.org

💻 www.cambodia.idp.com/ace.aspx

NUMBER OF TEACHERS: 55 foreign teachers in Phnom Penh and Siem Reap. Number set to increase with opening of second school in Phnom Penh at end of 2010.

PREFERENCE OF NATIONALITY: Any native English speaker is acceptable, though Australians preferred.

QUALIFICATIONS: Undergraduate degree plus CELTA or equivalent. 1 year teaching experience, with proven ability to work autonomously.

CONDITIONS OF EMPLOYMENT: 21–23 hours of classes a week, but teachers are expected to attend at the school 40 hours per week. Minimum commitment 6 months. Hours vary: the school is open 6am–8pm and on Saturday mornings. Teachers needed for general courses, English for Academic Purposes and ESP.

SALARY: $18–$25 per hour freelance, $1,700–$2,100 per month.

FACILITIES/SUPPORT: Advice given on affordable accommodation which is not hard to find in Phnom Penh (rents from $150 a month plus utilities). Assistance given before arrival on obtaining visas. The school is well equipped and resourced and a variety of professional development sessions are held at least once a month.

RECRUITMENT: Web advertisements, word of mouth. Interviews are required, but can be over the phone and are carried out in Australia from time to time. Professional references are checked.

CONTACT: Deborah Harrop, Coordinator; Louise FitzGerald, Director (louise.fitzgerald@acecambodia.org).

LAOS AND MYANMAR

Laos was the last country in the region to open its doors to foreigners. Over the past few years an amazing number of English schools have opened in the Laotian capital of Vientiane, ranging from well-established institutions to small, shop-front institutions staffed with locals or expats passing through on tourist visas. When English institutes first started opening in Vientiane, most were fly-by-night operations. But there are now several international English-medium schools such as the Lao-American College and the Vientiane International School (www.vislao.com), and also better organised private language schools.

The visa procedures have settled down in Laos. If possible, a letter of invitation should be obtained from your employer before arrival which entitles the holder to enter Laos on a B2 visa (non-immigrant, business visa) instead of a tourist visa. The B2 visa costs around $300 for a year, although 6-month and 3-month visas are available at a reduced rate. To extend the B2 visa if you are working at the same school costs the same each time. Only the most elite schools will cover the cost of the visa, although most will assist you in obtaining it.

In order to obtain the invitation, your sponsor needs a copy of your passport and probably copies of any educational credentials. Otherwise it is possible to apply for a tourist visa outside of the country (Bangkok is the closest and easiest place) for around $30 and enter the country on a one-month tourist visa. After arrival, the employer will have to make the invitation for a B2 visa. Then the teacher will be required to leave the country (usually across the border to Thailand) and re-enter on the B2 visa for a further fee. In addition to visas, work permits can be arranged by reputable schools at a cost of $120 per year.

Salaries and conditions of work can vary as much as the schools themselves. Vientiane College (see entry below) provides the best working conditions, staff development programme and benefit package. The majority of language schools pay by the hour, from as little as $5 up to $15 at the higher end of the range.

Demand for native English speakers also occasionally comes from bilingual schools such as the Vientiane Pattana School, a small primary school in Laos that has advertised internationally in the past. Teaching opportunities also exist in the larger provincial centres such as Luang Prabang and Svannakhet and, in Vientiane, in larger companies and ministries as in-house teachers. Again, conditions vary greatly and there are often delays with payments and payments may be made in the local currency (kip). It is possible to advertise on noticeboards around the town, or in the English language newspaper, the *Vientiane Times* (www.vientianetimes.org.la), in order to pick up one or two private students.

Some volunteer opportunities exist in Laos, for example with the Thai organisation Openmind Projects (mentioned below in the chapter on Thailand) and with the Sunshine School (see entry).

Not surprisingly, there is little scope for teaching English in reclusive repressive Myanmar (Burma). As Mark Vetare says of the country, '*it is truly a place to champion the poor not cater to the murderers and thieves who run the country.*' Many organisations recommend boycotting Myanmar completely to avoid bringing any wealth or comfort to the leaders. Interested teachers should find out more from Amnesty International or Tourism Concern in London (www.tourismconcern.org.uk). For information about a teaching programme for Burmese refugees in northern Thailand, see entry for Burma Volunteer Program in Thailand Directory.

LIST OF EMPLOYERS

21ST CENTURY SCHOOL OF ENGLISH

076/6 Sisangvone Rd. That Luang Tai, Vientiane Lao
PDR, PO Box 77

- +856 21 45 2500
- info@21centuryeducation.com
- www.21centuryeducation.com

NUMBER OF TEACHERS: 13.

PREFERENCE OF NATIONALITY: British, American, Australian, New Zealander.

QUALIFICATIONS: CELTA/TESOL.

CONDITIONS OF EMPLOYMENT: 1-year contract with 13.5+ teaching hours per week.

SALARY: $12–16 per hour.

FACILITIES/SUPPORT: School will arrange 1-year work visa but the teacher has to pay the costs.

RECRUITMENT: Usually via the internet or word of mouth. Interviews are essential and can be carried out from the UK or USA.

CONTACT: Kelly Kidson, Manager.

SUNSHINE SCHOOL

PO Box 7411, Vientiane

- +856 21 214522
- sunshinelaos@gmail.com

NUMBER OF TEACHERS: Volunteers only.

PREFERENCE OF NATIONALITY: English-speaking countries.

QUALIFICATIONS: Creative approach to working with the kids is important; experience in teaching or experience with young kids are both good assets.

CONDITIONS OF EMPLOYMENT: 1 week to 11 months. School hours include 7 teaching periods from 8am to 4pm on weekdays. Volunteers usually have 4–5 teaching periods a day (maybe less depending on the volunteer's needs), in kindergarten, primary or junior secondary classes. Volunteers may also be involved in creative activities with the children or teachers' classes or teaching village children and youth on the weekends

SALARY: Voluntary basis only. Long-term volunteers staying 6–12 months may get a small living allowance (max $100 a month) or help with housing, depending on the financial condition of the school at the time.

FACILITIES/SUPPORT: Long-term volunteers will be supported with working visas (which cost $250–$450). All volunteers get a vegetarian lunch provided on school days.

RECRUITMENT: Via www.go-mad.com and www.gurukul.com or by direct email to the school at sunshinelaos@gmail.com.

CONTACT: Cathy Lee, Director.

VIENTIANE COLLEGE

PO Box 4144, Vientiane

- 21 414873/414052/412598/416837/450049/450050
- info@vientianecollege.com
- www.vientianecollege.com

NUMBER OF TEACHERS: 40.

PREFERENCE OF NATIONALITY: Native English speakers from any region.

QUALIFICATIONS: Minimum bachelor's degree and CELTA. ESP/EAP experience preferred.

CONDITIONS OF EMPLOYMENT: Sessional and contract.

SALARY: From $1,500–$2,800 per month less 10% income tax.

FACILITIES/SUPPORT: Assistance with finding accommodation. School arranges and pays for work permit and residence visa. In-house training programme.

RECRUITMENT: Personal interview necessary.

CONTACT: Catherine M. Wood, Registrar; Denley Pike, Director.

TAIWAN

Taiwan remains a magnet for English teachers of all backgrounds and the ELT industry is booming. Part of the appeal of teaching in Taiwan is that the wages compare favourably with countries such as Japan, yet the cost of living is significantly lower. Equally important is that finding a job here is fairly easy. It used to be the case that schools were looking for only three things: a passport from an English-speaking country, a bachelor's degree and a pulse. These days, however, the better schools are becoming choosier, it is more difficult to get a working visa and many schools and local education departments are looking for an ELT qualification and prior experience. Nevertheless, the opportunities for teaching English in Taiwan are endless. For example, hundreds of private cramming institutes or *bushibans* continue to teach young children and high school students for university entrance examinations.

English language schools in Taiwan are becoming increasingly regulated. Only the reputable language schools, those who are fully licensed as foreign language schools, are permitted to employ English-speaking foreigners and sponsor them for visas, provided that they are willing to sign a one-year contract. Only native English speaker teachers with a university degree (in any subject) are eligible. Taiwanese consumers of English have a clear preference for the North American accent because of strong trading and cultural links between Taiwan and the USA. However, many schools will hire presentable native English speakers, whatever their accent. Few want their staff to be able to speak Chinese; in fact one teacher reported seeing a sign in a *bushiban* window boasting 'Teachers Not Speak Chinese'. Language teachers and tutors working in Taipei are predominantly American; native English speakers of other nationalities tend to gravitate to southern Taiwan. **Amanda Searle** from the UK felt only slightly discriminated against:

> *My employer claimed that they did not discriminate between people of different nationalities, but this is not what I have found. North Americans are the first choice when hours are allocated. I have had students complain that they wanted an American teacher because they wanted to learn 'real' English, though I have never had a student complain to me or the secretaries that my accent was difficult to understand.*

This has not been everybody's experience however, and some schools even boast 'English comes from England and so do our teachers'. Many non-Caucasians have experienced prejudice in Taiwan.

The market for teaching children from about age 3 seems boundless at the moment, so anyone who enjoys working with primary age children, i.e. likes to sing songs, play games and comfort little ones who miss their mums, may be able to find a job. However, recent government regulations require all kindergarten teachers to be fully qualified kindergarten specialists. While many CELTA trained teachers can no longer legally work in kindergartens, many still do so. English immersion kindergartens are all the rage and tend to pay their teachers very well. Women are often considered to have an advantage in this regard, and also tend to be preferred by the mothers of female pupils. Employers in this field generally provide detailed lesson plans which means that little time needs to be spent on lesson preparation.

FINDING A JOB

A few of the major organisations hire overseas either directly or via a North American agent. The Hess Educational Organization (see entry below), whose head office is in Taiwan, has a representative in Canada who can send out information to enquirers (Christian Derwee at hesscanadaeast@yahoo.com). Interviews are conducted either in Taiwan or by telephone from Taiwan. An agency that is gaining recognition is TEFLOne Recruitment (www.teflone.com) which recruits qualified teachers for posts in Taiwan as well as other countries in the Far East.

JAMES ROBINSON is one satisfied client of Teflone.com and he wrote in May 2010 from the small town of Taoyuan in Kaohsiung County in Taiwan's interior. After being made redundant as a welder/fabricator, he did a TESOL course which he describes as 'the best move I ever made'. Soon afterwards he met the chief recruiter for TEFLOne, David Coles, to hear about opportunities with the Shane School:

My interview was a very positive experience. I knew that Shane would offer peace of mind, a highly efficient service and above all a friendly interview. It is for these reasons that Shane stood out from amongst the rest. Many other interviewers from other organisations sounded a bit officious and none of them offered as realistic and honest information about life in Taiwan as Shane did. It also sorted out all the administrative requirements such as work permits and bank accounts and patiently answered questions they had probably been asked a hundred times before!

My hours are currently about 25 a week, a lot more if you include the preparation, but a million times more interesting than welding! Most of the children are so eager to learn and I was astonished how the really young children retained new information. Entertainment is the key.

Yes it was a learning curve and yes I made mistakes. But after a few weeks the preparation became far easier and it was a far more rewarding and positive experience. I think it's important to make things happen for yourself, e.g. to go climbing and cycling and participate in activities you like. This can be hugely rewarding for your inspiration as a teacher, to meet local people and get to know your new environment. As a result, my spare time is incredible. I still find it amazing that I can be out of the city and in the national park in 45 minutes, with its new aromas, wildlife and breathtaking scenery.

Another recruiter looking for candidates with a four-year degree is Asian Consultants International in Taipei (hr@asianconsultants.com; www.asianconsultants.com). Many websites contain a wealth of detail about Taiwan and what it's like to teach there. Jobs and lots of information about teaching in Taiwan can be found at www.tealit.com, www.taiwan-taipei.com and at www.aacircle.com.au. Also have a look at www.englishintaiwan.com. The Kaohsiung-based site www.taiwan-teachers.com is under new management and expects to be active in teacher recruitment from 2011. The US-based recruiter for Asia Reach to Teach (www.reachtoteachrecruiting.com) is very active in Taiwan where its main centre is located. Another possibility is ESL Dewey (www.esldewey.com.tw) which posts some ads, as does the *Tainan Bulletin* (www.tainanbulletin.com).

If using a recruitment agency in Taiwan, it is best to proceed with caution. In years gone by there have been reports of teachers accepting jobs before arriving in Taiwan, only to find that they have been placed not in Taipei as they agreed, but in some three-goat mountain village. Discrepancies also sometimes occur between the contracts agents have given to teachers in English, and those given to employers in Chinese.

Many people arrive on spec to look for work. Finding a *bushiban* willing to hire you is not as difficult as finding a good one willing to hire you. If possible, try to sit in on one or two classes or talk to another teacher before signing a contract. (If a school is unwilling to permit this, it doesn't bode well.) Read the fine print of the contract to find out what the penalties are for breaking a contract.

On the strength of the TEFL course she had completed at the American Language Institute in San Diego and a year spent teaching in Poland with ECSC, freelance photographer **Alicia Wszelaki** wanted a taste of teaching in the Far East. She joined a short summer teaching project in Taiwan for adolescent girls, run by the American Language Village (www.kidscamp.com.tw) that she had noticed on Dave's ESL Cafe. Teachers were housed in a hotel not far from the camp and she found working conditions to be very good although the hours were long over 10 straight days.

> *I realised a few days into the camp that this was indeed a summer camp and the kids were there not only to learn English but also to have fun. We played games, had lessons on pizza and hamburgers and other subjects that were more real world. The students really enjoyed these. There was lots of songs and dancing. If you choose to do a camp of this nature, bring lots of energy, smiles, optimism, an open mind, and water. It was a wonderful and rewarding experience. The students were great and the teachers were some of the most incredible people I have met – a truly great blend of personalities and experiences.*

The best time to arrive is at the beginning of summer (the end of the school year), when Chinese parents enrol their offspring in English language summer schools. Late August is another peak time for hiring, though there are openings year-round. Word-of-mouth is even more important in Taiwan than elsewhere because there is no association of recognised language schools.

If you want to meet foreigners who are clued up about the current teaching situation, try visiting well-known Taipei hostels or pubs. A good noticeboard is located in the student lounge on the sixth floor of the Mandarin Training Center of National Taiwan Normal University at 129 Hoping East Road. You might also make useful expat contacts in Taipei at the Community Services Centre (5 Lane 290 Chung Shan North Rd, Sec. 6, Tien Mu; ☎ 2836 8134; www.community. com.tw) or at the Gateway Community Centre (7Fl, 248 Chung Shan North Rd, Sec. 6, Tien Mu; ☎ 2833 7444).

Once you have decided to approach some schools for work, make contact by email or telephone in the first place. Next you must present yourself in person to the schools. Many schools in Taiwan are used to and expect cold-callers. In order to get around Taipei you should invest in the invaluable English language *Taipei Bus Guide* available from Caves Books (corner of Chung Shan Road and Minsheng E. Road) or Lucky Book Store in the university. Take along your university certificate and any other qualifications, and take the trouble to look presentable. **Peter McGuire** was told point blank that your appearance and how you conduct yourself at interview count for everything, and concluded that '*all your experience in life or teaching in other countries really doesn't mean a thing here*'. **David Hughes** specifically recommends paying attention to your feet:

> *Bring plenty of socks/tights. You have to leave your shoes at the door of Chinese homes, and it's difficult to appear serious and composed with a toe poking through.*

Anyone with a high level of education (i.e. a master's degree or PhD) might find work attached to one of the scores of universities and colleges, where working conditions are very good. Foreigners are also allowed to work in public high schools, though it is difficult to function without a knowledge of the language.

FREELANCE TEACHING

Work visas are valid only for employment with the sponsoring employer. However, many teachers teach private students, which pays handsomely from NT$700–$1,000 per hour. In a country where foreigners are sometimes approached in bars or on trains and asked to give English lessons, it is not hard to set up independently as an English tutor. **Peter McGuire** found the dream job of tutoring a travel agent three to six hours a day, seven days a week and then was invited to accompany his client on a trip to Hawaii:

> *Some of my lessons are given at private clubs, saunas, in taxicabs and fine restaurants. Actually, it's kind of unbelievable.*

Although it would be possible to make a good living by teaching privately, you will need to work for a school in order to obtain the visa. A helpful hint is to have business cards printed up, calling yourself 'English consultant'. It is even more lucrative if you can muster a small group of students and charge them, say, NT$300 per person. Women usually find this easier to set up than men. The main problem is finding appropriate premises.

Cancelled hours are a perennial problem. Freelancers will find it prudent to explain to students gently but forcefully that they will be liable to pay if they cancel without giving sufficient notice; most will not object. You can even request one month's fees in advance. Once you are established, other jobs in the English field may come your way such as correcting business faxes, transcribing lyrics from pop tapes or writing CVs and letters of application for Taiwanese students hoping to study overseas.

REGULATIONS

Tourists who arrive without any visa are allowed to stay in Taiwan no more than 14 days. People who intend to look for work can apply for the resident visa after arrival; however, they will need to enter the country on a visitor's visa valid for 60 days (an extension may be granted, but this isn't easy). To apply for this visa you need proof of a return air ticket and a document verifying the purpose of your visit, or a recent bank statement. During those 60 days, you must find a job and organise all the paperwork described in this section. If time runs out you will have to leave the country.

Information on visas should be requested from the Taiwan overseas office in your country of origin which is also where you apply for the visitor's visa. Do not reveal on any form that you are considering looking for work. You will have a choice of a single-entry visa (£32) and a multiple entry visa (£64), although to apply for the six-month multiple entry visa you need a letter of confirmation from your UK employer stating the purpose of your visit. The Taipei Representative Office in the UK is at 50 Grosvenor Gardens, London SW1W 0EB (020 7881 2650; www.taiwanembassy.org/uk). Details may be obtained in the USA from TECRA (4201 Wisconsin Avenue NW, Washington, DC 20016–2137; 202 895 1800; www.roc-taiwan.org/us) and in Canada from the Taipei Economic & Cultural Offices in Vancouver and Toronto (www.taiwan-canada.org). To stay legally in the country, teachers need to obtain an Alien Resident Certificate (ARC) from one of the many national immigration offices. Once you arrive and find a school offering a one-year contract, your school applies to the local education authority for a working permit for which they will need a copy and translation of your degree diploma, contract, medical certificate (requiring various tests) and passport. Once that is processed you can apply for a resident visa at the Ministry of Foreign Affairs; the fee will be NT$1,000 (about £21.50). Up to two weeks later your resident visa will be stamped in your passport. You are then obliged to apply to the Foreign Affairs police within two weeks for an ARC and a multiple entry permit. Some schools may make a contribution towards permit costs when the contract is renewed for a further year. If your tourist visa is due to expire before you have arranged a resident visa, you will also have to leave Taiwan to renew your tourist visa, and have a plausible reason why you want to remain in the country. If you claim to need an extension because you are studying Chinese, you can expect a spot test in Mandarin. (It is not clear if the same applies if you're a student of Kung Fu.)

TAX

After the work visa has been issued, tax will be withheld from your pay. The tax rate for foreigners who stay in Taiwan for less than 183 days in one calendar year (category A) is 18%. After six months, the rate of tax drops to between 5% and 13% but only on income beyond the standard exemption of NT$76,000.

CONDITIONS OF WORK

Most jobs are paid by the hour, and for the past three or four years, the minimum hourly rate a teacher should expect is around NT$550 (approximately US$17). For a monthly salary you should expect to receive around NT$55,000 (approximately US$1,700) for 25 hours per week. Occasionally the rate for cushy morning classes drops below and unsociable hours are rewarded (if you're lucky) with a premium rate of NT$600–NT$700. Rates outside Taipei (where the cost of living is lower) tend to be slightly higher due to the relative scarcity of teachers.

As usual some schools are shambolic when it comes to timetabling their teachers' hours. In a profit-driven atmosphere, classes start and finish on demand and can be cancelled at short notice if the owner decides that there are too few pupils to make it economic. When you are starting a new job, ask your employer to be specific about the actual number of hours you will be given. It is not uncommon for teachers who have been promised a full timetable at the point of hiring to find them-selves with fewer hours than promised and a considerably lower pay packet.

Although exploitation of teachers (and pupils) is not as rife as in Korea, you should be prepared for anything, as **Rusty Holmes** had to be:

> *The real reason there was such a high turnover rate of staff at one school was because of the supervisor's habit of barging into class at unpredictable moments and accusing the teacher (especially my Scottish colleague) of mispronouncing words, when she herself could barely speak English. The worst incidents occurred when she beat her own children in the face for getting poor grades, when she engaged a parent in a fistfight over a tuition dispute, and when she physically ran her husband out of the school, all right in front of our students.*

Having discovered the joys of world travel at age 30, **Steph Fuccio** from the USA took the plunge and fixed up a teaching job with an English school in Tainan via the internet. She found that good money could be earned and the cost of living was really low, which had the disadvantage that many of the foreigners there were focused on money to the exclusion of everything else. Her low overheads included US$200 a month for a small apartment all to herself and a used scooter bought (nowadays expect to pay between NT15,000 and NT$20,000 for a second-hand scooter). Meanwhile she was earning US$17 an hour despite having no teaching certificate or experience. She stayed for most of an academic year but left a little early having tired of teaching only young children. She concludes that '*the whole country is simply gone mad with learning English*'.

The usual problems which bedevil TEFL teachers occur in Taiwan, such as split shifts, often ending at 10pm, and compulsory weekend work, especially if you are teaching children. Few schools provide much creative training or incentives to do a good job. Like the educational system of China and so many other countries, Taiwanese state schools rely heavily on rote learning, making it difficult to introduce a more communicative approach, especially at the beginner level. Whereas some schools offer no guidance whatsoever, others leave almost nothing to the teacher. What is termed a 'training programme' often consists of a paint-by-number teaching manual. Here is an extract from the Teacher's Book of one major chain of schools:

How to teach ABCs (e.g. the letter K): Review A-J... Using the flash cards, say 'A – apple, B – boy, C – cat... J – jacket'. The whole class repeats after the teacher. Then say, 'A-B-C-D-E-F-G-H-I-J' and have the whole class repeat. Show the letter K flashcard. Say 'K' having the whole class repeat it each time you say it. Say 'K' 4 or 5 times.

And so on. This certainly makes the inexperienced teacher's job easier but possibly also very boring. Not everyone will be comfortable with such a regimented curriculum.

LEISURE TIME

Flats are predictably expensive in central Taipei so many teachers choose to commute from the suburbs, where living conditions are more pleasant in any case. Rents tend to be in the region of NT$7,000–NT$12,000 per month. There are so many foreigners coming and going, and the locals are so friendly and helpful, that it is not too difficult to learn of flats becoming vacant. You will have to pay a month's rent in advance plus a further month's rent as a deposit; this bond or 'key money' usually amounts to £400+. Several schools will appoint a Chinese member of staff to chaperone new arrivals and translate on house-hunting trips.

Taipei has a rapid transit system which is far more enjoyable (and cheaper) than running a motorbike. Some teachers stay in hostels near the central station and commute to work in a satellite city where wages are higher than in Taipei (e.g. Tao Yuan and Chung Li). Without doubt, the biggest inconvenience and danger in Taiwan is on the roads. Taiwanese drivers often commit driving manoeuvres that would result in lynching in other countries. Red lights and traffic laws are more often than not ignored and foreigners compound the problem by riding too fast on scooters, with little experience, and often under the influence.

Not a single visitor to Taipei, which is one of the most densely populated cities in the world, fails to complain of the pollution, second only to that of Mexico City. Not only is the air choked with the fumes and noise of a million motorised vehicles, but there are occasional scares that chemicals have infiltrated the water table contaminating locally grown vegetables. The weather is another serious drawback. The typhoon season lasts from July to October bringing stormy wet weather and mouldy clothes. The heat and humidity at this time also verge on the unbearable.

Taipei is not the only city to suffer from pollution; Taichung and Kaohsiung are also bad. Even Tainan with two-thirds of a million people has some pollution; 100 new cars are registered here every day adding to the problem. (This is a statistic which rather detracts from Tainan's appeal as the most historic city on the island with many old temples, etc.) Kaohsiung on the south-west coast is a large industrial city with a high crime rate but has the advantage of being near the popular resort of Kenting Beach and within reach of mountain campsites such as Maolin. The geographical advantage of Taichung further north is proximity to the mountains as well as a good climate and cultural activities. The east coast is more tranquil, though some find it dull.

Wherever you decide to teach, one of the highlights of living in Taiwan is the hospitality of the locals. In fact some people report being smothered by kindness, since the Taiwanese will not accept a refusal of any food or drink offered, and even paying for meals or drinks can be a struggle. In general, apart from some petty crime, corrupt politicians and fairly well hidden gang activity, Taiwan is virtually crime free, so you are free to pursue your leisure pursuits without worry. Taipei has a 24-hour social scene which can seriously cut into savings. Heavy drinking is commonplace. Films are usually shown in English with Chinese subtitles. For the truly homesick there are some English-style pubs with pool tables and darts boards. For **Rusty Holmes**, the food was a highlight:

Eating out is just as much a pastime in Taiwan as it is in Hong Kong. There are countless little mom-and-pop restaurants which offer delicious and inexpensive food. My favourite is the US$4 black pepper steak. Considering the high price of food in supermarkets, it would be cheaper to eat out than to cook at home. Taiwan is also a fruit-lover's paradise, though most are expensive by American standards. My favourite is the outstanding sugarcane Taiwan produces.

LIST OF EMPLOYERS

GLORIA ENGLISH SCHOOL
26 Alley, 17–14, Lane 66, Huan-Nan Road, Ping-Jen City, Taoyuan
+886 3 491 1751
gloria@glo.com.tw or younggges@gmail.com
www.glo.com.tw/e_employment.html

NUMBER OF TEACHERS: 100 for 18 branches in Taoyuan County (near Taipei).
PREFERENCE OF NATIONALITY: American or Canadian.
QUALIFICATIONS: Bachelor's degree, or 2-year college diploma and TESOL/TEFL certificate.
CONDITIONS OF EMPLOYMENT: 12-month contracts. Most classes are between 4pm and 9pm on weekdays and all day Saturday.
SALARY: NT$600 per hour for teachers without previous teaching experience (approximately US$18.50). Deductions vary from 0% to 10% depending on length of employment. End of contract bonus of NT$25,000 plus other bonuses given throughout the year.
FACILITIES/SUPPORT: Rent-free accommodation at one of the school's dormitories provided for 15 months. School will provide assistance with all related visa paperwork, but teachers are responsible for paying for their work permits. Training given.
RECRUITMENT: Online job postings, newspaper job postings, referrals by current or previous employees. Phone interviews are mandatory. If the applicant is already in Taiwan, in-person interviews are preferable.
CONTACT: Anita Yang, Hiring Manager.

HESS EDUCATIONAL ORGANIZATION
No 107, Section 2, Minquan E Road, Zhongshan District, Taipei City 104
2 2592 6998
hesswork@hess.com.tw
www.hess.com.tw

NUMBER OF TEACHERS: 500 native English speaking teachers in more than 120 branches throughout Taiwan. About 200 new teachers hired each year.
PREFERENCE OF NATIONALITY: American, Canadian, British, Irish, Australian, New Zealander and South African.
QUALIFICATIONS: Bachelor's degree (in any subject) plus desire to work with varied age groups and to experience Chinese culture.
CONDITIONS OF EMPLOYMENT: 1-year renewable contract. 2 contract options are available to suit each teacher's preference. Contract A – 20 hours/week minimum. Teaching hours are generally between 4:30pm and 9:00pm, Monday to Friday and Saturday mornings. Students aged 5–15 years old. Classes are 100 minutes. Contract B – 25 hours/week minimum. Students aged 3–15 years old.
SALARY: NT$560 per hour (gross). Tax rate is 18% for first six months then drops to 6%. A raise and bonus system is also part of the pay structure.
FACILITIES/SUPPORT: Airport pick-up and free hotel accommodation during initial 9-day training period. Full TEFL and curriculum training provided with four follow-up training sessions at 1, 3, 6 and 9 months. Assistance given to obtain work permits and accommodation. Application process

should be started 3 months in advance to allow time to collect visa and work permit documents.

RECRUITMENT: Apply online through Hess website or contact Rhein Hein; 4 major new teacher intakes per year. Applications accepted all year round.

CONTACT: rhein.hein@hess.com.tw.

INTERNATIONAL AVENUE CONSULTING COMPANY
13F-2, No. 1846, Jien Chen Road, Taichung City 403
4 2285 5139 or Mobile 918 003514
iacc.jobs@gmail.com or service@iacc.com.tw
www.iacc.com.tw

Recruitment agency with partner offices in Canada.

NUMBER OF TEACHERS: Dozens for elementary, high schools, private language schools and kindergartens in Tainan County, Taichung City, Chunghua County and Keelung City.

PREFERENCE OF NATIONALITY: Native English speakers: American, Canadian, British, Australian and New Zealander.

QUALIFICATIONS: Bachelor's degree. Government recognised provincial/state teaching certificate.

CONDITIONS OF EMPLOYMENT: 1-year contract, many starting July to September for the academic year. 25 teaching hours per week (approximately 40 working hours per week). IACC offers extra services for which a service charge is payable in instalments (which is refunded on successful completion of the contract).

SALARY: NT$60,000–NT$71,000 per month. Performance bonus.

FACILITIES/SUPPORT: Airport pick up and temporary accommodation for the first days. Assistance in finding an apartment and signing the contract with the landlord. Assistance in processing the work permit, ARC and NHI cards. Help in opening a bank account. Online teacher management system.

RECRUITMENT: All interviews carried out in Taiwan.

CONTACT: Apply online or email CV for the attention of Gina Wang.

KANG NING ENGLISH SCHOOL
No. 39 Park Road, Jhudong310, Hsinchu County
3 594 3322
serenachutung@gmail.com
www.kangning.com.tw

NUMBER OF TEACHERS: 11 (8 for the Language Department and 3 for the Kindergarten Department).

PREFERENCE OF NATIONALITY: British, American, Canadian, Australian, South African and New Zealander.

QUALIFICATIONS: Minimum bachelor's degree or two-year associate's degree (from US community colleges) and at least 6 months' teaching experience.

CONDITIONS OF EMPLOYMENT: 1-year contract. Working hours in the Language Department 1pm–9.30pm. Working hours in the Kindergarten Department 8am–5pm.

SALARY: NT$64,000–NT$70,000 per month (less 6% for taxes and social security) for the first year, depending on qualifications and experience. Contract fulfilment bonus of NT$30,000 (minimum).

FACILITIES/SUPPORT: Fully formed curriculum cuts down on preparation time. Free meals and accommodation for the first month during compulsory training and assistance to find suitable housing thereafter. KNES will also help teachers to obtain an ARC.

RECRUITMENT: Via website. Interview and demo lesson required. Occasional possibility of interviews in the US.

CONTACT: Serena Wen, Principal.

KNS LANGUAGE INSTITUTE
24 Chiuchang Rd, Niaosung Hsiang, Kaohsiung Hsein
7 370 6565
knschris@yahoo.ca
www.kns.com.tw

NUMBER OF TEACHERS: 45 for a number of branches.

PREFERENCE OF NATIONALITY: North American, though all native English speakers accepted (American, Canadian, British, Irish, Australian, New Zealander and South African).

QUALIFICATIONS: At least a bachelor's degree. Teaching experience, TESOL certification or BEd preferred. Applicants must pass a medical examination.

CONDITIONS OF EMPLOYMENT: 1-year contracts. Full-time hours 2pm–9.10pm, Monday to Friday, in one location.

SALARY: $NT585/hr plus end-of-contract bonus of NT$15,000.

FACILITIES/SUPPORT: Assistance with accommodation, no-interest loans, one-week paid training, paid work permit fees, health insurance, 3-week summer vacation.

RECRUITMENT: Via internet, university placement offices. Interviews in Taiwan or at KNS office in Canada. Telephone interviews also possible. Deadlines are 15 January for spring intake, 15 July for 1 September start and 15 April for summer. Teachers must arrive 2 weeks early for training and set-up.

CONTACT: Chris Aitken, Director of Teacher Recruitment.

KOJEN ELS

10F-2, No. 200, Roosevelt Road, Sec. 4, Taipei

✆ 2 8663 8287

🖰 luisarecruit@hibox.hinet.net

NUMBER OF TEACHERS: Around 300 (16 locations in Taipei plus 5 in Kaohsiung and 1 in Taichung).

PREFERENCE OF NATIONALITY: American, Canadian, British, Irish, Australian, New Zealander and South African.

QUALIFICATIONS: Minimum bachelor's degree. ESL experience and/or TESOL/TEFL certificate will increase chance of employment.

CONDITIONS OF EMPLOYMENT: 1-year contracts. Afternoon, evening and Saturday work. Pupils range in age from 13 to 60.

SALARY: Starting wage NT$580–NT$590 per hour. Bonuses paid at end of contract, calculated according to number of hours taught for hourly teachers.

FACILITIES/SUPPORT: 1 week free accommodation in shared apartments. Training provided.

RECRUITMENT: Direct application/walk-ins. Local interviews compulsory for some applicants. Applicants may be asked to teach a sample lesson. A photocopy of bachelor's degree must be brought to Taiwan.

CONTACT: Luisa Sia, Recruiter/Consultant.

JUMP START

6F, No. 3, Lane 334, JianGuo S Road, Sec 2, Taipei 106

✆ 2 2369 4128

🖰 jean@jumpstart.com.tw

🖳 www.jumpstart.com.tw

English immersion schools for children aged 2–12.

QUALIFICATIONS: Native English speakers. Early childhood education/elementary teachers needed, e.g. with degree, preferably BEd (especially early childhood or elementary specialists). Must be enthusiastic and enjoy teaching children.

CONDITIONS OF EMPLOYMENT: To start mainly from 1 July or 1 September but other dates possible. Guaranteed hours with extra hours available. Planned curriculum with complete teaching materials. Teachers should arrive a week in advance in order to receive a 2–3 day induction.

SALARY: Depends on qualification and experience.

FACILITIES/SUPPORT: Work visa and health insurance. provided. Airport pick-up. Accommodation provided on arrival.

CONTACT: Jean, Human Resources Representative.

LINDA YEE RECRUITING

No 59 5/F Percival Street, Causeway Bay, Hong Kong

✆ +852 8191 1623

🖰 asiaconnections@gmail.com

NUMBER OF TEACHERS: 50–100 teachers placed per year. Also in Hong Kong and China.

PREFERENCE OF NATIONALITY: None.

QUALIFICATIONS: Degree or diploma holders perfected. Must be aged under 55.

CONDITIONS OF EMPLOYMENT: 1 year. 25 hours per week.

SALARY: NT$45,000–$50,000 per month.

RECRUITMENT: Via partner recruiting offices.

CONTACT: Linda Yee.

MICHAEL'S ENGLISH SCHOOL

261 Tong-Nan Street, Hsin-Chu 300

🖰 michaelenglishschool@hotmail.com

A privately owned school managed by a Brit and his Taiwanese wife since 1985.

NUMBER OF TEACHERS: 3 Native English speakers.

QUALIFICATIONS: Native English speakers with recognised university degree. Teaching/coaching experience/EFL qualifications an advantage. References required. A genuine interest in teaching is essential. (Ideal for candidates considering teaching as a career.)

CONDITIONS OF EMPLOYMENT: Minimum 1-year contract. Afternoon and evening work only. Student-centred classes for 7–17 year olds. 80/115 hours per month.

SALARY: NT$600 per teaching hour.

FACILITIES/SUPPORT: One month (paid) induction course. 15 days paid holidays, 5 days unpaid. Gratuity fund. Free airport pick up. Assistance finding accommodation. Work visa, national healthcare, ARC, all available through school.

RECRUITMENT: Via UK education newspapers and the internet. Interview (in Taiwan or by telephone).

CONTACT: Michael Weatherley, Proprietor.

REACH TO TEACH

21 Everett Road Ext, Albany, New York 12205, USA

✆ +1 201 467 4612

🖰 info@reachtoteachrecruiting.com

🖳 www.ReachToTeachRecruiting.com

For contacts in other countries, see entry at beginning of Asia chapter.

NUMBER OF TEACHERS: 200+.

PREFERENCE OF NATIONALITY: American, Canadian, British, Irish, Australian, New Zealander and South African.

QUALIFICATIONS: Positive, enthusiastic, dedicated and flexible attitude are the most important qualifications. Teaching experience and/or a 120-hour in-class TEFL qualification will often lead to a higher salary or more job placement options. Teaching experience is a plus, but not a requirement.

CONDITIONS OF EMPLOYMENT: 1 year full-time. Schedules are generally either morning/afternoon (preschool) or afternoon/evening (elementary school). Preschool positions start twice a year (February and August) and applications are needed 3 months in advance. Elementary school positions can be applied for year round.

SALARY: Salaries are competitive with most elementary and preschools in Taiwan. Salaries vary depending on teaching experience, qualification, location and benefits. Salaries usually range between NT$55,000 and NT$70,000 per month.

FACILITIES/SUPPORT: Taiwan visa guidance and airport collection are provided plus teacher orientation/training (when available). Teachers have the option of continued support and contact with Reach To Teach throughout their year-long placement. Agency hosts teacher social events and gatherings (mostly in Taipei).

RECRUITMENT: Applications submitted via website. In-depth interviews conducted over phone and occasionally in person.

CONTACT: Email Director of Recruiting – Taiwan.

SHANE ENGLISH SCHOOL
6F-1, 41 Roosevelt Road, Section 2, Taipei
2 2351 7755
info@shane.com.tw
www.shanetaiwanjobs.com/index.htm

NUMBER OF TEACHERS: 180 in over 50 language schools and 3 English immersion kindergartens.

PREFERENCE OF NATIONALITY: Must be citizen of native English-speaking country.

QUALIFICATIONS: TEFL/CELTA/PGCE (dependent on position applied for).

CONDITIONS OF EMPLOYMENT: 1-year renewable contracts. Guaranteed salaries. 5 days per week schedule.

SALARY: NT$42,400–$60,000 per month depending on position, location and experience. Outward flights also paid.

FACILITIES/SUPPORT: Up-to-date facilities and teaching resources. Work permits, assistance with accommodation, and comprehensive initial and ongoing training provided.

RECRUITMENT: Applicants should contact the Principal directly and telephone or face-to-face interviews will be arranged.

CONTACT: Dave Roberts, Principal.

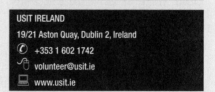

USIT IRELAND
19/21 Aston Quay, Dublin 2, Ireland
+353 1 602 1742
volunteer@usit.ie
www.usit.ie

PREFERENCE OF NATIONALITY: None.

QUALIFICATIONS: No degree necessary.

CONDITIONS OF EMPLOYMENT: 1-year contract with the possibility to renew. Between 4 and 6 hours per day.

SALARY: €14,160–€19,800 per year depending on qualifications.

FACILITIES/SUPPORT: Some schools will organise accommodation for the teachers, free of charge. Otherwise, coordinator in Taiwan will assist with finding accommodation and obtaining work permits.

RECRUITMENT: Interviews essential and can be held using Skype.

CONTACT: Alan Byrne, Volunteer and Paid Teach Abroad Coordinator.

THAILAND

Following a period of political and civil unrest in the first half of 2010, the situation in Thailand is once again generally calm and foreign teachers will be warmly welcomed. The same advice applies here as anywhere, that visitors should avoid demonstrations, specifically by anti-government ('Red Shirt') protestors which, even at the height of the crisis, was easy to do since they congregated in specific areas. Prospective teachers can keep abreast of the situation by checking the UK government's advice on http://ukinthailand.fco.gov.uk/en.

As confidence and stability return to Thailand, the English teaching scene is flourishing, especially in schools that teach English to children. For several years the government has been making efforts

Gap Year Thailand

Really having such a great time. I've done what I'd intended and gained more than I ever thought possible

... that's what **Stephanie Stinson** said of her programme with Gap Year Thailand, which organises placements for volunteers teaching English in schools in Thailand.

Julia Bowler reflected at the end of her stay:

The time has just gone too quickly for me. Saying goodbye was a lot harder than I had anticipated. My main teacher friend Neeang went back to her family home for a few days. I found it very hard saying goodbye to someone who has become a sister. I had to hold back the tears. She has been with me since first arriving and I will miss her incredibly. The teachers have said I'm welcome to come back and visit whenever I want. I know I will be returning to Thailand - I have fallen in love with it so much.

Some people use a volunteer placement to 'test drive' a career - before committing funds to train, to try TEFL to see if they like it (and perhaps take a TEFL qualification part-time while overseas).

Andrew Hynd said:

Gap Year Thailand appealed to me because it is not a massive for-profit organisation. It is a smaller organisation focused on making the volunteer's experience personal and genuine. David allowed me to customise my own programme, from the type of school, to the size of town I stayed in, to the length of time I was at the school.

Thailand is an easy place to start teaching. Respect for teachers - by pupils and parents - is very high (Wan Wai Kru - National Teachers' Day - is a moving experience); and English language is seen as of major importance.

Stephanie, Julia, Andrew - and others - give their stories in full at www.gapyearthailand.org.uk

to extend the instruction of English in state schools, by introducing 'EP' (English Programme), a bilingual stream within Thai state schools which involves the teaching of English and other subjects, preferably by native speaker teachers willing to accept a modest wage.

A knowledge of English is eagerly sought by most urban young people and, in the context of Thailand, 'urban' is almost synonymous with 'Bangkok' which is more than 20 times larger than its nearest rival Nonthaburi. The *Bangkok Post* is still a source of vacancies, and the Thai-specific website www.ajarn.com described below is a treasure trove of teaching information, contact details and job advertisements.

In its aim to improve the quality of English teaching in Thailand and to ensure that 'fake' teachers cannot be so easily accepted into the expat community, the government has recently tightened up the visa regulations and issuance of teachers' licences, which might provide an incentive for more people to consider joining one of the many volunteer teaching schemes that operate throughout the country.

PROSPECTS FOR TEACHERS

Only a small percentage of recruitment takes place outside Thailand. The major schools use foreign recruitment agencies and the internet to make contact with potential teachers, but most organisations depend on finding native-speaker teachers locally, including Thai universities and teachers' colleges, as well as private business colleges which all have EFL departments. Hundreds of foreigners graduate from one of the many TEFL training courses offered in Thailand (see Directory of Training Courses) and many of them have links with local schools. One of the most active is See TEFL (http://seetefl.com) which actually guarantees employment if job-seekers follow nine steps.

Thailand also appeals to English speakers who would like a career break and find that teaching is the best job going. **Ed Reinert** worked as a salesman for 25 years before becoming a teacher in Thailand; **Carlos Vega** was a computer technician who thinks that his teaching job is the best he can get in Thailand, '*there is nothing else you can do here but be a teacher, even if you are not a teacher.*'

Thais are exuberant and fun-loving people and their ideas about education reflect this. They seem to value fun and games (*sanuk*) above grammar, and an outgoing personality above a teaching certificate, although this attitude may be changing. Of course, there is already a nucleus of professional EFL teachers working at the most prestigious institutes in Bangkok. Many international and Thai bilingual schools look for individuals who can teach art, maths and science through the medium of English. Originally set up as teacher training colleges, there are 36 Rajabhat Institutes around Thailand which are autonomous and hire their own English teachers (though you can obtain more information from the central office in Bangkok; 2 628 5281 90). The institutes are listed at www.piatom.com/91.

Some schools and language institutes may be more keen to hire women on the assumption that they are less likely to become engrossed by the seamier side of Thailand's night life. However, all teachers now have to pay for a criminal background check, so this gender bias may be less relevant.

One thing to consider is that Thai salaries have not really increased in the last few years, even though the government wants to attract more professional teachers. This is something of a sticking point, and teachers who want to make a good living in Asia would be better off looking at Korea or Taiwan. However, living costs are still fairly low in Thailand (Bangkok and tourist resorts excepted) and many teachers have such an exciting time that they don't give a thought to savings, or indeed to coming home.

FINDING A JOB

IN ADVANCE

Among the many teacher placement agencies attempting to place suitably qualified candidates in schools throughout Thailand, try the following:

JP Education (Thailand) (www.JPTEACHERS.com). JP Education's tagline is 'Your Gateway to Teaching in Thailand' and the company invites online applications. During the recent hiring period, for the term beginning mid-May, the owner Tom Peterson recruited at least 70 teachers, mainly by conducting interviews on open days in his Bangkok office, for native English speakers with or without a degree. Candidates applying from overseas must hold a bachelor's degree.

Teach to Travel, Bangkok (+66 85 998 5900; teachtotravel@gmail.com; www.teach-to-travel. com). This Thai company recruits paid teachers, normally with a degree and a TEFL certificate, and volunteers. Placements to teach children are made in schools in central and northern Thailand and pay about 30,000 baht per month for 12 months. Guidance is given on obtaining a non-immigrant visa and most of the schools provide or assist with accommodation.

TLS Language School, 48/9 Ramkhamhaeng Road 60/3 Ramkhamhaeng Road, Bangkapi, Bangkok 10240 (+66 2 735 0956; www.tlslanguageschool.com). Licensed teaching agency that either employs about 40 teachers directly or places them in educational establishments. Assistance is given with work permit applications. TLS has satellite offices in Nonthaburi and Pattaya. The company also offers cultural courses such as the 20-hour course that is a requirement for obtaining a teacher's licence, and also a 200-hour Thai language and culture course that facilitates another long-stay visa, the ED (Educational) Visa.

Training Consultant Center (TCC), Bangkok (+66 86 402 5285; training_tcc@yahoo.com). Part-time and full-time teachers recruited for 10-month contracts, for example in Phaya Thai area. The offered hourly wage is around 400 baht.

BFITS (Bright Future International Training & Services), Suite 401–2, Chao Phraya Tower, 89 Soi Wat Suan Plu, New Road, Bangrak, Bangkok 10500 (+66 2 630 6622/3/4; info@bfitsthailand.com; www.bfitsthailand.com). BFITS is an agency that runs educational programmes in both private and public schools, rather than a teacher recruiter.

AYC Intercultural Programs Thailand, GOT Building, 9/197, 7th floor, Ratchadaphisek soi 29, 10900 Chatuchak, Bangkok (+ 66 2 556 1533; ayc.thailand@gmail.com; www.aycthailand.com). Native English speakers with a bachelor's degree are recruited for more than 20 schools in Thailand, and also for summer language camps.

London-based exchange travel companies such as IST Plus (see entry) and Global Nomadic (www.globalnomadic.com) arrange paid teaching jobs in Thailand but charge an administrative fee for their services. Global Nomadic's programme involves a TEFL training and job placement package costing €750 plus a placement fee of £145.

The British Council (www.britishcouncil.or.th/en) stipulates that it will consider only candidates who have a degree and at least 200 hours post CELTA experience teaching EFL to kids (7–11) and/or teens (12–16). The downside is that since the recent change of government, stricter regulations have been enforced with regard to the recruitment of foreign teachers. If you have a degree you should be able to find work, particularly as schools have had difficulty attracting foreign teachers because of the low wages and red tape issues. Certified teachers will fare even better.

The Anglo-Pacific (Asia) Consultancy (Suite 32, Nevilles Court, Dollis Hill Lane, London NW2 6HG; 020 8452 7836) is an educational consultancy which concentrates on recruiting teachers for schools, colleges and universities in Thailand as well as other Asian countries. Teachers are placed every month by APA, which welcomes graduates with a CELTA or Trinity certificate but also tries to place people with any TEFL background and/or appropriate personalities as long as they have a university degree. Their recruits are given briefing notes on their country of destination and a follow-up visit in their schools if possible. Recruits are guaranteed a salary, regardless of time table fluctuations, something which can be incredibly valuable when schools and institutes promise to pay 35,000 baht for 28 teachings hours, which then fails to materialise.

One of the best all-round sources of information about teaching in Thailand with an emphasis on Bangkok and on inside information about the main hiring companies is the website www.ajarn. com – *Ajarn* is the Thai word for teachers – with stories and tips and current job vacancies posted on www.AjarnJobspace.com. The site is run and constantly updated by a teacher, Philip Williams, who has been in Thailand for many years. Various online recruitment sites such as www.totalesl.com carry current vacancies in Bangkok and beyond. Icon Group Thailand (IGT) is a group of TEFL/TESOL websites providing educational resources and information to teachers, schools and students around the world with a special focus on Asia and the Middle East.

BARRY O'LEARY taught from October to May at Our Lady of Perpetual Help School in Bangkok (Nawamin 48, Klongchan Bangkapi, Bangkok; 2 733 4060 9; school@pramanda.ac.th) which he found on www.tefl.com:

The application was straightforward. I applied online, my references were checked and then I received an email with details of the job, school and general information about Bangkok. When I was greeted at Bangkok by the agency director, I was shocked because I had been expecting a man and found a tiny Thai lady. I was even more shocked when I was led out to meet two small nuns who were to become my bosses. During my interview with the Head Sister the following day, she asked me about my social habits including drinking and smoking and what I thought about Thai women. She then warned me of the dangers of Thai women. I was provided with a flat just outside the school which was great but I wasn't allowed any guests, not even colleagues. This was because a former teacher had abused the rules by taking 'ladies' back to his room. I was also asked to get my hair cut in order to be seen as a respected teacher (I didn't have much choice on that one).

There were many good features about the job: I loved the students, they were so much fun and interested in the lessons. There were a few discipline problems, which was why there was always a Thai teacher standing by with a cane, which I didn't agree with at all. At times it was difficult to get them to talk in English. I found that they responded much better to a game or competition to get them talking. Over seven months teaching the same class, I really got to know the students and their English improved immensely.

Although Barry had previously been just a TEFL teacher, in this job he was expected to teach English, Science, Art, Maths and Swimming to a class of 9 and 10 year olds. He had to follow lesson plans and a set syllabus, preparing and marking exams at the end of term.

Melanie Drake is another young teacher who landed a job in Thailand with ease, this one with ECC (see entry), after gaining a TEFL qualification at TEFL International Corinth in Greece:

I was contacted by my soon-to-be boss after he had spotted my CV on tefl.com. After several emails and a simple visa application process I was in Thailand. Culture shock all-round. My job required me to teach in businesses, poor government schools with cramped, sometimes a bit unsanitary conditions and also in a local private language school. My tiny, basic but clean apartment was free and came with the job. My wages were more than satisfactory to save some as life was incredibly cheap. I was pretty lonely before I got to meet the other members of staff. I was living alone quite far out from the school and was unable to communicate with anyone due to language difficulties. I was terrified of dogs and it turns out that my city, Ayutthaya, had some of the highest numbers of stray dogs in the country, and dealing with this was easily my biggest hurdle. Classes were also over-populated in the schools, sometimes 60 to a class - plus never air-conditioning. Students were for the most part quite lazy and more interested in the novelty of a foreigner than learning English. But, in hindsight, they showed more respect than the average British/American kid probably would.

VOLUNTEERING

For those who do not qualify for a salaried teaching position, the option of volunteering is attractive. Many worthy agencies operating internationally or at a grassroots level supply volunteer teachers to local schools who would otherwise not be exposed to native English speakers. To take one example, Gap Year Thailand (see entry) has a flourishing programme. The director, David Lancaster, explains: '*In our experience in Thailand, schools particularly want help from volunteers in spoken English. They usually have local teachers who are reasonably competent in grammar, vocabulary, spelling, teaching reading, etc, but value help from first-language speakers of English.*'

A charity founded by an American, Volunthai (www.volunthai.com) runs a teaching programme in rural north-eastern Thailand. Teachers' accommodation is provided as homestays, and the participation fee is a modest $375 for two months. Small-scale charities such as this can respond flexibly to individual requirements. For example, not so long ago Volunthai was able to incorporate an American family with four children aged 3–13, all of whom participated in school activities. Looking back on their experiences of travelling around the world, the **Battye** family concluded that becoming part of a rural Thai village through Volunthai was the highlight of the year for them.

In rural parts of Thailand, schools cannot afford to pay salaries to foreign teachers, and local children have little or no exposure to fluent English. Yet the children who dream of going to university and into the professions need to achieve a certain standard of English. To meet this need various organisations such as Volunthai, Dragonfly and Thai-experience.org (see entries) enlist the help of volunteer teachers.

Mundo Exchange Organization, 1435 NW 30th Ave, Portland, Oregon 97210, USA (503 227 8442). Volunteers teach English and computer skills to disadvantaged children and/or adults mainly in Isan province in north-eastern Thailand. Volunteers can be placed at short notice but 2–3 months' advance warning is preferred. The placement costs are €200 for 1 week, €500 for 1 month, €250 per month if staying 6 months or more. Fees include orientation, pre-arranged accommodation, travel within the project and support before and during the stay.

Openmind Projects, 856/9 Moo. 15 Prajark Rd, Amphor Muang, 43000 Nong Khai (+66 42 413 678; www.openmindprojects.org). The fee range for this volunteer teacher programme is from €495 for a fortnight to €1,955 for 24 weeks.

Starfish Ventures (0845 004 8010; www.starfishvolunteers.co.uk). UK organisation that places volunteers of all nationalities in development projects in Surin, a town northeast of Bangkok and off the tourist trail. The current fee of £1,270 covers three months' homestay accommodation and in-country supervision as you teach in a primary or secondary school or an orphanage.

Travel to Teach, T2T, 1161/2 Soi Chita Panya, 43000 Nong Khai (UK 020 8816 7592; www.travel-to-teach.org). Thai-based organisation which provides volunteer teaching opportunities (among others) in various locations. Fees start at €550 for a month.

VESL (Volunteers For Educational Support & Learning), Derbyshire SK23 7TA, UK (0845 094 3727; www.vesl.org) is a charity with an expanding programme in Thailand. All applicants pay a programme fee ranging from £900 for summer placement to £1,350 for 3 months.

Volunteer Teacher Thailand, Khao Lak, Phang Nga 82190 (+66 845290616; www.volunteerteacherthailand.org). This charity continues the work of the now disbanded Tsunami Volunteer Centre. Registration fee of 3,000 baht and volunteers can join programme any Sunday.

The Karen Hill Tribes Trust, York, UK (01904 411891; www.karenhilltribes.org.uk) sends self-funding volunteers, including gap year students, to northwest Thailand to work in upland and hill communities of Karen tribespeople, sometimes as language teachers for three or six months (fees respectively £1,000 and £1,750).

Barbara Darragh also saw for herself how extremely popular English teachers are and sent this account in May 2010:

My first volunteer trip to Thailand was with an organisation set up after the tsunami. I then went to Chiang Mai for six months and after completing a month's TEFL course with See TEFL I offered my services to a local school. I loved working there and made many Thai friends who are always emailing me and asking me when I plan to return, which I hope to do again in September. It is very easy to find good cheap accommodation and the Thai people are so friendly. The children are a delight to teach and are so excited when you go into the school. The poorer schools where I volunteer would never normally be able to afford an 'English' English teacher. There is also plenty of paid work and I did have a private student and if I had wanted I could have had a lot more. As soon as people realise that you are an English teacher they want you to teach them or their family. I have never felt so rewarded in a job before and the fact that I want to go back every year and work for nothing must say something.

ON THE SPOT IN BANGKOK

Any new arrival in Bangkok would be well advised to spend a week getting his or her bearings and asking foreigners living in the city for inside information about possible employers. Many people say that the teaching scene has become somewhat exploitative and life in the city so unpleasant that it is better to leave Bangkok as quickly as you can.

For those who feel strong enough to survive in Bangkok, language schools are very easy to locate, to approach on spec. The best place to start is around Siam Square where numerous schools and the British Council are located. The Council has a list of private and public universities, institutes, teachers' colleges and international schools throughout the country which have English departments and therefore possible openings for a native English speaker, but most people rely on the *Yellow Pages*, which include dozens of language school addresses. Note that the Thai school year ends in mid-March and restarts the second week of May.

The English language daily newspaper, the *Bangkok Post,* is an excellent source of job vacancies, especially the site www.JobJob.co.th, which is supported by the *Bangkok Post* and *Post Today.*

DILYS EWART *discovered that the divide between voluntary and paid teaching is not absolute when she went as an unqualified volunteer to Thailand through Gap Year Thailand. Within two months Dilys had had three job offers for paid employment as a teacher:*

During my introduction week in Thailand, we were shown many different aspects of the Thai culture. We were introduced to Thai food, Thai language, and Thai schools. On our fourth day in Thailand we went to a nursery school based in Bang Saen; there were eight classes in the school with 15–20 students in each class. When we arrived we were given ideas and examples to make a lesson plan for a class. I had only ever done one lesson plan before and it was for a different subject. After an hour of preparation time I was given a classroom of 16 students for 45 minutes. There were 3 assistant teachers there to help with the translation for the students. I got the students to play English games and write letters from the alphabet. At the end of the day I was invited into the Director's office and was offered a job as an English teacher, with a contract for 1 year; she told me how much she was willing to pay me and also discussed accommodation. As I was going to my placement as a volunteer teacher a few days later I declined her offer.

In my volunteer placement, during lunch breaks I helped a 6th year girl for an English speaking competition which she was entering. When competition day came I went along with her for support and last minute preparation. While she was being judged I was sitting outside on a bench when I was approached by a Thai teacher from another school. She asked what I was doing here in Thailand and where I was teaching. Then she asked me directly if I was interested in a job at her school as an English teacher. Once again she said how much they were willing to pay and said they would supply accommodation and some meals, with a six-month contract. I was very surprised, as she hadn't even seen me teach a class. As I was only a couple of weeks into my placement I declined the offer, but they insisted in giving me a number to call if I changed my mind.

I taught as a volunteer at Suan Pa Kao Cha Ang School for two months, through Gap Year Thailand. In my last week at the school I was offered a job with a year's contract with accommodation and reasonable pay, but again I declined the offer as I had plans for travelling. I feel if I need a job in Thailand I would be able to go out and use one of my job offers if I want. What can I conclude from this experience? Well, firstly, that there is massive enthusiasm in Thailand for learning English; secondly, that the schools are very keen to have first-language speakers of English as teachers; and thirdly that is it obviously possible to start as an unqualified volunteer teacher of English and easily get offers of employment. I had thought I would go to Thailand and get some teaching experience but I never thought I would come home with three job offers – and one of the best memories of my life.

craigslist (http://bangkok.craigslist.co.th/edu) serves Bangkok and publishes Situations Vacant. A favourite teachers' hangout is the Hole-in-the-Wall pub on Khao San Road. Or try the Hard Rock Café in Siam Square.

If the Siam Square schools are not short of teachers, which may be the case in the slack season, you will have to try schools further afield. Travelling around this city of 5.7 million is so time-consuming and unpleasant that it is important to plot your interview strategy on a city map before making appointments. Also be sure to pick up a map of the air-conditioned bus routes, particularly if you are contemplating a job which involves travelling to different premises.

It may not be necessary to do much research to discover the schools with vacancies. Many of the so-called back street language schools (more likely to be on a main street, above a shop or restaurant) look to the cheap hotels of Banglamphu, the favourite haunt of Western travellers in the northwest of Bangkok. There is such a high turnover of staff at many schools that there are bound to be vacancies somewhere for a new arrival who takes the trouble to present a professional image and can show a convincing CV. As usual, it may be necessary to start with part-time and occasional work with several employers, aiming to build up 20–30 hours in the same area to minimise travelling in the appalling traffic.

The teaching of children is an expanding area; if you don't want to teach the alphabet, don't accept pupils under the age of 5. On the strength of her claim that she had experience of 'working with children', **Alison Eglinton** was soon earning a reasonable wage (and she suggests that anyone teaching young children should master at least one word of Thai: *hong nam*, which means toilet).

Ajarn (teachers) are particularly respected in Thailand and are expected to look respectable. As well as dressing smartly for an interview, try to maintain a reserve in your manner while still project-ing a relaxed and easy-going image. Too many gesticulations and guffawing are considered impolite and immature and will not earn you the respect of Thai people. When visiting a school, wear your posh clothes and carry CVs and passport photos to clip onto the application forms; otherwise you'll be asked to come back with the correct documents. Don't be surprised if the application form asks some weird questions, such as asking you to give the name, age and profession of every member of your family. You won't be hired on the spot but may well be contacted by phone within a day or two. Everyone who has ever had anything to do with teaching English in Thailand emphasises the need to dress smartly, as **Bruce Lawson** describes:

> *The Thais like their pet farangs (i.e. foreign teachers) to look as much like currency dealers as possible. I bought a suit in Bangkok for £50 especially for the job hunt. Men should take out all earrings and wear a tie, thus risking asphyxiation in the heat and humidity of the hot season. Women should wear a decent skirt, not trousers.*

Appropriate dress was also a problem for **Susannah Kerr** who had been told by her sending agency (i-to-i.com) that T-shirts and flip flops would be appropriate. But this was not the case at her school in Nakhon Nayok (pop 25,000), and she was promptly taken on a compulsory shopping expedition and obliged to spend money on smarter clothes which she didn't care for.

> *The busiest season for English schools is mid-March to mid-May during the school holidays, when many secondary school and university students take extra tuition in English. This coincides with the hot season. Vacancies continue to be advertised through June, July and August. The next best time to look for teaching work in private schools is October, while the quietest time is January/February.*

ON THE SPOT IN CHIANG MAI

According to **Annette Kunigagon** who has made her home in Chiang Mai and is something of a resident expert in teaching in her adopted town, far more people have been coming to Chiang Mai to look for work than was the case a few years ago, since no one wants to live in Bangkok. She co-owns the Eagle Guesthouse at 16 Chang Moi Gao Road, Soi 3 (53 874126/235387; mail@eaglehouse. com; www.eaglehouse.com). She even organises unpaid teaching work as part of her Helping Hands Social Projects scheme (see her website).

Teaching opportunities crop up in branches of the big companies such as ECC and AUA and in academic institutes. There are lots of bilingual programmes at EP schools. Some of these schools are Anubaan Chiang Mai School, Wattano Payap School, Waree School and Fatih School. When approaching the bilingual schools, seek out the director for the 'bilingual' section of the schools.

Teachers are recruited for all levels from nursery school to kindergarten, primary to secondary, though usually a master's degree in education or a teaching degree will be required. When applying for jobs, it is best to visit the schools directly as they don't have time or the aptitude to answer endless emails. Most schools do now have websites, though they are not always professional or helpful.

There are five international schools which employ English teachers, though most are recruited abroad e.g. at international teachers' fairs such as those sponsored by the thorough and professional Search Associates (www.search-associates.com) rather than locally. Other jobs are available in the school holidays at summer and weekend camps held at resort hotels or at Chiang Mai's international schools and attended by rich children from Bangkok and other parts of Thailand. Getting in to these and the summer camps run by the British Council and YMCA is by word of mouth, friends or advertisements. Annette's advice is to be brazen, knock on doors, try hotels, shops catering to tourists, companies which export or have to deal with foreigners, pubs, restaurants, computer shops, large shops in the Night Bazaar area, etc.

Many private language schools can be found in the vicinity of Chiang Mai University and also in the area near the prestigious Thai secondary schools such as Montfort, Paruethai, Regina, Dara and Prince Royal College. The expanding expat community in Chiang Mai comprises many nationalities, most of whom use English as their second language and want to improve their skills.

ON THE SPOT IN THE PROVINCES

The number of teaching opportunities outside Bangkok has escalated, however, not many foreigners show an interest since the pay is much less than in Bangkok. The estimated four-fifths of teachers who are single males enjoying the nightlife in Bangkok are unwilling to move to a less exciting country town.

Competition for work is almost non-existent in lesser known cities such as Nakhon Sawan, Khon Kaen, Udon Thani, Ubon Ratchathani and Pathumthani. For a job in a university you will probably have to show a higher degree or teaching certificate. The best places are Hat Yai and Songkhla. Hotels are always worth asking, since many hotel workers are very keen to improve their English. If you find a place which suits and you decide to stay for a while, ask the family who run your guesthouse about local teaching opportunities. Sometimes the happiest and most memorable experiences take place away from the cities and the tourist resorts. **Brian Savage** returned to England after a second long stint of teaching in Thailand and describes one of the highlights for him:

> *My most rewarding experience was my week teaching English conversation in a rural high school in Loei province in northeast Thailand. These children had rarely seen and had certainly never spoken to a farang (foreigner in Thai) before. My work during that week and a subsequent second visit was really appreciated by the pupils. The first visit came about after I was introduced to a teacher at the Chiang Mai school where I was teaching. If travellers get away from Bangkok and the resorts, they too can have experiences such as this, especially in the friendly towns of the north and northeast. A little voluntary teaching can really boost the confidence of students who are usually too poor to pay to study with native speakers.*

REGULATIONS

The goal posts keep shifting on the question of visas, but enforcement is far stricter than it used to be. The preferred alternative for people who have already found a job is to apply for a non-immigrant B visa from any Thai Embassy. For this you will be asked to provide a copy of your degree certificate (now essential), various documents from your prospective employer in Thailand such as a contract of employment, and police clearance. With this visa, the applicant can stay in Thailand for no longer than 90 days unless his or her employer obtains a teacher's licence for which you will need a bona fide four-year university degree in education or any degree plus a TEFL certificate. A recent added requirement is that applicants must attend a 20-hour course with the unwieldy name 'Training Program for Foreign Teachers on Thai Culture and Teacher Professional Code of Ethics' which will cost between 4,000 and 8,000 baht. According to some, this is a means by which the government can add all teachers to a database in order to be able to check the legitimacy of work permit applications.

In the old days some job-seekers would arrive on a double-entry tourist visa and continue to extend it by crossing in and out of the country on 'visa runs'. However, the immigration authorities have clamped down on this and now people re-crossing the border are stamped in for a stingy 15 days only. However, it is possible to upgrade a tourist visa to a non-immigrant B if you have a guaranteed job, the correct paperwork, patience and 2,000 baht for the fee. It is usually easier to apply for the non-immigrant B at a Thai embassy in another country. In this case the applicant must stay overnight and pick up the visa the next day. Most people take the overnight bus from Bangkok and arrive at whichever border town they're going to early the next morning which makes the whole trip take at least three days.

The processing of the teacher's licence takes about a month. The documents needed for the teacher's licence and work permit include: a recent medical certificate, up to 24 photos of differing sizes, original or certified copies of your degree certificate and any TEFL certificates. Once the licence has been obtained, your school will help you to apply for a work permit which will take a further month. If the work permit is granted, you will get a one-year stamp in your passport. The wording of some of these demands is loose to say the least. A teacher is probably best advised to find out as much as they can from their prospective school/institute or voluntary organisation, who may well be prepared to help with the paperwork/interpretation of the paperwork. The visa forum of www.ajarn. com is a very good place to read about the evolving red tape situation and its practical (rather than theoretical) implications.

Once a work permit is granted, tax will be withdrawn at a very modest rate, sometimes as low as 2%. Thailand's national health scheme applies to visitors and so not all teachers worry about private insurance. Current Thai Labor Law demands that '*all people who work in The Kingdom of Thailand must be covered by The National Health Care Program, no exceptions, and regardless of nationality*'. Many employers may not even know this or keep it to themselves, in order not to have to pay any insurance fees. The monthly maximum an employer can charge you is 750 baht.

CONDITIONS OF WORK

In Thailand, the wages for *farang* teachers tend to be low. The basic hourly rate has risen only slightly over the past couple of years and is now in the 250–350 baht range (roughly £5–£7.50). Company work can pay more depending on location, but in-company contract work has greatly diminished. The norm is for schools to keep their staff on as part-time freelancers while giving them full-time hours; this is primarily to avoid taxes. Most language institutes pay weekly in cash, but beware of schools which turn pay day into a moveable feast.

The best remuneration is available from international schools such as the Bangkok Patana School (643 Soi Lasalle, Sukhumvit 105, Bangkok 10260; 2 398 0200; www.patana.ac.th). Note that the pay at international schools in Bangkok is as much as twice that paid by international schools elsewhere in the country. For a list of international schools in Thailand go to the website of the International Schools Association of Thailand and to register for vacancies fill out the form at www.isat.or.th/employment.asp.htm.

Carlos Vega works at Sathit Rangsit Bilingual School, in an inner suburb of Bangkok, which has all the modern facilities of a Western school. He is able to save about half of his income. Few employers help with accommodation which does not matter much since vacant apartments are not hard to locate and rental deposits not crippling as they are in Japan. According to **Helen Welch**, teachers in Bangkok are increasingly likely to want to live in foreigners' compounds, patrolled by armed guards. Things are more relaxed in Chiang Mai where a group of people can rent a house or live Thai-style in a studio room with attached bathroom for very affordable rents.

Remember never to touch a student on the head, which is difficult if you are teaching children. In class a show of anger will soon lose the students' respect since the Thais value a 'cool heart' (*jai yen*) and go to great lengths to avoid displays of negative emotion. Calm, smiling and enthusiastic personalities make all the difference. **Carlos Vega** thinks that there are two types of pupils, '*Primary are nice and ready to learn every day. Secondary students mostly don't care and don't want to learn anything in a system that makes it impossible for any student to fail. No one really has to do any work in order to pass the grade, so why bother? Usually if the parents are involved with the school the student tends to do well.*'

LEISURE TIME

It has to be said that Bangkok may be an exciting and lively city but it is not beautiful. It has very few parks, bad traffic congestion and polluted air – in fact Bangkok's carbon emissions rival New York's. There is also a great deal of what some might consider moral pollution, and there is a certain element of the teaching fraternity in Bangkok who are there primarily for the easy availability of sex in the notorious Patpong district (despite the AIDS crisis in Thailand). Thai Labor Law stipulates that '*any employees who comport themselves in a manner which would embarrass or cause serious damage to employers' reputation may be terminated immediately, by employer, with no legal recourse available to employee*'. This applies on AND off the clock. Many a *farang* man has been spotted in a 'night time establishment' and been fired the next day.

With the ratio of foreign men to women teachers at least six to one, many women (although in great demand as teachers) do not enjoy the atmosphere in the city and leave as quickly as they can. Fortunately for teachers earning a low wage, the more innocent pleasures of Thailand come cheap. **Felix Poon** wrote from Bangkok to say that the extremely low cost of living makes even a low salary enough for a very comfortable lifestyle. You can eat a good street meal for about 45 baht and a beer is 35–65 baht in a supermarket (twice as much in bars). Even part-time teachers should be able to afford to travel round the country, visiting jungle attractions such as Kanchanaburi, where you can ride an elephant along the banks of the River Kwai, and islands such as Koh Samet, Koh Samui and Koh Phangan where life is slow and the beaches are wonderful. Try to learn a little Thai as **Bruce Lawson** did after getting fried battered banana when he thought he had ordered garlic chicken. He recommends organising word-swaps with students, which will also illustrate to them that they are not the only ones who have to struggle with alien sounds. Wherever you end up teaching you are sure to discover that Thailand is famously welcoming.

LIST OF EMPLOYERS

THE AMERICAN ENGLISH LANGUAGE SCHOOL

79/29 Warabodin Village, Tambol Bang Pood,
Amphoe Muang, Pathumthani 12000

📞 924 3163

✉ teacherfinder@hotmail.com

NUMBER OF TEACHERS: 162.

PREFERENCE OF NATIONALITY: America.

QUALIFICATIONS: At least a bachelor's degree from an internationally accredited academic institution. BEd (or higher) degree holders will receive preference.

CONDITIONS OF EMPLOYMENT: 1-year contract, Monday to Friday, 8am–4pm.

SALARY: Starts at 35,000 baht per month with no real ceiling. The AELS sends teachers to many levels of schools where top earnings are 45,000 baht–90,000 baht. Taxes are from 1,000 baht to 1,750 baht per month and 750 baht per month for Social Security.

FACILITIES/SUPPORT: Company helps teachers find a place that has a good location, for a good rent, with good amenities, and takes them to all the necessary offices, every step of the way, to get the necessary papers (but doesn't pay for them).

RECRUITMENT: By personal interviews and teaching demonstrations, followed by credential checks. Company rarely hires directly from overseas: three videoconferencing interviews have led to only one hire so far.

CONTACT: Jason Alavi, Owner.

AMERICAN UNIVERSITY ALUMNI LANGUAGE CENTER

Bangkok: 179 Rajdamri Road, Lumpini, Patumwan, Bangkok 10330

📞 2 650 5040

✉ branches@auathailand.org

🖥 www.auathailand.org

Chiang Mai branch: AUA, 73 Rajadamnern Road, Amphur Muang, Chiang Mai 50200

📞 53 278407

✉ chiangmai@auathailand.org

17 branches throughout Thailand (5 in Bangkok, 12 provincial).

NUMBER OF TEACHERS: About 200 in total: 50–60 at main branch, up to 20 at other branches. Offers SIT TEFL certificate course in Bangkok and Chiang Mai.

PREFERENCE OF NATIONALITY: American, Canadian, British, Australian and New Zealander.

QUALIFICATIONS: Bachelor's degree and CELTA (or equivalent).

CONDITIONS OF EMPLOYMENT: 1-year commitment preferred. 4–6 hours teaching daily (considered to be full-time). Teaching year consists of 7 6-week terms separated by 1 free week (unpaid). Courses aimed at professionals aged 18–35.

SALARY: Starting rate is 330 baht+ per hour depending on experience/qualifications. Annual bonus paid after completion of Professional Development Program, free health insurance, work permit obtained but paid for by the teacher for first 2 years.

FACILITIES/SUPPORT: Participation in pre-service training session (32 hours) is preferred before teaching hours are assigned. Mentoring programme for new teachers, 15,000 titles in resource library.

RECRUITMENT: Adverts in the *Bangkok Post*, the internet and word of mouth. Apply online.

BELL EDUCATIONAL TRUST

UK: Hillscross, Red Cross Lane, Cambridge CB2 0QU

✉ jobs.thailand@bell-worldwide.com

🖥 www.bell-worldwide.com/locations/thailand

Thailand: 18th Floor, Wave Place, 55 Wireless Road, Lumpini, Pathumwan, Bangkok 10330

📞 2 655 4901

✉ Jobs.Thailand@bell-worldwide.com

🖥 www.bell-worldwide.com/jobs

NUMBER OF TEACHERS: 30+ for 3 independent language centres in Bangkok.

PREFERENCE OF NATIONALITY: None, but must be native English speaker.

QUALIFICATIONS: Bachelor's degree and CELTA (better still PGCE and/or DELTA). Experience of and/or interest in teaching English to young learners preferred. Candidates should be dependable and culturally sensitive team players.

CONDITIONS OF EMPLOYMENT: 1/2-year renewable contracts. Up to 21 contact hours per week (Monday to Friday or Tuesday to Saturday). Much of the work is with young learners.

SALARY: Gross salary 48,000 baht –58,000 baht per month (for degree and CELTA) or 54,000 baht –58,000 baht (PGCE).

FACILITIES/SUPPORT: Flight for teachers recruited outside Thailand. Hotel accommodation on arrival. Assistance in finding suitable accommodation. A loan for accommodation is made available, repayable over initial 3 months of employment. Work permit arranged. End of contract gratuity. 8 weeks' paid holiday per year plus public holidays. Health and medical insurance cover provided. Commitment to in-service training and professional development.

RECRUITMENT: Bell website (www.bell-worldwide.com/jobs), internet, newspapers, telephone and face-to-face interviews.

CONTACT: Louisa Bird, Logistics Manager (Contracts Department).

BRIGHT FUTURE INTERNATIONAL TRAINING & SERVICES (BFITS)
Suite 401–2, Chao Phraya Tower, 89 Soi Wat Suanplu, Bangrak, Bangkok 10500
✆ 2 630 6622 24
✆ info@bfitsthailand.com/hr@bfitsthailand.com
🖥 www.bfitsthailand.com

NUMBER OF TEACHERS: 120+ for about a dozen full curriculum partner schools.

PREFERENCE OF NATIONALITY: American, Canadian, British, Australian and South African. Primarily looking for native English speakers; non-native English speakers must provide TOEFL/TOEIC score.

QUALIFICATIONS: Bachelor's and TEFL certification. TEFL certification is not required for licensed teachers, teachers with degrees in education or English, or for teachers teaching content subjects such as mathematics.

CONDITIONS OF EMPLOYMENT: 1 year. 20–25 teaching hours per week for English conversation.

SALARY: 33,000 baht –35,000 baht per month for English Conversation Teachers; 38,000 baht for English Programme (Content) Teachers. All positions come with yearly bonuses. Thai taxes are deducted at a rate of approximately 1,300 baht per month.

FACILITIES/SUPPORT: Assistance given in locating accommodation and translating/negotiating lease, if needed. Teachers are given necessary documents with instructions on how to obtain a non-immigrant B visa plus 2 paid working days to travel to obtain it. BFITS takes care of all costs and processing of the work permit.

RECRUITMENT: Via TotalESL.com, TESall.com, ESLjobfeed.com and TeachOverseas.ca, partner sites of BFITS. Applications with CV, photo, degrees/certificates and professional references can be emailed with contact information. Date of availability (or relocation date to Thailand) must be specified. Interviews by Skype or in person.

CONTACT: Michael G. Hines, Assistant Director.

BOONYARAT COMPUTER AND LANGUAGE SCHOOL
73–75 Old Petchakaseam Road, Klongkrachang, Muang, Petchaburi 76000
✆ br.language@hotmail.com

NUMBER OF TEACHERS: 15 native English speakers.

PREFERENCE OF NATIONALITY: None.

QUALIFICATIONS: No preferences. However, by law, teaches must have a degree to get a work permit. Homestay tutors without degrees will not be eligible for work visa.

CONDITIONS OF EMPLOYMENT: 1-year contract. 18–25 teaching hours a week.

SALARY: 20,000 baht –35,000 baht a month for full-time teacher, less 3% for taxes.

FACILITIES/SUPPORT: Assistance given to teachers to find cheap accommodation and to obtain work permit if eligible. Internet access provided at school.

RECRUITMENT: Interviews not always necessary or can be conducted by phone. Written applications sometimes acceptable.

CONTACT: Noavarat Tosuwan (Nana), Manager.

BRITISH-AMERICAN
1730–1732 Ladprao Road, Wangtonlang, Bangkok 10310
✆ 2 933 5635/6/7/8 mobile 89 482 3577
✆ british_american2000@hotmail.com
🖥 www.british-american.ac.th

NUMBER OF TEACHERS: About 25.

PREFERENCE OF NATIONALITY: Native English speakers.

QUALIFICATIONS: Enthusiasm and positive attitude are essential.

CONDITIONS OF EMPLOYMENT: Usually part-time, 4–6 teaching hours per day.

SALARY: Earnings usually approximately 30,000+ baht per month. Local rent for an apartment is approximately 3,000 baht monthly.

FACILITIES/SUPPORT: Provide details of recommended apartments. All the visa paperwork is done by the school, but the teacher pays for visa and out of pocket expenses.

RECRUITMENT: Advertising in national newspapers.

NUMBER OF TEACHERS: Volunteers accepted on a rolling basis as needed.

PREFERENCE OF NATIONALITY: None.

QUALIFICATIONS: Teaching experience, interest in the Burma issue, creativity, and comfort with ambiguity. Minimum age 21 years.

CONDITIONS OF EMPLOYMENT: 3-month stays. Teaching 3 hours per day, 5 days per week.

SALARY: Accommodation and food are generally provided.

RECRUITMENT: Application, reference and phone interview.

CONTACT: David Weber, Volunteer Coordinator.

NUMBER OF TEACHERS: 40 to cover all of the university's short courses, including off-campus teaching and large university contractual courses. Note that the Faculty of Humanities at CMU also employs English teachers.

PREFERENCE OF NATIONALITY: None.

QUALIFICATIONS: University degree relevant to teaching English as a second language, native English speakers, teaching experience in ESL.

CONDITIONS OF EMPLOYMENT: 1-year contracts. 9–15 teaching hours per week.

SALARY: Rates of pay at the CMU Language Institute (June 2010) are 400 baht ($12.25) per hour for weekday classes and 450 baht ($13.75) for weekends. At the Faculty of Humanities, teachers earn about 20,000 baht per month and 8,000 baht for monthly rent (full-time positions); 300–350 baht per hour for part-time positions.

FACILITIES/SUPPORT: No assistance with accommodation. Help given with work permits, visa extension fee and insurance.

RECRUITMENT: Direct applications. Interview required.

CONTACT: Matthew John Kay, Director of International Programs Department (Language Institute).

Nation Education, a subsidiary of Nation Multimedia.

NUMBER OF TEACHERS: 3–5 full time with a number of part-time.

PREFERENCE OF NATIONALITY: Native English speakers.

QUALIFICATIONS: Minimum bachelor's degree with a recognised teaching certificate. 2 years' experience in teaching adults (preferably in Thailand) or experience of teaching Business English is an advantage.

CONDITIONS OF EMPLOYMENT: 6–12 months. Hours are between noon and 9pm for in-centre classes or 11am–8pm for corporate classes.

SALARY: At least 35,000 baht per month with 2 days off per week plus other company remunerations, such as medical and dental care, social security, etc. About 5% deducted for tax plus 750 baht for social security.

FACILITIES/SUPPORT: Can possibly recommend accommodation but teachers must find and pay for accommodation themselves. HR department will assist candidates who sign a 1-year contract and who have a non-immigrant B visa, and later in contract will subsidise the expense.

RECRUITMENT: Evidence of qualifications to be presented at first screening. Later, a teaching demonstration, lesson discussion and a personal interview in Bangkok are needed.

CONTACT: Thanakorn Thongprayoon, Academic Manager.

NUMBER OF VOLUNTEER PLACEMENTS PER YEAR: 150.

QUALIFICATIONS: Good working knowledge of English (or Thai!), flexibility and an open mind.

CONDITIONS OF WORK: 1–52 weeks. On most projects, volunteers work full days, 5 days a week.

SALARY: None. Volunteers pay a participation fee of £300 for 4 weeks, and £25 per week thereafter to cover project administration and their own expenses while volunteering.

FACILITIES/SUPPORT: Introductory 3-day course and longer TESOL courses available through local providers; choice of online option and courses based in beach towns in Thailand.

RECRUITMENT: Preliminary contacts online; application forms processed by email.

CONTACT: Dan Lockwood, Project Manager.

ECC (THAILAND)

Teacher Service Centre (English & Computer College), 5th Floor, 97/11 Big C Rajdamri, Rajdamri Road, Lumpini, Patumwan, Bangkok 10330

✆ +66 2 253 3312

✐ jobs@ecc.ac.th

💻 www.eccthai.com

50 schools in Bangkok and in most major centres outside Bangkok (including Chiang Mai and Phuket). Largest private language school in Thailand.

NUMBER OF TEACHERS: Around 500 native English speakers (usually recruit 10–15 new teachers each month).

PREFERENCE OF NATIONALITY: None.

QUALIFICATIONS: Bachelor's degree plus TEFL certificate (CELTA, Trinity or equivalent).

CONDITIONS OF EMPLOYMENT: 100–120 hours per month (average 25–30 hours per week), 6 day week, mostly in evenings and weekends. BUPA medical insurance, end of contract bonus, location allowance in Bangkok (3,000 baht –5,000 baht per month). 5 days' paid holiday plus 13 statutory holidays.

SALARY: Depending on qualifications and experience 30,000 baht –35,000 baht per month in Bangkok, 20,000 baht –30,000 baht in the provinces.

FACILITIES/SUPPORT: Work permit and 1-year visa applied for after arrival. Assistance (non-financial) given with finding accommodation. Professional development with regular workshops, including a number of short courses which are free to ECC teachers: Teaching English to Young Learners and Teaching Business English. ECC offer the Cambridge CELTA course and an Introduction to TESOL course.

RECRUITMENT: Adverts on the internet and qualified walk-ins.

CONTACT: Tely Kalambaheti, Teacher Recruitment Manager (jobs@ecc.ac.th).

ESCD ENGLISH CENTRE

8/36 Sukhumvit Road Siracha, Chonburi 20110

✆ 38 328203

✐ wnschool@cscoms.com or escd_thailand@yahoo.com

💻 http://eec.escd.or.th/vacancies.htm

NUMBER OF TEACHERS: 20 per year.

PREFERENCE OF NATIONALITY: Australian, European, American and Canadian.

QUALIFICATIONS: Degree plus TEFL. Aged 20–40.

CONDITIONS OF EMPLOYMENT: 12-month contracts to teach in local Catholic schools. 16–25 hours per week.

SALARY: 30,000 baht per month. Free flight at end of contract (up to 12,000 baht).

FACILITIES/SUPPORT: Accommodation 2,500 baht per month. Help with visas given; teachers must bring original of their degree certificate.

RECRUITMENT: Interviews essential.

GAP YEAR THAILAND

1 Vernon Avenue, Rugby CV22 5HL, UK

✆ 01788 552617/07899 887276

✐ david@gapyearthailand.org.uk

💻 www.gapyearthailand.org.uk

Professional education organisation whose key team members have a background in teacher education in universities in UK or in the Rajabhat universities (teacher training universities) in Thailand. The programme is approved and endorsed by the South East Asian Ministers of Education.

NUMBER OF PLACEMENTS PER YEAR: 10+ volunteers to work as assistant teachers, teaching English (particularly conversational English) in schools or universities.

QUALIFICATIONS: Minimum age 18, average age early 20s. Must speak English as a first language. Teaching qualification not needed.

CONDITIONS OF EMPLOYMENT: Minimum 2 months up to 6+ months.

SALARY: None. Programme cost: £980 including accommodation, which can be homestay with family or in a teacher's house.

RECRUITMENT: Applications accepted throughout the year. Telephone interviews. Pre-departure briefing weekend with

some TEFL training, and further training in the orientation programme on arrival.

CONTACT: David Lancaster, Chief Executive.

INLINGUA INTERNATIONAL SCHOOL OF LANGUAGES
7th Floor, Central Chidlom Tower, 22 Ploenchit Road, Pathumwan, Bangkok 10330
✆ 2 254 7028 30
🖱 chidlom@inlinguabangkok.com
💻 www.Inlinguabangkok.com

NUMBER OF TEACHERS: 140 full-time, 100 part-time.

PREFERENCE OF NATIONALITY: Native English speakers: American, Canadian, British, Irish, Australian, New Zealander and South African.

QUALIFICATIONS: Candidates must have at least 2 of the following: bachelor's degree, TESOL/TEFL/CELTA, experience.

CONDITIONS OF EMPLOYMENT: 1 year. Children's classes are on Saturday/Sunday 9am–6pm. Teachers work a 6-day week or 5 for corporate work.

SALARY: Guaranteed minimum 35,000 baht for full-time contract teachers. Possibly more, depending on workload.

FACILITIES/SUPPORT: Try to point staff in the direction of suitable accommodation. Full support given in work permit/visa applications. BUPA medical insurance.

RECRUITMENT: Internet adverts on www.ajarn.com. Applications welcomed on above email address. Mostly local hires.

CONTACT: Fraser Morrell, Director of Studies (fraserm@inlinguabangkok.com).

IST PLUS - TEACH IN THAILAND PROGRAMME
Rosedale House, Rosedale Road, Richmond, Surrey TW9 2SZ, UK
✆ 020 8939 9057
🖱 info@istplus.com
💻 www.istplus.com

NUMBER OF TEACHERS: 20–30 each year for two programmes, one for paid teachers in state schools, supported by the Overseas Education Group (www.overseasedu.com), and the other voluntary.

PREFERENCE OF NATIONALITY: None, although non-native speakers of English must have near-native proficiency in English.

QUALIFICATIONS: University degree in any field essential. TEFL training or experience is not essential but preferred. Maximum age 65.

CONDITIONS OF EMPLOYMENT: 5- or 10-month renewable contracts starting in either May or October, teaching 22 classes a week, which works out at a working week of 35–40 hours.

SALARY: Minimum salary 14,000 baht–15,000 baht per month.

FACILITIES/SUPPORT: Free accommodation (usually on-campus), all-inclusive 7-day orientation in Bangkok on arrival including basic EFL training, accommodation, sight-seeing and airport transfer. IST Plus arrange school placement, visa and work permit, insurance and 24-hour emergency hotline.

RECRUITMENT: Deadlines for application are 21 March for May departure and 15 July for October departure. Teach in Thailand Programme fees are £895 for 5 months, £995 for 10 months. Teachers who complete 10 month contracts starting in May will have their one-way flight home paid for by the host school. All teachers who complete their contracts will receive a TEFL certificate.

CONTACT: Ralph Allemano, Director (rallemano@istplus.com).

KING'S COLLEGE OF ENGLISH
1093/19–21, 5th Floor, Central City Tower I, Bangna-Trad Road, Bangna, Prakanong, Bangkok 10260
💻 www.kingsthailand.com

Part of group of King's English Language Schools based in Bournemouth, UK.

NUMBER OF TEACHERS: 45 for 3 schools in Bangkok.

PREFERENCE OF NATIONALITY: Native English speakers: British (majority), Canadian, American, Australian, New Zealander.

QUALIFICATIONS: University degree (any subject) plus CELTA or 120-hour equivalent. Preference given to applicants with qualifications or experience teaching young learners, however, experience not essential since support and extensive materials are supplied.

CONDITIONS OF EMPLOYMENT: 1-year contracts. Contractual arrangement is 112 contact hours per month; preparation time is extra. Saturday and Sunday are working days. 2 consecutive days off a week.

SALARY: Approximately 34,000 baht per month depending on qualifications and experience. Yearly increment, paid holidays (13 days plus 13 statutory public holidays). End-of-contract bonus of 25,000 baht and flight contribution.

FACILITIES/SUPPORT: Assistance with accommodation; loan can be given for deposit and deducted from monthly salary. Basic private health insurance provided by school.

Free Thai language lessons plus Thai cookery and boxing programme.

RECRUITMENT: Local and web adverts and UK recruitment agency. UK applicants should send CV and photo in the first instance to John Hudson (hudson.111@virgin.net). Interviews may be arranged at the King's School in Beckenham, Kent.

SIAM COMPUTER & LANGUAGE INSTITUTE
471/19 Ratchawithi Road, Bangkok 10400
- 2 247 2345 ext. 361–364
- bhudeb@siamcom.co.th or hrd@siamcom.co.th
- www.siamcom.co.th/english_teach.php

NUMBER OF TEACHERS: 37 at 35 school locations in the greater Bangkok area and 49 at 38 external locations in the greater Bangkok area.

PREFERENCE OF NATIONALITY: Native English speakers.

QUALIFICATIONS: College degree required; CELTA or equivalent and experience preferred.

CONDITIONS OF EMPLOYMENT: 1-year contracts. Full-time internal teachers 6 days per week in air-conditioned facilities; 15 or fewer students per class. All ages. Full-time external teachers 5 days per week in Thai classrooms. 50 students per class from kindergarten to high school level.

SALARY: 30,000+ baht per month based on experience. Bonus plans for external teachers. Hourly rates for part-time internal and external teachers.

FACILITIES/SUPPORT: Assistance with finding local accommodation. 15 paid Thai vacation days per year, assistance in obtaining a teacher's licence, work permit and 1-year visa. Complete teacher orientation and teacher training before starting in the classroom, with bimonthly teachers' meetings.

RECRUITMENT: Adverts in the *Bangkok Post* and on the worldwide web, and contacts with schools in Australia and the USA. Interviews in Bangkok required.

CONTACT: Patrick or Mr. Bhudeb.

SPENCER INTERNATIONAL
1st Fl., Muangthai Phatra Complex, 252/193 Rachadapisek Rd., Bangkok 10320
- +66 293 2901
- stephen.l@spencer.co.th
- www.spencer.co.th

NUMBER OF TEACHERS: 60.

PREFERENCE OF NATIONALITY: None.

QUALIFICATIONS: Degree holders are preferred, but positions for non-degree holders are also available.

Inexperienced and unqualified teachers have opportunities to undergo formal or in-house training through a staff development programme.

CONDITIONS OF EMPLOYMENT: 10-month contract. Usual hours 7:30am–3:30pm Monday to Friday. Evening and weekend work are offered as overtime.

SALARY: Starting salary 32,000 baht with increments after 3 months, 6 months and 1 year. Tax is deducted at source.

FACILITIES/SUPPORT: Training in ESL is provided on-site. Assistance given with finding accommodation in the school vicinity to suit teacher's lifestyle. School takes care of all work permit requirements for teachers who wish to transfer their visa status. Process can take up to 2 months, so short-term teachers are encouraged to get visas equivalent to their length of stay before arrival in Thailand.

RECRUITMENT: Via TESOL training programmes or the internet. Spencer International provides TEFL and TESOL courses in Bangkok, accredited through Chichester College, UK. Interviews can be conducted by email or telephone.

CONTACT: Stephen Louw, Academic Coordinator.

SUPER ENGLISH
38/1–2 Bandon Rd., Talad, Muang, Surat Thani 84000
- 77 213395
- teach@superenglishsurat.com
- www.superenglishsurat.com

NUMBER OF TEACHERS: 12.

PREFERENCE OF NATIONALITY: None, but must be a native speaker of English.

QUALIFICATIONS: University degree essential. Must have the right attitude: a willingness to learn, be flexible about living in an Eastern culture, able to think creatively and be patient. Must enjoy working with children and have a sincere desire to teach them English and to have an impact on their lives.

CONDITIONS OF EMPLOYMENT: Standard 1-year contract. Schedules vary greatly but usually less than 25 hours per week (and hours above 25 are paid overtime rate of 300 baht). Some teachers work in the morning and have their afternoons off; others prefer late mornings and continuing through the early evening. Classes finish at 6.30pm.

SALARY: 250–300 baht per hour. Current average salary is around 28,500 baht per month less tax deductions of about 200 baht per month.

FACILITIES/SUPPORT: Shared, furnished house in an ideal location of Surat Thani is provided for teachers, who all have a private bedroom. Paperwork provided pre-arrival for a

3-month non-immigrant B visa. School will process that visa into a 1-year non-immigrant visa and will obtain a 1-year labour permit and 3-year teacher's licence.

RECRUITMENT: Adverts on www.eslcafe.com and via recruiter in Canada: Ian Davidson of Davidson Recruitment Services (www.iandrs.com/Thailand/thai_index.htm). Interviews via Skype are essential.

CONTACT: Peter C. Meltzer, Owner and Director.

RECRUITMENT: Application can be made online. Volunteers can be placed at short notice but 2–3 months' advance warning preferred.

COST: €350 for 1–2 weeks, €450 for 3 weeks, €500 for 1 month, €1,380 for 24 weeks. Fees include orientation, pre-arranged accommodation, travels within the project, cultural outings and support before and during the stay.

CONTACT: Sabine Lindemann, Project Manager.

THAI-EXPERIENCE.ORG
1133/4 Kaewworawut Rd, Meaung District,
Nongkhai 43000
84 44 92 022
www.Thai-Experience.org

USIT
19/21 Aston Quay, Dublin 2, Ireland
+353 1 602 1742
volunteer@usit.ie
www.usit.ie

PROGRAMME DESCRIPTION: Teaching English, computer skills or vocational skills to disadvantaged children and/or adults in north-eastern Thailand (Isan province). Maintaining computers.

NUMBER OF PLACEMENTS PER YEAR: 80.

QUALIFICATIONS: Minimum age 18. Good command of English language. Computer trainers need computer skills, open mind and patience to deal with the different environment. No TEFL certificate needed as volunteers do not replace teachers but assist them, encouraging students to use their English language skills to speak, practise and motivate them to learn more.

CONDITIONS OF PLACEMENT: 1 week to 1 year; typically 2–3 months.

PREFERENCE OF NATIONALITY: None.

QUALIFICATIONS: Degree; otherwise a 4-week orientation and training course is needed on arrival.

CONDITIONS OF EMPLOYMENT: 5–12-month renewable contract. Teaching 4–6 hours per day.

SALARY: €8,500–€11,000 per year.

FACILITIES/SUPPORT: Schools will organise accommodation for the teachers, free of charge. Otherwise coordinator in Thailand will assist with finding accommodation and obtaining work permits.

RECRUITMENT: Interviews essential and can be held using Skype.

CONTACT: Alan Byrne, Volunteer and Paid Teach Abroad Coordinator.

Spanning 75 degrees of latitude, the mammoth continent of South America together with the Caribbean islands and the eight countries of Central America, offer an eclectic range of teaching opportunities. With the important exception of Brazil where Portuguese is spoken, South American countries have a majority of Spanish speakers and, as in Spain itself, there is a great demand for English teaching, from dusty Mexican towns near the American border to Punta Arenas at the southern extremity of the continent, south of the Falkland Islands.

The countries of most interest to the travelling teacher are Chile, Argentina, Colombia, Ecuador, Venezuela, Brazil and Mexico. Certain patterns emerged during the research for the various editions of this book, though sweeping generalisations are of limited value and will not apply to all countries and all situations. After problems with inflation, most countries (apart from Venezuela) have brought the problem under control, which means that salaries do not lose their value as quickly as they used to. Although pay scales are sometimes quoted in US dollars, wages are almost always paid in the local currency.

Urban life in the big cities of Brazil, Argentina and Chile is more like that of Europe than of developing countries. In such cities, the greatest demand for English comes from big business, and because of the strong commercial links between the two American continents, the demand tends to be for American English, though an increasing number of British and Australian teachers are finding work in these countries.

Among the most important providers of the English language are Bi-National Centers and Cultural Centers, the American counterpart of the British Council. There are scores of these centres in Latin America, including nearly 40 IBEUs (Instituto Brasil-Estados Unidos) in Brazil alone including the sub-network. Many of these centres are engaged in the teaching of English, some on quite a large scale employing upwards of 20 teachers. While some want a commitment from teachers to stay for two years, others are happy to take someone on for shorter periods or part-time. While the English Language Fellow Program administered from Washington requires teachers with an MA in TESL from a US university, there may be local opportunities for others. A good point of contact is the relevant Regional English Language Officer (http://exchanges.state.gov/englishteaching/reg-el-officers.html).

Britain also has cultural representatives in several Latin American countries; the longest established Culturas Inglesas are in Argentina, Brazil, Chile, Mexico, Peru and Uruguay (listed at www. aaci.org.ar/bienv.htm#lista). These Cultural Associations aim to teach English within the framework of British culture and work closely with the British Council and represent the elite end of the market. Usually they require their teachers to have specialised ELT training and experience. Only a few recruit abroad so it is worth making local enquiries on arrival.

Several South American nations have a number of British or American-style bilingual schools and *colegios*. Although this book is not centrally concerned with English-medium schools, which are usually looking for teachers with a PGCE or full teacher accreditation, international schools in South America are mainly for local nationals (rather than expatriates) who want a bilingual Spanish-English education and have a very strong emphasis on English language teaching. Despite the prestige of these schools, some are willing to consider EFL teachers who have not done teacher training. For example, many of them accept school leavers participating in gap year projects.

Finally, there are private and commercial language institutes from International House (Argentina, Chile, Colombia, Costa Rica, Mexico and Uruguay) through to Berlitz (which is strongly represented in Latin America) to the cowboy operations where standards and wages will be extremely low. **David Hewitt**, a computer programmer from Yorkshire with no TEFL training or experience, was surprised not only to walk into a teaching job in Brazil but also to find himself giving lessons to the director of the school. In whatever kind of school you teach, or if you just give occasional private lessons to contacts, you will probably find the local people extremely friendly and eager to help. The ethnic diversity and Latin warmth encountered by foreign teachers and travellers throughout the continent usually more than compensate for low wages and (in the big cities) a high crime rate.

PROSPECTS FOR TEACHERS

In a land where baseball is a passion and US television enormously popular, American (and also Canadian) job-seekers have an advantage. The whole continent is culturally and economically oriented towards the USA. There is a decided preference among language learners for the American accent and for American teaching materials and course books, which explains why so many language institutes are called Lincoln and Jefferson. Business English is gaining ground throughout the region, particularly in Argentina, Chile, Venezuela, Colombia, Brazil and Mexico, and anyone with a business background will have an edge over the competition.

The academic year begins in February or early March and lasts until November/December. In the southernmost nations of Chile and Argentina, January and February are very slack months for language schools; while further north in Bolivia, for example, the summer holiday consists of December/January. The best time to arrive to look for work is a few weeks before the end of the summer holidays. But many institutes run eight- to 12-week courses year round and will be eager for the services of a native English speaker whatever the time of year.

FINDING A JOB

Speculative enquiries from EFL teachers are much less likely to work if sent before arrival than after, although sending a 'warm-up' CV may help your job search. What the principal of a girls' school in Lima wrote is echoed by many other institutes. '*Anyone interested in a job is welcome to write to me at any time. If they happen to be in Lima they are equally welcome to come into school.*' Unless you are very well qualified or have met your prospective employer before, you are unlikely to be offered a contract while out of the country. This is unfortunate since work visas are best applied for in the country of origin of the teacher (see below).

IN ADVANCE

Not many Latin American language schools advertise internationally. Even the most prestigious schools complain of the difficulties they encounter recruiting teachers abroad, mainly due to the low salaries they can offer and the bureaucratic procedures for obtaining a work permit. Some British Council offices in South America keep lists of schools, as do some embassies and consulates in London and Washington. When 20-year-old **James Gratton** was making plans for his first trip to South America, he wrote to all the embassies in London and received quite a lot of literature, including a number of lists of language schools, for Paraguay, Uruguay, Peru, etc. He claims that the Argentinian embassy was particularly helpful and friendly at that time. Serious candidates might ask the cultural attaché for advice.

Language school chains and organisations which might be of assistance to qualified British TEFL teachers are International House, Berlitz, EF English First and Wall Street Institute. Saxoncourt Recruitment is occasionally active in Peru and one or two other countries of South America and sometimes recruits on behalf of Culturas Inglesas and international schools. For language school listings and teaching information check the splendid site http://thelajoblist.blogspot.com. TEFL training colleges in the USA often have close ties with Latin American language schools. The training centres in the USA such as Transworld Teachers send large numbers of their graduates to posts in South America.

The British Council arranges for language assistants to work in six Latin American countries for an academic year: Argentina, Chile, Colombia, Ecuador, Mexico and Paraguay; details at www.britishcouncil.org/languageassistants-latin-america.htm. Applicants must be undergraduates studying Spanish or graduates with a Spanish A level. The level of placements and the nature of the duties are more suited to graduates than undergraduates. Deadlines for application vary among the different countries.

The Association of American Schools in South America (AASSA, 1911 NW 150 Avenue, Suite 101, Pembroke Pines, Florida 33028, USA; 954 436 4034; info@aassa.com; www.aassa.com) co-ordinates teacher recruitment for its 40 members, all American-international schools in 14 Latin American countries. Candidates who attend a recruiting fair in December must have a degree and generally be state-certified teachers. There is a $110 registration fee and if you are hired your school pays a further placement fee to AASSA.

South American Explorers (formerly the South American Explorers Club) keeps lists of schools that employ English teachers. They have a volunteer database for members to access with information about volunteering opportunities throughout South America. Many of the organisations listed will take on English teachers without a TEFL certification. Membership costs US$60 per year ($90 for a couple). Contact the South American Explorers for further details (admin@saexplorers.org; www.saexplorers.org).

Lots of commercial volunteer agencies have programmes in Latin America such as: i-to-i (www.i-to-i.com), which sends people to teach in Argentina, Brazil, Costa Rica, Ecuador and Peru; Travellers Worldwide (www.travellersworldwide.com) with a programme in Argentina, Brazil, Bolivia, Peru and Guatemala; and Africa, Asia & Americas Venture (www.aventure.co.uk) with a teaching scheme in Mexico. MondoChallenge (www.mondochallenge.co.uk) sends volunteer teachers to projects in the Elqui Valley of Chile, the Andes and on the coast of Ecuador as well as Quito. Knowledge of Spanish may be expected on some of these programmes and accommodation is usually with host families.

WorldTeach at Harvard (617 495 5527; www.worldteach.org.) places paying volunteers as teachers of EFL or ESL in Costa Rica, Ecuador, Venezuela, Chile and (unusually) Guyana. AmeriSpan in Philadelphia (215 751 1100; www.amerispan.com) is primarily a language training organisation but it arranges internships in education and other fields, lasting two weeks to six months, in many Spanish-speaking countries.

ON THE SPOT

The concept of 'job vacancy' is very fluid in many Latin American language institutes and, provided you are willing to work for local teaching wages, you should be able to create your own job almost anywhere. As throughout the world, local applicants often break into the world of language teaching gradually by teaching a few classes a week. Non-contractual work is almost always offered on an unofficial part-time basis. So if you are trying to earn a living you will have to patch together enough hours from various sources. Finding the work is simply a matter of asking around and knocking on enough doors. For those who speak no Spanish, the first hurdle is to communicate your request to the secretaries at language schools since they invariably speak no English. Try to memorise a polite request in Spanish to pass your CV (*hoja de vida*) and letter (in Spanish if possible) to the school director who will know at least some English. Check adverts in the English language press such as *The News* in Mexico City or the *Buenos Aires Herald*. English language bookshops are another possible source of teaching leads.

Ask in expatriate bars and restaurants, check out any building claiming to be an 'English School' however dubious-looking, and in larger cities try deciphering the telephone directory for schools or agencies which might be able to use your services. There is more competition as well as more opportunities in the major cities (for example, it is said that up to half a million Americans live in Mexico City), so if you are having difficulties rounding up work, you could try smaller towns and cities off the beaten track.

The crucial factor in becoming accepted as an English teacher at a locally run language school may not be your qualifications or your accent as much as your appearance. You must look as neat and well-dressed as teachers are expected to look, at least when you're job-hunting. Later your standards might slip a little; **Nick Wilson**, who taught for two years in Mexico, says that it is easy to spot the English teachers in banks and office buildings; they're the ones wearing jeans, T-shirts and carrying cassettes.

FREELANCE TEACHING

In most Latin American cities, there is a thriving market in private English lessons, which usually pay at least half as much again as working for an institute. It is not uncommon for teachers to consider the language school which hires them as a stepping stone to setting up as a private tutor. After they have familiarised themselves with some teaching materials and made enough contacts among local language learners, they strike out on their own, though this is far from easy unless you can get by in the local language and have access to suitable premises. Clients can be found by advertising in the quality press, by placing notices on strategic noticeboards or by handing out business cards. If the latter, use the local method of address and omit confusing initials such as BA after your name: teachers often call themselves '*Profesor*' or '*Profesora*'.

REGULATIONS

Of course requirements vary from country to country but the prospects are dismal for teachers who insist on doing everything by the book. It is standard for work visas to be available only to fully qualified and experienced teachers on long-term contracts. Often you will have to present an array of documents, from university certificates and transcripts to FBI police clearance, which have been authenticated by your consulate abroad or by the consulate of the host country. Although many schools will not offer a contract before interview and then will make it contingent on a work permit, the procedures should be started in the teacher's country of origin, which makes the whole business very difficult. All of this can take as long as six months and involve a great deal of hassle and expense, not least for the employer.

The upshot is that a high percentage of teachers works unofficially throughout Latin America. It is hardly an issue in some countries, for example virtually no one gets a work permit in Brazil, not even long-resident language school teachers and no one seems to worry about it. Teaching on a tourist visa or as a 'tourist' in countries where you don't need a visa, is a widespread practice in Mexico and Peru. There are ways round the regulations, for example to work on a student/trainee/cultural exchange visa (as in Ecuador or Venezuela).

CONDITIONS OF WORK

Very few schools offer perks such as an extra month's salary or return flights to teachers who stay for a two-year contract. Contracts are fairly hard to come by and always require a minimum commitment of a year. The advantages are that you are guaranteed a certain income and you have a chance of applying for a work permit. Teachers without the CELTA or Trinity certificate are not greatly disadvantaged, partly because this qualification is not as widely known in Latin America as it is in Europe, although you can take the Trinity TESOL course at the Dickens Institute in Montivideo (Uruguay), and Stael Ruffinelli de Ortiz English in Asuncion (Paraguay). Many institutes offer their own compulsory pre-job training (to be taken at the teacher's own expense), which provides a useful orientation for new arrivals.

One of the seldom-mentioned perks of teaching in Latin America is the liveliness and enthusiasm of the pupils. Brazilian students have been described as the 'world's most communicative students' and classrooms around the continent often take on the atmosphere of a party. You may also be dazzled by the level of knowledge of Western pop culture, and should be prepared to have your ignorance shown up. Also be prepared to lose their attention if a lesson coincides with a major sporting event.

LEISURE TIME

Whether you are a serious student of Spanish or a frivolous seeker after the excitement generated by Latin carnivals, South America is a wonderful place to live in and travel. Women teachers may find the machismo a little hard to take, but will soon learn how to put it in its place. If you want to travel around, the annually revised *South American Handbook* definitely justifies the initial outlay of £22.50.

ARGENTINA

The teaching market in Argentina is ticking over without being really buoyant. Hundreds of institutes operate at varying standards. The economy is recovering well, with average growth forecast at between 3% and 4% (2010). The exchange rate is quite convenient for both European and American citizens with roughly 4 pesos to the US dollar and 5 pesos to the euro. Although language schools, many of which specialise in the business market, have not quite made a full recovery from the last deep recession at the turn of the century there is cause for some optimism. Teachers are more likely to secure a job once they are in Argentina.

Cultural exchange programmes will appeal to those willing to teach as volunteers in rural areas, normally in state rather than private schools. For example, Connecting Schools to the World (see entry) invites university graduates to live for one or two semesters in a *pueblo* or city in the Argentinian province of Córdoba. The programme fee of $500 covers homestay accommodation with a local family and a modest monthly stipend. Road2Argentina in Buenos Aires (11 4821 3271; www.road2argentina.com) places ESL interns for one to six months as part of a cultural exchange and language immersion programme. International interns are accepted without relevant training or experience to help in private or public school classrooms. Programme fees start at $975 for one month and include accommodation. (Road2Argentina also offers ELT training courses – see entry). As with all these programmes, participants are encouraged to take up various extra-curricular activities such as tango lessons, cookery and photography.

Other possibilities include:

Colonias de Inmersión al Idioma (CII), Casilla de Correo 044, Sucursal Plaza Italia, 1425 Buenos Aires (+54 11 4831 8152; www.ecolonias.com). Recruits language facilitators to work in schools. Participants must have a university degree, speaking knowledge of Spanish and TEFL certificate. TEFL Placement Express fee is US$200. Other cultural-cum-teaching programmes are available for higher fees but with fewer prerequisites.

EBC Servicios Lingüísticos, Buenos Aires (+54 11 6379 9391; toll-free numbers in English speaking countries listed on website www.teflgap.org or www.ebc-tefl-course.com). Offers a month-long TEFL training course for $1,599 followed by a job placement programme. EBC claim to have contacts with 200+ language schools in Buenos Aires.

Expanish, Buenos Aires (+54 11 4322 0011 or 1 888 EXPANISH; Tefl@expanish.com; www.expanishtefl.com). Operates regular 120- or 150-hour TEFL courses in Buenos Aires, which incorporate a local job facilitation programme in Buenos Aires. Expanish also offers an add-on week of Spanish tuition.

GIC – see entry.

Many companies are located in the outskirts of Buenos Aires, a city whose area is larger than London's. It can sometimes take more than an hour to reach some companies from downtown (where teachers might live) by bus, so make sure you negotiate a block of three hours minimum in one place, or it may not be worth your while. Language schools are linked from www.inglesnet.com, which also has a decent community section. Courses in Argentina tend to start in March and finish in December. The hourly wage for starting teachers is normally between 30 and 34 Argentine pesos, currently equivalent to $7.50–$9.

Job-seekers can try the *Buenos Aires Herald*, which accepts adverts for English teachers, or check community noticeboards such as craigslist. There is a useful noticeboard in El Ateneo, the English language bookshop at 340 Calle Florida (the main shopping street). For information on other English language bookshops, often good places to meet native speakers and to discover informal opportunities, download *Buenos Aires' Brilliant Bookshops* (http://argentinastravel.com/downloads/

bookstore-guide.pdf). Another contact point is the Instituto de Lengua Espanola para Extranjeros or ILEE, where many foreign residents take Spanish classes.

Some of the 16 bi-national Centers or Instituto de Intercambio Cultural Argentino-Americano (listed at http://argentina.usembassy.gov/binational_centers.html) offer English courses, as do the three International House schools in the capital (located in Recoleta, Belgrano and San Isidro). To work at one of these, you usually have to have worked for IH before. A large number of full-curriculum private schools prepare students for Cambridge and other exams, such as the Belgrano Day School (Juramento 3035, (c1428doa) Ciudad de Buenos Aires; 11 4781 6011; www.bds.edu.ar), which has pupils from kindergarten to school leaving age.

It is commonplace for Americans and Britons to move from learning Spanish to teaching English as **Richard Ferguson** did, a New Zealander who has travelled extensively in South America:

> *There are heaps of English schools in Buenos Aires and everyone wants to learn English. I made a few basic signs in Spanish advertising conversational classes, stuck them around Palermo (a wealthier suburb) and sometimes I'll stand on a busy corner and hand out leaflets. I'm charging about 30 pesos an hour and have a few students already so it's a good bet. I think any native speaker can teach here, better with experience and better still with qualifications. Either do as I did, approach some schools or look in the papers in the jobs section. I saw at least 15 in one edition of the* **Buenos Aires Herald.**

Luke McElderry from Texas and his girlfriend **Jenny Jacobi** spent hours researching potential teaching employers in Buenos Aires on the internet. After completing a training course locally, he sent a mass email with CV attached to at least 40 addresses and waited for responses to trickle in, and ended up hearing from about a quarter. He describes his job-hunt:

> *The first interviews were varied, some in English, one in Spanish, but all fairly casual. Most take 30 minutes and they seem to care more about your availability than your experience. I was asked a couple of times if I had any visa/permit and said no, and the employers didn't seem to care at all. I have heard the biggest institutes are the ones who care, and ironically pay the least!*

Before long, they were working for an institute, Speak Spanish, which, confusingly, also teaches English (www.speakspanish.com.ar). They were sent out to teach one and half hour classes in businesses. Sometimes they were assigned to comfortable conference rooms with whiteboards, free photocopies, faxes and coffee. Luke and Jenny found that all went smoothly, apart from finding accommodation:

> *It is a real hassle finding an apartment as they want to charge you tourist rates and it is nearly impossible to get a lease as an ex-pat. Accommodation prices depend on your ability to find a rental agency that doesn't require a* **guarantia** *from an Argentine property owner saying that you will pay the entire rental term in full; some places will let you pay everything up front, usually 6 months or more, but these places are very few and far between.*

Alicia Meta of ACM Business English, Buenos Aires, explains how the letting market works:

> *A one-bedroom apartment in a decent neighbourhood might now cost U$S1,000 if it is furnished, if not, around U$S600. If it is a short contract the agents will ask you to pay in full. For a short-term contract you also have to pay a commission to the real estate agency of about 8% of the total amount. For a one-year contract the commission is the equivalent of one and a half months of the rent to be paid. The deposit for a long-term contract (one year) is equal to two months rent. It is always returned once the deal is over.*

It is difficult for tourists to rent an apartment and unfortunately I believe that there is no other way out. My advice would be to get some feedback before coming to Argentina, go to a hostel and then calmly try to look for the best option. Usually, apartments in the outskirts of Buenos Aires can be cheaper but the payment method might not differ.

If you want to cast your net wider you can move to smaller cities where there will be fewer vacancies but also fewer applicants competing for the jobs. For example, Bariloche in Patagonia in the deep south of Argentina has an unexpectedly large market for English teachers because of its role as an international ski resort.

RED TAPE

Working papers can be obtained from the National Direction of Migrations by employers, though a school will be willing only for long-term propositions. It will be necessary for the applicant to provide a contract of employment for a minimum of a year, and birth certificate (notarised by a notary public in Argentina), as well as passport. Non-British passport holders must also provide a certificate of good conduct from the police authorities in his or her country or countries of residence in the five years prior to applying.

The Argentine embassy in London states on its website that British nationals (and also US nationals) do not need a tourist visa to enter Argentina for up to 90 days, which can be extended for another 90 days at the *Dirección Nacional de Migraciones*.

Most teachers are paid hourly by the language institutes employing them. Self-employed people are obliged to register with the DGI (tax office) and pay approximately 15% of their full-time earnings in tax.

LIST OF EMPLOYERS

ACM BUSINESS ENGLISH
Viamonte 2660, Buenos Aires
☎ +54 11 5025 4752
✉ info@acmbusinessenglish.com.ar
🖥 www.acmbusinessenglish.com.ar

NUMBER OF TEACHERS: 3–4.
PREFERENCE OF NATIONALITY: American, British and Canadian. Note: A strong Australian accent is usually difficult for Latin Americans to understand.
QUALIFICATIONS: TEFL, ESL or equivalent. Experience teaching ESL to adults in companies needed. Candidates with a teaching degree are the most sought after. General knowledge and high intellectual level needed for training executives who will be dealing with native English speakers at headquarters.
CONDITIONS OF EMPLOYMENT: No contracts. Part-time work so people are self-employed. Most teachers intend to stay in the country for at least 1 year, starting in March. Courses in Argentina start in March and finish in December. Usually 2–3 hours twice a week teaching in different companies. Many companies are located on the outskirts of Buenos Aires, so it can take more than an hour to reach some companies from downtown (where most candidates live) by bus. In these cases, a block of 3 hours minimum in one place is offered.
SALARY: Between 32 and 35 pesos per hour, paid at the beginning of the following month.
FACILITIES/SUPPORT: No training given. No assistance with accommodation.
RECRUITMENT: Word of mouth/posting on international websites, and in *the Buenos Aires Herald* (local English newspaper). Interviews in Buenos Aires.
CONTACT: Alicia Meta, Director.

COLONIAS DE INMERSION AL IDIOMA (CII)
Casilla de Correo 044, Sucursal Plaza Italia,
1425 Buenos Aires

✆ 11 4831 8152

✉ experienceargentina@ecolonias.com

💻 www.ecolonias.com

NUMBER OF TEACHERS: 25–35 TEFL interns per semester who spend 20 hours per week assisting with English in a local school, a few hours a week tutoring members of their host family and one weekend a month at a language camp for children and young people.

PREFERENCE OF NATIONALITY: Citizen of any English-speaking country.

QUALIFICATIONS: University students and graduates aged 20–26, no specific qualifications or experience required.

CONDITIONS OF EMPLOYMENT: 3–12 months, preferably starting 10 March or 25 July. Most schools prefer applicants who can commit to at least a semester. Schedules vary from school to school. Total of 25 hours a week.

SALARY: Monthly stipend of 280–350 pesos plus 200 pesos for participating in weekend language camp. Programme fee of $1,750 for up to 6 months, $2,000 for up to 12 includes homestay accommodation throughout with full board, Spanish coaching and opportunities to travel.

FACILITIES/SUPPORT: 60-hour Bridge TEFL online certificate course is compulsory for those who do not have a TEFL qualification (at a cost of $325).

RECRUITMENT: Through cooperating universities and the internet. Interviews sometimes carried out in the UK and Ireland.

CONTACT: Maria Laura Dominguez, Placement Coordinator; Fernando Damian Carro, CII Director.

CONNECTING SCHOOLS TO THE WORLD
Luis Maria Campos 545 1 D; 1426 Buenos Aires

✆ +54 11 477 26724

✉ connectingschools@gmail.com

💻 www.connectingschools.com.ar

NUMBER OF TEACHERS: 20 teachers per year. All placed in different towns in the interior of Argentina for a period of one semester.

PREFERENCE OF NATIONALITY: People from any English speaking country.

QUALIFICATIONS: College graduates.

CONDITIONS OF EMPLOYMENT: Teaching periods of one or two semesters. 25 hours of work per week. First semester starts in mid February and second in July. Participants must wish to become part of the community and to make a contribution. They must also wish to learn the Spanish language.

SALARY: Homestay in Argentine family, private Spanish tutoring, round trip bus ticket from Buenos Aires to location, $100 monthly stipend.

FACILITIES/SUPPORT: Two weeks of intensive ESL training on arrival. Supervision and help with lesson planning throughout the teaching period.

RECRUITMENT: Via internet. Resumé, list of references and a telephone interview with director required.

CONTACT: Cristina Rapela, Director.

GIC ARGENTINA
Av. de Mayo 1370, 3er piso of. 30, Buenos Aires
C1085ABQ

✆ +54 11 5353–9497/ USA: 202 552 1081/ UK: 020 7193 2270

✉ info@gicarg.org

💻 www.gicarg.org

NUMBER OF TEACHERS: 10.

PREFERENCE OF NATIONALITY: None.

QUALIFICATIONS: None.

CONDITIONS OF EMPLOYMENT: 3-month contracts offered. To work 20 hours per week.

SALARY: Unpaid (internships).

FACILITIES/SUPPORT: Accommodation provided in a student dorm, with host families, shared apartments.

RECRUITMENT: Interview required.

CONTACT: Graciela Cerquatti, Director.

INTERACTION LANGUAGE STUDIO
Av. L. N. Alem 428 6 I, Buenos Aires 1003

✆ 11 4311 7220

✉ info@interactionls.com

💻 www.interaction.ls

NUMBER OF TEACHERS: 5–8 foreign teachers and 40 local teachers.

PREFERENCE OF NATIONALITY: American and British.

QUALIFICATIONS: TEFL certificate and some teaching experience.

CONDITIONS OF EMPLOYMENT: Contracts from March to December. Usual hours from 3 to 20 a week.

SALARY: 31 pesos per hour (around $8).

RECRUITMENT: CV by mail, interview and mock lesson. Interviews essential.

CONTACT: Professor Virginia López Grisolia, Director of Studies and Owner.

SWITCH LANGUAGE SCHOOL

Avenida Presidente Roque Sáenz Peña 615, 7° Off. 716, Buenos Aires

☎ +54 11 4393 4125/4902 3437

✉ consultoraswitch@yahoo.com.ar

🖥 www.switchschool.com.ar/
www.consultoraswitch.com.ar

NUMBER OF TEACHERS: 10.

PREFERENCE OF NATIONALITY: None.

QUALIFICATIONS: Recognised TEFL Certificate.

CONDITIONS OF EMPLOYMENT: 9-month minimum contract.

SALARY: 35 pesos per hour.

FACILITIES/SUPPORT: No help given with work permits or finding accommodation.

RECRUITMENT: Interviews with a mock class carried out at the school are essential.

CONTACT: Mara France Garcia, Headmistress.

BOLIVIA

Even the poorest of Latin American nations offers reasonable possibilities to EFL teachers, provided you are prepared to accept a low wage. In contrast to the standard hourly wage of $15–$20 per hour in Santiago or Brasilia, the wages paid by language schools in Bolivia are about 14 bolivianos ($2 at the time of writing). However, a lot of businesses choose to pay their employees in dollars. Many teachers touring South America prefer Bolivia to many other countries for cultural reasons. La Paz is a city with a low cost of living and a colourful social mix. The class structure is immediately apparent with the upper class consisting of people of Spanish descent, the middle class or *mestizos* of mixed Spanish/Bolivian ancestry and the underclass of Indians still wearing their traditional costume. Bolivia may have preserved its traditional culture more successfully than other Latin American countries, but the inequality of wealth distribution has led socialist president Evo Morales to implement stringent wealth distribution measures, including nationalising much of the energy industry. Four of the country's wealthiest regions, including Santa Cruz, have been threatening (or declaring) autonomy in protest.

Only a handful of language schools and a couple of *colegios* (private schools) are listed in the La Paz *Yellow Pages* (www.guia-amarilla.com) and they are unlikely to commit themselves to hiring a teacher without meeting them first. Terms normally last from early February to early September, resuming at the end of September to the beginning of December. The biggest language school in the country is the ultra respectable Centro Boliviano Americano or CBA (Parque Iturralde Zenón 121, La Paz; 2 243 0107; http://cba.edu.bo) with three other locations in La Paz, plus schools in other cities such as Sucre, Cochabamba (www.cbacoch.org) and Santa Cruz (see entry below). Despite its name it hires British and Irish native English speakers as well.

Colegios employ native English speakers for their English departments and tend to pay as much as twice as much as the private language schools. Also, the hours of 8.30am–1.30pm are more convenient.

Mike Martin is one teacher who has fallen under the spell of Bolivia:

I love it here and get on very well with Bolivians. It's only fair to point out, though, that unrest is always here, and there are periodic protests and outbreaks of violence. I should also mention that I now teach free. I am in the fortunate position of being able to do this as I took early retirement and receive a pension, which goes a lot further here than at home. I reckon that you could live reasonably comfortably here for about $600 a month, allowing $150 for an apartment. But be prepared for lots of hassles with the immigration paperwork. When I was charging my students, I charged $3 an hour if they could afford it. A young woman joined and wanted 4 hours a week tuition. A few weeks later I asked her what she was earning and she was paying me about 70 percent of her salary as a part-time professional, so I halved her fees and later halved them again. It's because of stories like this that I eventually decided to teach free. I do think that if you advertised in the local press, you would have a plentiful supply of students as most want to learn English.

Among the volunteer teaching programmes active in Bolivia, WAVA's Language Assistant Bolivia scheme (www.workandvolunteer.com) allows participants to live in a host family and teach them English; the programme fee is £550 for 4–10 weeks. Volunteering Solutions (www.volunteeringsolutions.com/bolivia/volunteer_teaching_english_bolivia.htm) is a new agency based in India but with a global reach. It places volunteer teachers in kindergartens, primary and secondary schools all located in the city of Santa Cruz for up to six months. Inexperienced volunteers with little knowledge of Spanish work as classroom assistants alongside the regular teachers, but more adventurous people may be given a chance to teach a class independently. The application fee here is $200 plus approximately $200 a week to cover living and other expenses.

JONATHAN ALDERMAN was happy to put up with low pay in exchange for the excellent quality of life he found in Bolivia, which he says 'can feel like an idyllic paradise sometimes, because of the climate'. He did things that would be unimaginable at home such as swimming in a pool (in Oruro) whose waters were heated underground by a volcano, attending one of the many carnivals in February and throwing water balloons at the locals.

I first went to Cochabamba as a volunteer to give conversation classes in the city's public university, San Simon. This was through Projects Abroad (www.projects-abroad.co.uk). Everything was organised for me before I arrived, including accommodation and Spanish lessons. This was a great gentle introduction for someone new to the city and to teaching. In the university it is easy to settle in and make friends very quickly.

That only lasted for a few months, but I was sufficiently taken with Cochabamba to want to go back the following January. Before arriving, I had already fixed myself up with a job teaching at the Pan American English Center, which was a genuinely enjoyable place to work because of the relaxed atmosphere. But I became fed up with being paid late and left after only a couple of months to travel a bit. I wasn't breaking any contract, as there was none.

I came back to Cochabamba after a little while exploring South America and took a job in another institute, El Britanico Boliviano de Cultura (BBC, Calle España 171, Cochabamba; 422 0936). This was much better paid, at \$3.50 an hour. The lessons were mostly in the evening, but I was lucky to get some one-to-one classes through the school to teach during the day as well. This school was professionally run and the director paid me on the last day of the month without any hassle. In this school I also taught mostly adults rather than kids. One thing that makes this school stand out from the many others in Cochabamba is the strong emphasis on British rather than American English (as the name would suggest). This is the only institute in Cochabamba where students can take Cambridge exams. BBC often finds it quite hard recruiting teachers, simply because it is difficult to attract teachers to Bolivia due to the low salaries.

I would highly recommend staying and working in Bolivia – and if you are staying in Bolivia, it just has to be Cochabamba, because of the perfect spring-like climate. Teaching Bolivian students can be very fun, though the kids can be boisterous (I especially found teenage boys to be a pain in the arse). When teaching adults, it was nice to be able to establish friendships with the students. I obviously made a very positive impression with one class of students I taught for 4 months at the BBC, because when I left they presented me with a most ornate chess set (with many of the pieces in the shape of native Americans or llamas) – it was the best present I think I have ever received!

Later Jonathan went back to Cochabamba to concentrate on teaching private classes and doing some translation work, while still teaching an hour and a half a day in the Britanico. He concluded, 'if someone wants to earn a decent wage teaching English in Bolivia, one has to turn to private classes.' When he first arrived, he advertised in the local newspaper for private classes charging 30–35 Bolivianos an hour. He says you can expect to be approached in shops and restaurants as well as by your pupils and asked about private classes, but these will generally come from people who would find it a hardship to pay even \$2 an hour. The best place to advertise private English lessons is the Sunday edition of the newspaper El Diario (www.eldiario.net).

Most teachers arrive on a tourist visa and should in theory apply for a work visa. As Jonathan admits, most simply continue to work on a tourist visa:

This is illegal, of course, but there doesn't tend to be a great problem with it, as you are allowed four 90-day stamps in a year. In fact, schools tend to encourage their teachers to work this way, from my experience. One simply has to leave the country and return to get another tourist stamp. If I were asked questions at immigration I would say that I was working on a voluntary project in Bolivia and they would accept it. Of the people I knew who did get a long stay visa they did it off their own bat with no help from their school as far as I know.

LIST OF EMPLOYERS

CAMBRIDGE COLLEGE
Residencias del Norte, Av. Beni entre 4to y 5to Anillos, Santa Cruz de la Sierra
- +591 3 3416541
- esolacademic@cotas.com.bo/ direcciong@ cotas.com.bo/ cambridgecollege@cotas.com.bo
- www.cambridgebolivia.com.bo

NUMBER OF TEACHERS: 12.
PREFERENCE OF NATIONALITY: British.
QUALIFICATIONS: CELTA and 10 years' classroom experience.
CONDITIONS OF EMPLOYMENT: 2-year contract with working hours between 7am and 11am then 5pm and 9pm Monday to Friday.
FACILITIES/SUPPORT: Assistance given finding apartments near the school and the school organises all the relevant paperwork for work permits.
RECRUITMENT: Usually via adverts on TEFL websites. Candidates submit their CV and a model lesson plan and an interview is conducted through video conferencing.
CONTACT: Maria Renee Canedo Landivar, Headmistress.

CENTRO BOLIVIANO AMERICANO – COCHABAMBA
PO Box 1399, Cochabamba
- +591 4 425 6721/ +591 4 422 1288
- www.cbacoch.org

NUMBER OF TEACHERS: 2.
PREFERENCE OF NATIONALITY: American and British.
QUALIFICATIONS: Proficiency in English. Work experience in schools/universities. International Examination Diplomas/ TESOL/TEFL certificates.
CONDITIONS OF EMPLOYMENT: 2-year renewable contract. 6 hours chosen from the following teaching hours: 7–8.30am, 8.30–11.45am, 1.45–5pm, 2.30–3.45pm, 3.45–5pm, 5–6.30pm, 6.45–8.15pm, 6.35–9.45pm.

SALARY: Average of $4 per hour. Varies depending on academic background and teaching experience. Income tax of 13% is not deducted when the teacher submits invoices for the same amount each month. Social security deductions 12.21%.
FACILITIES/SUPPORT: Help given on finding accommodation at orientation. Healthcare provided. Assistance given with work permits. Teachers should come with a *visa de objeto determinado* valid for 30 days to start the paperwork for a work visa. If the teacher comes with a tourist visa, he/she has to change it to a *visa de objeto determinado* at a Bolivian Consulate in a neighbouring country. After that he/she may start with the paperwork for a one- or two-year work visa. School also helps with additional procedure for a work permit which incurs an extra fee.
RECRUITMENT: Via adverts in newspapers. Local interview necessary.
CONTACT: Mery Blum de Schwarz, Academic Director.

SPEAKEASY INSTITUTE
Av. Arce 2047, La Paz
- 2 244 1779
- speakeasyinstitute@yahoo.com
- www.speakeasyinstitute.com

NUMBER OF TEACHERS: 8.
PREFERENCE OF NATIONALITY: None.
QUALIFICATIONS: Minimum CELTA qualification or equivalent plus 1 year's experience.
CONDITIONS OF EMPLOYMENT: 6-month to 1-year contracts available. Maximum 40 teaching hours per week. School open from 7.30am to 9pm Monday to Friday.
SALARY: Bs 3,200 (£225) per month.
FACILITIES/SUPPORT: Help provided with finding accommodation and getting visa.
RECRUITMENT: Via internet. No interview required.
CONTACT: Alix Shand, Coordinator.

BRAZIL

The growth in Brazil's economy in recent years has encouraged the market for English teaching, which is not confined to the major cities of São Paulo and Rio de Janeiro. The upcoming World Cup in 2014 and Olympics in 2016 mean that the education authorities in Brazil are making English language teaching a priority.

There are dozens of Culturas Inglesas in the Associacao Brasileira de Culturas Inglesas (www.culturainglesa.com.br) and many IBEUs (Instituto Brasil-Estadios Unidos) scattered all over the fifth largest country in the world employing 234 teachers to serve 12,000 students. Qualified teachers can send their CVs to teach@ibeu.org.br to find out about vacancies.

Schools in smaller places often notify cooperating institutes in the big cities of any job vacancies for native English speakers. But speculative visits to towns of any size are likely to succeed eventually. Any of the four British Council offices in Brazil (Brasilia, Recife, Rio and São Paulo) may be able to supply a list of Cultura Inglesas and other established schools to people who call on them. The distinguishing feature of Brazilian EFL is the high proportion of well-qualified Brazilian English teachers. Recruiting teachers from overseas is seen to be unjustifiably costly and also very difficult from the visa point of view. Only individuals with very specialised expertise are invited to work in very senior posts.

Visas are a major headache. You are permitted to stay no more than six months on a tourist visa after which you will have to leave the country (usually across the Paraguayan border) or get an extension from the Federal Police. Training visas are an option for some. The Administrative Director of one of Rio de Janeiro's upmarket schools describes the difficulties:

> *Unfortunately, teaching English is not an area the government considers a priority in issuing visas. There are only two situations in which foreigners can teach in Brazil. The first is to work illegally, since there are numerous small schools who can afford to run the risk of hiring illegal foreigners. As a result, pay is usually bad and employment unstable. The alternative is available only to specialists, and is extremely rare. Because we have a webpage, I get requests from foreigners all the time. I basically tell them that it is an adventure here, only for the strong of stomach, and you have to be willing to subject yourself to the unsavoury experiences that go along with working without proper papers. I have come across dozens of foreigners who have been promised work-related visas. In 27 years of living in Brazil, I have never, not once, seen this happen. The only cases I know of where a person has taught legally, it has been when they enter the country with visas issued at the Brazilian consulate in their country of residence.*

Otherwise it will be a case of looking around after you arrive, by using the *Yellow Pages*, expatriate networks or informative websites such as www.gringoes.com, run by expats based in São Paulo. In São Paulo a good source of teaching jobs is the newspaper *Folha de São Paulo* on a Sunday. When job-hunting, expect to go through quite a rigorous interview procedure, as **Jon Cotterill** discovered:

> *When you drop your CV in, the school may ask you to take a written English test on the spot. This can consist of anything up to 100 questions plus a composition section. If you pass the test, you may get invited to a group interview, a 'dinamica de grupo'. This consists of a group of potential teachers (usually Brazilians) and you have to perform various tasks in small teams or pairs. If you are successful then you may be asked to do a two-week training course (usually unpaid). Only after all of this will you be offered work.*

An easier route in is through a 12-month exchange scheme for graduates. The enterprising student youth exchange agency Student Travel Information in Belo Horizonte (+55 31 3261.3035; www.stinter.com.br) runs a Teach & Travel – Work in Brazil programme for English-speaking university graduates to spend a year in one of many locations throughout Brazil. Participants work as language teachers at private language schools and state schools at primary, secondary and college level. The academic year runs from February to December, though the programme start dates are January and July. The salary earned will differ among employers but as a guideline will be R$1,500–R$3,000 (approximately $800–$1,600) per month.

Richard Jenkins, a New Zealander who has learned Portuguese, spent time in Brazil but didn't pursue his idea of looking for teaching work since he decided to move on to Argentina. However, he did meet an American who gave private English lessons in São Paulo charging 50 reais an hour (more than $30 at that time). But he bemoaned the fact that the city was hard to get around (the Metro area has a population of about 20 million) and he insisted that you need to have the students pay in advance for a few lessons. This is because Brazilians are notorious for not showing up, being late or cancelling at the last minute (which they don't see as a problem) so you need to take some precautions so as not to waste your time.

If you want to study Portuguese, you can apply for a student visa which would make it easier to stay on. For example, many foreigners register at the Pontifícia Universidade Católica in Rio de Janeiro (Extension Department, Casa 15, Rua Marques São Vincente 225, Gávea, 22453–900

BARRY O'LEARY, well-travelled TEFLer, arrived in Salvador (northern Brazil) just before Carnaval. (The best time to start work is following the Carnaval, which takes place during the week over Ash Wednesday every February.) He bought a map, borrowed a telephone directory from his hostel and walked round all the 25 language academies with his CV. His luck wasn't as quick as it had been in Ecuador (described later) because most academies couldn't tell how many students they would have until after Carnaval. But Barry managed to find an evening job at an academy outside Salvador and later found two other jobs.

I taught in three Institutes, PEC (www.pec.com.br), Okey Dokey and AEC Idiomas. The business academy sent me to various offices which were all fully equipped and well organised. Generally working conditions were excellent and so was the pay; I received about $8 an hour which was a good rate for Brazil. The pupils were a mixed bag, yet they all had a great sense of humour and participated in the lessons, though some students were there only because their boss wanted them to be and had little interest.

I worked at another academy one afternoon a week. The approach here was to teach English through music, followed by group conversation lessons. Each week the director would translate two or three songs for the students to sing along in English. The students enjoyed this immensely, and I thought it was a very original way to learn. Most students seemed to be more interested in asking me questions about England and my life rather than pay attention to the lessons, but it was a good way for them to improve their fluency. I found Brazilian students very happy-go-lucky people, they were always smiling and interested in learning English.

I was lucky enough to live in the old quarter of Salvador called Pelourinho, which was the hub of the nightlife, but also the hub of any trouble. I lived in a house with 15 people including Brazilians, Nigerians, French and Irish, for which I paid $20 a month and had a brilliant three months.

Rio; 21 529 9212). This is an excellent place to link up with students and advertise classes if you want to offer private lessons (which pay much better than working for an institute).

John Buckley, owner of a printing business in Blackpool, is just one traveller who was surprised at how welcome he was made to feel by a language school when he had no TEFL training or experience:

When I was in Brazil for Christmas and New Year, I thought I would go to the local English school to see what went on, armed with a bunch of roses for the teacher (luckily female) and a little knowledge of Portuguese. Before I knew it, I was teaching English, words, pronunciation, slang and English life in general. This carried on for a few days with the class getting bigger and bigger. I felt like an alien landed from Mars, but what a buzz. I have found my vocation in life and am now looking for a good TEFL training course.

LIST OF EMPLOYERS

ENGLISH ON DEMAND
Rua Paraisopolis 52, Santa Tereza, Belo Horizonte - MG 31010–330
- +55 31 3309 5590
- eod@mail.com
- www.englishondemand.com.br

NUMBER OF TEACHERS: 2.

PREFERENCE OF NATIONALITY: Native English speakers: American, British, Canadian and Australian.

QUALIFICATIONS: Minimum bachelor's degree. Must enjoy teaching even if lacking experience. Preference given to those with teaching experience.

CONDITIONS OF EMPLOYMENT: Minimum 12 months.

SALARY: Minimum $10 per hour. Extra payments depend on experience, attitude towards learning to teach and the commitment to the students.

FACILITIES/SUPPORT: One-bedroom house attached to the school can be made available to a qualified and approved teacher.

RECRUITMENT: Via internet. References will be taken up. Initial interview can be via Skype and also face-to-face interviews.

CONTACT: Val Nogueira (Managing Director) or Maxine Khan (Co-Director).

NEW START COMUNICACOES
Rua Uruguiana 10/1211, Centro, 20050–090 Rio de Janeiro
- 21 2508 6917
- newstart@newstart.com.br
- www.newstart.com.br

NUMBER OF TEACHERS: 10–20.

PREFERENCE OF NATIONALITY: Must be a native English speaker.

QUALIFICATIONS: Preferably CELTA or Trinity TESOL certificate and some classroom experience.

CONDITIONS OF EMPLOYMENT: Minimum 5 months' work.

SALARY: R$30 (£11) per hour.

FACILITIES/SUPPORT: Training in Business English.

RECRUITMENT: Direct application by CV via email and telephone.

CONTACT: Stephanie Crockett, Director of Studies.

SCHUTZ & KANOMATA ESL & PSL
Rua Galvao Costa 85, Santa Cruz do Sul 96810 170
- 51 3715 3366
- sk@sk.com.br
- www.sk.com.br/guests/sk-lcb.html

NUMBER OF TEACHERS: 3 every semester on Brazilian Language and Culture Program.

PREFERENCE OF NATIONALITY: Canadian, American and British.

QUALIFICATIONS: Main qualification is personality; must be communicative, considerate and interested in making friends. ESL teaching experience desirable.

CONDITIONS OF EMPLOYMENT: 5 or 10-month contracts. 20 hours per week, mostly in the evenings.

SALARY: Average net income above the cost of living.

FACILITIES/SUPPORT: Programme provides accommodation, meals and occasional weekend tours. Advice given on appropriate visas, e.g. visitor visa acceptable for 5-month programme and trainee visa for 10-month one.

RECRUITMENT: Strong internet exposure. Also former teacher in Canada acts as agent.

CONTACT: Ricardo Schütz, Principal.

SPEAKING - CENTRO DE CULTURA AMERICANA

R. Cel. Renno, 321 Centro, Itajuba, Minas Gerais
37500 050

☎ +55 35 3621 3354

✉ speakingidiomas@yahoo.com.br

💻 www.speaking.com.br

NUMBER OF ESL TEACHERS: 2–3 per year.

PREFERENCE OF NATIONALITY: American, Canadian and British.

QUALIFICATIONS: TESL or similar.

CONDITIONS OF EMPLOYMENT: Standard commitment February to December. 38 hours per week, Monday to Saturday.

SALARY: R$16 ($8) per hour net. Wage is enough for living in a small town in Brazil.

FACILITIES/SUPPORT: School provides a small furnished studio flat with utilities, housekeeper, laundry and internet connection; or helps with living expenses.

RECRUITMENT: By email or via ESL websites.

CONTACT: Dagmar Andrade, Director.

STI - STUDENT TRAVEL INFORMATION LTDA

Rua Bernardo Guimarães, 911- Loja 25 - Belo
Horizonte MG 30140.081

☎ +55 31 3261 3035

✉ info@stinter.com.br

💻 www.stinter.com.br

Teach and Travel in Brazil programme managed by student travel agency and culture exchange organisation.

NUMBER OF TEACHERS: 50 teachers for language schools, elementary and high schools and colleges, in small or large cities in one of four regions of Brazil where programme operates.

PREFERENCE OF NATIONALITY: American, British, Canadian, Irish, New Zealander and Australian.

QUALIFICATIONS: Must have a university degree plus work experience that satisfies certain criteria, e.g. 1 year of work experience in the same field as your education, or have done a 360+ – hour postgraduate training course or have 3 years of professional experience in a cultural or artistic position.

CONDITIONS OF EMPLOYMENT: Minimum 1-year contract, maximum 2. Normal 8-hour working day. Start dates July and January (for terms beginning August and February).

SALARY: R$1,500–R$3,000 (US$800–US$1,600) per month. Each school offers different benefits. 4-weeks paid vacation for 12-month contracts. Extra month's salary (*décimo terceiro*) paid as bonus in December.

FACILITIES/SUPPORT: 2-day pre-term group training on arrival, held in São Paulo or Belo Horizonte, plus 1–2 week training at destination school. Most schools assist teachers with accommodation. STI assists with visas which must be applied for at a Brazilian consulate abroad. Medical insurance provided.

RECRUITMENT: Candidates can be interviewed by Skype. Applications due at least a month before departure.

CONTACT: Marco Costa, Director.

CHILE

Chile's dynamic economy is flourishing and is still attracting foreign (mainly American) investment. In terms of market competitiveness, Chile ranks most highly among South American countries. As commercial, touristic and cultural contacts with the outside world have increased, so has the demand for the English language. The most booming market is for business English, though there is also demand for teachers of children, created largely by the Chilean government lowering the age at which English is taught in state schools from 7th grade to 5th grade.

The ongoing drive to raise the level of English language teaching throughout the country continues with the Chilean Ministry of Education's major initiative, the *Programa Inglés Abre Puertas* ('English Opens Doors'). This ambitious programme aims to provide English immersion courses in state schools in small towns and villages throughout Chile and enlists the help of many native English speakers. Foreign graduates (or non-graduates in the case of summer placements) work alongside local teachers in classrooms to help improve listening and speaking skills among pupils. Volunteers receive a small monthly stipend of 85,500 pesos (US$150) in addition to free room and board. Prospective volunteers can apply directly via the Volunteer Centre in Santiago (+56 2 487 5091; Skype EnglishOpensDoors; voluntarios@mineduc.cl; www.puntonorte.cl/voluntarios) or through partner organisations in North America such as those listed here.

TEFL Institute, 1906 W. Irving Park Boulevard, Chicago, Illinois 60613, USA (773 880 5141; www.teflinstitute.com). Participants must enrol in a TEFL Institute online or 4-week TEFL training course. Chile summer programme fee is US$50–$250 depending on date of registration.

Cultural Embrace, Austin, Texas, USA (+1 888 214 8570; www.culturalembrace.com).

Bridge-Linguatec (www.bridgetefl.com/english-opens-doors.php).

Centre for Cultural Interchange, Chicago, Illinois, USA (www.cci-exchange.com/teachinchile. aspx).

Note that the Open Doors programme does not enjoy universal acclaim. One prominent ELT recruiter in Canada, Footprints Recruiting, took the decision not to recruit for this programme on the grounds that teachers were not fairly remunerated and supported in a serious way; the argument can be read at www.footprintsrecruiting.com/all-teaching-jobs/teaching-jobs-in-chile/97/no-teaching-jobs-in-chile-with-footprint. Apart from this programme operating in state schools, most of the opportunities are in the commercial sector and the majority of those are in the capital Santiago where there are scores of private language schools. Some relevant institutes can also be found in the Valparaiso-Viña del Mar area. There will be less competition for teaching vacancies and a lower cost of living in smaller places such as the aptly named La Serena in the dry north of the country, or other towns such as Arica, Iquique, Antofagasta, Talca, Concepción, Valdivia, Osorno and Punta Arenas, all of which have possibilities for teachers, albeit on a smaller scale. Some course providers in Santiago serve clients in Valparaiso and their teachers either commute to 'Valpo' twice a week or live there.

The Instituto Chileno-Británico de Cultura in Santiago recruits only qualified teachers, and has a good library which incorporates the British Council's resource library for teachers; anyone prepared to pay the membership fee can borrow materials, though many schools in Santiago have good libraries themselves. Native English speaker teachers are also hired by the Institutos Chileno-Britanico de Cultura in Concepcion (britanico@ibritanico.com), Arica (www.britanicoarica.cl) and Viña del Mar (www.institutochilenobritanico.cl).

South American language schools tend to prefer face-to-face meetings rather than emails and phone calls. **Heidi Resetarits** typed 'English schools in Santiago' into a search engine, came up with a huge list of language schools in areas she wanted to apply to and then dropped off resumés in person.

I actually got an interview on the spot at the second school I applied to... and I happened to just walk by it – it wasn't even on my list! Santiago is a very modern city and new schools are popping up all the time. It's worth it just to walk around town and see what's there. I know that South Americans appreciate face-to-face meetings rather than emails and phone calls, so I walked in and asked to meet with a director. I decided to stay and chat a bit with the receptionist, and he made me an appointment for the next day.

The interview was a face-to-face with the director of the school [Comunicorp, included below]. After we talked about my resumé and a bit about my teaching experience, we set up a teaching practice (he chose a topic and a student) for the next day. I got the job within 3 days.

Doug Burgess went job hunting in Santiago, armed with a CELTA he had acquired at home in Cambridge and some experience. He had an interview with both Burford Corporate Training (www. burford.cl) and EF English First (see entry). Burford works exclusively from its own site, whereas about 60% of English First's classes are in offices. English First offered Doug a contract for 12 months with work visa and a rate of 5,500 pesos an hour, more if he had to travel more than two metro stations or worked at their other campus. Burford did not offer a contract: their rate of pay was 4,000 pesos an hour which would have gone up to 6,000 after a three-month probationary period. In the end, Doug accepted another offer from the prestigious Instituto Chileno-Británico de Cultura, paying 5,400 pesos an hour, more if he teaches high level classes, on Saturdays or in another branch of the British Institute. His contract is for 15 hours which is enough to secure a work visa, although he has the option of working up to 30 hours or more. Before Doug secured a full-time teaching job, he participated in an exchange programme run by Woodward School, Providencia. For every Spanish lesson he received, he gave an English lesson, and went from being a complete beginner in the language to fairly competent. Another school that operates an exchange programme is the Chileno Swiss Institute.

A further possibility is to teach at English-medium *colegios*, where a longer commitment will be necessary and a reasonable salary paid. Although they employ mainly certified teachers, often hired at recruitment fairs and through international advertising, they do need some native English speakers for their English departments. For example, **Eleanor Padfield** from Cambridge was determined to work abroad after finishing her A levels but did not want to go through an agency where she would be with lots of other British students. After spending the first half of her year in Salamanca, Spain, she sent emails in Spanish all over the world to find something to do, preferably in Latin America. Of the many schools and language schools she contacted, one of the few to reply was the Redland School, an upmarket private school. Although they told her that they didn't usually accept gap year students (since so many previous gappers had left prematurely to travel), they made an exception for Eleanor when she promised to stick it out till the end of the term beginning in March and ending in August. When June rolled round, she was tempted to leave early but her conscience (or her mother's exhortations) persuaded her to keep her promise, trying to see as much of the country as she could in her days off.

Heidi Resetarits was an English teacher for both the Universidad de Las Americas and Comunicorp, Santiago simultaneously:

I had two sets of students. My students from the institute were mainly businessmen who needed to learn English for work. These men were preoccupied with work but used their lunch breaks to take classes. They do want to learn, but more often than not, work took priority. I had a few women who were very dedicated and learned rather quickly.

I also taught 4th year college students how to write essays and give public speeches. They were at a different level than my business students (they were majoring in Teaching English) and they had a better grasp of the language. They were about 50–50 with effort and participation, but I could also have higher expectations for them. I really enjoyed working with these students.

The commercial institutes in Santiago vary greatly in size, reliability in their treatment of employees and teaching methods. Newcomers to the city quickly learn which are the better schools and gradually acquire more hours with them. In-company teaching usually takes place early in the morning; middle-ranking staff tend to be taught before the official working day begins while directors and higher-ranking executives take their classes at a more civilised mid-morning hour. Most teachers enjoy the variety of off-site teaching rather than classroom teaching which tends to be more textbook-based.

After completing the TEFL certificate course at the American Language Institute in San Diego, **Brianna Antman** heard about vacancies teaching business people at Comunicorp in Santiago, Chile. She sent her CV to the director and after a phone interview was given a contract to work for the standard academic year:

> *Most of my classes were one-on-one with managers, CEOs and other employees of large companies held in their offices. We were given a course summary sheet for each level which described the grammar points and functions that we were supposed to cover. Since we worked in a business atmosphere we were required to dress formally and adapt to the professional/business world.*
>
> *I found accommodation in the local newspaper 'El Mercurio'. However, most teachers found their accommodation through word of mouth and/or friends who were already here. Because the school is one of the higher paying institutes in Santiago, the wages of 6,000 pesos an hour were quite decent, enough to live off and travel. The school had a teacher's room filled with a plethora of resources, books, shared lessons on the computer, CDs, and incredibly experienced people in the field. All of the books were scanned onto the computer, thus making it quite easy to find/plan lessons.*

The academic year runs from March to December with a two-week winter holiday in July and one week recess in mid-September, so the best time to apply for a contract is the end of February. There are 19 British curriculum schools listed on the website of the Association of British Schools in Chile (www.absch.cl). The Santiago *Yellow Pages* are a useful source; look up Instituto de Idiomas or check online www.chilnet.cl/rc/port_select_companies.asp?acti_code=779.

Non-contractual work is usually paid by the hour, starting at 5,000 pesos and rising to 8,000 pesos. Established teachers working for universities such as UNIACC in Providencia can top 15,000 pesos but this is rare. The cost of living is higher than in many other places on the continent but teachers can still support themselves. **Heidi Resetarits** says that '*you won't be able to do much saving in South America in general*', and recommends that you don't move to Chile without savings if you want to have fun and money to travel. Normally 10% of earnings must be paid in tax, which in some cases can be reclaimed the following April/May.

Usually the CELTA certificate or equivalent is a minimum requirement for anyone considering working in the private sector. However, those looking to work within the state system of education will find that CELTA qualifications will not be accepted. In Chile a teaching degree takes five years, and school directors tend to look quite disparagingly upon one month/120 hour courses. A worthwhile volunteer teaching scheme is run by Voluntarios de Esperanza (VE; Carabineros de Chile 33, Santiago; 2 717 99 37; www.ve-global.org). VE works with partner institutions to place volunteers to work with children, including teaching English, for a minimum of four months beginning in September, January and May. The application process is competitive and no registration fee is charged.

RED TAPE

Most job-seekers arrive on a tourist visa valid for 90 days. Note that on entry some nationalities (not Britons) will have to pay a one-off 'reciprocity tax', e.g. $100 for Americans, $55 for Canadians. Once you find a job, the most common visa to apply for is the *Visa Sujeta a Contrato* (subject to contract visa) for which you will need to take a notarised copy of a contract from an employer that shows a minimum salary of 100,000 pesos a month to the *Departamento de Extrajería*. The cost varies among nationalities: in this case Americans get it for free whereas Britons pay $74. If you are able to commit yourself for a year, your employer may be willing to help you obtain the more flexible temporary residents visa. Many teachers who enter the country on a tourist visa end up working for employers who will not assist. Before their 90 days is up, they simply get a new tourist visa by crossing the border to Mendoza, Argentina. Good detailed visa information is available on the website of the TEFL training centre, the TEFL Academy, in Santiago (www.tefl-academy.com). If you are from New Zealand, Australia or Canada you can apply for a working holiday visa which allows you to work anywhere and to live and work without a contract for one year.

Rarely, people are offered a job before arrival. If this is the case, there are two ways to obtain the appropriate visa permit. Either your employer submits the application at the Ministry of Foreign Affairs in Chile (Direccion de Asuntos Consulares y de Imigracion, Bandera 46, Santiago) or you apply at the Chilean Consulate in your country of origin. You will need a signed and notarised work contract and a full medical report. If granted, the visa will be valid for one year. After that you may be eligible for a *visacion de residencia* which allows an unlimited stay.

ADVERTISING FOR PRIVATE CLIENTS

The average rate for private lessons is about 10,000–12,000 pesos per hour. There are many ways to meet the expatriate community from playing cricket at the Prince of Wales Club to frequenting the English language bookshop Books and Bits on Av Apoquindo in Santiago (www.booksandbits.cl).

You can advertise for private clients in *El Mercurio*, the leading quality daily. Other newspapers such as *La Epoca* and *La Tercera* have classified ads sections which will cost slightly less than *El Mercurio*. There is a magazine called *El Rastro*, consisting of nothing but advertisements, to which you can phone in a small advert free of charge (though the response may be less than spectacular).

Advertising at your embassy has helped some teachers. A useful option is to find a supermarket which has a noticeboard for small advertisements in their entrance halls. For example the Lider and Jumbo chains of stores have such noticeboards. Lider is located on the corner of Avenida Pedro de Valdivia and Bilbao, while Jumbo is on the corner of Portugal and Diagonal Paraguay. If you can translate between English and Spanish, it will be worth advertising yourself as a translator as well. The best way to find private clients, however, is by word of mouth.

LEISURE TIME

Although Santiago is cosmopolitan and modern, there are pockets of poverty and the men can be aggressive, shouting across the street at women. The quality of life however, is enviable. **Brianna Antman** points out that, 'Chile has a lot of beautiful places to visit and enjoy nature. Since the Andes are so close, there are a lot of activities in the mountains (horseback riding, trekking, white water rafting, etc). **Heidi Resetarits** managed to keep herself pleasantly busy in her spare time:

> I planned trips all over Chile at least once a week. I wrote for a magazine. I joined a gym and a swim team. I bought a bike and rode around town. I also spent a lot of time drinking coffee, pisco sours and/ or wine on patios, reading or just enjoying the day. Santiago is a great city to spend time in, and it is very easy to get around in and relatively safe. The people are friendly and want to know who you are and where you are from. My favourite days were spent walking to a random café, meeting a friend and letting that meeting go into a warm summer Santiago night.

LIST OF EMPLOYERS

ACADEMIA DE IDIOMAS DEL NORTE
Ramirez 1345, Iquique
+56 57 411 827
secretaria@languages.cl
www.languages.cl

NUMBER OF TEACHERS: 4.
PREFERENCE OF NATIONALITY: Native English speakers.
QUALIFICATIONS: Recognised TEFL certificate.
CONDITIONS OF EMPLOYMENT: 6–9-month contracts with
6 working hours per day.
FACILITIES/SUPPORT: Information on homestay families,
flats, hotels, etc. is given. Shared apartments with other
teachers sometimes available. Work contract provided in
order to get work permits.
RECRUITMENT: Interviews are essential and usually held in
Chile but can be conducted by telephone or Skype.

CHILENGLISH
Ramón Carnicer 81, Of. 607, Providencia, Santiago
+56 2 655 1676
chilenglish@chilenglish.com
www.chilenglish.com

NUMBER OF TEACHERS: 15.
PREFERENCE OF NATIONALITY: None.
QUALIFICATIONS: TEFL-certified teachers with previous
experience.
CONDITIONS OF EMPLOYMENT: Contract length is negotiable.
Full-time is 25–30 hours per week with classes between 8am
and 9pm, Monday to Friday. Some Saturday work available.
SALARY: Average 500,000 Chilean pesos per month.
FACILITIES/SUPPORT: Assistance given with work permits
and guidance when filling in relevant paperwork.
RECRUITMENT: Interviews essential.
CONTACT: Craig Wilson, Director.

COMUNICORP
Las Urbinas 68, Providencia, Santiago
2 234 1010
dgreenst@comunicorp.cl
www.comunicorp.cl

NUMBER OF TEACHERS: Approximately 30.
PREFERENCE OF NATIONALITY: None. Company prefers
to have a wide variety of cultures and accents represented
on the staff.
QUALIFICATIONS: At least one of the following: CELTA,
TEFL certificate, MA in TESOL, MA in Education, MA in
Communicative Disorders, and at least one year of
classroom EFL experience, preferably with adult Business
English students.
CONDITIONS OF EMPLOYMENT: Standard contract is
6–9 months. Hours are usually spread out during the day.
Most business students prefer to have classes at the peak
hours which are: 8:30–10am, 1–2:30pm, 6–7:30pm. Other
students, who are more flexible, take classes during the off-
peak hours from 10am to 11:30am and from 3pm to 4:30pm.
SALARY: Varies according to classroom experience, degree
held, and time with the company. The lowest salary would be
475,000 Chilean pesos per month up to 580,000 Chilean
pesos per month. There are additional benefits such as a
travel bonus at the end of the contract for those hired from
abroad and a monthly transportation budget. Taxes are less
than 5% and social security is not an issue if the teacher has
a home pension plan.
FACILITIES/SUPPORT: Assistance with finding accommodation. School assists with processing the work visa.
RECRUITMENT: Internet and word of mouth.
CONTACT: Diane Greenstein, Academic Director.

EES EXECUTIVE ENGLISH SOLUTIONS
Luis Thayer Ojeda 0130 of. 707 -708 Providencia-
Santiago
2 3357781
hspencer@ees.cl
www.ees.cl

NUMBER OF TEACHERS: 20–30.
PREFERENCE OF NATIONALITY: None.
QUALIFICATIONS: 4+ year degree, TSOL, CELTA or TEFL
and 1+ year's experience preferred.
CONDITIONS OF EMPLOYMENT: Standard contracts are
6–12 months. The usual hours are mornings, lunch time and
evenings, Monday to Friday.

SALARY: 6,000 to 8,000 Chilean pesos per hour, 25–30 hours per week. Deductions of 10% refundable with filing of tax return.

FACILITIES/SUPPORT: Company will provide proof of employment for lease and rental agreement. All foreign employees receive a Chilean work visa.

RECRUITMENT: In person interview.

CONTACT: Howard H. Spencer, Director of Studies.

EF ENGLISH FIRST
Hernando de Aguirre 215, Providencia, Santiago
☏ 2 374 2180
and Av del Condor 844, Ciudad Empresarial, Huechuraba, Santiago
☏ 2 242 8380
🖱 chile@ef.com
🖥 www.ef-chile.cl/www.englishfirst.com

NUMBER OF TEACHERS: 35–40.

PREFERENCE OF NATIONALITY: None (native English preferred).

QUALIFICATIONS: TEFL/TESOL/CELTA (preferably not online). At least 1 year's EFL experience preferred.

CONDITIONS OF EMPLOYMENT: 9, 12 months or unlimited contracts. Full-time 20–30 hours per week or part-time flexible hours.

SALARY: 500,000 Chilean pesos a month. Part-time 5,500–10,000 pesos per hour, depending on location. Minimum 10% tax deducted.

FACILITIES/SUPPORT: Advice given on accommodation and help with visa procurement from Extranjeria for full-time teachers. Free unlimited internet access and Spanish lessons at a minimum cost.

RECRUITMENT: Locally only (no advance contracts).

CONTACT: Erik Petko, School Director (erik.petko@ef.com).

ENGLISH FOR LIFE
Av. Tobalaba 1829, Santiago
☏ 2 415 0416
🖱 dos@englishforlife.cl
🖥 www.englishforlife.cl

Associate Member of International House.

NUMBER OF TEACHERS: Around 15.

PREFERENCE OF NATIONALITY: None.

QUALIFICATIONS: CELTA, Trinity TESOL or IH certificate are preferred and English for Life also offers its own teacher training programme. More experienced teachers have the possibility of moving into more senior roles or teacher training.

CONDITIONS OF EMPLOYMENT: Contract is initially for one academic year (9 months). The contract specifies an agreed number of contact (teaching) hours.

SALARY: Varies with number of contracted hours. Bonus may be paid depending on location of teaching in Santiago. Teachers are guaranteed a base salary, for example, for an 18 hour contract with extra hours and bonuses paid in addition. 7% deduction for health insurance. Overtime paid on hours worked over 24 per week.

FACILITIES/SUPPORT: Accommodation and flights are not paid for by the school, although help and advice are given in finding suitable accommodation. Teachers enter on a tourist visa and then apply for a work permit/visa when they have signed the contract. Teachers are entitled to paid holiday and sick leave on a pro-rata basis. Full academic support is given, e.g. employer pays for teachers to attend meetings and teacher development sessions which are run once a week by in-house teacher trainer. The school is easily accessible by metro and bus. School has a garden available to staff for lesson preparation, barbecues, etc. Free wifi access and computers. DOS willing to supervise teachers who wish to do the online DELTA or other career development courses.

RECRUITMENT: Through IHWO (www.ihworld.com/recruitment), www.tefl.com or direct application throughout the year. CVs should be sent to the DOS (dos@englishforlife.cl) who will contact suitable candidates for interview.

CONTACT: Serina Gafoor, Director of Studies.

FISCHER ENGLISH INSTITUTE
Cirujano Guzmán 49 Providencia, Santiago de Chile
☏ 2 235 6667/2 235 9812
🖱 contacto@fischerinstitute.cl
🖥 www.fischerinstitute.cl

NUMBER OF TEACHERS: 30.

PREFERENCE OF NATIONALITY: USA.

QUALIFICATIONS: University degree and TEFL certificate or similar and 1 year's experience in teaching.

CONDITIONS OF EMPLOYMENT: Minimum 1-year contract, 20 hours a week.

FACILITIES/SUPPORT: None.

RECRUITMENT: References, preferably from school abroad. Interviews essential, carried out in Santiago.

CONTACT: Celsa Contreras, Academic Secretary.

INSTITUTO CHILENO-BRITANICO DE CULTURA
Huerfanos 554 (Santa Lucia), Santiago
- ☎ 2 413 2350
- 🖰 mcuevas@britanico.cl
- 💻 www.britanico.cl

Other branches in Las Condes, La Florida, Nuñoa, Maipu and Providencia.

NUMBER OF TEACHERS: 10.

PREFERENCE OF NATIONALITY: None, but should be native English speaker.

QUALIFICATIONS: A degree in English or Modern Languages, plus a TEFL qualification. However, experience is valued more than TEFL qualification.

CONDITIONS OF EMPLOYMENT: 1 year, March to February. 30 teaching hours per week mostly evenings.

SALARY: £700 per month.

FACILITIES/SUPPORT: Help with finding accommodation is provided. Teachers are provided with a settling-in grant towards their accommodation.

RECRUITMENT: Usually on the spot.

INSTITUTO CHILENO-NORTEAMERICANO DE CULTURA
Moneda No. 1467, Santiago
- ☎ 2 696 3215
- 🖰 info@norteamericano.cl
- 💻 www.norteamericano.cl

NUMBER OF TEACHERS: 15–20.

PREFERENCE OF NATIONALITY: American and Canadian.

QUALIFICATIONS: BA in Education or TESL/TEFL and 6 months' teaching experience, or a bachelor's degree in related field with certificate in TESL/TEFL and 2 years' teaching experience.

CONDITIONS OF EMPLOYMENT: 1-year contracts starting in March. 30 hours per week. Peak hours of work early morning and early evening, and some Saturdays. Classes for adults, children, teens, business and academic English.

SALARY: Equivalent of US$1,100 per month in Chilean pesos.

FACILITIES/SUPPORT: Assistance given in obtaining visas. Training provided. Teacher's room with computers, email access and cafeteria privileges.

RECRUITMENT: Direct application by mail, email, phone or fax. Applicants should send cover letter, resumé, recent photo, copy of diplomas/certificates and letters of reference from recent employers.

REDLAND SCHOOL
Camino el Alba 11357, Las Condes, Santiago
- ☎ 2 959 8500
- 🖰 secretaria_rector@redland.cl
- 💻 www.redland.cl

NUMBER OF TEACHERS: 72 in total.

PREFERENCE OF NATIONALITY: British or other nationalities with English as a first language.

QUALIFICATIONS: University degree and teaching qualification. Pre- and post-university students also considered for gap year placements.

CONDITIONS OF EMPLOYMENT: 1–3-year contract. Classes run from 8am to 3.30pm or 5pm. Pupils aged 4–18.

SALARY: On application.

FACILITIES/SUPPORT: Assistance finding accommodation can be offered.

RECRUITMENT: Via email in first instance.

TEACHING CHILE
Av. Vitacura 3355, Dept 113, Santiago
- ☎ 720 221 3831 (US phone number routes calls to Santiago office); 020 8150 6981 (UK phone number routes calls to Santiago office)
- 💻 www.teachingchile.com

NUMBER OF TEACHERS: Approximately 90 native English-speaking teachers per year.

PREFERENCE OF NATIONALITY: None. To date, TeachingChile have placed teachers from Australia, Canada, England, Ireland, New Zealand, Scotland and the USA.

QUALIFICATIONS: Varies among schools. Overall, applicants should be a graduate of a university or in their final year of undergraduate studies, ESL/TEFL/TESOL certification and teaching experience are desired but not required. Spanish language skills are not required for classroom instruction but elementary conversational language skills are recommended for the teacher's cultural enjoyment.

CONDITIONS OF EMPLOYMENT: Minimum 6-month contract. The majority of teachers choose a 1-year contract. All contracts are renewable directly with the teaching institution assuming the school has positions available and the teacher has a good rapport with the employer and students.

SALARY: Minimum 335,000 Chilean pesos per month for a base of 15 hours of classroom time per week. For longer hours teachers can earn up to 450,000 pesos. Some schools deduct 13% for tax and an optional 7% for medical insurance, but salaries are adjusted accordingly and teachers make about the same net salary.

FACILITIES/SUPPORT: Guaranteed work contract, visa processing assistance, and accommodation arrangements are in place before the teacher leaves home. TeachingChile provides assistance with accommodation and a pre-paid transfer from Santiago airport to the first night's accommodation.

RECRUITMENT: Via the internet, universities and ESL/TEFL/TESOL job placement websites. Applicants submit an application package available from TeachingChile's website and are interviewed by telephone.

CONTACT: Bruce Thompson, Managing Director.

COLOMBIA

Since most people's only associations with Colombia are with crime and violence, it is not surprising to learn that teaching institutes in that country sometimes have trouble attracting qualified foreign teachers. Foreign teachers are extremely unlikely to become involved in any drug-inspired tensions but are guaranteed to be welcomed by the locals. Memories will be of a local carnival rather than of a neighbourhood shoot-out. **Dave Crowder** takes strong exception to knee-jerk negative reactions to his adopted country and to the warning contained in US and UK embassy literature:

I have found the people of Colombia to be universally friendly and helpful to strangers. Unlike the USA, the welcome here is genuine, open and amicable, and the people are genuinely interested in the novelty of a stranger among them. There is no more drug trafficking in Medellín where I live than in any other major city anywhere in the world (I used to live in Miami where there is much more drug gang activity). As a matter of fact, I will extend my comments about Medellín to every part of the nation that I have visited, which is everywhere but the few FARC/ELN-controlled areas in the boondocks.

With the expansion of trade (called *Apertura*), interest in English has increased, as evidenced by the popularity of English language media like newspapers and radio stations. However, a local law prohibits more than a 30%+ participation of foreign nationals in a school, so jobs for native English speakers are fewer than demand would seem to suggest. First Class English (see list of organisations) employs about 24 teachers, but can only offer 6 jobs to native English speakers without dual citizenship.

Colombia is more strongly oriented towards the USA than elsewhere in South America, with an extensive network of Colombian-American Cultural Centers around the country. However, **Charles Seville** from Oxford, who spent a year as an English language assistant at the University de Los Llanos in Villavicencio, was struck by how keen Colombians were to learn British English. There is a British Council Teaching Centre in Bogotá, whose market is primarily university students and young learners (www.britishcouncil.org.co) but which also runs conversation clubs. At the time of writing it was hiring teachers for an August 2010 start, offering a salary of between about 4,300,000 to 5,760,000 Colombian pesos per month; the contact email was mhairi-anne.gonzalez@britishcouncil.org.co.

It is possible to access the Colombian *Yellow Pages* on the internet (www.quehubo.com) which might provide a starting place for finding school addresses. The website www.poorbuthappy.com contains a long list of language schools in Medellín, though as of April 2010 the website has closed and is only useful as an archive. Some global EFL companies have a strong presence in Colombia. EF Education First is based at the World Trade Center (Calle 100 # 8a-55, Torre C – Oficina 801, Bogotá; 1 616 1130; www.ef.com.co) and Berlitz runs 11 centres, including five in Bogotá.

The main newspaper *El Tiempo* carries adverts for language schools in the capital. There are plenty of local language schools where untrained native English speakers can find work, but there are two main disadvantages. Wages and conditions can be very poor; many schools offer a few thousand pesos an hour (possibly about US$3.50), though the schools listed below offer more attractive salaries, with an upper limit of 18,500 Colombian pesos per hour (US$9). The second problem is the red tape. As usual, temporary working visas must be applied for in your country of residence. The Colombian Consulate in London has information about the requirements on their website (www.colombianconsulate.co.uk), which includes an undertaking by the employer to bear the cost of repatriation if the visa is cancelled and a letter from the Ministry of Work & Social Security testifying that the Colombian employer is not exceeding the legal limit on foreign employees. The visa fee is £130. If a teacher intends to stay in Colombia longer than six months, he or she must register in person at

DAS, the Colombian equivalent of the FBI, within 30 days of arrival. Approval will mean that you are entitled to acquire a *Cédula de Extranjería* (foreigners' ID).

Several TEFL training courses are offered in Colombia. ISSO in Bogotá, Cali, Medellín and Barranquilla (see Directory of Training Courses) is affiliated to ILCA (International Language Academy of Canada) and promises free job placement in Colombia.

LIST OF EMPLOYERS

FIRST CLASS ENGLISH
Carrera 12 # 93 - 78 Oficina 407, 407 Bogotá
✆ 1 6232380
🖰 gerencia@fcecolombia.com
🖥 www.fcecolombia.com

NUMBER OF TEACHERS: 24+ native English speakers (a proportion grant is required due to the local laws that prohibit a 30%+ participation of foreign nationals in the school). On average the school has space for at least 6 foreign national teachers who do not have dual citizenship.

PREFERENCE OF NATIONALITY: American and British.

QUALIFICATIONS: At least 1 year's teaching experience, preferably with executives/professional, CELTA, ICELT certification is a plus. But the bottom line is that the candidate must have 3+ year college/university degree, hopefully in business or related areas.

CONDITIONS OF EMPLOYMENT: Minimum 1 year, if volunteering a minimum of 4 months. Up to 8 hours of teaching within the hours of 6am to 9pm.

SALARY: Contracted hourly pay from $15,000 to $18,500 Colombian pesos per hour, disbursed every 15 days. The *retencion* (tax) deduction, specific to this type of contract, is about 7% of income.

FACILITIES/SUPPORT: Can assist with accommodation if necessary on a case-by-case basis. School provides paperwork for working visa, however the teacher is required to activate the visa by travelling to a vicinity country and going to the local consulate. This process can take up to 60 days in total from the moment the visa is requested.

RECRUITMENT: Email requests and walk-ins. An interview – possible by phone – is followed by 20-hour mandatory selection process. The process includes training, simulated class, teaching crash course and administrative instruction.

CONTACT: Andrew Diaz, Director.

INSTITUTO DE IDIOMAS (UNIVERSIDAD DEL NORTE)
Km 5 Via Pto Colombia, Barranquilla
✆ 5 3509736/5 3598852
🖰 arey@uninorte.edu.co
🖥 www.uninorte.edu.co/extensiones/idiomas

NUMBER OF TEACHERS: Around 5 a year.

PREFERENCE OF NATIONALITY: None.

QUALIFICATIONS: Master's degree in TESOL, Linguistics, Psychology, English, Elementary/Bilingual Education, or related areas. Must have certified experience teaching EFL, preferably outside the USA. Must be a native English speaker; be able to teach and evaluate students effectively; and have experience using language lab equipment.

CONDITIONS OF EMPLOYMENT: Minimum 1 year. 8 hours a day depending on classes assigned. Most likely 9am–5pm.

SALARY: Depends on qualifications. Other benefits include a living allowance of around $200 for rent, ticket and visa issuing costs. The university pays in Colombian pesos.

FACILITIES/SUPPORT: University recommends a rental agency and will serves as a guarantor. When teachers arrive, the university pays for a hotel for 1 week. The university also provides transport and documentation needed for the working visa.

RECRUITMENT: Via internet websites such as www.studyabroad.com. Interviews through Skype or videoconferencing are required. References are also checked.

CONTACT: Lourdes Rey, Academic Coordinator.

ECUADOR

Compared with its neighbours, Peru and Colombia, Ecuador represents an oasis of political stability. The economy has benefitted since it was forced to adopt the US dollar as the national currency. Teaching wages are still low, but obviously EFL teachers do not go to Ecuador to save money and it is still possible to live on the wages paid. For example, a night in a budget hotel costs from $9 and a tasty meal costs $5.

Demand for English continues to thrive, particularly for American English, in the capital Quito, the second city Guayaquil and in the picturesque city and cultural centre of Cuenca in the southern Sierra. The majority of teaching is of university students and the business community whose classes are usually scheduled early in the morning (starting at 7am) to avoid the equatorial heat of the day and again in the late afternoon and evening. Many schools are owned and run by expatriates since there are few legal restrictions on foreigners running businesses.

BARRY O'LEARY, on arriving in Quito visited a tourist agency that had the addresses of all the possible academies and institutes. He started his first TEFL job-hunt armed only with a basic TEFL certificate and speaking very little Spanish. As luck would have it he found two jobs in 24 hours just by walking round the city with copies of his CV:

I can still remember the buzz I felt when José, my first employer, said 'Yeah we're looking for someone to start next week.' I couldn't quite believe it. With this institute there wasn't really a formal interview or application process. With another school I had a basic interview to make sure I could speak and wasn't a monster, they didn't even ask for my TEFL certificate. In Ecuador everyone I knew was working without a work visa. I remember being worried about telling them I was only staying for three months but they were just happy to have a native speaker teaching their students.

The teaching varied. In one school I was responsible for conversation classes. I had no guidance with the type of lessons they wanted so had to use resources from my course, the internet and my imagination. In every lesson a local teacher was there to help with any language barriers. The working conditions were very relaxed, no lesson plans or meetings, I was just given a timetable and left to get on with it. As long as the students were smiling I was seen to be a good teacher.

I was lucky enough to find an apartment with an Ecuadorian family through an advertisement in an internet café. I made enough money to pay for my rent, food and some social activities and even managed to travel a bit with my last pay packet – and the dollars went much further in Peru. The students were all great, the teenagers tending to be cheeky, a few times they changed the theme of the lessons to 'Make the teacher dance like a fool' before they did any work, but this was all part of the fun. It was a very relaxed atmosphere most of the time. I really enjoyed working with local teachers and they were all very open and friendly and interested in my life in England since many of them had never left Ecuador.

The highlight of Ecuador was helping my first students to prepare a presentation for the Directors on their chosen topics of hooliganism, pollution and anorexia. The looks on their faces when they received their certificates was definitely worth all the hours of hard work we put in. The low point of my experience was unfortunately when I was held at knife point outside my house. Luckily I was not hurt and they did not steal anything but it should be known that certain areas of Quito are dangerous.

Wages are not as high as in Chile but higher than in Colombia, and usually allow teachers to enjoy a comfortable lifestyle since the cost of living is low. A qualified teacher can expect to earn about $700 a month. Accommodation is harder to find in Quito than in Cuenca. Qualified TEFLers should not accept less than US$6 an hour though the private institutes that accept unqualified teachers pay accordingly less. All teachers (both contract and freelance) have taxes withdrawn at source of between 5% and 12%. Quito is not as large and daunting a city as some other South American capitals and it should be easy to meet longer-term expats who may be able to give advice on teaching. The helpful British Council will give you a list of ELT schools throughout the country and will (unofficially) indicate which offer the best teacher support and modern teaching methods and resources. One possible source of information is the South American Explorers clubhouse (membership costs $60). In Quito the Club is at Jorge Washington 311 y Leonidas Plaza (Apartado 17 21 431). It includes language schools in Ecuador on its database and has a useful noticeboard.

As throughout the continent, charitable schools for children can always use voluntary help. **Nick Branch** worked in Quito at a Don Bosco Catholic preschool for disadvantaged children where he did some teaching from the front as well as painting, PE activities and games with the children. Another programme is Children of Ecuador based in the coastal town of Bahía de Caráquez. Volunteers receive a week of supervised in-class training, and are expected to teach six hours from 7.30am, Monday to Thursday, helped by the class instructor. The cost of a minimum four-week homestay is $1,290, a third of which is donated to the programme. Spanish classes and other extras are provided (www.childrenecuador.org).

RED TAPE

Technically you shouldn't work on a tourist visa but there is little control. Britons and Americans can stay 90 days. If possible, teachers should get a 12-IX non-immigrant visa in their country of origin for stays of three to six months (fee $200), which can be extended by visiting a neighbouring country, usually Colombia. Most employers will help teachers who commit themselves for a reasonable stay to obtain a cultural exchange visa, normally valid for a year. The requirements are as follows: two letters attesting to good character, a notarised copy of a police report, health certificate (including HIV test) and birth certificate, letter of invitation from an Ecuadorian employer, letter of financial support from a backer and a return airline ticket.

LIST OF EMPLOYERS

CENTRO DE EDUCACIÓN CONTINUA DE LA
ESCUELA POLITÉCNICA NACIONAL
Edificio Araucaria, Baquedano 222 y Reina Victoria,
Quito
☎ 22 500068
✉ henryguygooch@yahoo.com
🖥 www.cec-epn.edu.ec

NUMBER OF TEACHERS: 150+.
PREFERENCE OF NATIONALITY: American and British.

QUALIFICATIONS: BA in English, Applied Linguistics, TEFL, Drama, International Studies or a related field. TEFL certificate, one-year experience.
CONDITIONS OF EMPLOYMENT: Minimum 1 year (40 weeks of teaching). 6 hours per day.
SALARY: Volunteers are not paid a salary, but are provided with a monthly subsistence allowance of $605–$726 net as required by law and written agreement.
FACILITIES/SUPPORT: Teachers must find their own accommodation. Instructors are contracted as Cultural Exchange Volunteers under the agreement the university

maintains with the Ecuadorian Ministerio de Relaciones Exteriores.

RECRUITMENT: Word of mouth. Telephone interviews are conducted.

CONTACT: Henry Guy Gooch, Director of Linguistics and Cultural Exchanges.

CENTRO DE ESTUDIOS INTERAMERICANOS/CEDEI
Casilla 597, Cuenca
  7 2839003
  English@cedei.org
  www.cedei.org

A non-profit institution dedicated to the study of American languages and cultures.

NUMBER OF TEACHERS: 40

PREFERENCE OF NATIONALITY: Native English speakers.

QUALIFICATIONS: Minimum university degree in related field and TEFL/CELTA/TESOL certificate or university degree in TESL/TEFL. Experience in teaching EFL/ESL.

CONDITIONS OF EMPLOYMENT: Minimum 6-month stay, preference given to year-long commitments. Courses run from January to mid-March, early April to early June, mid-June to mid-August and early October to mid-December. Teachers teach on average 20 hours per week. Most classes meet Monday to Thursday and there are also Saturday Intensives. To teach both classroom courses and individuals. In addition to classroom classes, teachers may elect to give tutorials and conversation classes to supplement their income.

SALARY: Approximately $275 per teenage/adult course, $220 per children's course, and $234 per Saturday class. Courses are 40–50 hours long and teachers are given 3–4 courses per term (10 weeks). This is a high salary by Ecuadorian standards.

FACILITIES: Apartments are very reasonably priced. Cost of living is low. Average rent for a shared apartment/house is between $90 and $140 per month. Free Spanish classes, dance classes and internet access for teachers. Beautiful school building. Very charming city in an Andean setting.

RECRUITMENT: Via the website www.cedei.org.

CONTACT: Elisabeth Rodas, Academic Director of English Programs.

EF SCHOOL OF ENGLISH – QUITO
Catalina Aldaz No. N34–267 y Portugal, Quito
  +593 2 224 8651 ext 105
  steve.tomkins@ef.com
  www.ef.com

NUMBER OF TEACHERS: 20.

PREFERENCE OF NATIONALITY: None; school aims to have a mixture of nationalities and accents.

QUALIFICATIONS: CELTA or equivalent teaching qualification.

CONDITIONS OF EMPLOYMENT: 6 months to 2 years. 35 hours per week.

SALARY: Average $700+ per month after deductions of 12% for tax.

FACILITIES/SUPPORT: Accommodation arranged in local hostel, EF residence or with host family. Pre-arrival pack contains detailed information about the options. Free transfers on arrival.

RECRUITMENT: Via internet or worldwide network of EF schools. Teachers also recruited locally. For senior positions and long-term posts applicants may be asked to present themselves at a local EF centre.

CONTACT: Steven Tomkins, English School Director.

INLINGUA
Sebastian Quintero N37–12 y Jose Correa
(behind the Atahualpa Olympic Stadium), Quito
  2 245 8763
  inlinguaquito@inlingua.com
  www.inlinguaquito.com

NUMBER OF TEACHERS: 25–30

PREFERENCE OF NATIONALITY: None, but native English speakers only.

QUALIFICATIONS: Recognised TEFL/CELTA and/or teaching experience (particularly Business English).

CONDITIONS OF EMPLOYMENT: Minimum 6-month part-time/full-time contracts. Hours vary. Full-time position totals 20/25 hours per week.

SALARY: $6.15–$7.35 per hour depending on experience and/or qualifications.

FACILITIES/SUPPORT: Full training on Inlingua's international programme and teaching resources provided. Spanish classes and health insurance offered at discounted rates for teachers.

RECRUITMENT: Applications by email, interview and induction in Quito upon arrival.

CONTACT: Danni Walters, Academic Coordinator (academic@inlingua.com)

NEXUS: LENGUAS Y CULTURAS
PO Box 01011013, Cuenca
  +593 7 409 0062
  mcarrasco@nexus.edu.ec
  www.nexus.edu.ec

NUMBER OF TEACHERS: 3 or 4 teachers per term.

PREFERENCE OF NATIONALITY: None.

QUALIFICATIONS: Teaching certification (CELTA or similar at least). Teaching experience of at least 1 year.

CONDITIONS OF EMPLOYMENT: 6-month contracts. 3 regular terms per year plus a summer session. 18 hours per week.

SALARY: $288 per month.

FACILITIES/SUPPORT: Assistance given to teachers in getting cultural visas by sending them the necessary invitations and certificates. Spanish classes at special price.

RECRUITMENT: On-site interview or via email.

CONTACT: Marcela Carrasco, Director.

MEXICO

The lure of the USA and its language is very strong in Mexico. The frenzy of American investment in Mexico after the North American Free Trade Agreement (NAFTA) saw a huge upswing in both the demand for English by businesses and the resources to pay for it. That boom is now over, but the market for English is still enormous in universities, in business, almost everywhere. Proximity to the USA and a tendency towards what Australians call the cultural cringe (in Mexico called Malinchism after the lover of Cortès who betrayed her people) means that there will always be an unquenchable thirst for English taught by native English speakers in Mexico. Foreign teachers are automatically respected and are often promoted almost immediately.

Companies of all descriptions provide language classes for their employees especially in the early mornings and evenings (but seldom on weekends or even Fridays). **Roberta Wedge** even managed to persuade a '*sleek head honcho in the state ferry service*' that he needed private tuition during the sacred siesta and that busy executives and other interested employees of a local company needed English lessons at the same time of day.

It is not surprising that enrolment in English courses is booming when some employees have been threatened with dismissal unless they master some English. A vet going to Dubai, a stockbroker doing deals with the New York Stock Exchange, housewives who have to go to parties with their executive husbands, teenagers with exam worries, all are keen to improve their English. After each six-year presidential term of office, the top layers of management in companies (especially oil and banking) are replaced by new staff who need new training, especially English. Elections always boost the demand for English not only in Mexico City and the border cities to which US industries looking for cheap labour have relocated, but throughout the country, including the Yucatan Peninsula and other unlikely places, at least one of which must remain nameless in order to preserve Roberta Wedge's dreams:

> *After doing a 'taster' ESL course in Vancouver, I set out for Nicaragua with a bus ticket to San Diego and $500 – no guide book, no travelling companion, no Spanish. On the way I fell in love with a town in Mexico (not for worlds would I reveal its name – I want to keep it in a pristine timewarp so I can hope to return) and decided to stay. I found a job by looking up all the language schools in the phonebook and walking around the city to find them. The problem was that many small businesses were not on the phone. So I kept my eye out for English school signs. I had semi-memorised a little speech in Spanish, 'I am a Canadian teacher of English. I love your town very much and want to work here. This is my CV.' Within two days I had a job at a one-man school.*

The British Council in Mexico City can provide the addresses of the 25 or so language centres attached to state universities and also keeps the *Yellow Pages* which has a few pages of language schools. Also check the website of the Unión Nacional de Escuelas de Idiomas AC (www.unei.org.mx). The British Council runs English teaching centres in Mexico. For more information visit www.britishcouncil.org/mexico. Mexican-American bi-national centres employ scores of native English speakers, mostly on a local basis. The school year starts in early August and lasts for 11 months.

With a TEFL qualification and a year's experience in Indonesia, Canadian **Bruce Clarke** was in a good position to make use of the Mexico forum on eslcafe.com, where he learned of the vacancy at a state university in Oaxaca which he went on to fill. He reports that his students were pleasant and fun-loving, though not particularly energetic or keen to complete homework. A further possibility is to work at English-medium schools modelled either on the American or British system. Many of these advertise internationally for certified teachers or recruit through recruiting fairs but, as in Chile, Peru and elsewhere, some are willing to interview native English speakers locally to work in the EFL department. Without a TEFL background or at least a solid university education you are unlikely to break into any of these more upmarket institutes.

THE PRIVATE SECTOR

A host of private institutes supplies language training to business either on their own premises or in-company. The norm is for teachers to freelance and work for a combination of companies. There are also full-time school-based jobs with teaching companies such as Harmon Hall and Interlingua which have a national network of branches. Hours can be unpredictable and a lot of time is taken up travelling from office to office. Getting three hours of work a day (early morning and early evening) is easy. Anything above that is much trickier. Freelance teachers must be prepared for frequent holidays cutting into earnings. Normally institutes do not pay for public holidays, sickness or annual leave. For example attendance goes into a sharp decline after Independence Day on 20 November in the month leading up to Christmas and there are no classes over Easter. Most courses run for three months and there may be a lapse of one or two weeks before another starts. Usually freelancers are paid cash in hand with no deductions for tax.

The spectrum of institutes varies enormously. At one extreme there is the employer who pays the equivalent of $5 an hour, never pays on time, and who employs only Mexicans with poor English or native English speakers who have just arrived with their backpacks and no interest in or knowledge of teaching. The top of the range pays $15–$18 an hour, offers free training and gives contracts that aren't cancelled. These institutes are of course a lot more choosy about their teachers. Whereas a few companies want to control their teachers completely and send inspectors into classes, most leave teachers alone as long as the clients are happy. The typical institute consists only of four people: the owner who gets the contracts, a teacher coordinator, a secretary and an office boy.

One company with an office in the USA offers prospective teachers a job in Hermosillo or Monterrey, a Mexican visa, room and board in secure area, paid travel and modest pay; try contacting teachers@goenglish.com.mx. On arrival in Mexico City, a good place to meet foreigners is the famed Quaker-run peace and service centre in Mexico City, Casa de los Amigos, which has information on a variety of volunteering opportunities throughout Mexico City and Mexico. The Casa also has its own volunteer programme for those who speak Spanish and are able to commit for at least six months to a year, working for peace and social justice. The Casa is at Ignacio Mariscal 132, 06030 Mexico, D.F., Mexico (+52 55 5705 0521; amigos@casadelosamigos.org) and provides simple accommodation starting from 100 pesos (US$7.50) per night.

Obviously a TEFL qualification is an advantage though few employers are concerned about whether it is from a 130-hour or a 30-hour course. Business and financial experience is also beneficial, possibly more than a university degree. An ability to make a class interesting and patience are the two key qualities that many employers are looking for. As one of **Nick Wilson**'s bosses said, '*The most important thing is that the students enjoy their classes and think that they are learning English; don't just teach or we'll lose customers.*' Word-of-mouth recommendations are very important in Mexican culture, and jobs are seldom filled by postal applications.

Michael Tunison contacted half a dozen major teaching organisations from the *Yellow Pages* and was interviewed by Berlitz and Harmon Hall. Both offered tentative positions based more on his native English speaking than his American university degree and journalism background. The starting wage at both schools was the peso equivalent of US$350–$400 per month which seems typical of the large chains. One problem here is that these organisations do not pay cash in hand and therefore they want to hire only teachers with working papers. Another international chain of language schools represented in Mexico is Wall Street Institute (www.wallstreetinstitute.com.mx) with 18 schools; the ones in Mexico City, Cordoba Veracruz, Monterrey, Puebla and Chiapas had vacancies in 2010.

> *Guadalajara and resorts such as Puerto Vallarta, Cancun, Acapulco and Mazatlan are places where a great many locals need to master English before they can be employed in the booming tourist industry, though wages tend to be lower than in the capital. Several independent US training organisations have set up TEFL training centres in Mexico.*

American **Bradwell Jackson** is funding his round-the-world travels by teaching English:

After reading **Work Your Way Around the World**, *I made the decision to quit my job, leave my home, give most of my belongings to charity and sell my car, so that I could wander the earth freely. I wondered if it was really possible to get a job teaching English so easily. Well I found out that it is. I was sitting at a metro stop in Mexico City, trying to figure out what school to go to for my first planned job enquiry. After I decided that the particular school I had in mind was too far away, I looked up and saw an English school right across the street. Providence, I thought. I was right. I sauntered on upstairs, cheerfully asked if they needed an English teacher, and about an hour and a half later, I was told when to start my training. It really was that easy.*

I teach a range of students including some teenage girls. For them I came up with the idea of asking them to talk about a television programme **Rebelde**, *which is very popular among teens here. I also got them to pull out a teen magazine and tell me about the stars in it. I have also asked my students about popular Spanish songs and asked them to translate them into English for me.*

Mexico is the first country I have visited on my world wanderings and I can't believe how lucky I've been. The people are top-notch and I certainly must count my blessings.

WORKING FOR YOURSELF

Private lessons are in great demand, and may be given informally in exchange for board and lodging. But it is also possible to teach on a more business-like footing. With so many clients seeking one-to-one tuition through institutes, it is worth considering setting up as an independent tutor and offering private lessons at a rate which undercuts the institutes. Teachers who are tempted to poach students from the organisation they work for should bear in mind that employers who find out have been known to set the immigration department on errant teachers. However, it is legitimate to advertise yourself in the press and distribute printed business cards. **Elizabeth Reid** based some of the material in her book *Native English Speaker: Teach English & See the World* (now out of print) on her experiences of teaching in a small Mexican city. She started by developing her own private classes in borrowed premises (a disused shop). She recommends approaching the local community centre (*casa de cultura*), chamber of commerce or public library and offering one free sample class before signing up paying students. To increase goodwill she offered 'scholarships' to a limited number of students who really couldn't afford to pay.

Teaching in companies sometimes produces lucrative spin-offs in the field of translation and editing documents in English. Clients may offer other kinds of work too; for example **Nick Wilson** was asked to set up a Mexican-British arts foundation through a bank trust by someone he tutored in English. Anyone willing to pay a fee to have a job arranged for them should investigate the website www.teach-english-mexico.com. The programme fee is $950, though special offers of $650 have recently cropped up.

REGULATIONS

The red tape situation in Mexico is a difficult one. Visitors are not allowed to work or engage in any remunerative activity during a temporary visit. The Free Trade Agreement makes it somewhat easier for Americans and Canadians but still not straightforward. British citizens can stay in Mexico for 180 days without a visa as a tourist, according to the consulate website (http://mexico.embassy-uk.co.uk). As has been mentioned, established schools are not usually willing to contract people without an employment visa, unlike private institutes. The most respectable schools may be willing to help full-time contracted teachers with the paperwork but won't pay the cost (estimated to be up to $700). Among the required documents are a CV in Spanish, notarised TEFL and university certificates that have been certified by a Mexican consulate.

LIST OF EMPLOYERS

BERLITZ (CENTRO INTEGRAL DE IDIOMAS)

Av. Benito Juarez No. 2005, Local Sub Ancla M Plaza Sendero, Colonia Estrella de Oriente, C.P. 78396

- 444 166 35 70
- elvia.rico@berlitzslp.com.mx

NUMBER OF TEACHERS: 20.

PREFERENCE OF NATIONALITY: None.

QUALIFICATIONS: TESOL, TEFL, CELTA certification or a university degree in education.

CONDITIONS OF EMPLOYMENT: Standard 1-year contract. Hours mainly 7am–9am and 6pm–9pm, Monday to Friday, 8am–2pm Saturday.

SALARY: 60 pesos per 45 minutes of class.

FACILITIES/SUPPORT: School makes sure that the applicant has a place to stay after arrival.

RECRUITMENT: By email and telephone interview.

CONTACT: Elvia Rico, Language Instructor Supervisor.

BERLITZ (CENTRO INTEGRAL DE IDIOMAS) CULTURLINGUA JALISCO

Reforma #31, Col. Centro, Tlaquepaque, Jalisco

- +52 33 33 44 91 39
- info@culturlinguagdl.com
- www.culturlinguagdl.com/teaching

NUMBER OF TEACHERS: 4.

PREFERENCE OF NATIONALITY: Native English speakers.

QUALIFICATIONS: TEFL/TESOL certificate is essential.

CONDITIONS OF EMPLOYMENT: Standard length of contract is 15 weeks with maximum 32 working hours per week.

SALARY: 4,500 pesos per month.

FACILITIES/SUPPORT: Fully furnished accommodation is provided for teachers and included in the salary.

RECRUITMENT: Via internet sites such as Dave's ESL Cafe. Candidates with successful CVs are asked to submit a sample lesson plan and then a telephone interview will be organised.

CONTACT: Greg Davies, Owner.

DUNHAM INSTITUTE

Avenida Coronel Urbina 30, Chiapa de Corzo, Chiapas 29160

- 961 61 61498
- academic-coordinator@dunhaminstitute.com
- www.dunhaminstitute.com

NUMBER OF TEACHERS: 4.

PREFERENCE OF NATIONALITY: Native English speaker.

QUALIFICATIONS: ESL certified.

CONDITIONS OF EMPLOYMENT: Minimum 5 months. 3–4 hours in the afternoon and study Spanish in the mornings.

SALARY: None. Exchange of English teaching for free accommodation with a local family and 2 hours of Spanish tuition a day.

FACILITIES/SUPPORT: Work permits not required.

RECRUITMENT: Interviews not necessary.

CONTACT: Joanna Robinson.

EXPERIENCE MEXECO LTD

38 Award Road, Fleet, Hampshire GU52 6HG, UK

- info@experiencemexeco.com
- www.experiencemexeco.com

English teaching projects, among other volunteer opportunities, on Pacific coast of Mexico.

QUALIFICATIONS: All nationalities and ages (average 19–26). All backgrounds welcomed as any necessary training is provided. Spanish is not a necessity as local staff speak English and Spanish.

CONDITIONS OF PARTICIPATION: 1–3 months.

SALARY: None. Programme fee £799–£899 for 1 month, £1,899–£1,999 for 3 months which covers accommodation (homestay or private) and food throughout placement plus insurance and 24-hour in-country support, but excludes flights.

CONTACT: Daniel Patman, Director.

FAST ENGLISH INSTITUTE

Tlalpan 1525, Col. Portales, Mexico City 03300

Mobile 4455 4225 1840

fastamericanenglish@yahoo.com.mx

NUMBER OF TEACHERS: 12.

PREFERENCE OF NATIONALITY: None.

QUALIFICATIONS: Ability to communicate effectively in English, spoken and written.

CONDITIONS OF EMPLOYMENT: Teachers may sign a contract after 3 months (no contract required at the beginning). Hours can fall any time between 7am and 10pm.

SALARY: From US$7 an hour. Maximum US$14 per hour.

FACILITIES/SUPPORT: Some teachers stay at school's residential facilities.

RECRUITMENT: Interview and written exam.

CONTACT: R. Alaiyo Moreno Academic Director.

ROBINSON SCHOOL

Blvd. Everardo Marquez #200 Piso 2, Colonia Periodistas, Pachuca, Hidalgo 42060

USA mobile 208 241 6493

luke@therobinsonschool.com

www.therobinsonschool.com

NUMBER OF TEACHERS: 3.

PREFERENCE OF NATIONALITY: None, must be native English speaker.

QUALIFICATIONS: ESL certificate preferred. Must be enthusiastic and politically and culturally open-minded.

CONDITIONS OF EMPLOYMENT: 10 weeks. Individual schedules vary. Classes begin at 7am and finish at 8:30pm.

SALARY: 2,000 Mexican pesos per week (net).

FACILITIES/SUPPORT: Housing and/or furnishings can be provided and monthly rent deducted from pay cheque. Teachers will be assisted in acquiring necessary documents.

RECRUITMENT: Internet, word-of-mouth, newspaper adverts. Interviews are sometimes carried out in person in the USA but mostly conducted by phone.

CONTACT: Luke Robinson, CEO & Head of Recruitment.

UNIVERSIDAD DEL MAR

Bahias de Huatulco, Oaxaca 70989

958 587 2559

umarmxjob@yahoo.com

www.umar.mx

NUMBER OF TEACHERS: 16.

PREFERENCE OF NATIONALITY: None but must be native English speaker.

QUALIFICATIONS: Degree level education, TEFL teaching qualification (or an MA in TOEFL or related field) plus at least 1 year's experience working in a foreign country.

CONDITIONS OF EMPLOYMENT: 1 year commitment. Teaching hours are 8am–1pm and 4pm–7pm, Monday to Friday.

SALARY: 14,881 pesos gross (more for candidates with an MA in TEFL or Education plus 2 years' experience), plus free medical service, Christmas and vacation bonuses, savings scheme and monthly shopping vouchers. Monthly deduction of about 2,000 pesos for tax and social security.

FACILITIES/SUPPORT: Teachers must arrange their own accommodation. University files paperwork for work permit on arrival; processing can take up to 3 weeks and teachers cannot start work without work visa.

RECRUITMENT: Most via internet ads and emailed CVs. Telephone interviews essential; short-listed candidates are telephoned.

CONTACT: Caryl Coffey, Director of Languages (caryldelaney@hotmail.com).

PERU

Lima has in the past been considered one of the most stressful and dangerous South American cities in which to live, however, threats from guerrilla groups have largely passed and Peru has returned to the mainstream of destinations for English language teachers. Continuing low wages and the difficulty of obtaining working papers mean that few professional teachers can be attracted to the private EFL sector. For those who are, it is worth sending a CV to the English Language Officer at the British Council, who will send a list of British schools and language teaching institutes to anyone sufficiently well qualified or alternatively pass the CV to potentially interested institutions such as the 10 Lima branches of the British-Peruvian Cultural Association, known familiarly as Britanico (www. britanico.edu.pe).

Yet the range of opportunities in Lima is enormous because the stampede to learn English is unstoppable. Many company employees have been told by their bosses to learn English or risk demotion. Some employers organise a course at their place of work, but most expect their staff to fix up private lessons making the freelance market very promising at the moment. In-company training courses in all industries are often offered in English, so knowledge of the language is becoming essential for all ambitious Peruvians. The Peruvian economy is not in dire straits at present, as evidenced by the stability of its currency, the new sol.

A very useful online resource is the Ultimate Peru List (http://the ultimateperulist.blogspot.com) compiled by a young EL teacher, Sharon Hinojosa, who until recently was teaching in Lima and researched all the schools. Although she has now left the continent to teach at a university in Korea, she intends to keep the site up to date. She stresses how much easier it is to find teaching hours once you are in Peru than when you're trying to fix up a job from home.

Many temporary visitors to Peru who lack a TEFL background end up doing some English teaching once they have established a base in the capital, usually earning $5–$10 an hour. Some employers offer a free or subsidised training course to new potential recruits, at which native English speakers usually excel over the locals, whose knowledge of English is often very weak.

James Gratton arrived in Lima to take up what had sounded like a dream job. He had contacted the institutes included on the list sent by the Peruvian embassy in London and was contacted enthusiastically by one (on the strength of a certificate earned from a one-week intensive TEFL training course in London and nine months of living and teaching in Venezuela the year before). High wages and many perks were offered, including a promise to meet him at the airport. His new employer's non-appearance at the airport was just the first promise they broke, and the lesson he learned over the next few months was that in Peru (and probably more widely in the continent), you must confirm and reconfirm any arrangements. He lasted only six weeks with this company (and was told that this was a record stay for an expat teacher) but concluded that such bad employers can be used as stepping stones to better opportunities.

For those who prefer to organise in advance, a safer bet might be to join a work placement scheme organised by Projects Abroad (01903 708300; www.volunteer-teaching-peru.org), which has a programme in Peru for volunteer teachers supervision and back-up from local staff. The minimum stay is a month and the cost for up to three months is £1,895 which includes food and lodging. A similar price is charged for a volunteer/intern teaching role through the TEFL training institute Maximo Nivel in Cusco (www.maximonivel.com/volunteer).

Eco Trek Peru does not sound like a volunteer teaching programme but this ecotourism travel agency based in Cusco sends volunteers to remote Peruvian community schools for up to six months. Participants must be over 25, know Spanish and be adventurous (+51 84 247286; www. ecotrekperu.com).

FREELANCING

Setting up as a freelance tutor is potentially lucrative. A standard fee is $10–$20 a lesson, though this can be reduced for clients who want to book a whole course. James Gratton put a cheap advertisement (written in English) in the main daily *El Comercio* and signed up two clients. This was possible in his case since he was staying at his girlfriend's house where he had free access to a telephone. His new students were both employees of Petro-Peru, and soon other clients contacted James for lessons. He admits that freelancers do lose out to cancellations, though some of his students willingly paid for missed lessons. Freelancing is a continual process of advertising and getting new students to replace the ones that fall by the wayside.

REGULATIONS

Peruvian work visas are very rare and most people teach as tourists. British and Irish nationals, as well as US and EU citizens, do not require tourist visas for Peru, neither do nationals from EU countries. They are allowed to stay in Peru for up to 90 days, although they are required to possess an onward/return ticket. After that it is necessary to cross the Peruvian border. One reason which many people use to extend their stay is that they have formed a romantic attachment to a local woman/man. James Gratton felt that the authorities were not interested in rooting out illegal workers. When he approached the immigration office about the requirements for a work visa, they knew he was working but took no steps to stop him.

In his quest for a work visa, James gathered together all the necessary documents, including contract (the duration does not matter particularly), notarised certificates and documents translated into Spanish. All of this cost him a lot of money and time, and he still didn't succeed. He concluded that it would be possible only if you knew someone in the immigration department who could give your application a safe passage without having to pay fines (bribes) at every stage. Making key contacts is more important than gathering documentation. Care must be taken to keep on the right side of the tax office (SUNAT) to which about 15% of earnings are supposed to be paid. James obtained a tax number even though his passport clearly indicated his status as tourist, but ended up paying virtually no tax.

LIST OF EMPLOYERS

ENGLISH LIFE
La Paz 434, Oficina 602, Miraflores, Lima
+51 1 446 1968
englishlifeperu@gmail.com
www.englishlifeperu.com

NUMBER OF TEACHERS: 20 on self-employed basis.
PREFERENCE OF NATIONALITY: None.
QUALIFICATIONS: TEFL certificate or similar, plus some experience is desirable.

CONDITIONS OF EMPLOYMENT: 6 months. Casual teachers usually given part-time hours, on a class by class basis (3–15 per week).
SALARY: $8–$10 per hour.
FACILITIES/SUPPORT: No accommodation provided but advice can be given.
RECRUITMENT: People are invited for interview after submitting their CV. Interviews are essential.
CONTACT: Valerie Watson, Directora General & Owner.

INSTITUTO CULTURAL PERUANO NORTEAMERICANO

M.M.Izaga No. 807, Chiclayo

74 231241/233331

www.icpnachi.edu.pe

One of a dozen or so Bi-national Centres in Peru.

NUMBER OF TEACHERS: Fluctuating. North American students come as unpaid interns.

PREFERENCE OF NATIONALITY: American and Canadian preferred; others considered.

QUALIFICATIONS: University degree that qualifies candidate for teaching EFL/ESL. Experience not a necessity.

FACILITIES/SUPPORT: Can find apartments for teachers or arrange homestays. Help given with work permits for long-stay teachers.

RECRUITMENT: Via TESOL conferences and internet. Interviews not essential.

VENEZUELA

Proximity to the USA and the volume of business which is done with El Norte result in a strong prefer-ence for American accents and teaching materials in Venezuela. Oil wealth abounds in the business community and many corporations hire in-company language trainers through Caracas-based agen-cies. But work is not exclusively for Americans, as **Nick Branch** from St Albans discovered, nor is it confined to the capital:

> *Merida is very beautiful and a considerably more pleasant place to be than Caracas. The atmosphere and organisation of the institute where I worked were very good. But alas, as with all the English teaching institutes in Merida, the pay is very low. Merida is three times cheaper to live in than Caracas, but the salaries are 5–6 times lower.*

Nick investigated most of the schools and agencies in Venezuela and worked for several of them including one based in the Oriente coastal resort of Puerto la Cruz. Once again the pay was less than in Caracas but advantages such as easy access to the Mochima National Marine Park compensated. Opportunities for English teachers even exist on the popular resort island of Margarita. Check adverts in Caracas' main English language organ, the *Daily Journal*. Most give only a phone number. A typical advert might read:

> *We need English teachers and offer remuneration according to the market, stable incomes, paid train-ing, organisation in the work, more earnings according to commissions. Excellent working condition. Work with best team. Punctual payment.*

The last item is worth noting, since many institutes do not pay as much or as often as they promise at the outset. In fact, Caracas has more than its fair share of shady characters running language schools, so that newcomers should take their time about signing any contracts.

REGULATIONS

Most people work on a tourist card which is valid for 90 days and non-extendable. It is also at least possible to apply for a multiple entry visa if you can provide proof of employment, sufficient funds and a return ticket. A combined work/study contract (internship in American parlance) is the solu-tion which the Centro Venezolano Americano and Venusa have come up with (see entries) but this is available mainly to US citizens.

Most long-stay foreigners take brief trips to Curaçao or Trinidad and Tobago and get an extension of their tourist card when returning to Venezuela. Work permits are available only if the employer has obtained approval from the Ministry of Internal Affairs (DEX) and sent the necessary papers to a Venezuelan consulate in the teacher's country of residence. Even with a backer as well established as the British Council, the visa problem looms large.

Nick Branch describes the process of getting a work permit in Caracas as a nightmare:

> *On no account attempt to get one on your own, since this involves dealing with the DEX, a truly horrific organisation housed in what resembles a prison and with appalling disorganisation. I heard that they lost 3,000 passports of people who were applying for work permits. It was later discovered that they had been sold on the black market.*

James Gratton obtained a definite job offer from a university extension department on Margarita Island (address below) and presented the letter to the Venezuelan embassy in London. His application was turned down. His main complaint was that you hear a different story from every official. Even renewing his tourist card at the Immigration Office took a week and involved his having to present a typed letter in Spanish (and why would a bona fide tourist be expected to do that?) Yet he managed to stay legally in Venezuela for nine months, leaving the country when necessary and returning without once being asked to show a ticket home as proof of his intention to leave the country. His most serious problem occurred when one of his employers threatened to report his tourist status to the police if he quit to look for a better job (James did quit and the police were not called.)

LIST OF EMPLOYERS

CENTRO VENEZOLANO AMERICANO DEL CARACAS

Av. Principal José Marti, Edf. CVA, Urbanización Las Mercedes, Caracas 1060-A

📞 212 993 7911/8422

📧 cva@cva.org.ve

🖥 www.cva.org.ve

CVA also located in the state of Zulia: Calle 63, No. 3E-60, Maracaibo, Estado Zulia

📞 261 718 0842 5

🖥 www.cevaz.org

NUMBER OF TEACHERS: 100+.

PREFERENCE OF NATIONALITY: American, Canadian, Venezuelan.

QUALIFICATIONS: Bachelor's degree or teachers with EFL/ESL experience. A written and oral test is given to all non-native English speaking applicants.

CONDITIONS OF EMPLOYMENT: Minimum 6 months with renewals up to 2 years. Choice of children's courses (for ages 9–11), teens (12–15) and regular and Saturday courses for adults. Minimum 30 academic hours per week.

SALARY: Hourly rate plus housing bonus.

FACILITIES/SUPPORT: Assistance with obtaining accommodation, health insurance and visas. 2-week pre-service training course for interns is paid. Free Spanish course. Computer lab and access to cultural centre activities.

INLINGUA VENEZUELA

Caracas: Av. San Ignacio de Loyola, Edif. Milano, piso 4, ofic. 401, Chacao, Caracas

📞 +58 212 421 90 33

Valencia: Centro Tarbes 138, Edif. de ladrillos, piso 8, ofic. 8.6. Valencia

📞 +58 241 823 99 35.

📧 Email: vzla@inlingua.com

🖥 www.inlingua.com

NUMBER OF TEACHERS: 40 (about 8 of whom are native English speakers).

PREFERENCE OF NATIONALITY: Native English speakers from major English-speaking countries: UK, USA, Canada, Australia or New Zealand.

QUALIFICATIONS: Formal qualifications are less important than enthusiasm, ability and business experience, which are assessed through the application process. Candidates must be dedicated to providing good quality contractual teaching hours and be adaptable and honest. A year's teaching experience in a non-English speaking country would be desirable as would TEFL/CELTA/TESOL or equivalent and business experience.

CONDITIONS OF EMPLOYMENT: 8-month commitment. To work irregular hours in 3 primary shifts, starting 7am, noon and 5pm. However, teachers must be available from 7am to 7pm, Monday to Friday.

SALARY: $650 gross per month, paid in the local currency (bolivares).

FACILITIES/SUPPORT: As part of the induction, training in the inlingua methodology is given. Airport pick-up on arrival. Accommodation in shared teachers' apartment when available or assistance in finding accommodation. Assistance in obtaining a cell phone. Internet access is provided at the school. Spanish language lessons are provided. Initial and ongoing training, assessment and support.

CONTACT: Joe Rebbeck, Academic Supervisor.

IOWA INSTITUTE

Avenida 4 con Calle 18, Merida Edo. Merida 5101

📞 +58 274 2526404

🖥 www.iowainstitute.com

NUMBER OF TEACHERS: 7 native English speakers.

PREFERENCE OF NATIONALITY: None.

QUALIFICATIONS: University degree in Education, Linguistics, Modern Languages or some related field. If degree not in TEFL related field then a TEFL certificate or teaching experience is essential. All teachers must attend a 4-day seminar on school teaching methods held during September and again in January. Jobs for the less qualified (i.e. native English speakers who have not yet completed their degree) also possible. Those with experience working in children's camps for example, have been ideal for helping in the children's programme.

CONDITIONS OF EMPLOYMENT: Minimum 10 months. Full-time posts 6–8 hours a day. Part-time can be as few as 2 hours a day.

SALARY: By the hour, always a bit above the standard rate.

FACILITIES/SUPPORT: No accommodation assistance. Group Spanish lessons are free, private classes at cost price.

CONTACT: Cesar Gonzalez, through the web page.

VENUSA COLLEGE

Venezuela: 49–49 Avenida Urdaneta, Merida

USA: 6586 Hypoluxo Rd, Suite 324, Lake Worth, Florida 33467

274 263 7631

venusa@earthlink.net

www.venusacollege.org

NUMBER OF TEACHERS: 25–40 interns a year.

PREFERENCE OF NATIONALITY: American, British and Canadian.

QUALIFICATIONS: TESL certification and experience preferred but not required.

CONDITIONS OF EMPLOYMENT: 3-month to 1-year contracts. Hours vary.

FACILITIES/SUPPORT: Homestay or room option offered (some meals included). Visa application and information provided.

RECRUITMENT: Internet, alumni. Interviews not essential. Apply electronically. $50 application fee.

CENTRAL AMERICA AND THE CARIBBEAN

If you keep your ears open as you travel through this enormous isthmus squeezed between two great oceans, you may come across opportunities to teach English, especially if you are prepared to do so as a volunteer, Salaries on offer may be pitiful but if you find a congenial spot on the 'gringo trail' (for example, the lovely old colonial town of Antigua in Guatemala), you may decide to prolong your stay by helping the people you will inevitably meet who want to learn English.

COSTA RICA

As the wealthiest country in Central America, Costa Rica is a good starting (and perhaps finishing) point for many native English teachers. The Education Ministry is pursuing a national plan to improve English instruction and produce a bilingual workforce for the nation's growing economy. Although such rhetoric can never be completely relied upon, it does at least suggest that English is seen as an important economic asset. The English language newspaper *Tico Times* (www.ticotimes.net) corroborates this, and ran a series of articles headlined 'Learning English is a good investment' and 'Tourism will grow thanks to English speaking cops'. It is also government policy to teach English in primary schools, which has greatly increased the demand for English teachers. Although state schools can't usually afford to import expat teachers, they are often willing to accept an offer of voluntary assistance. The school year runs from 1 March to 1 December. The *Tico Times* publishes its job classified ads online at www.ticotimes.net/costaricajobs.htm. A recent one ran: '*The Swan English Learning is looking for Native English Teachers, for Heredia, San José & Ciudad Colon. Part and full time. Call 2249 3598; info@theswanenglish.org*'. Other places to look for teaching job ads are www.minuevotrabajocr.com and craigslist for Costa Rica.

There are plenty of private language academies in the capital San José. Temporary six-month re-newable working visas are issued to teachers working for established employers such as the Instituto Britanico (now International House) where **Jane Roberts** worked. After deciding that she needed a complete change from Hounslow and an office job, Jane signed up for a CELTA course and had to decide where she wanted to job-hunt. Her course tutors at International House London had told her group that they would probably have to work in Eastern Europe to start with:

> No thank you I thought, I want to work in a hot Latin country. IH had said don't expect to get a job straightaway in your dream destination, but I have proved this wrong. I got the address of Instituto Britanico, emailed them my CV and a covering letter, within two weeks was offered a job and a couple of weeks later I was here in Costa Rica.
>
> The working conditions are fine with a very well equipped library, cassettes, all necessary equip-ment for the classroom, and free email and internet access (when it works). My students are very mo-tivated, lovely to work with, keen to learn, really want to speak a lot. I have the greatest admiration for them as they often come after a hard day at work to a 3-hour lesson and put a lot into it. I have to ensure that it is as interesting as possible for them. My advice is to smile, relax, be nice to people. I have not found any problems with Latin Machismo, no hassles with men. They love my accent but have not been pushy or offensive. Costa Rican people are so friendly and helpful. It's a very chilled country.

If teachers wish to stay longer, the red tape becomes a little more painful. International House in San José advises: '*Candidates must have copies of their birth certificate and a police report certified by their foreign ministry or state department and the Costa Rican consulate in their country of birth. This involves some expense on the part of the candidate. After arrival, IH completes all necessary paperwork and applies for permission at their expense.*'

Bryson Patterson made use of contacts from the TEFL course he did at ALI San Diego to get his first job in Costa Rica at Pro-Language (entry below).

During my first job, I spent a lot of time on the bus going from class to class. This was a drawback. On the plus side, San José is right in the middle of Costa Rica and for a $4 bus ride of two hours you can be on either the Pacific or Caribbean coast. Shorter bus rides and less money get you to great mountain and volcano locations. Pro-Language was really cool about giving teachers time off to travel as well. Most of the other people working down here as English teachers are young people travelling around or older people doing the same thing. It is kind of a nice mix. As far as the students go, Costa Ricans are great. In an economy so closely linked to the US many people realise that it is imperative that they learn English.

Afterwards I moved to a town called Jaco on the Pacific Coast where I worked at a high school and then at the Marriott Hotel. I was teaching English first to high school students (that was hell) then to the hotel staff which was cool. A lot of people will tell you that there are no ESL jobs on the coast but they are wrong.

LIST OF EMPLOYERS

CENTRO CULTURAL COSTARRICENSE NORTEAMERICANO
Apartado Postal 1489–1000, San José
℡ +506 207 7500
✉ reclutamiento@centrocultural.cr
🖥 www.centrocultural.cr

NUMBER OF TEACHERS: Varies. Teachers also needed for centres in San Pedro, La Sabana, Alajuela and Cartago.
PREFERENCE OF NATIONALITY: None, but must be native English speaker.
QUALIFICATIONS: Experience in ESL and/or EFL is indispensable.
CONDITIONS OF EMPLOYMENT: Standard 1-year contract. Minimum 16 hours per week.
SALARY: $5 an hour paid in local currency (colones). Deduction of about $15 a month for voluntary insurance.
FACILITIES/SUPPORT: No assistance with accommodation or work permits.
RECRUITMENT: Via newspaper adverts, work fairs and internal recommendations. Interviews carried out at CCCNCR sites in Costa Rica after applications have been processed centrally.
CONTACT: Eloisa Quesada Colton, Head of Recruitment and Professional Development.

ENGLISH TO GO - INGLES SIN FRONTERAS
Apartado Postal 271–3007, San Joaquin de Flores
✉ academics@english2go.co.cr
🖥 www.english2go.co.cr

NUMBER OF TEACHERS: 15–25 contracted staff.
PREFERENCE OF NATIONALITY: Americans and Canadians, others can also apply.
QUALIFICATIONS: 2 years' classroom experience teaching ESL in a foreign country; certified ESL through CELTA (preferred) TESOL, TEFL or others.
CONDITIONS OF EMPLOYMENT: Standard 6-month contract. Hours vary according to needs of students or companies with whom English to Go contracts.
SALARY: $6–$10 per classroom hour.
FACILITIES/SUPPORT: If needed on arrival, English to Go will help with finding housing but does not pay rent.
RECRUITMENT: Ads in craigslist, ESL sites, newspapers, and website. Interviews essential.
CONTACT: Robert Holloway, PhD, Academic Director (+506 2588 2204; mobile+506 8914 1402; Skype: robaholloway).

INTERCULTURA LANGUAGE AND CULTURAL CENTER
Apdo. 1952–3000, Heredia
℡ +506 2260 8480 (ext 21)
✉ info@interculturacostarica.com
🖥 www.interculturacostarica.com

NUMBER OF TEACHERS: 26–29 (depending on the semester).
PREFERENCE OF NATIONALITY: Native English speakers: American, British, Canadian, Irish, New Zealander and Australian.
QUALIFICATIONS: Minimum bachelor's degree, and TEFL/CELTA certification. At least 1 year's teaching experience is preferred.

CONDITIONS OF EMPLOYMENT: 1 year starting in July and January. Average 20 hours teaching per week. Classes last 1.5–2 hours and are held in mornings, evenings and some afternoons. Hours of teaching mainly Monday to Thursday plus some Saturday mornings.

SALARY: $700–$1,000 per month net.

FACILITIES/SUPPORT: Local housing arrangements to help teachers find accommodation. Free Spanish lessons for full-time teachers. Mentor programme for new teachers, ongoing training and professional development opportunities.

RECRUITMENT: TEFL websites, local adverts and phone interviews. Applications should be sent in April and October in time for the start of the semester.

CONTACT: Bethany Kirk, English Department Director (bethany@interculturacostarica.com).

INTERNATIONAL HOUSE COSTA RICA – INSTITUTO BRITANICO
Apartado 8184–1000, San José, 10102–1000
✆ 2234 9054
🖂 britanico@amnet.co.cr
💻 www.ihcostarica.com or www. institutobritanico.co.cr

NUMBER OF TEACHERS: 40.

PREFERENCE OF NATIONALITY: None.

QUALIFICATIONS: Minimum qualifications are CELTA, CertTESOL Trinity College London, IHCTL, BA in Education with TEFL component, PGCE with TEFL. Global TESOL, TEFL International or online qualifications are not accepted. Minimum 12 months' experience.

CONDITIONS OF EMPLOYMENT: 12 or 24 months. 24 contact hours per week.

SALARY: Minimum for 2010: CRC 377,000, more for teachers with longer than minimum experience and higher qualifications.

FACILITIES/SUPPORT: First 2 weeks free accommodation, then secretarial and logistical help in finding somewhere suitable. Foreign hire teachers are also paid an overseas allowance of CRC 110,000 (2010). Candidates must have copies of their birth certificate and a police report certified by their foreign ministry or state department and the Costa Rican consulate in their country of birth. This involves some expense on the part of the candidate. After arrival, IH completes all necessary paperwork and applies for permission at their expense. Country specific details are made available to candidates during the recruitment process.

RECRUITMENT: Through IHWO recruitment, occasionally TEFL.com. Interviews essential, usually by phone, although sometimes IH affiliates interview in the country where the candidate is living.

CONTACT: Ben Naismith, Director of Studies, English Department.

PRO-LANGUAGE CORPORATE LANGUAGE SOLUTIONS
Edificio Langer, Of. #3, Zapote, San José
✆ +506 2280 6053 ext 11
🖂 cm@prolanguage.org
💻 www.prolanguage.org

NUMBER OF TEACHERS: 40.

PREFERENCE OF NATIONALITY: None, but native English speakers.

QUALIFICATIONS: TEFL certification or equivalent and a minimum of 6 months' experience.

CONDITIONS OF EMPLOYMENT: Minimum 4 months. Lots of part-time opportunities.

SALARY: $7 per hour.

FACILITIES/SUPPORT: Assistance with accommodation and work permits. Free Spanish lessons and free training.

RECRUITMENT: Newspaper adverts, internet, alliances with teacher training organisations.

WHITTEMORE DE COSTA RICA
300 este de Universidad Interamericana, San Pablo Heredia 00107/4000
✆ +506 2560 4100
🖂 teachers@inglescostarica.com
💻 www.inglescostarica.com

NUMBER OF TEACHERS: 12–18.

PREFERENCE OF NATIONALITY: North American and British.

MANDATORY: Must be native English speaker.

QUALIFICATIONS: TESL/TESOL/CELTA certified. Prefer 2 years' experience teaching English as a second language. Prefer minimum age 30.

CONDITIONS OF EMPLOYMENT: 6-month stay.

SALARY: $8 per hour (net).

FACILITIES/SUPPORT: Initial hotel booking arranged and suitable condo at $225 per month fully furnished including free colour TV, internet and cable.

RECRUITMENT: Via internet. Interviews essential via Skype.

CONTACT: Michael J. Whittemore, General Manager.

GUATEMALA AND HONDURAS

There are perhaps about a dozen institutes in the capital Guatemala City. But it is not nearly as appealing a destination as Antigua. Many travellers find that Lake Atitlán is the perfect place to use as a longer-term base. The small villages around the lake are all interconnected by launch boats, and the variety in atmosphere among these villages means that you can choose one that suits. Well known party town, San Pedro, attracts many foreigners who come to attend one of the many Spanish schools. Rooms are available for 15–35 quetzals (£1–£3) and food is also very cheap.

ANNA LING, 20 years old and from Cambridge, headed to San Pedro last year on her world travels, as she pursues her main interests, writing and performing music. She decided to stay for a while:

I am based at the Iguana Perdida hostel (www.laiguanaperdida.com), the first building near the launch stop. The local village is a wonderful place and home to the Amigos (www.amigosdesantacruz.org), a charity that has brought medical care and an outreach programme to the more remote villages. They have also built a library and a school offering free education to all children under 12, and scholarship programmes for older children. They are in the process of building a large new centre for vocational education. I went up to the village to see Pam, the current brains behind the operation, and within the hour I was teaching an English class. I was soon given a classroom and started an enrichment afternoon with the local kids, doing arts, craft and music projects. The organisation is so well run that anyone willing to give some time will be put to good use, whether in teaching, construction or any other interests.

Visas are not a problem at all, neither for work nor volunteering. No one even asks to see a passport. Language is no problem either. Personally I'm trying to live very much on a tight budget and paid language lessons (25–50 quetzals per hour) would push me way over my daily price watch. But volunteering at the school has been the best opportunity for learning Spanish I could imagine. I take up a dictionary and the kids speak really slowly and clearly and it has helped so very much.

Volunteer teachers who wish to go to Honduras can arrange a placement in Ceiba, the third largest city, through the fee-charging agency Volunteering Solutions (http://volunteeringsolutions.com/honduras/volunteer_teaching_english_honduras.htm), helping local people trying to get ahead in the burgeoning tourist industry. The cost is $1,450 for eight weeks.

NICARAGUA

ABC SCHOOL
519 Calle El Consulado, Granada
📞 55 2552 0812
📧 marlonabc@hotmail.com

NUMBER OF TEACHERS: 5 volunteers.
PREFERENCE OF NATIONALITY: North American.
QUALIFICATIONS: TEFL or equivalent, minimum 2 months' EFL teaching experience, some Spanish, some travel outside country of origin, interest in Nicaragua.

CONDITIONS OF EMPLOYMENT: Minimum stay 3 months. 20 hours per week on week days between 3pm and 8pm and on Saturday mornings and afternoons.
SALARY: Contribution of $160–$240 per month for housing.
FACILITIES/SUPPORT: Teachers are helped to find rooms to rent, or homestays.
RECRUITMENT: Internet and word of mouth. Phone interviews.
CONTACT: Marlon Gutierrez, Owner/Director.

EL SALVADOR

CENTRO DE INTERCAMBIO Y SOLIDARIDAD (CIS)

Melida Anaya Montes Language School, Avenida

Bolivar #103, Colonia Libertad, San Salvador

volunteer@cis-elsalvador.org

www.cis-elsalvador.org

NUMBER OF TEACHERS: 4–10 volunteer teachers at any one time.

PREFERENCE OF NATIONALITY: None.

QUALIFICATIONS: No teaching experience or certification needed. Must be committed to social justice and reciprocal learning between students and teacher.

CONDITIONS OF EMPLOYMENT: Minimum stay 9 weeks for complete English cycle. Time commitment includes teaching English 3 days a week (Monday, Tuesday and Thursday) 5.15pm–7pm, weekly 2 hour teachers meeting, plus time spent on lesson planning. Please contact for more details about rural volunteer placements and longer-term placements.

SALARY: None.

FACILITIES/SUPPORT: Help given in finding but not paying for accommodation. The CIS has a host family network with whom volunteers can live. Training for teachers provided. tourist visa ($10 at border) is sufficient.

RECRUITMENT: Word of mouth, internet, travel publications.

CONTACT: Daniel López, English School Coordinator.

DOMINICAN REPUBLIC

A major tourist destination, the Dominican Republic (DR) provides some opportunities for native English teachers, although these may well be low paid (or volunteer positions) because the DR is still one of the poorest countries in the Caribbean. A useful resource is the Dominican Republic One news and information service (www.dr1.com) in English, which has a classified section (including teaching vacancies), a blog, and a messageboard where you can ask the online community for information. The *Listín Diario* (www.listin.com.do), in Spanish, is a large circulation newspaper with a strong classified section, online and in print.

Possible leads include the Instituto Cultural Dominico-Americano (www.icda.edu.do) and Universidad APEC's English Department, (+809 686 0021; http://unapec.edu.do). There are also plenty of English speaking or bilingual schools that you can try.

Another option is to take part in the TESOL Exchange Program of the American Language Partnership International (Calle San Luis #83, Santiago, DR; +809 971 1422; info@alpinternational.com; www.alpinternational.com). Teachers are able to exchange ideas and activities through workshops, seminars and in the classroom, and work with ALPI's Dominican students of English. Those with little experience can 'cut their teeth' on lessons with the guidance and full support of the faculty. ALPI assists incoming participants with securing affordable housing (homestay or apartment-studio) before arrival together with airport transport.

NORTH AMERICA

Just about every university and college in the major cities has an ESL programme, as do a range of government and charitable organisations. Commercial schools offer a wide variety of classes but tend to focus on survival ESL and EAP (English for Academic Purposes) with writing as a major component. Berlitz and Inlingua are represented throughout the USA and are a completely different type of commercial school, concentrating on conversational skills and foreign languages for business people. Embassy CES (330 Seventh Avenue, New York 10001; 212 629 7300; www.embassyces. com) has adult English schools in Boston, New York, Fort Lauderdale, San Diego, Los Angeles and Seattle, plus one in Vancouver. These are worth applying to, although they often recruit locally.

Bilingual/bicultural classes are run in thousands of high schools across the country. Many require staff who are not only state-certified teachers but also bilingual in exotic languages like Hmong or Gujarati. Most larger cities have at least one free or low-cost workplace literacy/vocational ESL programme which caters for immigrants needing assistance with the basics of English. Some of these programmes operate in outposts (e.g. churches, libraries) and many depend on local volunteers as tutors. Volunteer positions can conceivably lead to better things.

GEMMA PIRELLI tried to think of ways of achieving her desire to travel after finishing a degree in psychology, and spend time with people from different cultures. She carried out lots of research on the internet and made contact with the director of Teachingenglishinitaly.com, Sheila Corwin, a fellow American. Not only did she enrol in a distance learning course, but took steps to get some practical experience:

In addition to putting together a portfolio of all coursework I'm doing for my distance TEFL course (the International Certificate for Applied Linguistics), I tried to find some volunteering opportunities and classroom observations here in New Jersey. Therefore I began to research local colleges/universities in my area as well as community centres accepting volunteers. I went back to my alma mater (Seton Hall University) and arranged a couple of classroom observations with the ESL adjunct. Because I wanted more involvement in the classroom, I decided to become a volunteer at a local community centre where they have programmes for adult learners. After connecting with the Director, she was able to accommodate me in a Monday evening class, and have me float around different classrooms to observe various levels. I was able to teach one class of learners at intermediate level which went very well and I was able to use my knowledge from the course as well as lesson planning guided by Sheila. Eventually I was put in charge of advanced learners (only one to three at a time). There are no set books and little structure so I had to arrange lessons on my own... There is no doubt in my mind that this experience will lead me to grand frontiers.

Although the demand for ESL teachers is enormous, it is very difficult for foreigners who do not have a 'green card' to obtain the necessary working visa. The J-1 visa is available to university students participating in an approved Exchange Visitor Programme (which are mainly for the summer) and to researchers and teachers whose applications are supported by their employing institution in the USA. Similarly it is extremely difficult to obtain the H-1B 'Temporary Worker' visa which is available for prearranged professional or highly skilled jobs for which there are no suitably qualified Americans, an increasingly unlikely circumstance as more and more Americans are becoming qualified to teach ESL/EFL. Although more US organisations now recognise the Cambridge Certificate than before, the MA in TESOL still dominates the American EFL scene. Even for qualified American teachers, part-time work is the norm, often referred to as being hired as an 'adjunct'. Many contracts are not renewed, creating a transient English teaching population. Pay is hourly and varies according to region, for example $25–$32 in Chicago, a little more in San Francisco. Part-timers almost never get benefits which means no health insurance or vacation pay. Even full-time teaching openings may be for just nine months with pay as little as $20,000 in the Midwest.

One possibility might be to teach at summer courses or work on summer camps attended by young people from overseas. For example, the Council on International Educational Exchange recruits ESL instructors for language camps on the east and west coasts, responsible for teaching English language classes to high school age international students in July and August. Even for such short appointments they look for an MA in TESOL or at least a strong background in ESL.

Canada has a flourishing ELT industry, however, the difficulty of getting a visa is a major stumbling block for foreign teachers. People with experience might have expected to be able to do some casual one-to-one tutoring of new immigrants, but stiff competition makes this difficult. When **David Hughes** arrived in Vancouver after a lengthy stint of teaching English in Taiwan, he felt fairly confident that with his experience he would be able to acquire a few fee-paying students from among the huge Chinese population in the area. But he didn't get a single reply to his advert. Two sources of possible contacts are Languages Canada (www.languagescanada.ca) and TESL Canada (www.tesl.ca). Member institutes will usually consider only Canadian citizens or those with work permits or landed immigrant status. The hourly wage starts at C$25 per hour.

AUSTRALASIA

While Europeans tend to have a somewhat Eurocentric view of the world, the Antipodean English language industry has built itself into a giant. TEFL has a very high profile in both Australia and New Zealand. There are no fewer than 17 Cambridge CELTA training centres in Australia and nine in New Zealand, most of them attached to flourishing English language colleges. There are a further four Trinity TESOL centres in New Zealand, despite its tiny population of about four million. **Gareth Lewis** of International House Sydney's Teacher Training Centre has generously provided an assessment of the ELT scene in Australia.

PROSPECTS FOR TEACHERS
IN AUSTRALIA

The growth in student numbers and ELT schools has resulted in strong job prospects for TESOL qualified teachers. Each year approximately 80,000 students study English in Australia on student visas and the Australian immigration department estimates that another 60,000 students studied on other visas, such as working holiday and tourist visas. This is an increase of 80% over the past 10 years. For obvious reasons of geography, the majority of Australia's international students are from Asia, although there are a growing number of students coming from further away including Italy and elsewhere in Europe.

Australia is a strong and growing market for longer-term students e.g. Academic English students (20+ weeks) and English for high school students (20–30 weeks) who need to improve their English skills for entry into an Australian university or high school. This longer-term student market has resulted in relatively steady student numbers year round. Whilst Australia does experience a peak in student numbers over the warmer months (September to May) due to an influx of study tours, there is not the same dramatic seasonal fluctuation as in Europe.

There are approximately 100 English language colleges in Sydney alone, around 70% of which are accredited by the National ELT Accreditation Scheme (NEAS). The profession is strictly regulated in Australia and standards are high in both the private and public sector. The minimum acceptable qualification to teach at an Australian NEAS-accredited language school is a degree in any discipline (or 3-year full-time diploma) plus a recognised TESOL qualification and 800 hours of teaching experience. Alternatively you may be considered with or a higher-than-pass grade in the TESOL qualification or if you can show references from your TESOL course director about your performance.

An acceptable TESOL qualification must have a practical component including at least six hours supervised and assessed practice teaching in TESOL and involve no fewer than 100 contact hours in total (or the equivalent in Distance Education programmes). To check the current requirements and a list of accredited language schools see the NEAS website (www.neas.org.au). Some non-accredited schools will employ TESOL trained teachers who do not hold a degree or diploma. It is interesting to note that due to the strong demand for TEFL qualified teachers in Sydney, job-seekers with the CELTA but without a degree have still been offered positions by accredited schools.

Candidates (whether Australians or foreigners on working visas) are regularly offered employment in Sydney and in other Australian cities within a week or two of completing the Cambridge CELTA course. Generally teaching contracts are short term and renewable. Once a relationship has been built between school and teacher the teacher can opt to work long term with one school or short term with a number of schools. Annual salaries range from around A$40,000 for a newly qualified graduate teacher without experience to A$60,000 for a head teacher.

Many foreigners teach English on a working holiday visa. Travellers aged between 18 and 30 years can apply for working holiday visas for up to 12 months. For further information visit www.immi.gov.au. When **Barry O'Leary** arrived in Sydney with a working holiday visa, he had very little money left so needed a job fast. He had emailed a number of language institutes in Sydney in advance and fixed up an interview the day after he arrived. In addition to walking round all the schools he could find, he used Australian search engines such as www.seek.com.au, www.jobsearch.gov.au and www.mycareer.com.au. Soon he found a job with Maewill English College in an outer suburb of Sydney (which has since closed):

This was my first full-time job and I was thrown in at the deep end. Initially I was doing maternity cover and working 15 hours a week, but this later increased to 45 including preparation time. The wages were fantastic, I wasn't paying any tax because I set myself up as a contractor and I was paid A$30 an hour (the going rate then) and $300 every two weeks for the evening business course I taught. I managed to save about A$8,000 in three months which paid for a brilliant trip up the east coast of Australia. There was always a laugh in the staff room and a lot of banter between England and Australia. I really enjoyed the mixed classes because there was such a range of opinions and at times more challenging because each nationality would have different weaknesses.

LIST OF EMPLOYERS

ACCESS LANGUAGE CENTRE
72 Mary Street, Surry Hills, New South Wales 2010
2 9281 6455
english@access.nsw.edu.au
www.access.nsw.edu.au

NUMBER OF TEACHERS: 16.
PREFERENCE OF NATIONALITY: None.
QUALIFICATIONS: Bachelor's degree plus TESOL certificate. Some experience essential.
CONDITIONS OF EMPLOYMENT: 4 weeks renewable to start.
SALARY: Depends on qualifications and experience.
FACILITIES/SUPPORT: No assistance with accommodation.
RECRUITMENT: Advertising and will respond to general enquiries about work while in Australia.
CONTACT: Blake Compton, Director of Studies.

EMBASSY CES
Level 1, 63 Oxford Street, Sydney, New South Wales 2010
2 9291 9300
enquiries@embassyces.com

Schools also in Brisbane, Gold Coast, Perth and Melbourne.
NUMBER OF TEACHERS: 15 in Sydney, 20 Brisbane and Melbourne, 14 Gold Coast, 10 Perth.

PREFERENCE OF NATIONALITY: None.
QUALIFICATIONS: NEAS minimum qualifications.
CONDITIONS OF EMPLOYMENT: Permanent, sessional (yearly or 3-monthly) or casual depending on area.
SALARY: Depends on experience and qualifications. Current average hourly rate is around A$35.
FACILITIES/SUPPORT: Excellent academic environments. Computer labs, wireless internet and email access, student common room. Homestay and lodge accommodation available.
RECRUITMENT: Local advertising.
CONTACT: Bradley Muller, Manager; Vernon Spain, DOS.

INTERNATIONAL HOUSE BRISBANE
126 Adelaide St, Brisbane, Queensland 4000 (Postal address: PO Box 13393 George St, Brisbane 4003)
7 3229 3389
neil@austlang.com.au
www.austlang.com.au

NUMBER OF TEACHERS: Approximately 20.
PREFERENCE OF NATIONALITY: None.
QUALIFICATIONS: CELTA or equivalent and minimum 1 year's experience.
CONDITIONS OF EMPLOYMENT: Variable length contracts. Up to 25 hours per week.
SALARY: Australian award rates.

RECRUITMENT: CV and interview. Interviews occasionally conducted overseas.

CONTACT: Neil Preston, Director of Studies.

MILNER INTERNATIONAL COLLEGE OF ENGLISH

379 Hay Street, Perth, Western Australia 6000

© 8 9325 5444

dos@milner.wa.edu.au

www.milner.wa.edu.au

NUMBER OF TEACHERS: 25–35.

PREFERENCE OF NATIONALITY: None. Teachers from the UK and Canada can come on a working holiday visa if they are under 30.

QUALIFICATIONS: Degree plus CELTA (or equivalent).

CONDITIONS OF EMPLOYMENT: No contracts for casual teachers. School hours 9am-3pm.

SALARY: There is an award scale for EL teachers ranging from A$27 to A$35 per hour.

FACILITIES/SUPPORT: Teachers find their own accommodation.

RECRUITMENT: CV and interview.

CONTACT: Deborah Pinder, Director of Studies.

PROSPECTS FOR TEACHERS
IN NEW ZEALAND

The English language teaching market in New Zealand is fairly similar to Australia; highly developed, although subject to demand fluctuation. Several years ago Chinese students, attracted by the favourable exchange rate and a liberalisation of the immigration regulations governing foreign students, swamped the market and with a CELTA and several years' experience, **Mr Roy** found himself in a very strong position:

When I came here a year ago, I've never felt so popular. I was amazed how many jobs I got offered cold-calling with a CV. I entered the country on a visitor visa which, as a British passport holder, gave me six months in the country. Before coming here I had looked on the internet for the addresses of English language schools and I brought a stack of CVs with me too. I just typed 'English language schools New Zealand' into the Google search engine and clicked on the second link www.english-schools.co.nz/ which gave me some useful information. I didn't jump at the first three jobs I was offered in Auckland because I wanted to check out Christchurch, the other main centre for EFL schools. There I was offered a few more jobs and decided to take up a post at Aspect [now Kaplan] at 116 Worcester Street in the city centre. The students are mainly Chinese, Korean and Japanese but there are notable groups from Taiwan, Switzerland and South America too. My school was helpfully willing to aid me with the visa bureaucracy and now I have residency. My school has a core of staff with open-ended contracts and a larger number of casual/part-time staff including some British people with working holiday visas who work for some months and then continue travelling.

Today, demand is not quite so high, as the number of Chinese students has decreased. However there are plenty of Saudis/South Americans, etc. who can see the appeal of learning a foreign language in this beautiful country. Private language schools are regulated by the New Zealand Qualifications Aurthority or NZQA (www.nzqa.govt.nz/providers/index.do). Its website lists all the educational establishments in New Zealand, but is worth looking through for leads (or search for 'language' to narrow it down). The national organisation of English language teachers, TESOLANZ, (www.tesolanz.

org.nz) provides a free listing to job-seekers, while English New Zealand (www.englishnewzealand. co.nz) is a group of schools which has its own accreditation process and a central contact for teacher recruitment (admin@englishnewzealand.co.nz).

British citizens aged between 18 and 30 can work in New Zealand through the working holiday visa scheme (www.immigration.govt.nz/migrant/stream/work/workingholiday).

LIST OF EMPLOYERS

BUCKSWOOD ST NOVA INSTITUTE

7 Auburn Street, Takapuna, Auckland

9 488 7777

info@novanz.com

www.novanz.com

NUMBER OF TEACHERS: 12.

PREFERENCE OF NATIONALITY: None.

QUALIFICATIONS: TEFL/CELTA minimum. Summer school experience an advantage.

CONDITIONS OF EMPLOYMENT: Renewal of contract done term by term. 25 hours per week.

SALARY: NZ$27 per hour plus 6% holiday pay plus meeting allowances.

FACILITIES/SUPPORT: Help with finding accommodation given occasionally. Job offer provided for teacher to take to NZ Immigration Service to apply for work visa.

RECRUITMENT: Via newspaper and internet. Telephone interviews acceptable if backed up with references. Some UK interviews possible at partner school.

DOMINION ENGLISH SCHOOLS

Auckland: PO Box 4217

9 377 3280

dos@dominion.school.nz

Christchurch: PO Box 3908

dos@dominion.school.nz

www.dominion.school.nz

NUMBER OF TEACHERS: Up to 20.

PREFERENCE OF NATIONALITY: None but must be native English speakers.

QUALIFICATIONS: Minimum Cambridge/RSA CELTA or Trinity CertTESOL or recognised equivalent. Preferably also university degree and experience.

CONDITIONS OF EMPLOYMENT: Flexible contracts. Part time hours 12.5 per week from 9am to 12pm. Full-time hours 25 per week, 9am–4pm.

SALARY: Starting wage approximately NZ$30 per hour.

FACILITIES/SUPPORT: Applicants must hold a valid work visa/permit.

RECRUITMENT: Local interviews essential.